Unrepresented Nations and Peoples Organization

YEARBOOK 1997

Unrepresented Nations and Peoples Organization

YEARBOOK 1997

J. Atticus Ryan (Editor)
Christopher A. Mullen (Series Editor)

KLUWER LAW INTERNATIONAL
THE HAGUE / LONDON / BOSTON

A C.I.P. Catalogue record for this book is available from the Library of Congress.

ISBN 90-411-1022-4
ISSN 1385-3546

Published by Kluwer Law International,
P.O. Box 85889, 2508 CN The Hague, The Netherlands.

Sold and distributed in North, Central and South America
by Kluwer Law International,
675 Massachusetts Avenue, Cambridge, MA 02139, U.S.A.

In all other countries, sold and distributed
by Kluwer Law International, Distribution Centre,
P.O. Box 322, 3300 AH Dordrecht, The Netherlands.

Printed on acid-free paper

Printed in the Netherlands

ACKNOWLEDGEMENTS

Unless we uncover and examine the many contexts in which international affairs occur we condemn ourselves to situations that perpetuate ignorance and indifference. The pages that follow represent continuing efforts intended to provide insight into the situations of the nations, peoples and minorities, as they themselves view and present them, as well as the policies of their collective representation through the UNPO. Further, the events and policies presented in this Yearbook express the difficulties inherent in bringing about change in a world where nonviolent voices must compete with the strident tones of conflict and the attention such violent tacits garner.

Although countless hands have assisted in the compilation of this volume, the following individuals deserve special attention for a number of reasons: Christopher Mullen for providing guidance, support and no small amount of hands-on assistance; Jet Nauta for her months of team coordination and sharing her knowledge of political geography; Isobel Buiter, Allison Comp, Karen Ernst, Orsalia Lambropoulou, Linnart Mäll, Kathy Voyles, Albertine Zanting and Erica Zwaan for working tirelessly to produce the Member Reports; Tsering Jampa and Michael van Walt for entrusting me with this responsibility, helping me come to terms with the rudiments of diplomacy and for final editorial review; Frank Wijnandts, Eliane Provó Kluit, Saskia Kerdel, José Amorim Diaz and Heidi Krieger for their patience and understanding during the various hectic stages of the Yearbook's production.

It has been my privilege to play a small a part in the significant international effort to promote human rights and specifically the rights of those nations, peoples and minorities left outside the corridors of power and prosperity. May we all one day recognize that ignorance and indifference are no substitute for an understanding that knowledge can bring freedom from oppression and justice out of inequity.

J. Atticus Ryan
Editor

TABLE OF CONTENTS

Documents

Appendices

PREFACE

Claiborne Pell

Chairman, Committee on Foreign Relations,
United States Senate 1987–1995

Eleanor Roosevelt, the driving force behind the Universal Declaration of Human Rights, the 50th anniversary of which will be celebrated in December 1998, once said that "the destiny of human rights is in the hands of all our citizens in all our communities." The UNPO has exemplified the spirit of that exhortation by mobilizing support for and dramatizing the plight of some of the most vulnerable nations and communities on planet Earth. During its seven years of existence, the UNPO has played an indispensable role in helping nearly 100 million people in some 50 or so nations and communities to gain a voice and representation that they would not otherwise have.

I have always been interested in small nations and peoples. In part, this interest was kindled by a knowledge of the suffering endured by the people of an American Indian forebear of mine. My interest was also nurtured by the deep appreciation and respect that I developed for the many contributions that small communities have made to enrich our lives despite the repression they have suffered. Most of all, however, it was the spirited work by my father, Herbert C. Pell, the U.S. Representative on the UN War Crimes Commission following World War II, to support the effort to have genocide considered a war crime that caused me to become involved in the promotion and defense of human rights everywhere.

I am pleased that many of the peoples that I have worked to help, first as a private citizen and then as a politician, have been among the beneficiaries of the UNPO's concern and advocacy. These include the Kurds of Iraq, the Albanians of Kosova and Macedonia, the East Timorese, the Taiwanese and the Tibetans. Hopefully, these and other member peoples of the UNPO will one day emerge from the darkness of repression or discrimination as have the peoples of the Baltic states and Hungary, which were of particular interest and concern to me and the organizations I worked with during the Cold War.

I was very pleased and honored to have been selected as a recipient of the first UNPO Award in early-1996. I was particularly grateful to be included in this Award along with José Ramos-Horta, the 1996 Nobel Peace Prize Laureate from East Timor. I have had the great pleasure of meeting Mr. Ramos-Horta and discussing his inspiring work in East Timor.

Unconscionable violations of human rights continue to occur in East Timor and in other regions of the world. Too often, democratic governments in America,

Europe and elsewhere react to these violations by looking the other way or pleading that nothing can be done. *Realpolitik* and commercial avarice cloud the conscience of otherwise civilized and enlightened governments. It has been the UNPO's mission to remind these governments, both directly and through public opinion, that in the pursuit of national interests there is room to insist that the weak, the powerless and the minorities of the world be guaranteed what has been solemnly promised to them in the Universal Declaration of Human Rights.

The UNPO and its member groups are committed to pursuing their objectives through nonviolent means. In furtherance of this principle, the UNPO convened a conference in July 1997 in Tallinn, Estonia entitled *Nonviolence and Conflict: Conditions for Effective Peaceful Change*. At that conference, the UNPO's member groups debated such questions as: Does nonviolence pay? How effective is nonviolent action? What are the conditions necessary or conducive for nonviolent action to be effective? Conference participants also wrestled with the uncomfortable reality that the international community often seems to pay more attention to groups that use violence than to those committed to nonviolence. It is also an uncomfortable reality that nonviolent movements can be sustained only if key members of the international community come to the aid of the victims of injustice.

The UNPO is often referred to as the 'alternative United Nations', because it is composed of representatives of distinct societies and communities instead of governments of internationally recognized nation-states. Indeed, the UNPO's General Assembly reminds me very much of the UN General Assemblies in which I have been privileged to participate as a member of the U.S. delegation. I began my career in public service on the staff of the Secretariat at the San Francisco Conference in 1945. As a result, the UN is very near and dear to my heart, and to this day I always carry with me a copy of the UN Charter, parts of which I helped to draft. Despite my love for the UN, I realize its limitations. I am comforted, however, by the fact that the UNPO provides a complementary forum for groups that have not yet achieved nation-state status to air their grievances and lobby for change.

In 1997, the UNPO provided critical hope and support to the many peoples seeking self-determination or even just simple relief from daily acts of oppression. The progress made by these peoples with the assistance of the UNPO is detailed in this Yearbook, as are the new challenges that have arisen to command our attention and spur us to action. This Yearbook chronicles, as have earlier Yearbooks, the advances and setbacks in reversing man's inhumanity to man. As such, it is both sobering and inspiring.

FOREWORD

Seif Sharif Hamad

Chairman of the General Assembly

In July, the 50 Members of the Unrepresented Nations and Peoples Organization held their fifth General Assembly in Otepää, Estonia. It is no coincidence that the fifth General Assembly should be held in Estonia, for it was there that the founding Members conceived the organization in 1990. Among the founding Members, Armenia, Estonia, Latvia, and Palau are no longer unrepresented, now being full members of the United Nations.

This is only one of the many achievements of the UNPO. But, among its ranks the UNPO has Members from a broad range of different cultural, religious, and linguistic backgrounds, each possessing its own particular objectives. Some desire full independence, while others desire the protection of their respective identities, cultures, and environments. Within this variety, the common unifying factor is that every Member nation and people suffers from oppression, exploitation, deportation, persecution, the occupation of their lands, or the denial of their human rights. In their hearts, all of them aspire to have their choices respected by the international community, and, under the UNPO banner, these nations and peoples have begun to assert their identities by confidently pursuing their right to self-determination and to express what makes them distinct cultural, linguistic, or religious groups.

One of the underlying principles of the UNPO is the use of non-violence as a tool to achieve the Members' objectives. The principle of non-violence is, within the Membership of the UNPO, taking root—for every Member *must* be committed to finding a non-violent means in achieving their goals—and nearly all have been able to shun the use of violence in their struggles. There are, nonetheless, the exceptional cases where the people have been forced to take up arms in response to state initiated violence, as witnessed in Chechenia, West Papua, and Nagaland.

What now encourages us is the fact that the voice of the minorities, indigenous peoples, and occupied nations of the world can no longer be ignored. The UNPO and its Members actively participate in international fora in order to highlight the problems of the unrepresented. It is through such interaction that UNPO Members benefit. What we look forward to by addressing the many and serious problems facing UNPO Members is to make the world aware of their plight and urge the United Nations to take concerted action in support of their aspirations.

As Chairman, I look forward to the maximum use of modern communications, such as the Internet, in shedding a brighter light on the aims and objectives of the UNPO, the reasons for which its Members struggle for the more than 100 million people they represent, and in campaigning for moral, diplomatic, and material support of the UNPO and its Members. It is, indeed, my sincere aspiration that the international community lend a hand in seeing to it that the Members of the Unrepresented Nations and Peoples Organization attain their objectives in the shortest possible time.

DIRECTORY

GENERAL ASSEMBLY

Chairman:

Seif Sharif Hamad (Zanzibar)	1997–

Vice-Chairmen:

Atner Khuzangai (Chuvash)	1997–
Göran Hansson (Scania)	1997–

Previous

Chairmen:

Erkin Alptekin (Eastern Turkestan)	1993–1997
Dr. Linnart Mäll	1991–1993

Vice-Chairpersons:

Senator John Nimrod (Assyria)	1993–1997
Ka'Aina Mililani B. Trask (Hawai'i)	1995–1997
Ken Saro-Wiwa (Ogoni)	1993–1995
Erkin Alptekin (Eastern Turkestan)	1991–1993
Helen Corbett (Aboriginals of Australia)	1991–1993

STEERING COMMITTEE

President:

Dr. Parris Chang (Taiwan)	1993–

Vice-Presidents:

Akhyad Idigov (Chechenia)	1997–
Chungdak Dawa Koren (Tibet)	1997–

Members:

Circassians
Eastern Turkestan
Greeks in Albania
Inkeri
Iraqi Turkoman
Lakota Nation
Nagaland
Ogoni
Scania
South Moluccas
General Assembly Chairman, Vice-Chairmen (non-voting)

Previous

President:

Kasur Lodi G. Gyari (Tibet)	1991–1993

UNPO SECRETARIAT

Acting General Secretary:
Tsering Youdon Jampa (Tibet)

Assistant General Secretary for the Americas:
Senator John Nimrod (Assyria)
Assistant General Secretary for Eastern Europe:
Dr. Linnart Mäll (Estonia)
Assistant General Secretary for Asia Pacific:
Helen Corbett (Aboriginals of Australia)
Assistant General Secretary for the Environment:
Victor Kasiëpo (West Papua)

Councillor for Political Affairs
Dr. Michael van Walt van Praag (former General Secretary, 1991–1997)

Director, UNPO Americas Coordination Office:
Karen Onthank
Director, UNPO Tartu Coordination Office:
Dr. Linnart Mäll

UNPO OFFICES

Office of the General Secretary
Javastraat 40A, 2585 AP, The Hague, The Netherlands
Tel: +31 70 360 3318 Fax: +31 70 360 3346
email: unpo@unpo.nl
Internet: www.unpo.org

Americas Coordination Office
444 North Capitol Street, Suite 846
Washington, D.C. 20001-1570, U.S.A.
Tel: +1 202 637 0475 Fax: +1 202 637 0585
email: unposf@igc.apc.org

Tartu Coordination Office
P.O. Box Tartu 414
EE 2400 Estonia
Tel/Fax: +372 7 406 651
email: unpotart@estpak.ee

INTRODUCTION TO THE HISTORY AND PRINCIPLES OF THE UNPO

The Unrepresented Nations and Peoples Organization was born out of a feeling of frustration at the exclusion of nations, peoples and minorities which do not constitute independent states from access to international fora and organizations. Many peoples, especially the relatively small ones, have a long history, much of which is marked by oppression, discrimination and sometimes deportation at the hands of outside powers. Their primary concern is to protect their people from extermination, assimilation, or oppression. Many times the states of which they form a part do not respond to their concerns. Their only recourse is through the international community and access to these organizations.

The first meeting of what would become the UNPO took place in Tartu, Estonia in September 1990. The meeting was hosted by Dr. Linnart Mäll on behalf of the Congress of Estonia, the representative body of Estonian citizens, then still under Soviet occupation. The gathered leaders decided to create an organization which would embody and promote the values of democracy, self-determination, tolerance and nonviolence. The UNPO would provide a legitimate international forum for the world's voiceless peoples and assist its members in bringing change by effective, democratic, diplomatic and nonviolent means. This, the participants believed, would, in time, reduce the need of many oppressed peoples and minorities to resort to violence in order to draw attention to their causes or to achieve their legitimate aspirations. Immediately, work began on the drafting of a treaty or charter of the organization to be presented to a founding assembly. A solemn protocol was drawn up and signed by all present to formalize the intent to found the UNPO. A Steering Committee was formed, which consisted of one representative from each of the peoples present. It would be the responsibility of that committee to organize the first and founding assembly of the UNPO.

The standing mission of the UNPO is to assist its Members in advancing their interests effectively through nonviolent means, including diplomacy, the use of the United Nations and other international procedures for the protection of human rights, the development of public opinion and other action-oriented strategies, and the exploration of legal options available in defending their rights. The UNPO is an organization set up and run by its Member peoples, in order to empower themselves and to participate in the international community.

As a non-aligned organization dedicated to nonviolent programs and solutions, the UNPO offers an international forum, media and information services, participation at the United Nations, training in diplomacy and conflict resolution, strategic planning, election and referendum monitoring, the promotion of human rights, research services, and a means of cultural preservation and promotion. Its Members also created a Peace Action Council in 1995.

Participation in UNPO is open to nations and peoples who adhere to the following five principles, which form the basis for the Covenant of the UNPO:

1. The equal right of self-determination for all nations and peoples;
2. Adherence to internationally accepted human rights standards;
3. Adherence to the principles of democracy;
4. Promotion of nonviolence and the rejection of terrorism;
5. Protection of the natural environment.

In addition, applicants must show that they constitute a "nation or people" as defined in the Covenant of UNPO and that the organization applying for membership is representative of that nation or people. The Unrepresented Nations and Peoples Organization is currently comprised of 50 member participants representing nearly 100 million people.

COVENANT

of the

UNREPRESENTED NATIONS AND PEOPLES ORGANIZATION

~

Founding Assembly
The Peace Palace
The Hague
11 February 1991

~

COVENANT OF THE UNREPRESENTED NATIONS AND PEOPLES ORGANIZATION

~PREAMBLE~

~*Whereas* all Nations and Peoples possess the right to self-determination; by the virtue of that right they freely determine their political status and freely pursue their economic, social and cultural development;

~*Whereas* many Nations and Peoples suffer under alien or colonial occupation or are otherwise denied the exercise of their self-determination;

~*Whereas* the rights of the individuals and the collective rights of people are inextricably linked;

~*Whereas* the protection of the natural environment is similarly linked to the rights of Nations and Peoples to determine their own destiny;

~*Whereas* many Nations and Peoples are victims of human rights abuses, discrimination, persecution, population transfers, forced assimilation, deprivation of land or other natural resources and sometimes genocide;

~*Whereas* the unprovoked use of all forms of violence by States against Nations and Peoples is to be condemned;

~*Whereas* the non-recognition of a majority of Nations and Peoples by intergovernmental organizations and the absence of meaningful venues for the expression and enforcement of their aspirations and rights often leads to the use of violence;

~*Whereas* the ends sought by the Nations and Peoples differ depending on their individual situation, history and goals, and range from the recognition and protection of basic human rights including cultural and religious rights, within existing States, to the recognition of their sovereignty or statehood on an equal basis with other States;

-*Whereas* it is not the intention to create an alliance or common front of participating Nations and Peoples against established States or against any individual State or groups of States;

-*Whereas* an effort is needed to address effectively the legitimate issues raised by unrepresented Nations and Peoples in order to increase stability, and to promote peace based on genuine respect and understanding for one another and for each other's diversity.

Therefore,

by the present Covenant, the Participating Nations and Peoples, represented by the undersigned Representatives, establish among themselves the UNREPRESENTED NATIONS AND PEOPLES ORGANIZATION (the 'Organization').

TITLE I
General Provisions

Article 1

It shall be the aim of the Organization, by assisting Participating Nations and Peoples ('Participants') to express their positions, needs and grievances in legitimate forums and by providing a community of support, to advance the fulfillment of the aspirations of Participating Nations and Peoples by effective non-violent means.

Article 2

For the purposes set out in Article I, the activities of the Organization shall include, but shall not be limited to:

(a) the facilitation of consultation, exchange of views and experiences, and cooperation with each other, to the extent desired by the Participants;
(b) assistance in effectively utilizing available procedures of United Nations bodies and specialized agencies and of other international and regional organizations;
(c) training in bilateral and multilateral diplomacy, including United Nations diplomacy and the principles of international law;
(d) training in negotiation skills and professional assistance in conflict management and resolution;
(e) training in non-violent strategies and professional assistance in the development of strategic plans and policies;
(f) professional legal and public relations advice;

(g) providing an information service for the dissemination of information provided by Participants to the public and among their own people;
(h) assistance in the development of democratic institutions and processes and in the monitoring of elections and referenda;
(i) assistance in the the development and implementation of measures designed to protect the natural environment and the creation of sustainable development projects.

Article 3

(a) The achievement of the tasks entrusted to the Organization shall be ensured by:

- an Assembly
- a Steering Committee
- a Secretariat

Each of these institutions shall act within the limits of the powers conferred upon in this Covenant.

(b) The institutions listed in subsection (a) of this Article may be assisted by an Advisory Council, acting in a consultative capacity, and various specialized bodies such as a Legal Council, an Environmental advisory Committee or an Agency for Conflict Management and Resolution acting under the direction of the Secretariat.

Article 4

Each Participant shall take general and specific measures which are appropriate to assist the Organization in achieving its aims and shall refrain from actions intended or reasonably expected to harm the Organization or impede its activities.

TITLE II
PROVISIONS GOVERNING PARTICIPATION

Article 5

Participation is open to all Nations and Peoples who are not adequately represented at the United Nations and whose Representative Body, as defined in Article 6 of this Title, fulfills all requirements set out in this Title and declares:

(a) Belief in the equality of all Nations and Peoples and in their inalienable right to self determination;

(b) Adherence to the internationally accepted human rights standards as laid down in the Universal Declaration of Human Rights and the International Covenant of Civil and Political Rights and Economic, Social and Cultural Rights;

(c) Adherence to the principles of democratic pluralism and rejection of totalitarianism and any forms of religious intolerance;

(d) Rejection of terrorism as an instrument of policy;

(e) Respect for all peoples and population groups, including minority or majority populations within territories inhabited by the Participant but belonging to different ethnic, religious or linguistic groups.

Article 6

For the purposes of this Covenant:

(a) A Nation or People shall mean a group of human beings which possesses the will to be identified as a nation or people and to determine its common destiny as a nation or people, and is bound to a common heritage which can be historical, racial, ethnic, linguistic, cultural, religious or territorial. A section of a people constituting a minority, living on a portion of its ancestral territory, incorporated into a Sate other than a State represented by that People, is included in this Article's definition.

(b) Representative Body shall mean a government, legislative body, liberation movement or other organ of leadership, whether in the territory of the Nations or People or in exile, recognized as such by a substantial section of the people which the Representative Body claims to represent; a Representative Body can also mean a coordinating organization or other form of association of two or more organs of leadership of one Nation or People or an organization or association of two or more Nations and Peoples.

Article 7

A Nation or People, through its Representative Body, may apply to become a Participant in the Organization by submitting the following information to the Secretariat for consideration by the Steering Committee:

(a) a brief history of the Nation or People;

(b) the reasons for the desire to become a participant in the Organization;

(c) adequate evidence of the recognition of the Representative Body as an organ of leadership by the people it claims to represent;

(d) a formal declaration of adhesion to the present Covenant;

The Steering Committee, on recommendation of the General Secretary, will decide on all applications. The Assembly may overrule this decision by a vote of two-thirds majority.

Article 8

Participation in the Organization does not in any way imply agreement among Participating Nations and Peoples on each other's objectives, policies, or allegiances and does not require any form of cooperation or solidarity beyond what is contained in this Covenant.

Article 9

Participants favor the use of peaceful means to achieve their goals. Participants shall not use the Organization or any of its bodies, specialized agencies or services in its name, to promote the use of violence.

TITLE III
PROVISIONS GOVERNING INSTITUTIONS

Section I: THE ASSEMBLY

Article 10

The Assembly, which shall be composed of delegations representing participating Nations and Peoples, shall exercise the powers of deliberation and control which are conferred upon it by this Covenant.

Article 11

Each delegation shall have the right to one vote in the Assembly.

Article 12

The Assembly shall hold regular sessions at least once every two years. The Assembly may meet in extraordinary sessions at the request of a majority of Participants or at the request of the Steering Committee. The Assembly shall elect its Chairperson at the beginning of every session. The Chairperson shall serve in the function until a successor is elected.

Article 13

The Assembly shall adopt the agenda at the start of each session on the basis of recommendations of the Steering Committee and the General Secretary.

Article 14

The Assembly shall act by a simple majority of votes of delegations present, unless stated otherwise in the Assembly Rules of Procedure. The quorum shall be laid down in the rules of procedure.

Article 15

The Steering Committee or the General Secretary may invite individuals, governmental or nongovernmental organizations or States to attend as Observers to the regular sessions of the Assembly, subject to the approval of the Assembly. The Assembly shall decide on the rights and duties of Observers by a simple majority.

Section II: The Steering Committee

Article 16

The Steering Committee shall be composed of five to fifteen persons, each representing one Participant, who will serve for a term of three years

Article 17

The Steering Committee shall meet at least twice a year. The Steering Committee shall adopt its own rules of procedure.

Article 18

The Steering Committee shall implement the overall policy of the Organization as determined by the Assembly. The Steering Committee shall possess all of the powers delegated to it by the Assembly.

Section III: The Secretariat

Article 19

The Secretariat shall consist of a General Secretary and assistant appointed by him or her. Members of the Secretariat need not belong to a Nation or People represented in the Organization. The General Secretary shall serve as the executive director of the Organization, and shall be elected by the Assembly for a three-year, renewable term.

Article 20

The duties of the General Secretary shall include:
(a) to direction the day-to-day operations of the Organization;
(b to represent the Organization;
(c) to establish and operate bank accounts for the benefit of the Organization;
(d) to maintain proper and regular books of accounts of all receipts and payments of the Organisation, including the creation of an annual balance sheet;
(e) to present status reports annually to the Participants and to the Steering Committee. These reports shall include the following information: the names and addresses of representatives of Participants and of members of the Steering Committee, and a description of the overall financial situation of the Organization and a description of the activities of the Organization during the previous year, including any additions, changes or amendments to the Covenant;
(f) to coordinate the activities of Regional Chapters in order to better accomplish the aims and objectives of the Organization; and
(g) to perform any duties delegated or requested by the Assembly or Steering Committee.

Section IV: REGIONAL CHAPTERS

Article 21

The Regional Chapters shall be established for the purpose of supporting the Organization and its activities, including the solicitation of funds. The statutes and bylaws of each of the Regional Chapters shall ensure that they shall exist for no other purpose, and shall expressly incorporate this Covenant by reference or otherwise.

TITLE IV
Financial Provisions

Article 22

Funding for the Organization shall come from Participants, and from international organizations, corporate or private contributions and fundraising activities.

TITLE V
TERMINATION OF PARTICIPATION

Article 23

Participants may terminate their membership in the Organization if they desire upon sending formal notice to the General Secretary. Termination shall be effective upon receipt of notice by the General Secretary.

Article 24

A Nation or People which becomes a member of the United Nations has the moral duty to remain a supporting member of the Organization and to take part in the work of the Assembly without a vote.

TITLE VI
LIQUIDATION OF THE ORGANIZATION

Article 25

The Organization shall cease to exist if
(a) Participants unanimously so decide; or
(b) In the event all Participants obtain independent representation at the United Nations.

TITLE VII
AMENDMENTS TO THE COVENANT

Article 26

Amendments to the Covenant shall be approved by three-fourths of the Participants.

(Covenant amended: Article 14 in March, 1995, and Article 26 in August, 1991.)

OVERVIEW OF 1997

STATEMENT BY THE
GENERAL SECRETARY

THE YEAR IN REVIEW

ANNUAL REPORT OF THE
GENERAL ASSEMBLY CHAIRMAN

ANNUAL REPORT OF THE
STEERING COMMITTEE PRESIDENT

STATEMENT BY THE GENERAL SECRETARY

Dr. Michael C.van Walt van Praag
General Secretary of the UNPO
February 1991–July 1997

Since its founding in 1991, the Unrepresented Nations and Peoples Organization has matured to become the effective forum and service organization of 50 nations, peoples and minorities who together represent nearly 100 million people in all parts of the world. It is today a player in the international community. For many peoples and minorities the UNPO is the only international organization where they are recognized and respected for who they really are. It does not matter how large or small a people or its territory is; or how wealthy or poor a minority is; or how independent or oppressed a nation is: in the UNPO each nation, people or minority has a right to its distinct existence and to determine its own destiny. There are no superior cultures or backward peoples. There is only the capacity to recognize and appreciate the wealth in diversity of civilizations, religions, and traditions or the sad inability to do so.

Seven years is not a long time, yet for me it has been a lifetime of learning, experiences, emotions, risks, fears and joys. The joy of experiencing the end of the Soviet occupation of Estonia; the intensity lived in the mountains of Chechenia with Dzhokhar Dudaev during the cruel Russian war; seeing the devastation of the Batwa survivors of the genocide in Rwanda; the lasting pain of losing a noble and extraordinary friend, Ken Saro-Wiwa, hung at the gallows; the inspiration obtained from His Holiness the Dalai Lama, whose wisdom and compassion never ends; the frustrations experienced at the table of peace talks between Abkhazia and Georgia and the hopes shared with Bougainvillian leaders meeting to seek to end an eight year war; the anger at the treatment of Aboriginal people by Australia's colonizers; the beauty of Assyrian dancers; the courage of Jumma students in the Chittagong Hill Tracts; the strength of the Crimean Tatar leader Mustafa Jemiloglu; the outrage felt when witnessing the show trial of the Omonia Five in Tirana; the celebration of the Nobel Peace Prize awarded to East Timor's Bishop Belo and my friend José Ramos-Horta; the disappointment at the election results in Chuvash; the tensions shared with Albanians in Macedonia; the hospitality of Ingush refugees chased from their homes in the Prigorodniy Rayon; the determination of the Kanaka Maoli of Hawai'i; arrests by Serbian police in Kosova; spiritual kinship with the Lakota; touched by the warmth of the reindeer herders in the vast snow-laden expanses of Sakha in Siberia; the satisfaction at the first talks to end 50 years of war in Nagaland; the enthusiasm of thousands of electors in the streets of Taiwan as true democracy was celebrated in that island state; the urge to help the people of Zanzibar in their desire to enjoy the democracy they were promised; the deep respect I felt for the greatness and the humility of President Manusama of the South Moluccas and of Isas Iussuf Alptekin of Eastern Turkestan. These feelings and many more were experienced with a rare intensity: the courage, suffering, and pride I have seen and experienced among so many exceptional people in all corners of the world has enriched my own life in a way that is hard to fathom. The gratitude and humility I feel towards all of the individuals, peoples and minorities I have had the privilege of being associated with is impossible to express.

I am convinced that our organization has indeed matured to the stage where a change in leadership will strengthen it, even if the process of getting there will have its difficulties. This is the primary reason that I decided not to seek a third term as General Secretary. But, also because I wish to dedicate more time to working with those for whom the UNPO was created—the people who struggle on the ground. That requires a re-arrangement of my time within, but not a departure from, the organization.

Seven years ago few people believed that the UNPO would have achieved as much as it already has. Not only has the organization grown tremendously, but the respect it commands enables it to contribute substantially to the participation of its Member nations and peoples on the international stage, and to assist in the prevention of conflicts or their resolution, albeit in a quiet and limited way. What has been achieved is due not only to the leaders of the peoples and minorities who represent their people in the UNPO, but also to the trust which the people on the ground have placed in the organization. I am proud and grateful for the opportunity I have been given to serve this organization and for the trust that its members placed in me. In the next seven years, we must deepen our collective efforts to assist one another and to sensitize and educate the world at large. Change is coming, but only because women and men everywhere believe in the need for it and are prepared to struggle for this belief.

May the inner peace that comes from such a sense of purpose and the power that comes from solidarity among peoples lead all Members of the Unrepresented Nations and Peoples Organization, and our brothers and sisters elsewhere, to the freedom and dignity which each of them yearn for. InshAllah, God willing!

THE YEAR IN REVIEW

The General Secretary

In July 1997 the fifth UNPO General Assembly was held in Otepää, Estonia. The General Assembly is a rare opportunity for the leaders of disenfranchised nations and peoples around the world to gather in order to get to know one another, share experiences and develop solidarity.

The General Assembly elected its new Chairman, Mr. Seif Sharif Hamad, a leader from Zanzibar, and two Vice-Chairpersons, the Chuvash leader, Mr. Atner Khuzangai, and Mr. Göran Hansson of Scania. The General Assembly also elected several new Steering Committee members, deciding these persons would henceforth also constitute the Board of the *Stichting* (foundation) UNPO. The Steering Committee now consists of the following members: the Chechen Republic Ichkeria, Circassia, Eastern Turkestan, the Greeks in Albania, the Inkeri, the Iraqi Turkman, the Lakota Nation, Nagaland, the Ogoni, the South Moluccas, Taiwan, and Tibet. The Chairman and Vice-Chairmen of the General Assembly are also non-voting members of the Steering Committee.

The UNPO has now existed for seven years. It is, therefore, still a young organization. But, in its short existence it has acquired a remarkable degree of credibility and authority. The organization is widely respected—other international organizations and governments listen to what we have to say, and increasingly take our views and recommendations seriously. The strength and power of the UNPO lies in the fact that its Members represent so many of the leading and lesser-known nations, peoples and minorities struggling for recognition and freedom. Collectively, representing approximately 100 million people.

In a world where the whole question of the relationship between states and their governments on the one hand, and peoples, nations and minorities on the other, has become central and where over 90% of armed conflicts concern this very issue, the Members of the UNPO have become an essential party in the search for peace and stability. Simply, they can no longer be ignored as a group, and therefore the UNPO cannot be ignored. For too long, unrepresented and often oppressed peoples and minorities have been viewed by the outside world as sources of trouble, instability, and even conflict. The time has come, to use former Tibetan Foreign Minister Kasur Tenzin Tethong's words, expressed during the UNPO Conference on Conflict Prevention, "For the world to realize that indigenous or non-self-governing peoples, minorities and occupied territories, and we as an organization, are not the problem. Instead, we can be part of the solution."

This message, if understood, will have a profound impact on the course of history, and, of course, in the first instance, on the situations of UNPO Member nations and peoples and others outside the organization. But, for this message to be conveyed with clarity, persuasiveness and power, it is important to stand together and dedicate time and resources to the joint struggle, in addition to continuing our dedication to the specific peoples we work for and with.

This was a year of contrasts and challenges for the UNPO's 50 Members. In *Zanzibar,* the Peace Action Council (PAC) was asked to assist in the search for a peaceful solution to the political stalemate in Zanzibar before violent conflict breaks out. It sent an initial fact-finding mission in April, which met with all of the top leaders and with the affected people. PAC Co-chairman Rodrigo Carazo headed a delegation, which met with the President of Tanzania, Benjamin Mkapa, and its former President, Mwalimu Nyerere. Partly as a result of the visit some progress was made towards a dialogue between the ruling and opposition parties to discuss differences and to seek a solution. Nevertheless, in November, there were renewed arrests of leaders of the opposition Civic United Front.

For the *Batwa,* following the UNPO's assistance of the President of the Association for the Promotion of Batwa (APB), Mr Zepherin Kalimba, at the UN in Geneva, the growth of outside support for development projects has continued. At an October meeting in London, NGOs interested in providing assistance agreed to coordinate their efforts to better assist the Batwa people.

For the *Ogoni,* the intimidating activities of the Nigerian special forces in Ogoniland continued in 1997, though their presence has become less blatant. The UNPO has continued to assist the Movement for the Survival of the Ogoni People (MOSOP) in developing and implementing new strategies, and to this end facilitated a training session for 45 MOSOP leaders in November. The UNPO has always called for dialogue and negotiations between Royal Dutch Shell and the MOSOP leadership. Despite increasing international pressure Shell's behavior and activity on the ground displays little or no significant change. This continues to make it extremely difficult for MOSOP to conduct a dialogue with the corporation.

Cabinda was welcomed for the first time at the General Assembly. Cabinda, a former Portuguese protectorate, is today struggling to free itself from Angolan rule. The territory has, in effect, never been decolonized, instead it was handed over from one colonial power to another, newly independent, one. The heavy fighting in neighbouring Democratic Republic of Congo and in Congo-Brazaville has increased the tensions in the region and intensified the pressure on the people of Cabinda.

In the Americas, a 50-day Peace Ride was once again conducted in May and June by the *Lakota Nation* spiritual leader, the Keeper of the Sacred White Buffalo Calf Pipe, Dr. Arvol Lookinghorse. At the UN in July and August, the UNPO assisted Chief Germaine Tremmel in drawing international attention to the plight not only of her people, but also that of the Nuxalk Nation of British Columbia.

The *Mapuche* in Chile continue to face the loss of land and evictions as hydro-electric plants and roads are constructed by the government and multinational corporations (MNCs) without meaningful consultation with the local Mapuche communities. In Argentina, the Mapuche intensified protests against forcible evictions of Mapuche communities which are threatening their land-base. The European Parliament passed a resolution in March calling on the Government of Argentina to protect the rights of the indigenous peoples. In Chile, the movement continues to struggle due to a lack of funds and facilities.

In Asia, an agreement was finally signed between the Jana Sanghati Samiti (JSS), representing the Jumma peoples of the *Chittagong Hill Tracts,* and the Government of Bangladesh on 2 December 1997. The agreement was reached after numerous rounds of negotiations with the National Committee set up by the government to conduct negotiations. The main opposition party of Bangladesh protested against the agreement. But, it is hoped that, despite the shortcomings which many Jummas also feel the agreement has, it can serve as the basis on which to build a new peace and move forward. At a major international conference in Bangkok in February, very concrete recommendations were made to the international community, including aid-donating countries, to step-up pressure on the Bangladesh government.

In India and Burma, the *Naga* conflict, though continuing, has entered a new phase. Since the Indian government's announcement of their willingness to negotiate, limited talks have taken place at the highest level, including discussions held to determine the modalities for formal negotiations. The conflict with India has existed since the respective declarations of independence of Nagaland and India in 1947. On 1 August a ceasefire was announced by both sides, and this ceasefire has been extended into 1998.

The State Peace and Development Council (SPDC), formerly the State Law and Order Restoration Council (SLORC), military dictatorship in Burma maintained its policy of population transfer—conducting deportations of *Karenni* out of and Burmese into Karenni State territory. The *Mon People* suffer a similar fate, with many civilians performing hard labor for SPDC troops. The *Shan State,* a new Member of the UNPO, shares the SPDC as a common adversary in its struggle for freedom and democracy. Although the international community continues to express its concern, the effectiveness of such expressions should be critically assessed. Economic sanctions were announced by the United States, but barring joint action by other countries, including the European Union but also India and other leading Asian states, the effects are certain to be limited.

In *Tibet,* the death of Deng Xiao Ping inspired some hope that the leadership would 'turn a new leaf' and respond to the Dalai Lama's persistent calls for dialogue and negotiations. So far, though, no such moves have been made by the Chinese government. His Holiness the Dalai Lama and the Tibetan Government-in-Exile continued the international campaign to highlight the abuses of human rights in Tibet. A UNPO fact-finding mission was sent to Tibet in April to investigate whether

China's rule in Tibet could be considered colonial. The mission's verdict, that China's rule in Tibet fulfills all the major criteria of colonialism, was presented to the UN Sub-Commission on Prevention of Discrimination and Protection of Minorities in August by Professor Cees Flinterman, the leader of the mission. (*The full mission report is contained in this volume.*)

This year also saw the worsening of the situation in *Eastern Turkestan*. Repression inside Eastern Turkestan increased late in 1996 and early this year with the arrest of thousands of 'splitists' and the execution of approximately 140 persons. Uprisings against Chinese rule, fuelled by massive population transfer of Chinese to Eastern Turkestan, led to massacres by the Chinese authorities. Largely in response, incidents of violent resistance against the Chinese authorities increased. But, a heightened interest in events surrounding the uprisings provided new opportunities for the UNPO and others to focus attention on the situation in the region.

November in *Taiwan* witnessed victories for the Democratic Peoples Party (DPP) in municipal elections, with most local governments now under their leadership. The UNPO continues to making its services available to this founding Member.

The UNPO continued to support the *Cordillera* Peoples Alliance (CPA) in the Philippines through the promotion of the issues and policies the CPA pursues. Despite agreements reached regarding local autonomy for the region, tensions are again growing between the CPA and the Government of the Philippines due to the expected increase in MNC mining activity. The CPA is effective at the UN Working Group on Indigenous Populations and participates in many other international fora, while the struggle on the ground continues.

Reports of arbitrary detention, summary executions and torture continue to come from *Acheh/Sumatra*, and during the year a number of Achenese refugees in Malaysia were threatened with forced repatriation or deportation to Indonesia. Fortunately, through tremendous effort, the Acheh movement was able to prevent this from taking place. Again in 1997, in *West Papua*, renewed tensions occurred with regard to the increasingly capacity of the Indonesian-supported operations of foreign-owned mining companies. Emerging solidarity among the Indonesian-focused UNPO Members (Acheh, East Timor and West Papua) with the Netherlands-based Government-in-Exile of the *Republic of South Moluccas* (RMS) allowed for the continuing development of a unified strategy begun in 1996. More arrests of East Timorese freedom campaigners and fighters occurred in 1997 in Indonesian-occupied *East Timor*, with some sentenced to death for alleged involvement in attacks on military personnel. Developments within the U.S. legislature, regarding restrictions on military aid to Indonesia, provided another sign that perhaps the tide is turning in favor of the oppressed within Indonesian controlled territories.

This year saw the start of serious peace talks regarding the conflict on *Bougainville*. The initiative and its facilitation resulted from the involvement of New Zealand. Several rounds of talks have been held and the declaration of a truce is anticipated. The *Maohi* people have continued to work on strengthening the organization within the islands of French Polynesia, and as such conducted little activity directed associated with the UNPO.

Earlier this year, the Australian government refused to officially apologize to the *Aboriginals of Australia* for the genocide committed against them, despite the publication by the Australian Human Rights Commission of a report which confirms that past Australian policies were genocidal. Deaths in custody of Aboriginal detainees are again rising and there are clear signs of increased racism. In *Hawai'i* the plebiscite, or 'Native Hawaiian Vote', which took place in 1996 despite opposition by Ka Lahui Hawai'i and other indigenous organizations, remained one of the primary issues, and the uncertainty which the vote created remained unchanged in 1997.

In the Middle East, *Assyrians* continue to be affected by constant fighting and violent conflict among Kurdish parties. The *Iraqi Turkoman* were similarly affected, and with the assistance of the UNPO, representatives of the Iraqi Turkman are presenting their case to United Nations human rights bodies.

In Europe, the situation in the Balkans has seen no remarkable change. Serbian repression remains unchecked, and incidents of police violence increased in 1997. Only a concerted international effort (such as a Dayton-type conference on the future of Kosova) can provide hope for a change on the part of the Serbian authorities. The lack of progress in easing tensions is leading to an increasing number of people in Kosova demanding more radical methods in regaining their freedom. In late-1996, the people of *Sanjak* took part in the first elections, monitored by the UNPO, and the President of the Muslim National Council of Sanjak (MNCS), Dr. Sulejman Ugljanin, returned from exile. But, this year Serbian authorities once again took control of the local government in Novi Pazar in what can only be described as a coup. Repression is on the increase after what seemed to be a short period of lenience before the 1996 elections.

For the *Greeks in Albania* the chaos and conflict leading to new elections 1997 put them under intense stress. It is hoped that, following these elections, peace can be restored to an Albania which has seen so much suffering in past decades. It is felt that the development of democracy within a peaceful framework would provide the Greek Minority with the best chance of improving their situation. Among the *Albanians in Macedonia* new laws banning the display of the Albanian flag have exacerbated relations with the government yet again, with several incidents breaking out between the authorities and Albanians.

Following improvements in the political situation in 1996, during 1997 the *Hungarians in Romania* were represented in the government by several ministers. They hope this coalition government will implement a change in the situation of the Hungarian minority. Though many are taking a 'wait-and-see' attitude, at this time most signs are positive. Finally within the European region, the Stiftelsen Skånsk Framtid (SSF) in *Scania* stepped-up its well-coordinated activities throughout the course of 1997.

In the Commonwealth of Independent States (CIS) and adjoining regions, following a visit to the region by the UNPO General Secretary in September 1996, President Aushev of *Ingushetia* requested the UNPO's assistance in sponsoring an international conference on the refugee issue to be hosted in the capital, Nazran. As a result, in February 1997, the UNPO co-sponsored the conference and Senator John Nimrod (Assyria) represented the organization.

In *Chechenia,* the UNPO monitored presidential and parliamentary elections in January, visiting more polling stations and districts than any other observer mission. They found the election to be free and fair, despite the very difficult situation which the Chechens faced. (*The monitoring report is contained in this volume.*) Since the elections and the installment of the government of President Maskhadov, Russia, though continuing negotiations, has instituted a blockade of the Republic

The *Circassians* and the International Circassian Association (ICA) mourned the passing of its first leader, Mr. Kalmukov, a man of great experience and integrity. In the Northern Caucasus, the UNPO also welcomed the *Kumyk* people, who have long struggled to preserve their identity and to protect it from assimilation policies and deportations. Parliamentary elections were held in *Abkhazia* in late-1996, and Senator John Nimrod and Lord Eric Avebury represented the UNPO as election observers. (*The full monitoring report is contained in this volume.*) A truly comprehensive political settlement remains elusive despite the dramatic gesture made by President Ardzinba to visit Tbilisi to meet personally with Georgian President Shevardnadze. Additionally, at the request of the Abkhazian government, the UNPO commissioned a legal opinion on the validity and interpretation of the 4 April 1994 agreement signed by Abkhazia and Georgia. *Bashkortostan,* was admitted as a Member of the UNPO in 1996, but only recently has contact provided the ability to undertake activities with respect to the Republic.

In the Volga region, economic development continues but criticism is growing from the opposition in the UNPO Member *Tatarstan*—an issue which the UNPO will explore. Presidential elections were held at the end of the year in *Chuvash,* while the *Udmurt* continue to experience declining economic productivity. Presidential and parliamentary elections in *Mari,* held late in 1996, unseated former President Vladimir Zotin, and the UNPO continues to assist the Mari when possible.

In the Crimea, the Organization for Security and Cooperation in Europe conducted two missions and members of the Council of Europe and parliamentarians from Estonia, Sweden and Denmark visited. It is hoped this will highlight the poor situation of the *Crimean Tatars.* With tremendous effort the *Komi* continue their three-year environmental recovery program. And, in the *Sakha Republic (Yakutia)* it is hoped that efforts by the United Nations Development Program (UNDP) to provide technical and financial assistance, based on a joint UNPO–UNDP mission conducted in 1996, are indeed beginning to provide benefits for the disadvantaged peoples of the Republic.

In *Tyva,* 1997 saw the establishment of the Kamby Lama (High Lama), the highest spiritual leader of the Buddhists in Tyva. Additionally, September brought the first election of the Kamby Lama at the All-Tyva Congress of Buddhists. This election together with the new institution displays the revival and consolidation of the religion of the Tyvans. A new leadership was elected in *Buryatia* and a parallel structure, the Congress of Buryat People was put in place to assist in the leadership's structural aims.

Programs within the UNPO Secretariat are maturing. The *Effective Participation at the United Nations and other International Fora Program* (EP) provides assistance to UNPO Members in gaining access to, and effectively utilizing, the appropriate UN and international bodies. For five years the EP has facilitated UNPO Member participation in the UN system, and now provides five forms of assistance: 1) training in diplomacy and the UN system, 2) preparatory seminars prior to UN sessions, 3) technical and advisory assistance, 4) information dissemination, and 5) an internship program. The latest training program took place at the United Nations in Geneva from 26 July–8 August. Through the EP, approximately 25 Members have gained greater and more effective access to the UN.

Another aspect of prominence for the EP during 1997 was the publication of the *UNPO Monitor*, a daily English and Spanish summary of debate during the sessions of the Working Group on Indigenous Populations and the Inter-sessional Working Group forming the draft Declaration on the Rights of Indigenous Peoples. The *UNPO Monitor* allows non-Members to acquire important information regarding developments within these forums.

For years, the organization has worked to develop a support-network for its *Conflict Prevention and Management Program*. To a degree, support has been successfully obtained and is used for activities designed and intended to help detect, prevent and resolve violent conflicts of two types: 1) conflicts between minorities, peoples and other populations and the state governments in whose borders they reside, and 2) internal conflicts among and between the population groups themselves. It is under the guidance of the Conflict Prevention and Management Program that many of the activities (election monitoring, fact-finding and diplomatic missions, and negotiation training, etc.) of the UNPO are conducted.

As the UNPO has consistently highlighted, the close of the Cold War has experienced the rise of 'intra-state' conflicts. Increasingly, the international community must find new methods to first prevent, and if necessary contain, these conflicts. The most frequent causes of a substantial number of such conflicts is the suppression or violation of the rights of smaller peoples and the often concomitant refusal to take their aspirations seriously. The UNPO organizes conferences and seminars with experts and representatives of governments and international organizations for senior representatives of nations, peoples and minorities intended to examine and explore ways to improve conflict prevention and resolution. To facilitate effective conflict prevention and management, the UNPO utilizes long-standing relationships of trust with its Members; the growing respect of governments, international organizations and NGOs; and, its reputation in helping to prevent conflicts of an intra-state nature. The investment involved in developing trust with affected groups, as well as their education and training in the techniques and tools of diplomacy and negotiation, has thus far reaped increasingly successful results. Throughout 1997, the UNPO has increased its contacts with other organizations working in the field of conflict prevention, preventive diplomacy and early-warning. UNPO representatives have attended a number of conferences and seminars on the topic, often as speakers, including the European Conference on Conflict Prevention held in Amsterdam in February. The UNPO is also on the Steering Committee of the Dutch Center for Conflict Prevention and is part of the Netherlands Platform for 50 Years of the Universal Declaration of Human Rights.

In efforts to keep both the Members and the wider-public informed, during 1997 the *Media and Information Center* issued more than 25 news-releases (*summaries of a selection of these are contained in this volume*), as well as providing continued coordination of press conferences and the facilitation of Member-press relations. The *UNPO News* was published quarterly in both Russian and English.

Despite all of these considerable efforts, a more effective means of keeping the disparate Members informed and involved in one another's struggles and activities must still be developed. Solidarity can be an extremely effective tool, but it is one which is being insufficiently used by the UNPO and its Members. With the help of Scania, the UNPO has expanded both the amount and scope of information regarding its activities and members on the organization's Internet-site, and advances made late this year will continue into 1998.

The UNPO has come of age. It has successfully passed the tests and obstacles of birth and childhood. Today it is widely recognized as a positive force on the international scene and it has a performance record of which it can be proud. Expectations are consequently high for what the UNPO can do to assist its Members and to prevent or help resolve conflicts now that the voice of many of its Members is, some for the first time, being heard. The challenge is to build steadily and securely on what has been achieved. In the process of doing so, it is for the Members of the organization to determine what the UNPO can best contribute to the achievement of their individual and collective aspirations—and the aspiration of world peace.

ANNUAL REPORT OF THE GENERAL ASSEMBLY CHAIRMAN

Seif Sharif Hamad

The General Assembly, composed of delegations of all participating nations and peoples, is the highest organ of the UNPO. As required by the UNPO Covenant, the General Assembly holds its regular session at least once every two years. In July, the fifth UNPO General Assembly was held in Otepää, Estonia.

UNPO Members used this Assembly to share their experiences, successes and problems, and, in doing so, drew support from each other. After considering reports from all Member participants, the General Assembly passed a number of resolutions aimed at alleviating the plight of individual participants. At the same time, the General Assembly took stock of achievements and shortcomings in the organization's performance since the previous Assembly (held in January 1995) and laid down strategies that would guide the Steering Committee and the Secretariat in performing its functions over the next two years.

In addition, the General Assembly elected a new Chairman, two Vice-Chairmen, and a number of Steering Committee members. The election of a successor to the first General Secretary (Dr. Michael van Walt) was postponed until a special March 1998 extraordinary General Assembly. Dr. van Walt has served as a very able and committed General Secretary since the founding of the UNPO in 1991, and the General Assembly paid him a glowing tribute for his dedication in serving UNPO Members and their causes. Dr. van Walt indicated his willingness to continue serving the organization should the new General Secretary wish, and it is my anticipation that he will continue to be of service to the UNPO in the years to come.

The meeting in Estonia did draw almost all Member nations and peoples. But, unfortunately, it did not attract the desired turn out of international media—essential in bringing to the world's attention the little known accounts of the struggles waged by the participants in their respective environs. Hence, in the future it is imperative that the use of modern communications technology be a matter of priority in informing the world of our individual plights.

Every UNPO Member in attendance received the satisfaction of knowing that they were not alone in their suffering. In meeting face-to-face with others possessing similar experiences, the Members confirmed their belief and hope that their voices must and will be heard. Each Member was made more conscious of the importance of the UNPO in uniting them in their common struggle. It became more apparent that, if strengthened further, the UNPO would serve as a collective tool to champion the individual as well as collective cause of the Members. The spirit prevailing by the end of the fifth General Assembly was that 'united we stand, divided we fall.'

I look forward to cherishing that spirit.

ANNUAL REPORT OF THE STEERING COMMITTEE PRESIDENT

Dr. Parris Chang

In 1997, the Steering Committee (SC) underwent a significant change in both its operation and function. It is now required that the 12 SC Member nations and peoples send the same delegates to every meeting. Each of these individuals is still the representative of the UNPO Member, but it becomes their responsibility to fully participate in the SC on behalf of the Member. Such a change was deemed imperative because the SC must make decisions on a number of issues at each meeting, and, therefore, delegates to the SC must be consistently knowledgeable regarding previous deliberations and general UNPO functions and policies.

At the fifth General Assembly (GA) in July, the organization and the decision-making process of the UNPO were also restructured. As a result, an Executive Committee consisting of the SC President, the General Secretary, and the Treasurer now discharge the regular responsibilities of the organization. The SC President has overall responsibility in leading the organization and, as such, convenes the Executive Committee, sets priorities and oversees the operations of the Secretariat. In doing so, he carries out these functions on behalf of, and reports to, the SC. The SC held three regular sessions during 1997, and, in Bonn on 17–18 April, admitted three new UNPO Members.

A primary responsibility of the SC during the second half of the year was the task of searching for qualified candidates to replace Dr. Michael van Walt, who stepped down as General Secretary in July after six years of service. Additionally, the SC worked on the organization of an extraordinary GA, planned for March 1998, to elect a new General Secretary. The SC has worked closely with the Election Committee to establish the criteria and search procedures for the candidates, with the Election Committee screening applicants, interviewing those qualified and reporting to, and consulting with, the SC. At its 16th meeting in the Hague on 5–6 December, the SC also set up a committee for the second UNPO Awards.

The SC has 12 full members elected by the General Assembly according to a formula (taking the need for regional representation in account) developed by the fourth General Assembly. Each is represented at the SC by a senior official of the Member's choosing. *Ex officio* non-voting members of the SC are the Chairman and Vice-Chairmen of the General Assembly, with the General Secretary and the Assistant General Secretaries also invited to participate in the deliberations as non-voting members. The current SC President has appointed Mr. Akhyad Idigov (Chechenia) and Ms. Chungdak Koren (Tibet) as Vice-Presidents.

UNPO MEMBERS
(as of 31 December 1997)

SUPPORTING MEMBERS*

Armenia
Latvia
Estonia
Palau

REGULAR MEMBERS**

Abkhazia
Acheh / Sumatra
Assyria
Batwa (Rwanda)
Buryatia
Chechen Republic Ichkeria
Chuvash
Cordillera (Phillipines)
East Timor
Gagauzia
Hungarian Minority in Romania
Ingushetia
Ka Lahui Hawai'i
Komi
Kurdistan (Iraq)
Lakota Nation
Mapuche
Mon
Ogoni
Sanjak
Scania
Taiwan
Tibet
Udmurt
Zanzibar
Aboriginals of Australia
Albanians in Macedonia
Bashkortostan
Bougainville
Cabinda
Chittagong Hill Tracts
Circassians
Crimean Tatars
Eastern Turkestan
Greek Minority in Albania
Inkeri
Iraqi Turkman
Karenni State
Kosova
Kumyk
Maohi
Mari
Nagaland
Sakha Republic (Yakutia)
Shan States
Republic of South Moluccas
Tatarstan
Tyva
West Papua

* Georgia was suspended as a Supporting Member in 1996.
** Chameria was suspended as a Regular Member in 1996.

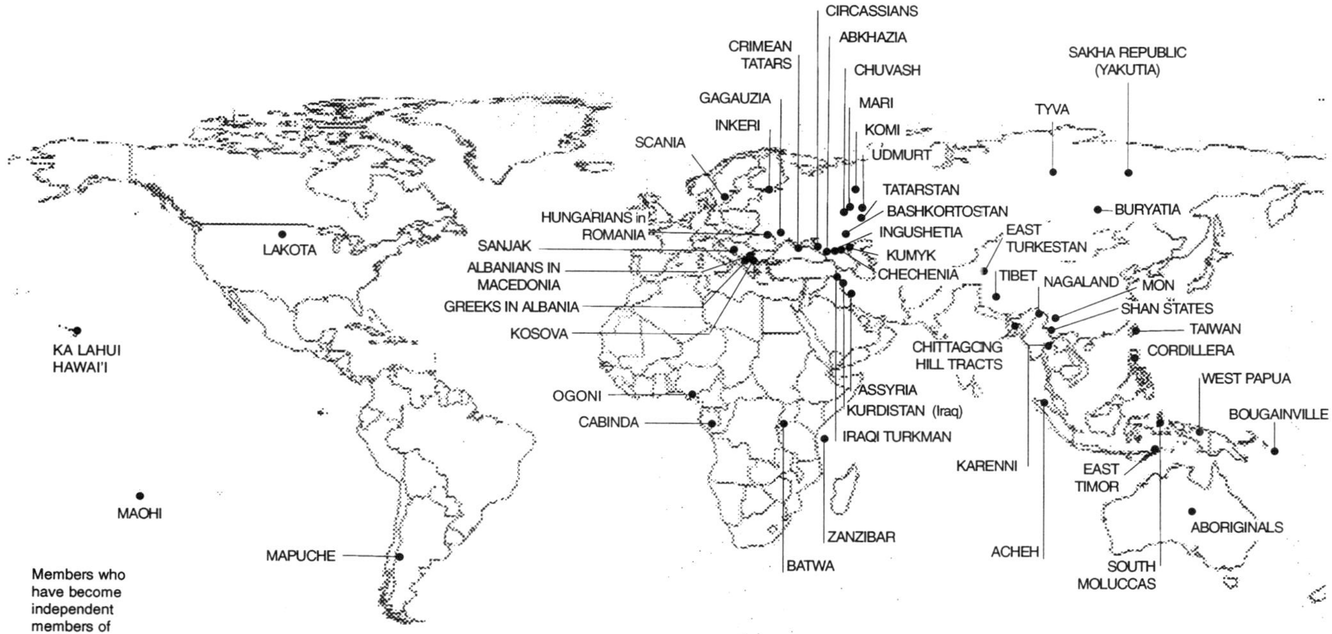

Members who
have become
independent
members of
the United Nations:
ARMENIA
ESTONIA
LATVIA
PALAU

Note: The borders shown above are used solely for geographic reference.

UNPO MEMBERS ANNUAL REPORTS

Preface to Member Reports

The following reports reflect the positions and views of the respective UNPO Member nation, people or minority. The positions taken or views expressed are not necessarily supported by the other Members of the organization.

The reports for new UNPO Members—Cabinda, Kumyk and the Shan States—include general histories and background information. The annual reports for previously accepted Members focus on activities and occurrences for 1997, but also include a short summary history. More comprehensive histories for those who became Members in 1991–1996 can be found in the editions of the *UNPO Yearbook* from 1995 and 1996.

The information for the Member reports comes from the Members themselves as well as secondary sources. This information is compiled, edited and prepared by Secretariat staff for the final report. While every effort is made to verify the information contained herein, due to the difficult situations in which many UNPO Members find themselves, it is possible that errors may occur.

SUPPORTING MEMBERS

All four of the Supporting Members below were among the original 15 founding Members in February 1991. As stipulated in Article 24 of the Covenant, after each achieved independence between 1991–1994 and were admitted into the United Nations, they subsequently assumed the role of supporting member of the UNPO. Georgia, although a founding Member, was suspended in 1996.

Armenia

Armenia declared its independence from the Soviet Union in September 1991 and was shortly thereafter admitted into the United Nations.

Estonia

Two years following its declaration of independence from the Soviet Union in 1991, Estonia was admitted to the United Nations. Estonia continues to be a principal supporter of the work of the UNPO.

Latvia

Following the August 1991 coup attempt in the Soviet Union, Latvia gained full independence. In September 1991 Latvia became a recognized member of the United Nations.

Palau

On 1 October 1994, Palau achieved independence from its status as a United States administered UN Trust Territory of the Pacific Islands and was admitted to the UN as a full member.

REGULAR MEMBERS

ABKHAZIA

Location:	Western Transcaucasia
Religion:	Christianity (Orthodox) and Islam (Sunni)
Language:	Abkhazian
Population:	525,000

Since the 13th century, Abkhazia has exercised significant political autonomy until its incorporation into Russia in 1810. After the Russian revolution, Abkhazia proclaimed its independence and, in 1918, entered the North Caucasian Republic. In 1919–1920, Russia annexed the North Caucasian Republic and, in 1921, Abkhazia was proclaimed a Soviet Socialist Republic. In the same year, under pressure from Georgian Bolsheviks, it was united with Georgia. The 1925 Constitution of Abkhazia declared SSR Abkhazia a sovereign state exercising state power on its territory independently from any other power. In 1931, the political status of Abkhazia was degraded to an Autonomous Republic within Soviet Georgia. This occurred without a referendum or any form of popular consent of the Abkhaz people. The years from 1933–1953 were marked by wide-scale 'Georgianization': cultural institutions were destroyed, the Georgian language imposed and mass population transfer from Georgia to Abkhazia was conducted.

On 20 June 1990, the Georgian Supreme Soviet passed a resolution which declared all documents adopted during the Soviet era as void. In response, on 25 August 1990, the Abkhazian Supreme Soviet declared "The State Sovereignty of the Abkhazian Soviet Socialist Republic". Political tensions with Georgia became armed conflict in 1992 as Georgian troops marched into Abkhazia. In 1993, Abkhazian troops re-took the capital, Sukhum, and expelled the Georgian troops. In April 1994, an agreement was signed which foresees the elaboration of proposals on restoring state-legal relations between Georgia and Abkhazia. Russian peacekeeping troops acting on behalf of the Commonwealth of Independent States (CIS) and under UN observation, were stationed between the two sides.

On 15 February 1996, the mandate of the Russian peacekeeping forces expired. After joint-meetings, Russian Minister of Defence, Pavel Grachev, said that although on some points the opinions of the sides had become closer, serious disagreements still remained. President Ardzinba, however, declared that Abkhazia had made a substantial step towards Georgia in its compromise concerning the establishment of federative relations between them. If earlier Abkhazia insisted on confederative relations with Georgia, now Abkhazia agreed to base relations with Georgia on the basis of a Federative Union within the borders of the Georgian SSR as of 21 December 1991.

According to Abkhazia, by 1997, 60,000–70,000 Georgian refugees had returned to the Gali region; some 80% of the total number of refugees. These refugees are not registered by UNHCR and are therefore not recognized as returnees. This imposes an extra burden on the Abkhazian administration in terms of registration and humanitarian help. In spite of the April 1994 Agreement measures to restore the Abkhazian economy, the Decision of the Council of Heads of States of the CIS of 19 January 1996 adopted measures on the political and economic isolation of Abkhazia. The conditions in Abkhazia today are inappropriate not only for the return of refugees but also for the current population.

Attached to the 1994 Agreement was a Quadripartite Agreement on the voluntary return of refugees and displaces persons. The Agreement provided for the creation of relative conditions of safety for refugees and also for the economic assistance. However, the Georgian side insisted on the unconditional return of Georgian refugees to Abkhazia, whereas Abkhazia maintained that such mass and uncontrolled return of refugees would seriously destabilize the situation in Abkhazia. As the situation in the Gali region began to stabilize, the refugees spontaneously started to return to Abkhazia. In spite of requests by the Abkhazian side to UNHCR and the Russian Foreign Ministry for support in registering the refugees, no assistance was given.

In March 1997 the CIS countries agreed to having peacekeeping forces in the region around Gali as well. Abkhazia does not agree to this extension of the mandate of the forces, fearing loss of control over the region. In response, Georgia declared in June 1997 that the Russian peacekeeping forces should leave as of 1 August, if the scope of the mandate wouldn't be extended. It was decided, however, that the troops would remain until the CIS meeting in September 1997. At that meeting, the mandate of the peacekeeping forces was again prolonged until the next CIS summit in the spring of 1998.

During 1997, several attempts were made at breaking the deadlock of the negotiation process. Negotiations in Moscow that took place on 13–14 June under the mediation of the Ministry of Foreign Affairs of the Russian Federation resulted in the preparation of a protocol to be signed on the settlement of the Georgian–Abkhazian conflict, based on the Agreements reached earlier envisaging the repatriation of the refugees as well as the problem of the state-legal relations between the sides. The Georgian side, however, has so far refused to sign. On 14 August 1997, the Abkhazian President Vladislav Ardzinba and President Eduard Shevardnadze of Georgia met in the Georgian capital Tbilisi. Russian Foreign Minister Yevgeny Primakov accompanied President Ardzinba and acted as a mediator during some of the talks. The two sides signed a statement agreeing not to use arms to resolve differences and under no circumstances to allow a resumption of bloodshed. Though the two sides managed to agree on a series of key measures for resolving the conflict, significant differences remain concerning the refugee question and the status of Abkhazia.

Throughout 1997 there have been reports regarding attacks on civilians and Abkhazian police, the laying of mines and kidnapping in the Gal, Gulrypsh and Ochamchira Districts. As noted in the UN Secretary General's report of 25 April 1997, the activities of groups trained in Georgian camps are aimed at personnel of the CIS peacekeeping forces, the Abkhazian militia and the local population. Cases of hostage taking of Abkhazian civilians and their subsequent interrogation by the Ministry of Internal Affairs of Georgia seem to substantiate the Georgian involvement in planning and cooperation with these actions. More than once, the Abkhazians have appealed to the UN Secretary General, the UN Security Council, the Government of the Russian Federation and the OSCE to look into Georgia's actions that use terrorism as an instrument to put pressure on Abkhazia. President Ardzinba has also appealed directly to Georgian President Shevardnadze to take effective measures against such terrorist acts, which have so far led to the killing of over a hundred people.

The severe economic blockade imposed by the Russian Federation continues to affect the Abkhazian economy in addition to the destruction inflicted by the war. The mainstays of the economy are agriculture (citrus fruits, tea, tobacco) and tourism. Other industries are coal, iron and mining, and in 1997 the economy saw some liberalization of the sale of agricultural products to Russia (mainly mandarines and other subtropical fruits). The telephone system in and outside Abkhazia is again operating.

As of late-1997, the U.S. Congress had yet to approve the sum of $5 million for a rehabilitation project. A UN delegation is expected to arrive in Sukhum as well to assess the humanitarian needs. The European Union has developed a project for the reconstruction of the Ingur arch electrical power station. As well, some western companies are working on de-mining the Gali district.

Abkhazia become a Member of the UNPO in August 1992.

ABORIGINALS OF AUSTRALIA

Location:	Australia
Religion:	Christianity, "Dreamtime" view of life
Language:	Some 500 languages belonging to 31 language groups, with Pama-Nyungan most commonly used
Population:	300,000
Ethnic diversity:	Korris, Murris, Noongars and others

The Aboriginals have resided on the continent of Australia for over 100,000 years. Aboriginals identify themselves as Korris, Murris, Noongars and other tribal and clan names. A large majority of Aboriginals reside outside of urban areas. The Aboriginal view on life and religion is defined as 'Dreamtime' which characterizes their daily life and religious rituals.

The Aboriginal way of life came to an end with the beginning of the European invasion on 26 January 1788, when the British landed on the east coast of Australia. Anti-Slavery International instigated the establishment of the Aboriginal Protection Society in the 1880s. Nevertheless, an assimilation policy to eliminate any sense of a separate Aboriginal identity was aggressively implemented. Between 1880 and 1960, as many as 100,000 aboriginal children (known as the "Stolen Generation") were taken from their families and placed in church-run institutions . The assimilation policy came under heavy criticism in the 1960s. Following a referendum on the subject in 1967, the Commonwealth of Australia was given the power to legislate on matters concerning Aboriginals.

In 1972, The Aboriginal Land Right Commission was established and by the Aboriginal Land Rights Bill of 1976 handed about 30% of the land over to Aboriginal hands. In Queensland, where most of Aboriginals live, a more limited Land Rights Act was established. The lands of the Aboriginals have been exploited by Australian mining companies for a long time, ignoring 'native' title rights or the negative environmental impacts the mines could have.

On almost every index of social well-being Aboriginals score lower than other Australians: lower life expectancy, higher infant mortality, poor housing conditions, lower access to education and employment. A major issue is the high rates of Aboriginal arrests and imprisonment and especially of Aboriginal deaths while in official custody. According to Amnesty International report of June 1997, a disproportionate number of Aboriginals continue to die in custody, despite the initiative of the Australian government, six years ago, to implement a national program to combat the high incidence of Aboriginal deaths in custody.

In April 1997, one of the major Aboriginal groups in Australia, the Northern Land Council (NLC), presented a Human Rights Dossier to the European Commission. The dossier was prepared in reaction to the Australian refusal, in 1996, to sign a trade agreement with the EU because of the inclusion of a human rights clause. The aboriginal people of Australia feared that Australia's refusal to sign may reflect ulterior motives especially after the government said it would ignore the "Wik decision" - a ruling of the Australian High Court in December 1996 which acknowledged aboriginal land rights.

On 26 May 1997, Prime Minister John Howard made his personal apology to the Aboriginal community for Australia's historical policy of forced assimilation. The apology was made at a Conference on Reconciliation with Aboriginals, following the example of the Uniting Church of Australia which in September 1996, had apologised for Aboriginal suffering in the name of the church.

Only a few hours before the Conference started, the Australian Commission for Human Rights had released a human rights report stating that the forced assimilation policies in Australia have been equivalent to ethnic genocide. According to the UN Convention on Genocide, adopted by Australia in 1949, the Australian government is held responsible for rehabilitating victims of the "Stolen Generation"and compensating their families. Nevertheless, Mr. Howard ruled out any possibility for government compensation although he admitted to an audience of Aboriginal delegates that the forced assimilation policies "involved both systematic racial discrimination and genocide as defined by international law." An official parliamentary apology, as recommended by the Human Rights Commission, was not made.

In late May 1997, a widespread discontent against the Aboriginal population broke out, particularly among the farmers whose leasing rights were at stake after the Wik decision of December 1996. The farmers, manifested their discontent to the government and demanded that the latter responded somehow to the implications of the High Court decision.

The "Wik decision" refers to the first title claim ever taken to the High Court, in relation to a ruling of 1992. This ruling recognized the native title in Australia's common law and in addition agreed that Australia was not "uninhabited" when the colonizers arrived. This 1992 ruling, known as the Mabo case, paved the way for the Native Title Act which was passed by the Australian government in 1993. The Act legally recognized and protected the native title but it did not clarify issues such as whether the pastoral leases, granted in the meantime by the Australian government, could extinguish native titles or not. It was in the Wik case in December 1996 that the Australian High Court ruled that previously granted pastoral leases do not always extinguish native title rights on the same land. The judges found that when the rights and interests of native-title holders and pastoral-lease holders conflict, the rights of the pastoral-lease holder prevail ; however, when there is consistency as to the rights and use of the land, then the two sets of rights could co-exist.

Eventually, the "Wik decision" caused a stir among farmers but also miners who already held leases on pastoral land. In June 1997, Prime Minister Howard, in an effort to ease the minds of the alarmed pastoralists, proposed legislation which amends the implications of the Wik decision. The proposed legislation is vague regarding most of its stipulations; it combines proposed amendments to the 1993 Native Title Act with a so-called "10 Points Plan".

The main feature of the proposed legislation is that the government enables lease-holders to upgrade pastoral leases by authorising other activities such as tourism and forestry, etc. Authorising such upgrading will convert the land-leases to freehold, perpetual or "exclusive" leases, and thus, will wipe out the native title. In this case, the government acknowledges the right to compensation for indigenous people—which is expected to entail a massive compensation bill for Australian tax-payers. Another feature of the proposed legislation is to impose severe limits to negotiation powers of indigenous people with respect to their native title on land, especially to areas where mining development plans have been proposed by lease-holders. The proposed legislation has already passed in the House of Representatives but met the strong opposition of the Senate when it was presented to them on the 1st of December. The opposition Labor Party, the Greens and the Democrats rejected most of the bill's "anti-aboriginal" clauses. The Prime minister threatens now to dissolve the parliament and call a general election, thus making aboriginal rights *the* voting issue.

Aboriginal and Islander organisations participated again in 1997 in the UN Commission for Human Rights Working Group and the Working Group on Indigenous Populations and in many other international fora.

The Australian Aboriginals are a founding Member of UNPO. They are represented by the National Committee to Defend Black Rights (NCDBR), which represents in the UNPO a coalition of national and key regional Aboriginal organizations.

ACHEH / SUMATRA

Location:	South-east Asia
Religion:	Islam
Language:	Achehnese, Gayo and Malay
Population:	5 million

Acheh makes up the northern most side of the island of Sumatra, bordered on the North by the Malaca Straits. In the 16th and 17th centuries, Acheh was one of the most powerful kingdoms in the region. Unlike many countries in Southeast Asia, Acheh resisted Western imperialism. The Dutch waged a colonial war for control of Acheh which lasted 69 years, ending unsuccessfully in 1942. The newly independent state of Indonesia, based on the island of Java, annexed Acheh with the help of the Netherlands in 1949, without a referendum and against the principles of international law and the law of decolonization. On 4 December 1976, Tengku Hasan di Tiro, the president of the Acheh-Sumatra National Liberation Front (ASNLF), proclaimed independence of Acheh. Since that time at least 50,000 Achehnese have been killed and many more tortured and imprisoned by the Indonesian occupation forces. Because foreign journalists are prohibited from visiting Acheh, human rights violations have gone largely unreported or reports have been ignored on the grounds that they could not be confirmed.

Acheh produces 50% of Indonesia's oil and gas. In addition, Acheh's economy relies on agricultural production, timber and other natural resource extraction. Despite the enormous natural wealth of the country, the Achehnese live in dire poverty. Much of Acheh's raw materials are exploited by and removed to Java, leaving no wealth creating activities for the Achehnese. Such projects are often carried out in conjunction with multinational corporations, whose profits are transferred to abroad. Moreover, this activity often leads to environmental destruction resulting from deforestation and pollution.

Due to the heavy military presence in Acheh, the human rights situation in 1997 has deteriorated. The population continues to be subjected to Indonesian military control, to arbitrary arrests, to imprisonment, to summary executions. Freedom of movement is seriously constricted and travellers must show an identity card. Night patrols in villages have been intensified and suspected members of the Free Acheh movement continue to be arrested. Social gatherings are prohibited and there is no freedom of expression. Achehnese experience discrimination in their own country and are excluded from good jobs which mainly go to Javanese who have migrated to the area under government encouragement.

Under the code name *Operasi Jaring Kikis*, or Operation Network Extermination, the Indonesian armed forces began a new wave of military operations in January 1997. Firearms were confiscated and 14 people arrested for alleged involvement in the Free Acheh Movement. According to the Indonesian Human Rights periodical *Tapol*, the military activity in Acheh had reached a new pitch.

Roadblocks were set up on main roads to check on the travelling public, who are subject to identity card checks, questioning and body searches. The armed forces justified their intensified presence by a series of bank robberies in January and February.[1]

One of these robberies, committed in February, was randomly attributed to a commander of the Free Acheh Movement, Mr. Rahman Paloh. Many Achehnese were arrested and later pictures of the dead Mr. Paloh and his lieutenant were printed in the local newspaper. It was reported that they had been ambushed and killed by the Indonesian military. Witnesses to the robbery said the two did not at all resemble those who had actually committed the crime.

Due to the human rights abuses perpetrated by the Indonesian regime, many young Achehnese are forced to leave the country for asylum in Malaysia. Due to threat of forced repatriation, 30 Achehnese members of the ASNLF scaled the security perimeters of nine embassies in Kuala Lumpur, Malaysia, in January 1997. Those who had entered the United States British, Italian and French embassies were later arrested by the Malaysian police with the help of the respective embassy guards. The remaining eight were detained in the Swiss and Dutch embassies, where they asked for resettlement in a third country. In March, word was received that, through mediation of the authorities from Switzerland, the Netherlands and the UNHCR, an understanding was reached with the Malaysian government which would allow the eight to stay in Malaysia, without fear of arrest.

According to the written account of the eight asylum seekers who were removed from the British High Commission, they were not able to get past the High Commission's Malaysian security guard, to whom they made their intentions clear and to whom they displayed the Achehnese flag. They believe security misinformed the eight that their case could not be handled due to Christmas holiday absences (many staff live on the premises). As the guard left them for a brief period, the eight assumed their request was being reported. However, within a half an hour Malaysian police arrived. In the presence of two British diplomats, who remained inside the Commission's compound, the Achehnese were forcibly removed despite their repeated calls to meet the British ambassador.

International law provides that diplomatic premises not be used by police to identify and detain people seeking asylum. The British Foreign Office, claims the men did not make their intentions clear. However, the Achehnese were only able to speak to the Malaysian security guard in Malay and not without risk to their safety. If Malaysia recognizes the Achehnese as political refugees, this could be seen as acknowledging the ongoing war in Acheh. This, in turn, would jeopardize relations between Malaysia and Indonesia.[2]

The Malaysian government has been carrying out a policy of placing illegal immigrants in detention centers to await repatriation to Indonesia. These include many Indonesians who are seeking work. However, the Achehnese immigrants are seeking refuge and face danger if repatriated. In September, the ASNLF reported that Achehnese asylum seekers who were being detained in such Malaysian immigration 'depots' were being mistreated by the police and denied medical treatment. In February and November respectively, two Achehnese died in detention centers from injuries incurred during an uprising against forced repatriation in December 1996. These injuries, received from the Malaysian police, were never properly attended.[3]

In an August press release from the Acheh/Sumatra National Liberation Front, it was disclosed that the military commander for North Sumatra and Acheh, Major General Sedaryanto, offered money or a job in exchange for illegal or confiscated weapons. According to the ASNLF, this would incite people to kill suspected members of the Free Acheh Movement without proof or investigation.

Acheh/Sumatra became a Member of the UNPO in August 1991.

ALBANIANS IN MACEDONIA

Location:	(Former-Yugoslav) Republic of Macedonia
Religion:	Islam and Christianity (Orthodox)
Language:	Albanian
Population:	700,000 (approximate)

Before the independence of Macedonia in 1992, the Albanians enjoyed the same constitutional rights as all other Yugoslavs. After 1992, Macedonia changed its constitution at the expense of the non-Slav people living in Macedonia. The Macedonian government asserts that Albanians are one of the minority populations in Macedonia and cannot, therefore, make claims of equality as a people. Nevertheless, the Albanians in Macedonia wish to be treated equally.

Tensions between the Albanians and Macedonians in Macedonia started well before the republic's declaration of independence. Since 1981 many Albanians have been dismissed from their jobs by the Macedonian authorities. The army, the police, the judiciary and the economy have largely been dominated by Macedonians and they have generally decided who is to get jobs or licenses.[4] A large portion of Macedonia's population was forced to seek work abroad since there have not been enough job opportunities in the FYROM. This is particularly true for emigré Albanians, who, as a negative consequence, have lost their right to vote.

In January 1992, the Albanians in Macedonia organized a successful referendum on territorial autonomy. The Macedonian government interpreted that as a first step toward secession and declared the referendum illegal. Shortly afterwards, the Council of Albanian Political Parties in the Former Yugoslavia—an umbrella organization of ethnic Albanians in Kosova, Montenegro, Serbia proper and Macedonia—decided that autonomy would only be an option for the Albanians in Macedonia if other democratic efforts to gain political and cultural rights fail.

The Albanians in Macedonia have long demanded higher education in the Albanian language, but without success. Admission to middle and higher education is made very difficult for Albanians; most higher education is in the Macedonian language. In reaction the Albanian population mobilized support, selected a building in Tetovo and proceeded to create an Albanian language university. The Albanian demand of 1995 to legalize the University in Tetovo has still not been met. The University is still considered illegal by the Macedonian authorities, however, at the same time it is condoned. In May 1997, the Tetovo University again received support from the Albanian community and its political Leaders. Since the first students will graduate soon, it is expected that new difficulties will arise, as it seems highly unlikely that their diplomas will be recognized by the State. [5]

There are some possibilities for Albanians to receive higher-education at the

Skopje Faculty of Arts and in Albanian language and literature courses at the Skopje Faculty of Philology. In 1997, at the Skopje Pedagogical Faculty, instruction in Albanian was introduced, a possibility which already existed in Bitola at their Pedagogical Faculty.[6]

Until recently, Macedonia, has been able to avoid the ethnic tension and bloodshed that other former Yugoslav states have suffered. The elections at the end of May 1997 resulted in a leftist coalition government including five ethnic Albanians. In Albania, elections are based on a district system which, according to Albanians, are being gerrymandered by the Macedonian authorities in order for the number of Albanians in Parliament to be minimalized. Albanians are currently represented in the 120-seat Macedonian Parliament by 19 members from three different political parties. Five of the 20 ministers in the government are Albanians (Party for Democratic Prosperity). Although Albanians received increasingly more representation in the state administration, proportionally Macedonians are still over-represented. For example, Albanians now constitute only 2.9% of Ministry of Defense civilians.[7]

Due to the collapse of the pyramid schemes in Albania, many weapons stolen during the chaos that followed were smuggled in Macedonia. This poses a threat to the relative stability in Macedonia. The smuggling also led to several incidents at the Macedonian-Albanian border, which further decreased stability.

The elections in Macedonia were followed by ethnic disturbances. Tension culminated on 9 July 1997, when the new mayors of Gostivar and Tetovo, both Albanian nationalists, insisted on flying Albanian flags on their respective town halls. This had become illegal the day before by the passage of a law on the use of minority flags. As a consequence, special anti-terrorist forces removed the flags which resulted in demonstrations by a few thousand Albanians. During heavy riots, involving excessive force against demonstrators by the police, three Albanians were killed and hundreds including children were injured in what has become known as the 'Gostivar incident'.

Mr. Rufi Osmani, the mayor of Gostivar, was charged with inciting racial hatred and accused of plotting for a 'Greater Albania'. The rising tension is partly a result of increasing Albanian nationalism and a revival of Islam. It has led to opposing national feelings among the Slav majority, beginning a vicious circle termed by President Gligorov, President of Macedonia, as "the rising ghosts of nationalism". Among some Macedonians there is a call for a "Greater Macedonia". In March 1997 a group of Macedonian students chanted "Albanians to the gas chambers", during a demonstration in Skopje.[8]

Although tensions rose because of the above, the government of the FYROM has advanced the human rights situation of the country somewhat in 1997. Macedonia ratified the European Convention on Human Rights and several of its Protocols. Other measures were also taken, such as the installment of an

Ombudsman in March. A new Law of Criminal Procedure was passed as well, which requires the police to have a court order before they can take someone for "informative talks". This is a notable achievement. However, this law was already violated in the Gostivar incident.

The Special Rapporteur of the UN Commission on Human Rights, Ms. Elisabeth Rehn, recommended to the Macedonian government that police should receive a strengthened training programme, supervised by the United Nations Preventive Deployment Force (UNPREDEP). She also expressed her concern that the Gostivar incident was not investigated properly, with no police officers incriminated, while legal proceedings for the demonstrators and the mayors advanced rapidly.[9]

The Albanians in Macedonia became a Member of the UNPO in 1993.

ASSYRIA

Location:	Middle East (present-day Iraq, Iran, Turkey and Syria)
Language:	Assyrian (Aramaic)
Religion:	Christianity
Population:	3,305,000 (home-region and diaspora)

The Assyrians are an ancient and distinct people, who today live in more than 40 countries, with over 2.5 million still living in the Middle East. The region from the Hikkari mountains to the Mosul district is the Assyrian nation's ancestral homeland, with Ninevah as its historical capital. The homeland, formerly known as Mesopotamia, is in present day Iraq.

The Assyrians are credited with the first alphabetically written language, a form of Aramaic. Although living in a predominately Muslim region, the Assyrians are Christians. In the first century they were among the first people to embrace Christianity. Living apart from the Christian world the Assyrians came close to losing their identity as a nation. It was not until the middle of the 19th century that they came into direct contact with the western world and their existence attracted attention from the outside world. Experiencing a cultural renaissance, they built modern schools, colleges and technical institutions in Iran and Iraq during the 19th and 20th centuries.

Assyrians suffered destructive blows because of their religion and ethnicity. They fell victim to the wholesale massacre inflicted upon Christians under the Ottoman Empire. Those who escaped the massacres fled their homeland to join the Assyrians living in Iran. At the end of World War I, the Assyrians were left without any support and no choice but to retreat from Iran in order to reach the British forces in Baghdad. In this long and costly exodus, the Assyrians lost more than two-thirds of their population. In return for the loss of their homeland in Hikkari (Turkey) and in compensation for great losses inflicted on them during World War I, Assyrians were promised by Britain, France and Russia a safe and independent homeland. This promise was not fulfilled and Assyrians were again betrayed and left unsupported in a situation that culminated in the massacre of a non-combatant population in Simeil, Iraq in 1933. From this time on, the Assyrian diaspora started and they fled in all directions as refugees to find a safe haven and protect themselves from total elimination.

Prior to the Gulf War more than 400 Assyrian villages were obliterated by the Iraqi government and much of the Assyrian population in the north of Iraq were forcibly transferred to the larger cities such as Baghdad. The 1991 Gulf War further aggravated the situation of the Assyrians; more than 250,000 Assyrians fled Iraq. The incursion of the Turkish army into northern Iraq in an attempt to end PKK armed activities in 1995 took its toll on the civilian population including the Assyrians.

Although the Kurds and Assyrians had joined forces at the time, their relationship has since deteriorated. Many Assyrian villages and farmlands are being occupied by their Kurdish neighbours. The continuous internal fighting between the two parties of Kurds, the Patriotic Union of Kurdistan (PUK) and the Kurdistan Democratic Party (KDP), which flared up again in September 1996, has led to several armed conflicts and general unrest in the region. The attack on the city of Erbil by KDP forces supported by the Iraqi army resulted in the killing of many Assyrians, the looting of Assyrian offices, cultural centres and schools and a manhunt for members of the Assyrian Democratic Movement. Since the Assyrians have not taken sides in the conflict between the KDP and PUK, their future in the areas is uncertain.

Currently, there are thousands of Assyrians still stranded as refugees in Jordan, Turkey, Greece, Austria, Spain and several other countries. Their families have been separated and sent to different countries and continents. There are over a million Assyrians scattered and living in over 40 countries. It should be said of the Assyrians today that although they are scattered all over the world, as descendants of a great nation they live in peace and dignity in each country in which they become citizens. As a result of this attitude they have gained the respect of their fellow countrymen. In most of these countries, for example, in the U.S., Australia, Iran and Syria they have run for public offices and have been elected to important positions.

For 1998, the AUA in co-sponsorship with the UNPO is planning a world conference of Assyrians in Geneva in an effort to tell the world who the Assyrians are, to tell about their plight and endeavour to gain support and understanding of the Assyrian situation by the United Nations and Government Officials. The AUA has accepted an invitation of Iran to hold its 1998 Congress meeting in the capital of Teheran. The AUA is also planning to continue its presentation about the Assyrian people to the UN Working Group on Minorities and its Commission on Human Rights.

The Assyrian Universal Alliance (AUA) became a Member of the UNPO in 1991. The aim of the AUA is to spread, uphold and enhance the Assyrian name in the world and to secure the human rights of the Assyrian people in their homeland.

BASHKORTOSTAN

Location:	Russian Federation
Religion:	Islam
Language:	Bashkir and Russian
Population:	4.1 million

The Republic of Bashkortostan is situated in the South Ural mountains and borders Tatarstan, the Udmurt Republic and the provinces of Perm, Yekaterinburg, Chelyabinsk and Orenburg. As one of the largest agricultural regions in the Russian Federation, it contributes significantly to Russia's GNP.

Bashkirs were first noted historically in the 9th century, living as farmers and hunter-gatherers. Later they formed several mini-states in the Turkic valleys of the Middle Volga, the Povolgie Basin and the southern steppe. Genghis Khan's forces invaded in 1224 and afterwards the region was ruled by the Golden Horde until 1557, when part of the Bashkirs fell under the rule of Nogay Orda of the Siberian and Kazan Khanates. There followed two centuries of struggle between the Russian government and the local population. Bashkirs were subjected to serfdom and forcible Christianization.

Between 1905–1915 Bashkirs lands were plundered. Local historians cite the deaths of more than half a million Bashkirs in 1917–1921 as being a direct result of starvation caused by civil war. During this period Bashkortostan became an official Autonomous Soviet Republic, accepting the constitution of the USSR in 1937 and becoming a state that same year. However, Bashkortostan possessed no sovereign rights to pass its own legislation or to set financial budgets. In 1978, a new constitution was adopted further reducing sovereignty and allowing no independence in the management of its natural resources. As *glasnost* swept through the USSR in 1980, a movement calling for more autonomy for the Republic was formed. A mass collection of signatures from all nationalities helped usher in economic independence and a new federal state.

In 1990, Murtaza Rachimov was elected as the new Chairman of the Supreme Council of the Bashkir Republic. That same year Bashkortostan declared its state sovereignty and on 3 August 1994, a treaty of accord was signed between the Republic of Bashkortostan and the Russian Federation. Under this treaty, the sovereignty of Bashkortostan was partially recognized by Russia. The highest representative body of Bashkortostan, a two-chamber parliament, was elected in 1995 and an all-Bashkir Assembly (*Kurultay*) was held in Ufa marking a milestone in political development.

Elections and a Congress of the Peoples of Bashkortostan are due to take place in 1998. It is expected that Moscow will seek to erode the new-found political status of the Republic to that of a provincial level. The Bashkirian President Murtaza Rakhimov remains in power as the head of the government. The working language of the government is Russian although various organizations are campaigning for

Bashkirian to also become an official language at government level. The Secretary of the All-World Kurultary of Bashkirs is currently developing education in the Bashkir language

On the agrarian front, Bashkirs are against the privatisation and sale of state farms, given that collective ownership is traditional to their culture and that much has been lost with speculative land deals in the past. The government is supporting the agricultural sector with fuel vouchers and other assistance and rural life has improved in relation to other parts of the former USSR.

Contact with foreign governments and organizations is on the increase. On 22 October the Government of Bashkortostan signed an agreement with the Government of the Netherlands to provide non-economic technical assistance in support of the social transformation process. In addition to this, economic support will come from the Dutch Programme for Co-operation in Eastern-Europe. In Estonia a delegation unveiled a statue of the Bashkirian hero Salavat Yulyayev in Paldiski. In May, a youth delegation participated in the Finno-Ugrian Peoples Youth Assembly in Estonia and, in July, the Chairman of the Bashkortostan National Center, Mr Akhtar Buskunov, participated in the UNPO General Assembly in Estonia.

The recent decade has seen a rebirth of interest in Bashkirian culture and religious life. Bashkirs from all over the former Soviet Union are returning to their homeland. Education in the Bashkirian language is now available at high school level and the creation of terminology for specialty courses is in development. Courses in the Bashkiri language are optional.

The Republic of Bashkortostan became a Member of the UNPO in 1996, represented by the Government and Parliament of the Republic of Bashkortostan.

BATWA

Location: Rwanda
Religion: Christianity and traditional religion
Language: Kinyarwanda
Population: 19,000

The Batwa are the indigenous inhabitants of Rwanda, in Central East Africa, and currently make up a small segment of Rwandan society.[10] Originally, the Batwa lived as hunters and collectors in the rain forests (Gishwati and Nyungwe) that covered Rwanda. In the course of the centuries, due to deforestation by farmers and cattle herders, the Batwa were driven out of their natural habitat. Nowadays, the Batwa of Rwanda can roughly be divided into two groups: the semi-nomadic Batwa of the forest and the sedentary Batwa. Their traditions are rich in song, dance and music, and cultural gatherings are firmly integrated into Batwa society. The Batwa form an isolated and marginalized group in Rwandan society. Traditionally looked down upon by the other groups as backward and dirty, there is little economic and social integration. Access to education, health care, media and housing is limited.

With some 7.3 million inhabitants, Rwanda was one of the world's most densely populated countries before the genocide and war in 1994. The Batwa made up only 0.4%, some 29,000 people, whereas the Hutu and Tutsi comprised 85% and 14% respectively of the total population in Rwanda. It is estimated that between 500,000 and one million people, mainly Tutsi, were killed during the genocide and another two million fled the country. Rough estimates for the present Batwa population, based on a provisional census carried out by the UNPO in late 1994, indicate that up to 10,000 Batwa died. Another 8,000 to 10,000 fled, leaving the post-war Batwa population in Rwanda between 10,000 and 20,000.

In order to defend the rights and interests of the Batwa, the Association for the Promotion of Batwa (APB) was created in 1991. In May 1995, the Batwa founded the Community of Indigenous Peoples of Rwanda (CAURWA), uniting the three existing Batwa organizations, the Association for the Global Development of the Batwa (ADBR), the Association for the Integration of the Orphans (APEDE) and the APB.[11]

In 1996, a Batwa representative attended the UN working Group on Indigenous Populations and the UN Sub-Commission on Prevention of Discrimination and Protection of Minorities, in Geneva. The UN Sub-Commission passed a resolution on the human rights situation in Rwanda, calling upon "the Government of Rwanda to devote particular attention to the situation of the Twa (...)".[12]

During 1997, the situation for the Batwa has not changed much, since no Batwa was admitted to the central administration at community, prefectoral or ministry level. No constructive action has been taken by the government to protect the

Batwa and they still are a minority that live on the margins of Rwandan society.

Since 1996, the Rwandan government has made efforts to facilitate the process of voluntary and safe return, resettlement and reintegration of the large number of refugees in the neighbouring countries. In 1997, the situation of the returnees has improved somewhat and the Batwa have established co-operation with several international governmental and non-governmental organizations, such as UNHCR, the European Union and most notably the World Rainforest Movement. Specific investigations by international organizations into the situation of the Batwa, however, were hardly carried out .

The human rights situation in Rwanda for the Batwa differed from region to region in 1997. In some regions Batwa were forced from their property. Acts of intimidation and violence continued unabated, particularly by former Rwandan soldiers and militia living in the refugee camps. Based on a resolution by the UN, the Rwanda Tribunal was set up to punish those responsible for the genocide. In 1997, 3,000 Batwa remained in prison (since 1994), without being charged or tried and there was no indication of a chance for them to be released in the near future.

Because of their poverty, over 4,000 Batwa families live in inadequate housing. Although the Rwandan government has adopted a housing policy, the Batwa are not well informed about it. The APB, therefore, travels throughout the country to persuade the Batwa to accept this offer from the government. The Rwandan Minister of Social Affairs gave his approval to a Batwa project, which enabled the Batwa to apply for aid from the UNHCR.[13] This APB/Femmes Nsanabandi project operates in six prefectures (urban Kigali, rural Kigali, Gitarama, Kibungo, Byumba and Umutara). The project enabled 52 women to form co-operatives, by financing farming tools.

Of the Batwa population, 98% are illiterate and 68% of Batwa children do not attend school. To stimulate school attendance the APB opened an account to help children to visit the schools more frequently. The aforementioned APB/Femmes Nsanabandi project also provided equipment for primary education. In January 1997, the APB has also established a scholarship programme for secondary education. Additionally, a project for adult education will commence in 1998.

In January, a roundtable organized by the APB, was held in Rwanda, at which the Batwa discussed issues that related to the economic, social and legal situation. The roundtable requested a national conference to be held, bringing together all ethnic groups of Rwanda to discuss their problems. Furthermore, the roundtable asked for legal assistance for the Batwa accused of having taken part in the genocide. It also urged the state to stop arbitrary arrests of the Batwa and to protect the Batwa minority in Rwanda, by fulfilling the international human rights standards which the Rwandan government has signed or says it supports.

CAUWRA hosted a presentation of Batwa at a National Commercial Exhibition in Kigali in 1997, in order to raise awareness for the Batwa. This gave the Batwa the opportunity to demonstrate their skills in pottery, one of their traditional crafts. The UN High Commissioner for Human Rights expressed willingness to support the Batwa, by assuring that a permanent exhibition site will be launched in Kigali.

All of these projects have raised the awareness of the relief agencies in the field towards the Batwa and some are willing to assist or are already assisting the Batwa in small projects.

The Batwa, with the APB as its representative body, joined the UNPO in 1993.

BOUGAINVILLE

Location: South Pacific
Religion: Christianity
Language: English and Pidgin
Population: 160,000

The island which would later be called Bougainville was first sighted in 1768 and was later annexed by the German New Guinea Company. The Agreement of 1899 between Germany and Great Britain separated Bougainville from the other Solomon Islands which fell under British control. Bougainville remained under German control until after World War I, when the German New Guinea territories became Mandate Territories of the League of Nations and were placed under Australian administration. Bougainvillians objected to their separation from the Solomon Islands. During World War II, Bougainville was the scene of fierce fighting and was again put under Australian administration, this time as a United Nations Trust Territory. Two weeks before Papua New Guinea (PNG) gained statehood in 1975, Bougainville unilaterally declared its independence, emphasizing its wish to remain separate from PNG. Despite appeals to the United Nations, Bougainville was incorporated into PNG territory against the wishes of its people.

By 1988, tensions had escalated into violence as it became increasingly clear that mining profits from an Australian joint-venture on the island were not benefiting the people of Bougainville and that the mining activity was seriously damaging the island's environment. That year, an organized group of traditional landowners, later known as the Bougainville Revolutionary Army (BRA), forcibly closed the mine and demanded the re-negotiation of contracts. PNG responded by sending in the Police Riot Squad and the Defence Forces, displacing some 24,000 villagers.[14] In May, 1990 Bougainville declared its independence officially for the second time and established the Bougainville Interim Government (BIG). Forced to withdraw from the island, PNG officials retaliated by enforcing a complete economic and communications blockade. In the nine-year conflict the number of lives lost to fighting and the blockade has been estimated at 15,000, almost 10% of the total population.[15]

Since 1990, no less than six serious attempts have been made to reach a political settlement to the conflict. Nearly every year for the past eight, peace talks between the BIG and the Government of PNG were initiated but have consistently deteriorated into the recommencement of violence. In September 1994, the Margini Charter led the way to the establishment of the Bougainville Transitional Government (BTG), under the auspices of the PNG. As the BIG boycotted this meeting, PNG saw the opportunity to select BTG representatives. However, in 1996 the BTG Premier was assassinated, with independent inquiries verifying the involvement of the PNG security forces.

In 1997, this history of failed peace accords degenerated to the extent that, in February, it was announced that PNG Prime Minister Sir Julius Chan had approved the use of foreign mercenaries to wipe out the rebel leadership in Bougainville. A

South African based mercenary establishment was hired to plan and execute the operation.[16] Within a month, international uproar and domestic opposition, led by the PNG defence commander himself, led to a capitulation on the part of PNG and the stepping down of the Prime Minister. Elections in July designated a new Prime Minister, ushering in a new era in PNG-Bougainville relations.

During the 53rd meeting of the UN Commission on Human Rights in April, the New Zealand delegation approached the BIG Secretary, Martin Miriori, in order to express New Zealand's interest in reinstating the peace talks. Representatives from the BIG and BTG met with New Zealand government officials in Wellington from 13–15 June, where they arranged the preliminary round of peace talks which would take place in July.

At Burnham Army Base, near Christchurch, New Zealand, members of the BIG, BTG and the BRA met from 5–18 July. The meeting culminated in a joint declaration which called for a ceasefire and the complete demilitarisation of the island, as well as the installation of UN peacekeeping forces on Bougainville. A commitment to set up a process of negotiation toward ending the war was also included in the declaration.

Various follow-up visits were made by the BIG Secretary to gain support for the peace process, in particular the issue of a peacekeeping force. At the invitation of the UN, Mr. Miriori met with the President of the UN Security Council and other permanent missions to the UN and the Members of the Security Council, including those from the Pacific. Following the ACP–EU 1997 resolution on Bougainville, which had called for a fact-finding mission to Bougainville, Mr. Miriori met with Dutch, Danish and British MEPs to brief them on the situation. Mr. Miriori also carried out ongoing consultations with the Foreign Ministry of the Netherlands, where he lives in exile and who are supportive of the BIG's efforts to promote peace.

In support of the Burnham Declaration, visits to Bougainville were made in August by the new PNG Prime Minister and the New Zealand Foreign Minister Don McKinnon. In this way, they displayed their support of the aims of the Declaration. The second round of Burnham talks, between senior officials, took place from 1–10 October, and included the PNG representative Robert Igara. This meeting resulted in the signing of a truce, which reaffirmed the principles contained in the preceding Declaration and called for the immediate cessation of the fighting. The real test of sincerity will lie with the leaders if the PNG, BTG, BIG and BRA who are set to meet in January 1998. This meeting of high-level officials will give the leaders the opportunity to give the final endorsement to the agreement, thereby beginning the demilitarization of the island and institution of a permanent ceasefire. The PNG Prime Minister, Bill Skate, said that if the truce is successful, his government would consider a formal ceasefire agreement.[17]

In the meantime, a Truce Monitoring Group, comprised of unarmed military personnel from New Zealand, Australia, Fiji, Vanuatu and Tonga was sent, at the end of November, to monitor the implementation of the Burnham Truce. Moreover, several monitoring teams, including PNG, Australian and New Zealand defence personnel, have visited the island to assess the ongoing peace process.[18] The people of Bougainville founded the Special Steering Committee of the Burnham Declaration in order to monitor the peace process on the ground and promote unity among the BIG/BRA and the BTG/Resistance groups.[19] The various factions are also involved in "reconciliation meetings" between the parties involved in pursuing peace talks on the island.[20] The PNG Prime Minister also directed the PNG security forces to help create an atmosphere of peace, in order to develop trust and confidence between themselves, the BTG and the BRA.[21]

Although the Burnham Declaration and the Truce enshrine the principle of self-determination for the people of Bougainville, the implementation of this principle remains to be ironed out. For the time being, the cessation of fighting and the strengthening of positive relations with the government of PNG are the primary concerns of the BIG.

Bougainville, represented by the BIG, became a Member of the UNPO in August 1991.

Buryatia

Location: Russian Federation
Religion: Buddhism
Language: Buryat and Russian
Population: 450,000

Buryat tribes are first mentioned in a Mongolian chronicle from the beginning of the 13th century, where they are referred to as the "wood people". Their ethnic origins are believed to stem from a mixture of Mongol, Turkic, Tungus, Samoyed and other peoples. Ties between the Mongol and Buryat peoples have remained close through the centuries. Organized into communities of clans, tribes and *kagants*, the Buryats converted to Buddhism around the 13th century, a religion which forms the core of their cultural and spiritual life today.

Their fertile lands and the prosperous trade routes of the region were threatened from two sides as the Russian and the Manchu Empire sought to expand their territories in the 17th century. By 1727, Russia and China had signed an agreement based on the establishment of borders and trade routes. Large numbers of Russians immigrated to the region making the Buryats a minority. Heavy taxes and the practice of serfdom led to acts of resistance by both Buryats and Russians. General disaffection and the privileged life of the Cossacks led to a revolution in 1917 and the brief existence of a Buryat National Committee.

In 1923, the Buryat-Mongol Autonomous Soviet Socialist Republic was founded consisting of all the traditional Buryat lands. The constructive approach to both social and cultural issues and a realistic approach to agricultural problems made this period a milestone in Buryat history. However in 1937 the Republic was split into three: the Buryat-Mongol ASSR, the Irkutsk and the Chita provinces. Soviet policies of forced industrialization, collectivization of the rural economy and population transfer were then introduced, leading to a loss of Buryat culture. During World War II, a large number of Buryats were killed fighting for the Soviet Union. The Buddhist clergy and Buryat intelligentsia were all but annihilated and in the 1970s it was forbidden to teach the Buryat language in school.

In recent years the Buryats have sought to regain their native culture and language in order to recreate a sense of national consciousness. The All-Buryat Association for the Development of Culture (ABADC) was formed to address these issues and has been active in developing a number of initiatives. Currently the organization is striving to solve ethnic problems and to establish contact with Buryats living outside the republic. The second Congress of the ABABC was held in April 1996 in order to establish the main goals of the organization up to 2001. Their aims and tasks include the following: The revival and development of the culture and spiritual life of the Buryat people, the protection of the rights and aspirations of Buryats living outside the Buryat Republic and the Aga and Ust-Orda Autonomous Districts (Chita and Irkutsk), the unification of Buryats to work for a common goal of the revival and the development of a Buryat-Mongol Nation. Other goals are the protection of the ecological balance in Lake Baikal and the surrounding country and the development of close ties with the international community and with other members of the UNPO. In June 1996, The Russian parliament passed a bill concerning legislation of the State Nationality Policy of the Russian Federation. ABADC expressed high hopes for this bill since it makes reference to national ethnic interests of ethnic groups living in different administrative territories in Russia.

In 1997, a new leadership was elected and a parallel structure, The Congress of Buryat People was put in place to assist in these aims. The Council and Presidency of ABADC organized a 1997 All-Buryat prayer day which was held wherever Buryats live. Seminars, roundtable conferences and competitions were facilitated in this period. Further to this, the ABADC participated in a session for the Parliament of the Russian Federation concerning social problems and in a Congress of Peoples of the Buryat Republic. A series of volumes on Buryat-Mongols and an encyclopedia "World of Baikal" will be published and included in the school reading list. ABADC is at present taking an active role in the preparations of documents for the Buryat Republic and continues to make proposals at both local and state levels. ABADC believe that it is possible to solve every conflict by negotiating in a peaceful manner: All peoples and nations in the world are equal and must be sovereign forever and in every sense.

The Buryats became a Member of the UNPO in February 1996, represented by the All-Buryat Association for the Development of Culture which represents all Buryats inside and outside the Buryat Republic in the Russian Federation

CABINDA

Admitted to UNPO Membership in 1997

Location:	Central Africa
Religion:	Christian
Language:	French and Portuguese
Population:	500,000

The territory of Cabinda is situated in Central Africa between the Republic of Congo in the north and the Democratic Republic of Congo (the former Republic of Zaire) in the south and east. In the west it borders the Atlantic Ocean. Cabinda covers an area of 7,270 km^2. A 60 km-wide strip of land of the Democratic Republic of Congo separates Cabinda from Angola. The capital of Cabinda is Tchiowa which is situated on the shore of the Atlantic Ocean and is the most important port in the whole territory.[22] Cabinda has a damp tropical climate with two seasons during the year: a dry/cool season from June until September and a rainy/hot season from October until the middle of May. Cabinda has huge forests, especially in the wet regions in the vast Maiombe area, where gorillas still live under protection. These forests have the second richest variety of trees in the world after the Amazon region in South America and the woods growing there, such as black wood, ebony and African sandal wood are of great value. High mountain ranges, up to 2,600 m high, run through the Maiombe forest.

The population of Cabinda is approximately 500,000 of which only one third is resident on the territory of Cabinda. The other two-thirds of the people live in several other African and European countries due to the repression by former Portuguese colonists and the occupation of Angola. More than 20,000 Cabinda people live in refugee camps in the Democratic Republic of Congo and in the Republic of Congo. About 80% of the population speak French and 20% speak Portuguese, although the latter is the official language. The majority of the Cabinda people are Christians, mainly Catholics and Protestants.

The Enclave of Cabinda originates from the old Kingdoms of Makongo, Mangoyo and Maluangu. These regions were attractive to colonialists for many reasons and disputes regarding influence and possession arose among European countries such as France, Holland, Germany and Portugal in the 18th and 19th century. Due to the existence of ancient and continuing relations with Portugal (since 1482), Cabinda formally became a protectorate of Portugal following signing by the old kingdoms of three treaties : the Chinfuma Treaty of 1883, the Chicamba Treaty of 1884 and the Simulambuco Treaty of 1885. From the time the Simulambuco Treaty came into force, until 1956, all problems concerning Cabinda were directly handled by the Portuguese government in Lisbon. After the Treaty of Berlin in 1885, at the

Berlin Conference in Germany, Cabinda was internationally considered as an integral part of the 'conventional basin' of the Congo and was officially recognized as a protectorate of Portugal. Tchiowa was chosen as the capital of the territory and, in 1887, Portugal sent its first representatives. They established a society based on western-european socio-political and economic concepts. Trade relations with the Dutch, French and Spanish people as well as with the Italians, Germans and Greeks during the pre-colonial period enabled a good number of the local population to find employment among shipping companies and to travel to Europe, particularly to France, England and Portugal. Other local people became specialists in trades which are still followed today, such as shoe-making, carpentry, woodworking, masonry and textile printing.

In 1956 the Portuguese government created an administrative union between Cabinda and Angola, an action which was contrary to the spirit of the three former treaties. But despite this event, Cabinda remains distinct from Angola, according to the version of 1971 of the Portuguese Constitution of 1933 (Chapter I, Article I *DA NACAO PORTUGUESA*) which has not been amended since its signing. In 1946, numerous people in Cabinda already promoting independence from Portugal, were deported to Baía dos Tigres in South Angola where they were detained and tortured by Portuguese colonialists. In the 1960s, with the wind of African independence blowing in from the two neighbouring Congos, large numbers of Cabindans sacrificed themselves for independence, freedom and the dignity of the Cabindan people. In 1962, at the 4th Commission of the UN on Decolonization in New York, the issue of self-determination was raised and in 1964, Cabinda was admitted to the Organization of African Unity (OAU) as the 39th African country to be decolonized.

At the beginning of the 1960s, three liberation movements—the Mouvement de Libération de l'Enclave du Cabinda (MLEC), the Comité d'Action Nationale des Cabindais (CAUNC) and the Alliance du Mayombe (ALLIAMA)—were founded. In 1963, these movements joined together to form the Front de Libération de l'Enclave du Cabinda (FLEC). In 1974, following the Salazarista regime in Portugal, the new Portuguese Government appeared willing to deal with the question of Cabinda. On 30 June 1974, FLEC was allowed to establish its seat in Tchiowa. On 1 August 1974, the Portuguese Minister of Foreign Affairs of the Spinoza Government raised the question of decolonization in New York. He declared that his Government intended to organize a referendum on self-determination for Cabinda but the process of decolonization came to halt when the Government of General Spinoza fell on 30 September 1974. The government leaders who replaced the General were sympathetic to the Mouvement Populaire pour la Libération de l'Angola (MPLA). In 1975, the Portuguese governor, Mr. General Themudo Barata was arrested through a *coup d' etat* by the Mouvement Populaire pour la Libération de l'Angola (MPLA), which had been massively armed by the former Soviet Union. The Angolan military forces occupied the capital of Cabinda and other ports claiming to be the only true representative body of Cabinda and backed by propaganda from Moscow. In the end, Portugal and three Angolan liberation movements—the Front National pour la Libération de l'Angola (FNLA), the MPLA and the National Union for the Total Independence of Angola (UNITA)—signed the so-called Alvor Agreement in 1975, in which Cabinda was declared as "an integral and inalienable part of Angola".[23]

The characteristics of this annexation were repression, corruption, bribery and nepotism and many fundamental human and political rights were violated. As a result, Cabinda slid into a time of chaos and became afflicted by violence and lack of stability. Angola's dependence on the former USSR was made official by the signing of a "friendship treaty" in October 1976. After Cuba and the former Soviet Union, the former German Democratic Republic (GDR) was the main supporter of the Angolan regime. Since the onset of the Angolan occupation and the Alvor Agreement, which violated the right of self-determination of the Cabinda people, over 70,000 people have been killed and more than 30,000 have fled overseas as refugees. Tens of thousands were detained and deported to Baía dos Tigres in southern Angola and many Cabindans were executed after summary trials and thousands of unarmed civilians were extrajudicially executed by Angolan security forces.

Wood and oil are by far the most important resources for economic development in Cabinda. About one third of the country is covered with tropical forests, especially with the vast Maiombe Forest. Wood is the oldest product and is exported to Portugal and as well to Germany, Italy, the Netherlands and other countries. The most important resource for Cabinda is oil which was found under the sea at Malembo, about 40 miles from the coast. Today the Cabinda Gulf Oil Company in association with Sonangol, Agip Angola Ltd. and ELF Petroleum Angola Ltd. is operator of the offshore concession of Cabinda and the present oil drilling rate is approximately 410,000 barrels per day.[24] As a result, Cabinda is considered as the "African Kuwait".[25] The most active oil companies in Cabinda at the moment are Sonangol (41%), Chevron (39,2%), Elf (10%) and Agip (9,8%). But whereas the drilling of oil has risen in the last twenty years, the living-standard of the Cabindans is still very poor since Angola receives all the money (almost US$ 4 billion) every year from the oil companies. The FLEC/FAC has never shown particular interest in the oil companies operating in Cabinda but always wished to establish a mutual understanding with them.[26]

At the beginning of the war in 1975, a large proportion of the rural population fled Cabinda, becoming refugees in the neighbouring countries. Subsequently, their homes were destroyed, their fields were ravaged and many families were left without a roof over their head. Today, there are still people who are forced by circumstances to live and sleep outside. To date, several dirt roads, abandoned at the beginning of the war, have remained in a state of disrepair. The agricultural activity which previously had produced most of the food supplies collapsed and could no longer ensure Cabinda's self-reliance on food. This lack of adequate food supplies has caused hunger and malnutrition and is one of the causes of Cabinda's high infant mortality rate.[27] Despite the presence of spring water, there is a shortage of drinking water and no provision for its distribution to areas of need, the Cabindans are forced to walk long distances to fetch water. The Medical Centres in Cabinda are in a bad condition as they were not modernized when the former colonialists left Cabinda and Angola occupied the territory. Consequently, the Cabindan population is forced to cross the border to Congo (Brazzaville) or Congo (Kinshasa) for medical care.[28]

Currently the situation in Cabinda is tense because of provocative actions by the Angolan military. In September 1997, the Angolan Government sent military planes carrying soldiers and heavy weaponry to Cabinda. Planes constantly landed at the airport of Tchiowa, unloading heavy military vehicles. The vehicles headed towards the region of Massabi and Miconge where Cabinda borders Congo Brazzaville, and in the direction of Ncuto, bordering Congo Kinshasa, in the equatorial forest of Maiombe. On 14 October 1997, the Angolan military forces crossed the border to Congo Brazzaville in order to occupy the city Pointe-Noire in Congo Brazzaville. This happened under the pretext that the president of Congo Brazzaville, Mr. Lissouba, supported the Cabindans in their demand for independence. On 15 October, the Angolan military forces occupied the FLEC/FAC office in Pointe-Noire and removed the staff. During this incident, two officers of the FLEC/FAC were seriously beaten by the Angolan military forces and suffered injuries requiring hospitalization in Pointe-Noire.[29]

The political and military turmoil in Congo Brazzaville and in the Democratic Republic of Congo and especially the intervention of Angola in these internal conflicts, created an atmosphere of great insecurity among the Cabindans and especially among the Cabindan refugees in both Congos. Presently, there are five refugee camps in the Democratic Republic of Congo and four camps in Congo Brazzaville. The offensives by the Angolan MPLA against the positions of the FLEC/FAC in the Cabindan territory resulted in the emigration of nearly 10,000 Cabindan refugees to the Democratic Republic of Congo, particularly to the Kouilou region.[30] The life in these camps is miserable due to the high density of refugees and the scarcity of food. The communication lines are difficult to maintain effectively.[31]

Already in September 1995, an Angolan UN official, Mr. Suza, visited a refugee camp in Kondi-Mbaka in the Democratic Republic of Congo for the first time in twenty years. This camp opened in 1993 and it gives shelter to more than 5,000 refugees. During his visit Mr Suza said in an interview at the Radio Congo that "the difficulty according to the Angolan president, Mr. Jose Eduardo dos Santos,[...] is that many leaders talk in the name of Cabinda but that their points of view do not agree with each other. The Cabindan leaders should agree with each other and find a mediator who would discuss the [Cabindan] question with the Angolan authorities." In Cabinda itself, the Angolan military tried to break the resistance of the FLEC/FAC. In Tchiowa, the capital of Cabinda, the Angolan police has arbitrarily arrested and executed Cabindan civilians who demanded independence of Cabinda. Because of the ongoing fighting, it is estimated that over 40,000 Cabindans fled to the vast Maiombe forest, which is mainly controlled by the FLEC/FAC.[32]

There have been reports about human rights violations in Cabinda. On 21 February 1997, a Cabindan fisherman was killed without an apparent motive, but presumably the Angolan soldiers considered the fisherman to be a member or supporter of FLEC/FAC.[33] In early January, following an attack on Ngomongo village in northeastern Cabinda by FAC, government forces beat Cabindan villagers severely and looted and burned at least ten houses.[34] On 11 December, Angolan military forces invaded the Cabindan refugee camp in Kondi-Mbaka in the Democratic Republic of Congo, where they caused panic among the Cabindan refugees and threatened to repatriate them to Angola by force.[35]

Cabinda, represented by the FLEC/FAC, joined the UNPO as a Member in April 1997. Its goals are the expulsion of all Angolan military forces and authorities from the Cabindan territory, a referendum on self-determination of the Cabindans and the installation of a parliament and a government in Cabinda.[36]

CHECHEN REPUBLIC ICHKERIA

Location:	Northern Caucasus
Religion:	Islam (Sufi)
Language:	Chechen and Russian
Population:	1 million (100,000 diaspora)

In 1859, Chechenia was conquered by Russia. Pockets of resistance continued and in the decades following the Russian revolution Chechens repeatedly rose against their rulers. In December 1936, the Chechen-Ingush Autonomous Republic was formed and later dissolved in 1944. In this same year, the entire Chechen and Ingush populations were deported to Central Asia. On their return, in 1956, many found their houses occupied or destroyed and their possessions taken. The Chechen-Ingush Republic was re-formed in February 1956.

A Chechen national movement for self-determination emerged in 1990. In that year, more than a 1,000 delegates met for a Chechen congress in order to "put pressure on the local authorities to speed up political change and celebrate Chechen culture."[37] On 1 November 1991, Chechenia officially declared its independence and the name of the republic was changed to the Chechen Republic Ichkeria. After three years of lack of dialogue as to the status of the Republic, the Russian military invaded on 11 December 1994. Attempts to destabilize the pro-independence Chechen government (including an assassination attempt and mercenaries sent in by Russia) preceded the invasion. The ensuing war lasted almost two years, with estimates of casualties ranging from 50,000–100,000. These figures include soldiers and civilians, men, women and children.

In 1996, a *Medecins sans Frontier* report described the conflict as "the world's cruellest war". It reported that civilians were systematically and repeatedly targeted by the Russian military. It also said that aid workers were prevented from entering bombed villages. In April 1996, President Dudayev appealed once more for an end to the war in Chechenia. On 26 April, during a satellite telephone conversation with a Russian official regarding the negotiation process, President Dudayev was killed by a rocket attack. In June, during the build-up to the Russian elections, a cease-fire was signed in Moscow, by acting-President Zelimkhan Yandarbiev and Russian Prime Minister Victor Chernomyrdin. However, following the re-election of President Yeltsin the war resumed as before, with the Russian military leaders apparently confident of victory. Chechen fighters then recaptured Grozny and other main cities in early August 1996. The newly appointed Secretary of the Russian Security Council, Alexander Lebed, met with Aslan Maskhadov, then Chechen Chief of Staff, to find a solution to the increasingly unpopular war. The offensive was subsequently cancelled and a cease-fire signed in Khasav-yurt on 31 August by Lebed and Maskhadov.

The situation in the devastated Republic remained extremely difficult following the 1996 cease-fire. The restoration of stability is now a major concern in the Republic. In December 1996, six members of the International Red Cross were murdered. The case remains unsolved and the majority of aid agencies pulled out of Chechenia following the killings.

Elections were held in January 1997, and were monitored by a mission from the UNPO and the OSCE. During his inauguration speech the new President Aslan Maskhadov swore on the Koran to defend Ichkeria's independence. Various foreign delegations were denied Russian visa's to attend his inauguration. In May Presidents Maskhadov and Yeltsin signed an agreement in which both sides agreed to reject the use of force in resolving disputes. An additional agreement decided that economic cooperation would be maintained between both sides and that the Republic would remain in the 'ruble zone' for one year.

Currently, little substantial progress has been made in negotiations on the future status of the Chechen Republic: disagreement remains on key issues such as the compensation for material losses during the war. Moscow had promised to invest some US$ 133 million, but the Chechens believe twice that amount is the true cost. Although it is claimed a first installment has been paid, the Chechens have not received it. The unofficial blockade impedes any sort of economic improvement. According to reports the situation on the ground is desperate, with little supplies, medicine or treatment available to those ill or injured. In the countryside villagers eat what they can produce, those in the cities fare worse. Little international aid apparently reaches those in need being either held up in Russian territory or because there is no infrastructure in place to channel it.

The Chechen Republic became a full Member of The UNPO in 1991.

CHITTAGONG HILL TRACTS

Location:	South-eastern Bangladesh
Religion:	Buddhism and traditional religion
Language:	10 languages respective to tribe
Population:	974,445
Ethnic diversity:	10 tribes, collectively known as the Jumma peoples

> Until 1860 the Chittagong Hill Tracts was an independent territory. In 1860 it came under British colonial rule but even then the Jumma people enjoyed self-rule and had collective ownership over the entire lands of the CHT. In 1900, the Regulation 1900 was enacted by the British and designed to protect the rights and interests of the indigenous people and to preserve their cultural identity. After the partition of India in 1947 the CHT was annexed to Pakistan. After Bangladeshi's war of independence from Pakistan in 1971, the CHT became part of Bangladesh. Constitutional amendments enacted in 1972 deprived the Jumma people of the protection as a distinct tribe and policies of population transfer and military repression followed.
>
> Since 1979 about 400,000 Bengali settlers have been transferred into the CHT, while Jumma families (20% of the total indigenous population) have been internally displaced under development programs which hardly meet the actual needs of the target groups. The atrocities conducted by the Bangladesh military and the miserable economic life have led almost 70,000 of Jummas to flee into squalid and crammed camps in southern Tripura, India.

In March 1997 a repatriation operation began which is still in process. An attempt has begun to repatriate some 7,000 Jumma refugees to the CHT from Tripura, India. The failure of the Bangladesh government to ensure the security of life and property of the repatriated Jumma refugees led them to refuse leaving Tripura, which resulted in forced repatriation. The first problem that repatriated people face is that they cannot have access to their homes and land because either the army or the Bengali settlers have occupied them in the meantime. Moreover, they cannot be reinstated into their former jobs despite the Bangladeshi government's commitment to the contrary. Other refugees are facing trial on their return (on charges mostly fabricated by the Bangladeshi Security Forces). The Jumma refugees are demanding a political solution to the CHT crisis to ensure their proper repatriation. They have been demanding involvement of UNHCR and the International Committee of the Red Cross for a proper rehabilitation in CHT.

Earlier this year, on 23–26 February 1997, a Peace Conference on the CHT was held in Bangkok, Thailand. Seventy country delegates and peoples from throughout Asia, the Pacific, the Americas, Europe and Australia met in Bangkok to review the situation in the CHT and explore ways of assisting in the process of peace and reconciliation between the indigenous peoples of the Chittagong Hill Tracts and the Bangladesh government. The participants called for peaceful and effective negotiations between the Bangladesh government and the Jumma people in order to promote regional autonomy with constitutional guarantees for the CHT.

The UNPO General Secretary attended the Conference and later met with Bangladesh governmental officials in order to plead for negotiations and renew a request for permission to visit the region. The Bangladesh government remained reluctant to allow a UNPO mission in the CHT. On 20 November 1997 the European Parliament passed a resolution on the CHT in which it calls on the government of Bangladesh to recognize the crucial demands of the Jumma people for regional autonomy, to demilitarize the CHT region and demands from the Bangladesh government to allow free access to international humanitarian and development organizations to the CHT region. As to the relocation of the Bengali settlers from CHT to other areas, the European Parliament encouraged the Bangladesh government to make full use of the financial assistance that the European Union has offered to Bangladesh.

On 2 December 1997, a long anticipated agreement[39] was signed between the Bangladesh government and the leaders of the CHT political wing, Jana Samhati Samiti (JSS). By the time this report was written, the contents of the agreement were not yet known. According to the international press[40], the prime minister of Bangladesh, Sheikh Hasina, has agreed to let three elected district councils control the area's land management and local police. The district councils will in turn elect a 22-member regional council, 13 members of which will be from the local tribes while seven members will be muslim migrants. It is evident that the councils will be dominated by tribes, which account for two-thirds of the region's 800,000 people. Nevertheless, nothing is known yet with respect to the rest of the JSS crucial demands (land rights, demilitarization, withdrawal of Bengali settlers and repatriation of refugees). While the Jumma people fear that Hasina government has offered too little, the opposition parties fear that the government gave away too much. The agreement will soon be introduced to the parliament for discussion.

The Chittagong Hill Tracts have been a Member of the UNPO since 1991.

CHUVASH

Location:	Russian Federation
Religion:	Christianity (Orthodox)
Language:	Chuvash
Population:	1.4 million

> The ancestors of the Chuvash were semi-nomadic tribes of Bulgars and Suvars who lived in the steppes of the North Caucasus in the 5th–8th centuries. During the 7th–8th centuries one part of the Bulgars left for the Balkans, while another part moved to the mid-Volga region providing the ethnic basis of the Chuvash and Kazan Tatars. The Volga-Bulgar state was founded and flourished until the beginning of the 13th century when it was destroyed by Tatar and Mongol conquerors. Under the dynasties of the following centuries, Bulgar traditions survived. Together with the Mari, the Chuvash fought fiercely against Ivan the Terrible until their defeat and incorporation into Russia in 1552. Under the Russian empire, Chuvash culture and language suffered as a result of Russification policies.
>
> In 1868, the revival of Chuvash culture began. In Simbirsk, a school was opened which became the center of the resurrection of the Chuvash people. In 1920, Chuvash became an Autonomous Republic within the Russian Federation of the former-USSR and gained some measure of political independence. In the course of the formation of this Republic, Simbirsk and 52% of the Chuvash population were excluded from the new republic's territory.
>
> The emerging political independence and cultural revival disappeared under Stalin. Although the centralization and Russification policies weakened somewhat after the death of Stalin in 1953, Chuvash culture and language continued to suffer. By 1985, 40% of all Chuvash children were not taught in their native language. The Chuvash Republic is now an autonomous republic within the Russian Federation.

In 1989, the Chuvash Public Cultural Center was founded, representing another revival of Chuvash culture. In 1992, the representative organ of the Chuvash nation—the Chuvash National Congress—was elected. In January 1993, the Chuvash National Congress joined the UNPO, with its goal being the continued revival and preservation of the Chuvash culture and identity. Drafts of a new constitution have been in progress since 1994 and in September 1995 opponents of the Chuvash President, Nikolai Fedorov, collected 25,000 signatures in favor of a referendum to abolish the presidency in the republic because of political differences.

On 27 May 1996, an agreement was signed between the Chuvash and Russian governments. This agreement laid-out divisions of authority and power with respect to the rebuilding of the Chuvash economy, the development of the regional agriculture and the destruction of stock-piled chemical weapons on Chuvash territory (pursuant to international treaties). The Chuvash Republic has considerable deposits of mineral resources, and in conjunction with lumber-based industries, this forms the primary basis of economic activity. Chuvash exports include a wide-range of agricultural and industrial products and consumer goods. At this time economic recovery and restructuring continues.

The Chuvash became a Member of the UNPO in January 1993.

CIRCASSIANS

Location:	Russian Federation
Religion:	Islam (Sunni) and Christianity
Language:	Circassian
Population:	4 million

Historic Cherkessia occupied the territory from the Black Sea in the west to the River Sunzhi (in present day Chechenia) in the east until the Russian conquest in the 1860s. Documents show the existence of a confederated Circassia in 1830 with more than 4 million people. As a result of genocide and deportation, at present, 3 million Circassians are scattered over 50 countries throughout the world. Adyge, the name the Circassians give to their nation, represents a number of different ethnicities such as Adyge, Kabardians, Shapsugs, etc.

It is said that 90% of the population perished as a result and the 10% of the population that still live on their ancestral land is divided into three separate republics. In the Republic Adygea, they make up 22.1% of the population (125,000); in the Kabardino-Balkarian Republic they make up 48.2% of the population (390,000); and in the Qarachay-Cherkess Republic they make up 9.7% of the population (60,000). In the respective republics they are called Adyge, Kabardian or Circassian. Other minorities belonging to the Circassian people are even more scattered, such as the Shapsug Adyge near Sochi, a small group near Mozdok and some villages near Uspensk in the region Krasnodar. The vast majority of Circassians live outside the Russian Federation: over two million Circassians live in Turkey and about 100,000 in Jordan, Syria, Israel, the United States and Europe.

The Russian-Caucasian war (1711–1864), was a brutal expression of the colonialism of Tsarist Russia that brought hardship and suffering to all the peoples of the Caucasus, including Circassians. In the years 1918–1920, the Bolsheviks halted the wave of Caucasian nationalism with the promise to restore their state and sovereignty. It was in spite of these promises that the Circassian nation was divided into three republics. The Circassians were forced to abandon their native language in favour of Russian in a policy intended to lead to assimilation. Presently, the Circassians are striving to reunite their nation and have managed to maintain a strong national consciousness, language and culture alive in exile, in part because of an old, unwritten epic, the *Adyge Khabze*, that expresses a philosophical and moral code which binds the people together.

The political, socio-economic and ethno-cultural problems that the Circassians are facing at the present time are a direct result of the Russian-Caucasian War and the subsequent genocide and deportations. Founded in May 1991, the International Circassian Association has set out to obtain recognition of the genocide which occurred. The Russian Federation, as an heir to the Russian Empire, has not recognized or condemned the genocide committed against the Circassian people. Although the Supreme Soviet of the Soviet Union adopted a law on the rehabilitation of oppressed peoples in 1989, the Circassians have so far not been included and therefore do not enjoy the status of 'people-in-exile' with the legal right to return to their ancestral lands. They consequently lack the official support needed to revive their language or to promote the return of their fellow people from exile.

In 1994 the International Circassian Association, with its headquarters in Chevkessk, became a member of the UNPO in order to stand up for the interests of the Circassian people living in different countries through non-violent means. In order to take the first steps towards the reunification of the Adyge people in the Russian Federation, the third Congress of the International Circassian Association (ICA) initiated a program to revive and re-develop the Circassian and Abazinian culture. It addressed the leaders of Adygea, Kabardino-Balkaria and Qarachay-Cherkessia to form a joint research centre to be presented to the Russian Federal Government for financial support. Throughout 1997, the ICA has been working on increasing the coordination of the activities of the various Circassian public organizations. In July 1997, Mr Teuvezh Kazanokov of the ICA was elected as a Member of the UNPO's Steering Committee.

A positive development at the political level was the inter-parliamentary agreement that was reached in 1997 between the three Republics where the majority of the Circassians now live: Adygea, Kabardino-Balkaria and Qarachay-Cherkessia. The agreement proposes the further development and strengthening of the traditional friendly relations between the three republics. Furthermore, it foresees strengthening contacts and dialogue between the Parliaments and coordination of legislative initiatives of joint social and political action, both on regional as well as on Federal affairs.

The Parliament of the Republic of Adygea adopted a law on the repatriation of Circassians regulating the legal position of the repatriants. A similar law was submitted to the Parliament of Kabardino- Balkaria and is hoped to be adopted in the near future. After the elections in Kabardino-Balkaria, scheduled for 1998, a similar law will be presented to their Parliament as well.

The economy of this region was so well integrated into the economy of the former Soviet Union and subsequently of the Russian Federation that it has become independent of the natural environment and is now incapable of developing on its own. There are some initiatives to establish new companies, joint ventures and to find new opportunities. Unfortunately, the unstable situation in the Caucasus, with the recent war in Chechenia, an economic blockade around Abkhazia and large-scale refugee problems all around, is little encouragement to potential investors.

Unemployment in the North Caucasus is very high and a large part of the Adyge working population move north to work in Russia. Their children can barely speak their native tongue. Although historic Cherkessia occupied fertile soils with large forest areas and is rich in oil, gas and gold, the bond with nature that was so typical for the Adyge people has been cut as a result of the diversion of rivers, the building of gigantic industries and the irresponsible use of the natural resources. In the 1970s, over 20 Circassian villages were resettled to create a huge reservoir, the so-called Kuban reservoir or Adygean sea. Due to the serious environmental consequences of this project, a federal program was created to drain this reservoir. However, due to lack of financial support from the Russian Government, the program has not been put into effect. Moreover, in spite of protests, the plans to re-route the Great and Small Zelenchuk Rivers into the Kuban reservoir continue. Several commissions have confirmed the technical and economic impossibilities of this project and the dangers for the environment.

The Circassians became a Member the UNPO in 1994.

CORDILLERA

Location: Philippines
Population: 1.1 million

The Cordillera Peoples' Alliance (CPA) is a grouping of some 120 indigenous Igorot peoples organizations from the five provinces which make up Cordillera. CPA was founded in 1984 in response to the murder of a local activist Macliin Dulag, who was instrumental in the protest against the Chico Dam project, which subsequently has never been implemented.

The Igorot differ in their perception of land ownership from the majority of the Philippine population, viewing it as a source of life which can neither be owned nor sold. However, this perception is persistently disregarded by the Philippines government which undertakes development projects in the region. The implementation of the Medium Term Philippine Development Plan (MTPDP), which aims to qualify the Philippines as a Newly Industrlialized Country by the year 2000, has so far only served to further violate the rights of the indigenous people of Cordillera.

Energy forms an integral part of the Philippines' development plan, as exemplified in the Department of Energy's Development Plan 1993–2005. This plan has, among other things, instituted 14 mega-dam projects in Cordillera, which will displace thousands from their ancestral lands. The San Roque Dam Project formed the focus of Cordillera Day 1997, which took place from 23–24 April in Dalupirip, Benguet province, one of the communities affected by the project. According to government estimates, the San Roque Dam will help decrease dependence on oil, irrigate thousands of hectares in Pangansinan and Central Luzon (the island on which Cordillera is located) and supply water to tourism centers. It will also submerge an 18 km stretch along the Agno river, including rice fields, ancestral lands and burial sites. As a consequence 316 households will be relocated.[41]

Although the San Roque Dam has been touted as the world's largest dam, plans for an even larger dam in the Apayao province of Cordillera have been revealed. Having only been granted provincial status in 1995, Apayao is considered Cordillera's 'last frontier'. Even provincial officials, including the governor, are opposed to the project due to the severe environmental and cultural damage it will inflict. The dam will submerge 11 villages and, according to provincial estimates, 1,800 families. In addition, the river on which the dam will be situated is the area's main source of fish and the only passageway to interior villages. Moreover, the project will be situated in an area prone to earthquakes. Nevertheless, the National Power Corporation (NPC) expects to begin laying the foundation in 1998.[42]

Despite assurances of resettlement from the NPC for both dam projects, the people in the affected areas do not have much faith in these promises. The NPC has in the past reneged on resettlement agreements in completed dam projects in Cordillera. Moreover, the NPC has not even presented preliminary resettlement plans for some projects before commencing with the dams' preliminary operations.

Political activity has accompanied the MTPDP, taking the form of Acts which are intended to facilitate the government's development plans. The Mining Act of 1995 made it possible for foreign mining concerns to fully own, operate and repatriate 100% of their profits. Other benefits accruing from the Act include a tax-carry forward of losses for 10 years and exemption from realty as well as environmental taxes.[43] At present, nearly two-thirds of Cordillera's land area is under application by foreign mining companies. Moreover, CPA estimates that almost half of Cordillera's land area is in effect 'owned' by foreign mining concerns, who could evict indigenous peoples from their ancestral lands.

In 1997, a national organization of indigenous leaders was created to follow-up on a series of consultations conducted in six areas in the Philippines with a view to creating an indigenous peoples' act. The CPA was invited to the consultations, but declined to participate because it felt that the present government would not enact laws which "would truly serve the interest of the people."[44] The Indigenous Peoples Rights Act (IPRA, or Senate bill 1728) came into force on 22 November 1997. A commission for indigenous peoples is to be established by February 1998, which will be responsible for defining the more unclear elements of the act. Mining executives with interest in the region believe these elements include the exact ownership of minerals on ancestral lands, as well as what constitutes ancestral lands. They are afraid that the IPRA will be interpreted as giving indigenous peoples the ownership of the minerals on their land. Because they are fearful of laying themselves open to litigation concerning ownership rights, mining companies are postponing projects until some clarity on the IPRA is forthcoming. This may be further delayed by presidential elections in May and a subsequent new administration taking office.[45]

On the other hand, the CPA believes that the IPRA will lead to the disintegration of indigenous peoples' concept of land ownership and use. In order to avoid conflict with the constitution, the IPRA must exempt strategic mineral resources already covered by the 1995 Mining Act, which ignores the indigenous peoples' rights to their natural resources. According to the CPA, "the [act] specifically asserts national interest over indigenous peoples' rights."[46] The IPRA also recognizes all property rights over ancestral lands organized before the act. The Mining Act combined with the 1992 National Integrated Protected Areas System (NIPAS), which delineated four national parks in Cordillera without reference to indigenous peoples' rights, have left indigenous people very little land to claim under the new IPRA. In addition, the provision for self-government in the IPRA requires all "indigenous systems" of government to be recognized by the government according to its compatibility with the national legal system and international human rights standards.[47] The CPA feels this is tantamount to forcing indigenous people to assimilate their system of government to the national one. The CPA believes that the government will use the IPRA as proof of their attention to indigenous issues. Moreover, they fear it will be a divisive force between those indigenous people who oppose the Act and those who support it.

A new bill on Cordillera regional autonomy was drafted in March. The last attempt at regional autonomy was rejected in 1990 by the people of Cordillera because they were not adequately consulted in the drafting of the Autonomy Act and they felt the issue was being used by politicians for personal gain. Although the new bill has only reached the House of Representatives' Committee level, politicians are already vying for positions in the Cordillera Autonomous government which will be created. The bill is expected to be approved in 1998. The autonomy provided by the bill does not address the question of ancestral land rights, which the indigenous people see as the foundation of self-determination. Indeed, increasing conflicts in 1997 centered around the issue of land and resources. The Armed Forces of the Philippines (AFP) and the Phillipines National Police (PNP) have been deployed in the Cordillera countryside to ensure implementation of government projects.[48]

A report published by the umbrella human rights organization, KARAPATAN, and one of its members, the Task Force Detainees of the Philippines, stated that the military are deployed in areas pending mining operations, dam sites and other energy projects. Concessions which affect the indigenous people are consistently supported by a heavy military presence. Moreover, the AFP continue to commit human rights abuses as they intensify their counter-insurgency operations in the Phillipines. According to the report, Cordillera is "one of the most militarized regions in the archipelago...[and] remains essentially brutalized by the AFP and the [PNP]...." The CPA believes that without recognizing the inherent rights of national minorities to their land, life and livelihood, nothing will be done "to address the basic issues of injustice, poverty and underdevelopment."

Cordillera is a founding Member of the UNPO.

CRIMEAN TATARS

Location:	Ukraine
Religion:	Islam
Language:	Tatar, Ukrainian and Russian
Population:	272,000

The Crimean Tatars are the indigenous people of the Crimea and are a Muslim Turkic people. The geographic position of the Crimean Peninsula has made it a key cross-road throughout history, providing transport and trading links between East and West, North and South. The invasion of the Golden Horde in the 1220s ensured the supremacy of the Islamic and Turkic-speaking tribes on the northern steppes of the Crimea over their Slav and Indo-Iranian counterparts.

Between the 14th and 18th centuries the Crimean aristocracy formed its own Khanate. As a part of the Ottoman empire this Khanate played a powerful role in relations between Moscovy Poland and the Ottomans. In 1783, this came to an end as Russian Cossacks occupied the Crimea forcing more than 142,000 Crimean Tatars to flee between 1785 and 1861. In 1917, the Crimea briefly declared its independence, only to have it cancelled by the Bolsheviks in 1918. In the years that followed approximately 1–1.25 million people fled to Turkey, Romania and the Caucasus. In 1921, there were no more than 130,000 Crimean Tatars left in their native country. In 1941, German troops invaded the Crimea. On 9 May 1944, Soviet troops reconquered the peninsula and deported the entire Crimean Tatar population nine days later; 46% of the population did not survive. The official reason given for the deportation was alleged collaboration with the Nazis. In fact, 4,400 Crimean Tatars fought against Stalin, while 50% of the more than 60,000 serving in the Red Army, died for the Soviet Union.

In 1988, the Crimean Tatars were officially allowed to return to their homeland. By the end of 1991, 166,000 Crimean Tatars had returned to the Crimea. In June 1991, at a meeting of the Crimean Tatar Movement, the Crimean Tatars Parliament (*Milli Mejlis*) was founded and national sovereignty declared. While the (primarily Russian) Crimean local administration regarded it as illegal, national democratic parties of the Ukraine, Tatarstan, Lithuania and Latvia recognized it as the legitimate representative body of the Crimean Tatars.

Since the Ukraine gained independence from the former Soviet Union, the government has not specifically refused the Crimean Tatars the right to return to the Crimean peninsula from exile but it does refuse them the full citizenship they need to truly integrate into society. As a people, the Crimean Tatars are structurally discriminated against by the Ukrainian government and this discrimination has allowed for little or no improvement in their situation—either politically, socially, or economically within the past year. In 1997, the Ukrainian parliament refused to pass amendments to the constitution, guaranteeing the representation of Crimean Tatars in local governments and the official use of the Crimean language.

Economically and socially, the returned Crimean Tatars have been facing difficulties in 1997 as they have in the previous years. The local authorities in Crimea still remain hostile towards the return of the Crimean Tatars. From the 262,000 Crimean Tatars who have returned to Crimea by late-1997, only 133,300 resettled and 128,700 still have no permanent homes. Initially, Crimean Tatars had to live in temporary buildings, often tents, without electricity or water. The local administration distributes land only to Russians and encourages them to build summer homes, but at the same time it puts up obstacles for Crimean Tatars to obtain land and build homes for themselves. On many occasions homes built by Crimean Tatars were destroyed by the authorities. Schools for Crimean Tatars are hardly available. No monuments of the Tatar history remained as they were destroyed by the Russians. The Ukraine is the only government within the CIS which is obliged to finance the return and resettlement of hundreds of thousands of people, who where deported during the era of the former Soviet regime. However, because the Ukraine faces great economic difficulties itself, it has so far not been able to provide the resources which are necessary for the settlement of the repatriates.

The most serious problem of the Crimean Tatars, however, remains the high unemployment rate among the population which was 49.6% by the end of 1997. Only 66,873 of 133,106 people who are able to obtain a permanent, temporary or seasonal employment. Most Crimean Tartars work in the agricultural sector (50,564) and the remainder in industry, the educational sector and the health-care system. Part of this high unemployment rate is due to the reluctance of Ukrainians to employ a Crimean Tatar who does not possess Ukrainian citizenship. In 1997, the Organization for Security and Cooperation in Europe conducted two missions, headed by Mr. Max van der Stoel, to the Crimea. In addition, members of the Council of Europe, parliamentarians from Estonia, Sweden and Denmark visited the Crimea.

The Crimean Tatars, represented by the *Milli Mejlis*, are a founding Member of the UNPO. Their goal is to resettle their ancestral homeland in the Crimea.

East Timor

Location:	South-east Asia
Religion:	Christianity (Catholic) and traditional religion
Language:	Tetum, Portuguese and Bahasa Indonesia
Population:	450,000

East Timor comprises the eastern half of the island of Timor, including the smaller islands of Atauro and Jaco and lies 640 km north-west of Australia. Sovereignty over West Timor was officially ceded in 1859 to the Dutch by Portugal, who retained East Timor. Following the overthrow of the Salazar regime in 1974, Portugal relinquished control over East Timor. A period of decolonization was instituted, with a view toward eventual self-determination.

Following a brief civil war, the Revolutionary Front for the Independence of East Timor (FRETELIN) gained control and asked Portugal to continue the decolonization process. The refusal of Portugal to become involved and the threat of Indonesian invasion led FRETELIN to unilaterally declare independence on 28 November 1975. Nine days later, East Timor was invaded by Indonesia. Since then, the original East Timorese population of 550,000 has decreased by 35%. State-sanctioned killings, forced sterilization, nativity control and population transfer of Indonesians all contribute to the depopulation of the indigenous people.

In 1987, the National Council for Maubere Resistance (CNRM), an umbrella organization for a wide range of East Timorese organizations advocating independence, was founded. The CNRM is internationally recognized as the legitimate organ of international representation of the East Timorese.

The award of the prestigious Nobel Peace Prize in 1996 to the people of East Timor through Dili's Catholic Bishop Carlos Filipe Ximenes Belo and José Ramos-Horta, Special Representative of the National Council of Maubere Resistance, helped renew the will of the East Timorese people and lent an increased degree of legitimacy to the international campaign for their right to self-determination. The prestige garnered from the Peace Prize has aided both Bishop Belo and Mr. Ramos-Horta by facilitating meetings with various governments and international organizations. One such example was the first meeting between a U.S. President and an East Timorese leader, when Bishop Belo and President Bill Clinton met briefly in the White House in June. The President, who earlier in the year declined to meet with Mr. Ramos-Horta, "stopped by" during a meeting between the Bishop and National Security Advisor, Sandy Berger. During the meeting, Mr. Clinton expressed his willingness to raise the issue of human rights with the Government of Indonesia. In November, legislation was passed which bars the United States from selling weaponry to Indonesia which the U.S. expects will be used in East Timor. The terminology used makes clear that Indonesia is obliged to refrain from using U.S. weapons in East Timor.[49]

A new Catholic diocese was created in 1997, in addition to that of Nobel laureate Bishop Belo. The new bishop of Baucau, Dom Basílio de Jesus Nacimento, was consecrated in Rome in January and took up his post in March. The new diocese will cover the eastern half of the territory. Dom Basílio reaffirmed his intention to use his position to promote the fundamental rights of the people of East Timor.[50]

In March, the UN Special Representative for East Timor, Mr. Jamsheed Marker, paid a visit to East Timor, where he met with Bishop Belo and civil and military officials. During his stay, a group of 200 university students, who felt he had not met with East Timorese people, gathered peacefully at Mr. Marker's hotel to ask for a meeting. They were allowed into the hotel foyer, where a UN staff person allegedly collected documentation from them about the current situation in the country. However, the Indonesian police then attempted to disperse the demonstration by firing warning shots and rubber bullets into the crowd. The police arrested 48 people, many of whom were subjected to beatings. Eleven had to be taken to a military hospital for treatment due to torture perpetrated by the police. Presently, 17 Timorese face charges of "sowing hate against the government," while 14 others are charged with expression of hatred or contempt through public media. Sixteen face charges of assault. Mr. Marker also met with the jailed resistance leader Xanana Gusmao before leaving Indonesia.[51]

At a meeting of the UN Commission on Human Rights, a resolution on East Timor was passed in April, which condemned Indonesian government for their human rights record. The resolution was co-sponsored by, among others, the European Union, the U.S. and Canada. Expressing deep concern for continuing human rights abuses, the resolution called upon Indonesia to co-operate fully with the Commission's thematic rapporteurs and working groups, and to respect human rights particularly with reference to East Timorese detained and in custody.[52]

Following Indonesian elections in late May, violence erupted in East Timor. Operations carried out by the East Timorese resistance army FALINTIL in protest of elections held in illegally occupied territory led to heavy retaliation by the Indonesian military. For this purpose, a new military commander, Colonel Slamet Sidabuter, was installed. Without delay, he launched a military offensive entitled *Operasi Tuntas* (Operation Finish Them Off). Since then, reports of disappearances, arbitrary detention and torture of East Timorese citizens have been common place.[53] Up to 125 people were arrested or detained and many were taken to interrogation centers where torture was often used to force information about or confessions of being a member of FALINTIL. The majority of the detainees were rounded up in the district of Bacau, where the military headquarters are located. The capital Dili has also been the sight of many arrests. Due to the massive military and intelligence presence in these areas at night, most people did not feel safe to leave their homes at night in fear of arrest or worse.

David Alex, the second in command of FALINTIL, was captured by the

Indonesian military on 25 June and was pronounced dead within 24 hours. An air of deception surrounds his death, as the military claim he died from wounds incurred during the apprehension, before reaching the hospital. This claim is discredited by a hospital nurse who confirms he was alive and in stable condition upon arrival. Moreover, the military buried Mr. Alex at 8:30 a.m. in Dili on 26 June without contacting any of his relatives who resided in the capital.

On a more positive note, South African President Nelson Mandela paid a visit in July to the jailed leader of the East Timorese resistance movement, Mr. Xanana Gusmao. With the consent of President Suharto, Mr. Gusmao was allowed to leave prison, where he is serving a 20-year sentence, and dine with Mr. Mandela at the State Guest House. Mandela later offered to mediate between the Government of Indonesia and the East Timorese resistance in order to put an end to the 22-year conflict.

A group of Nobel laureates and other eminent persons sent a letter in early September, appealing to President Suharto to support new attempts to resolve the conflict in East Timor. Signatories included former South African president F.W. de Klerk, who negotiated that country's transition from apartheid to democracy, and Gareth Evans, the former Australian foreign minister. This open letter was in response to both Mr. Mandela's initiative and an interview on Portuguese television with Konis Santana, the FALINTIL leader. There Santana indicated that in place of full independence, they would be willing to accept a form of autonomy similar to that of Puerto Rico in relation to the United States. In this case, Indonesia would take responsibility only for the defense and foreign affairs of East Timor. [54] Indonesia's foreign minister, Mr. Ali Alatas, ruled out even this option. Indonesia insisted that East Timor's incorporation into Indonesia is non-negotiable. However, Mr Suharto is scheduled to visit South Africa in November, where Mr. Mandela's suggestions will no doubt be discussed.

East Timor, represented by the CNRM, became a UNPO Member in 1993.

EASTERN TURKESTAN

Location:	Central Asia
Religion:	Islam
Language:	Turkic
Population:	16 million

Eastern Turkestan lies in the heart of Asia, bordering Kazakhstan, Kyrgyzstan, Tajikistan, the Mongolian Republic, Afghanistan, Pakistan, India, Tibet and China. The Uighurs, the indigenous people of Eastern Turkestan, comprise the largest group of the total population in Eastern Turkestan. Overthrown by Manchu invaders in the late 19th century, the country finally fell under Nationalist Chinese rule in 1911. Through various uprisings against the Chinese, an Eastern Turkestan republic was set up twice, in 1933 and 1944.

Eastern Turkestan has been under Chinese Communist rule since 1949. Though Eastern Turkestan (*Xinjiang* in Chinese) is considered an "Autonomous Region", the Uighurs have no say in governing the region. In addition to a policy of assimilation, political oppression and economic exploitation, the Chinese government has carried out countless nuclear tests at Lop Nur in the east of the country; the latest known test occurring in mid-1995.[55] Through a policy of population transfer, the number of Chinese inhabitants has increased from 5% of the population in 1949 to 40% in 1995. In the capital, Urumchi, this percentage has now reached 85%.

In a year of rising tension and numerous Uighur demonstrations, in which nearly 1,000 people lost their lives, a "Ten-Point Program" for security in Xinjiang was adopted in 1996 by the Chinese Communist Party Central Committee. This Program called on the Communist Party, the army, the public and state security forces in Eastern Turkestan to carry out a "pitiless struggle" against Uighur separatists. A wave of arrests and executions followed. Various reports indicate that up to 57,000 Uighurs were arrested and over 100 Koranic schools were closed.[56] In February, tensions erupted in violence in the town of Ili, near the Kazakh border. Reports said a large group of women had gathered in a mosque to pray on Holy Night during the month of Ramadan. After inspecting the gathering, the police tried to force the women to go home, an action against which the women protested. When the situation escalated into pushing and hitting Uighur men attempted to intervene and two of them were shot dead. This incident resulted in days of demonstrations which deteriorated into riots. Widely varying reports claimed between 30–300 dead and 100 injured, both Chinese and Uighur.

Two weeks later, a number of bombs exploded on public buses in Beijing, which were attributed to Uighur separatists. However, there was no proof to establish this connection. It was felt that the Chinese government may have even planted the devices themselves, in order to discredit the Uighurs and, according to Uighur leader Erkin Alptekin, "create a pretext for even more severe repression" in the region. The ensuing crackdown by the Chinese military was indeed harsh. Reports suggested from 1,000–2,000 Uighurs were arrested following the demonstrations, some of whom have been executed.[57] In June, three Uighurs were publicly executed for their alleged participation in the demonstrations. This took place in a stadium in front of a large crowd. Shortly after, as the Chinese authorities attempted to transport 27 more Uighur prisoners from the stadium to jail, two more Uighurs were killed by Chinese police who opened fire on a crowd blocking the convoy.[58] Up to three executions, 12 death sentences and 20 lengthy jail sentences were reported, all related to the February demonstrations.[59] Further disruption occurred in October, when bombs exploded in three locations in Eastern Turkestan. One bombing leveled a Chinese military building, killing 30 military personnel, while a second took place at a police department, killing nine officers. Lastly, an industrial oil site was targeted. No one has yet claimed resonsibility.[60]

The Chinese authorities are loath to discuss incidents of violence in Eastern Turkestan, particularly because China wants to boost its international image by glossing over its human rights record. However, the *Hong Kong Standard* newspaper reported in August 1997 that police had crushed an Uighur separatist group as part of a plan to "unleash a wave of terror" in Eastern Turkestan. That same month, the Chair of the Xinjiang Communist Party's Standing Committee, Mr. Amudun Niyaz, was quoted as stating his aim to "wipe out" Muslim secessionists in Eastern Turkestan.[61] Eastern Turkestan is China's gateway to Central Asia and the region's vast oil and gas reserves. In September, China signed a number of oil agreements with Kazakhstan, the largest of which requires the building of a 3,000 km pipeline to Eastern Turkestan, from where the oil can be shipped further afield. The railway system connecting Eastern Turkestan and the rest of China is currently being extended. There are already plans to extend and improve rail and road links with other Central Asian neighbours.[62] This expanding network may serve to further solidify China's relationship with Central Asia, as well as its dependence on Eastern Turkestan as the crucial link in an increasingly important association.

The effects of this policy on the Uighur's desire for self-determination remain to be seen. However, a ten-point resolution on Xinjiang, adopted by the Standing Committee of the Chinese Communist Party's Central Committee Political Bureau in 1996, stated China's intention of targeting Central Asian countries, in particular Kazakhstan, with diplomatic pressure and intelligence activities. This would be done in order to convince those countries to suppress Uighur separatist activity on their soil.[63] Closer economic integration between China and Central Asia may therefore work to strengthen China's influence on those countries in this respect.

The Uighurs themselves feel they are forced to choose between national extinction through gradual assimilation, or a mortal struggle to defend their cultural identity. The Uighurs have repeatedly called on the Chinese leadership to meet with representatives of Eastern Turkestan to find peaceful solutions to the ongoing problems. Although the goal is complete independence, the Uighurs are willing to begin with a negotiated and genuine autonomy.

Eastern Turkestan is a founding Member of the UNPO.

GAGAUZIA

Location:	Republic of Moldova
Religion:	Christianity (Orthodox)
Language:	Gagauzian, Moldovan and Russian
Population:	185,000

Gagauzia, officially *Gagauz Eri* (the land of Gagauzians), is an autonomous territory in the South of the Republic of Moldova. The Gagauzians are the descendants of the once numerous Oguzian tribes that settled in the south-western part of Europe in the 11th century and are a Turkic-speaking people. Most Gagauzians settled in the Budjak steppe of southern Bessarabia after Russia's annexation of the area in 1812. Territorial changes in the region put Gagauzia under Moldovan-Romanian administration from 1856–1878.

At the beginning of World War II, the entire territory was divided between two Soviet republics: the Moldovian SSR and the Ukraine. Thereafter, it was repeatedly subdivided into smaller administrative regions which resulted in a break of ethno-cultural links between the various Gagauzian villages. Moldova experienced a stirring of national sentiment during the final years of the USSR and this spurred the Gagauzian campaign for self-determination in the late 1980s. Discussion of separation from Moldova intensified soon after a law on languages was enacted in 1989. This law was perceived as discriminatory by the Gagauzians. In several southern districts of Moldova an independent Gagauzia was proclaimed in August 1990.

On 23 December 1994, following extensive negotiations, Gagauzia was recognized as an autonomous republic within Moldova. This was done through the adoption of the law "On the Special Status of Gagauzia" by the Parliament of Moldova. On 28 May 1995, the elections for the National Assembly of Gagauzia were conducted. On 11 June of that year, George Tabunshik was elected President of Gagauzia. On 1 August 1995, an end to the five-year conflict between Moldova and Gagauzia was officially declared.

During 1997, the Constitutional Commission of Gagauzia, founded in August 1996 by the National Assembly and comprised of 29 members and 10 experts, continued its working on the constitution of Gagauzia, which will be the first one for the autonomous region. Some improvements in 1997 can be seen in the cultural sector of Gagauzia: on 26 December 1997, the first professional Gagauzian theatre was founded and the first issues of a Gagauzian magazine, *Sabaa Yildiz* (Morning Star), were published. National scholars continued creating Gagauzian terminology since it is expected to replace Russian as the primary language in Gagauzia. Because of the current lack of exact terminology, the Russian language is still being used in schools and universities. The Gagauzian language is only taught as a separate course in schools and universities. Already in 1996, the Gagauzian language was transferred to the Latin alphabet. The Komrat State University, with 1,500 students, now has faculties of Gagauzian culture, economy and agriculture and, in 1997, the faculty of law was established. Historians of the Komrat University are working on a course about the history of Gagauzia and they hope that in the near future the fundamental national history can be published.

The economy of Gagauzia is primarily based on agriculture, especially wheat and other grain production, cattle-breeding and viticulture. Industry is not developed in Gagauzia. As is the case in Moldova, Gagauzia suffers from a major breakdown of its economy. Due to heavy rains in 1997, the production in the agricultural sector was very low. The land property still belongs to the state although farmers can rent it. There exists a bill on privatization which has yet to be passed in the National Assembly.

The Republic of Gagauzia, represented by its legally elected representative body, the Supreme Soviet of Gagauzia, was admitted to the UNPO in December 1994. Gagauzia wished to become internationally active and adhere to international treaties on human rights and other agreements.

Greek Minority in Albania

Location:	Southern Albania
Religion:	Christianity (Orthodox)
Language:	Greek
Population:	400,000

In 1913, Northern Epiros came under Albanian control. The Greeks had lived in that region since the third century BC and it had been a part of the Ottoman Empire for almost 500 years until the beginning of the 20th century. The decline of the Ottoman Empire created drastic changes in the Balkans. In December 1912, the Great Powers' Ambassadorial Conference in London declared Albania an autonomous state. A year later, the *Florence Agreement* divided Epiros, conceding the northern part to Albania. A new boundary between Greece and Albania was drawn by the International Commission for Definition of Boundaries. The signing of the *Protocol of Corfu* in 1914 insured that the Northern Epiros region would have its own administration and government. This protocol also recognized the rights of the Greek Minority and provided self-government under nominal Albanian sovereignty.

In 1920, Albania was admitted to the League of Nations under the condition that its government would give formal assurances that the rights of ethnic and religious minorities would be fully respected. This was undertaken in the form of the Albanian Declaration on the Protection of Minorities, proclaimed on 2 October 1921. These assurances, however, were not respected and by 1934 all non-state schools had been closed. Greece brought the issue to the Council of the League of Nations, which referred it to the Permanent Court of International Justice and, in 1935, the court decided that Albania had to restore the right of its minorities to establish their own schools.

Gross violations of human rights were committed against all citizens of Albania under the communist dictator, Enver Hoxha, who wielded total power from 1941 until his death in 1985. His Prime Minister, Ramiz Alia, held power from 1985 until the communist regime collapsed in 1991. The Greek minority suffered extensive persecution and the denial of its national and cultural identity. When, in 1992, Sali Berisha was elected the new president of Albania, many ethnic Greeks in Albania were eliminated from civil service jobs, the military and the police force as part of his suppression of the Greeks in Albania.

The political situation in Albania during the first half of 1997 was extremely unstable due to the collapse of "pyramid" investment schemes. Hundreds of thousands of Albania's 3.2 million people, for decades the poorest in Europe, invested in the funds, which the government later outlawed as pyramid schemes. The funds offered extremely high interest rates with the first investors paid from the deposits of later investors. The schemes eventually failed when no new investors were brought in and later investors lost their money. In demonstrations, particularly in the southern city of Vlore, thousands of Albanians demanded the full refund of their savings. The protests took on an anti-government focus because many people believed that the former President of Albania, Sali Berisha and his Democratic Party either benefited from the investment schemes or should have acted sooner to control them.[64] The protests erupted into violent ones, especially in southern Albania. In Tirana, the capital of Albania, warehouses of weapons were forced open and civilians removed a variety of automatic weapons. The southern part of Albania, which is known to Greeks as Northern Epiros and where most of them live, was controlled for a period by mafia gangs. Because of this situation many Greeks fled to Greece abandoning their homes and villages. The Albanians living in the North of Albania were not so much affected by the collapse of the pyramid schemes because they did not have so much money to invest in the schemes, whereas the Greeks and Albanians living in the southern part of Albania had access to the labour market in Greece and therefore were able too accumulate some savings, which most of them invested in the pyramid schemes. This is the reason why the violent outbreaks originated in South Albania and why they did not expand to the North. The economy is bankrupt and new credits will only be granted by the International Monetary Fund upon the condition that the affair with the fraudulent pyramid investment schemes is completely investigated.[65]

The parliamentary elections in Albania on 29 June 1997, supervised by monitors of the OSCE and other international organizations, resulted in a democratically elected government, headed by Fatos Nano of the Socialist Party. At this election, four members of the Greek Minority were elected. In the short time since the new president took over, he revoked Berisha's law restricting the freedom of the press and he allowed Greek schools to open in Albania, something which had been prohibited under the previous government of Berisha. In addition, Nano's government has so far guaranteed the freedoms of movement and speech and religion.

The Greek Minority in Albania has declared its support of the new government of Albania conditioned upon its working towards the democratization of Albania and its respecting and guaranteeing the rights of all Albanians, including the Greek Minority, according to the prior bilateral agreements between Albania and the Greek Minority. It is still too soon to foresee wether President Nano's government will be able to improve the conditions and the living standard of the Albanian people but if it succeeds, then the ethnic Greeks believe that they will also benefit and prosper.[66]

The Greek Minority in Albania is supported in its struggle for the recognition of its rights by the U.S. and Greek governments, the European Parliament, the UN Subcommission on Prevention of Discrimination and Protection of Minorities. This support emphasizes that the human rights of the Greek Minority in Albania must be respected and, among other aspects, has taken the form of pressure on the Albanian government to enact reforms. In September 1997, a concurrent resolution was submitted before the U.S. Congress urging *inter alia* that the new Albanian government embrace pluralism and foster cooperation and reconciliation among the political forces in Albania. The resolution also declared that the U.S. should assist the Albanian government in efforts to build durable democratic institutions, bring about economic reform and promote the rule of law.

The Greek Minority in Albania are a founding Member of the UNPO and are represented by the Democratic Union of the Greek Ethnic Minority in Albania (OMONIA). Its goal is to achieve cultural, linguistic and educational autonomy with a degree of self-government as was provided by the Corfu Protocol of 1914.

HUNGARIANS IN ROMANIA

Location:	Romania
Religion:	Christianity (various)
Language:	Hungarian and Romanian
Population:	1,625,000

The Hungarians first entered Transylvania in the late 9th century. Until the early 20th century, Hungarians had historically constituted the dominant nation in Transylvania. Although being an integral part of the Hungarian crownlands, Transylvania was organized as a semi-autonomous duchy for an extended period. Its local government and representative institutions were largely staffed by Hungarians. In the 16th and 17th centuries, Transylvania acquired a limited degree of independence. At that time it was ruled by its own elected Hungarian princes who significantly promoted Transylvanian-Hungarian literature and culture. In 1920, Transylvania was ceded to the Kingdom (later Republic) of Romania. As a consequence of this alteration in Transylvania's status, the Hungarians living in the region lost their political predominance. Over the last 77 years, the Hungarian community in Transylvania has experienced population loss as a result of emigrations to Hungary, Western Europe and America. This dispersal and the assimilation of the Hungarian population was strongly promoted during the period of communist rule from 1946 until 1989.

Following Transylvania's incorporation into Romania, the Hungarian population suffered discrimination, with harassment of the Hungarian minority increasing substantially under communist rule. With the fall of the communist government in 1989, the Democratic Alliance of Hungarians in Romania (DAHR) was founded to represent the interests of Romania's Hungarian minority and to aid the process of democratic transformation in Romania. The DAHR participated as a political party in elections held in 1990 and 1992, but, although the DAHR was one of the largest political parties in Romanian Parliament, it had never been included in the ruling coalition nor had its representatives been given any ministerial office.

This situation changed in 1996 when parliamentary and presidential elections were held in Romania in November. In this election, the DAHR won 7.5% of the seats in parliament. For the first time in the Romanian history, an ethnic Hungarian ran for the presidency and obtained 6.02% of the votes.[67] Also for the first time in Romanian history, the DAHR, led by Béla Markó since 1993, now takes part in the governmental coalition. Together with the Christian Democratic Peasants Party, the National Liberal Party and the Social Democratic Union, they form a stable majority.[68]

Following the negotiations among the governmental parties and political organizations, the DAHR could nominate two ministers,[69] eight state secretaries, two prefects and deputy prefects in seven counties in Romania, including the State Capital of Bucharest. The new Romanian government has fast developed a bilateral cooperation with Hungary and signed already more than 20 inter-ministerial treaties, including those concerning internal affairs, justice, education and health care. The issue of minority rights can be regarded as the most important success of the new political leadership in Romania.[70] On 18 May 1997 the Romanian government approved amendments to the Law on Education, providing for instruction in the mother tongue at all levels of education and abolishing the provision which stated that subjects such as history and geography must be studied in Romanian.[71]

In July, bilingual Hungarian-Romanian signs were installed in Targu Mures, a town with a 52% Hungarian majority. The installation of bilingual signs was based on government ordinance; the signs can be bilingual in municipalities where ethnic minority groups make up more than 20% of the population.[72] The Department for Protection of National Minorities (DPNM), set up in January, is led by a Hungarian minister and a German state secretary (nominated by the German Democratic Forum in Romania) and includes a special Office for the Social Integration of the Roma, which is run by a Roma representative.

Toward the end of the year, the situation of the minority rights in Romania seemed to develop in a positive direction however, the Senate of Romania did not pass those paragraphs of the governmental ordinance which eliminated the restrictions from the Law on Education. Since many Romanian senators of the government coalition voted for the maintenance of the restrictions together with the nationalist opposition, it can be stated that the solution of the problems of the minorities mainly depends on the Romanian majority.[73]

The international community reacted very positively to the development of the Romanian-Hungarian relations and considered that they can become a pillar of stability in central Eastern Europe. The deputy secretary general of the Council of Europe, Peter Leuprecht, has remarked, that the Romanian-Hungarian basic treaty represents "a major contribution to peace, reconciliation and the security of democracy on the continent". Regarding the inclusion of the DAHR in the Romanian Government, the U.S. President, Bill Clinton, expressed two times publicly his acknowledgements to the Romanian president, Mr. Constantinescu. The warming of the political relations between Romania and Hungary, including the democratic changes in Romania and the presence of the DAHR in the Romanian government opened new possibilities such as the setting up of joint military units based on the French-German experience. This cooperation is made stronger by the fact that for the first time in history, Hungary and Romania and the Hungarians in Romania have common aims, namely the European and Euro-Atlantic integration.

Romania's economic reform began in earnest only after the elections in November 1996, leaving the economy as much as five years behind other former Communist countries such as Poland, Hungary and the Czech Republic, which started reforms in 1990. Within months the new government slashed spending, freed prices, stabilized the currency and brought inflation down to 0.7% in July

1997.[74] However, since then, political spats between key reform ministers have blocked laws on investment protection, privatisation, tax reform and banking that could stimulate the economy and help start a recovery. As a result of this, inflation rose to 6.5% in October 1997 for a rate of 145% for the year.[75]

The Hungarian Minority in Romania, represented by the DAHR, became a Member of the UNPO in July 1994. The goals of the DAHR include the recognition of national minorities as constitutional elements of the state on the basis of the constitutional principle of equality and non-discrimination, the enactment of a law regarding national minorities, based on the principles of personal autonomy, local self-government of special status and regional autonomy. According to the DAHR, this law should include legal guarantees for national minorities to use freely their mother tongues in private and public as well as in legal matters, the establishment of an independent system of cultural institutions and an education, guaranteeing the development of an independent native-language school system.

INGUSHETIA

Location: Russian Federation
Religion: Islam (Sufi)
Language: Ingush
Population: 300,000

Once the Russian conquest of the North Caucasus was completed in 1864, large numbers of the indigenous North Caucasians, including many Ingush, were forced to emigrate, while large numbers of Russians were resettled in the region. Following the Russian revolution and the expansion of Bolshevik power, the North Caucasus peoples declared the establishment of the Autonomous Soviet Mountain Republic, of which the Ingush formed a part. However, by 1924 all parts of the Republic had been annexed to the Soviet Union as autonomous districts and, with the start of the Soviet program of collectivization, the political and intellectual leadership of Ingushetia was deported.

On 23 February 1944, the entire Ingush population was deported to Soviet Central Asia, accused by Stalin of collaborating with the Germans. The deportations resulted in the death of tens of thousands of Ingush. One third of Ingush territory, the Prigorodniy Rayon, was transferred to North Ossetia and land owned by Ingushetians was given to settlers. The Ingush historical heritage, including the mountain villages with their distinctive towers (*Gawash* or *Bous*), the cultural buildings and mosques were destroyed or damaged. Twelve years later, under Khruschev's de-Stalinization, rehabilitation of the Ingush and other peoples began. However, Ingush demonstrations in the Prigorodniy Area in 1970, demanding the return of the region to Ingushetia, were put down and in 1980 Ingush were forbidden to take residence in North Ossetia. After the disintegration of the Soviet Union, the Ingush held a referendum and, in June 1992, the Republic of Ingushetia formally became a Republic within the new Russian Federation.

In November 1992, the North Ossetian armed militia (OMON) attacked Ingush homes and villages in the Prigorodniy Rayon supported by Russian tanks and armoured vehicles, killing up to 1,000 people and causing some 65,000 to flee to neighbouring Ingushetia. Today, only 6,100 Ingush have returned to what is left of their homes. Although President Boris Yeltsin has issued decrees regulating the repatriation of these displaced persons, the Russian authorities are not actively encouraging their implementation. Negotiations between North Ossetian and Ingush delegations concerning the return of the displaced Ingush to the Prigorodniy Area, including an agreement signed by both presidents in July 1995, have not led to any substantial return of displaced persons.

Since the beginning of 1997, 30 people of Ingush nationality were killed in the Prigorodniy region and towards the end of the year an intensification of provocative activities by armed units of the Republic of North Ossetia was noted. Despite 39 official documents of the Federal Government of the Russian Federation concerning the return of the Ingush refugees, their return has been directly and indirectly hampered by the North Ossetian President Galazov, the Ministry of Internal Affairs and the

Russian troops that are stationed in the region. On 4 September 1997 a mutual agreement regarding the regulation of the relationship and cooperation between the Republic of North Ossetia-Alania and the Republic of Ingushetia was signed in Moscow by both Republics. On 15 October a program to this effect was adopted under the patronage of Russian Prime Minister Chernomyrdin.[76] However, it seems that neither the Government of North Ossetia nor the Federal Government of the Russian Federation fulfil their responsibilities following from these agreements. The main issues remain unsolved: the return of the Ingush people and compensation of material losses and the issue of the status of the Prigorodniy Region.

In February, the UNPO co-sponsored and attended an international conference organized by the Ingush Government in Nazran on "Refugees and Forcibly Displaced Persons: Problems and Ways of Solution". In a concluding address, the participants called upon the Member states of the Council of Europe, especially the Russian Federation, to assist in solving the refugee problem and to restore the constitutional rights and liberties of the Ingush citizens. The conference participants included representatives of international human rights and humanitarian organizations, academics and Members of the European Parliament. The European Parliament is drafting a resolution on the situation of the Ingush refugees which will be tabled early next year.

Ingush people within other parts of the Russian Federation have been discriminated against since the declaration of independence of the Chechen Republic in 1991, and especially since the outbreak of the Chechen war on 11 December 1995. This war greatly affected Ingushetia with Russian troops attacking and bombing Ingush villages resulting in significant civilian casualties. Ingushetia had to absorb more than 100,000 refugees from Chechenia in addition to the existing displaced Ingush population of 60,000. President Aushev never supported a military solution to resolve the Chechen question and presented a number of initiatives for a lasting peace in the area to the leaders of Kabardino-Balkaria, Dagestan, Qarachaevo-Cherkessia. President Aushev also initiated negotiations between the Russian and Chechen authorities for a cease-fire and peaceful settlement and for the release of all prisoners of war.

On 31 August 1997, the Russian Federation established a blockade of the Ingush Republic along its administrative borders, preventing the entry and exit of citizens with Ingush nationality and the delivery of goods. Since the Republic of Ingushetia is completely dependent on the supply of provisions and medicines from outside, as a result of the blockade the social and economic situation grew tense. It appears the blockade is related to the Russian policy of isolating Chechenia. Ingushetia has one of the highest unemployment rates among the republics of the Russian Federation—in January 1997 37% of the working population was unemployed. The unemployment rate among the refugees from North Ossetia is 9 out of 10. The exceptionally high rate is partially caused by the privatisation of state companies. The further privatisation of companies in 1997 has increased the unemployment rate even further.

Ingushetia became a Member of the UNPO in July 1994.

Inkeri

Location:	Russian Federation
Religion:	Christianity (Protestant and Orthodox)
Language:	Finnish and Russian
Population:	90,000 (20,000 in Ingermanland)

The Inkeri, or Ingrians, are a Finnish people originally residing in Ingermanland (or Ingria). The southern border of this region was established through the Russo–Swedish agreements of 1617, with the northern border the Finnish border of 1940, the western border running along the river Harva and the eastern border as lake Ladozhskoye. Most Ingrians now live within the Russian Federation, in the Leningrad *Oblast* and the city of St. Petersburg. The area where the Inkeri reside was for centuries the scene of the struggle between Swedes and Russians for control of the region. At the beginning of the 18th century came an end to the wars. In 1702, Peter the Great occupied the region and built the city of St. Petersburg. Ingrians were forced to build the new capital, at the same time as they relinquished their ownership of the region. The Inkeri developed as a nation towards the end of the 19th century and their numbers exceeded 150,000.

During the 1930s the majority of the Ingrians were deported to Siberia by Stalin's regime. In 1991, the repatriation to Finland began (about 20,000 Inkeri live there currently). In 1993, the Ingrians were rehabilitated by the Russians but still did not get the right to return to their home lands. In 1988, "Inkeri Liitto", an organization of Ingrians wishing to preserve the identity of the Ingrian Finns as a people, was created. The association has approximately 7,500 members and strives for all deported Ingrians to return to their native land so that they can become a major nationality in their own region again.

In general, Russian policy continues to violate the rights of the Ingrians. They are still denied self-determination and opportunity to receive education in their own language.Furthermore, they suffer social-economic deprivation due to a lack of employment opportunities. A promising governmental program entitled 'National cultural revival of the Ingrian Fins of Russia' does exist, but it remains only on paper. Though the freedom of expression and assembly is officially recognized, there is a lack of private regular journals. There is freedom of religious practice; the number of Lutheran parishes has increased to 14, new churches are being built and old ones are reconstructed.

While the political leaders of the association Inkeri Liitto remained in office during 1997, the president, Valerij Koj Vanen, sent in his resignation. Inkeri Liitto cooperated with different relevant governmental bodies in 1997. On 14–15 January the seminar 'Ingermanland Project 1997–2000' was held in St. Petersburg, with participants from government delegations from Finland and Russia. As a result of the seminar, the Russian government agreed to establish a special working group on Finno-Ingrian affairs. In order to face the problem of unemployment, under the auspices of the St. Petersburg department of Inkeri Liitto, a private labour exchange office started to work. With different organs of the government of Finland the complex programme of support for the Ingrian Fins in the region of their present habitat was discussed. From the same government the Inkeri received support in the field of education, and religious and social organizations from Finland rendered material support.

In 1997 the emigration of Inkeri to Finland, trying to build a new life there, continued and even increased. In the future this could mean the end of the Finno-Inkeri culture and language, which is of great concern to Inkeri Liitto. Activities undertaken by Inkeri Liitto in order to respond to human rights violations, include regular appearances of these issues in the press and on television (Russian as well as Finnish), the protection of the rights of Inkeri in courts and through legal consultation, and constructive work with the relevant authorities on the development of mutual understanding and cooperation.

On 24 January parliamentary hearings were held in St. Petersburg, on the concept of the Russian Federation National Policy as embodied in the Federal Programme for Revival and Development of Finno-Ugric Peoples of Russia. In August, the delegation of Ingrian Finns took part in the establishing session of the parliament of Finns living outside Finland, which took place in Helsinki. It also passed a proposal concerning support for Ingrian Finns for the preservation of their ethnic identity.

Inkeri Liitto is striving to promote conditions for the improvement of foreign investments, for example, by utilization of a longer-lasting tax policy. This would promote investments by multinational corporations in Ingermanland. The ecological problems of the region should be faced by allowing international control over the work of the area's nuclear power stations and introducing special measures for the construction of new harbours. In 1998, Inkeri Liitto will celebrate its 10th anniversary and it hopes to elaborate a precise plan of action for the coming decade. Furthermore the association expects to set up new concrete projects with the government of Finland and the Swedish Ingermanland Union aimed at supporting the language and culture of the Ingrian Finns.

Inkeri Liitto joined the UNPO in 1992, in order to receive support for their struggle for self-determination.

IRAQI TURKMAN

Location: Northern Iraq
Religion: Islam and Christianity
Language: Turkish
Population: 2.5 million

> The Turkman, originally from central Asia, began settling in the northern and middle regions of Iraq over a thousand years ago. The Turkman have suffered from both social and intellectual persecution under the various ancient and modern Iraqi regimes. Numerous villages in Turkman regions have been eradicated and their inhabitants expelled or forcibly transferred to remote areas in southern Iraq by Iraqi authorities. Although in 1970 the Iraqi administration granted very limited cultural rights to the Turkman within a narrow framework (including education in the Turkish language in primary schools, daily radio broadcasting for two hours and TV broadcasting for 30 minutes in Turkish) these rights were gradually taken away by the Iraqi authorities and by 1972 all Turkish schools were closed. The assimilation of the Turkman became state policy in 1971, when the General Assembly of the Baath Party decided to 'Arabize' Kirkuk until 1980.[77]
>
> Administrative boundaries were changed in 1974 to divide Turkman concentrations. Since the mid-1970s, Arabs have enjoyed special incentives and rights encouraging them to move to historically Turkman areas including the oil-rich cities of Kirkuk and Mosul. In the latter half of the 1970s, the names of several villages and places in the Governorate of Kirkuk (Tamin) were officially given Arabic names and in the 1980s Turkman societies, institutions and properties were officially 'Arabized'.[78] This meant that the Iraqi administration not only prohibited the people to speak Turkish in public but also punished those who spoke privately in the language. Hundreds of Turkman villages and towns were demolished under a number of pretexts. In Iraq's judicial system, the Turkman were ignored and the several Iraqi constitutions did not mention the Turkman. Article 6 of the present Iraqi constitution, dated 7 July 1990, only mentions Arabs and Kurds as the peoples in Iraq. The creation of the safe-haven by the United Nations, following the Gulf War of 1991, caused the division of the Turkman into separate communities in the Kurdish autonomous area and under the Iraqi administration.

The Iraqi Turkman continue tosuffer under the dictatorship of the Baath Party. They are prohibited from forming political parties, opening private schools, publishing books, magazines, newspapers or distributing pamphlets. Against these pressures, the Iraqi Turkman Cooperation and Cultural Foundation tried to gain international recognition. They presented the UN with a list of persons arrested by the Iraqi regime and whose whereabouts are unknown. The Iraqi government is guilty of violations of human rights, especially with regard to the various ethnic and religious minorities within its borders. The government, by its actions, considers ethnic minorities such as the Iraqi Turkman as being second-class citizens. The most repressive policy presently faced by the Turkman is that of forced displacement.[79]

In October 1997, Turkman organizations arranged a Turkman Assembly in northern Iraq. The assembly has secured unanimity among the Turkman organizations and determined the cultural, educational, information and social policies for the Turkman people. The groups who attended the assembly have adopted the "Declaration of Fundamental Principles" which is of binding nature for the Turkman people. A 30 member council was created, including the Turkman Co-operation and Cultural Foundation and various other Turkman organizations. In order to maintain the identities of the Turkman colonies and to ensure social solidarity, several associations and foundations have been established in Denmark, Sweden, Germany, the Netherlands, Turkey, Canada, the U.S. and Australia.

The Turkman region has large natural resources such as oil, gas and sulphur. In addition, there is an abundant production of wheat and cotton. Due to the economic embargo imposed on Iraq by the UN, there is little significant economic development in the Turkman region as well as in the whole of Iraq during 1997. This embargo has had serious effects on the social situation of the Turkman due to the resulting lack of food and medicine. Until the Gulf War, the Turkman did not have an unemployment problem, however, after the war the unemployment rate has risen tremendously due to the embargo and because the Iraqi regime denies the Turkman citizens jobs in the government, in trade and in agriculture.

Since October 1996, the Iraqi government has forced the Turkman citizens to alter their ethnic origin in the Civil Registers from Turkman to Arab. If a citizen fails to do so, he or she will be displaced to the Arab region in Southern Iraq and suffer the confiscation of all his or her belongings. This has resulted in widespread concern among the Turkman. Furthermore, Turkman are forbidden to buy and sell property or land among themselves, because legally they are required to sell it only to Arab citizens. In 1997, Turkman continued to be forbidden to buy or sell commercial transport vehicles.

Another form of suppression practiced by the Iraqi security forces is the assault on sellers, especially on the wandering hawkers in the markets of Kirkuk.[80] An example of this is the striking with truncheons of the peddlers and greengrocers at the Korya Bazaar in Kirkuk by the governor of Kirkuk who was dressed in a military uniform and accompanied by his guardians.[81] The Turkman are not allowed to practice their religion in public: religious ceremonies and prayers in the mosques in the Turkman language are forbidden. In mid-1997, religious lectures and sermons were also banned from all mosques.

So far, only that part of the Turkman region in Iraq, belonging to the UN security zone has obtained some aid and support from the UN, the Turkish Red Cross and other organizations. The rest of the Turkman community still strives for recognition and support from international organizations and through other assistance programs.

The Iraqi Turkman became a Member of the UNPO in 1991, and are currently represented by the Turkman Cooperation and Cultural Foundation. The foundation strives for a peaceful solution to the conflicts in Iraq and the establishment of a pluralistic parliamentary system which respects human rights and includes all ethnic groups within the territorial integrity of Iraq.[82]

KA LAHUI HAWAI'I

Location:	North Pacific
Religion:	Christianity and traditional religion
Language:	English and Hawaiian
Population:	240,000 (approximate)

Following the arrival of Captain James Cook in 1778, numerous missionaries and whalers settled in the region and eventually influenced the indigenous Hawaiians (the *Kanaka Maoli*). Thus, the traditional state religion of the chiefs, the institutions of *mana* (spiritual power) and the *kapu* system (privileges according to *mana)* ended and a new structure, similar to the British monarchy, was installed. From the middle of the 19th century, pressure from England, France and the U.S. saw to it that laws were changed to facilitate the ownership of land. Foreigners acquired most of the land in just one generation and began cultivating sugar, controlling the government in order to maintain control over their wealth.

In 1893, the U.S. overthrew the Kingdom of Hawai'i and in 1900 annexed it as a territory. Statehood was imposed in 1959. From 1946–1959, Hawai'i was listed as a non-self-governing territory under the United Nations. Kanaka Maoli are excluded from the U.S. policy by which American Indian and Alaskan Native governments are recognized and allowed legal and economic jurisdiction over their lands and natural resources. In 1991, the Hawai'i Advisory Committee to the U.S. Commission on Civil Rights issued a report documenting 73 years of civil rights' violations against Hawaiians. In 1993 the U.S. Congress passed Pub. Law 103-150, also known as "the Apology Bill", officially apologizing to the Hawaiian People for the illegal overthrow of their Kingdom in 1893. Most importantly, the Law acknowledged the right of the Kanaka Maoli people to self-determination, thus paving the way for a process of reconciliation.

From 1993–1996, the State of Hawai'i passed a series of laws creating an appointed body to oversee a process for the creation of a Hawaiian Nation. In June 1996, the state of Hawai'i organized a Native Hawaiian Vote in order to obtain a mandate for a process towards some form of native Hawaiian sovereignty. The state initiative was presented as an act of self-determination; nevertheless, questions about its validity under international law and the confusion as to what exactly is the voting issue led many native organizations to boycott the vote.[83]

Unrest continued in 1997 when the State Legislative vowed to initiate again a bill whose introduction last year was strongly opposed by native Hawaiians and had led to demonstrations. The proposed law virtually abolishes Hawaiian traditional rights to land and to access private land for gathering, fishing and other customary uses.[84] The proposed law has substantial support from real estate developers, banks and insurance companies.

Perfect Title Co., a small but successful title research company licensed to do business in Hawaii, began to issue, certify and file title reports which invalidate private property deeds in Hawaii based on the illegal overthrow of the Hawaiian Kingdom in 1893. Keanu Sai, the company's president, indicates that since the U.S has admitted the overthrow of the Kingdom was illegal, all deeds issued by the provisional U.S and State governments since 1893 do not convey legal title to native land. At the urging of insurance companies, private owners and corporate developers the State Attorney General seized the records of the company and arrested its officers. No actual fraud or legal violations have been proven to date.

In July, U.S. agents forcibly removed the Pai family from their traditional lands in Kona. The land has been sold to the U.S for a National Park. The family home, educational facility and bath area were destroyed and the fishing canoes and nets were seized. UNPO Steering Committee member Ms Germaine Tremmel, representative of the Lakota, witnessed and monitored the event. The State of Hawaii sent police and special agents to Makua Beach in Oahu Island to evict Hawaiian homeless families from tents in which they were living. Many Hawaiians were arrested and jailed. No homes or temporary shelters were provided by the state. Hawaiians have the worst housing conditions in the U.S. while over half of the Hawaiian population live in substandard or overcrowded conditions.[85] The economic and social situation of Hawaiian people declined even more in 1997 due to general budget cuts in state welfare, education and housing programs. In 1997 the first Hawaiian NGO (*Na koa Ikaika o Kalahui Hawaii*) was established to work in the intersessional Working Group on the UN Draft Declaration on the Rights of Indigenous Peoples, held in Geneva.

The Kanaka Maoli are a member of the UNPO through Ka Lahui Hawai'i. Founded in 1987, the organization is striving for a nation within a nation, to enable indigenous Hawaiians to negotiate with the U.S. and enforce their rights. Ka Lahui Hawai'i is recognized as the 'native government' of the indigenous peoples of Hawai'i by other native nations. As such, it has executed treaties with a number of other native governments in the Americas.This year, Ka Lahui Hawaii participated in an initiative to have Hawaiians reclassified from the Asian category to american native category; if this succeeds, they will no longer be considered as asia/pacific immigrants but native americans. Ka Lahui Hawaii representatives participate regularly in the UN Working Group Sessions of the Human Rights Commission held in Geneva.

Ka Lahui Hawai'i became a UNPO Member in 1993.

KARENNI STATE

Location:	South-east Asia
Religion:	Christianity and traditional religion
Language:	Karenni and English
Population:	300,000
Ethnic diversity:	Karenni sub-groups are Kayah, Kayan, Kayaw and Paku.

The Karenni are, with the Mon, the oldest indigenous inhabitants of present day Burma (Myanmar). Since 960 BC, the Karenni have lived along the Salween river in isolation from external influence. This strengthened their sense of independence and self-sufficiency. Karenni State, the mountainous area situated between Shan States, Karen State and Thailand, was independent before the British Empire annexed Myanmar in 1881. In 1948, it was annexed by Burma without the knowledge of the Karenni Supreme Council or the consent of the Karenni people.

For almost five decades the Karenni people have endured extreme Burmese persecution and have fought to retain their unique identity and sovereignty. The subjugation of the Karenni by the Burmese regime is exemplified by ongoing human rights abuses and racist policies under which the Karenni are forced to live, particularly since the State Law and Order Restoration Council (now known as the State Peace and Development Council, or SPDC) assumed control in Myanmar in 1989. While the Karenni economy is primarily agricultural, with rice as the main agricultural crop, much of this is either appropriated or damaged by SPDC troops. It is also used as payment for "porter's fees", which thereby releases a person from forced portering duties for the army. Due to continual forced relocation, Karenni lands are given to landless Burmese immigrants, the Karenni economy is stagnant.

From December 1996 to May 1997, 4,000 villagers were forcibly relocated, some of them several times, while those trying to escape the relocation were killed. In relocation camps, there was insufficient food, unsatisfactory sanitary conditions and few medical provisions. Villagers who are relocated often must leave behind their belongings, including much needed food supplies. Those who attempt to return to their former homes to collect such belongings are subject to torture and killing. In one particularly gruesome incident, a woman and several children were killed by having their heads smashed with a mortar and pestle used for pounding rice. Some refugees have reported that the SPDC troops encouraged them to go to Thailand. In another instance, the SPDC built a nine-foot high fence around a village relocation site and villagers were forced to get permission to visit their fields outside the perimeter, Villagers were sometimes denied permission for up 2 weeks.[86]

SPDC launched a new military offensive in June called *Myay Lan Sanit*

(Uprooting Area), in which SPDC forces were under orders to kill anyone, including women and children, found in specific areas. They also burned down more than 265 houses and destroyed countless acres of rice paddy. SPDC intended to clear the area of villagers without providing for their relocation. Out of fear for their lives, villagers hid in the forest and suffered from a serious lack of food and illnesses, such as malaria and dysentery.

In other areas, SPDC ordered everyone over the age of 10 to contribute labor to construction projects. Duties vary widely and include: infrastructure (such as roads, railways and dams) and military installation construction, brick making and work on confiscated farms. Forced laborers can usually go home at the end of the day, but are often too tired to fulfill their own labor duties. Moreover, forced laborers have to provide personal food and medicine at their own cost. Another abuse suffered by Karenni villagers is forced portering. This is said to be used as a means of "detain[ing] people ... for indeterminate periods of time."[87] Portering almost always entails a stay with soldiers, away from home for days or weeks, where laborers are often subject to ill treatment and beatings.

The Government of Karenni State was established in 1992, when the Charter of Karenni was drafted, in which all international treaties and Geneva Conventions were included. Situated at the Thai–Myanmar border, the government is constituted by the Prime Minister, who is the Karenni National Progressive Party (KNPP) Chairman, the President and Ministers of Interior, Health, Education, Finance, Foreign Affairs and Judiciary. The Karenni State is divided into three districts with 17 townships. In January 1997, 14 ethnic groups who reside in Myanmar, including the KNPP, met in order to construct a common program to end military rule and restore democracy. The resulting Mao Tha Raw Hta Agreement constituted the first comprehensive program agreed upon by ethnic groups, including those who have signed cease-fire agreements with SPDC and spelling out their common position. Most importantly, they vowed to strengthen the ties between the ethnic minorities movements and the National League for Democracy, headed by Aung San Suu Kyi. They also agreed to the establishment of a federal union wherein "national states [have] rights of national equality and self-determination."[88]

This year the KNPP has focused its efforts on obtaining financial support for the projects they carry out for the Karenni people. According to the KNPP, lack of finances has seriously limited the effectiveness of their endeavors to change their present situation. The Education Department received aid from various organizations, including the BBC, which was used for organizing events. The Karenni Social Welfare Committee (KSWC), founded in 1996 and organized by the KNPP, also received more attention. The purpose of the KSWC is to provide aid to Karenni who refuse relocation but are unable to travel to refugee camps in Thailand. As mentioned above, many of these people are forced to hide in the jungle, where conditions are poor. A mobile medical team with limited supplies was sent into the field to provide some relief. The KSWC also makes a record of human rights abuses and SPDC activities in Karenni State, for the information of the UN, NGOs and human rights groups. The KSWC also promotes educational opportunities for the youth.[89]

Contact with the outside world was facilitated by an Internet connection, through which the government of Karenni can now be reached by electronic mail. On the whole, the KNPP reports no improvement whatsoever in Karenni State. The European Commission, the Scandinavian countries and Switzerland have been approached for aid, but no response has been as yet forthcoming. Nevertheless, the EU tabled a resolution on Myanmar at the 53rd session of the UN Commission on Human Rights, which took place in April in Geneva. The resolution was adopted without a vote and expressed deep concern for the human rights violations against ethnic minorities. In 1998, the Government of Karenni hopes to engage external governments in negotiations and persuade the European Commission to consider diplomatic support and financial aid to Karenni State.

The Karenni became a UNPO Member in January 1993.

KOMI

Location: Russian Federation
Religion: Christianity (Orthodox and Protestant) and Islam
Languages: Komi, Russian and 70 other languages
Population: [census data not available]

During the Middle Ages the Komi were the merchants of north-west Europe. This situation lasted until 1472, when the Komi were conquered by the Russians and became a part of Russia. Before the Bolshevik Revolution of 1917 the Komi territory was divided among several *gubernia's* (provinces) in the Russian Empire. After the revolution of 1917, as a result of the Soviet nationality policy, the Komi autonomous region was proclaimed, later becoming the Komi Autonomous Socialist Soviet Republic (Komi ASSR). This nationality policy awoke the national consciousness of the Komi People. At present, around 75% of the Komi people speak their native language. Since 1992, the republic has been a sovereign within the Russian Federation. The Komi language and culture suffered a great deal from the forced Russification policies pursued during the years of Soviet rule and the Komi continue to rebuild their social, political and cultural identity.

In March 1996, the Government of the Komi Republic and the Russian Government signed an agreement on "defining the powers and responsibilities between the Russian Federation and the Republic Komi". In 1997, on the basis of this agreement the Committee for the Revival of the Komi People has elaborated new legislation to ensure possibilities for the Komi to stimulate their culture. Now, there are governmental programmes to preserve the languages and other modes of cultural expression within the framework of the nationality policy. Also, a ministry on Nationality Affairs has been established. Abroad, the Committee has been actively involved in activities for the International Decade of Indigenous Populations in the World and the Committee has participated in work on the draft resolution on Indigenous Populations.

On 5–6 December 1997, the 5th Congress of the Komi people was held in the capital of Syktyvkar. The Congress comprises 200 members delegated from regional conferences and representing over 50,000 people. The resolutions passed during this congress concerned the social and economic problems of the Komi people in the Komi Republic and the diaspora. This included the strong congressional opposition to plans by the Russian government to issue new passports of the Russian Federation without marking the ethnicity in them. In addition, the Congress demanded the Komi language be taught in all education levels, including pre-school and graduate education.

In presidential elections on 30 November 1997, Mr Yuri Spiridonov was re-elected as the president of the Komi Republic. Within the government, two Komis have been appointed as ministers. During 1997, the Committee has extended ties with NGOs in other countries with Finno-Ugric populations and governmental organizations, e.g. the Saami parliament and the Nordic Union. Foreign contacts, including permanent representations, have been established with Moscow and St. Petersburg.

The Komi Republic is dependent on the general social and economic situation in the Russian Federation. Economic growth is lacking and the situation in Komi is especially bad for the rural population. The land property still belongs to *kolkhozes* and *sovkhozes* (collective farms), although the privatization of it now is possible. However, all preconditions for successful economic development are present in the area. The vast forests can easily be exploited for timber and the natural resources of gas, oil and coal are so abundant that they will be profitable very soon after a start will be made on drilling. This touches upon another problem in the Komi Republic. Drilling for oil and gas has been going on for years now, but in the Soviet tradition, little attention has been given to maintenance of the oil pipes and its impact on the environment. In the Fall of 1995, an environmental disaster occurred in the Pechora river region when large spills of oil ended up in the rivers and marshes. To date, nothing has been done to ameliorate the ecological destruction from this accident and little or no attention has been given to preventing such occurrences in the future. During 1997, activity in oil-drilling and gas production increased marginally.

The Komi are represented by the Committee for the Revival of the Komi People, which joined the UNPO in 1992 in order to bring more attention to the subject of cultural revival.

KOSOVA

Location:	Balkans
Religion:	Islam and Christianity (Orthodox and Catholic)
Language:	Albanian
Population:	2.2 million

The Republic of Kosova is situated in the strategic crossroads of the Balkans, bordering Albania, Serbia, Montenegro and the Republic of Macedonia. The Albanian people are descendants of the Illyrians, inhabitants of the western Balkan peninsula since the third millennium BC. In 1913, as a result of the London Conference, one-half of Albanian territories, including Kosova, were taken away from Albania and granted to the Serb, Croat, Slovene Kingdom and to Greece. This was the starting point of the open and unsolved question of the Albanians in the Balkans. Forcefully included in the former Yugoslavia, the Albanians were subject to systematic depopulation in Kosova and a division of Albanian ethnic territories into four federal units: Kosova, Republic of Macedonia, Serbia and Montenegro.[90]

In 1943, the Conference of Bujan, attended by Allied representatives, recognized the Kosova-Albanian's right to self-determination. After the end of World War II, however, the Assembly of Kosova was forced to vote for an entry into Yugoslavia at its Convention in Prizren in 1945. In 1974, by reconfirming the Bujan Resolution, the federal status of Kosova was recognized in the Constitution of the Socialist Federal Republic of Yugoslavia. Kosova was represented in all elected bodies, including the presidency of the state, and had the right to veto. Kosova passed its own constitution, maintained a genuine constitutional government and had a territorial defence force.

During the 1980s, the Communist League gradually undermined Kosova's position, by illegally suspending Kosova's federal status and culminating in the military occupation by Serbia in 1989. The people of Kosova proclaimed Kosova's independence in July 1990, based on the right to self-determination and founded a nonviolent movement led by the Democratic League of Kosova (LDK).[91] The people of Kosova opt for independence, which is a compromise between the obvious solution of unification with Albania and the realistic political situation, which is based on the delicate geo-political balance in the region and compatibility with international principles. The Referendum on Independence in September 1991, and the internationally observed multi-party parliamentary and presidential elections of May 1992 convincingly show the existence of a shadow-state in Kosova.[92] The Kosova Assembly was never allowed to assemble and part of the Government of Kosova has been forced to operate in-exile. Since 1989, the Albanian nonviolent movement has built political and state institutions in Kosova and has sought international support for Kosova's case.

On 22 March 1998, the second multi-party parliamentary and presidential elections will be held. Human right abuses, such as extra-judicial killings, torture, intimidation, seizures, arrests, political 'show trials', property searches and forced evictions are occur frequently and are carried out by the Serb authorities. Approximately, 35,000 police and 40,000 military and paramilitary forces have been stationed in Kosova since 1989. Because of these oppressive policies more than 350,000 Albanians fled abroad.[93] The Council for the Defence of Human Rights and Freedoms (CDHRF) in Prishtina, the UN Special Rapporteur and other official sources, observed that the human right situation deteriorated dramatically in 1997. In comparison with 1996, killings nearly doubled to reach 35, and thousands of Albanians were tortured, wrongfully sentenced, harassed and evicted.

The schools and University have been closed for 450,000 Albanian pupils and students since 1991. As a temporary solution, Albanians organized education in private homes. In 1996, the Saint Egidio Community mediated an education agreement and Presidents Rugova of Kosova and Milosevic of Yugoslavia signed an agreement in September 1996. To date, the education agreement, granting Albanian education in the schools and university, has not been implemented. On 1 October 1997, thousands of Albanian students from the University of Prishtina demonstrated peacefully in demanding that the Prishtina University premises be returned to ethnic Albanians. Heavily armed Serbian police forces broke up the protests, using truncheons and tear gas to disperse the huge crowd. Several students and teachers got seriously injured. 29 October and 30 December saw similar actions, further increasing tensions in Kosova.

The economy of Kosova has gravely deteriorated, with over 70% of Albanians unemployed.[94] The Serbs have expelled 150,000 Albanian workers from their jobs; frozen enterprises' and citizens' financial assets in order to forcibly integrate Kosovan with Serbian companies; plundered equipment and resources; and have taken full-control of the mining industry. The national income has fallen from US$900 per capita to US$400 (statistically the lower limit of poverty according to UN standards). Many rely on hard currency, sent by the approximately 600,000 Albanian Kosovans who work and live in the diaspora. Similarly, the social situation and health care have drastically deteriorated following the expulsion of virtually all Albanian doctors and medical staff from health institutions.

As a result of the non-violent Albanian movement and President Rugova's peaceful policy, until now an outright war has been avoided. 1997, however, has witnessed increasing attacks on policemen, officials and pro-Serb Albanians, leaving many killed. Circumstances surrounding these attacks remain unresolved, but Serb officials, and increasingly other sources, such as the Western press, blame the Kosova Liberation Army (KLA).[95] Under this pretext, the Serbian police launched a new wave of killings and arrests. Framed political trials of groups of Albanians, resulted in draconian sentences; 52 Albanians were sentenced to 557 years of imprisonment.

The explosive situation in Kosova has reached a breaking point, also due to the prevailing crises in Serbia, Albania, FYROM, and recent turbulence in Montenegro.

In 1997 Kosova received increased attention and support from the international community. All relevant international fora including the U.S., the UN, the EU, the Contact Group, NATO, the OSCE, the Council of Europe, the European Parliament and the UNPO, seriously dealt with Kosova. Apart from the U.S. Information Center, the Serbian authorities refuse to permit other governmental, inter-governmental, or foreign media permanent representation in Kosova and attempts to open offices all failed.[96]

The United States has consistently supported a negotiated settlement of the Kosova issue, with international mediation. The U.S. will not recognize the FRY until the issue of Kosova is duly addressed and they have extended the outer walls of sanctions against Serbia for yet another year, as the Kosova issue remained unresolved. The UN adopted resolutions on Kosova, inter alia during the 52nd session of the General Assembly. It also expressed its concern on gross abuses of human rights and ethnic cleansing. The General Assembly urged implementation of the Education Agreement, unconditional return of OSCE monitors, respect of the peoples will and an urgent start with negotiations. The EU increasingly took an interest in Kosova and the issue remained one of key conditions for the EU–FRY relations. On 30 December, 1997 the EU removed the autonomous trade preferences to FRY for the year 1998, which were granted the previous year.

The OSCE dealt continuously with the question of Kosova in 1997. A Personal Representative of the Chairman in Office was appointed, but he was unable to work in Kosova, as Serbia refused to grant him a visa. In the NATO Ministerial Meeting (16 December) the security implications of the Kosova issue were discussed. The Final Communiqué stated the concern on the escalated situation in Kosova and called for a mutually acceptable solution through negotiations. The Bonn Conference on the Implementation of the Dayton Accord (9–10 December) focused specifically on Kosova. The Final Document expressed the increasing concern about escalation of tensions in Kosova and called for mutually acceptable solutions through responsible dialogue. The Serb side left the Conference as a reaction to the discussion of the Kosova issue. Germany has constantly been engaged in finding a peaceful solution. Germany co-sponsored (with the U.S. and France) two initiatives for an immediate start of negotiations between the two sides. In October, the German Bundestag adopted a resolution, assessing Kosova to be an international problem, which requires a negotiated settlement through mediation of a third party.

In October, the European Parliament adopted a resolution calling for the improvement of relations between the FRY and Kosova. The European Parliament, subsequently, urged the Serbian authorities to allow the opening of an EU office in Kosova. Additionally, in January the Italian Parliament stated that the solution of Kosova issue should be based on the right to self-determination.

Albanian–Serb roundtables were held in Rhodes, Munich, New York, Vienna, Ulqin and Athens, organized mainly by international NGOs. The New York roundtable, held on 7–9 April, brought together political representatives from both sides. Although the participants recognized the value of further discussion, no timetable was set.[97] Moreover, no representative of the Socialist Party of Serbia (SPS) attended the meeting. In April the UNPO assisted a delegation of Kosova during its visit in the Hague.

Throughout the year President Rugova had numerous meetings with statesmen and heads of international institutions, during which he sought recognition for the right to self-determination of the Kosovan people. He also called for a protectorate over Kosova as an interim solution, as well as for urgent start of a peace process regarding Kosova.

Kosova became Member of the UNPO in August 1991.

KUMYK

Admitted to UNPO Membership in 1997.

Location:	North Caucasus
Religion:	Islam
Language:	Russian and Kumyk
Population:	300,000

The Kumyk are an indigenous people of the North Caucasus. The Kumyk territory is separated into seven districts covering 12,000 km2, mainly in the plains and foothills of the present-day Republic of Dagestan (Khasavjurt, Babajurt, Kiziljurt, Bujnaksk, Lenin, Kajakent, part of Kajtag, Kizljarsk region). The plains region in the north is bordered by the Turek river while the Bashlychaj river to the south makes up the border of the more mountainous territory. The eastern border is formed by the Caspian Sea and in the west lies the region inhabited by the Avartsy people.

Although the Kumyk once dominated this region, massive migration has made them a minority. Dagestan itself is populated by no less than 19 different peoples, the Avars being the largest with 25% of the Republic's 2 million inhabitants. The Kumyk comprise 12% of the population. Of the total 300,000 Kumyk, 82% live in urban areas of Dagestan. The remaining Kumyk reside in the Chechen Republic Ichkeria, North Ossetia, Turkey, Iran and Syria.

Some scholars believe that the Kumyk are an intermingling of various indigenous Caucasian peoples with Turkic-speaking tribes who migrated to Dagestan. The Kumyk language includes elements of the languages of the Huns, Khazars and Kipchaks, who variously inhabited the region from the 4th through 12th centuries. The Kumyk consider themselves one of the indigenous peoples of Dagestan and acknowledge the influence of tribes who came to the region. The old Kumyk language was the language of correspondence with Russian czars, Russian officials, as well as the language of communication of the peoples of the North-East Caucasus.

Throughout much of their history, the primary focus of the economic activity of the Kumyk has been agriculture and livestock-breeding. Proximity to the sea and to numerous rivers created favourable conditions for fishing. Production of oil and salt also played a certain role in economy. Some mountainous parts of Dagestan were supplied with salt and oil produced by the Kumyk. The most important trade-routes of the East Caucasus passed through the Kumyk territory and this insured the key role of trade in the economy of the Kumyk.

Mentioned as early as the second century as one of the numerous tribes inhabiting the Caucasian region, the Kumyk culture and anthropological features resemble those of the other peoples of Dagestan and North Caucasus. Although the Kumyk people belonged to various kingdoms from the 4th–13th centuries, from c.1400–1867 they were united under the Kumyk Shamkhalat kingdom. This kingdom enjoyed protection from Turkey, Iran and Russia, although wars with the latter were frequent. Russia occupied the North Caucasus in 1867, however, and the Shamkhalat kingdom was divided into two Russian provinces.

During the period between the occupation and the Russian revolution in 1917 the Kumyk national movement was centered mainly in Turkey. Following 1917, the Kumyk joined forces with other North Caucasian peoples in the struggle for a North Caucasian Democratic Republic. However, the victorious Russian communists established an autonomous Dagestan in 1920, and Kumyk autonomy was suppressed. The Bolsheviks ignored Kumyk nationalists and the movement's leaders were killed or repressed.

Under Soviet occupation, a policy of ethnic reconstitution was implemented by which a new "historical community" was to be created: the Soviet people, in particular a singular Dagestan "people". Toward this end, massive population transfers occurred against the will of the people being transferred as well as the Kumyk. The scale of the population transfer was not economically justified and, in terms of national and language policy, it was aimed at forceful assimilation of the Kumyk and the transferred people. An unregulated migration of mountain dwellers to the plains led to the subsequent abandonment of numerous mountain villages. Because the new arrivals to the North Caucasus received a large portion of the Kumyk plains, land shortage among the indigenous Kumyk was widespread. The immigrants who moved to the plain in the last 50 years have had privileges such as higher purchase prices on agricultural products, larger private plots of land, easier admittance to Universities and better jobs. The introduction of monoculture agriculture and the exploitation of the soil and deforestation all contributed to the present situation of economic and ecological crisis in the area.

Land shortage and unemployment in rural areas, coupled with the inadequacy of basic social, cultural and economic conditions, aggravate the ever-increasing migration to towns. Since 1979, the percentage of the Kumyk population which lives outside Dagestan, and thus outside traditional Kumyk territory, has increased from 11–18%. Considering that the Kumyk are a small people, this increase is alarming. Because there is no single region left which is densely populated by Kumyk, the vast distances between Kumyk people make it increasingly difficult for the Kumyk to maintain their national traditions and language.

Since the 1930s, the Kumyk have been forced to use the Russian script instead of the traditional Arabic, thereby furthering the slow destruction of the Kumyk culture. In the regions where the scale of the population transfer was the largest, there are neither newspapers nor radio stations in the Kumyk language and many schools no longer teach in the Kumyk language. Moreover, the Kumyk are not able to represent themselves properly in the Russian Parliament because the Dagestani *nomenklatura* sends its own people to the representative bodies.

During the period of *perestroika*, the Kumyk national movement was revived. On 19 November 1989, during the First Congress of Kumyk People, the Kumyk People's Movement, *Tenglik*, was founded. The Congress is the highest representative body of the Kumyk people, while the Kumyk National Council is the representative body which works between the meetings of the Congress. The Movement is a public political organization of the Kumyk people, registered by the Ministry of Justice of Dagestan.

The main aim of *Tenglik* is to solve the problems of the Kumyk people: to create the conditions necessary for the development of the economy and cultural traditions, for a return to living in the ancient territory of the Kumyk and to form administrative bodies for self-government. In order to achieve this, the Tenglik feel that administrative reform in the Republic of Dagestan is necessary. Dagestan should be the federal state under which all nations, such as the Kumyk, can form their self-governed republics.

Tenglik joined the UNPO in order to establish relations with the international community and to be able to represent themselves properly in both international fora and the Russian Parliament. They also strive to preserve their traditional way of life, culture and customs of the people. They want to protect the Kumyk people against ethno-demographical aggression and avoid the discrimination that has been launched against them. Toward this end, *Tenglik* intends to radicalize the process of democratic reform by the use of non-economic means. The Kumyk people seek self-determination in the form of national autonomy.

KURDISTAN (IRAQI)

Location:	Iraq
Religion:	Islam
Language:	Kurdish
Population:	4 million in Iraqi Kurdistan

Kurdistan was for centuries the scene for disputes among regional and world powers. In 1245, the Mongolians conquered the territory and 250 years later the Ottomans followed. After the dissolution of the Ottoman Empire after World War I, the Kurds were promised their own state (Treaty of Sévres, 1920). Ultimately though, two Arab states, Syria and Iraq were founded. In the early 1980s, the Iraqi President, Saddam Hussein, began a systematic relocation and extermination of the Kurdish population. This so-called "Anfal" campaign led to the disappearance of over 180,000 Kurds. After being defeated in the Gulf War, the Iraqi forces withdrew from most areas of Iraqi Kurdistan in October 1991 and the United Nations created a safe-haven in the Kurdish area north of the 36th parallel (to protect the Kurdish and other civilian populations and provide humanitarian assistance). It also facilitated the formation of independent political structures.

In May 1992, parliamentary elections were held in South Kurdistan (Iraqi Kurdistan) which the UNPO monitored. A coalition parliament was formed dominated by the two largest parties, the Patriotic Union of Kurdistan (PUK) and the Kurdistan Democratic Party (KDP). Fighting broke out in 1994 between the PUK and KDP; the elected representatives of the Iraqi Kurds, the parliament and the regional government lost their power to the party militias. In practice, the parliament, which held its last assembly in May 1995, no longer has any influence. Iraqi Kurdistan is divided into two separate administrative units under the authority of the respective party militias.

During 1997, the Turkish military forces entered Iraqi Kurdistan on a number of occasions fighting the Kurdistan Workers Party (PKK). In October, the Turkish army carried out more than 20 air raids in the Iraqi Kurdistan region which resulted in casualties. Allegedly, napalm and cluster-bombs were used by the Turkish army during these attacks.[98] The policy of forced displacement applied by the Iraqi government was continued during 1997. According to a report by Special Rapporteurs of the UN, forcible relocations continued to take place in the context of a policy aimed at changing the demography of the oil-rich sectors of Kirkuk and Khanaquin by deporting ethnic Kurds and Turkman families. In order to increase the percentage of the Arab population in predominantly Kurdish areas, the Government of Iraq has forced entire communities to undergo internal deportation. The personal property left by the deportees was then given to ethnic Arabs coming from other parts of Iraq and several other villages have reportedly entirely been destroyed.[99] The Kurdish families being deported had been dispossessed of title to their properties as well as their food ration cards. In the city of Kirkuk, Iraqi troops have reportedly been conducting searches on a daily basis, with homes being raided late at night or at dawn.[100] The displacement left affected families in worse economic and social conditions: tens of thousands of Kurdish families from Kirkuk now live in tents and camps in the region from which the government withdrew its authorities in October 1991. These families live in extremely harsh conditions, particularly for small children and the elderly.[101]

In July, the Secretary General of the PUK, Jalal Talabani, met with some officials of the White House in Washington where the discussions focused on the situation in Iraqi Kurdistan and the efforts aimed at restoring peace to the region. In December, the UN General Assembly adopted a resolution in which it strongly condemned the massive and extremely grave violations of human rights and international humanitarian law by the Government of Iraq. It called upon the Government of Iraq "to cease immediately its repressive practices aimed at the Iraqi Kurd ... ."[102]

The state of emergency which lasted for ten years in several provinces in Turkey has been lifted for the provinces of Batman, Bitlis and Bingöl and prolonged for four months (until February 1998) in six other provinces. The constitutional ban on forming political organizations on religious or ethnic platforms does not permit a legal representation of Kurdish interests in the political and public life of Turkey. In Turkey, 152 laws and approximately 700 paragraphs regulate the freedom of speech concerning the Kurdish question.[103]

During 1997, the Turkish government continued attempts to solve the Kurdish question with military force, resulting in gross human rights violations. Kurdish villagers are bearing the brunt of human rights abuses committed by both government forces and armed members of the PKK. The authorities have reportedly tortured, abducted and extra-judicially killed villagers in the course of security raids on rural settlements.[104] On 13–14 December, at a meeting of European leaders in Luxembourg, Turkey was rejected as a candidate for membership in the European Union. The EU leaders cited as one reason for the rejection of its candidacy, the Turkish campaign against the Kurds.[105] According to the International Association for Human Rights in Kurdistan, a change of the present situation concerning the Kurdish question in Turkey is not in sight.[106]

Iraqi Kurdistan is a founding Member of the UNPO. It has been represented primarily by the PUK and KDP and the Association for the Rights of Kurdistan.

LAKOTA NATION

Location:	North-central North America
Religion:	traditional religion
Language:	Lakota (*Teton*), Nakota (*Yankton*) and Dakota (*Santee*).
Population:	100,000
Ethnic diversity:	79,000 Lakota, 5,000 Nakota and 28,000 Dakota

The Lakota, Nakota and Dakota Nation (also known as the Great Sioux Nation) descend from of the original inhabitants of North America. Following almost a half century of conflict and peace treaties between the Sioux and the westward migrating whites, the Second Fort Laramie Treaty was signed in 1868 between the U.S. government and the Sioux. The treaty established a Sioux reservation in their traditional territories surrounding the sacred Black Hills, "for the absolute and undisturbed use and occupation [by] the Indians." However, when gold was discovered in the Black Hills, six years later, white prospectors followed. In 1877, following clashes with the army, the U.S. government forced the Chiefs to transfer the Black Hills to white control and organized the partition of the Sioux Territory in violation of the 1868 treaty. More than a century later, in 1980, the U.S. Supreme Court ruled that the Sioux were entitled to US$122 million in compensation for the Black Hills. The Sioux refused to accept the money, which lies in trust in the U.S. capital.

The Federal government's institution designed to deal with Native American issues is the Bureau of Indian Affairs (BIA). Created in 1834, the BIA exercises political and economic power on reservations and as such remains the primary employment opportunity for many Native Americans (currently employing approximately 12,000 people). The BIA's bureaucratic power has allowed it to maintain a strong hold on the life of the community and has thwarted genuine attempts for economic self-control. Another government organ meant to deal with Native American issues is the Senate Indian Affairs Committee which has repeatedly brought up the issues of unemployment and poverty among Native Americans but which has consistent difficulty in mobilizing institutional support for many initiatives.

In 1994, the Lakota Nation Human Rights Organization was founded. The organization monitors the situation on reservations (i.e., tribal courts, social-service programs, communication between tribal councils and state and federal agencies, etc.) and prepares media presentations regarding the situation on reservations.

In 1996, the Lakota band of Hunkpapa, on Standing Rock Reservation, proclaimed inherent powers of sovereignty by using cultural resource laws relating to tribal landowners and tribes. The Hunkpapa Treaty Council strives for self-determination for the Lakota nation, pursuing international support for the UN Draft Declaration on the Rights of Indigenous Peoples. However, the enthusiasm of the Indians about the Draft Declaration is, by no means, shared by U.S government which is continuously lobbying for changes in the document especially to the provision that calls for the "restitution" of traditional indian lands.

The Lakota have formed several organizations for the development of tribal people, such as the Alliance of Tribal Tourism Advocates, whose overriding goal is to enhance prospects of tourism development in accordance with the traditional values and cultural integrity of the native people. Other self-help projects are the Oglala Lakota College and KILI radio, "the voice of the Lakota Nation", and the Lakota Fund which makes small loans to help entrepreneurs start businesses on the reservation.

In 1997 the Lakota once more protested for the misuse of Indian spirituality by new Age outsiders. The Pine Ridge reservation judge banned white people to be present at Sundance ceremonies and did not allow money to be paid for performing ceremonies. Although the first decision was revoked, the Oglala Lakota now consider holding a referendum about the issue. This conflict has once again focused attention to the question "who is an Indian"; many Lakota are married to non-Indians which would mean that their spouses and children would not be allowed to attend ceremonies. Also the question arose whether it would be a violation of human rights to refuse people access because of their race.

Mortgages became available this year to Indian home-owners on reservations in South Dakota. Restrictions to loans on lands held in trust were lifted and banks are now starting to fund housing on the reservations. In 1997, nine reservations voted for new chairmen to their tribal councils. On 21 June 1997, the Lakota Nation once again hosted a Prayer Day of Peace, as a chance for all peoples to come together in the name of peace and unity.

The Lakota Nation became a Member of the UNPO in 1994. Its leaders strive for the upholding of treaty-making powers as a nation with the U.S. and Canada and the right of inherent sovereignty.

MAOHI PEOPLE

Location: French Polynesia
Religion: Christianity (Protestant)
Population: 133,000

Almost 2300 years ago, the Maohi arrived on the coast of what is now known as French Polynesia and lived free of external influences until the 18th century. In 1767 the first Europeans arrived on Tahiti; in 1880 the islands became a French colony. The region was renamed French Polynesia in 1945 and assigned the status of *Territoire d'Outre-Mer* (overseas territory). At that time, the Maohi were granted French citizenship.

The Maohi managed to remain relatively self-sufficient despite French control, depending mainly on their traditional lifestyle for their livelihood. However, this changed drastically when France moved its nuclear testing program from Algeria to French Polynesia in 1960. The construction of the *Centre d'Experimentation du Pacifique* (CEP), France's nuclear testing center, was begun in 1963 and has been under the protection of the French army and navy. From the commencement of operations in 1966, 180 nuclear tests have been conducted. Following a three-year moratorium, the French government recommenced testing in 1995. By signing the 1996 Treaty of Rarotonga, the French promised to eventually discontinue nuclear testing and make the Pacific a permanently "nuclear-free zone".

French Polynesia is comparatively wealthy in relation to its Pacific neighbors, with an annual per capita income nearly three times that of Fiji. However, much of this affluence stems from the nuclear program upon which a large part of the population depends for employment. In 1995, the resumed nuclear program pumped $1.25 billion, over a third of the entire GNP, into the economy. Since the moratorium, unemployment has risen to 16% and jobs are increasingly scarce.[107]

The nuclear program continued to be the focus of Maohi activity in 1997. Abolition 2000, a global network of nearly 700 anti-nuclear organizations, held a conference on the island of Moorea from 21–27 January. Nearly 100 delegates from all over the world participated in the conference, which was hosted by Hiti Tau, the umbrella organization for Maohi non-governmental organizations. Although the conference's aim was to further the overall goal of total nuclear abolition by 2000, the focus remained the French Polynesian experience. Many first hand testimonies of miscarriages, birth defects and serious health problems were given by former employees of the test sites over the last 30 years.[108]

A resolution was adopted at the conference which addresses the inadequacies of the International Atomic Energy Agency (IAEA) study on the effects of French nuclear testing in the Pacific. The resolution cited the fact that the IAEA was established by the UN in order to promote nuclear power and that the study was heavily funded by the French government. Due to a "serious conflict of interest", the resolution requested that an ongoing comprehensive study be carried out and that adequate compensation be granted to those negatively affected by the tests.[109]

The resulting statement from the conference, the Moorea Declaration, supplements the original Abolition 2000 statement. The main addition centers around the need for the inclusion of the indigenous people in the abolition program.[110] Paragraph three of the Declaration states that "colonized and indigenous peoples have, in large part, borne the brunt of this nuclear devastation- from the mining of uranium and the testing of nuclear weapons on indigenous peoples' land, to the dumping, storage and transport of plutonium and nuclear wastes and the theft of land for nuclear infrastructure."[111] In other words, self-determination and independence are key to the indigenous peoples' ability to successfully oppose nuclear weapons.

Along these lines, Hiti Tau requested the return of French Polynesia to the list of the Decolonization Committee of the UN. They fear that because most of the world sees colonialism as a thing of the past, if their situation is not highlighted by joining the list, they will remain a colony indefinitely.[112] Another adopted resolution, addressing the IAEA study, also mentioned the "fact that the French nuclear program has seriously undermined the social, cultural and economic fabric of Polynesian life". This, states the resolution, is the effect of the islands' economic dependency on the nuclear program. Though the French have promised to subsidize the economy until 2006, many wonder what will happen thereafter.

The distortion of the economy is worsened by the fact that 36% of the workforce are public-service employees.[113] Although many Maohi reportedly desire independence, when it comes to a vote there is overwhelming support to remain a French colony. This apparent contradiction is due largely to the fact that French settlers comprise more than 50% of the population, but also, at least in part, because a vote for independence is a vote to rid themselves of the source of their livelihood.[114] This state of affairs was reflected in last year's elections in which the French-backed ruling party won 22 of 41 seats in the Territorial Assembly. However, the Tavini Huiraatira independence party, led by Oscar Temaru, won 11 seats, which was considered a substantial success. Many Maohi not only feel that they are treated like second class citizens in their own country, but also that France has done little to develop the local economy. Fishing, agriculture (vanilla and pineapples) and the famous black pearls are all traditional activities which have had scarce official encouragement. In addition, the European Union's labor policy will allow better educated EU citizens to obtain higher paying positions on the islands.

Also at the conference, Hiti Tau presented the preliminary findings from research being carried out by themselves in cooperation with the World Council of Churches and two academics from the Netherlands. These findings revealed widespread and severe health problems among the workers. Until now, health statistics have been tightly controlled by the French government, whose reporting has been internationally criticized as incomplete and inaccurate. The Hiti Tau study is the first independent and comprehensive study performed in French Polynesia since the nuclear tests began.

Presented in September, the study took the form of a sociological inquiry because no reliable medical or epidemiological statistics on the former test site workers' health situation were available. This was due to the fact that, among those involved in the study, 51.5% were never examined at the end of their stay at the test sites, 41% said that they had worked in possibly contaminated zones and, of these,54% said they "at times had to carry-out certain tasks against their will."[115] Many of those surveyed said that when they attempted to link possible contamination to health problems they or others were experiencing, they were threatened with with dismissal or declared unsuitable for their job.[116]

Due to the complete lack of health information, and the fact that most former workers were not tested following the termination of their employment, it was concluded that the French conducted no health-control system for their former employees. The French position that the nuclear tests were not harmful to the health of French Polynesians seemed to be upheld only by the fact that they had never actually collected data which could prove or disprove their claim.[117] Further epidemiological research toward a greater understanding of the effects of the nuclear program on the former workers and the population in general will be a follow-up activity, with 91.3% of those surveyed expressing the need for such a study.

Although the nuclear-free zone has been established on paper, the future continues to be dominated by the nuclear issue. The Treaty of Raratonga does not include any provisions against testing of delivery systems, basing of troops, mining uranium or the transport of nuclear weapons through the zone. Moreover, the clean-up and ongoing monitoring of contaminated sites, and support for test site workers affected by nuclear testing, is also unmentioned. The need to address these issues in more comprehensive legislation was called upon by the NGO Parallel to the South Pacific Forum, held in the Cook Islands in September, in their Pacific Islands Report.

The Maohi became a Member of the UNPO in 1994.

MAPUCHE

Location:	Chile and Argentina
Religion:	Traditional religion and Christianity (Catholic)
Language:	Mapudugun and Spanish
Population:	989,000

The Mapuche[118] are an indigenous people living in south-central Chile and Argentina along the Andes Mountain range, with the Bio-Bio River as a northern border. The Mapuche belong to the tribe of the Araucanians, whose ancestors moved to the region now known as Chile in South America 12,000 years ago. Against great powers such as the Incas, and later the Spanish conquistadors, the Araucanians always resisted. In the course of time, the Mapuche became the dominant group among the Araucanians, comprising 80% of the present indigenous population of Chile.[119] The Mapuche territory is divided into four main regions known as *Puelmapu, Pikunmapu, Lafquenmapu* and *Huillimapu.*[120]

After their second arrival in 1541, Spain signed a treaty in Quillin on 6 January 1641, recognizing the independence of the Mapuche and respecting the Bio-Bio River as the northern border of Mapuche lands. The Mapuche thereby agreed to return the Spanish prisoners of war and allow missionaries to remain. This situation was maintained throughout the period of Spanish rule on the continent. It came to an end in 1881 with the independence of Chile. Throughout this period the Mapuche nation was completely independent, territorially and politically, and it remained so until 1881. The situation was almost identical for the Mapuche in Argentina. In 1979, the Mapuche fell victim to an "Indigenous Peoples Law" instituted by the military regime under Pinochet, the aim of which was to destroy the traditional communities of the Mapuche.[121]

After more than 350 years of territorial integrity and signed and broken peace treaties, the Mapuche people have lost control of their territory to Argentina and Chile. The existence of the Mapuche people is not recognized by the Chilean constitution nor does Chile subscribe to international agreements that promote and protect human rights and rights of indigenous people such as the International Labour Organization Convention 169. This means that neither the legal nor the educational systems are obliged to make a distinction between the Mapuche and Chileans. As a result, the ancestral territorial resources of the Mapuche are continuously ignored and are legally taken into ownership by non-indigenous Chileans. Governmental politics and development projects have been pursued which have further eroded the Mapuche way of life. In Chile, for example, in the Bio-Bio region, the construction of six hydroelectric dams is under way and is threatening thousands of people with the loss of their homes and land. One of the dams has already been completed and a second one has just been given permission to be built. A new indigenous peoples' law designed to protect the land—under which development should not be possible without the agreement of the local communities—has been ignored in the first stages of the dam's planning. The Mapuche people most affected by the changes of the dam's construction live in the Santa Barbara district. The land that is to be lost under the waters of the dam, contains some very important archeological sites, including ancient cemeteries and the site of the historical settlement Chenques. The Mapuche assure that they are not against development, but they have very little legal representation on their behalf in order to achieve a settlement that will ensure a more equitable and sustainable development in which they can participate and by which they can benefit.[122]

Recently there have been plans made by the Chilean government to construct a by-pass in the ninth region. This will affect 28 Mapuche rural communities, where 3,000 people live. It is believed the planned road will lead to the destruction of many homes and widespread felling of the forest in that region, and it is certain that it will also cut through religious sites. In Argentina, the Mapuche are facing the threat of confiscation of 110,000 hectares of their land in Pulmari in the Alumine Region. This is due to the regional government, ignoring the Alfonsin administration's decision to award land rights to the local Mapuche in 1987 under National Decree No. 1410.

The conflict concerning the Pulmari region can be traced back to 1878 after the conquest of the Mapuche lands by the Argentinean army. In 1985 the former Argentinean president Raul Alfonsin announced that the Pulmari region would be returned to the Mapuche and in 1987 he founded the Corporation Interestadual Pulmari (CIP) by Decree No. 1410. The aim of this corporation was to achieve a socio-economic development of the region's indigenous peoples. The Mapuche were told that Pulmari would eventually be returned by the CIP, but this has not happened so far despite persistent requests by the Mapuche communities to the Argentinean authorities.

The regional government of Alumine does not respect the national decree. A Federal Judge has accused the Mapuche of encroachment on the land, which they consider to be their own. Some communities have been threatened with eviction while others are under surveillance by the authorities.[123] In March 1997, the European Parliament passed the "Resolution on the Situation of Human Rights and Indigenous Minorities in Argentina". This resolution expressed its concern on the safety and freedom of the representatives of bodies concerned with the protection of human rights or indigenous people. It also called on the Argentine Government to amend regulations to avoid misinterpretations regarding the rights of the legitimate land owners to defend the rights and interests of indigenous peoples and to avoid expulsion from their constitutionally recognized lands.

Since the beginning of October, the Pichi-Loncoyan and Pilin-Mapu communities of Lumaco municipality have been mobilising in defence of their land rights and the failure of the Chilean judicial system to deliver justice. Earlier this century, these communities were granted legal entitlement to an area of 3,000 hectares of their own ancestral land. Half of this area has now been confiscated by logging companies such as Arauco SA. The loggers occupied and exploited the forests in that region.[124] In an effort to regain their land and protect the forest, the Mapuche tried to stop the logging operations by non-violent actions but on 14 October, a police squad from Puren violently evicted the Mapuches, injuring many of them. Thirty-seven people were arrested and jailed for 20 days before being officially charged. Several other confrontations between the Mapuche and the Chilean authorities took place there, during which a total of 36 people was arrested and detained by the Chilean authorities.[125]

In an effort to add international weight to their efforts to preserve Mapuche culture and to exercise their rights to self-determination, the Mapuche joined the UNPO in January 1993, represented by the Mapuche Interregional Council, an umbrella body, uniting Mapuche organizations in Chile, Argentina and the United Kingdom.

Mari

Location:	Russian Federation
Religion:	Christian (Orthodox) and traditional religion
Language:	Mari (Volga-Finnic)
Population:	750,000

Mari is an autonomous republic in the Russian Federation, along the middle reaches of the Volga River and its tributaries. The Mari people have a long history of struggling against oppression. They have been conquered by Kazars, Volga Bulgars, Tatar Mongols and, in the 16th century, by Russia. Despite their defeat by Ivan the Terrible, Mari resistance against the Russians never ceased. In the 18th century, Mari cultural development was suppressed, with Tsarist Russia conducting a genocidal policy against them. At the end of the 19th century the first democratic movement was founded. In the first years after the Russian revolution, the area inhabited by the Mari became an autonomous region and later, in 1936, a republic. In spite of these developments, there was no improvement of the cultural situation with the Mari language eliminated from schools and the culture suffering from mass collectivization.

During *perestroika* the democratic-national movement of the Mari people was re-activated. In April 1990, the congress of the Mari people, *Mari Ushem* (Union of Mari), met in Ioshkar-Ola. In October 1990 the Supreme Soviet of Mari declared the sovereignty of the republic eliminating the word "autonomous" from the name—calling itself the Mari Soviet Socialist Republic. In December 1991, the first president of the Mari republic, V.M. Zotov, was elected. Due to the fact that the Mari have become a minority on their own land, the socio-political self-determination of this people remains more a declaration than a fact. In December 1994, the *Mari Ushem* activists formed a small political party, the Mari National Rebirth Party. The Mari Republic is headed by a chairman who is elected by the congress. Included among the statutory tasks of the Mari National Union are research into the economic, political and demographic situation of the Mari nation, and gathering and distribution of data on these issues.

During 1997 the political activities of the Mari people declined. This began with the second round of local presidential elections at the end of January 1997, in which Mr. Vyacheslav Kislitsyn was elected as the new president. He is Russian by nationality and does not know the Mari language. He reportedly won the presidential election by accusing the National Movement of the Maris in the local press of violating human rights in the Republic of Mari. In the new government only a few Mari are represented and nearly all ministers do not know the Mari language. Importantly, President Kislitsyn, did not appoint a Mari as the vice president as he had promised before his election. The Mari language is not supported in educational institutions in Mari, whereas in several Tatarstan and Bashkortostan schools, the Mari language is taught. About a third of the Mari people still live in Tatarstan and

Bashkortostan where, apparently, their culture and language is more recognized than in the Republic of Mari.

The main sources of economic development in the region are oil production, oil chemistry, forestry, agriculture and mechanical engineering. Tourism is a new branch of the economy currently being developed. There is unemployment in the Mari Republic but no restrictive prohibitions. Multinational corporations have not yet found their way to the republic and the land still belongs to the *kolkhozes* and *sovkhozes* (collective farms). In June, the Day of Mari Culture and in May–June the festival *Semik* were celebrated. Some improvement in the situation of the Mari people can be noted, since the level of national self-consciousness has improved. For 1998, therefore, the Mari Ushem hopes to increase the activity (the number of activists) of the population, in order for this process to continue.

In 1991, Mari Ushem became a Member of the UNPO, in order to seek support for the preservation and development of its national culture and identity. The goal of this democratic national movement is to resist the cultural linguistic assimilation of the Mari people.

MON PEOPLE

Location:	South-east Asia
Religion:	Buddhism
Language:	Mon and Burmese
Population:	1 million

The former Monland covers three regions stretching over the whole of southern Burma, namely Tenasserim, Pegu and Irrawaddu. The Mon people, along with the Khmer, migrated from China and established a common kingdom in the 1st century, later broken up into the Cambodian and Mon kingdoms. Bordering Thailand in the east and the Andaman Sea in the west, it includes many small islands along its coast line. While the natural resources in Mon State are enough to feed the local population, natural resources such as forest and onshore and offshore mineral resources are exploited only by top Burmese military leaders and foreign companies. At the present time one of the largest investments in the exploitation of natural gas reserves is in Mon State.

After World War II, the promise of independence by the British alerted all non-Burmese ethnic groups to speculate on the future of Burma after independence because all of them had suffered from bitter historical experience before the annexation of Burma by the British. Thus, they became politically active, looking forward to prospects and safeguards of their fundamental human rights in an independent Burma. The Mon presented a seven-point-demand in 1947 intended to safeguard their rights after independence. But, U Nu, the Prime Minister, rejected the Mon demands in saying that the Mon and Burmese were the same and no separate national rights for the Mons should be contemplated. When the demands became popular, and overwhelming support was given to the Mon people, the government imposed their will by force, which resulted in a civil war continues to this day. Though the Mon resistance movement has lasted more than four decades, the Mon have never lost hope and will not surrender their sovereign rights to the Burmese.

It has been over two years since the New Mon State Party (NMSP) and the SLORC (now renamed the SPDC) reached a ceasefire agreement on 29 June 1995. Although there is no fighting between NMSP and SPDC's troops, the human rights situation in Mon State has only worsened; the SPDC continues to violate human rights despite the conditions of the cease-fire agreement. 10,000 Mon refugees who had fled to Thailand were forcibly repatriated to Burma (renamed Myanmar) in 1996, after pressure from the Thai authorities. However, the repatriated refugees remained in camps near the Thai-Burmese border, controlled by the NMSP, because they feared returning to their villages. The situation in the camps is quite harsh; The chances to create farmlands and have self-suffiency are poor and international aid cannot reach them.

The international community has repeatedly condemned the SPDC for its bad human rights records. One of the most notorious instances is the Ye-Tavoy railway, the new "Death Railway". A total of 120,000 people have been forced to build 177 km of embankment, 2.43 meters high and 3.65 meters wide. The building of the Ye-Tavoy railway is linked to the agreement to build a gas pipeline taking Myanmar's gas into Thailand. In view of the Yadana gas pipeline project the entire local population of the Tenasserim Division is being subjected to hardship as a result of the forced labor imposed by the SPDC: forced relocations, arbitrary arrests, rape and executions have taken place in 1997. On 15 May 1997, the UNPO wrote an appeal letter to the government of Thailand urging them to consider delaying the project until progress could be made with respect to the establishment of tripartite dialogue between the SPDC, representatives of ethnic minorities in Myanmar and the democratic groups led by Daw Aung San Suu Kyi to promote national reconciliation.

In April 1997, 800 Mon fled the Tenasserim Division and crossed into Thailand, to a site near the border.[126] On 6 June 1997, with only 300–400 Mon remaining at the site, the Thai authorities repatriated the entire group directly into the hands of the local Burmese army commander. Television cameras and the UNHCR were invited to be present. It remains unclear whether the refugees were willing to return to Myanmar. The fact that they were given the chance to step aside if they did not want to embark on the trucks, does not establish free will to leave or stay.

The Mon became a UNPO Member in 1996 through the Mon Unity League.[127]

NAGALAND

Location:	South Asia
Religion:	Christianity and traditional religion
Language:	Dialects (Tibeto-Burmese), English spoken among minority
Population:	3 million

Nagaland is situated at the junction of present day China, India and Myanmar. The greater part of Nagaland is under Indian rule. It is divided and administered under the states of Assam, Arunachal Pradesh, Manipur and Nagaland. The portion of Nagaland on the Myanmar side has been placed under two administrative units, the Kachin state and Sagaing division. The population of slightly more than 3 million people is comprised of 16 major and 20 minor tribes, of whom about 90% are Christian.

Having migrated from Mongolia around the 10th century, the Nagas are racially and ethnically distinct people. Prior to 1881, the Nagas were living in permanently established village-states. By 1881, the British declared several parts of Southwest Nagaland as a British District. A set of regulations meant to "protect" the Naga, effectively isolated them from political movements in India. Following a 1929 Naga memorandum stating their opposition to possible incorporation into British India, the Naga Hills district was declared an "excluded Area" in 1935. On the eve of Indian independence, the Naga National Council (NNC) declared Nagaland's independence. Nevertheless, despite Mahatma Ghandi's assurances to the contrary, the Naga Hills District was declared a part of India according to the Indian Independence Act of 1947. The independence efforts continued in 1949, when India allegedly revoked the validity of an agreement recognizing the right to self-determination of the Naga people. In 1956, the Federal Republic of Nagaland was declared. In 1963, the state of Nagaland was created by the Government of India. The Armed Forces Special Powers Act of 1958 enabled the Government of India to consolidate its authority through military operations.

Indo-Naga talks resulted in the signing of the Shillong Accord in 1975, which stipulated the unconditional acceptance of the Indian constitution and the surrender of arms by the Naga forces. The accord was not accepted by most Nagas however, leading to the establishment of the National Socialist Council of Nagaland (NSCN) in 1980 with the mandate to pursue the struggle for freedom. The NSCN refuses to accept incorporation into India and continues to strive for the independence of Nagaland. In March 1995, the Indian government again declared the state of Nagaland a "Disturbed Area", empowering the armed forces under the Armed Forces Special power Act of 1958. The situation in Nagaland continued to be tense throughout 1995–1996, with recurring incidents of arrests, abductions causing disappearances, torture and summary executions. Indian forces present in Nagaland are estimated at over 200,000 according to the NSCN.

In 1996, the Prime Minister of India and other senior government officials expressed the need to seek a political negotiated solution to the conflict in Nagaland.

After extensive indirect and direct contacts between the Government of India and the NSCN, agreement was reached for unconditional dialogue at the highest level (Prime Ministerial). In February, then Prime Minister of India, P.V. Narasimha Rao, visited the north-eastern region of India and Nagaland. His successor, Prime Minister Deve Gowda, met secretly with the NSCN Chairman and General Secretary in March in Switzerland, where they reiterated the agreement reached with the previous Indian government for unconditional talks. This process was temporarily challenged by reports in early May of a large offensive by the Indian military against the NSCN. Although the offensive appeared to send a contradictory signal regarding the intentions of the Indian government, the new Prime Minister Gujral and the NSCN leadership promised to carry on the negotiation process.

Preliminary talks took place later in May in Geneva between senior Indian government officials and the NSCN leadership to discuss modalities for negotiations and the conditions necessary for its success. The result was a declaration of a cease-fire to enter into effect on 1 August. The cease-fire was extended on 1 October and it has been observed, despite a number of incidents involving both members of the Kaplan faction of the NSCN and Indian forces. The venue of the talks remains to be decided, but this will be outside of India. A cease-fire agreement mutually declared on 25 July for a period of three months was recently extended until 31 January 1998. The question of the venue for negotiations between the Government of India and the NSCN is under discussion.

Nagaland became a UNPO Member in 1993 through the National Socialist Council of Nagaland (NSCN) .

OGONI

Location: Southern Nigeria (Niger Delta)
Religion: Christianity and traditional religion
Language: Ogoni languages (Gokana, Eleme, Tai, Khana) and English
Population: 500,000

The Ogoni are a distinct ethnic group in south-eastern Nigeria. Archaeological and oral historical evidence suggests that the Ogoni have lived in the Niger delta for about 500 years. Until the advent of British colonial rule in Nigeria the Ogoni enjoyed self-determination. In 1914, Great Britain formed the Colony and Protectorate of Nigeria. On 1 October 1960, Nigeria became independent from Great Britain and, in 1963, the Federal Republic of Nigeria was proclaimed. Several attempts have been made by the Ogoni to reclaim autonomy, the latest being the submission of the Ogoni Bill of Rights to the Nigerian government in 1990 and the formation of the Movement for the Survival of the Ogoni People (MOSOP) in 1990. On 10 November 1995, Ken Saro-Wiwa (then President of MOSOP) and eight other Ogoni leaders were executed by the Nigerian regime. As a result, the Government of Sani Abacha was suspended from the Commonwealth.

In 1958 Shell Oil Company struck oil in Ogoniland, which set in motion a process that dramatically affected not only the Ogoni but Nigeria as a whole. About 90% of Nigeria's export income is obtained through the oil business, while the land of the Niger Delta where the Ogoni live is the source of over 90% of the resources. The social and environmental costs of the oil exploitation have been high for the Ogoni. Many Ogonis do not have access to the basic necessities of sanitation and health.[128] Additionally, Ogonis are still denied a share of the revenue from the oil business, as the distribution of oil revenues is controlled by the federal, state and local governments. The majority of the Ogoni suffer from a persistently high unemployment rate.[129] There are significant health-care problems in Ogoniland due to the limited supply of medicines available and little diagnostic equipment. People involved in MOSOP activities encounter problems in obtaining medical assistance because the staff at the clinics fear reprisals.[130] Arrests and extortion continue to pressure many and some families have resorted to selling their produce to release arrested relatives. Living standards have worsened in Ogoniland with restrictions on freedom of movement, the confiscation of goods and forced bribes paid to soldiers. Unemployment in Ogoniland has increased as more Ogonis have been forced underground or have been dismissed from jobs due to alleged sympathy for MOSOP.[131]

During 1997, human rights abuses continued with impunity in Ogoniland. The Nigerian military has both sustained and intensified efforts to stamp out protests. Several prominent MOSOP members and activists were targeted, causing many to abandon their jobs or to flee the country. In some areas in Ogoniland Nigerian troops set up road blocks and collected "tolls" from motorists, cyclists and farmers. There were three incidents, where the troops shot into moving vehicles, killing two persons. On 2–3 January 19 Ogoni communities were raided by the Nigerian army in an effort to stop traditional Ogoni Day celebrations planned for 4 January, as there is a general ban on all forms of assembly throughout Ogoniland. Throughout the year, burial ceremonies, family meetings, church services and other cultural activities were dispersed and participants arrested by Nigerian authorities. On 15 occasions gun-shots were used to disperse gatherings.

On 13 March, a delegation of the African Human Rights Commission of the Organization of African Unity visited the 19 Ogonis detained since 1995 in Port Harcourt prison. During the guided tour by the Nigerian authorities, the prisoners were neither asked questions nor allowed individual interviews. The defence lawyers of the Ogoni 20 (one more Ogoni was arrested and detained on the same charges) have suffered continuous harassment by the Nigerian military throughout 1997.

In July, Shell Nigeria announced plans to re-enter Ogoniland before the end of the year. (The company had withdrawn from Ogoniland in 1993 because of the hostile attitude of the local community to its activities). The statement by Shell suggested that the company is not sincere in its often repeated claim that it will not operate behind a 'security shield'. In their response, MOSOP categorically denied meeting and negotiating with Shell and insisted that for any dialogue to be useful, basic freedoms would have to be restored in Ogoniland first. In October, the Commonwealth Heads of Government decided during their meeting in Edinburgh that "Nigeria should remain suspended from the Commonwealth."[132] The Heads of Government expressed concern about the failure to observe fundamental rights, in particular the continued detention and imprisonment of many Nigerians.[133]

Despite difficult circumstances MOSOP was able to undertake various activities in 1997. Pictures and films on human rights violations were smuggled out of Nigeria and were used to show the situation to the outside world. On 10 November, the second anniversary of the execution of the Ogoni 9 was commemorated and led to a new wave of arrests. One of the most significant achievements of MOSOP in 1997 was the international assembly of MOSOP, attended by delegates from Nigeria, the U.K., US, South Africa, Italy and the refugee-camps in Togo and Benin. The meeting, held in West Africa in November and facilitated by the UNPO, focused on conflict resolution and training for grassroots activities, including international organization and the basic principles and skills of negotiation.[134] It was the first time since the 1995 executions that the entire MOSOP leadership was able to meet.. A resolution was adopted by the meeting to resolve differences and misunderstandings that had existed among some Ogoni activists.

The Ogonis, through MOSOP, joined the UNPO in 1993. The goal of the Ogoni is to end environmental in devastation of Ogoniland caused by oil companies, specifically Royal Dutch/Shell, respect for human rights and a measure of self-determination that will offer opportunity for economic emancipation, social advancement and the preservation of Ogoni languages and culture within the Nigerian federation.

SAKHA REPUBLIC (YAKUTIA)

Location: Russian Federation
Religion: Christian and traditional religion
Language: Yakut, Russian and distinct indigenous languages
Population: 1 million

The Sakha Republic (Yakutia) is the largest autonomous republic of the Russian Federation and contains over 80 nationalities. The Russians and the Sakha-Yakuts are the largest groups, with smaller indigenous groups (such as the Evenks, Evens, Yukagirs, Chukchi and Dolgans) comprising the rest. Yakuts are famous hunters, trappers, fishermen and reindeer herdsmen. Traditionally, there were two main types of economy: reindeer herding on the tundra, and fishing and hunting in the forests, tundra and sea. Reindeer herders were nomadic, while hunters and fishers were either permanent settlers or moved within a limited territory on a seasonal basis.

The history of the people of Sakha dates back to the 13th century, when the hordes of Genghis Khan invaded the Central Asian steppe. As a result of a major migration nomadic-pastoral tribes penetrated the North, driving away the Yakugir tribes. In 1632, Russian Cossacks established fortifications on the bank of the Lena river, which developed into the current capital, Yakutsk. This date is considered the mark of the incorporation of Yakutia into Russia. During the late-1980s and early-1990s, the Sakha Republic obtained a considerable amount of autonomy as a result of its geographical distance from Moscow and its mineral importance to Russia. In September 1990, the Declaration of State Sovereignty of the Sakha Republic (Yakutia) was adopted and the Republic's first and current President, Mikhail Nikolaev, was elected in December 1991. President Boris Yeltsin and Mikhail Nikolaev signed an agreement on 25 June 1995 delineating the division of powers between the Federal and Sakha Governments. The treaty is the fifth such accord signed between Moscow and members of the Russian Federation.

In December 1992, the Sakha Republic adopted a new constitution, marking the beginning of a new Sakhan society. In the constitution, the official status of Sakha is set out with respect to sovereignty, democracy, the legal system and the right to self-determination in the republic as a part of the Russian Federation. The new legal system is based on a generally accepted division of powers among the legislative, executive and judicial branches. It provides a demarcation of state and regional powers and, for the first time in the history of the Yakut state, it is understood that the natural resources within the territory of the Sakha Republic belong to its people.

In 1996, the Government of Sakha developed the "Yakutia in the 21st Century" program as a plan for the future economic development policy for the Republic. One of the most important developments in Sakha has been and is the reformation of the social security system. In recent years it was decided that an improved system capable of providing for the well-being of those living below the minimum standard of living was needed. The new system provides all people who do not have sufficient income (such as the unemployed, the disabled and the retired) with their basic living requirements.

On 23–24 April 1997, the Assembly of the Peoples of Yakutia was held in the capital, Yakutsk. As over 80 nationalities live in Yakutia, it is important for them to develop good relations with the government. So far, there have been no conflicts in Sakha during the last few years and good relation must be maintained. The role of the Sakha (Yakut) language is increasing in public life. Although lectures at universities are still held in Russian, the Sakha language is used in the faculties of Yakutian language and literature. In addition, many schools teach the Sakha language.

On 13–18 August 1997, the third General Assembly of the Northern Forum was held in Yakutsk, during which the President of the Sakha Republic, Mr Mikhail Nikolaev, was elected as the chairman of the General Assembly. This is an example for the increasing influence of the Sakha Republic in movements of northern peoples, as the former Chairman was Norwegian. Though the Sakha Republic remains a part of the Russian Federation, during 1997 the President continued to promote the independent relations and policies of the Republic (as evidenced in the development of economic and cultural relationships with foreign countries, including Japan, Ukraine, Latvia and Kazakhstan).

Until the end of the 19th century animal husbandry, hunting and grain production formed the basis of the economy. Today industry forms the most important part of the economy, contributing 43% of the gross national product. Industry stems primarily from mineral exploitation, the Sakha Republic being the sole supplier of gold and tin in the CIS market. The economy of the Sakha Republic is based on the transition to a market economy combined with the improvement of the social situation. The first steps have been made on the road to private property, privatisation of companies, decentralisation of production, the production of consumer goods and the introduction of the freedom to trade and competition. The major part of the national economy is still provided by exploitation and preparation of raw-materials. To make the industry and the financial situation of the republic more stable, measures to rebuild the structure of the economy have been taken. In this new structure the exploitation of raw-materials must be improved together with the establishment of a new industry for products meant for the internal market. To make the new structure work it is necessary that there be some infrastructural adjustments, especially with regard to railroads. The economic situation in Sakha stabilized in 1997 compared to previous years. There has been growth in the privatization of companies and in the agricultural sector the privatization is now finalized.

Sakha became a Member of the UNPO in 1993 in order to make the international community conscious of the state and people of the Sakha Republic and to develop international contacts.

Sanjak

Location:	Federal Republic of Yugoslavia
Religion:	Islam and Christianity (Orthodox)
Language:	Bosniac, Serbian and Montenegrin
Population:	530,000

Sanjak is situated in the centre of the Balkan peninsula in the Federal Republic of Yugoslavia (FRY), administratively divided between the two federal states of the FRY, Serbia and Montenegro. The Bosniacs living in Sanjak and other parts of the FRY are part of the same nation as the Bosniacs living in Bosnia and Hercegovina. Historically, the Bosniacs are a south Slavic people who settled on the Balkan Peninsula from the 6th to 7th centuries along with other Slavic peoples. The first Slavic states, Bosnia and Duklja, were created around 1000 on the territory of Illyricum, where later Serbia and Croatia were created.[135] Throughout the Middle Ages, Bosnia, Duklja, Serbia and Croatia were ruled by Byzantium, Hungary and Bulgaria, with Sanjak a constituent part of Bosnia and Hercegovina. It had special autonomy status until 1878, when it was separated from Bosnia and Hercegovina at the Berlin Congress. Sanjak existed as an independent political and territorial unit until 1912 when it was occupied by Serbia and Montenegro. During this period of occupation, 40,000 Muslims were expelled by Serbian authorities and 16,000 persons suffered a similar fate at the hands of the Montenegro authorities controlling Sanjak. When the Kingdom of Yugoslavia was established in 1918, Sanjak lost its legal status as an autonomous part of Bosnia and Hercegovina.

During World War II, an anti-fascist council was created which re-established Sanjak as an independent region. However, this right to autonomy was rescinded in 1945 by the communist regime and Sanjak was divided between Serbia and Montenegro. During this period, 15,000 Muslims were killed or tortured by Serbs and Montenegrins. Today, Sanjak is under direct military occupation of the Serbian armed forces. In 1991, Muslim citizens formed the Muslim National Council of Sanjak (MNCS), which strives for full political and territorial autonomy of Sanjak with the right of connection to one of the republics. In a referendum held by the MNCS in October 1991, 98% of the voters, representing 69% of the total number of registered voters, opted for autonomy. Since 1992 about 16,000 people have been victimized by varying forms of military-police terror.

Although a principal trade route ran through Sanjak until 1878, helping develop the region, Sanjak has since become one of the most under-developed areas in the region. Due to the lack of economic development, the local population has struggled to find employment with many living off the production of smallholdings. Before 1991, liberalization of the economy helped to boost economic welfare but the Bosnian war ended any further improvements.

The Bosniacs in the Federal Republic of Yugoslavia are consistently deprived of their right of being a constitutional part of Bosnia and Hercegovina and this status has remained unresolved as well as the status of Sanjak where the Bosniacs are the indigenous people, comprising a majority of the population. There are no mechanisms for the protection of the Bosniacs in the FRY and the government and the majority of the opposition parties deny the national identity of the Bosniacs in Sanjak. Hatred and intolerance against the Bosniacs is openly expressed by politicians scientific and cultural institutions through press releases and school books. There is no university on the whole territory of Sanjak.

In 1996, the UNPO sent a monitor to Sanjak to observe the federal and municipal elections on 3 November 1996 in the FRY.[136] The List for Sanjak Dr. Sulejman Ugljanin (LSSU) won two seats in the Federal Parliament, three seats in the parliament of the Republic of Montenegro and 136 seats in the local parliaments in the towns of Sanjak. A post-election report issued by the MNCS listed details of intimidation by ruling party supporters.

The political situation in Sanjak is deteriorating. Between 10–14July 1997 Serbian police forces entered the municipality of Novi Pazar, which was then put into receivership by the Government of Serbia. The Regular Assembly of the MNCS scheduled for 12 July was subsequently banned by an Order from the Serbian police. Dr. Sulejman Ugljanin, President of the Coalition LSSU and of the MNCS was required to appear in court on charges of secession and accusations that his political work endangers the state. He had previously been accused of the same offenses in 1993. These allegations are completely unfounded and on numerous occasions Dr Ugljanin has made it clear that he is not seeking separation of Sanjak from the state. These measures of the Government of the Republic of Serbia have greatly discouraged the Bosniacs in Sanjak after having taken part in the elections of November last year. It also dissuades refugees and displaced persons from returning since they are afraid to be harassed upon return as they were between 1992 and 1995.

On 1 August the UNPO appealed in a letter to all members of the European Union, the OSCE, the European Parliament, the Council of Europe, and the European Action Council for Peace in the Balkans. The UNPO urged them to express their concern to the Serbian government and to seek clarification for the disturbances in Novi Pazar. Following the appeal of 1 August 1997, the UNPO facilitated a visit from a delegation of the "List for Sanjak Dr. Sulejman Ugljanin", including Dr. Ugljanin and five other presidents of political parties in Sanjak (Mr. Esad Dzudzevic, Mr. Kasim Zoranic, Mr. Izudin Susevic, Mr. Ibrahim Djerlekand Mr. Fahrudin Kugic), to Western Europe, to bring further awareness to the situation in Sanjak. On 21 September 1997, the Coalition LSSU participated in the presidential and parliamentary elections in the Republic of Serbia. Whereas in the Parliament of the Federal Republic of Yugoslavia the LSSU won one seat, in the Parliament of the Republic of Serbia it gained three seats.

In 1997 the FRY authorities increasingly refused to let in Bosniacs returning from abroad. This means that Bosniacs who have to leave e.g. Germany, where they temporarily resided as refugees, cannot return securely to Sanjak. The FRY authorities do not give them the necessary papers, thus leaving many Bosniac refugees deprived of there right to live with their own people. This creates much tension and fear among Bosniacs outside as well as within Sanjak.

The Bosniacs of Sanjak, represented by the Muslim National Council of Sanjak, became a Member of the UNPO in 1993.

Scania

Location:	southern Sweden
Religion:	Christianity (Protestant)
Language:	Swedish, with a minority using Scanian
Population:	[census data not available]

Scanian written history extends back to the early part of the last millennium. Since then, Scania has experienced 430 years of independence, 850 years as part of Denmark, 62 years as an autonomous area under Sweden and 277 years as an integral part of Sweden. Sweden invaded Scania in 1658 and subsequent peace treaties guaranteed Scania the right to maintain its traditional self-rule. Self-rule was unilaterally nullified by the Swedish central government in 1719, though, and parliamentary authority was transferred to Stockholm. Scania is a subject of the Kingdom of Sweden, with proportional representation in the Swedish parliament.

Since Sweden's 1991 application for membership in the European Union, it has become clear to authorities that Sweden would have to adapt to the EU's regionalization policies. This process resulted in a Provincial Board for the province of Skåne, formally established on 1 July 1997. This provincial board, the *Regionfullmäktige* (Regional Board of Skåne), has very limited political powers.[137] It is a creation of the state authorities without the participation of the people of the region and the institution has limited popular support in Scania. The people are generally unaware of its composition, purpose and authority but are expected to vote for it at its first election in September 1998. The new regional body is geographically limited to only a portion of Scania—the province of Skåne. The two other provinces of Scania, Halland and Blekinge, are excluded, though the EU region consists of two Scanian provinces (Skåne and Blekinge). The citizens of Skåne did not show up for the inauguration of the Regional Board of Skåne on 1 July 1997, which illustrates the lack of support and legitimacy.

Seen from an international perspective, the economic situation in Sweden is generally very affluent and Scania is a part of this economic well-being. The economic situations in the various regions, however, vary, mainly because of a historic concentration of wealth and capital in the state capital Stockholm. The regional Research, Technology and Development Index (RTD) of 1993 serves as an illustration of this problem. While the RTD for Stockholm is 418 and 182 for the outlying regions surrounding Stockholm, the RTD for Scania is only 80 (the EU average is 100). Scania has its greatest development potential in the areas of agriculture, food industry and medical industry. About 25% of the population is engaged in the agricultural and food manufacturing sector. Other major sources of employment are found in mechanical manufacturing, trade and service sectors. Scania suffers under a relatively high unemployment rate, just as Sweden as a whole. There is a considerable 'brain-drain' from the region, since 15 of Sweden's 22 largest corporations and manufacturing companies, as well as a major part of organizational and public life, are situated in the Stockholm region.

The historic human rights violations, which are still embedded in the past and present re-nationalization policies in Sweden, are the major human rights problem in Scania. During the period of military invasion by Sweden at the end of the 17th century, more than 30% of the population in Scania was either executed or expelled. Some were forcefully conscripted by the Swedish military to the Baltics, from where only few returned. Although this incident belongs to history it is still something both the Scanian people and the State leadership must learn to come to terms with. The psychological situation is very troublesome with an extremely high level of self-censorship in the region. Scania is considered, treated and described as territory that has always belonged to Sweden—neglecting the distinctness of Scania's culture, language and history. This attitude is intimidating and discriminatory. There are frequent examples of individuals who do not accept the official view of the state myth regarding history, language, culture, etc., and they are treated in a discriminatory way. A number of pro-Scanian authors, historians, cultural personalities and the like, have become ostracised because of their views and opinions. The freedom of openly declaring loyalty to Scania exists formally but it creates problems at work, in career and business as well as in personal relationships with others.

Since the 1950s, many attempts were made to bring the Scanian issue to the attention of radio and television but without success. There are examples of historians who have been almost totally boycotted from mass media because of their pro-Scanian views. When Scania became a member of international organizations such as FUEN (Federal Union of European Nationalities, Flensburg, Germany) and the UNPO, it was ignored by the local mass media in the region. Paradoxically, the media in the Capital of Stockholm published extensively on the events which may illustrate the high degree of self-censorship in the region itself. Even persons such as the well-known Scanian poet Nils Ludwig, engaged in the writing of poetry, are showing fear of reprisals if their subject concerns Scania.[138]

The Scanian Future Foundation has this year been involved in a number of areas such as acting as an official advisor to the Swedish Government in the development of the Regional Board of Skåne, promoting the use of the Scanian flag, pressing the Government to sign the Council of Europe's Charter on Regional and National Languages of 1992 and promoting the Scanian language as one language to be recognized and protected under this Charter, promoting the concept of returning illicitly obtained objects of culture and art to their places of origin, i.e. from the State capitals to the Regions, and promoting the regional history to be taught in the region's schools.

Scania, through the Scanian Future Foundation, became a Member of the UNPO in 1993.

SHAN STATES

Admitted to UNPO Membership in 1997

Location:	South-east Asia
Religion:	Buddhism
Language:	Shan and Burmese
Population:	[census data not available]

The Shan States[139] are situated in the north-eastern part of present day Myanmar, bordering China, Laos, Thailand and the Karenni state (Kayah). It lies at an average of 610 meters above sea-level and the highest point, Mount Loilaeng, is at an elevation of 2,700 meters. The Shan States cover a surface of 160,000 km². Bisected north to south by the Salween river, most of the Shan States is composed of broad valleys and pine and evergreen forests. The main products derived from natural resources are: rice, tea, tobacco, vegetables and opium. Rich, also, in mineral resources and abundant in timber, the Shan States have the potential for a self-sufficient economy.

The history of the Shan people dates back to 650 BC, when they are said to have migrated from China to present-day Myanmar and settled in the area known as the Shan States. By the end of the 13th century, the Shan ruled all of Burma (then called the Ava Kingdom) and by the mid-14th century they had created an empire which stretched to Yunan region of China in the north, Tenasserim region of Burma in the south, Assam in the west and included parts of Laos and Thailand in the east. At the end of the 16th century, the Shan were defeated by the Burmese and 50 years later by the Chinese, thus bringing an end to the Shan monarchy. Even so, the Shan had been recognized by both the Chinese and Burmese as a separate entity. In 1887, the Shan States became a British protectorate. In 1922, the Shan were granted a distinct status and the"Federated Shan States" were established by the British rulers.

The historic Panglong Agreement in 1947 between Burma and the Shan paved the way for the "Union of Burma Constitution" which followed their joint independence from the British in 1948. In 1952, Burma invaded the Shan States under the pretext of fighting against a Chinese nationalists incursion. Ten years later the Burmese military staged a coup and abolished the Union Constitution. Since then, the Shan have been waging a resistance movement against the Burmese military oppression, striving for fulfillment of their right to self-determination.

In January 1996, the resistance group Mong Tai Army (MTA) led by Khun Sa surrendered to the Burmese military,[140] the SPDC. However, large numbers of ex-MTA troops refused to surrender and instead began to move north, along the Thai–Myanmar border, to join other Shan resistance groups who were under a ceasefire agreement with the SPDC, at the time. Soon, an alliance of forces was created and in February 1996 Shan troops penetrated into the Central Shan State. The Burmese military responded by implementing a policy of relocation in the area in order to cut off civilian support to the resistance groups.[141] The relocation is still in progress today.

The Shan Nationalities League for Democracy (SNLD) emerged as the largest political party in the 1990 national elections within the Shan States, representing the non-Burmese. SNLD, as well as NLD,[142] participate in the National Convention (NC) formed by the SPDC in 1993 to draft a new Union of Myanmar Constitution. Unlike NLD, SNLD has not been able to attract the attention of foreign powers and media, therefore the SNLD must be more moderate regarding their indictments of the SPDC policies outside the NC, but inside the NC they remain firmly and vocally committed to realising the fulfillment of the rights guaranteed by the Panglong Agreement of 1947.

With the SNLD having no voice outside the National Convention and the Shan resistance being cut off from Thailand, a traditional gateway to international media and public awareness, the need for a voice outside Myanmar was tremendous. On 16 November 1996, the Shan Democratic Union (SDU) was founded by key members of the Chiangmai-based Shan State Organization and the Bangkok-based Tai Union.

During 1997, there have been regular reports of serious human rights violations in the Shan State.[143] Numerous incidents of forced relocation, forced labour, illegal confiscation of goods and extra-judicial killings are reported. According to the Shan Human Rights Foundation, specific incidents of random shootings, murder and rape occurred in the villages of Namzarng and Murngpan, from June–August. Since the relocation began in February 1996, an estimated 200,000 villagers have been forced at gunpoint to abandon their homes and move to relocation sites near main roads and towns. Between May–July 1997, 200 villages were forcibly relocated. No food, medicine or clothing has been provided by the SPDC at these sites, and, dispossessed of their ancestral land, the relocated Shan farmers have been forced to survive as wage-laborers or transients. The result of the relocations and physical brutality has been a massive exodus of Shan refugees to Thailand. It is estimated that, thus far, no less than 500,000 people have fled to Thailand. Once in that land though, the Thai authorities refuse to grant them refugee status. The result is that refugee camps will not receive them, forcing them to work as illegal labourers, beggars and prostitutes, living at a subsistence level in work-sites together with their elderly dependents and young children.

In an appeal on 8 September 1997, the SDU urged the United Nations, as well as other international organizations and national governments to exert all possible influence upon the military regime of Myanmar to stop the implementation of " inhuman policies which are tantamount to the ethnic cleansing of the Shan people". In another appeal made to the UN General Assembly on 26 October 1997, SDU stated that the non-Burmese peoples policy is: "Democracy in Burma is meaningless without the recognition of the equality and right to self-determination of the non-Burmese peoples and vice-versa."

The Shan became a Member of the UNPO in June 1997 and is represented by the Shan States Organization (SSO), a member of the SDU.

Republic of South Moluccas

Location: South-east Asia
Religion: Christianity and Islam
Language: South Moluccan
Population: 1 million

The South Moluccan homeland, once colonized part of the Dutch Indies, is an archipelago of some 150 islands located in the Banda Sea. Its main islands are Ceram, Ambon and Buru. The spice trade brought the first Europeans to the area in 1513. In the 1600s the Netherlands invaded the South Moluccas and incorporated the region into the Dutch East Indies. The Dutch attempted to convert the indigenous people to Christianity and pressed them to serve in the colonial army, the Koninklijk Nederlands Indonesisch Leger (KNIL). Of all the East Indian peoples, the South Moluccans were the most receptive to Dutch influence.

At the end of the post-World War II decolonization process, and following increasing armed resistance against the Netherlands, the Dutch transferred sovereignty of their colony to the Independent Federal Republic of Indonesia. As soon as it became obvious that Indonesian President Sukarno intended to change the state's character from a federal into a unitarian state, the South Moluccans declared their independence from the component state of East Indonesia, one of the member-states of the Indonesian Federation. The South Moluccas democratically joined the state of East Indonesia in 1947 on the express condition that their national character and entity should remain guaranteed. Since the declaration of 25 April 1950, the South Moluccans have struggled politically for the recognition of their right to self-determination and independence as the free Republic of the South Moluccas (RMS). The RMS functions as a government-in-exile. There are currently 50,000 Moluccans living in the Netherlands. Dr. Manusama, who was President-in-exile from 1966–1993, passed away in December 1995, and is honored as the country's Second Father. He was succeeded by Dr. F. Tutuhatunewa as President.

The repression of the Moluccans has continued. The levels of education and health services provided by the state remain poor. Indonesia has established plywood factories in order to improve the economic situation of the Moluccas, however, at the same time many Indonesians have migrated to the region taking these job opportunities. Because of Indonesia's transmigration policy, the South Moluccans may become a minority in their own country. In addition, the policy jeopardises the balance between Muslims and Christians within the South Moluccas. Religious tensions might very well lead to conflicts in the future. Another consequence of the transmigration is increasing unemployment among the South Moluccan people.

An important issue in 1997 has been natural resource extraction and its effects on the environment and livelihood of the Moluccan people. The non-governmental organization Down to Earth, which focuses on Indonesian environmental issues, reported on the mining activities on Haruku island These islands won an environmental prize in 1985 for their sustainable management of fish based on the traditional system called *sasi*. However, since two mining companies have begun conducting exploratory operations on the island, the *sasi* system is being destroyed. Soil erosion has made the water of the Wai Ira river too muddy for human use and the fish which form the villagers' staple diet is declining. When letters to provincial officials yielded no response, the villagers decided to hold a meeting in April to discuss the matter. There they expressed their concern about lack of information and lack of understanding about what could happen to them if the mining companies decide to pursue their operations.[144]

A similar situation was highlighted by a campaign, initiated by the Netherlands Center for Indigenous Peoples, focused on the island of Yamdena. Although the Indonesian government designated Yamdena a nature reserve in 1971, due to the island's unique biological diversity, they granted large logging concessions in the area in 1991. Following local opposition to the logging, which resulted in repressive measures against the islanders, the company withdrew in 1994. However, in 1995, a new logging license was granted to a state company, meaning that resistance to the company can be interpreted by the government as anti-nationalist activity. In March 1997, the European Parliament adopted a resolution in which an appeal was made to the Indonesian government to put a stop to the lumber activity on Yamdena island. The people of Yamdena have taken their case to the national courts.[145]

As in the past, South Moluccan delegations visited Geneva during human rights meetings at the United Nations. Delegates have attended the Working Group on Indigenous Populations of the UN, the UN Commission on Human Rights and numerous international conferences. Many useful contacts have been established, including those with Indonesians who advocate human rights and a democratic system of government in their country.

The environmental and social impact of natural resource extraction was emphasized by the Moluccan government's statement submitted to the meeting of the UN Working Group on Indigenous Peoples, which took place from 28 July–1 August in Geneva. The agenda item on which they spoke, 5a, concerned the rights of indigenous peoples with special reference to the environment, land and sustainable development. The delegate pointed out that the Indonesian Mining Act of 1967 states that all natural deposits are considered to be the property of the state and are to be used to maximize the welfare of the state. In other words, all land on which natural resources are found are subject to governmental appropriation. This conflicts with the customs of the Moluccan people. The forced resettlement which takes place as a result of these policies disrupts the indigenous people's system of traditional law, called *adat*. The statement also stressed the widespread pollution caused by mining operations in the Moluccas. Mercury and gold used in mining contaminates the soil. Staple foods are no longer edible and the coral reefs and seaweed are also damaged due to the flow of contaminants into the ocean.[146]

The South Moluccas became a Member of the UNPO in 1991 and is represented by the RMS. The South Moluccas continue their struggle for international recognition and eventual independence.

TAIWAN

Location:	East Asia
Religion:	Taoism, Buddhism and Christianity
Language:	Taiwanese (Fukienese and Hakka) and Mandarin
Population:	21 million
Ethnic diversity:	Taiwanese, indigenous people and Chinese immigrants

The first major wave of Chinese immigration to Taiwan took place in the 17th century, when the island became a Dutch plantation colony. Loyalists to the fallen Ming dynasty expelled the Dutch in 1662 and established a rebel base on Taiwan, but were defeated by the Manchu Ching dynasty forces in 1683, which brought Taiwan under Manchu imperial rule for the first time in its history. Taiwan remained part of the Chinese empire until 1895, when it was ceded to Japan following China's defeat in the Sino-Japanese War. Japan renounced its claim to Taiwan in 1945, after its defeat in World War II. On behalf of the Allied Powers, the Kuomintang (KMT), then in power on the mainland, occupied Taiwan. Taiwanese resistance to KMT rule led to a rebellion that began on 28 February 1947, in which 10,000–20,000 Taiwanese were massacred.

When the Chinese communists defeated the KMT in 1949, the KMT and two million mainlanders fled to Taiwan. Led by Chiang Kai-shek, who remained president of the Republic of China (ROC) and Chairman of the KMT until his death in 1975, the KMT transferred its entire governmental structure to Taiwan, insisting (until June 1994) that it was the sole legitimate government of China. The KMT subsequently imposed martial law from 1947–1987, with those attempting to voice support for democratic reform silenced by censorship, arrest, or imprisonment.

Although opposition parties were prohibited under martial law, the Democratic Progressive Party (DPP) was formed in 1986. Since its formation, the DPP has been at the forefront of Taiwan's democratic reforms and endorses the right to self-determination for the people of Taiwan.

In March 1996, despite efforts by the People's Republic of China (PRC) to intimidate Taiwan with military force, the people of Taiwan held their first-ever democratic presidential election. The KMT's Taiwanese candidate, Lee Teng-hui, was re-elected. The direct election symbolized the success of Taiwan's transformation into a democratic nation. Despite losing its bid for the presidency, the DPP's popularity has continued to rise since then. With party membership doubling to 140,000 over the previous year, by mid-1997 it was leading the KMT in public opinion polls. In a by-election held in March 1997 for the Taoyuan County Magistrate, the DPP candidate easily won and the majority of Taiwanese now live in counties under DPP administration.

The reform process, still led by the DPP, continues. Constitutional amendments passed by the National Assembly in July began phasing-out the Taiwan

Province as a level of government, moving Taiwan another step toward nominal nation-state status. In elections for county chiefs in November, the DPP won 12 seats against the KMT's eight. This is the first time the DPP has received more seats than the KMT in national elections and the first time it has received more votes.

Taiwan's 1997 per capita GNP of US$14,000 and its huge foreign exchange reserves (second after Japan), make it an actor on the world's economic stage. With limited resources, Taiwan's economy is driven by trade (primarily machinery, electronics and textile exports). According to the Ministry of Economic Affairs, nearly 10% of the population is engaged in agriculture, fishing and forestry, 38.5% in industry (75% of this in manufacturing) and 51.8% in the service sector.

While China's pressure on its trading partners to isolate Taiwan diplomatically continues unabated, the KMT continues the effort to campaign for membership in the UN, where the Taiwanese have been voiceless since the Republic of China had its seat transferred to the PRC in 1971. Taiwan's sixth attempt in six years to gain UN membership met with failure again in September 1997, as did its campaign for entry into the World Health Organization. Admission into the World Trade Organization (WTO) seems likely as terms of Taiwan's entry are currently being negotiated with WTO member countries.

Taiwan is a founding Member of the UNPO and is represented in the organization by the Democratic Progressive Party.

TATARSTAN

Location: Russian Federation
Religion: Islam and Christianity
Language: Tatar and Russian
Population: 1.8 million Tatarstan

The Republic of Tatarstan is situated in the far east of Europe, in the middle of the Volga River basin. Tatarstan borders the republic of Udmurt in the north, the Mari-El and Chuvash Republics in the west, Bashkortostan in the east and the Samara Region to the south. Strategically situated in the middle of the Volga basin, Russia's main commercial artery, Tatarstan is of great economic importance to the Russian Federation. Seven percent of Russia's oil is produced in Tatarstan, along with most of Russia's heavy trucks and military aircraft. In terms of industrial output, Tatarstan ranks eighth among the territories of the Russian Federation.

With the collapse of the Soviet Union, Tatarstan was the first Republic to declare its sovereignty. This was, however, never accepted by the Russian Federation. Tatarstan did not sign the new Federation Treaty of 1992, but instead adopted its own republican constitution. The new constitution stated that Tatarstan was no longer a part of the Russian Federation, but was instead a sovereign republic associated with Russia. In February 1994, a bilateral treaty between Tatarstan and the Russian Federation was signed in which the relations between the two republics was settled. Tatarstan today has a limited sovereignty, with foreign affairs remaining primarily the domain of Russia. The treaty makes reference to both the Russian and the Tatarstan Constitutions, thus leaving some ambiguity as to the precise status of Tatarstan.

During 1997, the economy of Tatarstan grew by 3%, with a 7% improvement in the agricultural sector. Because of this continuous economic growth, the living standard in Tatarstan has become the highest in the Russian Federation. Problems remain, however, with the organization of market structures. Some growth of industrial production is noted, but this was achieved primarily in the field of oil extraction and oil chemistry. A new branch of economic development which is actively being developed is car production. In the town of Yelabug a factory for the production of Chevrolet Blazer is being built with investment and assistance from the U.S. multinational General Motors. Opel has also invested in car production in Tatarstan producing two models which are increasingly popular in Russia. The aircraft industry was also showing signs of success with orders for helicopters coming from abroad. Moreover, during the year, there were continued and new contacts with various countries such as Malaysia, Singapore and Brazil and which have important significance for the economy.

Tatarstan's main economic goal is to attract as many multinational corporations as possible to invest in various projects and to import the latest technology. It is also hoped that multinationals will provide much-needed jobs as unemployment increased in 1997 to a level of 60,000 people. For 1998, the Republic hopes to expand economic cooperation with different countries and to progress toward entering the World Trade Organization, which would stimulate foreign investment. Furthermore there are plans to introduce state securities (eurobonds) and to fully open commercial activities of Tatar enterprises to the international market.

Foreign contacts increased in the political sphere as well in 1997. Tatarstan now has representational bodies in many parts of the Russian Federation as well as in Turkey, Hungary, the United States, Australia and France among others. On 21 May, a delegation from the Chechen Republic Ichkeria, headed by president Maskhadov, visited Tatarstan. An agreement was made between the two as sovereign republics. Amongst other activities of the government in 1997 were three seminars on the settlement of international and national conflicts, held in The Hague with participation of the presidents of Tatarstan, Abkhazia and representatives of Chechenia. In 1997 there have been many negotiations with representatives of different countries, such as Egypt, Turkey and Kazakhstan.

The International Congress of Tatars was held in Kazan from 28–29 August. Aiming to promote Tatar unification world-wide, the conference was attended by elected representatives of Tatars from as far as Poland and Lithuania. Many among the Tatar diaspora are struggling for national or cultural autonomy. In places such as Moscow and St. Petersburg, Tatar schools and cultural centers have been opened. In Tatarstan, there are both Tatar and Russian schools where both languages are compulsory. Although university education is mainly in Russian the conditions for introducing Tatar-language higher education are good. Already many universities provide courses in Tatar, for example the faculties of philology and history at the University of Kazan and the Pedagogical University. A language law is in the process of being completed, on the basis of which mass media will effectively be available in both languages.

Tatarstan exhibits a high degree of tolerance and freedom for other ethnic groups. For example, in 1997 a building was handed over to the European Association for the construction of a synagogue and a German church was opened. Moreover, there is also mother tongue education for Udmurts and Maris and the only Udmurt secondary school in existence. In the Udmurt and Mari republics mother tongue education is not available. Aware of their advancement in this area, Tatars also study the history and languages of neighboring peoples. The Institute of History opened a department of Finno-Ugric peoples (e.g. Udmurt and Mari) and published the first issue of the journal *Finnougrica* in 1997.

Tatarstan became a Member of the UNPO to help foster its goal of achieving sovereign status and negotiations continue with the Russian government regarding increased self-determination or full governmental autonomy. Tatarstan has actively taken part, on behalf of the Russian Federation, in delegations which carried out work for the UN, the Council of Europe and several international organizations.

TIBET

Location:	Central Asia
Religion:	Buddhism, Bon (indigenous religion of Tibet)
Language:	Tibetan
Population:	6 million (more than 130,000 in exile)

When Tibetans speak of "Tibet", they refer to the three provinces of U-Tsang, Kham and Amdo. This differs from the Chinese "Tibet", or "Tibet Autonomous Region" (TAR), which is comprised only of U-Tsang and parts of western Kham provinces, or less than half the country. Most of Amdo province has been renamed Qinghai; the remaining territory has been annexed to the Chinese provinces of Gansu, Sichuan and Yunnan. Following Chinese occupation, Tibet was divided in order to break up the country and facilitate control over its population. In this update, the term "Tibet" is used to describe the situation in the entire country as it is known and recognized by the Tibetan people.

Since the establishment of a unified Tibetan state in 618, the nation has twice fallen under the influence of foreign powers: in the 13th century by the Mongol Empire and in the 18th century by the Manchurian Qing Dynasty. Tibet was offered military protection in exchange for religious teachings from Tibetan Buddhist lamas. Following these periods of external influence, Tibet resumed its independence in every respect. This situation changed drastically in 1949, when the People's Liberation Army (PLA) of the People's Republic of China (PRC) crossed into Tibet. A 17-Point Agreement was imposed on the Tibetan government in May of 1951, incorporating Tibet into the PRC. A national uprising in 1959, in opposition to persistent violations of the 17-point Agreement, was brutally crushed by the PLA and resulted in the death of 87,000 Tibetans. This situation prompted the flight of Tibet's head of state and spiritual leader, the Dalai Lama, and over 100,000 Tibetans into exile.

The aftermath of a series of repressive and intimidating policies implemented in Tibet in 1996 by the Chinese government, has been the continued violation of fundamental human rights. The Tibetan Centre for Human Rights and Democracy, located in Dharamsala, India, reports regularly on the countless numbers of Tibetans, particularly monks and nuns, imprisoned for "splittist" activities and the treatment they receive in confinement.

Following a disappearance of nearly two years, Chadrel Rinpoche, the former abbot of the Tashi Lhunpo monastery, was sentenced in April 1997 to six years for "plotting to split the country".[147] He is said to be the most senior lama and highest level official to be found guilty of a political offense in Tibet for 15 years.[148] Chadrel Rinpoche was head of the official Chinese-appointed search team for the 11th reincarnation of the Panchen Lama, Tibet's most important spiritual figure after the Dalai Lama. In attempting to get state and religious authorities to agree on the search for the reincarnation, Chadrel Rinpoche publicly asked the Dalai Lama for his assistance in 1993 with the endorsement of the Chinese. However, in 1994 the Chinese altered their policy of contact with the Dalai Lama, claiming that His Holiness was "no longer a religious leader". At the 3rd General meeting of the 8th CPPCC,[149] Chadrel Rinpoche refused to accept China's plan to install its own choice of Panchen Lama.[150] He was harassed and detained, until the Dalai Lama announced in May 1995 his official recognition of Gedhun Choekyi Nyima as the 11th Panchen Lama. Following this announcement, Chadrel Rinpoche was said by the Chinese authorities to be ill and hospitalized.

Shortly after the Dalai Lama's announcement, Gedhun Choekyi Nyima and his parents were reported as missing. The whereabouts of the now eight-year-old Gedhun Choekyi Nyima is still unknown. In response to the report of the UN Working Group on Enforced and Involuntary Disappearances, presented at the 53rd Commission on Human Rights in April 1997, the Chinese authorities claimed to be withholding the whereabouts of the boy and his family for their own protection and that they were being hidden at the request of his parents.[151]

Annual reports were also released by the UN Special Rapporteurs for Torture and for Religious Intolerance and the UN Working Group on Arbitrary Detention, all expressing concern at the human rights situation in Tibet. All the above reports indicated the wish to conduct a fact-finding mission in China. Despite the detailed accounts of human rights abuses in Tibet contained in the reports, a resolution on China was not debated or voted upon by the UN Commission on Human Rights. The discord among EU members, initiated by France's refusal to support a resolution on human rights in China, meant the resolution was introduced by Denmark alone. The Chinese delegation interrupted statements given by Denmark and the Netherlands in support of a resolution and proposed a "no action" motion which was passed with support from 27 of the 53-member commission.[152] This motion meant that the resolution was not discussed.

Despite this failure, various missions visited Tibet in 1997, both official and unofficial. The Norwegian government (15–17 April), the Swiss government, a group of German parliamentarians and senior members from the UN Working Group on Arbitrary Detention (6–16 October) visited Tibet at the invitation of the Chinese government. Unofficial missions were carried out by the UNPO (28 April–3 May) and U.S. Rep. Frank Wolf (9–13 August). In contrast to the official missions, the unofficial visits were able to use their own interpreters and speak relatively freely with Tibetans they met. Official missions complained of visits to monasteries and prisons arranged by the Chinese authorities, where they felt they were kept from viewing and speaking freely.[153]

A number of reports were published in 1997 which concerned Tibet. The Tibetan Centre for Human Rights and Democracy published its annual report for 1996, entitled *Tibet: one more year of political repression*. The "Strike Hard" (*Yan Da*) campaign, focused on the repression of freedom of religion, was highlighted along with many other human rights violations including: arbitrary arrests and detentions, disappearances, torture and racial discrimination.[154] The UNPO published *China's Tibet: The World's Largest Remaining Colony*, which clarified the internationally-accepted criteria for colonialism, against which China's relationship with Tibet was analyzed. Mission members used evidence from their experiences in Tibet to reach their conclusion that Tibet is *de facto* a colony of China.[155] High levels of torture were reported among Tibetan refugees in the report published by the U.S.-based Physicians for Human Rights. Among 258 new arrivals in Dharamsala, India, 15% reported personal experience with torture, while 47% said a relative or close friend had been tortured. Half of these reported the torture to have taken place since 1995.[156] A report published in December 1997 by the International Commission of Jurists (ICJ), entitled *Tibet: Human Rights and the Rule of Law*, documented the recent escalation of Chinese repression in Tibet and recommended that a referendum be held under United Nations supervision in order to verify the wishes of the Tibetan people with reference to their right to self-determination.

Another positive note was the appointing in the United States Department of State of a special Coordinator for Tibetan Issues, Mr. Gregory Craig, in October. The result of successful lobbying in the U.S., Mr. Craig's central mandate on behalf of the U.S. government is to promote dialogue between the Chinese government and the Tibetan government-in-exile.[157]

Tibet's spiritual leader and Head of State, the Dalai Lama, paid an important visit to Taiwan. In March, the Dalai Lama spent six days in Taiwan on a religious visit as a Buddhist spiritual leader. The Dalai Lama was received with honors of a Head of State and met with Taiwan's first democratically elected president, Mr. Lee Teng-hui. Several prayer meetings were held in stadiums in front of large crowds.[158] Although the Dalai Lama wanted to de-emphasize the political nature of the visit, many Taiwanese demonstrated in support of Tibetan independence.[159]

Another important visit was made to the United States in April, where the Dalai Lama met with U.S. President Clinton. To avoid offending China, President Clinton "dropped by" a meeting between the Dalai Lama and Vice-president Al Gore. President Clinton said he would encourage China to engage in high level talks with the Dalai Lama or his representatives.[160]

Tibet was a founding Member of the UNPO. The Tibetan people struggle to regain their independence. The Tibetan government-in-exile has stated its preparedness to agree to a genuine self-rule for Tibet in association with the PRC. They call for negotiations without pre-conditions with China, a goal supported by numerous governments, non-governmental organizations and a network of grass-roots support groups in over 60 countries.

TYVA

Location: Russian Federation
Religion: Buddhist
Language: Turkic
Population: 309,000

The Republic of Tyva lies at the upper reaches of the Siberian Yenisey river. The Tyvians are one of the oldest people to inhabit Central Asia. The first mention of Tyva in written sources dates from the 6th century. In 1207, Tyva was conquered by Genghis-Khan and for a time it came under the Yuan dynasty. The Mongol feudal system prevented the Tyvian culture from further development. Tyva freed itself of the Mongol rule in a series of small-scale wars from the 14th–16th centuries, and despite this the Tyvian people managed to form a cohesive nation with a strong identity. In 1914, Tyva became a Russian protectorate. During the Russian Civil War (1918–22) Tyvians joined Russians in their struggle against the White (counter-revolutionary) forces.

On 14 August 1921, the All Tyvian Hural (Gathering) proclaimed the sovereign Tyvian Peoples Republic. During the existence of the independent republic (1921–44), major achievements were made in socio-economic, political and cultural development. However, most of these occurred under strong ideological pressure from the Soviet Union. By the beginning of the 1930s, the Soviet Union started to overtly interfere in Tyva's internal affairs. In August 1944, in an extraordinary session of the Small Hural (Parliament), the Tyvian National Republic made the decision to "voluntarily" join the Soviet Union, a decision accepted by the Presidium of the Supreme Soviet of the USSR on 11 October. Tyva then became an autonomous province (*oblast*) of the Russian Federation. In 1961, the autonomous province received the status of Tyvian Autonomous Socialist Soviet Republic.

After the collapse of the Soviet Union in 1991, the Republic of Tyva (within the Russian Federation) was founded. The Tyvian government is making an effort to develop political and economic ties with other countries. In the Constitution of the Republic of Tyva, adopted by a national referendum, the Republic Tyva is described as a sovereign democratic state, possessing the right to self-determination and withdrawal from the Russian Federation and the determination of its own international economic and political relationships. The process of democratization of government institutions and public life continues: new political parties, a more pluralist society are developing and traditional ways of life are gaining renewed attention and acceptance. International conferences and symposiums are being held on subjects of importance to Tyvian culture and there are now public commemorations of historic events.

For many Tyvians, the most important event in 1997 was the establishment of an institution, called Kamby Lama (High lama), which is an institution for the highest spiritual leader of the Buddhists in Tyva. Tibetan Buddhism is the official religion of the Tyvian people since the latter half of the 18th century. Besides Buddhism, there also exists a traditional belief in Tyvian Shamanism and recently some sects have emerged but none of these beliefs has the right to call itself a 'state religion'. In September 1997, the first Kamby Lama, the 20-year-old Khertek Aganak, was elected at the All-Tyva Congress of Buddhists. This election together with the new institution indicates the revival and consolidation of the indigenous religion of the Tyvians and it shows the renaissance of Tyvian consciousness, spirituality and traditional culture.

During the presidential elections in Tyva, held on 16 March 1997, the incumbent president, Mr. Sherig-ool Oorzhak, won 70.5% of the votes and therefore remains president of the Republic of Tyva. He was supported by the Russian pro-governmental organization "Our Home is Russia". The government in Tyva, however, is mainly composed of Tyvian ministers. In an effort to improve the relationship with the Russian Federation, the Government of Tyva signed an agreement with the Ministry of Nationalities of the Russian Federation on 14 March 1997. According to this agreement, both sides are committed to resolving all problems that may occur in relation to the issues of local self government, cultural development, federate relations and nationalism. The Tyvian language is, according to the constitution, the official language of the Tyva Republic and Russian has the status as the language for the inter-ethnic relationships in Tyva. Although in the universities use of the Russian language is dominant, most schools in Tyva teach in the Tyvian language. But despite this agreement and the good cultural relationship between the Tyvians and the Russians, the political relationship in Tyva does not function effectively. This is due to the fact that all registered political parties and public organizations in Tyva are controlled by the president or are dominated by the Russian organization "Our Home is Russia". There is no movement in Tyva which opposes the authority of the president.

Due to the poor economic situation in Tyva, the standard of living worsened during 1997. This resulted in many emigrations of Tyvians and Russians from Tyva. At the present time, here is no foreign investment in Tyva. The Tyvian constitution does not allow ownership of private property but everybody is entitled to rent land for some period or a life-time with the right to bequeath it.

Tyva became a Member of the UNPO in February 1996, wishing to learn the procedures of diplomacy and foreign affairs as well as the means of non-violent struggle and to share the experiences of other nations and peoples.

UDMURT

Location: Russian Federation
Religion: Christianity and traditional religion
Language: Russian
Population: 747,000 (497,000 within Udmurt Republic)

The Udmurt are one of the Finno-Ugric peoples living inside the territory of the Russian Federation. The Udmurt Republic is situated in the western part of the Urals, bordering Tatarstan, Bashkortostan and the Perm and Kirov regions. From the 8th until the 13th century Udmurt was under the rule of the Volga-Bulgars. After the Mongol invasion of 1236, the southern part of Udmurt was placed under the control of the Kazan Khanate and the northern part under Russia. In July 1918, an Udmurt National Congress convened in Elabuga (south of present Udmurtia) and reconvened in September 1919, in an attempt to establish independence during the Russian Civil War. Following the Bolsheviks's consolidation of power, it was quickly disbanded and its very existence purged from Soviet sources. During Soviet rule, the Udmurt Republic became a victim of Russian population transfer policies. Many Russians were transferred to the region resulting in the Udmurt people becoming a minority in their own Republic. As a result of the Russification of Udmurt, the possibility to study the Udmurt language almost disappeared along with the Udmurt culture. Today the process of cultural rebuilding continues.

The political situation in Udmurt Republic showed little significant change in 1997; local elections are scheduled to take place in 1998. The Republic is now considered to be the republic of all the peoples living there, while the Udmurt are considered only to be the nation that gave the Republic its name. Russians now constitute the majority in Udmurt's administrative authorities and the official language is now Russian.

In August 1996, The Udmurt administration drafted a law on culture and took this to the Supreme Soviet of the Udmurt Republic for adoption. The law requires a project for the preservation and development of the language and culture of the Udmurts and the other nationalities living in the Udmurt Republic. The law is also meant to promote contact with Udmurts living outside the Udmurt Republic and provides for assistance in their education as well. To this end, on 5–6 November 1997 the Congress of All-Udmurtian Association, *Udmurt Kenesh*, took place. The delegations of 16 regions of Russia where Udmurt population lives participated. The delegations made requests to accelerate the process of adopting the several bills concerning the Udmurtian people with emphasis to the issues of ethnic education and culture. General education is now in the Russian language, whereas only in elementary education is the Udmurt language permitted. The goal of the Udmurt Kenesh is the application of the Udmurt language in all levels of education.

In October 1995, the Russian Federation government and the Udmurt Republic signed a series of agreements defining the respective responsibilities of the Federation and the Republic with regard to the division of state property, budget relations, law and order, defence industries, the use of oil and forest resources and environmental protection. Industry in Udmurt consists primarily of the 225 industrial enterprises which for a large part form part of Russia's military complex and are controlled by the Russian Federation. These enterprises include chemical warfare production facilities, which are being converted to other uses. The land still belongs to the kolkhozes and sovkhozes, in part because the Udmurt people oppose the privatization of land. The economic situation overall, is unstable. Industrial and agricultural production has fallen even more in 1997 despite an increase in grain production due to improved weather conditions this year.

In 1991, the Udmurt became a Member of the UNPO. The Udmurt are represented by the Udmurt Council (*Udmurt Kenesh*), the growing body of the All Union Udmurt Congress. It strives for a healthy environment, for equal education for the Udmurt, for the Udmurt children to be taught in their own language, for management of the economy in the interest of the indigenous Udmurt people and for the realization of the right of self-determination.

WEST PAPUA

Location:	South-Pacific
Religion:	Christianity and traditional religion
Language:	Papuan languages
Population:	900,000
Ethnic diversity:	240 distinct peoples

West Papua is the western part of the island of New Guinea and borders on the Moluccas in the West, Papua New Guinea in the East and Australia in the South. The Papuan people existed for thousands of years before the Spanish 'discovered' New Guinea in 1546. In 1828, the western half of the island became a Dutch colony, West New Guinea. To realize a self-governing Papua state, the Netherlands supported the Papuans in establishing their own institutions, such as the New Guinea Council. The New Guinea Council inaugurated the national symbols on 1 December 1961: West Papua as the name of the country, *hai Tanahku Papua* the national anthem and *Sampari* (Morningstar) the national flag.

On 15 August 1962, Indonesia and the Netherlands signed the New York Agreement to resolve a dispute over the future political status of the territory. In 1963, Indonesia succeeded in seizing control of the territory with the understanding that a referendum, the Act of Free Choice, would enable the Papuans to vote on their own future status. In 1965, the indigenous peoples of West Papua started a resistance movement against Indonesian occupation and established the *Organisasi Papua Merdeka* (OPM), the Free Papua Movement. In 1969, the stipulated referendum took place but it was "stage managed" by the Indonesians who, through bribery and intimidation, managed to secure the desired outcome: a unanimous vote for continuation of the Indonesian occupation of West Papua. On 19 November 1969, the UN General Assembly "took note" of the referendum and endorsed the Indonesian occupation. In the early 1970s, Indonesia renamed this territory Irian Jaya, their 26th province.

On 8 January 1996, an OPM group in the highlands of West Papua took 26 hostages, of which eight people were held until 15 May 1996. Although the resort to such kind of action was condemned by the international community, the OPM group was finally able to attract the world's attention to the ever deteriorating human rights situation and environmental destruction. West Papuans believe that the international community would still not have reacted if it was not for the British, Dutch and German citizens who were among the abducted. The OPM is still today an active liberation movement with supporters in West Papua and in the rest of the world, struggling for recognition to self-determination of the Papuan people through advocacy, diplomacy, non-violent action as well as armed resistance.

During the last 30 years, vast areas of West Papua have been granted as concessions to multinational, transnational and Indonesian mining, oil and logging companies without consultation with, or approval of, the indigenous peoples who have inherited these lands from their ancestors who held them for 40,000 years. Many indigenous communities—who have had little contact with industrialization or large-scale commercial activity—have been forcibly removed from their ancestral lands or made leave through intimidation and bribery and to make way for the exploitation of natural resources. Moreover, the operations of the mining companies, particularly PT FI[161] in West Papua, have caused enormous tension which has often led to wars between the tribes in the area.

In late-January 1997, two Amungme PT FI employees abducted and raped three Dani women in a container. This sparked violent conflict between members of the two groups in which six people died and 52 were wounded. The Indonesian troops stationed there did nothing to intervene, instead they attended the "spectacle", taking pictures. Less than two months later, more violence broke out involving hundreds of local people, when Nduga men tried to rob two members of the Amungme tribal council, LEMASA,[162] in Kwakmi Lama. The indonesian troops again did nothing to prevent the killings that followed (six or more people were killed), in a two days fighting.[163] These incidents are regarded by many people as a symptom of the social ills created by the mining companies' presence in the area.

Tension erupted into violence again on 21 and 22 August which resulted in two deaths, when a thousand tribesmen armed with bows, arrows and spears, blockaded the main PT FI road, in effect cutting off all connections between the mining company and the lowlands. The action flared up following a road accident the evening of 20 August, when two tribes people were killed in a road accident after accepting a ride with Freeport personnel.[164] The accident, which occurred under unusual circumstances, inflamed the already strained relations between PT FI and the indigenous groups effected by its mining activities. In 1996, PT FI set up the "1% Trust Fund", which was intended to compensate the tribal communities for loss of land and environmental damage. After negotiations with the Indonesian government, the one percent of PT FI's profits would, eventually, be funnelled into development projects determined by military needs in the area. The fund was rejected in March 1997 by the two local groups, the Amungme and Kamoro, who are most affected by PT FI's operations. These groups called on PT FI to fulfil its responsibilities with respect to human rights and environmental damage. PT FI ignored this message and instead dealt with other indigenous groups. In August, PT FI went ahead with the second phase of the 1% Fund.

On 7 October the Associated Press reported that famine and disease caused by the worst drought in a half-century have claimed at least 413 lives in Irian Jaya. Many of the victims were babies and infants living in drought-stricken villages where food gardens have withered and safe sources of drinking water have dried up. The Jakarta Post said communications with villages hit by the drought was difficult and a thick haze from hundreds of forest fires set by logging companies had hampered attempts to deliver emergency supplies.

Currently, the West Papua Peoples' Front (WPPF), based in the Netherlands, represents the West Papuan peoples in many forums and international conferences, such as the UN Working Group on Indigenous Populations, the UN Sub-Commission on Prevention of Discrimination and Protection of Minorities and the UN Commission on Human Rights.

West Papuans striving for self-determination helped to found the UNPO in 1991.

ZANZIBAR

Location:	East Africa
Religion:	Islam and Christianity
Language:	Kiswahili, Kiunguja, English and Arabic
Population:	800,000
Ethnic diversity:	Africans, Arabs, Asians and Comorians

In the 19th century, the ruler of Oman transferred his capital from Oman to Zanzibar. In 1890, Zanzibar was granted the status of British Protectorate and the British Foreign Office ran the administration through the sultanate and its Arab administrative institutions. In 1913, the British Foreign Office handed over the responsibility for Zanzibar's affairs to the Colonial Office, and, in 1926, the standard colonial system of government was introduced.

In 1963, Zanzibar became independent and was accepted as a member of the United Nations. In January 1964, however, the coalition government of the Zanzibar Nationalist Party and Pemba Peoples Party was overthrown by the Afro-Shirazi Party (ASP). It proclaimed the Peoples Republic of Zanzibar and consolidated ties with the mainland. Without consulting the people, the Presidents of Zanzibar and Tanzania signed a treaty on 26 April 1964, uniting the two states into the present United Republic of Tanzania. All political parties were subsequently banned and the ASP merged with Tanganyika's only political party to form Chama Cha Mapinduzi (CCM).

In 1992, a multi-party system was introduced in Tanzania, and in 1995 the first multi-party elections were held. Election monitors, from the UNPO and other international organizations, found that a number of irregularities occurred with respect to the election process and the result, a narrow victory for the incumbent President, Salmin Amour, were questioned by the opposition party Civic United Front (CUF) as well as western governments. Following these elections, many people who voted for the opposition CUF, were repressed by arrests and unlawful detentions.

The conflict, resulting from the 1995 elections, has played a predominant role on everyday life on Zanzibar. Most western donor countries have frozen their development assistance to Zanzibar after the fraud in the 1995 elections. This has had a devastating effect on the economic situation on the islands. The main sources of economic development are agriculture, trade and tourism, all of which have suffered greatly from the tense situation on Zanzibar. On the other hand, there are reports that the drug trade is flourishing, thus further contributing to a deterioration of politics on the islands.

On 26 July 1997, Mr. Salim Msabah Mbarouk, member of the Zanzibar House of Representatives of the CUF, left or was abducted from his house and was not seen in public until 3 August. On 1 August, Mr. Mbarouk resigned from his position as representative of the Mkunazini Constituency in Zanzibar city, a CUF stronghold. CUF believes he was forced to do so by the CCM government.

His resignation was followed by blatant violations of basic human rights by the Zanzibar Authorities. The attempts of Mr. Mbarouk and CUF to obtain a court injunction to stop the Mkunazini by-election until their case was heard and disposed of, were in vain. The High Court, allegedly under instructions of the Chief Justice of Zanzibar, refused them leave to appeal to the Court of Appeal of Tanzania and denied them any court proceedings.

During voter registration in September, nearly 200 CUF supporters were arrested and were denied bail for up to six weeks without the Tanzanian Government stepping-in. The Zanzibar Election Commission announced the programme for the by-election of 30 November. As happened in 1995, the CCM was accused of importing persons from outside the constituency and illegally registered CCM supporters in the Mkunazini Constituency. This led to clashes on the same day between CUF and CCM members in which three persons were seriously injured.

Just before the by-election day, on 29 November, seven prominent CUF leaders and supporters including two Members of the Zanzibar House of Representatives were arrested. After the CUF won the by-election from the CCM, even more CUF leaders and supporters were arrested and detained. Sixteen detainees were first charged with sedition, which was changed to treason in early-January, as only the latter charge could deny them bail. As the situation in Zanzibar deteriorated, the UNPO continued to maintain close contact with the leaders of the CUF and others. It held meetings with Seif Sharif Hamad, vice-chair of CUF and maintained contacts with several governments on the issue.

Several initiatives to get the two parties on Zanzibar to enter into a dialogue were embarked upon. The Peace Action Council (PAC), an independent organization, originally set up by the UNPO, sent two missions to Zanzibar and to the Tanzanian capital of Dar es Salaam, in order to assess the situation on Zanzibar and to facilitate dialogue between the two parties. The PAC, headed by its co-chair, former President of Costa Rica, Don Rodrigo Carazo Odio, had meetings with key-actors of the Tanzanian government.

The Union Parliament also initiated a model for dialogue. The President of Zanzibar gave his fiat to the Parliament's initiative in November 1997. Preparations were made, with the UNDP financing the initiative, and CUF presented itself in Dar es Salaam at the agreed date in December. Unfortunately, a message came at the last moment that CUF first needed to recognize President Amour, before any form of dialogue could start.

Most remarkably, Mwalimu Julius Nyerere has publicly acknowledged that indeed there exists a problem in Zanzibar. He also stated that the conflict concerned Tanzania as a whole and that both the Union Government and the Zanzibar Revolutionary Government should resolve it immediately. At the turn of the year the Commonwealth Secretary General, Chief Emeka Anyaoku, renewed his efforts to facilitate dialogue

Zanzibar became a Member of the UNPO in August 1991 and is represented by the Zanzibar Democratic Alternative in association with the CUF. The CUF wishes to recover its victory of the 1995 elections through nonviolent means.

NOTES TO MEMBER REPORTS

1. "Wave of arrests in Acheh", TAPOL Bulletin, No. 140, April 1997, pp. 17, 7.
2. "Achehnese asylum bid foiled by British diplomats", TAPOL Bulletin, No. 139, February 1997, pp. 11-12.
3. ASNLF Press Release, 16 November 1997, "The Incarceration of Achehnese Refugees in Malaysian Detention Centres Claimed Another Dead Victim".
4. Bart Rijs, in *de Volkskrant*, 21 November 1997
5. Elisabeth Rehn, *Situation of Human Rights in the Former Yugoslav Republic of Macedonia*, 30 September 1997 (E/CN.4/1998/12)
6. *Ibid.*
7. U.S. Department of State, *Country Reports on Human Rights Practices for 1997*, 30 January 1998
8. *The Economist* (26 July 1997)
9. Elisabeth Rehn, *Situation of Human Rights in the Former Yugoslav Republic of Macedonia*, 30 September 1997 (E/CN.4/1998/12)
10. Batwa is the plural form used to indicate two or more people of the Twa group. Mutwa is the singular form.
11. The APEDE withdrew from CAUWRA in January 1997
12. See (E/CN.4/Sub.2/1996/L.6)
13. The *Ministère du Genre, de la Famille et des Affaires Sociales* (MIGEFASO) is the full term for the Rwandan Ministry of Social Affairs
14. A "Manifesto" for the Independence Struggle of the People of Bougainville, M. Havini p.14.
15. *Onze Wereld*, May 1997, "Mee met de Rebellen van Bougainville", p.10.
16. News Release, BIG, 23.2.97, "Bougainville leader appeals to members of the International Community to urge PNG Prime Minister ... to immediately abandon his government's plan to hire foreign mercenaries to fight on Bougainville".
17. *Post-courier* (PNG) 13 October 1997, "The Burnham truce: three beautiful words"; Pacific Islands Report, 15 October 1997, "Burnham Talks Agree to a Peace-Keeping Force for Bougainville"; *The Guardian*, 15 October 1997, "PNG-Bougainville Truce"
18. *The National Newspaper*, 3 November 1997, "Panel to oversee B'ville truce"; "Unarmed Pacific peace force due in Bougainville", *The Straits Times*, 18 November 1997.
19. Update on Peace Process in Bougainville, M. Miriori, August 1997.
20. *The National Newspaper*, 30 October 1997, "Reconciliation talks continue in B'ville.
21. *The National Newspaper*, 3 November 1997, "Build Trust in B'ville, army told"
22. *Cabinda: The Tragedy of its People*, Committee for Action and Aid to Cabinda refugees (CAARC), Grenoble, France, II.5
23. Article 3 of the Alvor Agreement
24. Cabinda Gulf Oil Company Limited, May 1995
25. See *Cabinda: The Tragedy of its People*, II.6
26. Francisco Builo, representative of the FLEC/FAC in a briefing to UNPO, 20 November 1997
27. See *Cabinda: The Tragedy of its People*, II.9

28. See *Cabinda: The Tragedy of its People*, II.9
29. Antonio N'Zita in a briefing to Francisco Builo (see fn. 5) 31 October 1997
30. Antonio Meta Makosso in: *Rapport sur la vie des refugies Cabindais au Congo*
31. See Antonio N'Zita briefing, 31 October 1997.
32. See Francisco Buil briefing, 20 November 1997.
33. Amnesty International, MAGRAN Action, January 1997
34. See Cabinda Gulf Oil Company Limited, May 1995.
35. Antonio Nzita in an appeal to the Foreign Minister of the Republic of Congo 12/12/1997
36. President of FLEC/FAC, Henriques N'Zita in a meeting with the Angolan president Santos in Paris 25 February 1994
37. Gall and De Waal, *Chechnya, A Small Victorious War*. 1997.
38. *ibid.*
39. The peace process initiated in 1992, had led to no tangible improvement until now, other than repeated unilateral extensions of the cease-fire. The Agreement which was expected to be signed in July 1997 fell into stagnation after the uncompromising approach of the B'shi government on principal demands of the Jumma people and its focus only on minor issues.
40. *International Herald Tribune*, 3 December 1997
41. "Going Against the San Roque Dam", HAPIT, January-April 1997, pp. 17-19.
42. "Another Dam Project Met Stiff Peoples' Opposition", *HAPIT*, May-August 1997, pp. 12-13.
43. Tito Golote, "Tribal folk sacrificed for national interest: Dams and Mines Topped concerns of Cordillera People in 1996", *Manila Today*, January 9-15, 1997.
44. "Another Oppressive Law: The Indigenous Peoples Rights Act", *HAPIT*, May-August 1997, p. 1-4.
45. "Undermined in the Phillipines", *The Economist*, 29.22.97, p66.
46. "Another Oppressive...", *HAPIT*, May-August 1997, p4.
47. "Another Oppressive...", *HAPIT*, May-August, p4.
48. "At the Claws of Imperialist Globalization", *HAPIT*, Jan-April 1997, pp. 6-16, p7.
49. "Congress votes to bar use of US weapons in East Timor", Press Release, East Timor Action Network, 13 November 1997.
50. "Vatican creates new diocese in East Timor", Reuters, 29 December 1996; "Vatican creates second diocese in East Timor", *Maubere Newsletter*, June 1997, issue 12, p4.
51. "Students trying to meet envoy attacked," *Maubere Newsletter*, June 1997, issue 12, p5.
52. "UN resolution condemns Indonesia, *TAPOL Bulletin*, July 1997, pp23-24.
53. "Human Rights abuses hit a new low", *TAPOL Bulletin*, August 1997, pp15-16; *Summary and Events in East Timor and Internationally*, prepared by the East Timor Permanent Representation to the European Union.
54. "Notables Seek Solution to East Timor Rebellion", International Herald Tribune, 11 September 1997; "Verzet O-Timor voor oplossing a la Porto Rico", *de Volkskrant*, 25 August 1997.
55. *Chinese Policy, Human Rights Abuses and the Consequences*, Eastern Turkestani Union in Europe, 1995, p19.

56. *The Economist*, "China's rebellious west", 5 February 1997, pp57-58.
57. "Oeigoeren tarten China in strijd om staat", *NRC Handelsblad*, 15 February 1997; Floris Harm, "Oeigoeren machteloos tegen toevloed Chinezen", *de Telegraaf*, 27 February 1997.
58. "People's Republic of China, Xinjiang: Trials after recent ethnic unrest", Amnesty International, 21 March 1997, ASA 17/18/97.
59. "Three bombs exploded in northern Eastern Turkestan", Eastern Turkistan Information Center, 2.10.97.
60. *ibid.*
61. Peter O'Niell, "Central Asia, Beijing and the Uighurs", *Outsider Newsletter*, November 1997, pp4-5.
62. "China's rebellious province", *The Economist*, 23 August 1997, pp43-44; "Kazakhstan's pipeline to prosperity", *The Economist*, 11 October 1976, p77.
63. Point 8 of the translation of the 15-page Uighur-language document on Xinjiang, UNPO, September 1996.
64. *International Herald Tribune*, 11 February 1997
65. *Der Spiegel*, Nr. 37 1997 S. 160
66. Menelaos Tzelios, International Federation for the Protection of the Rights of Ethnic, Religious, Linguistic and other Minorities (UNPO member) in a letter to UNPO, 8 November 1997
67. Mr. György Frunda from the DAHR
68. Almost 60% of the seats
69. Minister of Tourism and Delegate Prime Minister for Ethnic Minorities
70. International Helsinki Federation for Human Rights: OSCE Implementation Meeting on Human Dimension Issues in Warsaw, 1997
71. *ibid.*
72. *ibid.*
73. Tibor Szatmári, the Counsellor on International Relations of the DAHR, in a Briefing Sheet to UNPO, 10 December 1997
74. *International Herald Tribune* 27 November 1997
75. See Tibor Szatmári, Briefing Sheet to UNPO, 10 December 1997
76. The program is entitled "Joint Activities of the Organt of Governmental Power of The Russian Federation, the Republic of North Ossetia-Alania and The Republic Of Ingushetia To Overcome the Consequences of the Ossetian-Ingush Conflict and to Bring the Situation In the Republic Into a Healthy State."
77. Ziyat Köprülü in *Turkish Presence in Iraq*, Ankara, 1996
78. *Report on the situation of human rights in Iraq* by Max van der Stoel, UN Commission on Human Rights, 1994, p49.
79. *Violations of Human Rights of Iraqi Turcomans*, Turkoman Cooperation & Cultural Organization, 1997, pp1 and 3.
80. Ziyat Köprülü in *Turkish Presence in Iraq*, Ankara, 1996, p. 2.
81. Dr. Muzaffer Arslan, member of the Chairman Committee of the Turkoman Cooperation & Cultural Organization, in a briefing sheet to UNPO, 18 December 1997.
82. Ziyat Köprülü in *Turkish Presence in Iraq*, Ankara, 1996.

83. The result of the vote, held in June 1996, revealed that over 60% of eligible Hawaiians boycotted the vote and only 27% supported the state initiative. A UNPO mission went to Hawai'i in 1996 to examine the political and economic status of the Kanaka Maoli and to investigate the state plebiscite.
84. These rights had been affirmed by a court ruling in 1995.
85. Hawaiians account for 80% of the state's homeless population which exceeds 3,000 families. Hawaiians are twice as likely to be homeless as are other ethnic groups in the State due to the high cost of an average house - US$ 360,000- which is unattainable for Hawaiians whose per capita income is under US$ 11,000 per year.
86. *MYANMAR: Ethnic minority rights under attack*, Amnesty International, 22 July 1997, ASA 16/20/97.
87. *ibid.*, pg 8.
88. "Mae Tha Raw Hta Agreement: Ethnic Nationalities Seminar", *Burma Alert*, February 1997, pp3-4.
89. *Karenni Independence*, 20 January 1997, Government of Karenni publication, pp1-4.
90. Dr. Millan Obradovic, *Agrarna Reforma i Kolonizacija na Kosovu 1918-1941*
91. The Constitutional Declaration of Independence was adopted by the Assembly of Kosova in July 1990. The Constitution of the Republic of Kosova was adopted in September 1990.
92. 99% out of those participating in the referendum opted for an independent and sovereign Kosova. Albanians, Muslims, Turks, Croats and Roma participated in the referendum. In the elections of May 1992, the LDK won 76% of the votes. Dr. Rugova was elected president of Kosova.
93. See resolution 1077 (1996) of the Council of Europe
94. European Action Council for Peace in the Balkans, *Kosova: From Crisis to a Permanent Solution*, 1 November 1997, p6
95. In Kosova known as *Ushtria Çlirimatare e Kosovas* (UÇK). Their support is said to be on the increase, thus endangering a peaceful outcome of the conflict in Kosova.
96. The OSCE long-term mission was forced to close in 1993 and efforts to redeploy it were in vain.
97. The jointly agreed positions state that: (1) Kosova constitutes a serious problem that requires an urgent solution, with the international encouragement and assistance; (2) The problem can only be resolved by mutual accord, reached through dialogue that is entered into with no preconditions or prejudgment of possible outcomes; (3) The agreement must be based on the principles of democratisation, mutual respect between the sides, respect for human rights, both individual and collective and promotion of regional stability through respect for the Helsinki principles concerning borders. An interim solution requires a democratic Kosova and a democratic Serbia.
98. *Kurdish Review*, November 1997
99. UN Reports of Special Rapporteurs and Representatives: *Situation of Human Rights in Iraq* A/52/476, 15 October 1997
100. *ibid.*
101. *ibid.*
102. UN General Assembly resolution 52/141 of 12/12/1997
103. Sertac Bucak, director of the International Association for Human Rights in

Kurdistan, in a briefing to UNPO, 15 December 1997
104. Amnesty International in *Turkey-Human rights and the health professions,* EUR 44/159/1997
105. *International Herald Tribune* 15 December 1997
106. UN General Assembly resolution 52/141 of 12/12/1997
107. Benchly, P. "Charting a New Course: French Polynesia, *National Geographic.*
108. IPB News March 1997.
109. Abolition 2000 Internet site
110. IPB March
111. Hiti Tau News 1997, Internet site.
112. IPB March
113. Hiti Tau Radio-Active, Internet site
114. See Benchly in *National Geographic*
115. Summary, 'Mururoa and Us', Hiti Tau *et al,* 1997, p2.
116. *ibid.,* pp3-4
117. press release, ECSIEP, 3 October 1997, "Children worked at French nuclear test-sites in Pacific; Authorities failed to set up adequate health control system for former workers."
118. "Mapu" means land and "che" means people, therefore, "Mapuche" means "people of the land"
119. *pogrom,* Nr. 187, 1996
120. Land of the East, land of the North, land of the Pacific coastal region in the West, land of the South
121. *pogrom,* Nr. 187 1996
122. Reynaldo Mariqueo, international coordinator of the Mapuche Inter-regional Council, in a statement at the UNPO Nonviolence Conference in Estonia, 22 July 1997
123. Mapuche International Link, 17 December 1997
124. Mapuche International Link, 22 December 1997
125. *ibid.*
126. Human Rights Watch/Asia Report.
127. The Mon Unity League (MUL) is an umbrella organization representing Mon people inside and outside Burma to their common struggle for restoring the entirety of the lost Monland.
128. *Africa International,* March 1996, p7
129. *Ogoni: the struggle continues,* World Council of Churches, Unit III, 1996, p24
130. *Africa International,* March 1996, p26
131. Meshach Karanwi in a briefing to UNPO, 1997
132. Communiqué by the Commonwealth Heads of Governments, 27 October 1997.
133. *ibid.*
134. See Karanwi briefing, 1997.
135. Elementa Montenegrina 1/90 Hrestomatija, Cetinnje 1992
136. See Monitor Report in *UNPO Yearbook 1996.*
137. Illustrated by the speech of the Minister of the Interior Jörgen Andersson at the inauguration day of the Board on 1 July 1997:" You must cease to use the name

Regional Parliament. The name Parliament is reserved for the Swedish Riksdag, the State Parliament. We are not accepting any more parliaments. Sweden is a nation state and will so remain."

138. Nils Ludwig in"Mitt Skåne": "Nils Ludwig knows the Scanian. He loves Scania. Through the book is an invisible red thread: Scania is a *Swedish* province, the Scanians are *Swedish*. The establishing of our cultural ties with Sweden is our most important contemporary goal and mission of life. This book of confessions does not give room for any uncontrolled provincial feelings, unnecessary knowledge or false profundity. It appeals just as much to the heart of the Scanians as to the enlightened love for King and Country of the Swedes."
139. The *Federated Shan States* became *Shan State* when the Union of Burma was formed and reverted to its old name in 1962 when the Burmese generals abolished the Union Constitution. On 11 June 1997, the new designation *United Shan States* was adopted; still, *Shan States* is most commonly used.}
140. SURA's statement, released by S.H.A.N, 3.4.97
141. The resistance groups fighting against SLORC still today are: The rebellious Shan United Revolutionary Army (SURA), the Shan States National Army (SSNA) and a common designation for their combined armed force the Shan States Army (SSA). The above armed groups have been bound together under the umbrella organization Shan States National Organization (SSNO).
142. The National League for Democracy (NLD) was the largest winning opposition party in the same elections, *within* Burma, led by Nobel Laureate Aung San Suu Kyi, representing Burmans
143. Situation in SHAN states, published by Shan Herald Agency for news (S.H.A.N), 22.3.97, Shan Human Rights Foundation (SHRF) monthly reports, The BurmaNet News, July 1997, Amnesty International reports on Burma, 1997
144. "Haruku islanders reject mine", *Down to Earth*, no. 34, August 1997, p. 9; "Indonesian gold company faces protests and five deaths", *Drillbits & Trailings*, vol. 2, no. 21, 7.11.97.
145. *Een Eiland Gaat Ten Onder*, NCIV.
146. *Homeland Mission 1950 Maluku*, Statement on agenda item 5: Review of development pertaining to the promotion and protection of human rights and fundamental freedoms of Indigenous Peoples; Statement on agenda item 5a: environment, Land and Sustainable Development, Mr. Nico Souisa, SIWA-RIMA descendant, submitted at the 15th session of the UN WGIP, Commission on Human Rights, Geneva, 28 July - 1 August 1997.
147. "Chadrel Rinpoche- the man who found the XIth Panchen Lama", *Human Rights Update*, Tibetan Centre for Human Rights and Democracy, vol. ii, no. 9, 15 April 1997, pp8-9; "Senior Lama Sentenced", *UNPO News*, April - July 1997, p10.
148. "Senior Lama Sentenced in Panchen Lama Search Dispute", *TIN News Update*, 9 Mary 1997.
149. Chinese People's Political Consultative Committee, the meeting commenced on 4 May 1995 in Beijing.
150. "Panchen Lama - a childhood lost", *Human Rights Update*, Tibetan Centre for Human Rights and Democracy, vol. ii, no. 9, 15.5.97, p. 2.

151. "UN Human Rights Investigators Express Concern on Tibet", *News Update*, 23 March 1997, The Tibet Bureau for UN Affairs, Geneva.
152. "Shame" and "UNPO Members at the United Nations", *UNPO News*, April - July 1997; "UN human rights body falls flat on China", *Tibetan Review*, May 1997, p6.
153. The escaped former prisoner Palden Gyatso explained in his book, *The Fire under the Snow*, how prisoners were made to clean up before official visits and high profile prisoners were moved out of view.
154. *Tibet: one more year of political repression*, 1996 *Annual Report: Human Rights Violations in Tibet*, Tibetan Centre for Human Rights and Democracy, February 1997.
155. *China's Tibet: the world's largest remaining colony*, UNPO, August 1997.
156. See "Doctor's Group Reports Widespread Torture in Tibet", *Tibet Brief*, 31 October 1997, p21.
157. U.S. Department of State, Office of the Spokesman, Press Statement, 31 October 1997.
158. Keith Richburg, "Calls for Independence Mark Start of Dalai Lama's Visit to Taiwan", *International Herald Tribune*, 24 March 1997, p4.
159. "Dalai Lama Turns to Taiwan's Politics", *International Herald Tribune*, 27 March 1997.
160. Alison Mitchell, "Clinton Visits Dalai Lama, Informally", *The New York Times*, 24 April 1997; Tom Carter, "To China's Dismay, Clinton Meets With Dalai Lama", *The Washington Times*, 24 April 1997.
161. The most infamous mining company operating in W.Papua for over 20 years now, is the PT Freeport Indonesia (PT FI) , subsidiary of the US-based Freeport McMoRan Copper and Gold Corporation.
162. The indigenous people in the area have established their own representative body, the Amungme-council LEMASA, to monitor, negotiate or counteract any further activities by the Indonesian government or PT Freeport Indonesia. LEMASA, however, faces increasing pressure from Freeport and Indonesian authorities. LEMASA has taken the risk in 1996 to file a US$6 billion court case in New Orleans, Freeport's hometown.
163. *Down to Earth*, May 1997.
164. *Down to Earth*, August 1997.

DOCUMENTS

Elections in Abkhazia and
the Prospects for Peace
November 1996
(presented December 1996)

Chechen Republic Ichkeria Election
Monitoring Report
January 1997

'China's Tibet': The World's Largest
Remaining Colony
April–May 1997

UNPO Fifth General Assembly
Summary Proceedings
July 1997

Nonviolence and Conflict:
Conditions for Effective Peaceful Change
July 1997

ELECTIONS IN ABKHAZIA AND THE PROSPECTS FOR PEACE

REPORT ON THE VISIT TO GEORGIA/ABKHAZIA
21–28 NOVEMBER 1996

Prepared by Lord Eric Avebury for presentation
to the Parliamentary Human Rights Group
of the United Kingdom
December 1996

TABLE OF CONTENTS

I. INTRODUCTION

Lord Eric Avebury and Senator John Nimrod visited Georgia and Abkhazia between 21–28 November 1996, at the request of the Unrepresented Nations and Peoples Organization. The opportunity was taken to pass through Tbilisi and spend a day there on the way out, and a day and a half on the way back, and to engage in discussions with the following persons:

Georgian Foreign Minister Mr. Irakli Menagharishvili;
Chairman of the Parliamentary Committee on Defence and Security, Mr. Revaz Adamia;
Director of European and American Affairs at the Foreign Ministry, Mr. Konstantin Zhghenti;
The Ambassadors of the USA, Russia, France and the UK, and the First Secretary of the German Embassy;
Representative of the ICRC Mr. Yves Daccord;
Legal Officer of the UNHCR Mr. Bayisa Wak-Woya;
Chairman of the Supreme Council of the Autonomous Republic of Abkhazia, Mr. Tamaz Nadareishvili;
Co-Director of Caucasia, Mr. Teimouraz Rekhviashvili;
Director of the Caucasian Institute for Peace and Democracy, Professor Gia Nodia;
Project Coordinator, Vertic Transcaucasus Office, Mr. Daniel Cousens.

This report comments on the elections, but is mainly concerned with the process of negotiations on the return of the exiles, and the settlement of the political dispute between Georgia and Abkhazia.

My warmest thanks are due to the British Ambassador in Tbilisi, His Excellency Mr. Stephen Nash, the Deputy Head of Mission, Mr. Michael Hancock, and members of the staff at the Embassy, who were enormously helpful in facilitating the meetings in Tbilisi, and with travel arrangements. Their friendly welcome and unstinting assistance was very greatly appreciated.

I was also grateful to the Georgian Embassy in London, who expedited my visa and gave me useful advice prior to the visit.

II. BACKGROUND TO THE VISIT

According to the most recent report of the United Nations Secretary-General, no significant progress has yet been achieved in spite of continuous efforts to seek a comprehensive political settlement of the conflict between Georgia and Abkhazia. The key unresolved issues remained the future political status of Abkhazia, and the return of the refugees and displaced persons.[1]

The Abkhazian authorities had announced their intention to hold parliamentary elections in the territory on 23 November 1996. These had been denounced as illegitimate by President Eduard Shevardnadze, and by the international community, and the Georgian authorities decided to hold a plebiscite among the exiles from Abkhazia in Georgia and elsewhere to demonstrate that a large number of qualified voters had been disfranchised by their inability to return to their homes.

In the security zone established on the Abkhazian side of the frontier with Georgia, low-intensity violence continued to be endemic. The Secretary-General's report mentions cases of murder, armed robbery, kidnapping and assault occurring frequently in the Gali region, together with mine-laying and attacks on the CIS peacekeeping force and Abkhaz militia checkpoints. The Georgians demand that police functions be included in an enlarged mandate for the CIS peacekeeping force.

The official program for repatriation of the exiles came to a halt because the Georgians were not satisfied with the Abkhazians' rate of processing of applications. However, between 40,000 and 60,000 refugees are estimated to have returned to the Gali region informally. These people can move freely backwards and forwards across the frontier.

The war caused immense damage all the way along the coast road, from the Ingur river crossing up to and beyond the capital of Abkhazia, Sukhumi. Most of the houses are uninhabitable, and there is no chance of repairing any of the damage because of the blockade imposed by the CIS. Some goods do enter Abkhazia via Turkey, and smuggling flourishes between the Russian Federation and Abkhazia, tolerated by Russian border guards who are allegedly easily bribed. However, the economic effects of the blockade are affecting not only the existing civilian population, but also the capacity of the territory to accept further returnees.

One hopeful sign had been the 15 November meeting between President Eduard Shevardnadze and Georgian Foreign Minister Irakli Menagharishvili on one side, and Abkhazian Foreign Minister Konstantin Ozgan and an Abkhazian Deputy on the other.

III. MEETING WITH GEORGIAN FOREIGN MINISTER, IRAKLI MENAGHARISHVILI, 21 NOVEMBER

Mr. Menagharishvili said at a meeting on 21 November that there had been contacts at an official level prior to the 15 November 'summit', and that there were ways of getting messages between the parties. The idea of the high level meeting had come from the Georgian side, he said. (President Ardzinba claimed, however, that he had proposed it).

With regard to the Russian participation in the peace process, he said: "*We have to be sure when and how the Russians should be involved, remembering that they took part in the conflict.*" On the role of Federal Councillor Edouard Brunner, he said "*We have no criticism of Mr. Brunner personally, but we are not satisfied with the role of the*

United Nations, and he is working on their behalf. They have taken a strange position as observers, leaving the process of negotiation to the Russians." (Other Georgians were less inhibited in their assessment of Mr. Brunner, which may simply indicate that he is impartial, and they are disappointed that he does not show the same preference for the Georgian side that is displayed by the Security Council, the European Parliament and the Council of Europe.)

Mr. Menagharishvili said that he had first met Mr. Brunner only a month previously. The Minister thought there should be no interruption in the negotiating process, and that the problems demanded systematic and regular work. It was not correct to describe the existing process as negotiation. "*We have to find out how to make the process permanent, otherwise there is no way out.*"

Moscow could not be depended on to accelerate or slow things down. On the other hand, Russia could not be separated from the process, and everybody would have to work on the formula. Mr. Ozgan had accepted, however, that there should be continuous working contacts.

Other factors to be considered were, according to the Minister:

* the role of the international community;
* the place of Russia in the process;
* economic restoration;
* repatriation of the refugees, including non-Georgians.

The objective should be to overcome one main difficulty: the fate of the Abkhazian people should not be subject to political manipulation. Abkhazia is one of the keys to the Caucasus. Not only is Russia manipulating events in the region, but there are also powerful forces involved, which have their roots in muslim countries.

On the Abkhazian elections, Mr. Menagharishvili said that they were unacceptable because one part of the population would be unable to vote. (That did not bother the international community in the case of Sierra Leone, where elections were held while there were 154,900 refugees in Guinea, and 120,000 in Liberia, to say nothing of 360,000 people internally displaced)[2].

"The whole population of Abkhazia must vote. This is the point from which we start. We are not expecting anything good from these elections. We told them, 'You will create a structure that has no legitimacy, you will create another gap between your population and the refugees. Better that we sit down together and narrow the gap. For example, that both sections of Parliament continue until there is a chance of allowing everybody to vote. Any step which is unacceptable to the international community, as this is, will make matters worse.'

"Ardzinba could have used the Security Council Resolution to prolong the life of the Parliament. I tried to send him that message. We need to neutralise negative influences and to reach agreement on the internal environment for a peaceful settlement. In the meetings on Ossetia, the OSCE played a useful role, and they could do so here too."

The Minister's suspicions of Russia, and his enthusiasm for bringing in other players, appear to be widely shared. One theory presented, though not by Mr. Menagharishvili, was that the Russians had an interest in keeping low-level conflicts going all over the 'near abroad', to give themselves a plausible excuse for prolonging their military presence in newly independent states, and thus exerting political pressure on them.

IV. MEETING WITH PRESIDENT ARDZINBA OF ABKHAZIA, 23 NOVEMBER

"*Georgia and the Friends of Georgia want to involve FOG in the negotiating process, and never to leave the table. When the FOG change their name, so that they are friends of both Georgia and Abkhazia, I would agree to their participation,*" President Ardzinba said at a meeting on 23 November.

The Ambassadors of FOG reminded me that their full title is Friends of the Secretary-General for Georgia. Since the title is a contentious matter, however, it would be helpful if it could be changed, say to 'Black Sea Group', or to any other form of words that contains neither Abkhazia nor Georgia. This question of the name has impaired the effectiveness of the FOG throughout its whole existence, and it was one of the complaints raised by the Abkhazians when I last visited the region in December 1994. It was, of course, not merely the title which prompted concern, but the title was seen to represent the point of view of the member states.

"*As to permanent negotiations, the outcome does not depend on the hours spent at the table or the number of pens worn out. An agreement could be reached in ten minutes if there was the political will. So there is no sense in continuing these negotiations under present conditions.*

"*I am ready to sign an agreement based on the Declaration of 4 April 1994, and on the principle of equality. There was a draft of the main principles—nine or ten points—on which a detailed agreement could be based. I told Mr. Brunner, we have no wish to return to being part of Georgia, taking into consideration what happened in the late war, and we are quite capable of living independently.*"

I asked Mr. Ardzinba whether he thought it would be helpful to ask an international lawyer to write an agreement, based on the Declaration of 4 April, setting up the institutions that would be necessary to operate the common functions identified in the Declaration, such as foreign affairs, customs and border posts. He agreed that this would be helpful. If the parties set aside the question of Abkhazia's constitutional status, allowing it to emerge as a by-product of an institutional framework, rather than defining the status first and deducing the institutions from it, I believe that progress could be made. I found it difficult with some on the Georgian side, such as Mr. Konstantin Zhghenti, Director of European and American Affairs at the Foreign Office, to get across the importance of this point as a psychological hurdle to be surmounted. Mr. Ardzinba insists that Abkhazia is *de facto* independent, while the Georgians—and the international community—continually emphasise "*the sovereignty and territorial integrity of Georgia within its internationally recognized borders,*"[3] and use pejorative language, referring to 'the Abkhaz separatist authorities.'[4]

President Ardzinba, on the other hand, points out:

> "*The main problem is the one-sided support of Georgia by the international community and by Russia. We are not a country that has been conquered; we are looking for an agreement after a war. People here asked me to conduct a referendum on total independence as part of these elections, but I rejected that because I wanted to reach an agreement. There is a minimum we can accept. We are not a part of Georgia and we can only have a treaty-based agreement. Even in Tatarstan their constitution calls the state a subject of international law. As for our position, Abkhazia and Georgia were equal in status when the Soviet Union first came into existence. We were both Republics, with the right to secede from the USSR. Then there was a treaty relationship between Abkhazia and Georgia, which continued up to 1932. At that point Stalin, who was of course a Georgian, altered the relationship and reduced our status to that of an autonomous republic within Georgia. Large scale transfer of the Georgian population into Abkhazia took place, with a view to making us subordinate. But after the downfall of the Soviet Union, it was the Georgians who abrogated their constitution, so that there was a return to the relationship between us which existed prior to the treaty of 1924. Under those circumstances, we had the same right to go back to the status we held at that time, and to formulate a new constitution just as the Georgians had done.*"

This is at least an arguable case, and Georgian spokespersons did not attempt to rebut it. When it was raised, they asserted that what had happened in the Soviet period was no longer relevant. Whatever the legal merits of the argument, however, it is no more useful, as a starting point for productive negotiations, than the Georgian assertion that Abkhazia is subordinate to Georgia, because that was the position from 1932 onwards, even though the instruments on which that relationship depended had been abrogated. It is surely more sensible to leave those questions aside and to see whether practical matters can be agreed, concentrating first on those which could be of mutual benefit to both parties, and others as well. The reopening of the railway from Georgia to Russia, which passes through Abkhazia, is an obvious example.

For the record, however, on 20 June 1990—when Gamsakhurdia was in charge—the Supreme Soviet of the Georgian SSR passed a resolution suspending Soviet laws connected with the leaving of the USSR by a union-republic, on the definition of rights existing between the Union and subjects of the Federation, and on the basis of economic relations and other matters. Since this affected the rights of the Abkhazian ASSR (defined in the 1978 Georgian Constitution) and since at the time autonomous republics within Russia itself were claiming to be full union-republics, the Abkhazians declared 'The State Sovereignty of the Abkhazian Soviet Socialist Republic' on 25 August 1990. The relationship between Georgia and Abkhazia was not spelled out by either party at that time, because the main preoccupation of the authorities in Tbilisi was to free themselves from control by Moscow.

After Gamsakhurdia's flight into exile, the Military Council of Georgia, which had come into power by a military coup, abrogated Georgia's 1978 constitution in February 1992 and reinstated the constitution of 22 February 1921 which had been introduced by the independent Menshevik-led government. Clause 107 of that constitution states that "Abkhasie (district of Soukhoum), Georgia Musulmane (district of Batum), and Zakhathala (district of Zakhatala), which are integral parts of the Georgian Republic, enjoy an autonomy in the administration of their affairs."[5]

Clause 108 states: "The statute concerning the autonomy of the districts mentioned in the previous article will be the object of special legislation." In other words, the nature of the relationship was never specified in the crucial 1921 constitution, and although Abkhazia had been militarily annexed by General Mazniev (Mazniashvili) on behalf of the Menshevik regime in 1918, its status under international law was indeterminate.

Left without any constitutional definition of their relationship with Georgia, the Abkhazians reinstated their own constitution of 1925 on 23 July 1992, under which Abkhazia was a Soviet Socialist Republic, co-equal with Georgia, and linked with Georgia by treaty. At the time this was viewed as a temporary measure until a new legal definition of relations between Abkhazia and Georgia could be agreed. A draft for such relations was published at the end of 6 July but Georgian forces invaded less than a month later.

V. MEETING WITH FOREIGN MINISTER KONSTANTIN OZGAN, 23 NOVEMBER

Mr. Ozgan began by drawing attention to the high turnout in the Abkhazian elections, particularly in the Gali region. He said the average for the territory as a whole was 85%, while in Gali it reached 90%. (According to the Abkhaz Central Electoral Commission Chairman, Vyacheslav Tsugba, in the first round of the elections 26 candidates won over 50% of votes, which entitles each of them to a seat in parliament. The total number of seats is 35, and therefore, around 65% of seats in the Abkhazian parliament have been filled. The turnout was 82%.) [7]

I briefed him on the meeting I had had with Foreign Minister Menagharishvili. Concerning the recent meeting in Tbilisi, he said he had been there to see Mr. Shevardnadze and that Mr. Menagharishvili had been present. There was also an Abkhazian deputy present. The meeting arose from an initiative by President Ardzinba, who asked him to go.

On the role of Mr. Brunner, Mr. Ozgan said he was aware that the Georgians were not fully satisfied,

> *"but we think that he has enough time to devote to the process and is well-informed on the conflict. I had a long talk with Mr. Brunner in late September, and I did not notice that he supported one or the other side. I thought he was very wise, and that being a special envoy, he has done more than others, such as the Security Council, the FOG, the OSCE or the European Parliament. The very reason why the Georgians are not satisfied with Mr. Brunner is that he does try to consider both sides' viewpoints. I am convinced that although he is very busy, he does have time to visit and to listen. It is the others I have mentioned who have no time for us. If they came and studied the case objectively, Georgia would not be satisfied with any of those actors either.*

"We are always ready for negotiations, any time. It is for the Georgians to decide when they are ready. If Mr. Menagharishvili says the word, we are ready to meet at any place and any time.

"As to the Russians as mediators, I think they do rather well. Russia has paid a lot of attention to the dispute. Strengthening the role of the United Nations, that would not be the way I would formulate the question. The UN has not studied the case since 1992, and we are now in 1996. If they do study the case themselves, their role could be strengthened." [I think he was referring to the members of the Security Council. Visits to Abkhazia by FOG Ambassadors have done something to remove the impression gained by the Abkhazian leadership that nobody except Mr. Brunner was interested in hearing their side of the story, and it is important to expand those channels of communication.]

"On the 'strange position of the UN in leaving the negotiations to Russia', the fact is that they are not equipped to deal with the process. Yes, we did agree that the negotiation process must be continuous, and we agree that leadership meetings should be held, with and without mediators.

"On the refugees, we signed an agreement in April 1994 and we are ready to implement it. The fact that 60,000 have returned to Gali demonstrates our good faith.

"The world community has to work with us so that they have an objective understanding of the problems. They have to make an effort, but so far they only listen to Mr. Shevardnadze. I have written to the Security Council, the Secretary-General and the European Parliament, and I hope they will study what we say.

"There is no state–legal relationship between Georgia and Abkhazia. All previously existing arrangements were made by Stalin and Beria. Stalin demoted Abkhazia to the status of an autonomous republic in 1931, but in 1990–91 Georgia declared all the treaties of that period as null and void. So, there has been a political vacuum since then, except for the agreement of 4 April 1994. Georgia demands her territorial integrity and we accept that, within her 1920s boundaries. In the same terms, Abkhazia is now an independent state."

The international community recognized the 15 union-republics of the former

Soviet Union within their 1991 borders. In doing so, they ignored the fact that these entities were artifacts of Soviet imperialism, and also that, within the parameters of the Soviet state–legal system, they were not immutable. If the dissolution of the ties which bound Georgia to other entities within the Soviet system was lawful, this should have been taken into account. There is an unfortunate inclination to substitute state practice for international law in these matters, undermining the rule of law in international affairs.

In the course of the discussions with both Mr. Menagharishvili and President Ardzinba, I asked whether they thought that a resumption of the refugee repatriation program might be coupled with economic incentives for the rehabilitation of damaged houses and infrastructure. Both said this was an idea that could be considered. Later, I found in discussion with the UNHCR Legal Officer, Mr. Bayisa Wak-Woya, that the UNHCR had reached an agreement with Abkhazia, under which the Abkhazian authorities would undertake a village by village survey and following which they would report on the state of repair of each village and the work needing to be done to repair damaged houses or infrastructure. The return program could then be coordinated with the timetable for physical rehabilitation, on which assistance would be needed from the international community. This seems a much more practical approach than specifying a fixed number of returnees per month, and it also has the advantage that refugees can return village by village, so that they would be accompanied by their neighbors.

Mr. Wak-Woya also said that all the refugees who had returned informally to the Gali region continued to be registered in Zugdidi, because they obtained free distributions of aid thereby. This means that the 40,000 or 60,000 informal returnees are being counted on both sides. The Abkhazians say that 60,000 have returned to the Gali region, and that in a recent head-count they enumerated 90,000 Georgians in Abkhazia altogether. There are certainly Georgians in other regions, since we met some in Pitsunda and in Gagra. Yet the figures quoted by the Georgian authorities assume that nobody has returned. It is unfortunate that the unofficial returnees were never registered, as recommended in the report on my previous visit dated 15 December 1994.

The chairman of the [Tbilisi-based] Supreme Council of the Autonomous Republic of Abkhazia, Tamaz Nadareishvili, said that there were 340,000 exiles altogether, of whom 220,000 were of voting age. He claimed that every single one of these persons had voted in the referendum conducted on the same day as the Abkhazian elections, and that every single one of them called for the reintegration of Abkhazia into Georgia.

The number of refugees who left Abkhazia as a result of the conflict has never been properly determined. The UNHCR[8] gives a figure of 250,000. However, the UNHCR's London office give a different picture. The UNHCR Office in Tbilisi has informed us that the number of persons the Georgian authorities claim have left Abkhazia as a result of the conflict in Abkhazia is as follows:

- 200,000 Georgians left Abkhazia for Georgia proper;
- 30,000 Georgians left Abkhazia for Russia;
- Up to 50,000 Russians and other minorities may have left Abkhazia for Russia;
- Some 30,000 Abkhaz left Georgia and went to Abkhazia or Russia, and 25,000 Abkhaz may be displaced inside Abkhazia;
- The figure of 285,000 represents all internally displaced persons, including Ossetians, in the country. This figure is often used in appeals for humanitarian assistance, but the Georgian government also used the figure 300,000[9].

Thus, according to the information given to the UNHCR by the Georgian authorities, which has not been independently verified, the maximum number of persons who left Abkhazia for Georgia, Russia or any other country of refuge, was 280,000. However, the last Soviet census of 1989 showed that there were only 240,000 'Georgians' altogether in Abkhazia, and by common consent the statistics were manipulated to increase the number of 'Georgians' and diminish the number belonging to other nationalities. Ethnicity had to be entered in pencil, and all the forms were taken to Tbilisi for processing. Many Mingrelians stated their nationality as such, but they were not so recorded in the official statistics. Even if the official total of 'Georgians' was correct, by no means all of them left, and the alleged figure of 230,000 'Georgian' refugees is impossible.

Although he did not make this point in the course of our discussions, he had said at a news conference held at the office of the Georgian Federation of Journalists, that *"by holding the elections, the separatists have themselves put an end to a peaceful settlement of the conflict."*[10] This was not true, since the Georgian government, whilst condemning the elections, had not said they would break off negotiations if they were held, and indeed they continued to emphasise the importance of more intensive talks. President Shevardnadze himself said that the talks would continue, two days after the poll. He said:

> *"As far as the visit to Tbilisi by Konstantin Ozgan and* [Abkhaz parliamentary deputy] *Daur Barganjia is concerned, there was an agreement that the meeting would remain confidential. Later, the Sukhumi authorities decided that it was not necessary to comply with the agreement on the confidentiality of the meeting, and neither do I view it as a tragedy that they had publicly divulged it. In itself, the meeting is significant because in a way it initiated a dialogue between Georgians and the Abkhaz. You may recall my visit to Gudauta* [in Abkhazia last spring]. *One of the aims of that visit was also to start a dialogue but unfortunately that meeting proved to be a one-sided dialogue and up until now, there has been no serious continuation of the dialogue. Now we have an initiative by the current leaders of Abkhazia, the Sukhumi leaders, who decided to hold a dialogue in Tbilisi. The dialogue will continue in future. At least this is what we agreed on. Meetings may be held in Moscow, Abkhazia or Tbilisi. These will*

> *mainly be bilateral meetings and talks. I regard a detailed review of the* [Tbilisi] *meeting as a little premature. What we agreed on needs elaboration, additional coordination and it is inexpedient to publicly divulge the contents of the talks. The next meetings will show how useful the Tbilisi dialogue has been. I would like to indicate that representatives of Russia were informed about the meeting in Tbilisi and only tactics of support can be expected from them ...*"[11]

So President Shevardnadze himself refuted Mr. Nadareishvili's alarmist prediction. The perception of these matters, and what people say about them, is often influenced by their strongly-held viewpoints. I experienced this in a minor way with Mr. Nadareishvili personally. During the course of my interview with him, he asked me whether I had represented the UK officially as an observer at the Abkhazian elections. I told him that I was there in my personal capacity, and that the UK government did not recognize the elections. I also said that he could repeat this to the media. This was reported as follows: "*From the very start, Lord Avebury expressed concern over reports in the Russian media claiming that he had been sent to Abkhazia as an official observer at the elections ...*"

VI. THE ELECTIONS IN ABKHAZIA

In assessing any election, it is necessary to consider not just the polling day arrangements, but also the registration of voters, selection of candidates, access to the media, freedom of assembly and expression, etc. Because we only arrived in Abkhazia on the eve of the poll it was not possible to form an opinion on most of these questions. There was no sign of electioneering in the form of posters or public meetings, but it has to be remembered that the population of Abkhazia is comparable with that of a London Borough, and we were told that everybody knew who the candidates were and what they stood for.

At the polling stations, there were lists of eligible voters on large sheets, also recording their addresses and identity card numbers. As a voter arrived, his or her identity card was checked against the register, and the voter would then sign against the name, following which a ballot paper would be issued. The papers listed the names of the candidates, and the voter was required to delete all the names except that of his or her preferred candidate.

If an unregistered voter turned up, with an identity card, the presiding officer would normally register that person on the spot.

Some voters turned up with more than one identity card, asking to record the vote of a relative. This was allowed, against the rules, in two of the polling stations we visited. It is not likely that this irregularity led to any distortion of the result, since presumably the relative had given the holder of his/her card the authority to act on his/her behalf.

According to the final report of the Central Electoral Commission of Abkhazia on Elections to the Popular Assembly (the Republic's parliament) 81% of the electorate turned out to vote and 30 MPs were elected out of a field of 83. Five seats in parliament remain vacant (because no candidate gained more than 50% of the poll), so there would be repeat elections in five constituencies in two weeks time. Of the 30 elected MPs, there are 19 Abkhaz, four Russians, three Armenians, two Georgians, one Greek and one Kabardin.

The Commission reported that observers issued complaints concerning some minor technical difficulties in the elections, but considered that everything else was fine. The elections have been declared democratic. And, the entire Georgian population of Abkhazia voted, they said.[12]

There were no acts of violence on election day itself, but two terrorist attacks occurred on the eve of poll. An armoured personnel carrier belonging to the [Russian] peacekeeping forces blew up on a mine, and it was reported that a Russian serviceman in the vehicle was severely injured. A bomb also exploded at the administrative building in Gali, destroying an office on the ground floor which had been occupied only two minutes earlier. As usual with these incidents, there was no evidence of the identity of the culprits, though it was believed by the Abkhazian authorities that the sabotage was perpetrated in order to disrupt the elections and intimidate voters.

The Georgian Ministry of State Security, however, said that the allegations made by the Abkhazians were "merely yet another political pre-election farce". The Georgians claimed that the worsened situation ahead of the "illegal elections" was "caused in fact by the extremely tense confrontation between the Gudauta and Ochamchire clans which turned into an armed conflict long ago." The Ministry said that it was "practically impossible to hold elections in Gali District, where there is complete chaos and impunity reigns. The population feels in a state of panic and is seeking shelter in forests as well as territories controlled by the legal Georgian authorities."[13] The turnout was, in fact, higher in the Gali District than in the rest of Abkhazia.

According to President Eduard Shevardnadze, over 99% of the refugees from Abkhazia voted in a plebiscite held in connection with the parliamentary elections in Abkhazia. "*Out of a total of 238,000 refugees who were eligible to vote,*" said the President, "*224,800 people took part in the plebiscite. This makes 93.8% of the refugees over 18 years of age. In Georgia, over 186,000 citizens took part in the plebiscite. Almost all the participants, that is, over 99% of the refugees, said no to the separatist elections in Abkhazia, that is, they deplored the elections.*" [14]

Other figures quoted by Mr. Shevardnadze were that some 16,000 people turned up at polling stations in Moscow, 5,200 in St. Petersburg, 1,800 in Podolsk [Russia], 2,700 in Kiev, 7,080 in Sochi, 530 in Trabzon [Turkey], 550 in Yerevan, 800 in Minsk, several hundred in Greece, and many, mostly Jews forced to leave Abkhazia, in Israel. Among the participants in the plebiscite were ethnic Georgians, Abkhaz, Armenians, Russians, Greeks, Jews, and others. Although it was claimed that the plebiscite was officially monitored by western observers, nothing was said to me about this by any of the FOG Ambassadors, and the nature of the claimed observation needs to be elucidated.

He also cast doubt on the statistics announced for the Abkhazian elections, saying that they "seem to be taken from outer space." He claimed that according to the United Nations, the current population of Abkhazia was no more than one-third of the pre-war population, making it a maximum of 175,000. The Abkhazians say that the figure is about 300,000. Part of the difference may be accounted for by the 60,000 returnees in the Gali region mentioned earlier, who are still treated by the Georgian authorities as living in Zugdidi, where they register for aid. There is still a substantial discrepancy between the statistics used be either side, and it would be useful if the parties could agree to commission an impartial joint study, so that reasonably accurate information could be made available to aid agencies and others on which to base their policies.

VII. CONCLUSION

The opening of conversations at the Foreign Minister level, and their probable continuation in Sukhumi in early December, are hopeful signs of a better atmosphere in which the twin problems (of the return of the exiles and the constitutional status of Abkhazia) could be progressed.

VIII. RECOMMENDATIONS

1. The Friends of Georgia should change their name, to, say, "The Black Sea Group".
2. Informal returnees should be registered.
3. It would be helpful if, as a sign of good will, the CIS blockade were lifted, and travel by Abkhazians facilitated, so that improved contacts could be achieved between Abkhazians and the rest of the world.
4. Other confidence-building measures ought to be adopted at the same time, including the opening of the railway line and Sukhumi airport.
5. The Abkhazians should actively undertake the village survey agreed with the UNHCR, so that the return of the exiles can proceed in an orderly manner.
6. The international community should be asked to commit resources to the rehabilitation of housing, water, sanitation, schools, clinics and the rest of the infrastructure of Abkhazia, so as to facilitate the return of the exiles.
7. The parties should commission, jointly, a survey of the population of Abkhazia, and of the exiles living abroad, so that accurate figures are available to aid agencies, the UNHCR, and the authorities of Georgia and Abkhazia.
8. The parties should concentrate on the methodology of establishing joint institutions to perform the functions listed in the Declaration of 4 April 1994, leaving the question of Abkhazia's constitutional status to be considered at a later date.

IX. NOTES

1. *Report of the Secretary-General concerning the situation in Abkhazia, Georgia,* S/1996/843, 10 Oct. 1996.
2. *The State of the World's Refugees,* UNHCR (1995), pp114 and 248–9.
3. United Nations Security Council Resolution 1077 of 22 Oct. 1996.
4. Parliamentary Assembly of the Council of Europe Recommendation 1305 (1996) on the humanitarian situation of the displaced people of Georgia.
5. Kandelaki, C., *The Georgian Question Before the Free World,* Paris, 1953.
6. Hewitt, G., *Central Asian Survey.*
7. ITAR-TASS news agency (World Service), Moscow, 0556 gmt 24 Nov. 1996.
8. Georgian Radio, Tbilisi, 0600 gmt 24 Nov. 1996.
9. Georgian Radio, Tbilisi, 0528 gmt 25 Nov 1996.
10. Russian TV channel, Moscow, 0500 gmt 26 Nov. 1996.
11. Georgian Radio, Tbilisi, 0600 gmt 24 Nov. 1996.
12. Kontakt News Agency, Tbilisi, 1330 gmt 22 Nov. 1996.
13. Georgian Radio, Tbilisi, in Georgian 0600 gmt 22 Nov. 1996.
14. Kontakt News Agency, Tbilisi, in Georgian 1330 gmt 22 Nov. 1996.

CHECHEN ELECTION MONITORING REPORT

SUMMARY OF THE UNPO MISSION
TO MONITOR ELECTIONS IN THE
CHECHEN REPUBLIC ICHKERIA
24–29 JANUARY 1997

by
L. Mäll, E. Alptekin, M. Tzelios, K. von Habsburg, F. Besson,
A. Khuzangai, A. Leontyev, G. Verblyudo, T. Kümmel, A. Talvik,
P. Volkonskiy

with
Yob van As and J. Atticus Ryan

TABLE OF CONTENTS

I. INTRODUCTION

A. Terms of Reference

In an invitation contained in a letter from the Minister of Foreign Affairs of the Chechen Republic Ichkeria, Mr. Rouslan Chimaev, (written on behalf of President Zelimkhan Yandarbiev and dated 9 November 1997) to the General Secretary of the Unrepresented Nations and Peoples Organization was invited to monitor the Presidential and Parliamentary elections in the Chechen Republic Ichkeria on 27 January 1997.

The outcome of these elections, which were held in accordance with the terms of the agreements reached between the Chechen Republic and the Russian Federation, were of great importance to the promotion of peace and democracy in the region. The former Commander-in-Chief, Aslan Maskhadov, was elected president by a majority vote of the people.

The Chechen Republic Ichkeria became a member of the UNPO in 1991, and the UNPO agreed to send a mission to monitor the elections in the Chechen Republic in accordance with Article 2(h) of the Covenant of the UNPO. The observer's terms of reference were:

a) To ascertain, in an impartial manner, whether the elections were free and fair and adequately represented the wishes of the people of the Chechen Republic Ichkeria.
b) The leader of the mission was responsible for leading the mission, coordinating the activities of all the members of the mission and for reaching agreement on the preliminary report of the mission.
c) The leader of the mission or someone designated by him was to keep the UNPO Secretariat informed of the progress of the mission and of developments in Chechenia on a daily basis.
d) Immediately upon the mission's completion, the mission was to deliver a preliminary report of its findings to the General Secretary of the UNPO and to the Government of the Chechen Republic Ichkeria.
e) A report was to be prepared as soon as possible, but no later than 14 days after the mission's completion and was to be transmitted to the General Secretary of the UNPO. The report would be forwarded to the Government of the Chechen Republic Ichkeria, to the Russian Federation, to the United Nations, the Organization for Security and Cooperation in Europe, to the European Union and others by the General Secretary of the UNPO and was to be made public by him.

B. Participants of the UNPO Mission

The participants of the mission were:

Dr. Linnart Mäll (UNPO Assistant General Secretary for Eastern Europe and Director of the UNPO Tartu Coordination Office);
Mr. Erkin Alptekin (Chairman of the UNPO General Assembly and Representative of Eastern Turkestan);
Mr. Menelaos Tzelios (UNPO Assistant General Secretary for United Nations Affairs and Representative of the Greek Minority in Albania);
Mr. Karl von Habsburg (Member of the European Parliament from Austria);
Ms. Frédérique-Jeanne Besson (French Institute of Anatolian Studies, Istanbul);
Mr. Atner Khuzangai (Representative of the Chuvash National Congress);
Mr. Aleksey Leontyev (Member, State Council of the Chuvash Republic);
Mr. Gennadiy Verblyudov (Journalist, Estonia);
Mr. Toomas Kümmel (Journalist, Estonia);
Mr. Artur Talvik (Journalist, Estonia);
Prince Peter Volkonskiy (Estonia).

II. SITUATIONAL BACKGROUND

A. Historical

During the 19th century, what is now known as the Chechen Republic Ichkeria was conquered by the Russian empire despite resolute Chechen resistance. Even with the dramatic changes following the Bolshevik revolution of 1917, the Chechens were unable to free themselves from Russian domination; they did, however, engage in numerous uprisings during the 1920s and early-1930s. In 1944, the Chechen people, together with the neighbouring Ingush, were deported to Kazakhstan on the accusation of collaboration during the German occupation. After the death of Stalin, Soviet Communist Party General Secretary Nikita Khrushchev rehabilitated the Chechens, allowing them the opportunity to return to their homeland.

As a result of perestroika in the late-1980s, a national revival movement led by the Vaynakh Democratic Party (VDP) began in Chechenia. During the coup attempt against Soviet President Mikhail Gorbachev in August 1991, the Chechen Communist Party and government supported the instigators of the coup, while the VDP condemned it. After the coup attempt was put down, massive rallies in Grozny forced the dissolution of the Communist government and the calling of new elections. Because of his position favoring independence for Chechenia, Dzhokhar Dudaev was elected the new President by an overwhelming majority.

On 1 November 1991 Chechenia officially declared independence. The Russian government subsequently ignored all invitations to negotiate a solution acceptable to both sides, and, on 7 November 1991, Russian President Boris Yeltsin declared a state of emergency in Chechenia. This political manoeuvre having failed, Russian forces subsequently withdrew.

In December 1991, Yeltsin declared the independence of Russia, which resulted in the disintegration of the Soviet Union, and on 31 March 1992 the new Federation Treaty of the Russian Federation was signed by a number of its existing republics. Chechenia refused to become a signatory, and in response the Russian government imposed an economic blockade.

On 11 December 1994, the Russian Army invaded Chechenia. It is estimated that as many as 120,000 civilians died from the resulting war, and a further 350,000 were displaced by the fighting.

B. Events Immediately Preceding the Elections

When, in August 1996, the Chechen resistance managed to recapture Grozny (in a battle lasting only three days) Russian Security Council Secretary, Aleksandr Lebed, negotiated a cease-fire agreement with the Commander-in-Chief of the Chechen Forces, General Aslan Maskhadov, signed on 31 August 1996 in Khasav-yurt. According to this agreement the Chechen government was to organize elections for a new parliament and president.

The general election was set for 27 January 1997, and was organized by the Chechen Central Election Commission in accordance with the Election Law published in the national newspapers, accessible in all polling stations, and prominently posted throughout the country.

III. THE MISSION

A. Itinerary

The UNPO mission was present in Chechenia from 26 January–29 January 1997. On 26 January it visited the election headquarters in Dzhokhar-Gala (Grozny), where it interviewed the chief election official. On the same day it also visited the headquarters of several prominent presidential candidates. The mission had an extensive meeting with Zelimkhan Yandarbiev (President since the death of Dzhokhar Dudaev in April 1996). Similar meetings were held with other candidates, including Shamil Basaev, Field Commander in the Chechen resistance, Movladi Udugov, and General Aslan Maskhadov.

On 27 January, polling stations opened at 7:00 a.m. and were to remain open until 8:00 p.m. The mission visited 29 polling stations in the Oktyabrskoye, Artskhoy, Alkhan-Kala, Kulari, Gekhi, Germenchuk, Argun, Sali and Vedeno Districts. In each polling station mission participants had conversations with election officials and examined the voter lists, as well as the progress of the voting process itself. In all polling stations the members of the mission met with the chairpersons of the commissions, observers and trustees of the presidential or parliamentary candidates. The vote tabulation continued throughout the night of 27

January, and on 28 January the mission was still observing the count.

B. The Candidates and Campaigning

Sixteen candidates ran for the post of President, with all candidates expressing support for independence. Every Presidential candidate had to register before 2 January 1997 by depositing the equivalent of US$100,000 with the Central Election Headquarters. Following this the candidate was granted 20 minutes of radio and 10 minutes of television time, as well as a full page in the national Chechen newspaper.

In the Parliamentary elections there were a total of 63 districts where 900 candidates from 36 parties ran individually for a seat in Parliament.

The day before the elections three presidential candidates withdrew their candidacy. This message was relayed to the polling stations, where officials from the election committees did their best to strike the names of those candidates from the ballots before distributing them to voters. Some of the more remote polling stations did not receive this message, and this predictably caused some confusion.

Many political parties, political and religious organizations, and citizen action groups participated in activities designed to highlight and explain the positions and points of view of individual presidential and parliamentary candidates. The most prominent campaigning was conducted by the Party for National Independence, the VDP, the International Committee for Human Rights, *Islaman Neq* (the Islamic Way), the Free Chechenia Movement, and the Peoples Union for the Revival of the Republic.

C. Voter Eligibility and Registration

After two years of war, the authorities experienced difficulty in registering all eligible voters. Nevertheless, between 4 December 1996 and 27 January 1997 election officials visited each accessible family in Chechenia (and in the Chechen refugee camps in the neighboring republics of Dagestan and Ingushetia) in order to register eligible persons over 18 years of age.

The vote was open to all citizens of Chechenia according to the criteria specified in the Election Law and in the Presidential Decree of 12 March 1995. Eligible voters were identified as Chechen citizens based on a passport registered in Chechenia (or, in the case of Soviet passports, specifying 'Nationality: Chechen').

During the war many Chechens lost their passports or had them confiscated upon entering Russian filtration camps. Those who did not have passports were issued provisional documents (Registration Form No.9) by the Chechen Ministry of Internal Affairs. Thus, voter lists were used flexibly in order to allow for late registration. The lists consisted of 400,000 names, though in some places turnout was as high as 130%, displaying the difficulty inherent in maintaining a thorough list of eligible voters.

D. Voting by Chechen Refugees and the Chechen Diaspora

The voter eligibilty criteria were also applied to Chechens living outside the Republic, who could exercise their right to vote if they came to Chechenia. The names of the Chechens of Dagestan (Akinians) were included on the voter registration lists by the National Chechen Council in Dagestan (operating under the supervision of the Central Election Commission). These lists were distributed to Chechen villages bordering Dagestan, as the Dagestani authorities would not allow the installation of polling stations on its territory (as was permitted in the neighboring Ingushetian village of Sleptsovsk).

At the time of the elections an estimated 30,000 Chechen refugees were residing in Dagestan, most of them in private houses in Akinian villages. For the elections, they generally voted at the same polling stations as the Chechens of Dagestan, but were registered on supplementary lists.

The Chechens in Dagestan (both refugees and residents) made widespread use of transportation provided by the Central Election Committee and the Chechen National Council in Dagestan. Each polling station had at its disposal a number of vehicles that performed a shuttle service from Dagestani villages to the polling stations across the border in Chechenia. In those border polling stations visited by mission participants a register of the number of shuttles to and from, and the number of people making use of them, was meticulously kept.

Although exact figures are not available, it was apparent that large numbers of Chechens from other Caucasian republics, the former Soviet Union, and Germany travelled to Chechenia for the elections, as well as a limited number from the United States.

E. Voting Regulations and Procedures

The election committees at the polling stations consisted of 11 prominent community members. The head and secretary of the each commission received special training if they had no previous administrative experience. One official, who did not have such experience, travelled to Grozny 16 times over the month prior to the elections to receive administrative training.

Voter registration lists were in alphabetical order and were divided among the members of the election commission. Two additional lists were kept: the supplementary list and the mobile ballot box list for those voting at home.

All voters were required to show proper identification and were registered either on the existing list or on a supplementary list. To include the name of an unregistered voter on the supplementary list a document of identification was required (a passport or Registration Form No.9), and each member of the election committee was authorized to register unlisted persons on this list.

In some instances the checking of documents was inconsistent: many unregistered voters came in groups but, as was repeatedly stated, "Chechens recognize each other." Registration of voters on the supplementary list was, therefore, done automatically and informally, though not illegally, as such a problem had been anticipated and decisions made regarding the criteria which would prove identity.

Each election committee was equipped with a mobile ballot box to enable the elderly and incapacitated to vote from home, and, thus, allow for greater participation. Voters who used the mobile ballot box were marked on a separate list as "voting at home."

The mission took note of those cases where people were not permitted to vote: some because they could not show proper identification, others because they had already voted elsewhere (identified by a fluorescent spray on their hand).

In voting two different ballots were used, one each for the Presidential and Parliamentary Elections. The ballots were kept in sealed boxes in close proximity to the voting centers and under police protection for the 24 hours prior to the election. Each of the 435 polling stations were given an amount of ballot forms corresponding to their voter registration list plus 10%. When more ballots were needed on election day they were, in general, promptly delivered.

The ballots for the Presidential elections were printed with the name and short descriptions of each candidate. The voters were to cross out the names of the candidates they did not support, a procedure not always clear to the voter.

In casting their vote, the ballot was folded and placed in the appropriate ballot box for the Presidential or Parliamentary elections. For those unable to read, accompaniment by a relative into the voting booth was permitted.

After voting, the left hand was sprayed with a substance visible under ultraviolet light, and, before voting, everyone had their hand checked with an ultraviolet lamp to prevent instances of multiple voting. Several election monitors tested various methods to remove the spray without success.

Several polling stations lacked basic facilities—an example being Argun, where there was no electricity and voting in the evening was done by candlelight. Many polling stations lacked telephone connections, and, therefore, the messages that three candidates withdrew their candidacy one day earlier and that voting was extended by two more hours on the election day had to be transmitted orally.

F. OBSERVANCE ON ELECTION DAY

The mission began its observation at 6:30 a.m. in Germenchuk (District 31, polling station 3). In this polling station none of the 11 members of the Election Committee was a member of a political party and none of them represented a presidential candidates.

During the mission's observation at polling station No. 18 in Grozny, (accompanied by two representatives from the Glasnost Foundation, the president and an observer from the Movement for Fair Elections and its Chechen branch), the ballot boxes were inspected by all observers, counted in public, and on the Presidential ballots the names of the three candidates which had withdrawn their candidacy were removed. The beginning of the vote was then delayed until the delivery of the ultra-violet lamp needed to identify those who had already voted. The procedure of signing the first ballot form by all the members of the local election committee was observed and the voting began.

The Chechen branch of the Movement for Fair Elections was represented in nearly every polling station visited. In many polling stations 'trustees' of the main presidential candidates were present. Additionally, representatives of groups of civilians who had nominated a candidate for parliament were present. In general, the mission witnessed no overt verbal propaganda or efforts to negatively influence voters.

Mission participants stopped in the Sunzha rayon in Ingushetia, bordering the Achkhoy-Martan rayon of the Chechen Republic Ichkeria, where preparations were made to enable participation by refugees in Troitskaya, Vognakievskaya and Asinovskaya. Organized transport to Grozny or other places allowed soldiers to cast their vote at home. Chechens from Dagestan voted in the villages of Koshkeldi, Girzel-yurt, Engel-yurt, and some polling stations in Novy Grozny and Nozhay-yurt.

On election day participation was so substantial, that, in accordance with the request of almost all local electoral commissions, the Central Election Committee decided to extend voting by two hours, until 10:00 p.m. This message spread quickly, despite communication difficulties, and did not cause excessive problems in most polling stations.

G. The Counting of Votes

At 10:00 p.m. the polls closed, and those voters inside a polling station at the deadline were given until 10:30 p.m. to vote. Following this, unused ballots were counted, cut at one corner, packed, sealed and signed by the members of the electoral commission.

The ballot boxes for the parliamentary elections were then opened in the polling station, and the results tallied in the presence of registered representatives of the candidates and election observers.

Once the results of the parliamentary elections were determined, the ballot boxes for the presidential election were opened and the number of ballots counted. All the materials were then taken to the Central Election Committee at the House of Culture in Urus-martan, where the ballots for the presidential election were counted by the same committee from the polling station. The hall was arranged in such a way that the election monitors and the representatives of each candidate could observe the counting of votes. The district results were then submitted to the Central Election Headquarters.

IV. MISSION FINDINGS

The mission concludes that, although the elections were conducted under very difficult circumstances, the election procedures met with international standards and accurately expressed the will of the people of the Chechen Republic Ichkeria. The mission observed that the greatest difficulties encountered in the election process were due to the complications inherent in establishing a comprehensive list of voters due to the overwhelming amount of refugees and displaced persons. The layout of the ballot sheet also led to some confusion and a disproportionate number of invalid votes. However, the mission found that despite the difficulties, the flexibility and goodwill of all parties concerned led to the smooth conduct of both the parliamentary and presidential elections.

'CHINA'S TIBET'
THE WORLD'S LARGEST REMAINING COLONY

REPORT OF A FACT-FINDING MISSION
AND
ANALYSIS OF COLONIALISM AND CHINESE RULE IN TIBET
APRIL–MAY 1997

Unrepresented Nations and Peoples Organization

In cooperation with
Tibet Support Groep Nederland
International Campaign for Tibet

TABLE OF CONTENTS

PREFACE

The United Nations declared 1990 as the start of the International Decade for the Eradication of Colonialism. Colonialism in its many forms has plagued the world for centuries. Much progress was made this century in securing the freedom of peoples who suffered under colonialism. In many cases the outcome of the decolonization process was the creation of independent states, in a few cases the establishment of associations between the former colonies and the former colonial powers. But in some regions colonialism persists, and it appears certain that despite the call for the acceleration of decolonization, we shall enter the 21st century without having rid the world of colonialism.

The largest territory to have lost its sovereignty since the Second World War is Tibet, which came under Chinese Communist rule in 1951, following a military invasion of the country. Resistance to Chinese rule has been considerable and continues to this day. The Chinese government characterises this resistance as a conspiracy of "splittist" Tibetans, headed by the "Dalai clique," to split the Chinese "Motherland":

> Maintaining stability is one of the two major tasks of our region. ...In the past decades, since the Dalai clique betrayed the Motherland and fled away, their sabotage activities of the conspiracy to separate the motherland have never stopped.[1]

But Tibetans view their movement as a liberation struggle. The government of Tibet, which went into exile in 1959, following a massive but unsuccessful revolt against China, strives to free Tibet from occupation. The 14th Dalai Lama, the political as well as spiritual leader of Tibet, stated in a speech at the European Parliament in 1996:

> The problem of Tibet is...fundamentally of a political nature. It is a problem of colonial domination: the oppression of Tibet by the People's Republic of China and the resistance to that domination by the Tibetans.[2]

This observation by the exiled Tibetan Head of State, is not the only reference to Tibet as a 'colony' of the People's Republic of China. The current situation in Tibet is described increasingly often as 'colonial'. These descriptions are based on the assumption that colonialism is a well-defined concept which needs no further explanation. Yet, it is by no means clear what it actually means and how it can be defined. Research on colonialism has mainly focused on concrete examples of European rule in Africa and Asia. Most people would agree, however, that the term colonial has a much wider meaning: it refers to a political system, to a set of beliefs, to an attitude of one people towards another. Little research has been done on the mechanics of colonial systems and their ideological underpinnings.

In the present report, the situation in Tibet is examined in terms of its relationship to China. The question is posed: is Tibet a colony of China? Stated differently: is China's rule over Tibet since 1951 a form of colonial rule?

In order to answer this question, which can have far reaching implications, the Unrepresented Nations and Peoples Organization, in association with the Tibet Support Group Netherlands and with the help of the International Campaign for Tibet, commissioned an independent study on colonialism and sent a mission to Tibet, Nepal and India, composed of three eminent and independent persons: two members of Parliament, one each from Ireland and the Netherlands (a former colony and a former colonial power, respectively) and a professor of International Law of Maastricht University, with extensive United Nations experience, who headed the mission. Their findings are contained in the Tibet Mission Report, which is the first part of this publication.

The second part of this publication. is an Independent Study on Colonialism and Tibet, which consists of a study, made up of two distinct parts: Part I is a study of colonialism. The author analyses the concept of colonialism and identifies the principal characteristics of or criteria for colonialism. The members of the mission to Tibet read this part of the study before starting on their journey, and adopted these criteria as the framework for their investigation. Part II of this study, which was written independently of the mission's work, is a study of the situation of Tibet in relation to the concept of colonialism analysed in Part I.

The observations of the mission members (contained in the mission report) and the conclusions reached by the independent. researcher compliment each other very well. What emerges from this body of work is astounding: the PRC, a state which has been on the forefront of the struggle against colonialism and which has been a champion of colonised peoples, is today undeniably a colonial power itself.

China's rule over Tibet since 1951 has all the characteristics of colonialism in the real sense of the word. This is evident not only from the manner in which Chinese authority was established and is maintained in Tibet. It is clear from the way in which the Chinese authorities decide on and implement economic and other development policies and exploit natural resources, and from the population transfer of million of Chinese into Tibet. It is clear also from the policies implemented by China regarding the Tibetan language, culture and religion. Mostly revealing is the attitude of the Chinese authorities and of the Tibetan people, whose perceptions of each other are typical of those of the colonial power and the colonised people.

This report is the first in-depth analysis of the de facto colonial status of Tibet. The implications of the findings contained in this report could be very significant. International law and practice, including especially the practice of the United Nations, condemns colonialism in all its forms and recognized the full right to self-determination of colonial peoples and territories. It prescribes decolonization as the means for exercising this right and requires of the administering power (usually the colonial power) to undertake all measures to facilitate its realization.

It is hoped that this report may contribute to efforts by the UN and others to accelerate the eradication of colonialism as we approach the end of the Decade.

TIBET MISSION REPORT

Prepared by Mission Members
Prof. Cees Flinterman
Ms. Josephine Verspaget
Senator David Norris

I. INTRODUCTION

Ever since the Chinese People's Liberation Army marched into Tibet in 1949-1950, the situation in Tibet has been the object of international concern. In the 1980s and 1990s, various fact finding missions have visited Tibet with a view to assessing allegations of violations by the Chinese authorities of the civil and political, as well as the economic, social an cultural rights of the Tibetan people. These missions have yielded much useful information on various aspects of the situation in Tibet. One of the issues which is often raised in relation to Tibet, but has so far not been researched in depth, is the question of whether or not Tibet can be regarded as a colony of the People's Republic of China. It is this question which the following mission report sets out to answer. On the basis of a short but intensive, fact finding mission to Tibet and to Tibetan centers in Nepal and India, the mission came to the conclusion that Tibet indeed displays the basic elements of colonialism as defined in chapter 5 of the report.

This report is based on an unofficial fact-finding mission to Tibet. The members of the mission would be most pleased to accept an invitation to return to Tibet as official guests of the People's Republic of China, in order to carry out a longer, more comprehensive mission, provided they are permitted to bring their own translators and are given unrestricted access to all areas of their own choice.

The mission would like to express the sincere hope that their findings and recommendations will help to bring about a relationship between the People's Republic of China and Tibet which is more satisfactory to the Chinese and the Tibetan peoples, inside Tibet as well as in exile. In this respect, a clear distinction is made between the Chinese authorities and the Chinese people, and the Chinese people are not held responsible for the concerns noted in this report. Moreover, the mission participants believe that the current situation in Tibet is not only of bilateral concern to the Chinese authorities and the Tibetan people, but also a matter which affects the international community at large. During their visits to Tibetan communities in Nepal and India, they were informed that thousands of Tibetans leave Tibet annually, in spite of the grave dangers of the journey. This was considered to be an important indicator of the level of dissatisfaction among Tibetans inside Tibet. Equally distressing was the fact that many young Tibetans are becoming increasingly frustrated by the fact that the non-violent protest against the Chinese regime in Tibet has so far failed to bring about substantial change. The participants are concerned by the indications that an increasing number of Tibetans are considering violent forms of protest. A prompt and effective resolution to the rising political tension in Tibet is considered to be of great importance to the maintenance of international peace and stability.

II. MANDATE OF THE MISSION

The mandate of the mission was to determine whether Tibet shows the characteristics of a colony in its relation to the People's Republic of China; to report on its findings objectively; and to formulate conclusions and recommendations.

III. PARTICIPANTS

The members of the mission were:

Professor Cees Flinterman (mission leader), Professor of International Law at the University of Maastricht, former Head of the Netherlands Delegation to the UN Human Rights Commission.

Ms Josephine Verspaget, Member of Parliament of the Netherlands, spokesperson of the Foreign Affairs Committee of the PvdA (Netherlands Labour Party), member of the Parliamentary Foreign Affairs Committee.

Senator David Norris, Member of the Senate of the Republic of Ireland, bureau member of the joint Oireachtas Committee on Foreign Affairs.

The mission was assisted by a senior representative of the UNPO, an interpreter and independent experts with extensive knowledge of and experience in Tibet.

IV. ITINERARY OF THE MISSION

28 April to 3 May: Visit to Tibet
Visits were made to the following places in and around Lhasa and Tsethang:

the Potala Palace (the former residence of the Dalai Lama), the Barkor (the Tibetan center of Lhasa), construction sites, Tibet University, primary and secondary schools in Lhasa and neighbouring areas, Ramoche Temple, Jokhang Temple, Cement Factory, Sera Monastery, Ganden Monastery, primary schools and small monasteries near Ganden , Tsethang city and Tsethang nunnery.

3 May: Kathmandu, Nepal
The mission met with the United Nations High Commissioner for Refugees in Kathmandu, Nepal. They also visited the Tibetan Welfare Office/Reception Centre for new arrivals from Tibet, where they interviewed recently arrived Tibetan refugees, the Jawalakhel Tibetan Handicraft Centre and Tibetan Old

People's Home.

4 May: Travel to Delhi and Dharamsala, India

5 to 7 May: Dharamsala (Northern India)

Meetings were held with His Holiness the Dalai Lama; the Kashag (the Cabinet of the Tibetan Government-in-Exile); officials from the Department of Information and International Relations; the Chief Justice Commissioner of the Supreme Justice Commission; the Director of the Election Commission.

The mission also met with members of the Tibetan People's Deputies (the Parliament of the Tibetan Government-in-Exile).

Visits were made to the SOS Tibetan Children's Village School, the Tibetan Institute of Performing Arts and the Transit School for new arrivals from Tibet.

Mission members interviewed new arrivals from Tibet, and met with a number of Tibetan NGOs (Tibetan Women's Association, Tibetan Youth Congress, Gu Chu Sum, National Democratic Party of Tibet, Tibetan Centre for Human Rights and Democracy).

9 May: New Delhi

Meetings were held with a number of Indian scholars to discuss the issue of colonialism, particularly in relation to Tibet.

V. METHODOLOGY

A. ORGANIZATION AND PREPARATION

The mission was organized and facilitated by the Unrepresented Nations and Peoples Organization, with the assistance of the Tibet Support Groep Nederland (TSG NL) and the International Campaign for Tibet (ICT). With the clear understanding that the three mission participants retained their full independence from the objectives and political affiliations of the above organizations, the mission was mandated to report its findings impartially and objectively.

B. CONCEPTUAL FRAMEWORK FOR ANALYSIS

Prior to the mission, the UNPO and the TSG NL commissioned an independent researcher to undertake an analysis of colonialism, which identified the nature and constituent elements of colonialism, (Independent Study on Colonialism and Tibet,

Part I). This provided the foundation for the mission's understanding of colonialism, on the basis of which the participants would be able to assess whether or not these elements could be detected in Tibet today.

C. ENTRY INTO TIBET, NEPAL, AND INDIA

Due to the politically sensitive nature of the current situation in Tibet, it was decided that the mission would keep a low and unofficial profile and that the mission members would operate as private individuals. Three of the mission members and the mission staff entered the People's Republic of China, Nepal and India without difficulty. The fourth mission member, an Eastern European Member of Parliament, was not able to enter the People's Republic of China. For unspecified reasons, he was not issued a visa and was therefore unable to participate in the mission.

D. USE OF EXPERTS

During the mission, the three members were assisted by two experts with extensive knowledge on Tibetan culture, language and history. One expert stayed behind in Tibet for three weeks to collect further data, which he later conveyed to the mission.

E. LIMITATIONS

The mission was subject to two types of limitations. The first type of limitation is inherent to any kind of fact-finding mission to Tibet: communicating with Tibetans entails the risk of reprisals against these Tibetans by the authorities. Therefore, contact with Tibetans was restricted to a minimum and has to be conducted with the utmost discretion.

The second type of restriction was the short duration and the limited geographical scope of the mission. This restriction was partly compensated by the fact that the aforementioned experts enabled the mission to use its limited time very effectively and to maximize its opportunities to collect information. Moreover, one of the experts stayed behind in Tibet for three more weeks. In addition, the mission brought its own translator and was thus able to communicate directly with Tibetans whenever possible.

F. USE OF TERMS AND ABBREVIATIONS

In this mission report, the term 'Tibet' refers to the Tibet Autonomous Region, as well as to the Tibetan Autonomous Counties and Prefectures outside the Tibet Autonomous Region (i.e. in the Chinese provinces Qinhai, Gansu, Sichuan and Yunnan)

TAR: Tibet Autonomous Region (comprising central Tibet and parts of eastern Tibet)
CCP: Chinese Communist Party
PLA: People's Liberation Army
PRC: People's Republic of China

VI. CRITERIA OF COLONIALISM

Prior to the mission the following criteria of colonialism, as identified in the Independent Study on Colonialism and Tibet, Part I, were adopted. It was on the basis of these criteria that the situation in Tibet was assessed:

A. Establishment of Colonial Rule

Colonial rule is established in one or more of the following three ways: military conquest and subsequent annexation; the conclusion of a treaty or contract; the creation of merchant enclaves followed by settlement.

Colonialism always involves the migration of people from a metropolitan state to a satellite region, but the magnitude of settlement differs from case to case.

B. Characteristics of Colonial Administration

The original population of the colonised territory is not, or poorly, represented in the colonial government. The interests of the original inhabitants are largely determined by the metropolitan, colonial power.

Colonial rule superimposes national borders. In most cases these borders do not correspond to the local community structure(s) or to the political history of the colonised territory. Often the territory in question had not been organized as a nation state before the advent of the colonial power.

Economic development is planned and imposed by the colonial power and often benefits the metropolitan state at the expense of the satellite region. Resources located in the colony are transferred to or used for the benefit of the metropolitan state and for further processing and marketing by that state.

Civilising mission: the colonial power undertakes to 'civilise' the original inhabitants of a colony. The underlying presumption is that the colonial power possesses a culture/civilisation which is superior in relation to the culture/civilisation of the colonised population(s). In addition, the colonial power often claims that the original population of the colonised territory is unable to rule itself for reasons of political immaturity or economic backwardness.

Cultural exchange between settlers/representatives from the metropolitan state and the original inhabitants of the colony is asymmetrical. The latter adopt more aspects of the culture of the former than vice versa.

C. Maintenance of Colonial Authority

The reactions of colonial powers to colonial resistance of colonised peoples are based on strategies to eliminate dissent. The maintenance of colonial authority involves a permanent military presence, consisting of soldiers from the metropolitan state or local soldiers under the command of officers from the metropolitan state. The maintenance of authority is often strengthened by a policy of population transfer.

D. Perceptions

Colonised people(s) experience colonial rule as alien. Similarly, citizens from the metropolitan state continue to make a distinction between themselves and the original inhabitants of the colony.

E. Outcome of the Colonisation Process

Colonisation may result in one or more of the following situations: 1) decolonization, 2) complete take-over of the colony by the metropolitan settlement community, 3) the continuation of colonial rule over a territory which retains most of its pre-colonial identity, or 4) integration into the metropolitan state.

None of the aforementioned criteria is essential in establishing that a certain situation can be described in terms of "colonialism". A combination of a number of these criteria is sufficient for determining that a situation is at least de-facto colonial.

VII. FINDINGS

In seeking to answer the question whether the relationship between China and Tibet displays the attributes of colonialism as discussed in section six of this report, the mission found that the Sino-Tibetan relationship does indeed display most of these attributes. Its findings with respect to each of these attributes can be summarised as follows:

A. Establishment of the current relationship between Tibet and the People's Republic of China

Military conquest and the conclusion of a treaty

The question as to how the current relationship between Tibet and China was established is largely a historical question which would require research beyond the scope of this report. It is an established fact, however, that the Chinese People's Liberation Army marched into Tibet in 1949-1950 and reached Lhasa in 1951. The Seventeen Point Agreement for the Peaceful Liberation of Tibet was signed in Beijing in 1951. The validity of this treaty is contested by Tibetans on the grounds of coercion.

Merchant enclaves and settlement

Commercial life in the urban areas visited by the mission was found to be clearly dominated by Chinese rather than Tibetan entrepreneurs. Commercial centres both in the urban areas and the countryside attract Chinese entrepreneurs from neighbouring Chinese provinces, in particular from Sichuan Province. While noting that there is a considerable number of wealthy Tibetan entrepreneurs in Lhasa, the mission gained the impression that the majority of wealthy enterprises in Lhasa and Tsethang are owned and run by Chinese entrepreneurs and that the conditions for economic success are set by Chinese rather than by Tibetans. The following examples reinforce this impression. On the compound of the Lhasa Cement Factory the majority of the owners of small make-shift grocery stalls and street vendors were all Chinese.

The mission observed that in Lhasa and Tsethang, the Tibetan part of town had been reduced to a small area on the outskirts of the new town. The Tibetan buildings were surrounded by a much larger area of new, modern Chinese style buildings. While noting that a number of Tibetans lived in these Chinese style, urban areas, it appeared that many of those buildings were owned by and/or inhabited by Chinese people. The mission noticed that the Tibetan city of Lhasa had been reduced to a Tibetan quarter, which resembles a folk-art tourist attraction, rather than a developing and self-reliant town. In Tsethang, it was observed that the center of the new city is dominated by modern Chinese style entertainment industries, such as brothels, beer restaurants and karaoke bars. The traditional Tibetan houses are now located on the fringes of the city.

In one shop in the eastern part of Lhasa, along the Beijing Dong Lu, a Tibetan shop girl explained that the Chinese owner preferred to have Tibetan rather Chinese shop girls behind the counter, suggesting that the owner attempted to create the appearance that the shop was Tibetan. The mission thus learned that a number of shops which may look as if they are run by Tibetans are in fact owned by Chinese.

In the areas visited by the mission, Chinese settlement in rural areas remained largely restricted to places of commercial interest, such as road side shops and restaurants, military bases, industrial sites, green house agriculture centers and major tourist attractions.

B. Administration of Tibet

Political representation

The Chinese Communist Party (CCP) plays a dominant role in the Chinese administration. The fact that the Secretary of the Tibet Autonomous Region branch of the CCP is Chinese is an important indicator that the ultimate decision making power in Tibet rests with the Chinese government in Beijing. This observation is reinforced by the fact that the People's Liberation Army in Tibet consists almost entirely of Chinese soldiers and officers.

It was noted that the authorities in Tibet are keen to highlight the role of Tibetans in the political decision making process. The following example reinforced this impression: the Chinese guide, who worked for the state-run travel agency CYTS and who appeared to be well-informed about current political affairs in China and Tibet, was asked who was the most powerful person in Tibet. The guide answered that this was Mr Ragdi (a Tibetan who is generally known for his pro-Beijing views). However, it is a well-established fact that Mr Chen Kuiyuan, whom the guide did not mention, is the most important and powerful cadre in Tibet, both in rank and in practice. Mr Ragdi is the deputy Secretary of the CCP (TAR branch), while Mr Chen Kuiyuan is the Secretary.

Recently arrived Tibetan refugees in Nepal and India expressed little trust in Tibetan high-ranking officials. They conveyed to the mission that, with a few exceptions, these officials are 'like toys in the hands of Chinese and hold no real power. Tibetans who speak out, such as the former mayor of Lhasa, are fired or demoted to low administrative jobs.'

Many aspects of life, such as travelling and communicating with foreigners, are controlled by the authorities rather than by the private individuals in question. The following examples will clarify this observation:

It was noted that contact with ordinary Tibetans at cultural heritage sites, such as the Potala Palace, is clearly monitored by officials. In the Potala Palace a monk pointed to one of the Tibetan officials, commenting that 'the Chinese' were very dangerous. This remark was considered significant as it suggested that the monk viewed the Tibetan official as part of the Chinese administration rather than as a Tibetan official.

The mission's visit to Tsethang was delayed by several hours because the (Tibetan) tourist guide who was to accompany the mission had to obtain travel permits from the Public Security Bureau authorities. For reasons not specified by the authorities, the guide, who has extensive experience on obtaining travel permits, was unable to obtain the permit at first. A Tibetan who overheard the conversation between the guide and the mission remarked: 'We have no control over these decisions.'

One of the mission members was told by a newly arrived Tibetan refugee, who used to live in a retreat in the mountains near Trayerpa Monastery (Takste), that he had been forced to change his life after the authorities had started to levy a monthly 'cave tax'. He remarked: 'The mountains no longer belong to us. Now we have to rent them from the Chinese.'

Many of the newly arrived farmers from Tibet mentioned that they had to pay heavy taxes. A number of farmers interviewed by the mission explained that they had to hand over part of their harvest to the authorities, sell part of it at a low price, and the part they were allowed to keep was not enough to live on. One Tibetan from a Tibetan Autonomous County in Qinghai who worked as a tax collector told the mission 'Whenever I went on my tour to collect taxes from the Tibetans I felt very sad because I know that the farmers had very little or not enough to feed their own families, but if I failed to collect the required quantity, they would deduct it from my monthly salary.'

Another farmer from one of the Tibetan Autonomous Counties in Qinghai Province explained that he had been forced to leave his home after the authorities decided to build a dam in the Machu River. He and approximately 500 other Tibetan farmers had been resettled in an area which was very isolated. There was no road fit for motor vehicles and the only way to cross the river was by boat. The area was too far away from any school for his children and therefore he decided to bring his children to India so they could be educated in one of the Tibetan schools in exile.

The authorities in Tibet regularly make use of unpaid laborers, e.g. for the construction of roads or government offices. New arrivals from Tibet in Kathmandu related that failure to participate in these projects results in having to pay a fine. They told the mission that the Tibetans who are working on these projects generally do not have a say in the planning and construction process and that the authorities are often the primary beneficiaries of these projects. This is particularly the case in the construction of roads leading to major mines.

Borders

The Chinese geographical definition of Tibet as one Tibet Autonomous Region and a number of Tibetan Autonomous Prefectures and Counties[I] incorporated in Qinghai, Yunnan, Gansu and Sichuan, is a unilaterally imposed administrative organization of an area which Tibetans perceive as one region consisting of the three provinces Utsang, Amdo and Kham. The current borders between the Tibet Autonomous Region and the Tibetan areas incorporated in the Chinese provinces Sichuan, Qinghai, Gansu and Yunnan partly correspond to the borders of the pre-1950 Tibetan provinces Utsang (Central Tibet), Amdo and Kham. But in a number of areas, e.g. in the case of the western border of Kham, the new borders cut across historical boundaries.

Control over and use of resources

Many centers of major commercial interest are dominated and/or controlled by Chinese entrepreneurs or the authorities. Apart from the Barkor, the Tibetan centre of Lhasa, the mission did not see any centres of commercial interest which were dominated by Tibetans.

The following examples reinforce this general observation:

In the Lhasa Cement Factory, the mission conducted a series of short conversations with the workers at the plant. The factory was built by the authorities, after the Chinese annexation of Tibet. It was noted that most of the ordinary workers of the Cement factory were Tibetans, while the higher level management consisted mainly of Chinese. The working conditions at the factory were unsanitary and the hands of a number of the workers had peculiar stains and scars as if they had been exposed to harmful chemicals. The mission discovered that the cement is mainly used for Chinese style new construction projects in urban areas. On the basis of cursory observation and conversations with workers at construction sites, the impression was that the main beneficiaries of these new buildings are Chinese officials and entrepreneurs.

A number of Tibetans mentioned that the Chinese authorities are involved in uranium mining in Tibet, and that the uranium is subsequently transferred to mainland China. The mission was told that the workers in these uranium mines come from mainland China for the mining, that these mines appear to be administered under the control of the military, and that Tibetans are denied entry into these mines. Although the mission was unable to carry out any on-site research on this subject, it took note of these remarks and was concerned that Tibetans are not given access to information on this subject. (see recommendation no. 9b)

There are many reports of large scale logging and export of timber to China. A recently arrived Tibetan couple from Chamdo and Bawa in eastern Tibet confirmed these reports. Tibetans in exile expressed concern that this deforestation (primarily in eastern Tibet) has a negative impact on the fragile ecosystem of Tibet and Central/South Asia at large.

A monk at the Potala Palace spoke about the current location of the original treasures of the Palace. The monk informed the mission that a selection of the most valuable books and other treasures from the Palace had been transferred to Beijing, for 'safe keeping' and 'conservation'.

The tourist industry, which is an important economic resource, is largely dominated by Chinese. The main and best-equipped tourist agencies are Chinese government institutions, such as the CITS and the CYTS. There are indeed some Tibetan run travel agencies, which are much smaller and which generally cater to low-budget travellers. The mission learned from a Chinese tour guide from Shanghai, that one of the incentives to come to Tibet was that he earned more in Tibet than in Shanghai for the same type of work. It was also learned that since December 1996 more than sixty Tibetan tour guides who had been educated in India had been fired and replaced by Chinese and Tibetan guides who had been educated in Tibet or China.

A foreign tour guide who had visited Tibet for many years, told the mission that the type of tourist industry which was being developed and promoted by the authorities resulted in turning the highlights of Tibet's spiritual heritage into an economic commodity and destroying Tibet's distinctive culture, identity, architecture and the traditional way of life of the Tibetan people. The tour guide complained that many tourists were losing interest in Tibet for that reason and that he considered relocating his tours to other parts of the world.

The mission noted that one of the rooms of the Potala Palace, which used to be an assembly hall for the monks, had been turned into a Chinese tea pavilion, with Chinese-style chandeliers of tinted glass. Compared to the normal prices in Lhasa's restaurants, the prices of tea and cold drinks were extremely high. According to one of the Potala monks the profit went to the authorities administering the Potala Palace.

On the basis of its own observations, the mission believes that the Chinese authorities try to exploit Tibet's economic potential and also permit private Chinese entrepreneurs to do so at the expense of the Tibetan population.

Civilising Mission

Some of the English speaking Chinese which the mission came into contact with were positive and sympathetic towards the Tibetan people and culture. However, they were all employed in the tourist business and were likely to have a vested interest in pleasing their customers. It was not possible to carry out in-depth interviews about their perceptions of and attitude towards the Tibetan people, but it was clear that the majority of the Chinese have come to Tibet to make money and that they show little or no interest in the Tibetan culture and lifestyle. Those Chinese with whom the mission talked considered the replacement of ancient Tibetan buildings by new Chinese-style structures as necessary and useful.

The views expressed by the official newspaper, the China Daily, were markedly different from those of the Chinese people contacted by the participants. During the mission's visit the China Daily denounced the Dalai Lama, who is perceived by the overwhelming majority of the Tibetans as the essence of Tibetan Buddhism, in aggressive and condescending terms. Among other things, the newspaper accused the Dalai Lama of not being a genuine, 'normal' Buddhist. The newspaper even accused the Dalai Lama of betraying Buddhist doctrine. On 21 April 1997 the China Daily reported:

By using Tibetan Buddhism as a political tool to incite separatism, the Dalai Lama has engaged in a number of activities to wreck Tibet and the Buddhist religion, to destroy the religion's normal order, and to wilfully violate religious disciplines. He has committed many evil acts that betray the religion's goals as well as Buddhist doctrines.[2]

The paradox of a declared atheist Chinese leadership defining the criteria for 'genuine Buddhism' was striking. It was noted that the China Daily articles on the Dalai Lama were not signed. This was interpreted to signify that the article expressed the official view of the Chinese government.

It was learned that during the mission's stay in Tibet, a series of political re-education sessions were being conducted in a number of the monasteries visited by the mission. On one of the main walls of the Jokhang temple in Lhasa, a large bright yellow notice was discovered which announced the results of the first series of exams which are part of the political re-education programme conducted at the temple. One of the Jokhang monks discreetly contacted was asked what he thought about the political re-education session which were being conducted in the afternoon. He answered that the classes were compulsory for all monks. He added that all monks had to study four books in the course of a period of three months. The first book, on law, had just been completed and the exam results were displayed on the yellow notice board on the wall. The monk explained:

> We have to study four books. The first one deals with legal issues. We did not have a real problem with this book. Now we have to study the second book, which deals with Tibetan history. This will cause problems, as we are not prepared to accept the Chinese version of Tibetan history.

In the same temple, the mission noticed a room full of modern, tubular chairs, in which, according to one of the Jokhang monks, re-education classes took place. It was noted that this room was markedly different from any of the rooms used for religious education, in which monks sit on the floor behind low, long wooden tables, facing each other. It was perceived as significant that the political re-education classes made use of furniture brought in from outside the monastery for this occasion. The fact that this happened within the context of political re-education reaffirmed the impression that the political re-education classes constitute the imposition of one (political) culture upon another.

The mission gathered some information booklets and brochures on Tibet in hotels and offices, which invariably portray the old pre-1949 Tibetan society as dark, feudal, primitive, superstitious and backward and describe the 'new' society as scientific, rational, practical and modern. The collected material shows that the Chinese authorities go to great length to explain that they have come to Tibet to help the area to develop economically, politically, culturally and socially. The following quotes from a tourist guidebook for sale in Lhasa illustrate this point:

> A reporter from the Italian news service asked high ranking official of the Chinese government in Beijing (an ethnic Tibetan), 'Do you think the Tibetan people could have got rid of the feudal serf system on their own, instead of letting the Han people liberate them?' Jigme Ngapoi Jigme replied: 'In old Tibet it would have been very difficult for the Tibetan people to liberate themselves, since Tibet had long been under the feudal serf system, which allowed the majority of the Tibetan people no political and social rights. If you really understand the actual social conditions at that time, you will comprehend that it would have been difficult for the Tibetan people to overthrow the feudal serf system without the help of the Central Government and the People's Liberation Army.[3]
>
> In a section on economic development, the guidebook states:

> Pests and weeds in the fields are also under control. In the past, since religious people thought that killing pests meant taking lives, they wouldn't accept the idea of using pesticides. Thus over 1 million mu were attacked by harmful insects and over 1.3 mu overrun by weeds (...) Meanwhile a large number of scientific and technical personnel have gone to the fields, explaining the necessity of destroying insects and teaching the farmers how to destroy insects and weeds.

And:

> Tibetans have gradually come to realise that animal husbandry will have a bright future only if they attach great importance to scientific and technological development.[4]

Cultural exchange/Acculturation

In the places visited by the mission a clear acculturation process is taking place, and cultural exchange is asymmetrical. In a number of cases this process was imposed, but in other cases it appeared to be unintentional.[5]

One of the clearest examples in this respect is that many Tibetans are living in the new Chinese style urban areas, e.g. Lhasa and Tsethang, while no Chinese person was encountered living in the traditional Tibetan quarters of these two cities.

It was noted that many traditional Tibetan buildings are torn down and replaced by new structures. Some of the new houses in the Barkor (the Tibetan centre of Lhasa) resemble the traditional architecture. The new buildings in other parts of Lhasa and in Tsethang bear little or no resemblance to Tibetan architecture. It was clear to the mission that the construction taking place in parts of Tibet largely consists of modern, Chinese style buildings which are superimposed on the Tibetan cities and towns.

Chinese is the dominant language which everyone is expected to speak. On the other hand, Tibetan is perceived by the Chinese as a 'minority language', which only those belonging to that 'minority' are expected to speak. It was learned that the presence of a handful of Chinese students in a classroom automatically entails that the language of education is Chinese. This demonstrates that Tibetans are expected to learn Chinese, while Chinese do not have to learn Tibetan, even though they live in Tibet. Tibetans are generally handicapped in the education system as they tend to lag behind their fellow Chinese students. Moreover, Tibetans who do not acquire sufficient command of the Chinese language face limits in finding a job after graduation.

The mission visited the University of Tibet and was welcomed by the staff members of the University who were helpful and friendly. After an extensive tour around the campus and visits to several classrooms, the mission noted that the dominant language of education is Chinese. As far as could be discerned, at least 95% of the lectures were given in Chinese. A student working at the computer department told the mission that the two languages used in the computer classes are Chinese and English. He added that experts were working on a Tibetan language programme, and it was about to be introduced at the University. Later it was discovered that Tibetan language programmes have existed for a long time and are in use in Tibetan communities in India and in Tibetan institutions in the West. This raised the question of why Tibetan language computer programmes were not yet used in Tibet itself, if these programmes were readily available in other parts of the world.

The mission conducted a series of conversations with students at the university and asked some specific questions about the language of education. It was noted that all university textbooks, with the exception of those used in the course on Tibetan language and literature, are written in Chinese instead of Tibetan.

The mission visited a number of student dormitories at the University of Lhasa and talked to a Tibetan student who shared his room with three others including one Chinese student. Although this Chinese student had been living in Tibet for a number of years, he did not speak a word of Tibetan and the Tibetan boy had to act as a translator between the Chinese student and the mission participants.

As far as the mission members could make out, most of the senior staff of the university were Chinese. The members were shown around by a Chinese woman who was born in Tibet and spoke some Tibetan. The mission's translator could make out that she did not speak it very well and that most other Chinese staff members did not speak it at all.

The mission attended an art class and noted that most of the drawings, some of which were very fine indeed, were painted in the classical Chinese style. The portraits of Tibetan nomads, however beautiful, were painted in a western European style. Whether students were indeed discouraged from producing art in the traditional Tibetan style, or whether it was their own choice to follow another cultural tradition, was questioned.

It was noted that each classroom had big portraits of Mao Zedong on its walls. The pictures were accompanied by a Chinese slogan with a translation in Tibetan.

The mission was struck by the fact that the University of Tibet does not have a law department. Lawyers in Tibet receive their legal education in China. This implies that only Chinese law as such will be applied in Tibet. No activities seem to be under way within the university of Tibet to codify the laws of an autonomous Tibet (e.g. family law, land law, etc.), let alone to set up a legal education programme with due respect for Tibetan national laws.

The Lhasa Traffic Middle school, which appears to have been part of a transport work-unit in the past, is now an ordinary middle school. Most of the pupils in the class were Chinese and the language of education was Chinese. When a mission member asked how many students in the class could write their names in Tibetan, it turned out that only one student was able to do so.

Aware of the official policy of bilingualism for public notices and signs, the mission checked carefully whether this policy was upheld in Lhasa and Tsethang. In the modern parts of Lhasa and Tsethang, most street signs and notices are in Chinese. Whereas most public signs are bilingual, the Tibetan letters are generally smaller than the Chinese ones and in some cases even absent. On several shops and restaurants, the Tibetan language signs are a direct transliteration from the Chinese rather than a Tibetan expression or name. In most cases the inscriptions and signs at military sites are only in Chinese. While most public notices were indeed in Chinese and Tibetan, it was noted that the inscriptions on military bases and military institutions were generally only in Chinese. The mission also noticed that certain traffic signs provided Chinese language warnings only. For example, on a road construction site on the road from Lhasa to Ganden, a sign which warned drivers of an upcoming road block was only in Chinese.

Tibetan language newspapers do exist, but they are hard to find. Chinese and English language newspapers on the other had are readily available in local shops and hotels. Mission members tried to find Tibetan language television and radio programmes in all hotels it stayed in and at many different moments of the day. However, they were not able to find these programmes. It appears that Tibetan language television and radio programmes are either few in number or transmitted at unusual hours or both.

The music played on the street, in restaurants, bars and other public places is pre-dominantly Chinese. Special attention was paid to the advertisements at the cinema, which were either in Chinese or in English. No Tibetan language videos were found. In a number of cases English films were dubbed in Chinese but not in Tibetan.

It was noted that very few Chinese in Tibet could speak Tibetan. Even those who were born in Tibet or had lived there for many years, rarely spoke Tibetan. Those who did speak Tibetan had extremely limited language skills. From conversations with Tibetans and Chinese on this subject, it was learned that Chinese and Tibetans believe that it is not necessary for Chinese living or working in Tibet to be able to speak Tibetan. Urban Tibetans on the other hand, need to learn Chinese in order to be able to function fully in their own urban society. In one Chinese restaurant on the Beijing Donglu, the mission tried to order food in Tibetan, but the Chinese waiters and waitresses were unable to understand. After several minutes a Tibetan girl working in the kitchen was asked to translate for the mission from Tibetan into Chinese. However, her command of Chinese was not sufficient for this task. As some of the staff spoke fluent English, orders were then taken in English. The Tibetan girl told the mission she was from a rural area and had recently started her job in the Chinese restaurant. When asked how much she earned per month, she answered she was rather uncertain about this. After her first month she had received RMB 300 while her colleagues earned around RMB 1000 a month. When asked why there was a difference between her salary and those of her colleagues, she answered that she did not know as her Chinese was not good enough to ask for an explanation.

It was clear that the girl was severely handicapped by not being able to speak and understand Chinese sufficiently.

C. Maintenance of Authority

Suppression of dissent

On many occasions Tibetans raised political issues, even though they were not formally interviewed on political subjects. It became clear that the level of political discontent is widespread in urban areas as well as in the countryside. As stated in the introduction of this mission report, it was alarming to learn that thousands of Tibetans leave Tibet annually, in spite of the dangers of the journey across the mountains as well as harassment by the Chinese and Nepalese police. This fact is a significant indicator of the dissatisfaction of the Tibetan people with the current situation in Tibet.

Given the well documented fact that the mere expression of political criticism of the Chinese authorities or policies, as well as support for the Dalai Lama, may lead to prison sentences ranging from two to ten years, the mission felt that any expression of dissent in Tibet was significant.

In the Potala Palace, the mission was secretly given a note by a monk, with the following text in English: 'Tibet is not China's territory. Tibet needs assistance from your country to regain its freedom.' The writer of the note decided to pass on the note regardless of the fact that a policeman was standing close to him, albeit with his back turned towards the monk. It was surprising that the monk had signed the note with his name. He was apparently willing to risk a prison term of several years if the note had been discovered by the authorities. His resentment against Chinese rule over Tibet was obviously very strong indeed. In order to protect the identity of the monk, it was decided not to include a copy of the hand-written note in this report.

Many of the main tourist sites are under heavy surveillance, both by video cameras and microphones as well as by officials. Particularly in the Potala Palace, the number of video cameras was extraordinarily high and most of the cameras are directly pointed at the seats of the monks rather than the books, statues or other cultural treasures.

In one of the main temples in Lhasa, a hand-written slogan in red chalk was discovered on the wall, which stated: 'Tibet is independent' The person who had written this slogan was apparently prepared to risk severe repercussions. Later, similar slogans were found elsewhere.

Criticism of the Chinese regime is being systematically silenced. It was learned that Tibetans speaking out for independence or criticising the Chinese regime face the risk of being arrested and detained for several years. The suppression of political dissent remains more or less invisible to those unable to speak or understand the Chinese language or without expert knowledge of the area. The flow of information on this subject is severely restricted, not only to foreigners but also to Tibetans themselves. It was striking that a number of extremely high profile Tibetan political prisoners had been sentenced in a secret trial in Shigatse, one of Tibet's main cities, but that no one in Tibet appeared to be aware that this trial had taken place. This is all the more remarkable since the trial took place immediately prior to the mission's visit and that it concerned an issue of major importance to all Tibetan people: the dispute over the succession of Tibet's second most important spiritual leader, the Panchen Lama.

In Tibet itself, the mission witnessed subtle acts of suppression of dissent. On 29 April the mission happened to witness a public, military ceremony in front of the Potala Palace. During the raising of the national flag of the People's Republic of China, a number of soldiers beat up a Tibetan onlooker, apparently in answer to a critical remark. These soldiers belonged to the music band of the PLA.

A discrepancy was observed between strong and widespread discontent with the current political regime in Tibet on the one hand, and a virtual absence of graffiti, wall posters or other forms of natural, popular protest on the other hand. The rare examples given in the previous paragraphs are the exceptions rather than the general pattern in this respect. The mission interpreted this discrepancy as an indication that the repercussions of discovered dissident views and activities prevent the open expression of criticism. This conclusion was strengthened on a number of occasions.

The absence of pictures of the Dalai Lama in the market, monasteries or other public places was noted. Several pictures of the Dalai Lama were discovered in private rooms and in some cases these pictures were covered by other pictures or wall carpets. Mission members were constantly approached by Tibetans who asked for pictures of the Dalai Lama. The fact that these pictures are not for sale at the market nor permitted to be on display in public places is part of the systematic restriction of religious and political rights of the Tibetan people to freely show devotion to and support for the Dalai Lama.

Despite the widespread if subtle expressions of Tibetan nationalism, the traditional Tibetan flag was entirely absent. The Chinese national flag, on the other hand was prominently displayed even in such traditional Tibetan places as monasteries and nunneries. It was concluded that the authorities in Tibet are strictly prohibiting any manifestations of Tibetan nationalism. This is corroborated by official statements of Chinese officials who repeatedly call for measures to combat 'splittism' in Tibet:

> Maintaining stability is one of the two major tasks of our region. (...) In the past decades, since the Dalai clique betrayed the Motherland and fled away, their sabotage activities of the conspiracy to separate the motherland have never stopped. We emphasise the Tibetan language, development, the improvement of the living standards of the masses, the importance of unity, prosperity, and the construction of a civilised Socialist Tibet. The basic condition for it is to stop and prevent the damaging acts of the Dalai clique

and create a social atmosphere in which we can concentrate our energy on economic development.[6]

Tibetans inside Tibet said that programmes from the Voice of America are frequently jammed, and expressed great concern about this to the mission. Some Tibetans complained that they were not able to find the Voice of America programme, nor the recently started Tibetan language service of Radio Free Asia on their new radios. It was not possible to verify whether this was due to a deliberate effort by the authorities to stop Tibetans from listening to the programme, but the mission noted that Tibetans are concerned about the lack of access to reliable information about Tibet and international affairs.

Military / Police

During the mission's visit, the PLA presence among civilians was rather discreet. On the other hand the PLA barracks on the outskirts of Lhasa and Tsethang are large. One of the main objectives of the heavy, army presence appears to be to deter potential unrest as well as to establish the physical reality of the Chinese regime in Tibet. The mission was informed that PLA presence is extremely heavy during times of political unrest as well as during sensitive dates, such as 10 March, the anniversary of the mass uprising in Lhasa in 1959. It was discovered that most of the daily monitoring of political protest is carried out by the Public Security Bureau or by the People's Armed Police.

A considerable number of military trucks and convoys were seen on some of the main roads in Lhasa, as well as on the road between Lhasa and Meldrokungar and between Lhasa and Tsethang. On 1 May, at least 46 east-bound military fuel trucks were counted on the road from Ganden to Lhasa.

The mission noted a clear difference between the Chinese People's Liberation Army (PLA) on the one hand and the Public Security Bureau (PSB) on the other hand. As far as could be discerned, the PLA consisted entirely of Chinese soldiers and officials, while the majority of the PSB personnel were Tibetans. One Tibetan commented: 'We do not like it if Tibetans join the PSB, but we can understand it. It is hard to find work and we need to feed our families.' No interaction was observed between the Chinese PLA and the Tibetan people. In daily life, there is little or no contact between the army and the Tibetan population. The army appears to be a garrison army brought in from outside, living in isolation from the local population on its own private compound with its own facilities. The PSB on the other hand is part of the local population, speaks the same language, and visits the same restaurants, shops and night clubs.

Population transfer

A clear pattern of continuous and intensifying Chinese migration into Tibet was discerned. In Tibet itself the mission was not in a position to verify whether or not the influx of Chinese settlers was the result of a deliberate policy by the Chinese government. However, statements were taken from Tibetans in Nepal and India that Beijing practices a policy of population transfer in Tibet. Moreover, it was learned that Tibetans regard this phenomenon as a serious threat to the preservation of their culture, religion and distinctive identity. They fear that the increasing presence of Chinese economic migrants from neighbouring provinces could place the Tibetan population in position of economic subordination.

Note was taken of the considerable amount of independent research which has been carried out on the subject of population transfer. A recent and in-depth report about population transfer in Tibet concludes:

Our research has demonstrated that the Chinese government is responsible for having set up a framework which facilitates and encourages migration to Tibet. (...) Immigrants to Tibet are dominating new market opportunities, encroaching on agricultural land and marginalizing Tibetans in their own economy. [7]

Chinese and Tibetan Perceptions of each other

Chinese perceptions—

Tibetans and Chinese view each other as foreigners, or 'alien' peoples. All Chinese contacted emphasised that they were different from Tibetans. They stressed that the Tibetan language was very different from Chinese, and that Tibetan was an extremely difficult language to learn. They added that the Tibetan culture and life-style were very different from the Chinese culture and lifestyle. Many Chinese said that they had come to Tibet purely for economic reasons, and that they would have preferred to stay at home if the economic prospects there had been more favorable. Many Chinese settlers in Tibet maintain strong links with their home bases in China, where they often spend the winter months. Many Chinese send their children to schools in their home provinces. Even those who have lived in Tibet for many decades continue to consider themselves residents of their hometowns in mainland China.

Tibetan perceptions—

It is significant that there are very few inter-marriages, despite the fact that many Chinese have lived in Tibet for more than one generation. Tibetans clearly perceive the Chinese residents in Tibet as outsiders, or strangers. Those Tibetans who were asked to comment on this said that the difference between Tibetans and Chinese concerned many aspects, including race, religion, language, traditions and lifestyle. One Tibetan commented that the fact that travelling inside Tibet is controlled by (Chinese) authorities clearly shows that Tibet is under foreign control.

D. Outcome of the Colonisation Process

It is clear that Beijing's policy on Tibet is to continue to absorb Tibet into the

People's Republic of China. Recognising that Tibet has so far largely remained economically, culturally and socially separate from the PRC, Beijing appears to be doing its utmost to integrate Tibet fully into China. For this purpose, it uses various political, economic, and educational/cultural tools:

It was observed that the word 'Tibet' on public signs is practically always accompanied by the word China. The title of the most widely sold tourist map and tourist guidebook in Lhasa reads: China's Tibet. A number of publications were found under the same name, including a magazine. Moreover, the large number of Chinese national flags in Tibet, both in the cities as well as in the countryside, was striking. For example, the number of Chinese national flags in Tibet was much higher than in Xian, where the mission stopped over en route to Lhasa.

The Chinese government attempts to integrate the Tibetan economy fully into the economic system of China proper. During the mission's stay in Tibet, the China Daily published an article which explicitly referred to economic development in Tibet as a way to undermine 'splittism'.

With respect to the issue of integration, the mission observed a difference between urban and rural areas in Tibet. In the areas visited by the mission, it was noted that the Chinese presence in the Tibetan countryside is limited to administrative centers, industrial sites as well as places of commercial interest, such as villages along the main roads. There were no Chinese farmers or rural settlers. It seemed that at present a dual track process is taking place, with Tibet's cities, major towns and road side villages becoming increasingly linked to mainland China, while Tibet's countryside remains more or less isolated. The further extension of the road network into rural areas will have a major impact in this respect.

Recently arrived Tibetans interviewed in Nepal and India clearly favored independence or at least a high degree of autonomy for Tibet. During an in-depth interview with the Dalai Lama in India, the mission learned that the Tibetan Government-in-Exile has presented the Chinese government with detailed proposals on a form of association between Tibet and China which would leave the Chinese government in charge of foreign affairs and defence and which would leave the responsibility for all other affairs with a locally and democratically elected Tibetan government in Lhasa. It was also learned that the Chinese government has so far not indicated any willingness to negotiate with the Dalai Lama and the Tibetan Government-in-Exile about any of these proposals, and continues to integrate Tibet further into the People's Republic of China.

VIII. CONCLUDING OBSERVATIONS AND RECOMMENDATIONS

On the basis of the foregoing assessment of the question of whether the characteristics of colonialism, as defined in the mission statement, apply to the current situation in Tibet, it was concluded that Tibet is a de-facto colony of the

People's Republic of China. This conclusion is based on the following findings:

Establishment of Colonial Rule

Communist Chinese rule over Tibet was established by means of a military intervention and the subsequent conclusion of a treaty. This was followed by a gradual process of establishing an administration under the strict control of the Chinese Communist Party and settlement of Chinese nationals in Tibet.

Administration of the Colonised Territory

Tibetans have little or no decision making power in the administration of Tibet. This observation extends to the political as well as social, economic and cultural aspects of administration.

The current division of Tibet in the Tibet Autonomous region and the Tibet Autonomous Prefectures/Counties runs counter to the Tibetan concept of Tibet as consisting of one unified territory divided into three provinces. In a number of instances the borders of the TAR do not correspond to the historic Tibetan provincial borders.

The Chinese government presents and explains its policies in Tibet in terms of a 'civilising mission'.

Intercultural exchange is asymmetrical: The Chinese residents in Tibet adopt hardly any aspects of Tibetan culture, while the influence of Chinese culture on Tibetans, in particular those living in urban areas, is strong.

Natural resources are 'exported' to China proper or used for industrial and construction sites which primarily benefit Chinese settler communities.

Chinese development projects in Tibet are imposed and Tibetans have little or no say in the planning and implementation of these projects.

A. MAINTENANCE OF COLONIAL AUTHORITY

Tibetan protest against Chinese rule, or any aspects of Chinese rule, in Tibet is systematically silenced.

The Chinese government maintains a heavy and permanent military presence in Tibet, in order to maintain control.

There is a clear pattern of continuous and intensifying Chinese settlement in Tibet. In spite of the concerns expressed by the Tibetan people, the Chinese authorities do not impose any restrictions on this process. On the contrary, there is well-researched evidence that the Chinese authorities are facilitating and encouraging Chinese migration into Tibet.

B. PERCEPTIONS

Tibetans and Chinese view each other as 'alien' peoples.

C. OUTCOME OF THE COLONISATION PROCESS

There is clear evidence that Tibetans in Tibet want independence from China or at least a high degree of autonomy within the People's Republic of China. The Dalai Lama and the Tibetan Government-in-Exile have proposed a form of association with China which would permit China to retain responsibility for foreign affairs and defence. However, until present the Chinese government has not indicated any willingness to negotiate with the Dalai Lama or the Tibetan Government-in-Exile. Meanwhile, the Chinese authorities continue to accelerate the political, economic, social and geographical integration of Tibet into China.

D. RECOMMENDATIONS

1 a. The mission believes that it is of the utmost importance that negotiations take place between the Chinese government and the Dalai Lama and the Tibetan Government-in-Exile at the earliest possible date. The mission is convinced that such negotiations should be unconditional.

1.b. The mission urges strictly non-partisan third countries, such as Norway or countries in the Middle East, to offer their good offices to facilitate such negotiations and to host such negotiations on their territory.

2. The mission supports the demand by the Tibetan Government-in-Exile for a referendum on the future status of Tibet, provided this referendum takes place in all Tibetan areas[8] and is conducted under strict international control.

3. The mission calls on the European Union establish a (joint) consular presence in Lhasa.

4. With due respect for cultural and ethnic diversity, the mission recognizes and is concerned about the impact of continued Chinese settlement in Tibet on the survival of Tibet's distinctive culture and religion.

   a. It urges the Chinese government to formulate and implement restrictions on the migration of Chinese to Tibet.

   b. It calls upon the Chinese government to allow an international and impartial commission to assess the formal legal status of Chinese currently in Tibet and suggests that the position of those Chinese who have no formal residence permit should be reassessed in the light of the preservation of Tibet's distinctive culture.

5. Without prejudice to recommendation number 2, the mission calls upon the Chinese Government at least give effect to the concept of genuine Tibetan autonomy, which is enshrined in the constitution of the People's Republic of China. In order to achieve this objective the Chinese government should transfer genuine authority to a locally elected, representative Tibetan government with full powers in all fields relating to local affairs and the preservation of Tibet's Buddhist culture. These powers should include but not be limited to the following fields:

   a. The local Tibetan government should be exclusively responsible for establishing and maintaining a system of education

   b. The local Tibetan government should be solely responsible for determining and implementing its im/migration policy.

   c. The local Tibetan government should be exclusively responsible for formulating and implementing a human rights policy based on the Universal Declaration of Human Rights.

   d. The local Tibetan government should be exclusively responsible for formulating and implementing economic policies, including tourism, mining and investment by companies from outside Tibet.

   e. The local Tibetan government should be in charge of and maintain a police force.

   f. The local Tibetan government should be entitled to issue local currency and stamps as well as passports to Tibetans. In this context, the mission would like to point out that the European Union passports retain their own national identity while being part of the larger unit of the European Unity.

6.a The mission calls upon the World Bank, the European Union, the United Nations Development Programme and other international or bilateral donors to refrain from giving development aid to projects conducted by the Chinese government in Tibet, unless there are verifiable guarantees that the project(s) will benefit the local Tibetan population and unless there is freely expressed agreement by the Tibetan population that the project will be to its benefit.

6.b The mission calls upon all foreign corporations not to invest in Tibet, unless there is clear well-researched evidence that the local population will benefit from these projects. Moreover, the mission calls upon those foreign corporations which have already established a presence in Tibet, to ensure that no human rights violations take place on their premises and within their control.

7. The mission calls upon the government of the PRC not to hinder the establishment of non-governmental human rights organizations and independent grassroots movements in Tibet.

8. The mission urges the Chinese government to establish a fully fledged law faculty at the University of Lhasa.

9.a Recognising the limitations of its own fact-finding capacities in Tibet, the mission calls upon the government of the People's Republic of China to provide full access to a well-equipped international fact-finding commission consisting of experts from all relevant disciplines, accompanied by translators of their own choice.

9.b The mission calls upon all relevant organizations such as the International Atomic Energy Agency, Amnesty International, Human Rights Watch, the Unrepresented Nations and People's Organization and others to request the government of the People's Republic of China to allow for an independent fact-finding mission to Tibet, on the condition that they are to be given full access to all areas and are permitted to bring their own translators.

10. The mission calls upon the international community to support the establishment of a democratic government in Tibet which is based on the rule of law, equality, a modern legal system, which respects the equality of all people without distinction with regard to race, gender and sexual orientation.

11. The mission calls upon the ICRC and the UNHCR to establish aid posts at the border of Tibet and Nepal

12. While respecting the intrinsically religious nature of the Tibetan culture, the mission supports the plans of the Dalai Lama and the Tibetan Government-in-Exile to establish a democratic regime in Tibet which is based on the secular state principle.

13. The mission calls upon the government of the PRC to halt any further unauthorised exploitation of natural resources in Tibet.

14. The mission urges the government of the PRC to ensure Tibetan language education at primary, secondary and tertiary levels in all disciplines with the exception of Chinese language and literature.

INDEPENDENT STUDY ON COLONIALISM AND TIBET

Prepared by
Francisca van Holthoon

Commissioned by the Unrepresented Nations and Peoples Organization
& the Tibet Support Groep Nederland

PART I: COLONIALISM IN FACT AND IN LAW

I. TYPES OF COLONIES

A. INTRODUCTION

The word 'colony' has its etymological roots in Greek and Latin. The literal meaning of the word 'colonia' in these languages is 'settlement'. One of the most important characteristics of colonialism is settlement: the migration of people from a metropolitan state to a satellite region, a 'new world'. Colonialism is not an easy concept to define, as it manifests itself in many different ways and degrees. Many writers on colonialism distinguish between 'settlement 'and so-called 'exploitation'[1] colonies. The main difference between these types of colonies is that settlers in settlement colonies tend to settle down permanently. They cultivate the land and take possession of it.[2] In exploitation colonies, the interests of the colonizers tend to be economic, political and strategic: metropolitan settlers manage and supervise the exploitation of resources or safeguard the geo-political interests of the metropolitan state, but they seldom stay on after the conclusion of their mission. The following section will briefly discuss the most important characteristics of both types of colonialism.

B. SETTLEMENT COLONIES[3]

Typical examples of settlement colonialism can be found in the Americas, Australia, New Zealand, South Africa and Southern Rhodesia. In these colonies the metropolitan settlers gradually ceased to identify with their metropolitan state and assumed an identity of their own, distinct from both the state they had left and the 'new world' as they found it upon their arrival. The colonial liberation struggles following this process were struggles of whites against whites. The original inhabitants of these territories played no (significant) role in this 'decolonization' process. Long after the white settlers had gained independence from their states of origin, they continued their own imperial mission: to conquer the original inhabitants of the region and take possession of their land. In many cases, the earlier inhabitants were systematically attacked and killed during these pioneering missions.

Most settler colonies were not founded by political leaders but by private individuals: religious dissidents, missionaries, commercial adventurers and jailers looking for prison sites.[4] Only after these private individuals had established a certain degree of control over the overseas territories, did the governments, of which the pioneers were nationals, get involved in the colonization process. For this reason it is often said that the settler colonies were founded in 'a fit of absent-mindedness'.[5] This absent-mindedness clearly refers to the state and not to the settlers themselves, who were determined to establish a 'new world'.

Colonial rule in the settlement colonies was mainly established by settlement. Metropolitan settlers arrived in great numbers and gradually gained control over the territory by concluding treaties with the original inhabitants or simply by cultivating barren, sparsely populated areas. In most settlement colonies, the metropolitan settlers became the new majority, the new local population, such as in the case of the Americas, Australia and New Zealand. In other cases they remained a small but influential minority, for example in South Africa and Southern Rhodesia.

In most settler colonies, the central administration of these new states was exclusively in the hands of the settlers; the original inhabitants were resettled in or confined to reserves, little islands of 'nativeness' in a sea of metropolitan settlers. The settler regimes determined the size and the locations of these reserves, or 'bantustans' in the case of South Africa. These reserves were generally infertile, isolated areas, without mineral resources and in most cases unsuited to the traditional modes of subsistence of the original inhabitants. Within the confines of these reserves the original populations enjoyed partial or full local autonomy, while outside these reserves they could not represent themselves politically.

The economic systems, infrastructure and development projects of the settlers exclusively served their own needs. In many cases land inhabited or used by original inhabitants was taken[6] for the purpose of building roads, railroads, dams, power stations, etc. These development projects did not only fail to benefit the original population but also often reduced them to poverty and structural dependence. As the wilderness was brought under control and cultivated by the settlers, the earlier inhabitants largely lost their own independent means of subsistence. They were forced to compete with the settlers on terms introduced and imposed by the latter. As many of the 'natives' were unable or unwilling to do so, they were pushed into the margin of society.

In most settlement colonies the maintenance of colonial rule involved very little effort. The fire arms of the settlers proved far superior to the arrows of the original inhabitants; after some initial fighting, heavy military presence was unnecessary. As many potential dissidents and protesters were killed in a very early stage, there was no large-scale organized protest to counter the settler regimes.[7]

In most settlement colonies the colonization process has resulted in the complete take-over of the 'new world' by the settlers. In the Americas, Australia, Canada and New Zealand, the indigenous populations have been reduced to a handful of small, 'exotic' minorities. Many of the original inhabitants were killed by white pioneers, while most of the remaining members were gradually assimilated into the new societies.

C. Exploitation Colonies

Exploitation colonies also involve settlement by metropolitan migrants, but the nature and the patterns of settlement in exploitation colonies differ from those in settlement colonies.

Many exploitation colonies were established by private companies, such as the Dutch East India Company in Indonesia, the British East India Company in India and the Belgian mining companies in Congo. In these colonies, the initial settlers were traders, who travelled back and forth between their home countries and the colonies. They rarely settled down permanently. In most cases the national governments of these entrepreneurs did not get involved in the colonization process until a substantial metropolitan presence had been established. Before the rise of nationalism in Europe, these governments were generally not interested in exercising national control over these overseas trading posts. In many of those exploitation colonies, territorial possession continued to remain of secondary importance to economic and strategic interests.

A clear example in this respect is India, large parts of which never fell directly under British control. British rule over India, even after it became a 'crown colony', was not really an end in itself but mainly served to safeguard vested economic, geopolitical and or strategic interests.[8] Similarly, large parts of the Netherlands East Indies (referred to hereafter as 'Indonesia') were never effectively ruled by the Dutch colonial regime.

The Dutch were mainly interested in Indonesia for its resources and for the fact that possession of Indonesia enabled the Netherlands to upgrade its status as a small country. The number of Dutch who immigrated to Indonesia was relatively small and very few of them settled permanently.

Some exploitation colonies were established by military conquest and subsequent treaties. Most of these colonies were established during late 19th century European imperialism.[9] Examples include Somalia, Uganda, Morocco, and Tunisia. In these colonies the first colonial 'pioneers' were soldiers, who paved the way for colonial officials and civil servants.

Unlike their counterparts in settlement colonies, most colonial regimes in exploitation colonies established local representative bodies at some point.[10] The powers of these representative bodies varied widely. In most colonies these bodies served as an outlet for the political ambitions of the original population without granting this population any substantial decision making power. A clear example in this respect is the 'Conseil du Gouverneur General' and the 'Conseil de Province' in Congo. After seemingly revolutionary reforms in the mid 1950s, a handful of Africans, who were carefully selected by the Belgian authorities[11], were granted representation in these councils which were mere consultative bodies. Real, effective power rested with the Belgian colonial authorities until the eve of independence.

During the second half of the 19th century, many colonial powers in 'exploitation' colonies started to justify their colonial rule in terms of economic development. In many cases, these colonial powers depicted themselves as benefactors who brought welfare and economic development to their poor colonial subjects. In Indonesia this policy was termed the 'ethical policy' as opposed to the earlier 'cultivation system' which was based purely on the mercantile exploitation of natural and human resources. The cultural counterpart of economic development was the so-called 'civilising mission': the idea the 'natives' needed to be 'civilised'. In many cases this 'civilisation' involved the conversion to Christianity.

Unlike the immigrants in most settlement colonies, the majority of settlers in exploitation colonies continued to regard themselves as outsiders, as citizens of the metropolitan state to which they would return after their term of duty was over. Unlike most settlement colonies, the overwhelming majority of non-settlement colonies has been decolonised by now.

D. Hybrid Colonies

It is not always possible or necessary to distinguish between settlement and exploitation colonies, as some colonies manifested both elements or gradually changed from exploitation colonies into settlement colonies. A clear example of such a 'hybrid' is Algeria. French colonial rule was established in 1830 when the first French troops landed on the Algerian coast. This rule was subsequently consolidated by settlement. At some point Algeria was home to one million 'colons'[12] (i.e. French colonial settlers). The majority of these settlers had no intention of returning to metropolitan France and considered Algeria to be their home. At the same time, France claimed that Algeria was not a colony, but a 'province outre-mer'. Algeria even came under the Ministry of the Interior. Pleven, the French Commissioner for the Colonies, stated:

> In [Algeria] there are no peoples to liberate, no racial discrimination to abolish... The overseas populations do not want any kind of independence other than the independence of [rather than from] France.'

Algeria was of great strategic significance to France as it was the gateway to Africa, a bulwark against the alleged pan-Arabic ambitions of the Egyptian president Nasser. Moreover, after the discovery of large oil deposits in the Sahara desert, France became even more insistent in its efforts to incorporate Algeria into metropolitan France. The French 'colons' in Algeria, on the other hand, gradually ceased to identify with the Paris government and attempted to steer an independent political course.

Similarly, Southern Rhodesia gradually changed from an exploitation colony into a settlement colony. Like their counterparts in South Africa, the white settlers started to consider Southern Rhodesia to be their home, rather than a temporary staging post in a foreign continent. Had Ian Smith's attempt to declare independence from the UK not been strongly condemned and blocked by the international community, Southern Rhodesia may well have remained a settlement colony.

The present-day French colonies in the Pacific show elements of both types of colonialism. French economic interest in New Caledonia is considerable. Caledonia's rich mineral deposits of chromium, nickel and cobalt have turned these Pacific Islands into important economic assets. In the case of Polynesia the French authorities are mainly interested in using the territory for nuclear testing.[13] In addition, both colonies house a significant number of permanent French settlers and 'demis'[14], who regard the French Pacific islands, rather than metropolitan France, as their home. Unlike the white settlers in South Africa and Southern Rhodesia, these French settlers in Polynesia and New Caledonia have not actively campaigned for independence from their metropolitan state[15], although many of them do not identify with Paris as their primary capital.

For the sake of clarity, this report will use the schematic three-part division into settlement, exploitation and mixed colonies. This approach may oversimplify an infinitely complex phenomenon, but for the sake of this report it is a useful organizing device.

II. DOCTRINES ON COLONIALISM

As stated in the Preface, colonialism is a rather elusive concept. It is both a political, a legal, an economic, a cultural and a social phenomenon which does not lend itself to a short and clear definition. While states have carefully refrained from defining colonialism, many scholars of various disciplines have written about the subject. A comprehensive review of all existing literature on colonialism is clearly beyond the scope of this report. The following section will look at a number of definitions of colonialism by historians and anthropologists.

A. SELECTED DEFINITIONS

Many writers have used the terms colonialism and imperialism interchangeably, as if there is little difference between these two phenomena. In his article A Definition of Colonialism, R.J. Horvath maintains that the important difference between the two phenomena appears to be the presence of a significant number of settlers from the colonizing power in the colonised state.[16] Whereas settlement may be the most important feature of colonialism, it is generally acknowledged that colonialism involves much more than the immigration of people from one region to another one.
In his book Modern Colonialism: institutions and policies, T.R. Adam defines colonialism as 'the political control of an underdeveloped people whose social and economic life is directed by the dominant power'.[17] This definition touches upon some important aspects of colonialism, but the element of 'alien domination' which appears to be at the heart of the colonial experience, is missing from this analysis..

According to Hans Kohn 'colonialism is foreign rule imposed upon a people'.[18] He emphasises that 'this phenomenon of foreign rule has nothing intrinsically to do with European control over portions of Asia or Africa. (...) Nor need colonial rule signify domination by white nations over dark-skinned peoples (...)'.

Colonialism to Michael Doyle is one of the possible outcomes of imperialism, which in turn is the process of establishing 'a relationship, formal or informal, in which one state controls the effective political sovereignty of another political society.'[19] This relationship, according to Doyle, can be achieved by force, by political collaboration, by economic, social or cultural dependence.

The Palestinian writer Edward Said endorses Doyle's analysis and adds that both imperialism and colonialism are supported 'and perhaps even impelled' by ideologies which maintain 'that certain territories and people require [emphasis added] and beseech domination, as well as forms of knowledge affiliated with domination'.[20]

Lee C. Buchheit, a legal scholar, explains colonialism in the following terms: 'the domination of a people by foreign governors (with its attendant injury to national and cultural pride) and the inability of the colonial subjects to control their own political destiny, often coupled with a degree of economic exploitation and denial of human rights.'[21]

B. The Salt Water Doctrine

Most scholarly writing on colonialism and decolonization is based on the 'salt water doctrine', according to which the term colonialism exclusively applies to the relationship between European colonial powers and their 'overseas territories'[22]. According to Hans Kohn, this is an 'emotional bias', as it is based on the 'widespread though unwarranted assumption, which had its origin in the fifteenth-century age of discoveries, that colonial empires are established by sea-powers, whereas expansion into contiguous land masses does not produce (...) colonialism'.[23]

Buchheit voices his criticism of the salt water doctrine as follows:

> International law is thus asked to perceive a distinction between the historical subjugation of an alien population living on a different part of the globe and the historical subjugation of an alien population living on a piece of land abutting that of its oppressors.[24]

According to a strict interpretation of this 'salt water doctrine'[25], territories need to be separated from the metropolitan state by sea in order to qualify as colonies. The doctrine relies on what has been referred to by some writers as the 'principle of distance' as an indispensable element of colonialism. The principle of distance is generally discussed in the context of the right to decolonization or self-determination. While it must be borne in mind that the criteria for colonization and those of the right to decolonization are not the same, as only a number of colonies have been recognized as possessing the right to decolonization, these criteria do overlap: if colonies do not need to be separated from the dominant metropolitan state by sea in order to possess the right to decolonization, it automatically follows that the principle of distance is not a constitutive element of colonialism.

At first glance, Article 22(6) of the Covenant of the League of Nations may seem to be a convincing legal source of the 'salt water doctrine'. This Article states inter alia:

> There are territories, (...) which because of their geographical contiguity to the territory of the Mandatory (...) can best be administered under the laws of the Mandatory as an integral portion of its territory.

However, this Article does not state that geographical contiguity involves (permanent) title to territory. It is a mere recommendation on the manner in which a Mandatory Power could administer a contiguous Mandate Territory.[26] Significantly, the United Nations Charter, which is the legal successor to the Covenant of the `league of Nations, does not repeat Article 22's reference to contiguity.[27]
UN General Assembly Resolutions 567 and 1541[28], which appear to come closest to supporting the principle of distance, suggest that this principle is a mere guideline which can be dispensed with if other factors are equally or more important.[29] The second part of the Annex to Resolution 567, describes Non-Self-Governing Territories[30] as territories 'on equal status with other component parts of the metropolitan or other country' and enumerates the 'factors indicative' of these territories as follows:

> 3. Geographical considerations: Extent to which the relations of a territory with the capital of the central government may be affected by circumstances arising out of their respective geographical positions, such as separation by land, sea or other natural obstacles.
>
> 4. Ethnic and cultural considerations: Extent to which the population is of different race, language or religion or has distinct cultural heritage, interests or aspirations, distinguishing them from the peoples in the country with which they freely associate themselves.[31]

In his book *A Concept of Nation*, Driessen notes:

> The use of the word 'indicative' in the title [of resolution 567] (...) leaves open the possibility of a Non-Self-Governing Territory bordering upon its metropolitan state.[32]

It is clear that the 'salt water doctrine' has played an important role in the way colonialism has been perceived and assessed. However, there is no convincing legal basis to support this doctrine. This suggests that the salt water doctrine imposes rather arbitrary restrictions on the conceptual scope of colonialism.

From this short overview a number of salient characteristics of colonies emerge: political, economic and social domination by a foreign metropolitan state and the presence of metropolitan settlers. Moreover, we have concluded that there is no legal rule which states that a satellite region needs to be geographically separated from the metropolitan state in order to qualify as a colony. Having established these basic facts, the next chapter will examine how colonialism has been dealt with in the international political arena.

III. COLONIALISM ON THE INTERNATIONAL AGENDA

A. Introduction

Until the end of the First World War, the existence of colonialism went more or less unchallenged. Hans Kohn writes:

> The Roman empire had been the model for Western political thought for over a thousand years. Americans at the end of the eighteenth century spoke proudly and hopefully of their 'empire'. The French revolutionaries proclaimed their 'imperial' expansion of their leadership. Modern Western civilisation was regarded as superior to other, comparatively stagnant civilisations and to bring higher civilisation to less developed countries was considered a praiseworthy enterprise. (...)[33]

The condemnation of colonialism has become almost universal by now. This condemnation tends to focus on a specific manifestation of colonialism, while other forms of colonialism continue to evoke a sense of heroism and courageous determination. Ironically, the United States of America, which has been among the strongest critics of 20th century European colonial rule in Africa, Asia and Latin America, recently celebrated the 500th anniversary of the discovery of America by Columbus, which paved the way for some of the most ruthless colonial conquests in the history of colonization.

The following section will sketch the 20th century development towards the internationalisation of colonial administration as well as delineate the limits which have been imposed on this development.

B. The League of Nations

After the First World War, the allied powers divided the German and Turkish colonies among themselves. At the same time, the idea that the simple annexation of these territories was incompatible with the ideals for which the Great War had been fought was starting to gain ground. President Wilson played a pivotal role in disseminating the principle that colonization by conquest was no longer acceptable. In doing so, he referred to the American Declaration of Independence: 'Governments derive their just powers from the consent of the governed.' Most probably, it was never Wilson's intention to apply his theories on self-determination beyond sub-state 'nations' within the conquered Ottoman and German empire in post First World War Europe. But once he had launched the principle of self-determination, it was soon adopted by those favouring decolonization all over the world. The fifth of Wilson's famous 14 Points recommended:

> free, open-minded and absolutely impartial adjustment of all colonial claims, based on the strict observance of the principle that in determining all such questions of sovereignty, the interests of the populations concerned must have equal weight with the equitable claims of the government whose title is to be determined.

This idea, though very unpopular among certain colonial powers, inspired the inclusion of Article 22 in the Covenant of the League of Nations, which reads:

> To those countries which as a consequence of the late war have ceased to be under the sovereignty of the States which formerly governed them and which are inhabited by peoples not yet able to stand up for themselves under the strenuous conditions of the modern world, there should be applied the principle that the well-being and development of such peoples form a sacred trust of civilisation and that securities for the performance of this trust should be embodied in this Covenant.
> (...)
> The best method of giving practical effect to this principle is that the tutelage of such peoples should be entrusted to advanced nations who by reason of their resources, their experience or their geographical position can best undertake this responsibility, and who are willing to accept it, and that this tutelage should be exercised by them as Mandatories on behalf of the League.

The Mandate system of the League of Nations, however limited in scope and application, constituted the beginning of a system of supranational supervision over colonial territories.

C. THE UN CHARTER: TRUST TERRITORIES & NON-SELF-GOVERNING TERRITORIES

The idea that colonial administration was no longer a strictly national and sovereign affair was further developed within the UN, the legal successor to the League of Nations.

The most important UN document on colonialism is the UN Charter itself. Chapters 11, 12 and 13 of the UN Charter deal with Trust Territories and Non-Self-Governing Territories (NSGTs). The UN General Assembly adopted a series of important resolutions on colonialism which will be discussed later.

Compared to the Mandate system of the League of Nations, The UN Charter represents an important step towards the internationalisation of colonial issues. In addition to the Trusteeship System, which replaced the Mandate system of the League of Nations, and which regulates the administering of colonial territories of conquered powers after the First and the Second World Wars, the UN Charter includes a Chapter on NSGTs. Article 73 of the UN Charter contains a short but interesting phrase on the nature of colonialism. It refers to colonial powers as:

> members who have or assume responsibilities for the administration of territories whose peoples have not yet attained a full measure of self-government'[34] [emphasis added].

Subsequent attempts by UN Secretary General Trygve Lie to clarify the factors to be taken into account in determining which territories qualified as NSGTs failed.[35] Notably absent in the texts adopted by UN organs is a clear and widely accepted definition of colonialism. This absence can be traced to the deliberate attempt by some UN member states to avoid a general definition by confining the scope of the term colonialism and its implications to a specific and exhaustive list of territories. The list of these so-called 'Non-Self-Governing-Territories and Trust Territories reflects the extent to which the international community was (and is) prepared to acknowledge the geographical scope of colonialism.

The UN has undoubtedly served as the principal international forum of discussion on colonialism and decolonization. The following section will give a brief overview of these discussions and select those elements which are relevant to this report.

1945-1960: Gradual Internationalisation

The distinctions between the rules governing Trust Territories and Non-Self-Governing Territories (NSGTs) was the subject of many heated debates in the decades following the Second World War. One of the main differences between these two legal regimes is that the Trusteeship System contains the phrase 'progressive development towards self-government or independence'[36],[emphasis added] Whereas the NSGTs system merely mentions 'self-government' as one of its objectives.[37] The Afro-Asian Block maintained that 'self-government' included the possibility to opt for independence, while most of the colonial powers claimed that 'self-government' merely implied internal self-determination (i.e. autonomy).[38]

Another difference between Chapter 11 and Chapters 12 and 13 of the UN Charter is that the latter two provide for extensive international supervision in the form of the Trusteeship Council, whereas Chapter 11 remains silent on the question of supervision. Between 1945 and 1960 the Afro-Asian Block successfully lobbied for the adoption of many General Assembly Resolutions which slowly but gradually eroded the distinction between NSGTs and Trust Territories and encouraged NSGTs to seek independence.

UN Supervision vs. Non-interference Principle

A number of states, notably the Netherlands, Spain, Portugal and France, attempted to circumvent international supervision by maintaining that their colonies were integral parts of the metropolitan state. They called these territories 'overseas provinces' or 'provinces outre-mer' instead of colonies. The ultimate failure of these states to avoid UN supervision shows very clearly that the relevant UN organs have not considered recognition by a metropolitan state of the colonial status of a territory (as opposed to its 'provincial status') to be a constitutive element of colonialism.[39]

The history of the Portuguese colonies is one of the clearest examples that the refusal by a metropolitan state to recognize the colonial status of its colonies did not prevent the UN from treating these territories as such. While most colonies had gained independence by the end of the 1960s, Portugal held on to its colonies much longer. The Portuguese dictator Salazar maintained that the Portuguese territories in Asia and Africa constituted integral parts of Portugal and that the independence of these territories would amount to the dismemberment of Portugal.[40], This did not deter the UN from strongly condemning Portugal's refusal to report[41] on its colonial policies in Angola, Mozambique and East Timor. Portugal's response to UN pressure to report on the situation in these territories was that 'the furnishing of information was conditional upon voluntary agreement of Member States that the principles of Article 73[42] applied to them'.[43] For the first time in the history of the NSGT system, the UN General Assembly) took the significant step of listing 9 particular territories as NSGTs, thus demonstrating that it considered itself competent to determine when Article 73 of the UN Charter applied in concreto.

1960: Rapid Changes in Colonial Relationships

Whereas the 15 years following the end of the Second World War witnessed a slow but steady pace towards international supervision over the administration of colonies and the development of an evolutionary right to self-determination for NSGTs, 1960 marked the beginning of a new era in the grand debate on colonialism and decolonization. From 1960 onwards the legal discussions were replaced by the political weight of the UN General Assembly resolutions.[44] Two General Assembly Resolutions set the tone in this new era: Resolutions 1514 and 1541[45]. Both of these resolutions, which are generally discussed in the context of decolonization, contain interesting phrases on the nature of colonialism. Therefore, they are worth examining in some detail.

Resolution 1514 and the Special Committee of 24

On 14 December 1960, the UN General Assembly adopted the by now historical resolution 1514: 'Declaration on the Granting of Independence to Colonial Countries and Peoples.' This political declaration, which is generally considered to reflect customary law and is as such binding on all states, constituted a powerful break through. Not only was the difference between Trust Territories and NSGTs finally eliminated, but a third category of 'all other territories which have not attained independence' was also added to the list of colonies.[46] The preambular phrase 'the necessity of bringing to a speedy and unconditional end colonialism in all its forms and manifestations' [emphasis added] also indicates a development towards a wider interpretation of colonialism. This conclusion is reinforced by the definition of colonialism contained in resolution 1514. The Declaration condemns 'the subjection of peoples to alien subjugation, domination and exploitation'[47]. It does not explicitly equate this phrase to colonialism, but the context implies that it defines colonialism in these terms. The Special Committee of 24 was established[48] to supervise the implementation of resolution 1514. It replaced all earlier ad-hoc committees. Compared to these earlier supervisory organs, the supervision regime of the Committee of 24 constituted an important break-through: it was granted the power to hear petitioners and carry out missions to gather first hand information.[49] In theory, the inhabitants of the territories in question were at last given some say in defining the actual substance of their 'paramountcy of interest'.[50] On paper these interests were no longer exclusively determined by their colonial rulers.

Resolution 1541

Whereas the Trust Territories constituted a well-defined, exhaustive list of regions, the term Non-Self-Governing Territories remained undefined. The colonial powers preferred to list these territories rather than to define them, and they came up with a list of 74 NSGTs. The Afro-Asian Block, fearing that this list would remain subject to the sovereign whims of the colonial powers, unremittingly attempted to specify which criteria should be used while determining which territories qualified as NSGTs, to which Article 73 of the UN Charter should be applied. On 15 December 1960 it finally succeeded in securing the passage of General Assembly Resolution 1541: 'Principles which should guide members in determining whether or not an obligation exists to transmit the information called for in Art. 73 of the UN Charter.' Principle IV of this resolution reads:

> Prima Facie there is an obligation to transmit information in respect of a territory which is geographically separate and is distinct ethnically and/or culturally from the country administe ring it.

Principle V adds:

> (...) additional elements may be, inter alia, of an administrative, political, juridical, economic or historical nature. If they affect the relationship between the metropolitan State and the territory concerned in a manner which arbitrarily places the latter in a position or status of subordination (...).

Two phrases warrant special attention. Firstly, the words prima facie suggest that the criteria mentioned in Principle IV are indicators, instead of hard and fast criteria.[51] Secondly, the words inter alia point out that the list of indicators is not finite and that other indicators may be relevant as well (see section 2.2).

The 'indicators' of colonialism emerging from this resolution are: geographical separateness, ethnic/cultural/historical distinctness and arbitrary legal/political/economic subordination of a territory by a Metropolitan State.

The International Decade for the Eradication of Colonialism

The issue of colonialism has not been entirely removed from the agenda of the United Nations. Although most former colonies on the list of the Committee of 24 had gained independence by the '70s, some colonies still remain. `A number of these colonies are on the list on the Committee of 24[52] while others are not and never have been on that list.

In 1990, at its 45th session, the General Assembly adopted a resolution announcing the beginning of the 'International Decade for the Eradication of Colonialism.' During this decade, the 'elimination of the last vestiges of colonialism by the year 2000'[53] was to be one of the priorities of the United Nations. Most states interpret this resolution as merely addressing the situation of territories listed by the Special Committee on Decolonization, although the language of the resolution itself does not explicitly impose this limit. It 'called upon the Administering Powers to take all necessary steps to enable the peoples of Territories concerned to exercise fully as soon as possible their right to self-determination, including independence.'[54]

In the course of the Decade of the Eradication of Colonialism, the General Assembly adopted a number of resolutions on the subject, reiterating its conviction of the need for decolonization of the remaining colonies. During its 50th session, the UN General Assembly adopted Resolution 50/39, in which it noted 'with concern the negative impact which the non-participation of certain administrating Powers has had on the work of the Special Committee [i.e. the Committee of 24]'. It confirmed once again that 'the continuation of colonialism *in any form or manifestation — including economic exploitation* — is incompatible with the Charter of the United Nations, the Universal Declaration of Human rights and the Declaration on the Granting of Independence to Colonial Countries and Peoples'. [emphasis added][55]

This chapter has outlined the process towards the internationalisation of colonial administration. This exercise has shown that the remarkable progress which has been achieved has merely applied to a limited group of territories recognized as colonies and thus subject to international supervision by the Committee of 24.

IV. NON-ALIGNED PERCEPTIONS: FROM DELHI TO CARTAGENA

As stated before, debates on colonialism tend to be loaded with emotions. Whereas colonial systems are strongly condemned by some as racist exploitation, others praise it as a system of good governance over those unable to rule themselves. This chapter will examine a selection of official statements on colonialism by representatives of colonised peoples.

The very first Afro-Asian Conference, which was one of the precursors of the later Non-Aligned Movement, was held in Delhi in 1947. Many of its participants were yet to be decolonised. Interestingly, Tibet also participated in this conference. The first official and most important inter-governmental conference of the Afro-Asian Block was held in Bandung, Indonesia, in 1955. This conference is generally seen as the founding meeting of the Non-Aligned Movement (NAM). Most of the 29 participating states had recently been decolonised and the anti-colonial sentiments expressed during the conference were very strong. The Final Communiqué of the Bandung Conference condemned colonialism on various grounds. It called colonialism a 'means of cultural repression' and defined colonialism as 'the subjection of peoples to alien subjugation, domination and exploitation'.[56] It is interesting to note that this definition reappeared five years later in the aforementioned UN General Assembly resolution 1514.

However unanimous those attending the Bandung Conference were in their condemnation of colonialism, there existed considerable divergence of opinion on its definition. The Ceylonese delegate, Sir John Kotewala, received strong support when he maintained that:

> There is another form of colonialism [i.e. other than western colonialism], however, about which many of us represented here are perhaps less clear in our minds and to which some of us would perhaps not apply the term colonialism at all. Think for example of those satellite states under Communist domination in Central and Eastern Europe - of Hungary, Rumania, Bulgaria, Albania, Czechoslovakia, Latvia, Lithuania and Poland. Are not these colonies as much as any of the colonial territories in Africa or Asia? And if we are all united in our opposition to colonialism, should it not be our duty to openly declare our opposition to Soviet colonialism as much as to Western imperialism?[57]

The strong support Sir Kotewala received reinforces the conclusion reached in section 2.2 of this report: that colonialism is not contingent on a 'salt water barrier', nor on European colonial rule in Africa and Asia.

Kotewala's strongest critic was Zhou En Lai, who represented the People's Republic of China (PRC). Zhou strongly rejected Kotewala's suggestion for the obvious reason that the PRC and the Soviet Union were allies at the time. Moreover, Zhou adhered to the Leninist doctrine on colonialism, according to which colonialism equalled 'capitalist exploitation'. According to Lenin socialist systems of government could therefore never be colonial.[58] Thirdly, Zhou might have felt threatened by the analogies between Russian 'new colonialism' and Chinese policies, not only in Eastern Turkestan, Inner Mongolia and Tibet, but also in other areas, such as Cambodia, Thailand and Laos.[59]

For these reasons Zhou objected to the inclusion of the phrase 'colonialism in all its forms', as proposed by the majority. He finally accepted the face-saving word 'manifestations' instead of 'forms', so the Conference as a whole could declare that 'colonialism in all its manifestations is an evil which must be speedily brought to an end.' As far as Zhou's rejection of Kotewala's observation was mostly based on reasons of a political rather than a conceptual nature, it had little bearing on the Conference's observations on the nature of colonialism as a system of 'alien domination, subjugation and exploitation.' Interestingly, the Constitution of the People's Republic of China states that 'China consistently opposes imperialism, hegemonism and colonialism, works to strengthen unity with the people of other countries, [and] supports the oppressed nations and the developing countries in their just struggle to win and preserve national independence (...).'[60] [emphasis added]

In spite of the fact that the world has changed dramatically since 1955, the Final Communiqué of the Non-Aligned Movement's summit in Cartagena in 1995 closely resembled the Bandung Declaration. The assembled governments 'reiterated the continued validity of the right of all peoples to self-determination, the exercise of which, in the case of peoples under colonial or alien domination and foreign occupation, is essential to ensure the eradication of all these situations and to guarantee universal respect for human rights and fundamental freedoms. The participants strongly condemned 'ongoing brutal suppression of the legitimate aspirations for self-determination of peoples under colonial or alien domination and foreign occupation in various regions of the world.' They reaffirmed 'the inalienable right of peoples of Non-Self-Governing Territories to self-determination and independence in accordance with GA resolution 1514 (XV) of 14 December 1960 regardless of the territory's size, geographical location, population and limited natural resources.'[61]

V. COMMON FEATURES OF COLONIALISM

In order to gain insight into the quintessential nature of colonial systems, this chapter will give a general overview of the ways in which colonies have been (and are) established, administered and maintained.

A. The Establishment of Colonial Regimes

Military Invasion and Annexation

Most colonies are established by military conquest followed by occupation and annexation. In the case of conquest, soldiers are the first to arrive in 'the new world', followed by civilian settlers. Both during the actual conquest and the subsequent annexation, military presence tends to be considerable and permanent. Unlike gradual colonization by settlement, colonization by conquest is a rather sudden, instant affair. Once military control has been established, the more gradual process of gaining comprehensive economic, cultural and political control of the territory starts to evolve. During this process control by military means tends to decrease and to a large extent gives way to the more subtle maintenance of control by the civilian and often indigenous police.

Settlement

In many European colonies the first visitors from the metropolitan state were missionaries, venturing out into the wilderness in order to convert and 'civilise' the natives. The mission stations established by these missionaries often started as small communities consisting of a church, a school and some houses. Most of these communities gradually developed into villages and towns which subsequently started to attract more and more settlers from the metropolitan state.

Some colonies started as a collection of planters' estates or trading posts. Capitalist enterprises from rich and technologically advanced countries set up new businesses in territories which were rich in natural resources, but lacked the technical expertise to exploit these resources. Most of these commercial settlements were initially isolated islands of a handful of foreign surveyors in charge of a large work force of natives, who provided cheap labor. These islands tended to grow into bigger settlements, and paved the way for colonial administrators who exercised effective rule over the territory.

Colonial officials typically arrived in the 'new world' when a certain metropolitan presence had already been established by missionaries, merchants or soldiers. They tended to be temporary residents, who rarely spent more than a few years in the alien territory. They were generally appointed by their metropolitan governments, which kept track of their whereabouts, activities and numbers. Some of these officials stayed on after their term of duty had expired and settled down permanently as planters, merchants or farmers.

In colonies which were not established by military conquest, soldiers tended to arrive along with administrators, or soon afterwards. In most cases their primary task was to protect the settler minority in the 'alien' territory. In some cases soldiers were directly involved in the establishment of commercial enterprises and institutions, in other cases soldiers merely protected the settler community.

Some imperialist powers sent scientific missions into uncharted territories in order to plant the first colonial seeds. In some cases these scientific missionaries primarily explored whether these territories were of potential economic interest, e.g. for the presence of (mineral) resources or fertile land. In other cases it was a purely imperialist exercise, motivated by reasons of prestige and political power.

Technical experts were often recruited from the metropolitan state in order to set up and maintain economic, industrial or agricultural development projects. As these projects tended to be based on metropolitan concepts of development and were tailored to metropolitan needs, the expertise required for these projects had to come from the metropolitan states. In most colonies this expertise was imported rather than developed locally. The industrial and agricultural development projects set up by these experts subsequently attracted more workers from the metropolitan state.

Most colonial pioneers who settled down as farmers in colonial territories were driven by a scarcity of (fertile) land at home. As they invested much time and effort into setting up a new farming enterprises and gave up their home bases in their own countries, they tended to settle down permanently and gradually became the new locals. They were a particularly significant category of settlers as they were closely linked to the land. After one or two generations, most of them had no home and/or land other than the farms they had established in the colony. Like farmers and merchants, metropolitan workers who migrated to the satellite region were often driven by economic motives. Lack of work and/or economic opportunities at home prompted them to trek to the 'new world', in search of a better life. Unlike farmers, they tended to flock to urban centers or industrial sites, such as mines or factories. Their presence was contingent on the availability of lucrative work.

In a limited number of cases, the first metropolitan settlers were criminals exiled to distant and 'barbarous' lands in order to be punished and 'reformed' through arduous labor.[62] The criminal origin of this community wore off with the arrival of the next generation(s), but few of these settlers and their offspring returned to their motherland.

Treaty / Contract

Many colonies are established on the basis of a treaty. In most cases these treaties are concluded after military invasion. They constitute so-called 'unequal treaties' imposed by (the threat of) military force. In other cases these treaties establish a protectorate regime[63] in which a dependent territory surrenders (part of) its sovereignty in exchange for military protection by a powerful metropolitan state. There are examples of territories which voluntarily concluded these treaties, on the basis of the principle of mutual benefit. Most of these treaties contain clauses guaranteeing a certain, if limited, degree of autonomy to the dependent territories, but more often than not, these autonomy clauses are violated by the more powerful party to the treaty.

Some colonies are established after the conclusion of a lease or a contract of purchase.[64] In these cases, it is the conclusion of such contracts which set in motion the settlement process by which effective rule is established over the region.

B. COLONIAL ADMINISTRATION

Once a colony has been established, the nature of the colonial regime will vary according to the style of colonial government adopted by the metropolitan state. The one overriding common aspect in these different colonial regimes is the element of 'domination' of the satellite territory by the metropolitan state. This 'domination' has various different and inter-connected aspects.

Political Representation

The political representation of the population of the colonised areas in the local and central administration tends to be limited to the lower administrative levels or to symbolic, 'rubber stamp' positions which involve little or no effective decision making power. The system of 'indirect rule', such as the style of government employed in some British and Dutch colonies, theoretically constitutes an exception in this respect, but in practice this system often amounts to the attribution of power to a small, carefully selected group of locals who are loyal to the colonial regime and exercise power on behalf of this regime. These figure heads are selected, instructed and often co-opted by the metropolitan rulers and do not represent the local population at large. Their power is largely contingent on their loyalty to the regime and therefore their positions cannot be said to constitute actual political participation of the local population. Moreover, the system of indirect rule often attempts to secure the loyalty of 'natural rulers'[65] such as state chiefs, religious leaders or members of the old elite, as intermediaries. These 'natural rulers' are in a unique position to function as vehicles of indirect colonial rule, provided they are willing to do so. In order to gain their support, colonial rulers tend to grant them considerable concessions.

Most systems of indirect rule are based on the idea that local 'chiefs' are responsible for the administration of small rural units or 'chieftancies'. This system of localised auto-administration holds an important political advantage for colonial powers. It provides colonised subjects with an important outlet for their political ambitions, while it does not threaten the central government's monopoly on the overall power.

In the system of 'direct rule', the process of co-option plays a relatively minor role. The system of direct rule does not attempt to put a 'native face' on the colonial administration and colonial rule is exercised without local intermediaries. In both systems, the central decision making power rests with the metropolitan power.

As stated earlier, colonised peoples perceive colonial rule as foreign. Similarly, colonial administrations tend to regard indigenous representatives from their colonial territories as 'outsiders', who may at best have a (limited) say in policies affecting their own region but who should not be granted any power on the level of national decision making.

The political justification which has often been used is that colonies are not capable of governing themselves and that they are better off with their colonial rulers than they would be with their own, natural leaders. The British High Commissioner in Egypt, Lord Lloyd, used this very argument when he maintained that what people wanted was 'not independence, but good administration'.[66] It was 'the white man's burden' to protect the backward, politically immature people from the exploitation, tyranny and corruption of their natural leaders.

Colonial powers often argue that their dependencies are politically immature and incapable of defining their own interests and governing themselves: In democracy the people really do take an active part in government, and the fact that one can find twenty [native] university graduates capable of forming a cabinet does not imply that the responsibility for governing their country can forthwith be handed over to them.[67]

This argument was used by progressive colonial rulers who genuinely intended to assist their colonial subjects in the process of their political emancipation as well as by conservative colonial governments who used it to justify their refusal to let go of their colonial territories.

Colonial Borders

Colonial borders often divide local communities in ways which reflect the political interests and spheres of influence of the colonial powers rather than the natural population patterns and political history of the territory.[68] Similarly, the administrative borders within one colony are often drawn with total disregard to the original community structures. Whatever the reasons behind this policy, it has often disrupted the social fabric of the local population and imposed artificial, arbitrary community structures. Emerson analyses this phenomenon as follows:

> Over the centuries the national heritage of many peoples has been diverted into new channels by the colonial experience which they have undergone. Indeed, the creation of nations themselves is in some instances (...) to be attributed primarily to the bringing together of diverse stocks under a single imperial roof. In this fashion inner unity has often been promoted by colonial rule, while at the same time the multiplicity of colonial systems has emphasised the diversities between peoples by forcing them into disparate colonial patterns.[69]

After decolonization, the principle of 'uti possidetis'[70] generally precludes restoration of precolonial borders. While it is beyond the scope and focus of the present report to discuss the problems arising from these inherited colonial borders in detail, it should be noted that this inheritance often contains the potential for violent territorial conflicts. At the same time, the restoration of pre-colonial borders is not necessarily the best solution in such cases, as this could create other, equally serious tensions in societies inevitably and permanently transformed by colonial rule.

Economic Aspects

Colonial powers often legitimise their presence in and their rule over their satellite areas in economic terms. They claim that it is the metropolitan state which brings development and progress to the dependent and underdeveloped colonies. Quoting the Covenant of the League of Nations and later the UN Charter, colonial powers consider it to be part of their 'sacred trust' to 'promote to the utmost, (...) the well-being of the inhabitants of these territories,'[71] who were 'not yet able to stand by themselves under the strenuous conditions of the modern world'.[72]In addition, it has been argued that the exploitation of mineral resources was not only a right but even a duty of colonial powers. The French writer Sarraut elaborates on this idea:

> Nature has distributed unequally across our planet a wealth and variety of raw materials; and while she has located in this continental extremity which is called Europe, the inventive genius of the white races and the technical expertise with which to exploit natural resources, she has concentrated the most abundant reserves of these materials in Africa, tropical Asia and equatorial Oceanea, towards which the developed countries in their need to live and to create, are directing their impetus and their drive (...) Must these immense expanses of land, which could produce so great a variety of foodstuffs, be allowed to lie fallow, abandoned to the thickets of indifference, ignorance and incompetence?[73]

It is the metropolitan state which represents modernity vis-a-vis the 'backward' populations of the colonies. At the same time, colonial rulers tend to exploit and export the mineral resources within their colonies at the expense of the local population. In the case of mineral resources, the processing of the resources mined in colonised territories often takes place in the metropolitan states. The economic spin-off from the mining of these resources is often low, whereas the processing of these resources creates a job-market for (semi) skilled metropolitan labourers and yields lucrative final products.

This pattern is basically the same in the case of other types of natural resources, such as cotton, rice, tea and coffee. 'Although the extent to which this exchange of natural resources for (professed) development benefits the metropolitan state at the expense of the colonised territory differs widely in each particular situation, the element of exploitation or the attempt to exploit is consistent.

The use of cheap labor in colonised territories by the metropolitan state in order to maximize national economic growth falls within this same pattern of exploitation: the local population needs the income, even if it is minimal, while the colonial powers need the cheap labor. Although there is mutual benefit in absolute terms, the colonial labourers are forced into a position of relative deprivation. Once this relationship has been consolidated, very few individuals let alone communities manage to break away from this position of structural dependence unless the entire political and economic system changes dramatically.

As has been noted in the previous paragraphs, development in colonies is generally planned and executed by the metropolitan state and responds to the needs of the latter rather than the former. It requires skills which are often new to the local population, which had no need for these skills until the arrival of the colonial settlers. Therefore skilled labor tends to be performed by experts recruited from the metropolitan state, whereas the unskilled labor is performed by locals. The practice of employing outsiders to plan, co-ordinate and supervise development has important economic implications, such as the difference in the salary level of skilled and unskilled labour and increased competition on the local job market.

The assumption underlying the patterns identified in this section is that the metropolitan state is in a better position to define and fulfil local needs in its 'backward' and underdeveloped colonies than the local population itself. Protest against the imposition of colonial economic policies and exploitative development is often portrayed by colonial powers as backward, short-sighted resistance to modernity.

Cultural Aspects

The cultural counterpart of economic development rhetoric, is the concept of the mission civilisatrice, the civilising mission. This idea was most prevalent in the French colonial policy, which encouraged the inhabitants of the colonised territories to become 'perfect Frenchmen'. At the heart of this policy is the paternalist idea that the 'backward', undeveloped inhabitants of the colonised areas need to be educated and brought up to the level of the superior culture and life-style of the colonizing power. This ideology is reflected in the Covenant of the League of Nations, which distinguishes between 'the peoples not yet able to stand by themselves under the strenuous conditions of the modern world' and 'the advanced nations', whom, 'by reason of their resources, their experience and their geographical position' should be entrusted with 'the tutelage of such peoples.'[74]

The fact that the Covenant merely takes note of the 'strenuous conditions of the modern world' imposed on colonised territories without addressing its root causes, clearly demonstrates the unquestioning, self-righteous attitude of those in charge of the 'mission civilisatrice'. An important aspect of the mission civilisatrice is the colonial power's language and education policy in its colonies. Whereas some colonial powers deliberately choose to restrict the teaching of the language of the metropolitan state to the elite[75], most colonial powers try to impose their own language on the local population at large.

> All the colonial peoples have been brought into the modern world under the aegis of an imperialism which superimposed a European language on the native tongue. This imperial language served three principal purposes which have an obvious bearing on the effort to secure national cultural identity. It was the language of instruction at least for higher education, it was the instrument through which intercourse of all varieties could be maintained with the advanced European and European descended peoples, and it was frequently the lingua franca within each of the several nations and between them (....) The white man (...) generally learned the local languages only as an act of grace or better to rule or trade with the subordinate peoples, whereas it was assumed that the natives who wanted to advance must rise to the level of the foreign language.[76]

It is the language of the metropolitan state which is associated with modernity, sophistication and social status, whereas oral and written fluency of the local language tends to be a useless asset for those in search of social advancement.

In most if not all colonies the language of the colonial power is used as the language of administration. For this reason, the education system needs to produce people who know this language well and who are capable of 'mediating linguistically between the metropolitan nation and the colonised peoples'.[77] In many cases these 'mediators' receive their education in the metropolitan state, which offers better educational facilities and more exposure to the language and culture of the colonial power. Colonial civilising missions often produced the so-called évoloué , the 'developed native' who had benefited from an education at a metropolitan school or university.[78]

The concept of the 'civilising mission' is in fact intertwined with the colonial concept of economic development and has often been invoked in order to justify the exploitation of the natural resources located in colonial territories:

> To colonise is to establish contact with new countries in order to benefit from their total range of resources, to develop these resources for the benefit of national interest and at the same time bring to the native peoples the intellectual, social, scientific, moral, cultural, literary, commercial and industrial benefits of which they are deprived and which are the prerogatives of the superior races. To colonise therefore, is to establish an advanced form of civilisation in a new country in order to achieve the twin aims we have just mentioned.[79]

In the United States of America the missionary zeal of the early puritan settlers played a formative role in the colonization process and later found its secular counterpart in the concept of Manifest Destiny: the United States was endowed with a historical duty to spread democracy and civilisation, up to the Pacific Ocean in the West and the Rio Grande in the South.

Geo-political Designs

Frequently, the geo-political and/or strategic significance of colonial possessions is equally if not more important to the metropolitan state than their economic profit. Obvious examples in this respect are the Polynesian and Melanesian islands in the Pacific, which are still French colonies. Gibraltar is another well known example of a small colony which is of little economic significance but of great strategic importance to the United Kingdom. The same holds true for the Pacific islands which are administrated by the United States.

A related but different element of the geo-political motives underlying colonial rule is the international power which the possession of colonies entails. Imperial prestige is particularly important for small states which would be rather insignificant without colonial possessions. This importance manifested itself particularly clearly in the European power struggle in Africa during the latter half of the nineteenth century. This struggle was fuelled mostly by the need for imperial status rather than for actual territorial expansion or economic profit.

Colonial powers often make use of geo-political and strategic arguments in justifying their colonial rule to their own citizens as well as to the international community. During the first decades of the Cold War, the preservation of African and Asian colonies was often equated with resistance to the 'communist menace'. Moreover, following the Second World War, European colonial powers felt that they needed 'to develop ..[their] own power and influence equal to that of the United States of America and the USSR'[80] and to show that they were not subservient to the two superpowers. Interestingly enough, geo-political considerations which have nothing to do with the interests of the local population and much to do with the maintenance of the global balance of power by the five permanent members of the UN Security Council, were codified in the UN Charter, which states that:

> There may be designated, in any trusteeship agreement, a strategic area or area which may include part or all of the trust territory to which the agreement applies (...). All functions of the United Nations relating to strategic areas, including the approval of the trusteeship agreements and of their alteration or amendment, shall be exercised by the Security Council.[81]

The fact that the Charter states that the interests of the inhabitants of these 'strategic areas' are subservient to those of the Security Council, which is effectively dominated by the United States., the Soviet Union (now Russian Federation), China, the United Kingdom and France, appears to run counter to the 'paramountcy of interests' codified in Article 73 of the Charter.

C. The Maintenance of the Colonial Authority

All colonial regimes face challenges to their rule by their colonial subjects. While the reactions of colonial powers to these challenges range from the bloody suppression of dissent to the (partial) accommodation of the grievances of the colonised subjects without relinquishing political control, these reactions share certain common elements.

Curtailment of Civil Rights

Colonial powers tend to curtail or violate the civil rights of colonial subjects who protest against colonial rule. In such cases, the violation of individual rights is a symptom of the more deep-rooted political problem of imposing and maintaining a colonial regime against the wishes of the local population. Some colonial powers have justified these violations by claiming that the colonised territory was not yet ready for self-government and that allowing individuals to voice their protest against colonial rule freely, would result in chaos and bloodshed. Other colonial regimes claim that the suppression of dissent is necessary to protect the population at large against a handful of irresponsible and ignorant elements who do not truly represent the people.[82] How could they represent the people, if the colonial rulers know best how to serve the 'paramount interests' of these people, how to bring them greater prosperity, development and civilisation?

Military Presence

The maintenance of colonial control often involves permanent military presence. This military presence should be distinguished from the military forces employed in colonies which are established by military conquest. The soldiers may be the same individuals but their mission is essentially different. In the case of military conquest, the metropolitan soldiers are pioneers, conquering a new territory, while soldiers who are in charge of protecting and maintaining colonial authority supplement the efforts of authorities whenever civilian means to subjugate the local prove insufficient. In some cases, the army plays an active role in crushing challenges to the colonial regime. In other cases, military presence may be a mere symbolic show of force, while the civilian police is in charge of maintaining public order on a day-to-day basis. Whereas the police force often consists entirely or partly of locals, soldiers are typically nationals of the metropolitan state. Among the lower military ranks there may be a handful of local soldiers, operating under the command of metropolitan superiors.

Mission

In some colonies, the civilising mission has strong religious dimensions and colonial powers claim that they have the 'divine right' to colonial authority. Missionaries set out to convert the 'natives' and save them from eternal damnation.

It is here that the 'sacred trust of civilisation' codified in the Covenant of the League of Nations becomes truly sacred. In many cases this 'colonization of the mind' has important political implications. Replacing a traditional belief system of a people by an alternative frame of reference often amounts to changing the entire identity of this people. As this distinct identity is often a vehicle of nationalist aspirations, the modification of this identity may be a means of diminishing (potential) political resistance to colonial rule.

D. PERCEPTIONS AND ATTITUDES

The Alien Concept

In the first place it should be noted that the phrase 'alien domination' has been coined by colonial peoples themselves. It is their own experience of colonial rule which inspired the member states of the Non-Aligned Movement to use the phrase 'alien subjugation, domination and exploitation' at the Bandung Conference. This phrase was subsequently repeated in a number of key documents, such as the Declaration of the Granting of Independence to Colonial Peoples and Countries. The fact that countries under colonial rule agreed on this definition of colonialism, provides an important insight into the nature of colonialism itself. It is the element of 'alien-ness' which distinguishes colonialism from other non-representative systems of government, in which one group of people controls and represses another group of people.

Interestingly enough, not only colonised peoples but also most colonial powers agree that their colonial subjects are foreigners from a foreign territory, who can never be entirely assimilated and always remain a separate class of citizens. Even the French government, which at some point seriously undertook to assimilate its colonial subjects and make them into perfect Frenchmen, never ceased to distinguish between native Frenchmen and those originating from their 'provinces outremer'.

It is this element of 'alien domination' which has often been automatically interpreted as involving geographical distance,. That, as has been shown in paragraph 2.2, has no valid basis in international law and does not do justice to the multiple ways in which 'alien-ness' might manifest itself. Cultural, ethnic, linguistic and historical factors may be of equal or even more importance in determining whether or not the rule exercised by a metropolitan state over a satellite region is 'alien'.

Paternalism

Colonial rhetoric often refers to 'the interests' of the local population. This rhetoric found its way into the Covenant of the League of Nations as the principle of 'sacred trust' and later into the UN Charter, which recognizes the principle that 'the interests of the inhabitants of these [non-self-governing] territories are paramount'.[83] Yet, colonial powers seldom or never clarify who is to determine the nature or the contents of these interests. Typically, it is the government of the metropolitan state which defines the interests of the inhabitants of the satellite state (i.e. the colony). This practice often finds its justification in the argument that the native population of the colony lacks the education and expertise which is required for the adequate determination and articulation of its own interests.

The observations of the famous explorer and colonial officer in British India, Sir Francis Younghusband, are typical in this respect. He wrote:

> The Chitrasis [indigenous population of a mountain area in northern Pakistan] are children. But the people who treat children best are English nurses. (...) These people will know quite well when they deserve a good sound smacking, and if it is given with no ill-feeling behind it, they will, like children, take it in good part and respect us.[84]

Colonial powers often refer to the original population as infants or children, who need strong authoritarian parents who can help them to grow up to be responsible adults.

E. Possible Outcomes of the Colonisation Process

Colonisation may result in a number of different situations. At one extreme end of the spectrum we find decolonization: the colonial power withdraws and the original population (re)installs its own government. At the other end of the spectrum we find territories which have been completely taken over by the colonial settlers or integration within the metropolitan state. In the latter case, the original population has been reduced to a marginal minority and the pre-colonial identity of these territories has been replaced by the identity of the settler society, which is dominant in every respect. In the case of integration within a metropolitan state, no new state is established, but the process of assimilation and/or marginalization of the original population is similar. Between these two extremes of decolonization and take-over or integration, there is a multitude of intermediate forms, such as the continuation of colonial rule over a territory which preserves a certain national identity of its own, as in New Caledonia or Samoa. There are also cases in which one colonial regime has been replaced by another colonial regime, such as in the case of East Timor, Western Sahara or Namibia.[85]

In some former colonies, the former colonizing power retains considerable economic, cultural, political or military influence. This phenomenon is generally referred to as 'neo-colonialism': the continuation of a colonial relationship after formal decolonization. In other decolonised territories the links with the former colonizing powers have been completely severed.

The various possible outcomes of the colonization process may be determined by external factors, such as political pressure by the international community on colonial powers to grant independence to their colonies as well as by internal factors, such as the attitude of the original population and/or of the metropolitan electorate, the size of the metropolitan settler community and the nature of the colonial regime.

F. CONCLUSION TO PART I

Having now established what the essential characteristics of colonialism are and how they manifest themselves, we now need to ask ourselves what the relevance of this effort is with respect to the two basic questions asked in the introduction of this report: what is colonialism and to what extent can Tibet be classified as territory under colonial rule?

As has been stated before, the terms 'colonialism', 'colonial' or 'colonies' are used frequently as if they need no further clarification. Moreover, it is often assumed that colonialism was abolished several decades ago. These assumptions are based on the idea that the term colonialism applies to a limited set of territories, most of which have gained independence by now. Yet, as the preceding chapters have shown, colonialism is in fact a complex phenomenon with many political, cultural, economic and social facets. In order to understand this phenomenon in all its complexity, this report seeks to look beyond the well-known cases and types of colonialism and identify the essence of colonialist systems of government. The elements enumerated in the following section do not only offer us insight into the system of colonialism, but also provide us with a diagnostic instrument which can be used to determine whether territories which prima facie display colonial features can in fact be classified as colonies.

The situation in Tibet is increasingly often described as 'colonial'. If Tibet is indeed a colony of the People's Republic of China, it will have to contain at least some of the following key elements.

Establishment

* Colonial rule is established in one or more of the following ways: military conquest and subsequent annexation, the conclusion of a treaty or contract, merchant enclaves and subsequent settlement. Colonialism always involves the settlement of people from a metropolitan state in a satellite region.

Administration

* The original population is not, or poorly, represented in the central government. The interests of the original inhabitants are largely determined by the metropolitan, colonial power.

* Colonial rule often superimposes national borders which do not correspond to

the local community structure(s) or the political history of the colonised territories. In most cases these territories were not organized as nation states before the advent of the colonial power.

* Economic development is planned and imposed by the colonial power and often benefits the metropolitan state at the expense of the satellite region. Resources located in colonies are transferred to the metropolitan state for further processing and marketing.

* Civilising mission: the colonial power undertakes to 'civilise' the original inhabitants of a colony. The underlying presumption is that the colonial power possesses a culture which is superior in relation to the culture/civilisation of the colonised population(s). In addition, colonial powers often claim that the original population of the colonised territory is unable to rule itself for reasons of political immaturity and economic underdevelopment.

* Cultural exchange between settlers/representatives from the metropolitan state and the original inhabitants of the colony is asymmetrical. The latter adopt more aspects of the culture of the former than vice versa.

Maintenance of Colonial Authority

* Reactions of colonial powers to colonial resistance are based on strategies to eliminate dissent. The strategies may vary from the suppression of dissent to accommodating the grievances of the colonised population without relinquishing political control.

* The maintenance of colonial authority involves permanent military presence, consisting of soldiers from the metropolitan state or local soldiers under the command of officers from the metropolitan state.

Perceptions

Colonised people(s) experience colonial rule as alien domination. Similarly citizens from the metropolitan state continue to make a distinction between themselves and the original inhabitants of the colony.

Outcome of the Colonisation Process:

Colonisation may result in one or more of the following situations: decolonization, complete take-over of the colony by the metropolitan settlement community, the continuation of colonial rule over a territory which retains most of its pre-colonial identity, or integration into the metropolitan state.

PART II: TIBET, A COLONY OF THE PEOPLE'S REPUBLIC OF CHINA?

VI. CHINESE RULE IN TIBET: ESTABLISHMENT, ADMINISTRATION, AND MAINTENANCE

A. INTRODUCTION

The Chinese government argues that Tibet became an integral part of China in the 13th century and has remained Chinese territory ever since. The Tibetan Government claims that Tibet was independent before the Chinese invasion in 1950.[1] Whatever the various arguments presented, it is generally accepted among scholars that Tibet existed and acted as an independent state from 1913 to the Chinese invasion in 1949/1950.[2] On the eve of the Chinese invasion, Tibet fulfilled all generally recognized criteria of statehood: a permanent population, a defined territory, a government and the capacity to enter into relations with other States.[3] Prior to the invasion, the Tibetan government established diplomatic relations with a number of countries and steadfastly refused to respond to repeated Chinese overtures to 'approve', 'accept' or 'join' the Chinese Republic, which had been established in 1911.[4] Chinese military intervention constituted an act of aggression against a state which at that point in time was neither part of the People's Republic of China, nor acted as such. In this second part of the independent study, the nature of China's rule over Tibet will be examined in light of the criteria of colonialism identified in Part I.

B. ESTABLISHMENT OF CHINESE AUTHORITY

Military Conquest

Shortly after the foundation of the People's Republic of China in 1949, after decades of turmoil and civil war in China, the Chinese People's Liberation Army (PLA) started its march towards Lhasa. Some heavy fighting took place between the Tibetan and the Chinese armies, in which the former were outnumber by the latter by many tens of thousands. In the first two weeks of fighting, which took place in and around Chamdo, some 4,000 Tibetans officers and soldiers were killed and the rest were forced to surrender.[5] By 1953 the Chinese authorities had consolidated their rule in most parts of Tibet. The Dalai Lama tried to find a modus vivendi with the Chinese authorities, given the impossibility of effective resistance in the face of the powerful Chinese PLA. Despite these efforts Tibetan protest against Chinese rule gradually mounted and culminated in a mass uprising against Chinese rule in 1959. In Lhasa the uprising was crushed, and according to Chinese figures at least 87,000 Tibetans were "eliminated".[6] In the course of the following year, the Chinese authorities crushed many Tibetan resistance movements and eventually established control over most parts of Tibet. Tibetans continued to wage a guerrilla war against the occupation forces and initially received some support from the U.S. Central Intelligence Agency. However, major revolts occurred in 1968 (the Nyemo rebellion which spread to 20 of the Tibet Autonomous Region's (TAR) 70 counties) and the early 1970s, none of which had any CIA involvement, in addition to hundreds of small revolts and protests which continue to this day.

Treaty

After the defeat of the Tibetan army, the Seventeen Point Agreement for the Peaceful Liberation of Tibet was signed by representatives of the Chinese and Tibetan governments in Beijing in May 1951. The Chinese government threatened the Tibetan representatives that failure to sign the agreement would result in the resumption of the military invasion of Tibet.[7] The Tibetan representatives preferred to sign the agreement rather than witness the further destruction of Tibet. The Seventeen Point Agreement states inter alia that 'the Tibetan people shall return to the big family of the Motherland - the People's Republic of China'.[8] Moreover it states that 'the Local Government of Tibet shall actively assist the PLA to enter Tibet and consolidate the national defences '. The Tibetan government , which had not given the Tibetan delegates full powers to sign any kind of treaty, rejected the Agreement as soon as it was broadcast by Radio Peking on 27 May 1951. Attempts by the Dalai Lama, who was 16 years old at the time, to re negotiate the treaty failed. Shortly after his escape to India in 1959, he stated publicly:

> While I and my government did not voluntarily accept the Agreement, we were obliged to acquiesce in it and decided to abide by the terms and conditions in order to save my people and country from the danger of total destruction.

On another occasion, the Dalai Lama stated that:

> The consent of the [Tibetan] Government was secured under duress and at the point of the bayonet. My representatives were forced to sign the agreement under the threat of further military operations against Tibet by the invading armies of China leading to utter ravage and ruin of the country.[9]

From a legal perspective, the Seventeen Point Agreement was void ab initio. According to Article 51 of the Vienna Convention on treaties, which is declaratory of international customary law, a treaty is without any legal effect if 'the expression of a State's consent to be bound by a treaty which has been procured by the coercion of its representative through acts or threats directed against him'. Article 52 adds: 'A treaty is void if its conclusion has been procured by the threat of use of force in violation with the principles of international law embodied in the Charter of the United Nations.'

The Seventeen Point Agreement continues to play an important role in Beijing's efforts to legitimise Chinese rule over Tibet, even though most of the treaty's substantive provisions have been violated by Chinese governments. The most relevant provisions in this respect are Articles 4 and 11 of the treaty. Article 4 reads: 'The Central Authorities will not alter the existing political system in Tibet. Neither will the Central Authorities alter the established status, functions and powers of the Dalai Lama. Officials of various ranks shall hold office as usual'. Article 11 reads: 'In matters related to various reforms in Tibet, there will be no compulsion on the part of the Central Authorities. The Local government of Tibet should carry out reforms of its own accord, and when the people raise demands for reform, they must be settled through consultation with the leading personnel of Tibet.' Interestingly, the TAR is the only autonomous region within the People's Republic of China which was established on the basis of a treaty (i.e. the Seventeen Point Agreement of 1951). This suggests that the Chinese authorities regard the TAR as different from the other four autonomous regions.[10]

Settlement

Before the Chinese invasion in the early 1950s, there were virtually no Chinese in Tibet, except in some border regions between Tibet and China. (These areas were later incorporated in the Chinese provinces Gansu, Sichuan and Yunnan, and in Qinghai.) Chinese colonists settled here as farmers, traders and shopkeepers in the decades preceding the military conquest and gradually gained control over large tracts of land that once belonged to Tibetan nomads.[11]

Up until 1934 there were no Chinese officials in Tibet. Earlier there had been Manchu, who had been expelled by the Tibetan government after the Manchu empire had collapsed in 1911. In 1934 China opened a diplomatic mission in Lhasa, the status of which was equal to the British mission in Lhasa, but lower than the Bhutanese and Nepalese missions. Soldiers of the Chinese People's Liberation Army were the first large group of Chinese frontier pioneers in Central Tibet. After they had established military control in the early 1950s, Beijing's comprehensive political rule in Central Tibet was mainly effected by Chinese government officials and Chinese Communist Party cadres. Many Chinese from all over China were moved to eastern Tibet in order to carry out the 'economic reconstruction work' outlined in the first 5-year plan. Some of these Chinese laborers settled down permanently. Not until Deng Xiao Ping's introduction of economic liberalisation policies in the early 1980s did a large number of Chinese merchants and entrepreneurs arrive in Central Tibet as well[12]

C. ADMINISTRATION

Political Aspects

As stated before, the government of the People's Republic of China has consistently claimed that Tibet constitutes an inalienable part of its territory, and that those who claim that Tibet was or should be an independent state are 'splittists' supported by foreign anti-China forces[13] and the 'Dalai clique' As detailed in Part 1, some European powers, notably France, the Netherlands and Portugal, similarly maintained that some of their colonies constituted integral parts of their metropolitan states. This did not prevent the international community from recognising these territories as colonies and treat them as such.

In the debates in the United Nations General Assembly, most states outside the communist block condemned China's rule in Tibet, and many referred to it as colonial rule. Interestingly, Tibet[14] was recognized as having a separate status within the PRC. Officially it enjoys a status which is equal to the other 4 Autonomous Regions within the PRC.[15] However, the government of the PRC unilaterally restricted the application of the Agreement to the area which it called the Tibet Autonomous Region. Leaving aside the illegality of this restriction of the treaty which was legally void ab initio, the TAR is the only Autonomous Region within the PRC which is based on a treaty.

Although most substantive provisions of this treaty have never been implemented, Chinese policies in Tibet are to a certain extent adjusted to local, Tibetan circumstances. Moreover, serious efforts have been undertaken to create a semblance of Tibetan local autonomy.

Political Representation—

In theory, Chinese law provides for Tibetan political representation by establishing a system of local autonomy. In practice these legal provisions are circumvented in ways which deny real autonomy.

Since 1949, China has maintained control in Tibet through Tibetan and Chinese Party and government officials. The erosion of the role of Tibetans started before the TAR was established. In the 1950s, the Dalai Lama was given important but nominal titles in the structures set up by the Chinese authorities, including the Chairmanship of the Preparatory Committee for the Autonomous Region of Tibet.[16] Following the 1959 rebellion, Tibetan involvement in the government was drastically limited and remained nominal. During the 1970s, China continued to transfer many Chinese cadres to Tibet, upon whom they relied heavily to govern Tibet. When Hu Yaobang, General Secretary of the Communist Party, visited Tibet in 1980, he ordered this trend to be reversed, so that greater levels of governance and authority be put back into the hands of Tibetans.[17] In a famous speech the Panchen Lama said:

> When Comrade Hu Yaobang visited Tibet in 1980, he decided to repatriate all the useless Chinese personnel from Tibet. We consider this a wise decision. What is the point of having useless personnel....Tibet has suffered greatly because of the policy of sending a large number of useless people. The Chinese population in Tibet started with a few thousand

and today is has multiplied manifold.[18]

Hu Yao Bang's personal efforts did not materialise, and there was no immediate policy shift, but the 1980s did see a period of relaxation which included the limited empowerment of Tibetans in government positions. By July 1994, even this very limited trend was officially halted. At the Third Work Forum on Tibet, the Central Committee of the Communist Party announced that "we should take effective steps to maintain the current ranks of Han cadres and transfer Han and other minority cadres from the hinterland to Tibet."[19] Today, the remaining upper level Tibetan cadres are concentrated in the United Work Front Department, a branch of the Communist Party, which only has the authority to give advice to the government and the Party.

The preamble of the Seventeen Point Agreement refers to the Tibetan people as the 'Tibetan nationality' and states that:

> All nationalities within the People's Republic of China shall enjoy national equality and the freedom to develop their spoken and written languages and to preserve or reform their customs, habits and religious beliefs."[20]

Its substantive provisions guarantee that "Tibetan people have the right of exercising national regional autonomy under the unified leadership of the Central People's Government, "[emphasis added][21] that "the Central Authorities will not alter the existing political system in Tibet [nor] the established status, functions and powers of the Dalai Lama."[22] It guarantees "freedom of religious belief"[23] and prohibits any form of compulsion on the part of the Central Authorities with regard to the introduction of reforms.[24]

A historical parallel can be drawn to the treaty-based French protectorate regimes in Tunisia and Morocco. In these two French protectorates, indirect rule by local representative bodies gradually moved towards direct rule by the French authorities. Similarly, the Chinese authorities have violated the very Agreement which, according to them, constitutes the legal basis for Chinese rule in Tibet.

The autonomy provisions in the Constitution of the People's Republic of China (1982) and the Law of the People's Republic of China on Regional Autonomy of Nationalities (1984) are much more limited and qualified than those in the Seventeen Point Agreement. According to the Law on Regional Autonomy, the autonomous organs have to operate under 'the uniform direction of the Central Government'[25] and remain 'subject to the approval by the Central Government[26] and the National People's Congress'.[27]

In assessing the current political representation of Tibetans within the political system of the PRC, three important points should be made. In the first place, the number of Tibetan representatives in the central government and central CCP organs is small.[28] As Hungmao Tien notes: 'While Peking can claim participation by all nationalities in the political process on the basis of percentage figures, their numbers have tended to be concentrated in less important organizations at the lower levels."[29] As the Chinese government and Party structures operate on a centralist basis, in which the lower level is subordinate to the higher level,[30] political representation on the local level involves little decision making power. TAR officials are subordinate to the central government, while Tibetan officials in the Autonomous Counties and Prefectures are subordinate to their provincial governments.[31]

Secondly, it is important to note that in reality it is the Chinese Communist Party (CCP) which makes policy and monopolises power, while the 'state implements policy and provides symbolic expressions of popular participation.'[32] As such, the CCP constitutes a semi-independent power block with a strong and pervasive influence on both the government and the army. CCP members dominate key government posts and have more real and effective power than non-Party government officials, even those with higher ranks. One of the Four Cardinal Principles on which Chinese politics is based is: Leadership by the Communist Party. Significantly, China's autonomy laws remain silent on the role of 'minorities' in the CCP. Whereas the 1984 Law on Regional Autonomy requires that Tibetans hold positions of authority in the TAR[33], no such requirement exists with regard to positions in the CCP. The highest, though still nominal, government position in the TAR is indeed occupied by a Tibetan[34], while the TAR Party Secretary post has never been occupied by a Tibetan. The official autonomy which Tibetans enjoy on a governmental level is subject to the ultimate, de facto control of the CCP.

Thirdly, the most important precondition for becoming a CCP member is political loyalty. Article 6 of the Party Constitution states:

> A probationary Party Member must take an oath in front of the Party flag. The oath reads: 'It is my will to join the Communist Party of China, uphold the Party's programme, observe the provisions of the Party Constitution, fulfil a Party member's duties, carry out the Part' decisions, strictly observe the Party discipline, guard Party secrets, be loyal work hard, fight for communism throughout my life, be ready at all times to sacrifice my all for the Party and the people and never betray the Party. [emphasis added]

In addition, Party Cadres have to 'fight against the hostile forces disrupting socialism and combat all erroneous tendencies inside and outside the Party.'[35]

Tibetan officials, and Party cadres a fortiori, are either genuinely loyal to the Chinese regime or try to reform the system from within. The leeway for such reform is extremely limited: cadres who are suspected of 'inconsistent thinking'[36], i.e. disloyalty, are sidelined or purged.[37]

It can be concluded that the political representation of the Tibetan people, on the local as well as on the central level, is structurally inadequate both in law and in fact, and is nominal at best.

Imposed Borders—

Tibetans were relatively unconcerned about the legal status of their country, until the Chinese started to lay territorial claims to Tibet. Religion, more than a nation state structure, was the organizing principle of Tibetan society. Like many of the pre-colonial territories, Tibet did not perceive itself in terms of a nation state until the early part of this century. In spite of the fact that Tibet defined itself primarily in religious terms until the beginning of this century, Tibet did function as a nation state, and fulfilled all the criteria for statehood, including a defined territory over which the Tibetan government exercised its jurisdiction.[38]

After the annexation of Tibet, Beijing divided Tibet into the Tibet Autonomous Region (TAR) and a number of Tibetan Autonomous Counties and Prefectures which were incorporated into Sichuan, Yunnan, Gansu and Qinghai Provinces. Some of these borders between the TAR and the other Tibetan regions had been imposed as early as 1950, but most of them were officially imposed by the Chinese government on 9 September 1965. By this time much of the original government structures of the pre-1949 Tibetan state had already been dissolved. The division of Tibet into the TAR and the Tibetan Autonomous Prefectures is a Chinese construction and does not reflect the Tibetan perception of Tibet as 'cholka sum' (three regions): Utsang, Kham and Amdo. Moreover, the borders between the TAR and the other Tibetan regions do not always correspond to ethnic, historical and cultural boundaries.

Not only did the Chinese authorities change the external borders of Tibet, but they also renamed or rearranged a number of internal administrative units inside Tibet. The military administration of the area is based on yet another structure. The eastern part of the TAR belongs to the Chengdu Military Region and the western part belongs to the Lanzhou Military Region. The fact that Tibet does not operate as one unified administrative and military unit appears to be at odds with the concept of 'autonomy' and Tibetan self-identification.

Economic Aspects

Imposed Development—

Ever since China annexed Tibet, Beijing has imposed development projects on Tibet without consulting the local Tibetan population. This practice was particularly obvious during the early decades of the Chinese occupation of Tibet, when Beijing imposed a system of collectivised farming on the Tibetan people, whose criticism of this system was crudely suppressed. During the 1970s and '80s the Chinese authorities unilaterally imposed large-scale wheat production in parts of Tibet. These projects failed completely, as wheat does not grow well in high altitude areas. (Tibetans traditionally did not eat wheat. Barley is the staple food of the Tibetans as Tibet's high altitude is particularly suitable for growing this crop.)

After the abolition of collectivised farming and the introduction of Deng Xiao Ping's policy of Reform and Opening Up in the late '80s, Beijing stepped up its efforts to explore the economic potential of Tibet and the possibilities to exploit this potential to the maximum extent. The shift from ideologically motivated to profit oriented development projects was not accompanied by increased participation of Tibetans in the planning and implementation of these projects.

A clear example of an imposed development project is the Hydro-electric power station in Lake Yamdroktso. Tibetans were adamantly opposed to the construction of this station for a number of religious and environmental reasons. Tibetans regard the lake as a sacred place, which would be desecrated by the construction of the power station. The project has serious environmental implications, as the water level will drop considerably each year. The late Panchen Lama managed to suspend the project, but after his death the construction work was resumed and the station is now functioning.

Another example of an imposed development project is the Panam Rural Integrated Development Project. This project aims to boost the grain production of the Panam area in central Tibet. In 1995, the European Union, relying on Chinese sources claiming that the project is to benefit local Tibetans and has the support of NGOs working in the field, was about to provide substantial funds for the project. When subsequent independent research revealed that neither local Tibetans nor NGOs were consulted, the EU (temporarily) suspended its funding proposals. To date the decision is still pending. The same research revealed that Panam has no need for increased grain production, as Panam is already one of Tibet's main 'bread baskets'. This suggests that, contrary to Chinese claims, the extra grain will be transported elsewhere, rather than benefit the local Tibetans. Moreover, local Tibetans have expressed concerns that the project may attract Chinese workers and/or farmers to the region. The Yamdroktso and the Panam Integrated Rural Development Project do not constitute exceptions: rather, they typify the development policy which is imposed by Beijing and which does not take Tibetan views and concerns into account.

In many areas in Tibet, economic development involves the use of forced labor: Tibetans are recruited on a regular basis to perform 'community services', such as constructing roads, government offices or irrigation canals. Generally, failure to show up results in fines or the imposition of extra work quotas. Most of these community services constitute compulsory labor as defined by the International Labour Organization (ILO): 'all work or service which is exacted from any person under the menace of any penalty and for which the said person has not offered himself voluntarily' and clearly do not meet the criteria set by the ILO for 'normal civic duties', in which case 'the members of the said community or their direct representatives shall have the right to be consulted in regard of the need for such services'.[39]

The economic development priorities set by the Third National Forum of Work on Tibet (1994) include irrigation, mining and infrastructure construction projects. Apart from a handful of individuals selected by Beijing, Tibetans have been systematically denied participation in determining these objectives. The fact that Tibetans lack effective political means to set their own economic development priorities as well as have a say in the practical realisation of the priorities set by Beijing, is directly related to their structural lack of political representation.

Progress or Exploitation—

Chinese sources invariably praise development projects in Tibet as selfless attempts by Beijing to modernise poor and 'backward' Tibet. This rhetoric is inspired by socialist ideology, which depicts the socialist paradise as a classless, prosperous, materialist society. Closely related to this theory, is the idea that Tibetan resistance to Chinese rule will disappear once Tibetans are wealthy. Both views reflect the importance of economic progress as legitimization and consolidation of the regime. Before going into the underlying reasons for the Chinese government's emphasis on economic progress in Tibet, it is necessary to examine whether Tibetans have indeed benefited from Chinese development projects and economic liberalisation policies.

During the Great Leap Forward and the Cultural Revolution, when millions of Chinese and Tibetans starved to death, socialist rhetoric on economic progress was blatantly at odds with reality both in China and Tibet. Following the introduction of Deng Xiao Ping's economic liberalisation policies, the Chinese authorities have sought to step up the exploitation of the economic potential of Tibet. All over China, the problem of the growing gap between the poor hinterland and the rich coastal areas is perceived by the Chinese government as a potentially serious source of instability. Tibet is not only a poor hinterland but also a politically sensitive area. Therefore, Beijing has attempted to enhance economic growth in Tibet by encouraging mainland Chinese and foreigners to invest in Tibet and improving the infrastructure in order to facilitate the transportation of natural and human resources. As a result, the overall standard of living has risen sharply, but the new wealth generated by 'market socialism' tends to be distributed among members of the new urban business elite, which is predominantly Chinese.

Transfer of Natural Resources—

The Tibetan plateau contains a wealth of natural resources, including gold, copper, uranium, wood and salt. There is no historical evidence to suggest that the presence of these resources played a major role in Beijing's decision to annex Tibet, but it is interesting to note that Xizang, the Chinese name for Tibet, literally means 'Western Treasure House'. Before it was annexed by China, most of Tibet's resources remained untapped, for technical as well as religious reasons. Since the Chinese take-over, Beijing has undertaken to locate Tibet's natural resources, exploit them and transfer them to China for further processing and marketing.

In many respects, Beijing's mining policies in Tibet are reminiscent of the ways in which European powers used to exploit the natural resources in their colonies in the name of (local) economic development.

In some mines heavy labor is performed exclusively by Tibetans, whereas other mining companies employ a considerable number of Chinese workers. Some mining enterprises in Kham and Amdo are reported to make use of forced or semi-forced labor. In some cases, Tibetan workers are summoned to construct roads connecting these mines to major roads to China. They have to work for a certain number of weeks per year for a negligible salary. Those who do not turn up have to pay a fine or have to work extra shifts. In some areas a 'gold tax' is imposed: locals have to mine a fixed quota of gold a year and sell it at a nominal price to the authorities.[40] If they fail to meet the set quota, they have to pay a fine. In some parts of Tibet, prisoners are forced to work in mines.[41]

The official reason why some mining companies employ Chinese rather than Tibetans is that in some areas there simply are not enough Tibetans who could do the work. In addition, there are reports that in certain types of mines[42], Tibetans are not allowed to work as the resources which are being mined there are very valuable.

Mined resources are transported to mainland China. This is clearly the case in the areas around Lake Kokonor where large scale salt mining takes place. Many truckloads of salt are transported to China on a daily basis. Little research has been done on uranium mining in Tibet as relevant data are not available, but a number of Tibetan refugees have reported that there are uranium mines in Tibet in which all workers are Chinese and where the uranium is transported to China as soon as it has been mined.

Logging takes place on a large scale in many parts of Tibet, notably in the east, and is devastating for the environment. Almost all of this wood is transferred to China. Very little is used for construction work in Tibet.

Stretching the concept of natural resources to include lucrative tourism, it should be noted that the kind of tourism which Beijing promotes in Tibet involves expensive Chinese operated tours and services, tailored to wealthy tourists.[43] Whereas Chinese tourist agencies employ a considerable number of Tibetan drivers, guides and hotel personnel, the main profit goes to these Chinese agencies. This pattern of discouraging and restricting individual tourists has no parallel in China.

Cultural Aspects

Civilising Mission—

Rhetoric on China's 'historical mission'[44] to liberate the Tibetan people from 'dark, medieval feudalism' and 'superstition' and to 'civilise' them can be found in almost any randomly picked Chinese book on Tibetan history. Tibetan rulers are described as merciless cruel exploiters, while the current Chinese authorities are portrayed as the embodiment of civilised, rational and modern rule:

As is well-known, Tibetan feudal serfdom was a reactionary, dark social system characterised by cruelty and brutality.... Following the peaceful liberation of Tibet, the people's government introduced a series of measures to help the Tibetan people in political, economic and cultural spheres and to improve the living standards.... Today the Tibetan people, freed of centuries-old feudal exploitation and oppression as well as of imperialist penetration, are working with renewed vigor for the building of a socialist new Tibet and contributing to the nation-wide effort to modernise China.'[45]

Chinese literature on Tibet tends to present Chinese culture as dominant and modern, while it presents Tibetan culture as peripheral, eccentric and medieval. In Chinese propaganda material, Tibetan Buddhism has often been referred to as 'feudal superstition' and ridiculed as the 'blind faith' of a backward people. China's legal newspaper Fazhi Ribao recently reported that in Tibet: 'Feudal and superstitious activities are rampant.... Shamanist witches dance into frenzies, geomancers search for auspicious locations.'[46] (The perception of religion as a manifestation of 'backwardness' is closely related to Marxist evolutionism, which views history in terms of stages of development towards the 'Socialist Paradise', which is 'prosperous, rational, scientific and atheist.' According to this socialist view, Buddhist devotion is simply a stage in the development of a society:

Religion is an historical phenomena which occurs at certain stages of human society. (...) The conditions for the natural extinction of religion are: the great improvement of social productivity and the abundance of social property, the establishment of high level socialist democracy and great improvement in education, culture, science and technology.'[47]

Beijing derives part of its official legitimacy for its rule over Tibet from its professed 'advanced stage of civilisation.' Its official rhetoric closely resembles the language on the 'sacred trust' principle used in Article 22 of the Covenant of the League of Nations:

The best method of giving practical effect to this principle is that the tutelage of such peoples should be entrusted to advanced nations who by reason of their resources, their experience or their geographical position can best undertake this responsibility (....) [emphasis added]

The PRC claims to 'assist' Tibet, politically, economically and culturally to overcome its 'backwardness'. Chinese literature tends to present China's policies in Tibet as self-sacrificing efforts to help a poor and backward area and protect it from 'western imperialism'.

Chinese rhetoric on education invariably refers to Chinese education as the path towards modernity and socio-economic progress:

'The results [of Chinese education policies] helped free the [Tibetan] people from ignorant and backward conditions created by serfdom, and enabled them to walk along the glorious path of modern civilisation.[48]

The economic counterpart of Beijing's civilising mission is its emphasis on the necessity to recruit technical experts from China in order to advance Tibet materially and build up its socialist market economy.

The Chinese government maintains that the overwhelming majority of Tibetans are grateful to their Chinese 'liberators' who freed them from oppression and lifted them into the 20th century. The Chinese government's technique of discrediting political resistance as a reactionary attempt to re-establish feudal society and as an imperialist threat to Tibetan society, enables Beijing to portray itself as the 'protector' of Tibetan interests against the harmful influences of a "mere handful" of pro-independence activists.

Asymmetrical Cultural Exchange—

Particularly in urban areas of Tibet, Chinese cultural influence is both visible and pervasive. Most young urban Tibetans are able to speak fluent Chinese and tend to adopt various aspects of Chinese culture. In certain parts of the Tibetan Autonomous Prefectures and Counties in, Sichuan, Gansu and Yunnan, Tibetan is no longer the language of communication among Tibetans. Very few Chinese settlers speak Tibetan, even those who were born in Tibet. Most of them continue to live according to the traditions and life-style they brought along from mainland China. They continue to identify with mainland China as their region of origin.

The Sinocization of the Tibetan people and culture is promoted by two types of assimilation: 'informal' assimilation resulting from the mere exposure to Chinese influence and institutionalised 'formal' assimilation resulting from explicit attempts by the Chinese authorities to assimilate the Tibetan people. The distinction between these two types is not always clear, as one could argue that 'informal' assimilation results from a deliberate absence of policies aimed at preserving the distinct Tibetan cultural identity.

As far as 'informal' assimilation is concerned, in most urban parts of Tibet, a considerable degree of assimilation has taken place. Generally speaking, the Chinese influence in the Autonomous Prefectures, most of which fell under Chinese control several years before the Autonomous Region, tends to be stronger than in most parts of the TAR. One of the reasons for this is that the Tibetan areas in Sichuan, Gansu, Yunnan and even Qinghai have become relatively small Tibetan regions in predominantly Chinese provinces, dominated by Chinese. Beijing's economic policy of Reform and Opening Up, its subsequent efforts to attract and facilitate Chinese investment in Tibet and to encourage Chinese migration to Tibet are likely to promote further assimilation. The education system in Tibet tends to reflect Chinese cultural, political and social values. Chinese students at Tibetan schools do not learn

Tibetan and are often placed in separate classes, while Tibetan students learn Chinese either as their first or their second language.

Beijing's educational policies in Tibet have gone through a series of changes. After the Cultural Revolution, during which manifestations of Tibetan cultural traditions were virtually outlawed, Tibetan language education underwent a revival. This revival was mainly a result of Chinese concessions to the late Panchen Lama, who continuously promoted the Tibetan language as the language of education and administration. In July 1988, Tibetan was declared the official language of the TAR. The "Regulations on the Study, Use and Development of the Tibetan Language", which were passed by the local People's Congress in March 1989, stated that "most" lectures in tertiary institutions should "gradually" be in Tibetan and that Tibetans must speak in Tibetan at important meetings, that official documents and signs should be written in Tibetan and Chinese, and that proficiency in Tibetan should be one of the qualifications for government employment.[49] This latter criterion is interesting, as its implementation would have amounted to the exclusion of Chinese from government posts in Tibet, as the number of Chinese who are fluent in Tibetan is negligible. Since the late Panchen Lama's death in 1989, the political mood has changed considerably.

Chinese rhetoric on education in Tibet reflects a return to the primacy of politics over education standards. Most of the measures promoting the Tibetan language have now been reversed. Except for some 40 special schools in Qinghai province, Tibetan is only taught for a few hours a week at secondary schools in Tibet, while all other subjects are taught in Chinese. Four Tibetan-medium secondary school classes, initiated by the late Panchen Lama in 1989 in three secondary schools in central Tibet, have now been dissolved, although they were extremely popular and successful. As most Tibetan children attend Tibetan medium primary schools, they score well below national averages at Chinese medium secondary schools and the drop-out rate among Tibetan students is high. Proficiency in the Tibetan language has little practical use except for those who wish to become teachers of Tibetan.

Therefore, more and more Tibetan parents encourage their children to concentrate on Chinese from an early age. The top 1,600 children aged 12 or 13 are selected each year to attend secondary schools in mainland China.[50] Many parents do whatever they can to have their children selected, believing that assimilation is the only key to a successful career.[51] At university level, a similar trend towards abolishing Tibetan language education is taking place. The original objectives of the University of Tibet in Lhasa, which was founded in 1985, was to provide training for both Tibetan and Chinese cadres who would advance Tibet's economic development. In the early years of the existence of the University of Tibet, which offered a number of classes in Tibetan language and art[52], Tibetan cultural aspirations played an important role. By now only one of the university's 17 courses is taught in Tibetan. The previous head of the University, who maintained that 'the ultimate goal [of the University] is the establishment of the centre of Tibetan culture in China', was recently replaced by a Chinese official who does not even speak Tibetan.

The fact that both at schools and within the administration, the Tibetan language promotion campaign of the mid-eighties has been substituted by policies affirming Chinese as the language of administration and communication, has raised concern among Tibetans.

"Without educated people in all fields, expressing themselves in their own language, Tibetans are in danger of being assimilated. We have reached a crucial point," one leading Tibetan intellectual told the South China Morning Post in 1992. "All hope in our future, all protection of our heritage depends on this."[53]

D. MAINTENANCE OF AUTHORITY

Restrictions on individual rights in colonial situations cannot be seen in isolation, but are part of a system of collective control and maintenance of colonial rule in the face of opposition. Cause and effect are closely intertwined and form a vicious circle: most restrictions are attempts to stifle protest movements and often spark off more resistance. In the case of Tibet, restrictions imposed on the rights and freedoms of individual Tibetans are inspired by Beijing's attempts to stifle and root out Tibetan nationalism. But these very restrictions often fuel the resistance to Chinese rule and the independence movement. In order to maximize its control over Tibet, Beijing cautiously combines severe restrictions on civil and political rights with selective concessions in other areas. The following sections will give an overview of the various methods employed to achieve this aim.

Curtailment of Civil / Political Rights

The Chinese Constitution and Criminal Procedure laws provide for a wide range of civil and political rights, including the right to freedom of expression, peaceful assembly, the right not to be tortured or ill-treated as well as the freedom of religious belief.[54] The wording of these provisions, however, tends to be vague and subject to serious restrictions, especially when the security of the state is deemed to be at stake. Both in China and Tibet, civil and political rights are systematically curtailed and violated. In mainland China, Beijing's human rights policies and practices often respond to challenges to the monopoly of power by the Communist Party. In Tibet, Chinese human rights policies respond to a different type of challenge: Tibetan protest seldom targets specific aspects of the Party or of Chinese rule, but generally rejects this rule altogether. Tibetan independence demonstrations are seen by the Chinese authorities as an attack on the Chinese state itself. The Chinese authorities at times regard Tibetan resistance as a more grave threat and affront to the system than Chinese dissent, which by its very nature is at least not anti-Chinese.

Religious Policies

Beijing's religious policies in Tibet show parallels to the attempts by some of the European colonial powers to convert their colonial subjects in order to consolidate their power. (See Part 1) Conversion amounts to substituting a certain belief system by another one. Similarly, Beijing's attempts to replace the Buddhist belief system by an atheist, socialist frame of reference constitutes a form of conversion. Realising that Buddhism is the organizing principle of Tibetan society and a vehicle of Tibetan nationalism, Beijing has systematically attempted to substitute Tibetan Buddhism by a state-controlled surrogate version of Buddhism referred to in Chinese propaganda as 'normal', i.e. patriotic, religious practice.

Beijing's policies on religion have gone through a series of changes. During the '60s and '70s, Buddhist practice was outlawed. Most Tibetan temples and monasteries were destroyed in the 1950s and early 1960s while the remaining ones were destroyed during the Cultural Revolution. Since the early 1980s, a number of monasteries and temples, including Sera, Ganden, Drepung and Tashi Lhungpo, began rebuilding, and greater religious freedom and tolerance was permitted. Pictures of the present (14th) Dalai Lama re-appeared in monasteries and private houses and for several years it was possible for Tibetans to worship the Dalai Lama as their religious leader as long as they did not openly support the political struggle which he represents. During the mid- and late 1980s, thousands of monasteries, temples and religious sites were being rebuilt by local villagers, with or without permission by the relevant government agencies which have tried to carefully manage and oversee the post Cultural Revolution religious opening.[55]

Analogous to its treatment of Tibetan party members and high government officials, the Chinese authorities treated the Tibetan religious 'upper strata'[56] with great circumspection, hoping they could co-opt these leaders and use them as intermediaries between Beijing's policy makers and the Tibetan people.[57] In his speech at the 1990 Work Conference of religion, CCP Secretary and PRC President Jiang Zemin stated:

> Senior figures in the religious sector have a certain influence among the masses of believers, so it is of great importance to do our work with them properly.[58]

Jiang's 1990 speech reflected Beijing's attempt to maintain stability and control by allowing a limited amount of freedom of religion:

> We must make it clear that Communist Party members are atheists, and that this does not in any way contravene the policy of religious freedom. We ought to step up education. However, we cannot interfere willy-nilly, if the masses believe in religion. If we do, it would be very easy to harm the party's relationship with the masses of believers, and harm stability and unity.[59]

Since the Third National Forum of Work on Tibet in July 1994, Beijing's policy on religion has undergone yet another clear shift.[60] Whereas the aim of maintaining 'unity and stability' has remained the same, political strategies now include active, hands-on management of monasteries by government or Party authorities, "intense re-education" of monks and nuns, and campaigns to root out support for the Dalai Lama. During the Third National Forum it was decided that the policy of allowing a limited degree of religious support for the Dalai Lama would be abandoned. Whereas earlier campaigns had targeted the 'Dalai clique', rather than the Tibetan leader himself, the Third Forum signified a shift towards direct personal attacks on the 'Dalai' himself:

> Although sometimes the Dalai speaks softly and says nice things to deceive the masses, he has never ceased his splittist activities. Even up to today he has never changed his standpoint of trying to gain Tibet's independence. We must always have a clear view of Dalai and reveal his double-faced true colour as much as possible. The focal point in our region's fight to oppose splittism is to oppose the Dalai clique. As the saying goes, to kill off a serpent, we must first cut off its head. If we don't do that, we cannot succeed in the struggle against splittism.[61]

The Chinese government justifies its current attack on the Dalai Lama by discrediting him as a religious leader and portraying him as a threat to Buddhism itself. The fact that the inherently atheist Chinese government has appointed itself the role of the very 'protector of Buddhism' manifests a significant technique of political control: instead of prohibiting religion altogether, Beijing tries to 'appropriate' Tibetan Buddhism by divesting it of its essence and replacing it with so-called 'normal' religion. This 'normal' religion is state-controlled, and 'patriotic.'[62] 'Normal' religious activities exclude worshipping the Dalai Lama and involves 'love for the great motherland':

> Religion has a wide-spread influence in Tibet. Our Party's external policy is freedom of religious belief, and protects the normal religious order. The State has invested substantially on the reconstruction of temples and supports the normal religious activities, while at the same time administrating temples in accordance with the law to prevent any manipulation to engage in any activities that are harmful to the interests of the public and the government. At present, the majority of monks and nuns in the region are law-abiding and patriotic religious devotees, but there are still some thoroughly convinced followers of the counterrevolutionary Dalai clique.[63] [emphasis added]

Beijing's reaction to the events leading up to and following the identification of the 10th Panchen Lama is another clear example of this technique of appropriation and subsequent control. The 10th Panchen Lama was the most important religious leader in Tibet after the Dalai Lama's flight to India in 1959. After the death of the 10th Panchen Lama in 1989, the Chinese government declared that Beijing would be in charge of finding the 11th Panchen Lama, and appointed a committee to search for the new incarnation. However, when the Dalai Lama announced in May 1995 that, according to religious practice, he had recognized the reincarnation of the 10th Panchen Lama from the candidates presented to him by the search committee, the Chinese government declared the Dalai Lama's pronouncement 'null and void' and prohibited Tibetans from worshipping the 6-year-old boy identified by the Dalai Lama as the 11th Panchen Lama[64] In November, the Chinese government announced that it had recognized another 6-year-old boy as the 11th Panchen Lama. The Panchen Lama recognized by the Dalai Lama was kept in detention and Chadrel Rinpoche, the Lama who headed the search committee, was arrested. The authorities went to great lengths to have an enthronement ceremony which, to all outward appearances, looked like a traditional ceremony but which was perceived by Tibetans as ridiculing Buddhism and Buddhist rituals.

The anti Dalai Lama campaign and the Chinese government's orchestration of the search for and enthronement of the 11th Panchen Lama are closely related developments which share an important common element: the Chinese government claims that it is protecting the religious interests of the Tibetans. In December 1995, China's official daily newspaper Xinhua News Agency noted:

> If [the Dalai Lama's] words are followed, Tibetan Buddhism will be led on a path of going against the interests of the people.[65]

At the same time, Beijing denies the Tibetan people any say in determining the actual contents of these religious interests. This policy is not an end in itself but a method of gaining and maintaining control over the central belief system of the Tibetan people. Until now Chinese policies on religious practice appear to have had little effect on the Tibetan people, who continue to practice religion on their own terms. The pressure on monasteries and nunneries to adopt 'normal' religion has been strong. Those resisting this pressure are frequently expelled from the institution, or if the resistance is too openly articulated, they face arrest and risk long prison sentences. In spite of these harsh punishments, resistance has been continuous and widespread.

Political Aspects

The Chinese government attempts to combine the nominal maintenance of Tibetan 'autonomous' government bodies with a strong central state structure. Tibet's formal autonomous status within the PRC has confronted Beijing with a serious dilemma: on the one hand, Beijing is not prepared to grant Tibet real autonomy as it fears it will lose its grip on the politically sensitive region. However, the complete denial of autonomy would be an embarrassment to the Chinese leadership, as it would obviously and visibly violate Chinese legal provisions on Tibetan autonomy. Moreover, it could be a source of further social and political instability among Tibetans and fuel pro-independence sentiments.

For many years, the Chinese authorities have attempted to create a group of 'loyal' Tibetan cadres and government officials who could bridge the gap between the Central government and the Tibetan people and provide a 'Tibetan face' on Beijing's policies. This is similar to methods employed by a number of European colonial powers. The Chinese government hoped that these 'hand-picked'[66] Tibetans would give up their pro-independence aspirations for positions of relative power and wealth. For a long time high ranking Tibetan government officials and party members were invariably portrayed as 'patriotic' and dissidents among them were seldom publicly punished. A former TAR government official and CCP member, who escaped to India in 1993, recounted the following experience:

> In 1983 the authorities started to suspect that I was taking part in pro-independence activities. [...] I was interrogated for 13 days without being beaten. [...] They told me: 'If you tell the truth we will reward you with money and you will be promoted.' I saw that they had brought torture equipment, but they didn't use it. They were very polite and said: 'Even Party members make mistakes. As long as you confess and repent, you don't need to worry.' After 5 days they got angry and shouted: 'We have tried to reform you because we think you are a promising man. You could have a bright future. You could have a top position in the TAR government.' They did not hurt me. It would have been a disgrace to the party to torture me. Finally I was released. I was quietly removed from the party and sent on 'early retirement.[67]

Recently the Chinese authorities have started to replace many high-ranking Tibetans by Chinese[68] as their strategy of instituting indirect rule appears to have failed. This shift manifested itself clearly in the decisions taken at the Third National Forum of Work on Tibet in July 1994, during which Beijing launched a campaign which aimed at 'purifying the cadre contingent'. By now, those cadres who 'did not have a firm standpoint' have been side-lined or dismissed.

Maintenance of Authority by Economic Means

Internal CCP documents suggest that economic development in Tibet is not only motivated by Beijing's wish to diminish the gap between its newly industrialised rich provinces and the poor hinterland, but also by it's attempt to break Tibetan resistance and eliminate support for 'splittism'. "Beijing is attempting to accomplish with wealth what force failed to do: undermine the independence movement and integrate long-rebellious Tibet," according to the Wall Street Journal which recently ran a front page story on the this theme[69]. In a speech at the 6th TAR Regional CCP

Congress, Chen Kuiyuan, the Secretary of the TAR branch of the CCP, stated:

> Our Central Party stands firmly by the guidelines given by comrade Deng Xiao Ping, to pay attention to 'grasping with two hands'. Both hands must be tough; while successfully handling the economy, the Party must also settle some big political waves. ... Thus we are not only able to competently raise the speed of economic growth but also fight effectively against the hostile power in the political dimension.[70]

Economic development policies in Tibet are both economically and politically motivated. Its political purpose is to strengthen Chinese rule in a politically sensitive region. The Chinese leadership appears to believe that the Tibetan demand for religious freedom and political independence will diminish as a result of an increased standard of living. According to Chen Kuiyuan:

> The fundamental interests of the Tibetan people are increasing development and maintaining stability. As communists are representatives of [the] Tibetan people's fundamental interests, the starting point and the end-result of all our work is to make the Tibetan people prosperous and help them thrive as soon as possible, so that they will live and work in peace and contentment. (...) While people continue not to clearly see their own fundamental interests, blind religious belief is unavoidable. (...) Communists should intensify the work of educating and guiding the people, so that they will become prosperous as soon a possible. People in richer areas usually do not take a great interest in religions, whereas the poorer people are, the stronger their enthusiasm for religions. Party and government leaders at all levels should pay attention and importance to this point.[71]

More than anything else, economic development provides the Chinese leadership with legitimization of Chinese rule over Tibet. Significantly, during the recent 1996 re-education campaigns, the monks at Sera Monastery were taken on visits to the Military Hospital in Lhasa, the restoration work at the Potala Palace, and the Traditional Tibetan Hospital, in order to illustrate the benefits of Chinese rule. The monks were later taken on a tour of modernization projects in Lhasa.

Economic development being one of Beijing's main legitimization devices for it rule in Tibet, demonstrations against price-rises, increased medical and tuition fees and taxes are in certain respects more threatening to the Chinese leadership than outright pro-independence demonstrations: they constitute a direct challenge to the Central Government's claim that Chinese rule has brought prosperity and development to Tibet.

Military Presence

A large contingent of the Chinese People's Liberation Army (PLA) troops is stationed in Tibet. The total number of PLA soldiers stationed in the TAR is difficult to establish with certainty, and estimates range from 40,000 to 200,000.[72] The overwhelming majority of PLA soldiers are Chinese from all over China. The official rationale for this heavy and permanent army presence is the defence of the international borders with India, Nepal, and Pakistan. But the heavy army presence also appears to reflect Beijing's concern with the potential for social and political unrest in Tibet. On sensitive dates, such as the anniversaries of major Tibetan demonstrations or uprisings as well as on Chinese national holidays, army presence tends to be particularly heavy.

The PLA functions mainly as a deterrent, the visible manifestation of China's authority in Tibet. As such, it performs important symbolic tasks, such as marching through the capital Lhasa on the anniversary of the foundation of the People's Republic of China. During the last few years, the presence of the PLA has become more inconspicuous, reflecting Beijing's shift in policy towards using more refined measures of control through the police and an inconspicuous network of informers. The PLA in Tibet is no longer directly in charge of suppressing Tibetan resistance. Ordinary policemen, the majority of whom are Tibetans, are responsible for identifying and dealing with individual cases of political opposition to Chinese rule. The People's Armed Police, which consists mainly of Chinese, is responsible for quelling mass demonstrations and using force where necessary.

Education / Language Policies

The 1990s have seen a regression with respect to the use of the Tibetan language at schools and universities as well as in the administration as compared to the 1980s.

One reason given for the decreased use of Tibetan as the language of education and administration is simply practical one. It is much easier and cheaper for the authorities to use existing Chinese school material than to have to produce Tibetan materials. The same goes for official documents: it is time consuming and expensive to translate documents. The Chinese authorities increasingly appear to be unwilling to invest time and money into providing Tibetan language education materials and official documents.

But, the decline in the use of Tibetan appears to be politically motivated. The Tibetan language is seen by some leaders as the proper target of both the current campaign against the pro-independence movement and the nation wide campaign to eradicate traditional beliefs. In October 1995 Communist Party leaders in the Tibet Autonomous Region are said to have circulated a document arguing that separatism was partly caused by schools teaching too much religion and using the Tibetan language.[73]

Beijing's rhetoric on education in Tibet has always reflected a concern with losing political control over the interaction process between teachers and their pupils. Teachers suspected of arousing pro-independence sentiments among their students have been systematically removed from their posts or detained and sentenced[74]. After the relatively liberal period from the mid 1980s to the early 1990s, education in Tibet has once again become more politicised. Current Chinese rhetoric on education bears some resemblance to the extreme language of the Cultural Revolution:

The success of our education does not lie in the number of diplomas issued to graduates from universities, colleges, poly-technical schools and middle schools. It lies, in the final analysis, in whether our graduating students are opposed to or turn their hearts to the Dalai clique and in whether they are loyal to or do not care about our great motherland and the great socialist cause. This is the most salient and the most important criterion for assessing right and wrong, and the contributions and mistakes of our educational work in Tibet. To successfully solve the problem, we must improve political and ideological work at schools and have political and ideological work run through all the teaching, study and work at schools.[75]

Population Transfer

The early influx of Chinese settlers during the process of establishing Chinese control over Tibet, should be distinguished from Beijing's more recent policy of population transfer. Beijing's current policy of population transfer in Tibet is a means of conquering a territory which has consistently opposed Chinese rule, by demographic rather than military means.

Beijing's methods of population transfer to Tibet have varied from forced resettlement, to active encouragement of Chinese citizens to settle in Tibet, to a passive laissez-faire policy towards spontaneous Chinese migration to Tibet. The following section will give an overview of these methods:

Forced Resettlement

All over the People's Republic of China forced resettlement of large groups of people to sparsely populated regions has taken place, notably during the 'rustication' (Chinese: Xiafang) programme during the 1950s. Tibet being one of the most sparsely populated areas under Chinese control, Tibet saw a large influx of Chinese during the early years of the PRC. New Chinese towns were created in Tibet, such as Bayi in the TAR and Golmud and Xining in Qinghai. [76] Many Chinese were transferred to the Xining area to build agricultural communes and most of them settled down permanently. Moreover, millions of Chinese prisoners were transferred to prison labor camps in North East Tibet, referred to as Qinghai.Many of these prisoners were forced to settle in this area after their release or simply had nowhere else to go.

Forced resettlement of the type described in the preceding paragraph, is largely a phenomenon of the past. However, another type of forced resettlement still exists.

Chinese Communist Party cadre and government officials who are transferred to Tibet often have no other option than to move to this high and remote area. Refusal to go and work in Tibet may result in disciplinary measures, such as demotion or dismissal.

Active Encouragement

Chinese migration to Tibet has been actively encouraged by the Chinese leadership, in order to accelerate the economic development and to consolidate Chinese control over Tibet. In August, 1994 Chen Kuiyuan, the Secretary of the TAR branch of the Chinese Communist Party (CCP) said that "to accelerate Tibet's development, (...) we (...) open our job market to all fellow countrymen.' Furthermore, he said:

> All localities should have an open mind, and welcome the opening of various restaurants and stores by people from the hinterland. They should not be afraid that people from the hinterland are taking their money or jobs away."[77]

Beijing's strategic attempts to employ 'loyal' Tibetans as government officials, both in the TAR and the remaining Tibetan areas, has failed and their positions are being filled with Chinese cadres. In February 1994, Xinhua , the official Chinese News Agency, reported that 1000 'outstanding leading officials and technicians' would be sent to the TAR 'to help boost the local economy and promote social progress'.(Decisions of this kind have repeatedly been announced and carried out since the early 1980s.)

Other examples of active encouragement of Chinese to settle permanently in Tibet include the policy to encourage PLA soldiers to settle in Tibet after their military service is over and engage in civil professions.[78]

Since Lhasa was given the status of a 'Special Economic Zone' within the PRC, Beijing has stepped up its earlier policies of offering financial incentives to Chinese entrepreneurs who set up businesses in Tibet. In 1992, the TAR Government issued a document entitled 'Certain Regulations on Encouraging Businessmen from Home [i.e. mainland China] and Abroad to invest in Tibet.' These regulations included the following incentives:

> For productive enterprises set up by businessmen from outside of the region, the incomes from their production and operation are exempted from local income tax. (...) Investment projects in tourism worth over US $5 million that last more than ten years are exempted from income taxes during their first three profit making years, and are required to pay only half of their income taxes in their fourth profit-making years. Businessmen who invest in Tibet may hire technicians and management personnel from outside the region and

these personnel may apply for multiple entry-exit permits.[79]

In addition to financial incentives, Chinese living in Tibet are sometimes exempted from the strict one child policies in force in mainland China.[80] Moreover, many Chinese recruited for specific development projects receive considerable hardship allowances in addition to housing and free education for their children. These policies and practices are referred to in numerous regulations and publications but nowhere are they more succinctly stated than in Poverty of Plenty, originally commissioned as an official report, and subsequently translated into English in book form:

> The personnel thus brought in from developed regions cannot be expected to live on the local fare of tsampa (roasted barely flour) and raw meat. They need good housing, hospitals, cinemas and schools for their children. Hence, in order to make use of the initial equipment [from developed areas], new personnel and machinery have to be continuously brought in, which in turn require the successive construction of buildings and other facilities.[81]

Laissez-Faire Policy

As a result of relaxation on the restrictions on movement, lack of economic opportunities at home and improved roads into Tibet[82], many more Hui Muslims and Chinese have migrated to Tibet, setting up petty business and semi-skilled service industries, such as bicycle repair, hairdressing, restaurants and hotels.

After the institution of Deng Xiao Ping's policy of Reform and Opening Up, a number of administrative measures controlling individual freedom of movement have been revoked in order to facilitate the emergence of a free market economy.[83] As a result of this relaxation, it became much easier for Chinese people to migrate to Tibet and start private businesses. Moreover, many existing roads into and within Tibet were improved and new roads were built. The road construction projects have attracted many (mostly unskilled) Chinese laborers from neighboring, overpopulated Sichuan Province and has facilitated the influx of Chinese migrants.

The overwhelming majority of those currently arriving in Tibet are part of the so-called 'floating population'. The introduction of mechanised farming in mainland China produced a large surplus rural labor force. Since the partial lifting of the restrictions on the freedom of movement, these surplus rural laborers have drifted to cities in search of work. In mainland China the Central Government has issued national guidelines in order to regulate and reduce this 'wild' migration to urban areas because of its potentially destabilizing impact. In Beijing rural migrants had to start paying large sums of money as 'city accommodation fees' in order to be allowed to stay in the city. In Tibet, which is classified as a 'rural' area, migration has not been restricted. The majority of the 'floating population' migrating to Tibet consists of small entrepreneurs, traders and unskilled workers. At present, there are few Chinese farmers in the TAR,(as opposed to Eastern Turkestan , where many Chinese farmers have settled), but this may change as a result of current agricultural developments. These types of projects initially attract a large number of Chinese workers and may in future attract Chinese farmers in search of arable land.

After 'liberating' Tibet, the PLA has played an important role in the colonization of Tibet. Not only does the army regularly take part in infrastructure building activities, agriculture[84] and industrial production, but it has also attracted many entrepreneurs who set up entertainment businesses catering to the army. Prostitution, which is officially illegal in the People's Republic of China, is rampant near army bases in Tibet, including in many cities such as Lhasa. A significant number of those running and working in the entertainment industry in Tibet are Chinese migrants from Sichuan.[85]

Forced resettlement, active encouragement and a passive laissez-faire policy are the three methods employed by Beijing to carry out what it has significantly called 'the final solution for Tibet'.[86] If implemented fully, this 'final solution' will complete the colonization process which started in the early 1950s and render the sinocization of Tibet irreversible. In Chinese controlled Mongolia (so called "Inner Mongolia"), this policy has already been "successfully" implemented: at present the ethnic Mongolian population constitutes less than 2% of the population of the area and has largely lost its distinct cultural identity. Another parallel could be drawn to the so-called 'white colonies' of European powers, in which the colonization process at some stage passed the point of no return and the original inhabitants have been reduced to negligible minorities.

E. PERCEPTIONS

There is no doubt that Tibetans, even those who accept the Chinese claims, experience Chinese rule over Tibet as 'alien'. In 1988 a by now well-known group of monks from Drepung Monastery issued a manifesto entitled The Precious Democratic Constitution of Tibet The manifesto, which describes the group's hopes for a future society based on a constitution guaranteeing democracy and human rights, states:

> If Tibetans continue to struggle with a courageous determination based on the force of established truth, we will not always have to remain under the foreign Chinese invaders.' [emphasis added][87]

The distinctness of the Tibetan culture and history was consistently recognized internationally. Thus, the UN General Assembly passed resolutions in 1959, 1961 and 1965 which expressly referred to the distinct culture and religion of the Tibetan people.[88] More recently, in 1991, the UN Subcommission on the Prevention of Discrimination and Protection of Minorities also adopted a resolution on "the situation in Tibet" in which it referred to the 'distinct cultural, religious and national identity of the Tibetan people'[89]

The fact that Tibetans perceive Chinese rule as 'alien', is based on a number of objective and subjective factors. The most important objective factor is that Tibetans are culturally and ethnically distinct from the Chinese. The Chinese and Tibetan languages are entirely different. At present Tibetans use a number of Chinese loan words, but the Tibetan language itself has nothing in common with Chinese. The Tibetan language is part of the Tibeto-Burmese language group, while the Tibetan script is based on Sanskrit. Tibetan Buddhism, which is one of the most essential elements of the Tibetan cultural identity and constitutes the central value system of the Tibetan people, is radically at odds with the atheism preached by the current Chinese leadership. Tibetan culture and its visible manifestations, such as architecture and clothing are distinctly different from their Chinese counterparts. Moreover, the physical features of the Tibetans are different from those of the Chinese.

Even more important than the aforementioned objective factors is the subjective perception of alien-ness. Neither the Tibetans nor the Chinese consider themselves as belonging to the same race or people. Interestingly, Dr Sun Yat-sen, the founder of the Chinese Republic, referred to Tibetans as belonging to the 'alien races'.[90] Most Chinese today would still agree with this observation. The overwhelming majority of Chinese living in Tibet retain their Chinese identity and their sense of being culturally and ethnically different from Tibetans. The amount of inter-marriage is marginal, even among Chinese who have lived in Tibet for a number of decades. In most Tibetan cities and towns, Chinese and Tibetan inhabitants live in separate quarters. The fact that Tibet is administered as a separate territory within the People's Republic of China reflects that Beijing regards it as distinct from its Chinese provinces. Tibet is the only 'autonomous' region within the current People's Republic of China with which Beijing concluded a treaty.

Tibetan resentment against alien policies imposed by the Chinese manifests itself in various ways. Pro-independence protest is the most obvious manifestation of this resentment, but by no means the only one. Many cases of economically motivated protest are fuelled by the same resentment and are increasingly interpreted by Beijing as a political threat. Mao Zedong's distinction between so-called 'antagonistic offenses against the people' and 'non-antagonistic contradictions' within the people,[91] appears to have become blurred. Traditionally, repressive policies were merely applied to the first category, whereas the latter 'offenses' were to be resolved by discussion and education. Over the past few years however, a number of essentially 'non-antagonistic contradictions', such as protest against tax increases or price rises, have been referred to in Chinese sources as 'hot topics' susceptible to 'manipulation' by political dissidents:

> Exploiting 'hot topics' in society, [the 'Dalai clique and 'international hostile forces'] incite the masses, sow dissension among various nationalities and create incidents in an attempt to undermine political stability and unity and to interfere with reform, opening up to the outside world and economic construction.[92]

This interpretation is reinforced by the fact that a considerable number of non-political, socio-economic demonstrations in Tibet manifest strong pro-independence undercurrents. This is related to the fact that Tibetans perceive Chinese policies as 'alien'. Social and economic dissatisfaction tends to be fuelled by general resentment against alien Chinese rule.

F. OUTCOME OF THE COLONIZATION PROCESS

Since the Chinese invasion, Chinese control over Tibet has steadily intensified. Until now Chinese influence has tended to be strong in low altitude, easily accessible, mostly urban areas, while it is absent in high altitude and remote places. Most European colonies showed this same pattern. For example, Many parts of what later became Indonesia never came directly under Dutch control, which was concentrated on the island Java. Similarly, many parts of India were never effectively controlled by Britain.

At present, parts of Tibet resemble settlement colonies and parts of it resemble non-settlement, or 'exploitation' colonies. In most parts of Amdo and Kham, Chinese settlers outnumber Tibetans. In these areas, colonization appears to be irreversible. The Tibet Autonomous Region shows characteristics of the 'hybrid' type of colony discussed in Part I. It bears some resemblance to Algeria during French colonial rule: a large and influential settler community in a colonised society which has retained a strong sense of distinct cultural and ethnic identity. Unlike the colonization process in the Americas, Australia and New Zealand, the colonization of Algeria was not irreversible. Like the French in Algeria, the Chinese maintain that Tibet constitutes an integral part of its territory. Where Tibet differs from the settlement colonies described in Chapter 1 is that the Chinese settlers in Tibet do not cease to identify with Beijing as their capital and metropolitan China as their state.

The colonization process in Tibet has not yet been concluded and continues to penetrate into areas of the Tibetan plateau which so far have remained more or less unaffected by Chinese rule. This increased accessibility of these areas resulting from the construction of a number of airports and major roads may well accelerate this development. 'Floating' Chinese migrants are now able to enter Tibet relatively easily. If this migration process continues at the current rate, the colonization process will become irreversible all over Tibet and its distinct cultural and ethnic identity will be permanently replaced by the identity imported by Chinese settlers.

PART III: CONCLUSIONS

The analysis of the meaning of colonialism and the development of the characteristics of or criteria for colonialism contained in Part I of this study allow us to ascertain whether Chinese rule over Tibet is indeed a form of colonial rule. The fact that the government of the Peoples Republic of China itself does not recognize Tibet to be a colony is not relevant to the issue of whether Tibet is de facto a colony of China. It is the substance of the Chinese rule and of relations between Tibet and China which is relevant.

The distinctiveness of the Tibetan territory and of its people from China and the Chinese people is not seriously contested. Scholars and many other authors from Tibet, China and other countries have written volumes about the distinct racial, ethnic, linguistic, cultural and historic identity of the Tibetan people. The Tibetan landmass, the Tibetan plateau, is geographically distinct from China, and its unique physical characteristics has kept the land and people of Tibet entirely separate from the land and people of China and those of other countries for centuries. This is not to say that there were no political contacts, wars, conquests or periods of close interaction with Tibet's neighbours, including the Chinese. But the two entities and peoples remained separate and distinct throughout. This is the reason that to this day, both the Chinese and the Tibetans regard each other as "foreign" or "alien" peoples. The Chinese authorities and many of the Chinese people may consider that Tibet "belongs to" China, i.e. is a possession of China. Hence the many Chinese publications entitled "China's Tibet." But this is perceived by both sides as the possession by one controlling and more powerful entity and people of the territory of a relatively weaker entity and people that is and remains distinct.

The present rule over Tibet was established in the way most colonial powers establish control: by military action and by a treaty which bears all the characteristics of an "unequal treaty."

The administration of Tibet has all the characteristics of a colonial administration. The Tibetan people's participation in government is little else than a "rubber-stamp" function, with all real decision-making and executive authority exercised by the Chinese, particularly through the Communist Party and the army. The most senior Tibetans in the Chinese government hierarchy (for example Ngapo Ngawang Jigme), are former aristocrats who have been co-opted, as was the case in most European owned colonies. But despite trying to give a semblance of autonomy, China mostly governs Tibet by direct, as opposed to indirect, rule.

Characteristic also of colonial relationships, China uses Tibet's economic "backwardness," and at times also its alleged social and cultural "backwardness" to legitimise its rule over that country. It develops the region by bringing in skilled labor from China and exploiting natural resources and undertaking industrial projects or "development" projects that are primarily beneficial to China or to

Chinese settlers in Tibet. This too, is typical of exploitation colonialism.

One of the serious charges levied against China is that it is carrying out a population transfer policy which has the effect of reducing Tibetans to a minority in their own land.

The movement of settlers to a colony from the metropolitan state is a central element of colonialism. For this element to exist it is not necessary that the migration occur as a result of a forced transfer or even a determined and consistent policy. The movement of Chinese from their homes in China to Tibet has taken place and is continuing at this time at a scale almost reminiscent of the settlement colonies.

As more settlers move in, the pressure on Tibetans to assimilate increases. At the same time, the Chinese authorities are once again repressing the use of the Tibetan language and other expressions of Tibetan national identity, including, in particular, religion. The Chinese language clearly dominates, and the education system is designed to further strengthen this trend.

As resistance to these policies and to what Tibetans perceive as alien rule increases, it is met by suppression of human rights and political freedoms. The military and armed police presence is there to remind the population of who is in control. Once again in characteristic colonial fashion, the officer corps of the army is controlled by the Chinese, while Tibetans serve primarily in police ranks or hold low status army jobs.

Tibet has the characteristics of exploitation colonies and also some characteristics of settlement colonies. In fact, it could be best characterised as a mixed, hybrid-type colony.

Tibet was not included on the United Nation's list of Non-Self-Governing Territories, which was designed for the decolonization of territories colonised by European and other Western states. But when one compares the situation of Tibet with that of settlement colonies and exploitation colonies, including those who were put on the UN list, the resemblances are striking.

Despite China's insistence that Tibet is an integral and inalienable part of China, the study which we have undertaken shows that at least de facto Tibet must indeed be regarded as a colony of China.

NOTES

PREFACE

1. Speech by Chinese Communist Party Secretary of the Tibet Autonomous Region (TAR) Chen Kuiyan during the 4th Plenary Session of the 6th TAR Regional Congress on 14 May 1996.
2. H.H. The Dalai Lama, Speech at the European Parliament, Strasbourg, 23 October 1996.

TIBET MISSION

1. In the Chinese Provinces Qinghai, Gansu, Sichuan and Yunnan, there are 11 Tibetan Autonomous Prefectures, consisting of a large number of counties and 3 Tibetan Autonomous Counties (including Xining City). The Autonomous Prefectures are: Dechen (Yunnan), Kartse (Sichuan), Ngaba (Sichuan), Kanlho (Gansu), Haidong (Qinghai), Tsojang (Qinghai), Tsolho (Qinghai), Malho (Qinghai),Tsolho (Qinghai), Malho (Qinghai), Golog (Qinghai), Yushu (Qinghai), Tsonub (Qinghai). In addition there are three Tibetan Autonomous Counties which are not part of a larger Tibetan Autonomous Prefecture: Mili (Sichuan), Pari (Gansu) and Xining City/County (Qinghai).
2. *China Daily*, Monday 21 April, p. 4.
3. *Potala,* New Star Publishers, Beijing, 1991, p. 6.
4. *Potala,* New Star Publishers, Beijing, 1991, p. 17.
5. It should be noted that it is often hard to establish whether assimilation is intentional or unintentional.
6. Speech by TAR Party Secretary Chen Kuiyuan during the 4th Plenary Session of the 6th TAR Regional Congress on 14 May 1996.
7. *New Majority, Chinese Population Transfer into Tibet,* published by Tibet Support Group UK, London Printing Press, London 1995, p157 and 159.
8. *i.e.* the Tibet Autonomous Region and all Tibetan Autonomous Prefectures and Counties.

INDEPENDENT STUDY ON COLONIALISM AND TIBET

PART I

1. Some writers use the term 'non-settlement' rather than 'exploitation' colonies. The term 'non-settlement colonies' seems to be somewhat misleading, as all forms of colonialism involve settlement. Therefore, this report will use the term 'exploitation' colonies'.
2. Interestingly, these 'settlement colonies' have never been recognized as colonies within international fora, such as the League of Nations and the United Nations. Within non-governmental fora, on the other hand, the permanent settlement of 'foreigners' has clearly been recognized as a form of colonialism. E.g. the Preamble of the Resolution on Imperialism and Colonialism which was

adopted at the non-governmental All Africa Peoples' Conference in Accra in 1958 reads: Whereas (...) two groups of Colonial Territories have emerged to exist: 1) Those territories where indigenous Africans are dominated by foreigners who have their seats of authority in foreign lands (...) 2) Those where indigenous Africans are dominated and oppressed by foreigners who have settled permanently in Africa (...). (quoted in 'Apartheid and Colonialism', Robert E. Gorelick, in CILSA (XIX), 1986, p.80.)

3. Some writers refer to these colonies as 'white colonies'.
4. The most well-known example of this type of colony is Australia.
5. See Huttenback, *Racism and Empire, White Settlers and Colored Immigrants in the British Self-Governing Colonies*, 1830 - 1910, (Ithaca, NY: Cornell University Press 1976), Introduction.
6. As land ownership was an unfamiliar concept in most native societies, the term 'expropriation' is rather problematic.
7. In the case of South Africa, the situation was radically different. In spite of heavy oppression, the black majority continued to challenge the 'alien rule' imposed by Dutch and British settlers.
8. In a number of non-settlement colonies, such as Angola, territorial possession did start to play a role of primary importance.
9. As military conquest is a national rather than a private act, it is not surprising that most colonial conquests coincided with the age of European imperialism.
10. In most cases this process started around the turn of the century, when evolutionist theories on stages of 'development' started to gain ground.
11. See Henri Grimal, *Decolonization: the British, French, Dutch and Belgian Empires, 1919-1963*, (London: Routledge and Kegan Paul, 1965), p. 323.
12. See Mc Williams and Piotrowski, *The World Since 1945, A History of International Relations* (Boulder: Lynne Rienner Publishers, 1993), p.130.
13. See Virginia Thompson and Richard Adloff, *The French Pacific Islands*, (Los Angeles: University of California Press,1971), p. 325.
14. *i.e.* French/Polynesians or French/Melanesians.
15. The pro-independence demonstrations in Tahiti during the French nuclear testing in the Pacific in 1995 constituted an example in this respect.
16. See R.J. Horvath, 'A Definition of Colonialism', in *Current Anthropology*, vol.13, no 1, February 1972, p.47.
17. T.R. Adam, *Modern Colonialism: Institutions and Policies*, (New York: Doubleday and Company, 1955), p. 3.
18. See R. Strausz-Hupe and H. W. Hazard, eds., *The Idea of Colonialism*, (Foreign Policy Research Institute, University of Pennsylvania, 1958), p. 11.
19. See M. Doyle, Empires, (Ithaka University press), quoted in E. Said, *Culture and Imperialism*, (London: Chatto and Windus, 1993), p.8.
20. See E. Said, *Culture and Imperialism*, (Chatto and Windus, London 1993), p.8.
21. See L. C. Buchheit, *Secession, the Legitimacy of Self-Determination* (Yale

University Press, 1978), p.18.

22. This geographic definition represent the so-called 'salt water orthodoxy'.
23. See R. Strausz-Hupe and H. W. Hazard, *The Idea of Colonialism*, (Foreign Policy Research, University of Pennsylvania, 1958), p. 7.
24. See L. C. Buchheit, *Secession, the Legitimacy of Self-determination*, (Yale University Press, 1978), p.18.
25. Some writers use the term 'blue water colonies' instead of 'salt water colonies'.
26. This conclusion is supported by the fact that the view which article 22 expresses on the destiny of South West Africa has proved to be untenable. The fact that Namibia, in spite of its contiguity to its Administrating State South Africa, has never been considered part of South Africa and has even been referred to as a colony of South Africa provides strong evidence to the irrelevance of the 'salt water' doctrine under international law.
27. The legal successor to article 22 of the Covenant is article 77, UN Charter. This article merely states that 'it will be a matter for subsequent agreement as to which territories (...) will be brought under the trustship system and under what conditions.'
28. A/Res/567 (VI) and A/Res/1541 (XV)
29. These ethnic and cultural factors are enumerated under consideration no 4 of the Annex of resolution 567.
30. This term is used in Chapter 11 of the UN Charter and refers to a certain category of colonies, which were only gradually recognized as possessing the right to decolonization.
31. Part 2, annex UN General Assembly Resolution 567.
32. See B. Driessen, *A Concept of Nation*, (The Hague, T.M.A. Asser Institute, 1994), p. 90.
33. See Hans Kohn, 'Reflections on Colonialism', in R. Strausz-Hupe and H. W. Hazard, eds., p. 2.
34. Article 73, UN Charter.
35. Yassin El-Ayouti, *The United Nations and Decolonization: The Role of Afro Asia*, (The Hague, Martinus Nijhoff), p. 39.
36. UN Charter, Art. 76.
37 . UN Charter, Art. 73(b).
38. *i.e.* adequate political participation and representation in the local and central government.
39. To a certain extent, this observation ties in with the development in the legal doctrines on the recognition of states, in which the 'declaratory theory' has gained ground at the expense of the 'constitutive theory'.
40. See McWilliams and Piotrowski, *The World since 1945*, Lynne `rinenner Publishers, Boulder (Colorado), 1993, p. 136.
41. See Art.73 of the UN Charter.
42. Article 73 (e) reads: '[Members of the United Nations undertake] to transmit

regularly to the Secretary General for information purposes, subject to such limitation as security and constitutional considerations may require, statistical and other information of a technical nature relating to economic, social, and educational conditions in the territories for which they are respectively responsible other than those territories to which Chapter XII and XIII apply.'

43. U.N. Doc., A/AC/100/1, 1969, p.43.
44. Important though the external pressure of the UN was, it was not until the dictatorship of Salazar was overthrown, that Portugal started to take steps towards granting independence to its African colonies.
45. A/Res/1514 (XV) and A/Res/1541 (XV)
46. A/Res/1514 (XV), Par. 5; in fact a number of colonies which had never been listed as Trust or NSG Territories had already attained independence by 1960. e.g. India/Pakistan, the Phillipines, Indonesia, Burma, Ceylon, Libya and Sudan.
47. See Res. 1514, Par. 1; NB This phrase has been taken from the Bandung Declaration of 1955. See *Asian-African Conference*, Publications division, Ministry of Information and Broadcasting, (New Delhi, Government of India Press, 1955), p. 29-33.
48. UN General Assembly Resolution 1654, November 1961.
49. The Trusteeship Council had already been granted this power in Art. 87.
50. UN Charter, Art. 73.
51. See also section 2.2 on the Salt Water Doctrine.
52. The list of territories to which the Declaration is applicable according to the committee of 24 is: New Caledonia (France), Tokelau (New Zealand), East Timor (Portugal), Western Sahara (Spain), Anguilla, Bermuda, British Virgin Islands, Cayman Islands, Falkland Islands, Gibraltar, Montserrat, Pitcairn, St.. Helena, Turks and Caicos Islands (United Kingdom), American Samoa, Guam, United Staes Virgin Islands (United States).
53. See UN General Assembly Resolution A/RES/4/47.
54. See UN General Assembly Resolution A/Res/4/47.
55. A/Res/50/39 (1995)
56. *Asian-African Conference*, p. 29-33.
57. Quoted in G. McTurnan Kahin, *The Asian-African Confernce*, (Ithaca, NY, Cornell University Press, 1956), p. 19.
58. See R. Strausz-Hupe and H. W. Hazard, *The Idea of Colonialism*, (Foreign Policy Research Institute, University of Pennsylvania, 1958)
59. This observation is supported by the fact that Prince Norodom Sihanouk of Cambodia and Prince Wan Waithayakon, Foreign Minister of Thailand, expressed concerns at Chinese 'infiltration' and 'subversion' in Cambodia, Thailand and Laos, thus undermining their independence and sovereign integrity.
60. Preamble of the Constitution of the People's Republic of China, 1982.

61. *Final Communique* of the 1995 Cartagena Conference of the Non-Aligned Movement, p.59.
62. The best-known example is Australia.
63. e.g. Tunisia and Morocco.
64. e.g. Hong Kong.
65. John D. Hargreaves, *Decolonization in Africa* (Addison Wesley, Longman, London,1988), p. 20.
66. Lord Lloyd, *Egypt Since Cromer*, 1933, p.5.
67. Quoted in Grimal, *Decolonization: the British, French, Dutch and Belgian Empires 1919 - 1963*, Routledge and Kean Paul, London 1965, p 293.
68. Some colonized islands constitute an exception to this basic characteristic of colonialism, but this is not true for all colonized islands or groups of islands. The case of Indonesia constitutes a clear example in this respect. Before the islands which make up today's Indonesia were colonized by the Dutch, Indonesia as such did not exist as one national entity.
69. Rupert Emerson, *From Empire to Nation: The Right to Self Determination of Asian and African peoples* (Cambridge, MA: Harvard University Press, 1960) p.60.
70. According to this principle, the exercise of self-determination has to respect colonial borders. Once a colony has been decolonized, its inherited an often artificial borders are fixed.
71. See Art. 73, UN Charter.
72. See Art. 22 of the Covenant of the League of Nations.
73. See A. Sarraut, *Grandeur et servitude coloniale*, pp.59, 111, 112.
74. See Art. 22(1) and 22(2) of the Covenant of the League of Nations.
75. The Dutch in Indonesia e.g. did not try to introduce Dutch as the national language, but stimulated the use of Malay as the local 'lingua franca'.
76. See Rupert Emerson, p. 136.
77. See B. Anderson, *Imagined Communities* (London: Verso 1993), p. 115.
78. Interestingly enough it was often this élite which was at the forefront of decolonization movements, familiarized as they were with the great ideals of western political philosophy.
79. Merignhac, *Precis de legislation et d'economie coloniales*, quoted in Grimal, *Decolonization: the British, French, Dutch and Belgian Empires 1919-1963*, Routledge and Kegan Paul, London, 1965, p. 2.
80. Bevin quoted in Hargreaves, p. 104.
81. See Art. 82 and 83 of the UN Charter.
82. e.g. the pro-independence demonstration in the Congo in January 1959 was initially described by the Belgian government as a riot by 'idlers' and 'unemployed'. See Grimal, *Decolonization: the British, French Dutch, and Belgian Empires 1919-1963*, Routledge and Kegan Paul, London 1965, , p. 335.
83. See UN Charter, Art. 73.
84. See *The Last Great Imperial Adventures*, Patrick French, Flamingo, London

1995, p.105.

85. i.e. before it gained independence in 1990.

PART II

1. *Tibet: Proving Truth from Facts,* Department of Information and International Relations, Tibetan Government in Exile (Dharamsala, 1993); His Holiness the Dalai Lama, The Collected Statements, Articles and Interview of His Holiness the Dalai Lama (Dharamsala, 1986).
2. See e.g. *Tibet: The Position in International Law, Report of the Conference of International Lawyers on Issues relating to Self-Determination and Independence for Tibet* , London 6 - 10, 1993 (London: Edition Hansjorg Mayer, 1994).
3. See *Montevideo Convention on the Rights an Duties of States,* Art. 1, which is commonly accepted as reflecting international customary law. See D.J. Harris, Sweet and Maxwell, *Cases and Materials on International Law,* (London, 1991) p.102-104.
4. See Melvyn Goldstein, *A History of Modern Tibet, 1913-1951* (Berkeley: University of California Press, 1989).
5. See Robert Ford, *Wind Between the Worlds* (New York: David McKay, 1957).
6. See Warren Smith, *Tibetan Nation* (Boulder: Westview Press, 1996) p.451, ft. 2.
7. The Dalai Lama, *My Land, My People* (New York: Potala Press, 1983): Goldstein, p. 769; M. van Walt van Praag, *The Legal Status of Tibet* (Boulder: Westview Press, 1987) p.147.
8. Seventeen Point Agreement, Article 1, quoted in in Michael van Walt van Praag, *The Legal Status of Tibet,* Westview Press, Boulder, 1987.
9. See The Dalai Lama, *My Land, My People,* (PotL Press, New York 1983)
10. Xinjiang, Inner Mongolia, Ningxia and Guanxi.
11. C.P. Fitzgerald, 'The Northern Marches of Yun-nan', in: the *Geographical Journal,* 1943.
12. Graham Clark, 'The Movement of Population to the West of China,: Tibet and Qinghai', in Judith M. Brown and Rosemary Foot, *Migration: The Asian Experience,* (New York: St.. Martin's Press, 1991) p. 246.
13. See *White Book Tibet, Its Ownership and Human Rights Situation,* (Beijing: Information Office of the State Council of the People's Republic of China), p.7.
14. The *Seventeen Point Agreement* was concluded with 'Tibet' without any references to its geographical delimitation.
15. *i.e.,* Xinjiang, Inner Mongolia, Ninxia and Guanxi.
16. See The Dalai Lama, *Freedom in Exile* , Hodder and Stoughton, London 1990) p. 104, 106-7.
17. For the full text of Hu's recommendations, see Xinhua News Agency in Chinese, 30.5.80
18. The Panchen Lama, Address to the TAR Standing Committee Meeting of the National People's Congress, Beijing (28.3.87), published as Department of

Info. and International Relations, Central Tibetan Administration of His Holiness the Dalai Lama, The Panchen Lama Speaks (1991), p. 5.

19. Speech given by Mr. Ragdi on September 5, 1994 at the Seventh Plenum of the 6th Standing Committee Session of the TAR Communist Party, also referred to as 'Document No 5':"The focal point of the policy of opening the door wider in Tibet should be towards the inner part of the country [i.e. towards the PRC]. While depending on our region's own good aspects of policy and production resources, we should combine these with the good aspects of the inner part of the Country [i.e. PRC.], its intellectuals, technicians, management personnel and communications. Mutual economic support and exchange in every field should be broadened. We should encourage traders, investment, economic units and individuals to enter our region to run different sorts of enterprises. We should turn our good production resources into economic [advantages] and join our region's economy with the nation's vast market."
20. See Preamble, *Seventeen Point Agreement*, cited in Michiel van Walt van Praag, The Status of Tibet, Westview Press, Boulder, 1987, p. 337.
21. See *ibid.*, par. 3.
22. See *ibid.*, par. 4.
23. See *ibid.*, par. 7.
24. See *ibid.*, par. 11.
25. 1984 Law on Regional Autonomy, Preface, cited in *The Myth of Autonomy: A Legal Analysis of the Status of Tibet*, International Campaign for Tibet and the Human Rights Law Group, (Washington, April 1994).
26. See 1984 Law on Regional Autonomy, article 20.
27. See 1984 Law on regional Autonomy, article 19.
28. A handful of Tibetans hold positions within the National People's Congress. e.g. Phuntsog Wangyal and Ngapo Ngawang Jigme are among the most high-profile Tibetans in the Central government, but their power is reportedly nominal at best. According to unofficial sources, Ngapo Ngawang Jigme appears to have been sidelined and there is evidence that the Chinese authorities no longer trust him.
29. See Hungmao Tien, 'Sinocization on National Minorities in China', in *Current Scene*, vol. XII, no. 12; see also *The Myth of Autonomy*.
30. Speech given by Mr. Ragdi on 5.9.94, 'The 5th Document of the 7th Plenary of the 6th Standing Committee Session'.
31. *i.e.* Sichuan, Qinghai, Gansu and Yunnan, respectively.
32. See Donald R. DeGlopper, 'Chinese Nationality Policy and the Tibetan Question', in Problems of Communism, November/December, 1990.
33. Article 17, 1984 Law on Regional Autonomy, cited in *The Myth of Autonomy, A Legal Analysis of the Status of Tibet*, A report by the International Campaign for Tibet and the Human Rights Law Group, p.11.
34 Gyaltsen Norbu.

35 Constitution of the Chinese Communist Party, art. 35.
36 Speech given at the meeting for party members of the Fourth Plenary Session of the Sixth TAR Regional Congress and the Youth Plenary Session of the Sixth Political Consultative Conference, by Chen Kuiyuan, 14.4.94.
37. *The Tibet Daily* (22.5.96) reported that a Tibetan member of the Chinese People's Political Consultative Conference and vice chairman of the Tibet branch of the People's Political Consultative Conference was dismissed as 'he lost the basic principle and political stand of patriotism'. The paper added that 'the conference decided to dismiss him from is post to purify the PPCC organization, which demonstrates its 'solemn stance on patriotism'.
38. See Warren Smith, *Tibetan Nation: A History of Tibetan Nationalism and Sino-Tibetan Relations* (Boulder: Westview Press, 1996), chapter 16, 'Tibet's Legal Status'.
39. ILO *International Labor Conventions and Recommendations 1919-1991*, Vol.1, ' Convention no. 29, Convention Concerning Forced or Compulsory Labor' (Geneva International Labor Office, 1992), p.116.
40. Interview with a farmer from Khanze, Dharamsala, 1995.
41. Notably in Amdo and Kham, areas now incorporated in Qinghai and Sichuan Province.
42. Interview with a farmer from Khanze, Dharamsala 1995.
43. Apart from these Chinese operated tourist agencies, a number of successful Tibetan tourist agencies have sprung up over the past few years. These tend to be small scale enterprises, catering to low budget travellers, while Chinese operated tours tend to tailor to wealthy travellers.
44. This term is used in many Chinese propaganda documents/speeches.
45. Wang Furen and Suo Wenqing, *Highlights of Tibetan History* (Beijing, New World Press, 1984), p.43 and p.179.
46. *Fazhi Ribao*, February, 1995.
47. Report by LAWASIA/TIN, *Defying the Dragon, China and Human Rights in Tibet*, London, 1991, pp. 108-9, citing the Ganze Propaganda Guide.
48. Speech by Chen Kuiyuan at the 5th Regional Meeting on Education, 26.10.94.
49. See Wang Hao and Duo Qiong, "Tibet Adopts Regional National Autonomy System," Xinhua, 30.5.90, translated by FBIS, 1.6.90. See also, Wu Naitao, "Languages: Pedigree of Ethnic Equality," Beijing Review, May 4-10, 1992, pp. 25-29.
50. See *TIN Update*, 31.12.96, 'Student Unease at Language Policies in Schools', Tibet Information Network (London).
51. However, as in many French and British colonies, assimilation is a condition but certainly no guarantee of social advancement.
52. See *TIN Update*, 31.12.96, Tibet Information Network (London).
53. *Ibid.*
54. See *Opening to Reform?: An Analysis of China's Revised Criminal Procedure Law,*

Lawyers Committee for Human Rights, New York, 1996.
55. See *A Season to Purge: Religious Repression in Tibet.* Washington, International Campaign for Tibet, 1996.
56. See *Cutting off the Serpent's Head,* Tibet Information Network / Human Rights Watch (London, 1996), p. 64.
57. See Ronald Schwartz, *Circle of Protest* (New York: Columbia University Press, 1994).
58. See official summary of the speech of CCP Secretary Jiang Zemin at the 1990 Work Conference on Religion, in *Xinhua,* 8.12.90.
59. *Ibid.*
60. "Work Forums" on Tibet are top-level Party and government meetings which determine long-term policies on Tibet. The first was in 1980, the second in 1984 and the third in 1994. The Third "Work" was attended by all seven members of the Standing Committee of the Party's Central Committee. At least two members, President Jiang Zemin and former Party Secretary of Tibet, Hu Jintao, gave substantive presentations.
61. Internal Party document entitled 'Seizing this Good Opportunity of Having the Third Work Forum [and] Achieve in an All Round way a New Aspect on Work in Tibet', given by Ragdi, 5.9.94, at the Seventh Plenum of the Sixth Standing Committee Session of the TAR Communist Party, cited in *Cutting off the Serpent's Head,* Tibet Information Network/Human Rights Watch, London, 1996, p. 32.
62. According to article 36 of the Constitution of the PRC, 'the State protects normal religious activities. No one may make use of religion to engage in activities that disrupt public order, impair the health of citizens or interfere with the educational system of the state.' This article implies that religious activities which are not deemed 'normal' are not protected by the state. It does not specify who is to determine whether a certain religious activity is normal or not. The Chinese authorities often legitimize religious repression in Tibet by claiming that the religious activities in question are not 'normal', that they 'disrupt the public order' and the integrity of the state.
63. Speech by Chen Kuiyuan (TAR Party Secretary), Sixth TAR Regional Congress and the Fourth Plenary Session of the Sixth Political Consultative Meeting, 14 May 1996.
64. Note that in July 1993 the Chinese authorities had allowed Chadrel Rinpoche, the head of the search party in charge of identifying the reincarnation of the 10th Panchen Lama, to meet the Dalai Lama's brother in Beijing and to send the Dalai Lama an official request for 'guidance' in the search.
65. Xinhua News Agency, Summary of World Broadcast (SWB), 2 December 1995.
66. This is the term J. Nehru used when criticizing the British.
67. Interview with an ex-government official in Dharamsala, January 1994.
68. e.g. in 1996 the Tibetan mayors of Meldrogonkar and Toelung have reportedly

been replaced by Chinese.

69. Marcus Brauchli, "To Integrate Tibet, China's New Approach Tries Economic Lures," *Wall Street Journal*, 14.7.97.
70. Speech by Chen Kuiyuan on the meeting for Party members at the Fourth Plenary Session of the Sixth TAR Regional Congress and the Fourth Plenary Session of the Sixth Political Consultative Conference, 14 `may 1996
71. Speech by TAR Party Secretary Chen Kuiyuan on 5 December 1994, SWB 5/12/94
72. See "170,000 Troops Deployed Near Lhasa", *Far Eastern Economic Review*, 19.11.92, p. 8; "Peking to Move Military Headquarters to Tibet", *South China Morning Post*, 8.3.89; Central News Agency, 5.12.92.
73. "Policy Shift in Teaching in Tibet," Tibet Information Network, 6.5.97.
74. e.g. Dawa Dolma, a teacher at the Lhasa Cement Plant primary school, Kunchok Tenzin from Sog district and Sonam Tering from Qinghai Province.
75. Speech by Chen Kuiyuan, TAR Party Secretary, at the 5th Regional Meeting on Education, held on 26 October 1994.
76. See Pu Ning, Red in *Tooth and Claw: Twenty-Six Years in Communist Chinese Prisons* (New York: Grove Press, 1994). The author chronicles his life on the Tibetan plateau as a prison laborer sent from China.
77. See "Chen Kuiyuan Exhorts Tibetans not to Fear Chinese Influx," Tibetan Environment & Development News, February 1995, No. 17, p. 8.
78. Quoted in TIN background briefing paper, no. 26, p.38, Tibet Information Network (London, 1995).
79. See Doc. 5, internal CCP speech given by Mr. Ragdi during the Third National Forum of work in Tibet, held in September 1994.
80. See H.S. Liao, 'Tibet's Economic Reform Since Deng Xiao Ping's South China Tour', in *Issues and Studies*, March 1994, Vol. 30, no. 8.
81. Chinese settlers have stated that they are allowed two children as a reward for being subjected to a very unpopular population transfer program. Some Chinese families in eastern Tibet can only have one child, or choose to have only one child, particularly if they are higher Party cadres who should set an example. Chinese who are sent to eastern Tibet for only one or two years are sometimes discouraged from having two children. One Chinese reported that the policy was that Chinese must remain in Tibet for 8 years before they could have a second child. Second generation Chinese who are born in eastern Tibet are reportedly always allowed to have 2 children, as if they have become de facto minorities by virtue of their length of stay. See *The Long March: Chinese Policies in Eastern Tibet*, International Campaign for Tibet (Washington, 1991), pp. 11-13.
82. Wang & Bai, *Poverty of Plenty* (New York: St.. Martin's Press, 1991), p. 148.
83. See Graham Clarke, 'The Movement of Population to the West of China: Tibet and Qinghai', in Brown and Foot, *Migration: The Asian Experience*, St.. Martin's Press, New York, 1991, p. 248.

84. *The New Majority: Population Transfer into Tibet,* Tibet Support Group UK (London, 1995), p. 56.
85. Several large farms such as the 1st August Farm belong to, and are administrated by, the PLA.
86. See Marcus Brauchli, "To Integrate Tibet, China's New Approach Tries Economic Lures," Wall Street Journal, 14.7.97.
87. *The Precious Democratic Constitution of Tibet,* a political protest document written by a group of monks from Drepung Monastery in 1988 and subsequently smuggled out of the country.
88. Resolution 1353 (XIV) called for 'respect for the fundamental human rights of the Tibetan people and for their distinct cultural and religious life'. Resolution 1723 (XVI) stated that the General Assembly was 'gravely concerned about the suppression of the distinct cultural and religious life which [the Tibetans] traditionally enjoyed'. Resolution 2079 (XX) declared its 'conviction that the violation of human rights and fundamental freedoms in Tibet and the suppression of their distinct cultural and religious life of its people increase international tension and embitter relations between peoples.'
89. UN Subcommission on the Prevention of Discrimination and Protection of Minorities, Resolution 1991/10, UN Doc. E/CN.4/1992/37.
90. 'The Chinese race totals 400 million people; of mingled races there are only a few million Mongolians, a million or so Manchus, a few million Tibetans, and over a million Mohammedan Turks. These alien races do not number altogether more than ten million, so that, for the most part, the Chinese people are of the Han or Chinese race with common blood, common language, common religions and common customs - a single, pure race.' Sun Yatsen, San Min Chu-i, 1927, p. 11 and p.12.
91. See Mao Zedong, *On Contradiction Among the People,* quoted in Cutting off the Serpent's Head, TIN / Human Rights Watch Asia, London 1996, p. 10-11.
92. See 1994 Report of the Government of the TAR quoted in *Cutting off the Serpent's Head,* TIN/ Human Rights Watch Asia, London 1996, p.11

FIFTH GENERAL ASSEMBLY: A SUMMARY OF PROCEEDINGS

Otepää, Estonia
15–19 July 1997

Unrepresented Nations and Peoples Organization

THE UNPO FIFTH GENERAL ASSEMBLY

From 15–19 July 1997 the Unrepresented Nations and Peoples Organization held its fifth General Assembly in Otepää, Estonia. Delegations from nearly all 50 Members attended the proceedings. In addition to the Assembly, a two-day conference on Nonviolence and Conflict was held (*the conference report is contained in this volume*).

Of key importance for the fifth General Assembly was the nomination and election of a new Chairman, General Secretary and members of the Steering Committee. Although, ultimately, a new General Secretary was not elected during this session, the work of the Assembly in this transitional phase in the organization's history is of importance and interest both to the Members and those who support the organization.

The following summary of the proceedings of the Assembly provides insight, understanding and transparency regarding both the working of the Membership as a whole and the organization as an entity in the international arena. In addition, it highlights the various positions and goals as put forth by the Member delegations among a body of peers and before the international community.

GENERAL ASSEMBLY PROCEEDINGS

General Assembly V: Tuesday, 15 July 1997

Morning session

Mr. Erkin Alptekin, Chairman of the General Assembly: Opens the Fifth General Assembly. Welcomes all. Asks for one minute of silent prayer for the success of the Assembly, and for those fallen in the struggle for the just cause of their peoples. Thanks all and welcomes distinguished guests: Mr. Enn Tarto, Member of the Estonian Parliament; Mr. Aivar Nigol, Mayor of Otepää; Mr. Rodrigo Carazo, former President of Costa Rica; and all new members of the UNPO. Thanks the Government and Parliament of Estonia for the opportunity given to the UNPO to hold the General Assembly in the newly independent Republic of Estonia. Thanks Dr. Linnart Mäll and his staff for their efforts. Calls on Senator Parris Chang to take the stand.

Senator Paris Chang, President of the Steering Committee: Welcomes all. Emphasizes the importance of the successful Estonian struggle, which set a precedent for all other unrepresented peoples. States that the UNPO is now a global organization, with members from all continents, and, therefore, with a global programme as well. Emphasizes the importance of cooperation, solidarity, and hard work of all members and expresses gratitude for all their efforts. Encourages members to create a solid base for the UNPO.

Dr. Michael van Walt van Praag, General Secretary: Welcomes and thanks all present. Highlights the fact that this is the largest General Assembly so far, and one of the most crucial. Observes the growth of the UNPO from a pioneer organization to an established and viable global organization. Remarks that in the past unrepresented peoples and minorities have been viewed as a source of instability and conflict. Quotes the words of Kasur Tenzin Namgyal Tethong, at the last Conference on Conflict Prevention: "It is time to realize that these peoples minorities are not the problem, but part of the solution." Notes this will have an impact on the course of international relations of states, nations and peoples. Welcomes all to Estonia, which as a founding member now enjoys its recovered status as an independent state, making it a meaningful place to hold this General Assembly. Proceeds to hand the 1996 Yearbook to the Chairman, the President of the Steering Committee, and the distinguished guests.

Dr. Linnart Mäll, Assistant General Secretary: Expresses pleasure to see all gathered in Otepää, near the holy lake, which was blessed by His Holiness the Dalai Lama. States that the struggle of unrepresented peoples is and will be one of the most important in the world. Reminds all that the preparatory meetings of the UNPO were also held in Estonia. Hopes all members enjoy their stay. Introduces Mr. Enn Tarto, who organized the school boys' freedom fighter group in 1956, and who was imprisoned three times for a period of sixteen years under Soviet rule. Recalls that Mr. Tarto, since his release in 1988, continued to play an active role in the independence struggle as Deputy Chairman of the Estonian Congress; and now serves as a Member of the Estonian Parliament.

Mr. Enn Tarto, Member of the Estonian Parliament: Welcomes all. Believes all Estonians of goodwill also welcome this General Assembly, especially the freedom fighters from Taiwan, Tibet, and Chechenia. Recalls the day, 5 September 1990, when the Founding Committee of the UNPO met here. Observes that many international organizations are trying to resolve human relations and conflicts by peaceful means, notably the United Nations. Remarks that the UNPO follows the principles of the Universal Declaration of Human Rights and the Declaration of the Peoples Rights of Self-Determination. Emphasizes that all organizations of this kind should insist on the enforcement of legal acts. Remarks that in political practice it seems that powerful states are immune to sanctions, thus not abiding by International Law. Calls for all legal actions to be implemented fairly. Wishes the UNPO members success in their endeavours to become represented nations and peoples. Questions whether the UNPO will continue to function when its members achieve representation. Emphasizes that the UNPO will continue since there are hundreds of peoples seeking freedom and the right of self-determination.

Mr. Aivar Nigol, Mayor of Otepää: Addresses all. Expresses that he is pleased to receive the Fifth General Assembly in Otepää, and on behalf of the local government wishes the General Assembly success in its endeavours. Observes that Otepää is the site of this General Assembly because previous events of the UNPO were also held here, but also because Otepää played an important historical role in the Estonian struggle for independence. Highlights that Otepää is proud to have had the national banner of Estonia blessed in the local church. Remarks that many relevant national events have taken place in Otepää since the independence of Estonia. Points out the existence of the Pühajärv Lake, considered holy by generations of Estonians. Hopes that all present receive the blessing of the Otepää spirit, and have success in the future. Wishes success to the leaders of the UNPO, the representatives of peoples, and the peoples themselves in their struggles. Invites everyone to enjoy the beautiful landscape of Otepää, to cherish their time here, and to return.

Mr. Erkin Alptekin, Chairman: Welcomes new Members again. Calls the representatives of the new Members to sign the Covenant of the UNPO:

Bashkortostan (not present)
Buryatia, represented by Mr. Dashi-Nima Dugarov
Cabinda, represented by Mr. Henriques Tiago N'Zita

Kumyk, represented by Mr. Salav Alijev
Shan, represented by Mr. Myo Min
Mon, represented by Mr. Sunthorn Sripanngern
Tyva, represented by Dr. Kara-Kys Arakchaa

Calls two more representatives of Members who joined the UNPO in the past, but have not yet signed the Covenant:

Komi, represented by Ms. Zhanetta Proshutinaskaya
Udmurt, represented by Ms. Nadejda Zolotariova

States that the UNPO now has 50 members, representing more than 100 million people world-wide. Welcomes new members and wishes them to fully collaborate with the goals and strengthening of the UNPO.

[Break]

Erkin Alptekin, Chairman: Announces several amendments to the agenda. The first amendment is that the nominations for Chairperson and Vice-Chairperson of the General Assembly should be handed in today. Nominations will take place tomorrow morning. The second amendment is that the reports by the General Secretary and by the President of the Steering Committee will be dealt with tomorrow morning. Hereafter the General Assembly adopts the Agenda. The new members are invited to give introductory statements. The representatives of Bashkortostan are not present at this moment and will give an introductory statement after their arrival.

Mr. Dashi-Nima Dugarov, All-Buryat Association of the Development of Culture: Greets the participants of the General Assembly after a short prayer in the Buryat language. Due to the occupations by various states, the Buryat people have lost a firm grip on their cultural and national identity. The Buryat people are a different and special population with their own traditions. In 1991, the Buryat people asked the United Nations for support of a cultural festival to remember and cherish their own culture, language and prayers. Ends with compliments to the organization and adds that great things are happening here, people are united in finding a path in peace, friendship and prosperity.

Mr. Henriques Tiago N'Zita, President of FLEC/FAC (Cabinda): Opens with extending greetings and gratitude for the admission of Cabinda within the UNPO. States that Cabinda is not Angola. It is situated in Central Africa, separated from Angola by a 60 km long coastal strip. Angola was a colony and Cabinda was a protectorate of Portugal. After the decolonization in 1975, Cabinda became a part of Angola instead of becoming an independent state. This was a clear violation of international law by Portugal and Angola. Cabinda is still illegally and militarily occupied by Angola.

States that the people of Cabinda want to negotiate with the Angolan Government in a peaceful and non-violent way in order to achieve a solution acceptable to all parties involved. Requests intervention of the UNPO and other international organizations to support the struggle for independence and the right to self-determination. Asks to bring an end to the human right violations and suppression in Cabinda.

Mr. Salav Alijev, Chairman of the Kumyk People's Movement: Expresses gratitude for the admission of Kumyk within the UNPO. The last hundred years have been catastrophic for the Kumyk people. Due to dispersal and mass migrations, the Kumyk people have become a minority in their own land (22% of the total population). The Kumyk people lack self-government and self-determination. Remarks that especially the young people want to solve the problems which they face through non-violent and peaceful means. The Dagestan Government ignores the wishes of the Kumyk people to control their own lives. Dagestan must act as an autonomous republic which respects the indigenous peoples in the same land.

Mr. Sunthorn Sripanngern, Mon Unity League: Introduces the Mon delegation. The seven million Mon people live in southern Burma and parts of Thailand. In 1757, the Mon people were conquered by the King of Burma and lost their independence. The Mon have been oppressed for a long time. They have struggled hard for the survival of their culture and language under enormous pressure of the ruling Burmese military junta (SLORC). States that the unity of the Mon people is necessary for the protection of the Mon national identity and pride. States that it is important for the Mon freedom struggle to gain international attention and recognition.

Mr. Myo Win, Representative of the Shan People: Expresses gratitude for the admission of the Shan people within the UNPO. States that the main problem of the unrepresented nations is the reluctance of the international community to recognize the rights to self-determination, especially within the context of non-state nations. The Burmese military coup and subsequent abolition of the "Constitution of the Union of Burma" on the part of the Burmese authorities frees the Shan people from contractual obligations to that union. Comments that the nature of the conflict within the Shan States has changed from an internal to an international crisis. Asks for support and guidance in gaining international attention to the situation within the Shan States.

Dr. Kara-Kys Arakchaa, Representative of Tyva: Expresses gratitude for being invited to the General Assembly of the UNPO. Explains that the autonomous Republic Tyva is located in the central part of Asia. The people of Tyva belonged to different Turkish emperors and were a Russian protectorate. In 1992, the Tyva Peoples Republic was created with its own parliament and president. States the main problems are self-determination of the indigenous people, cultural and economical development and deprivation of the right to use national resources. The Tyvan people still have few rights although it is a sovereign state with a fixed constitution. Questions the economic potential of Tyva; no investors are interested in Tyva. Suggests that the UNPO should look at ways to encourage the creation of economically self-supporting and independent people. Since 1993, Tyva has expressed support for the work of the UNPO. Wishes success for all the people in the world.

Senator Parris Chang, President of the Steering Committee: Requests a formal approval of the Report of the General Secretary.

[The report is approved by the General Assembly.]

GENERAL ASSEMBLY V: TUESDAY, 15 JULY 1997

Afternoon session

Mr. Erkin Alptekin, Chairman: Requests Senator Chang to select three persons to arrange the election of the Chairperson and two Vice-Chairs, who will be responsible for tomorrow's election.

Senator Parris Chang, President of the Steering Committee: Selects three members for the election committee: Dr. Robert Gyula Cey-Bert, International Ambassador of Karenni; Mr. Göran Hansson, member of the UNPO Steering Committee and representative of the Foundation for the Future of Scania; Mrs. Chungdak Dawa Koren, representative of H.H the Dalai Lama and member of the UNPO Steering Committee.

Mr. Erkin Alptekin, Chairman: Gives rules of procedure for nominations and indicates there are three positions: one Chairperson and two Vice-Chairpersons. Indicates that each of the positions will be voted separately and that it will be carried out tomorrow. Emphasizes there is only one vote per delegation. Asks Michael van Walt van Praag for legal advice.

Dr. Michael van Walt van Praag, General Secretary: Points out that nominations will be done today and the voting itself tomorrow. Proceeds to read Article 32, parts 2 and 3 of the Assembly Rules of Procedure: Article 32. Part 2: "The Chairperson is elected by a majority. In case none of the nominees obtains a majority, the nominee receiving the least number of votes will be dropped and additional rounds of voting will continue following the same procedure until a chair person is elected." Part 3: "First and second Vice-Chairpersons shall be elected in the same manner as the Chairperson." Clarifies then that the Chairperson is elected by majority.

Mr. Nadir Byekir, Representative of the Crimean Tartars: Asks Dr. van Walt van Praag if it is simple or absolute majority which the article mentions.

Dr. Michael van Walt van Praag, General Secretary: Clarifies that the article refers to an absolute majority, i.e. over 50% of all Members.

Senator Parris Chang, President of the Steering Committee: Urges the Election Committee to come forward. Requests the delegates to hand in their nominations promptly so that a list may be prepared. Nominations are submitted. Reminds all members that in case of an eventual nomination, persons who wish to decline the nomination may do so tomorrow.

Mr. Erkin Alptekin, Chairman: Reminds the Election Committee to organize the nomination papers and prepare the ballots by this evening. Remarks that two years have passed since the fourth General Assembly, therefore new issues always arise. Stresses that every member should deliver a statement in order to be up to date. Reminds all that the time limit for such statements is five minutes. Invites the representative from Abkhazia to the stand:

Mr. Muradin Khasambiyevich Urchukov, Representative of Abkhazia: Wishes the General Assembly to work hard in order to achieve all goals and be fruitful. States the importance of all members to be current on the Abkhazian situation. Informs the Assembly that a Russian Commission investigated their case and concluded that Russia had trapped Abkhazia, blocking all air, land and sea contact. Points out that some of the main challenges of Abkhazia are opening its borders, creating a viable economy. Emphasises that Abkhazia has no money and that they have not been recognized. Thanks UNPO for recognizing Abkhazia as a member. Hopes for Abkhazian independence in the future.

Ms. Rosemary Roe, representative of the Aboriginals of Australia: Introduces herself as a Yamatji Woman from Carnarvon in Western Australia, and representative of the Aboriginals of Australia through the National Committee to Defend Black Rights. States that seventy percent of the indigenous population in Australia is under 30 years old, as Aboriginals have a high mortality rate due to poor health, poverty, state persecution, injury and violence; giving them some of the worst life statistics of a Western democracy. Remarks on the ongoing racism and onslaught against this native people. Explains her statement is focused on indigenous youth, as they now constitute the majority of indigenous people.

Points out that the Australian Government violates these youths' rights in several ways: by severely denying them land rights, even though these have been protected in court; and by having practice d the forced removal of children from their homes. Refers to the Generation of Stolen Children, which publicised this long hidden truth. Points out that the Government does not take responsibility for any of these actions. Stresses that these children also suffer from mental, physical and sexual abuse committed by various authorities. Explains that aboriginal children are taught to believe they are inferior to others, and that they have no right to education, employment or access to services. Mentions Pauline Hanson, for her extremist campaign to reduce aboriginal rights and funding of aboriginal aid programmes. Refers to Hanson's arguments that aboriginal people should have no more rights than other Australians. Criticises the Law and Order Agenda, which puts property over people, eliminates the possibility of discretionary sentencing, and directs funds to the construction of jails rather than social programmes. Mentions the Australian Institute of Criminology, which stated that indigenous young people are being detained at an earlier age and are overrepresented in detention centers. Observes that these actions contravene the United Nations Convention of the Rights of the Child and the Beijing Rules. Remarks how some indigenous young people are being kept in adult jails. Emphasizes that the police have always been involved in harassing Aboriginal people. Stresses that, although a lot of money is spent on the research of these problems, the government remains inactive in their solution. Points out that the Australian government focuses on reducing its deficit by cutting funds for Aboriginal community programs, legal aid, and by defining youth as under 25, thus denying them the right to collect unemployment benefits. Adds that the government also intends to privatize services, therefore depriving Aboriginal communities of proper service. Laments that this results in mental health problems, drug addictions, alcohol abuse and suicide. Mentions the personal case of the suicide of her nephew of eleven years of age as a crude example of this tragedy. Requests a youth seminar allowing young people the right to speak and invites the UNPO Peace Action Council, especially Nobel Peace Prize winner José Ramos Horta, UNPO Assistant Secretary General for Asia and the Pacific, Helen Corbett and a representative of H.H the Dalai Lama and all other interested persons to attend.

Mr. Yusuf Daud, Representative from Acheh: Appreciates this opportunity to give an account of the history and the violation of human rights in Acheh. Emphasizes how the Kingdom of Acheh was powerful in the past, even resisting occupation by the Dutch colonial forces. Reminds that after Japanese occupation, the Dutch government did not interfere with the region again. Highlights that Acheh was forced to become part of Indonesia, without plebiscite or referendum. Points out that Acheh was re-declared independent on December 4, 1976, by His Highness Tengku Hasan di Tiro. Recalls that the Indonesian government retaliated heavily, causing great loss of life. States that between 1990 and 1993, approximately twenty thousand innocent civilians were murdered. Notes that these atrocities have been well documented by several international human rights organizations, such as Asia Watch and Amnesty International.

Points out that international observers have been denied entrance to the region, and that the United Nations Human Rights Commission in Geneva has not taken any concrete actions on their behalf. Observes that eleven Indonesian officers were given promotions in 1992 for their ruthless conduct in Acheh. Remarks that recently thousands of Indonesian troops were sent to Acheh in an attempt to suppress renewed political activities of the Acheh Sumatra National Liberation Front. Explains how the government has resorted to state-terrorism, arbitrarily arresting and torturing innocent civilians. States that such facts have been documented in a report by the United Nations Special Rapporteur on Torture. Adds that hundreds of Achehnese have fled to Malaysia where they face refoulement, since the Malaysian government does not consider them as refugees. Stresses that forced repatriation would cause the immediate execution of these people. Appeals to all international human rights organizations, especially the UNPO, to help Acheh, East Timor, Celebes, and West Papua in their struggle against the oppression and inhumanity of the Javanese Indonesian government.

Mr. Qenan Sheji, Representative of the Albanians in Macedonia: Gives the geographical location of the State of Macedonia in the Balkan. States that the Albanian indigenous people descend from the Illyrian people, and have a history of over three millennia. States that after World War II, half of Albania was wrongfully allocated to former Yugoslavia. Recalls that in 1946 the Albanian population was recognized as a people by the Yugoslav Federation within the statutes of the Socialist Federation of Macedonia. Adds that this status was changed to the one of nationality in 1974. According to the new constitution of 17 November 1991, Albanians in Macedonia are considered a minority group within the sovereign Republic of Macedonia, now completely run by the Slavic people despite the fact that Albanians constitute a third of the total population. Underlines that this situation is totally unacceptable to the Albanians in Macedonia, especially since the Albanian Republic has been divided against the peoples' will.

Points out that in 1992 two separate referenda were held, one among the Slavic people and one among the Albanians. Remembers how this resulted in contradictory objectives. Albanians demanded equal representation with political, cultural and economic autonomy. The Slavic people demanded a separate state. Emphasizes that during the formation of the Republic of Macedonia, an exclusive form of nationalism was enforced by the Slavic people, marginalizing other groups. Notes that Albanian Parliamentarians boycotted the draft constitution. Stresses that in the election process a Slavic vote counts twice compared to an Albanian vote. Adds that a centralist system has been implemented since then, limiting the activity of regional authorities. Remarks that the largest Albanian political parties have joined and propose the following programme to avoid further confrontation: 1) To achieve the right of self-determination without repression ensuring the right of complete independence in total peace and liberty. Explains that Yugoslavia was created by an agreement, and when it fell apart all peoples should have automatically gained the right to self-determination; 2) To achieve internal self-determination; 3) To create a bi-national and multi-cultural system. Continues to state that this new agreement should be based on the following criteria: a) hereditary rights, b) democratic rights, c) human rights according to European standards, and d) the implementation of western standards, allowing the situation in Macedonia to be considered in the existing Western European institutions. Warns that should such an agreement not be reached, Macedonia will end up in a negative spiral and a crisis situation similar to that of former Yugoslavia.

[Representatives of Assyria and Bashkortostan not present]

Mr. Zéphyrin Kalimba, Representative of Batwa: Presents greetings on behalf of the Batwa nation in Rwanda, a small country in Central Africa. States that Rwanda has three ethnic groups, of which the Batwa are the hunters and gatherers, the Bahutu the farmers, and the Batutsi the cattle raisers. Emphasizes that the Batwa live mostly from the environment. Recalls that in the history of the region, the Batwa were present since the fifth century, and were then followed by the Hutus and the Tutsis, in that order. Calculates that there are approximately thirty thousand Batwa people, representing 0.4% of the Rwandan population. Adds that the Batwa are short in size, approximately 1,5 meters, and live mainly off two activities: the making of handicrafts and hunting and gathering. Highlights that the Batwan people suffer from tropical diseases, do not have a sufficient diet or a decent supply of food, have a high mortality rate, and close genetic links between each other. Reminds that half of the population of Rwanda was exterminated during the recent civil war. States that ten thousand Batwa died from the war, three thousand were imprisoned and more than ten thousand women and children were widowed or orphaned. States that Batwa was accepted as member of the UNPO in 1993, with the aid of the Association for the Promotion of Batwa. Recalls that in 1994 a UNPO mission visited the country to asses the situation of the Batwa after the war. Adds that on August 15, 1996, the United Nations Sub-Commission on Prevention of Discrimination and Protection Minorities passed a resolution in which special attention was devoted to the Batwan situation. Hopes the UNPO will help with their situation and thanks all present.

Mr. Akhyad Idigov, Representative of the Chechen Republic Ichkeria: Starts with greeting members of the UNPO and expressing gratitude for the work of the organization. Thanks the General Secretary of the UNPO, Dr. Michael Van Walt Van Praag for his visit to the Chechen Republic during the war. Gives a brief statement on the current situation in Chechenia. In 1994 elections were held in Chechenia. The Russian Federation accused the Chechen people of violating the constitution. Russia feared that the secession of Chechenia and other republics would weaken the federation. States that Chechenia did not want to go to war but that the Chechen people would never allow forceful occupation. Reiterates that Chechenia wants peace with Russia, but shall never surrender and wants to be recognized by the Russian Federation as an equal neighbour. Proposes that the UNPO should adopt a resolution which defines a method to handle problems which arise between large states and small nations.

Mr. Pradhir Chakma, Representative of Chittagong Hill Tracts: Expresses that he is encouraged by the opportunity to participate in the General Assembly. Explains the recent developments concerning Chittagong Hill Tracts and the Jana Samhati Samiti, the only political party in Chittagong Hill Tracts. States that peace negotiations are being held. The fifth round is currently taking place in Dhaka. States that the government attitude at the peace talks show that the Bangladesh government does not want a lasting solution. The fundamental issues have not been negotiated. Stresses that the most important issues at hand are regional autonomy, traditional land rights and demilitarization. Refers to a resolution of the European Parliament which grants money for the withdrawal of Bengali settlers from Chittagong Hill Tracts. Clarifies that the Bangladesh government is not willing to welcome the resolution. Emphasizes that the withdrawal of Bengali settlers would simplify the whole negotiation process. Urges the government of Bangladesh to 1) negotiate a political settlement ensuring regional autonomy for the Jumma people, 2) withdraw the Bengali settlers, 3) involve the United Nations High Commission for Refugees and the International Committee for Red Cross to ensure the proper rehabilitation of the Jumma returnee refugees, and 4) welcome an international body or government to facilitate the peace process.

Mr. Atner Khuzangai, President of the Chuvash National Congress: Starts by stating that the Chuvash people are one of the Turkic people in the Russian Federation. 51% of the Chuvash people live outside the Chuvash Republic, an autonomous republic in the Russian Federation. Mentions that the Chuvash Republic has good relations with its neighbouring republics. Together with Bashkortostan, Mari, Tatarstan and Udmurt, they formed the Volga Peoples Assembly. States that the current situation in Chuvashia is very difficult, with the same economic problems as in other parts of the Russian Federation. In December, 1997, presidential elections will take place, with the danger of clashes between the two candidates. The Chuvash National Congress is looking for a third candidate. Explains the candidate should be democratic and of Chuvash origin. The candidate should offer native leadership with a modern point of view and respect the most important freedoms and the right to self-determination. Concludes by stating that the policy of the UNPO should be based on these two fundamental values.

Mr. Khaji-Mourat Khatoukaev, Representative of Circassia: Acknowledges the important work of the UNPO. Explains that after World War II, the United Nations was necessary in facilitating negotiations between big powers. The smaller and unrepresented nations remained outside the United nations. The UNPO filled that gap in an era when many new conflicts had arisen. States that the International Circassian Association stands for all the CIrcassians who fought against the Russian forces and for the majority of of Circassians living outside the homeland. In the course of the Russian-Caucasian war, lasting 100 years, a considerable part of the Circassians were decimated on the basis of their ethnicity and religion. More than 90% of the Circassian survivors were forcibly deported from their native country. States that at present, Circassians live in more than 45 countries, the majority of which are dispersed in the Krasnodar region, Adegei, Cherkess Republic, and the Kabardino-Balkar Republic. States that the aim of the International Circassian Association is to unite Circassians spiritually, politically and to preserve the ethnic unity of Circassians. Demands of the Russian Federation, which inherited the legislative right of the tsarist autocracy, to acknowledge the genocide against the Circassians, to recognize the status of exiled people, and to undertake efforts to let them return to their homeland and maintain dual citizenship (in their present country of residence and in Russia). Addresses the international community and the UNPO members to support their demands and expresses readiness to cooperate with the UNPO members within the framework of the organization.

Mr. Nadir Byekir, Representative of Crimean Tartars: Draws attention to the important work of the UNPO. Acknowledges the help the UNPO is providing in Geneva with the Working Group on Indigenous People and the Subcommission on Prevention of Discrimination and Protection of Minorities. Gives an example of the effect of the UNPO on the delegations from countries which commit violations of human rights. Stresses the importance of the training the UNPO provides to its members and the research conducted through the UNPO Secretariat. States that this encourages non-violent negotiations and conflict prevention. Continues with observations on the current situation of the Crimean Tatars. The Crimean Tatars hoped the new Ukrainian constitution would have been established in 1996. Until now nothing has happened. Adds that according to Ukrainian law, the Crimean Tatars are considered as less than a national minority without any power. Calls on the UNPO for help. Without support all attempts to improve the situation will be fruitless. Addresses all the members of the UNPO, especially the new members, to use the bodies of the UNPO to achieve their goals. Expresses gratitude to the staff of the UNPO for all its work.

Mr. Zacarias da Costa, Representative of East Timor: Greets all members of the UNPO and the people of Estonia. Adds that Estonia is an example for a lot of the UNPO members because it achieved independence notwithstanding its history of occupation by foreign powers. States that the 1996 Nobel Peace Prize was awarded to Catholic Bishop D. Ximenes Belo and José Ramos Horta, Special Representative of CNRM. The award is an acknowledgement of the just struggle of the people of East Timor. Expresses the believe that the United Nations can do much more for East Timor and hopes the new Secretary General, Mr. Kofi Annan will be able to achieve much. Welcomes the outcome of the talks between the Foreign Ministers of Portugal and Indonesia. Condemns the continued brutal violation of human rights by the Indonesian authorities and the killing of armed resistance leader. Stresses that East Timor is willing to find a peaceful and negotiated settlement. Expresses his solidarity with people from Acheh, West Papua and South Moluccas—all victims of the same Indonesian dictator. Pays homage to great men and women who have given their lives in the name of freedom and democracy, in particular to Ken Saro-

Wiwa. Concludes by thanking Dr. Michael Van Walt Van Praag, General Secretary of the UNPO and the staff of the UNPO for all their work.

Mr. Nigmat Bazakov, Representative from Eastern Turkestan: Starts by saying that he is very proud that a son from Eastern Turkestan, Mr. Erkin Alptekin, is the chairman of the General Assembly. Explains that Eastern Turkestan is situated in Central Asia. Eastern Turkestan has always had difficulties with its Chinese and Russian neighbours. Eastern Turkestan was occupied by China in 1949. The situation still exists today. States that the situation of Eastern Turkestan and its Uighur population is worsening. States that genocide is occurring and China is attempting to make Uighurs a minority in their own land. States that there are concentration camps in Eastern Turkestan. People are being arrested and killed and more than one million Uighur refugees are living in Kazakhstan. Provides examples of the human rights violations conducted by Chinese authorities. Adds that China is trying to isolate Eastern Turkestan from the rest of the world. The Chinese authorities are using the natural resources of Eastern Turkestan and continue to exploit its wealth. Reminds the General Assembly of the resolution on Eastern Turkestan, adopted during the last General Assembly. Since then the situation has worsened. Calls for a UNPO mission to Eastern Turkestan before the situation becomes even more dangerous and armed conflict breaks out. States that Eastern Turkestan has the right to self-determination and seeks the attention of the international community.

Ms. Kimberly "Kealoha" Pisciotta, Representative of Ka Lui Hawai'i: Thanks the UNPO for all its work. States that the Hawaiian people are getting tired and angry, especially after the "plebiscite" of last year which had the purpose of containing the Hawaiian people. Continues with explaining the philosophy of the Hawaiian word aloha. Explains that the literal translation of the word means love, but it is much more far-reaching. Explains that through aloha a person establishes relationships with family, loved ones, the whole of mankind and the creator. States that by offering aloha to the oppressors, even though they have put the word through extreme bastardization, this will eventually direct the oppressors to the right action. Adds that aloha is about resisting what is contrary to the spirit. Adds that aloha expresses forgiveness for the hurt. States that if they must perish in the process of the struggle, the people from Hawai'i will do so with aloha in their hearts.

Mr. Azamet Nalgiev, Representative of Ingushetia: Greets all participants of the General Assembly. States that during the last 150 years the people of Ingushetia have been deported five times. Recalls that the last deportation took place in autumn 1992. States that all of the Ingush population of the suburban region of North Ossetia had been forcefully deported in two days. States that the practices of forced migration have always been kept quiet. The 40,000 refugees in Russia are living in poor conditions. The people of Ingushetia demand full rights, prosperity and rehabilitation of their nation. States that the main problem is that small nations disappear and big nations survive. The UNPO should use all kinds of methods, fora and international bodies to help small nations solve their problems. The UNPO has a good reputation and should not be ignored but used in full scale.

Mr. Aleksander Kiryanen, Representative of Inkeri: States that the first declaration of Human Rights was signed after the Second World War. After 60 years of the United Nations, there are still no rights for indigenous people. Conflicts remain between States and the indigenous peoples living within their territory. Indigenous peoples have no statehood and are not supported by any government. This means that they will lose their own language, identity and status and will finally disappear all together. Inkeri Finnish is being taught in schools but it is at the expense of the Inkeri themselves. The Russian Government will not support the education of Inkeri children in their mother tongue. There should be an international non-governmental organization for indigenous people without statehood. In October 1996 this problem was discussed at the UNPO regional meeting in Tartu, Estonia. The proposal was approved and an appeal was sent to the United Nations General Assembly. States that dialogue between a government and indigenous people is necessary to solve existing problems.

Dr. Muzaffer Arslan, Representative of Iraqi Turkoman: States that 2.5 million Iraqi Turkman, of Turkic origin, live in Iran and are the third largest population in Iraq. The Iraqi Government continues to commit human right violations against the Turkman on a daily basis. Iraqi Turkman are treated as lower citizens, tortured, executed and forced to migrate. Mr. van der Stoel has made an accurate report during his mission. States that Iraqi Turkman are prohibited from buying and selling land. Adds that it is also forbidden for Iraqi Turkman to buy commercial transport. States that in the process of forced displacement, the Iraqi Turkman are not allowed to take any belongings with them. Adds that Turkman neighbourhoods are not maintained which provokes diseases, epidemics and a rapid death rate. The Iraqi Government indoctrinates imams and priests to impose their religious authority. States that Iraqi Turkman are forced to register as Arabs. In August 1996, the Front Organization building was stormed and destroyed. Adds that one month later a peasant was shot dead without reason. To avoid the racism and hostility in Iraq, the Turkman have turned to national and international organizations which support their struggle. The situation of the Turkman is evidence to violations of international law and resolutions of United Nations Security Council.

Dr. Robert Gyula Cey-Bert, Representative of Karenni: States that during the last two years the situation of the Karenni has worsened. The Karenni were over run by the Burmese army in 1948. States that the Karenni tried to resolve the problem by non-violent means. States that in 1995 the cease-fire was violated by SLORC. Riots, beatings, rapes and arrests are a daily routine. Due to forced displacements, villagers hid in the forest and were often shot on sight by the Burmese junta who also planted landmines around the forests. States that Karenni are forced to work for the Government or for the Burmese Army for poor wages and under bad conditions. Concludes that the Karenni will not give up and hopes that they will survive with the help of the UNPO. Thanks Dr. Michael van Walt van Praag for helping the Karenni people.

Ms. Zhanetta Proshutinskaya, Representative of the Komi People: States that Komi is an autonomous Republic within the Russian Federation. The Congress of the Komi people was founded in 1991. Within the Komi Republic there are only a few indigenous peoples and 70 different nationalities. States that the Komi seek to develop their culture and use their traditions, historical monuments and language. In 1991, there were laws established regarding the status of Komi language, education, culture and economy. Remarks that adopting laws in the Russian Federation is a slow process. Adds that any attempt to adopt laws affecting the Komi takes even longer. This brings about the danger of national catastrophes. The Komi children should be prosperous, know their mother tongue, and live within a democracy. States that the Komi people are employed in agricultural businesses, administrative bodies, and in the government of the Republic of Komi. People of other nationalities in the Komi Republic should have their own rights. Concludes that the Komi must resolve the cultural, economic and legal questions that pertain to their situation as a distinct ethnic group. Remarks that five minutes is not enough to mention all of the problems affecting the Komi.

Chief Germaine Tremmel, Head Hereditary Chief, Lakota Nation: States that this was a hard year. 175 years of colonization are behind the Lakota people, from "Turtle Island", the United States. States that the population diminished from 3,000,000 to 7,000. Mentions that since the last century land belonging to Lakota has reduced to 1.5 million acres. Nowadays the Lakota people live in reservations under federal or military control, which are called concentration camps by their inhabitants. Due to the "Doctrine of Discovery" the Lakota people are viewed as unable to determine their own destiny. States that the band of Lakota to which she belongs is called "Hunkpapa", which means 'Leaders of the sacred fires'. In 1990, the Lakota, the people of the sacred white buffalo calf pipe, declared their independence. States that the Lakota people are finding ways to challenge the Colonialism of the United States through peaceful means. June 21, 1996 was declared "World Peace and Prayer Day". People from around the world were united in peace and prayer. Adds that in 1996 the Lakota situation was presented to the UN Human Rights Commission. As a result, a special rapporteur was appointed to investigate "Religious Intolerance" in 1998. States that the Lakota Nation is working to establish its own bank for economic sustainability. Encourages members of the UNPO to form alliances that are strong, as this organization is moving towards a new vision.

Mr. Reynaldo Marique, International Coordinator, Mapuche Inter-regional Council:

Expresses appreciation for invitation. After more than 350 years of territorial integrity and signed and broken peace treaties, The Mapuche people have lost control of their territory to Argentina and Chile. States that the lack of recognition by Chilean law makes the Mapuche a non-existing and unknown nation. Six dams have been built in the Bio Bio region, forcing people to migrate, damaging the environment, and creating a loss of archeological sites and ancestral land. States that the Government has not replied to the letters of appeal sent by the Mapuche. Notes that Mapuche are not against development, but want equal and sustainable development. Construction of a new road will affect 28 Mapuche villages, 3000 Mapuches, and will affect the social, economical and cultural life of the Mapuche people. In the Pulmari region, the land of six communities was confiscated when a judge broke the promise to let the Mapuche live on their ancestral land. Other Mapuche villages are threatened by an oil company which pollutes the environment by constructing a road. No action has been taken by the Government. States that many Mapuche people suffer from brain damage, cancer, and damage of the immune system, etc. Acknowledges the strong relations between the Government and the powerful companies and the related violations of the rights of indigenous people. Emphasizes that changes should be achieved in a peaceful way.

[The Chairman closes the statements of the UNPO members. Requests announcement of nominees for the election for a new Chairman, Vice Chairman and Second Vice Chairman.]

Mrs. Chungdak Dawa Koren, Representative of His Holiness the Dalai Lama:

Nominations for Chairman:

Mr. Atner Khuzangai	(Chuvashia)
Mr. Akhyad Idigov	(Chechen Republic Ichkeria)
Mr. Erkin Alptekin	(Eastern Turkestan)
Mr. Azamat Azievich Nalgiev	(Ingushetia)
Chief Germaine Tremmel	(Lakota Nation)
Senator John Nimrod	(Assyria)
Mr. Seif Sharif Hamad	(Zanzibar)
Ms. Frieda Souhuwat	(South Moluccas)
Mr. Chope Paljor Tsering	(Tibet)
Ms. Tsering Jampa	(Tibet)

Nominations for the First Vice Chairman:

Senator John Nimrod	(Assyria)
Mr. Seif Sharif Hamad	(Zanzibar)
Ms. Kimberly Pisciotta	(Hawai'i)
Mr. Atner Khuzangai	(Chuvashia)
Mrs. Chungdak Dawa Koren	(Tibet)

Mr. Göran Hansson	(Scania)
Mr. Aleksander Kiryanen	(Inkeri)
Senator Parris Chang	(Taiwan)

Nominations for the Second Vice Chairman:

Mr. Nadir Byekir	(Crimean Tatars)
Mr. Göran Hansson	(Scania)
Ms. Frieda Souhuwat	(South Moluccas)
Senator Parris Chang	(Taiwan)
Mr. Salav Alijev	(Kumyk)

[Erkin Alptekin, Parris Chang, Nadir Byekir, Tsering Jampa, Kimberly Pisciotta, Reynaldo Mariqueo, Frieda Souhuwat, and Chungdak Dawa Koren withdraw their nominations. Final list of candidates is announced.]

Mr. Erkin Alptekin, Chairman: Names the final list of candidates.

Nominations for Chairman:

Mr. Atner Khuzangai	(Chuvashia)
Mr. Akhyad Idigov	(Chechen Republic Ichkeria)
Chief Germaine Tremmel	(Lakota Nation)
Senator John Nimrod	(Assyria)
Mr. Seif Sharif Hamad	(Zanzibar)

Nominations for the Vice Chairman:

Senator John Nimrod	(Assyria)
Mr. Seif Sharif Hamad	(Zanzibar)
Mr. Atner Khuzangai	(Chuvash)
Mr. Göran Hansson	(Scania)
Mr. Aleksander Kiryanen	(Inkeri)

Nominations for the Second Vice Chairman:

Mr. Göran Hansson	(Scania)
Mr. Salav Alijev	(Kumyk)

[Session adjourns]

GENERAL ASSEMBLY V: WEDNESDAY, 16 JULY 1997

Morning session

Mr. Erkin Alptekin, Chairman: Welcomes all to the second day of the General Assembly. Calls for the resumption of Member statements.

[Representative for the Mari is not present.]

Mr. Isak Chishi Swu, Chairman of the National Socialist Council of Nagaland: Expresses his gratitude for the time he has been given to address the General Assembly on the issue of Nagaland in India. Announces there has been a major improvement in the situation, as the Indian authorities have declared their willingness to seek a peaceful solution to the problem. Stresses the importance of nonviolence, and remarks that the Naga leadership has always supported this path. Regrets this has never been respected until now. Explains both sides have come to the following terms of understanding: 1) the talks should be unconditional; 2) the talks should be at the highest level, i.e., at the Prime Ministerial level; 3) the venue of the talks should be outside India. Expresses the Naga leaders will approach this process with sincerity and earnestness. Indicates that it is premature to predict any outcome. Emphasizes that both parties must acknowledge the history that has existed between them. Expresses gratefulness for the commitment and support of the UNPO, and praises its Covenant. Gives profound gratitude to Michael van Walt van Praag for his efforts to solve conflicts by peaceful means. States that Nagaland will abide by the UNPO Covenant, whatever turn the world may take.

Mr. Ledum Mitee, Acting President of the Movement for the Survival of Ogoni People (MOSOP): Expresses that the General Assembly offers a unique and emotional opportunity to explain the situation of the Ogoni and to express appreciation for the members' support, especially during the critical period, when Ken Saro-Wiwa and eight other Ogoni activists were brutally executed by the Nigerian military. Remarks that despite worldwide condemnation following the execution of his colleagues, no positive changes have occurred. Highlights the suffering of the Ogoni due to the activities of Shell Oil Company, which devastated the environment in Ogoniland, gravely polluting drinking water. Adds that hundreds of Ogonis are detained in military jails under inhuman conditions, twenty of whom await the same fate as Ken Saro-Wiwa. Highlights that all public activities, including religious ceremonies, have been banned. Emphasizes that the Ogoni will continue their struggle for justice, so the sacrifice of their leader and colleagues has not been in vain. Thanks the UNPO for its efforts for being the voice of the voiceless, the vision for the ignored, and the hope for the suppressed. Adds that as we march into the next millennium, the UNPO needs to change. Stresses that the UNPO should strive to become an effective alternative to the United Nations. Notes that next year is the 50th anniversary of the Universal Declaration on Human Rights. Underlines that the very existence of organizations such as the UNPO exposes the lack of accomplishment in the field of human rights. Considers that next year offers a good opportunity to highlight the cases of unrepresented peoples and for the UNPO to bring awareness on how to implement the protection of human rights.

Ms. Frieda Souhuwat, Representative of South Moluccas: Explains South Moluccas were known as the spice islands in the past, and explains their geographical location. Recalls South Moluccas as the first victim of Indonesian oppression, before West Papua, East Timor, and Acheh. Gives a historical account of the islands. Highlights that the conception of an Indonesian state never existed until the Dutch agreed to hand over the colony to Sukarno in 1949. Points out that Sukarno continued the same policy of colonization, without consulting the peoples involved. Recalls the proclamation of the free Republik Maluku Salatan (RMS) in 1950 after which South Moluccas was bombed, invaded by troops, and blocked from the outside world. Mentions the strategic position of South Moluccas in the Pacific. Informs on the devastating effects of Indonesian trans-migration policy, which might result in the South Moluccans becoming a minority in their own country. Adds that by establishing factories for foreign workers, the Indonesian government creates unemployment among Moluccan people. Observes the difficult situation of Haruku, where mining exploration has begun. Indicates the possibility of environment pollution, soil erosion, and forced removal of the people from their land. Comments that Indonesia behaves as a neo-coloniser, and that the colonization of Indonesia should be considered by international law. Proposes that the UN should be called upon to maintain international peace and security, to prevent and remove threats to peace, and to suppress acts of aggression. Admits the imperfection of the present international legal order, and encourages everyone to improve it. Reminds members of the importance of acting as a united front within the UNPO.

Göran Hansson, Representative of the Foundation for the Future of Scania: Gives the geographical location of Scania, in the south of the Scandinavian peninsula. Emphasizes that the people of Scania do not enjoy any form of recognition or legal protection in Sweden and that their culture and language are rapidly dying. Gives a historical account of major events in Scania and highlights the Peace Treaty of Roskilde of 1658 which transferred Scania from Denmark to Sweden and guaranteed the Scanian people self-rule with the right to their own legislature. Emphasizes that this self-rule was nullified by Sweden in 1720, with parliamentarian functions moving to Stockholm. Announces the positive changes in Scania since the integration of Sweden into the European Union in 1995, after which Sweden signed the European Convention of Human Rights.

States that Scania has no ambition to become an independent state, since they feel the institution of the state too archaic. Expresses Scania's wishes to have regional self-determination within the framework of the constitutions of both Sweden and the European Union. Points out that the following human rights must be respected by Sweden: a) recognition of Scanians as people or nation, b) creation of a regional parliament, with full negotiation authority, c) respect for the boundaries of the historic Scania when implementing European Community regional policies, d) signing and ratification of the European Language Charter of 1992 and acceptance of Scanian as a minority language, and e) fulfilment of the United Nations resolution of 1982 and return important cultural property to places of origin. States that he represents not only the Scanian people, but also a human virtue called regional identity and self-worth. Acknowledges that all people have the right to self-worth, self-esteem and self-confidence. Reports how the rate of disappearance of languages and regional cultures grows at the alarming rate of one language every two weeks. Laments this situation and states something must be done to reverse it. Considers the UNPO to be the correct organization to do such a thing, by helping to protect the interests of nations and peoples. Says he tries to support the UNPO financially, morally and physically; especially by paying fees on time, since all depends on it.

Senator Parris Chang, Democratic Progressive Party of Taiwan: Recalls Taiwan is a founding member of the UNPO. States that the DPP has played an active role in the democratization of Taiwan, including the abolition in 1987 of the martial law imposed previously by the Kuomintang (KMT) party, and in the creation of political and institutional reforms. Highlights that thanks to the democratization of Taiwan during the past decade, all representative authorities are now elected by public ballot. Stresses that DPP is supported by half the population of the island, and its members compose one third of the parliament. Informs that new municipal elections will be held in November 1997, parliamentary elections in 1998 and presidential elections in the year 2000. Forecasts a DPP president in the year 2000, thus ending KMT rule. Remarks that Taiwan must also be aware of the threat imposed by The People's Republic of China, as evidenced by the military practices and ballistic missiles test firings just off Taiwan's two major harbours, all which occurred during the election of 1996. Points out that the Taiwanese defied Beijing's intimidation by overwhelmingly voting (75%) against reunification with the PRC. Refers to the time of the Hong Kong handover when tens of thousands of Taiwanese held a mass rally to "Say No to China", emphasizing that Taiwan has a choice.

Expresses the opposition of Taiwan people to Chinese colonialism, as might come to be in Hong Kong. States that the Taiwanese will pay the necessary price to safeguard their freedoms and sovereignty. Regrets that even though Taiwan has a population of 21.3 million people and a world-class economy, it has been denied representation in international organizations due to Chinese interference. Remarks that the Taiwanese campaign for membership in the United Nations will continue, since Taiwan is an independent sovereign state. Adds that Taiwan plays an active international role, by providing humanitarian relief in Chechenia, Somalia, Azerbaijan, Cambodia and North Korea. Reminds all present that the use of violence to solve disputes and practising hegemony in international relations is not permissible. Highlights how Taiwan condemned Russian imperialism and barbaric behaviour in Chechenia as well as China's colonial conquest of Tibet, Eastern Turkestan and Taiwan. Warns that appeasement of China could create consequences similar to the Nazi regime before World War II and calls on all present to prevent history from repeating itself. Invites all members to hold the next General Assembly in Taiwan in due course of time.

Mr. Renat Kharisov, Vice-speaker of the Supreme Council of Tatarstan: Expresses gratitude for the invitation to this General Assembly and especially to Estonia for hosting the event. Rejoices at seeing the positive changes in Estonia since the Soviet days. Hopes the beauty and quietness of this land will never be interrupted again. Describes geographical location of Tatarstan as being in the European part of Russia. Explains Tatarstan has 68,000 km2 of land rich in oil resources. Explains Tatarstan has a population of 3.7 million, of which only 25% live in the area itself. Wishes close relationships to continue between all Tatars, especially after the collapse of the former Soviet Union. States that new conditions make it difficult to open schools in the Tatar language, or for Mari people, whose rights the Tatars also respect. Emphasizes Tatarstan has developed its own laws, i.e. the Declaration of Tatar Sovereignty. Expresses that Tatarstan has never signed an agreement which joins Tatarstan to the Russian Federation, but has signed agreements to split administrative functions with Russia. Proposes Tatarstan should be a subject of international law. Adds that their country has entered other agreements with Russia concerning cultural and economical rights.

Informs that Tatarstan has close ties with other countries such as the United States, Turkey and Romania. Remarks Tatarstan is still not a stable state, but is trying to create stable organs and establish good relations. Comments that Tatarstan has received a lot of foreign investment due to the fact that they have developed laws to protect the economy. Adds they have raised both productivity and production of the industry. Informs they are preparing the Second Congress of Tatar People, where they will try to incorporate the principles of nonviolence into their laws. Refers to how Tatarstan supported Chechenia in its struggle against Russia and emphasizes that such countries will be stable factors in the world in the future. Wishes the UNPO and its members every success. Proposes the next General Assembly to be held in Kazan, the capital of Tatarstan. Distributes memos, a map of the region, and the English version of the Constitution of Tatarstan to the present and newly elected leaders of the UNPO.

Kalon T.C. Tethong, Minister of Foreign Affairs, Department of Information and International Relations, Central Tibetan Administration of H.H. the Dalai Lama: States that as one of the founding members Tibet is proud to be present in this General Assembly and looks forward to hearing input from other members. Expresses his appreciation of the statements previously presented. Emphasizes that all members must act together for the effectiveness of the UNPO. Recalls the participation of his predecessor Mr. Tashi Wangdi in this forum. Hopes to work closely with all members and aid every one to achieve the UNPO cause. Wishes that he could give a positive report similar to Nagaland, but regrets that is not the case of Tibet. Remarks that the grave situation of Tibet has deteriorated even more since the last General Assembly. Notes that the Chinese government has increased its oppression, discrimination and marginalization of Tibetan people.

Exemplifies that Chinese authorities have stepped up their campaign against H.H. the Dalai Lama, even prohibiting the display of his photograph. Regrets the new leadership in China after Deng Xiao Ping's death has not brought new changes in the approach to Tibet. States that H.H the Dalai Lama has approached this new leadership, but so far there has been no positive response. Explains the government of H.H. the Dalai Lama maintains a high profile international campaign, holding hearings on the human rights situation in Tibet and on the illegitimacy of Chinese rule in Tibet. Recalls the demonstrations held in Brussels (1996) and Geneva (1997), where thousands of people expressed their support for the Tibetan cause. Expresses thanks for the support from the UNPO and the attendance of its members to these demonstrations. Adds that a secret UNPO mission visited Tibet in April this year to investigate whether the PCR's rule over Tibet could be considered a form of colonialism. Emphasizes that the mission's verdict was an unqualified 'yes'. Reports that cultural repression, genocide and other atrocities continue to occur with the characteristic arrogance of the Chinese leaders; and that when H.H the Dalai Lama asked for help from international bodies, China accused him of abusing politics under the pretext of religion and internationalizing the issue.

Notes that China continues to publish all kinds of falsities for propaganda. Stresses that the suppression of religious practices and the desecration of the Tibetan language are the most current sources of danger. Adds that mandatory primary school is in Chinese only, and that it is impossible for young people to enter higher education without knowing Chinese, if you are a lucky candidate. Hopes gatherings such as the UNPO will offer non-violent solutions to our problems and thanks all for their cooperation and friendship, especially the people of Estonia.

Ms. Inaria Kasiepo, West Papuan Peoples Front: Introduces herself and Ms. Grace Roembiak. Recalls that West Papua is one of the founding members of the UNPO and expresses happiness to be surrounded today by many people sharing the same aspirations. Recalls the Indo-Dutch agreement, signed 35 years ago in New York with the help of the government of the United States (which was worried about communism spreading through the islands), which allowed Jakarta control over West Papua. Explains that this treaty, by the elimination of the independent status of West Papua, was contrary to the fact that on December 1st, 1961 West Papua's national symbols, national flag (the Morningstar), and the name of their country had been inaugurated. Underlines that this occurred despite the fact that the rights of self-determination of the West Papuan people were implicitly mentioned in the New York agreement. Recalls that the rights of the West Papuan people were not taken into consideration during the preparation the treaty nor during its implementation. Underlines that the United Nations failed in its duties to protect West Papua. States that no concrete measures have been taken by the United Nations to restore peace in the region. Refers to the UNPO Yearbook for more information on historical facts. Adds that after November 19, 1969, the West Papuan right to self-determination has not appeared on the United Nations agenda. Points out that the West Papuan people work towards a re-examination of their case by the United Nations.

States that in 1965 the Organisasi Papua Merdeka (OPM) was established.

States that the OPM has turned into an armed and civil resistance movement and is used as a symbol for freedom. Adds that the Morningstar and the OPM have been used in non-violent actions as well, such as flag raisings and independence proclamations. Regrets the brutal retaliation by the Indonesian army, especially during the funeral of Dr. Thomas Wainggai, one of the leaders of non-violent action who died in prison. Adds that demonstrations involving West Papuans have been held in Jakarta since the last General Assembly. Stresses the complexity of the problem is increasing, now spreading to economic and environmental issues as well. Points out the severe effects of the market economy and trans-migration on the population of West Papua, turning West Papuans into second rate citizens in their own country. Stresses that this also has diversified the resistance movement which is not only directed against Indonesian occupation but also against any foreign occupation, such as that of multi-national corporations. Comments there are positive changes as well in the West Papuan situation, such as awareness and solidarity by international organizations, and the growing number of non-governmental organizations (NGOs) in the country. Mentions the hostage taking by the OPM in January 1996, which ended after four and a half months. Underlines that the OPM does not advocate violent methods, but that it recognizes some positive results of the hostage situation since it augmented international awareness of the movement. Laments that Indonesian troops used it as an excuse to send in more troops to track down the OPM at all costs. Comments that this resulted in the isolation of the area, raping of women and burning of villages after which thousands of people were displaced. Points out the Indonesian government does not give any space for negotiation and thanks the Secretary General Dr. Michael van Walt van Praag for his mediation during such a difficult time. Assesses the involvement of West Papua in the UNPO is in itself an act of self-determination which gives them the opportunity to challenge the international order and the United Nations system. Rejoices the increase of membership in the UNPO and its inclusive character. Emphasizes that the UNPO, due to its growth, should improve structure and effectiveness, in order to increase membership and member involvement. Proposes the creation of regional offices for these purposes and for practical reasons. Greets new members and thanks all.

Mr. Seif Sharif Hamad, Vice Chairman and Representative of the Civic United Front: Is honoured to be present in the Fifth General Assembly of the UNPO. Remarks the UNPO is a global organization, bringing together different peoples, who must work to create a just world. Recalls the UNPO was founded in 1991 to help people facing oppression of all sorts. Highlights that the UNPO stands on firm principles and therefore is a reputable organization. Stresses the importance of peoples to take their destiny into their own hand. Comments on the importance of timely fee payment by all members, since this is the main means of support of the UNPO. Adds that Zanzibar will do everything possible to make arrears. Extends thanks to the General Secretary and his staff for all their efforts. Expresses his satisfaction to see some former members of the UNPO now in the United Nations, congratulates them and requests them to always help out in the quest of all the other members who have not achieved such status. Expects that more members will become independent in the future. Reminds all of the importance of acting in unison to create world-wide awareness, and commends the UNPO for its efforts to sensitize the world. Believes that the UNPO has championed Zanzibar's cause most effectively. Stresses the non-violent strategy of the Zanzibari people, supported by the UNPO. Suggests that the Secretariat must be strengthened and be made more efficient, and see to it that the members obtain a means of implementing resolutions. Highlights the importance that all members should always be fully informed of each others situations, for which he fully supports the use of internet since "communication is power". Hopes that Zanzibaris will have attained at least a partial victory in the near future. Invites the UNPO to establish a regional office in Zanzibar, for all African affairs. Recalls unfair elections procedure and the great pressure exerted on the people of Zanzibar, who could resort to violence should their patience run out. Looks forward to hosting a General Assembly in Zanzibar and thanks all those present.

Mr. Menelaos Tzelios, Representative of the Greek Minority in Albania: Reminds all of the terrible situation in Albania during the last six months. Recalls that the ruling party abused its power in May 1996, by shutting down free press and media, thus receiving 95% of the votes in the elections. Explains the desperate actions of destitute Albanians, which followed the unveiling of the Pyramid games, fully supported by the government. Stresses that consequently 1,600 people lost their lives. Considers that if Albanians suffer, the Greek minority will suffer too, since they share a common history of 2000 years. Lists several goals of the Greeks in Albania: 1) the right to their own language, 2) to be included in civil jobs, police and armed forces, 3) that their churches and the property of the churches should be restored, after being taken by the communist government. Explains that the exact number of Greeks in Albania is not clear, since the government counts 58,000, the CIA 260,000 and the minority itself 400,000. Stresses that the respect of the rights of people should be carried out always, irrespective of their number. Proposes an internationally monitored census to be conducted. Thanks the UNPO for its support in the past, especially with the mission to Albania, and Dr. Michael van Walt van Praag for his participation in the trial of their leaders. Reports that the recent elections of June 29, 1997 were carried out freely and a new government has been democratically elected. Hopes this government will not commit the same mistakes as previous governments and informs that the European Community and the United States are eager to help the people of Albania.

Ms. Nadejda Zolotariova, Member of All Udmurt Association "Udmurt Kenesh": Indicates Udmurt is a new member, located in the western part of European Russia, with a population of 700,000 people. States they are hard working people, eager to create a new nation. States that they have two languages, Udmurt and Russian, both of which have been officially recognized in the Language Law, which has yet to be implemented. Stresses the critical economic situation of Russia, and the resulting economic reforms which have caused great suffering, especially in rural areas. Adds that this impedes the continuation of the mother tongue. Explains they have created a committee to preserve all cultures, with no special distinctions. Adds that draft laws have been prepared dealing with the future conditions for a multi-national society. States, however, that Udmurt should be a priority in order to keep the language alive. Invites all members of the UNPO to attend a Conference which focuses on the solution of the crisis, to be held on 11 November, in commemoration of the proclamation of the Republic in 1920. Presents books for the UNPO library, their flag and coat of arms.

[The process of electing new organizational officers begins.]

Mr. Erkin Alptekin, Chairman: Informs that Dr. Michael van Walt van Praag will explain the legal procedure of the election again. Allows nominees to give their statements briefly.

Addresses the participants for the last time. Commemorates his youth and his father. Being a youngster in Eastern Turkestan, he thought had all the problems of the world, but after meeting other people and members realised that they have even bigger problems. Refers to his father's struggles and achievements for the Uighur people. Was taught to be, act, live like and fight for the Turkish, Islamic, and Uighur cause and for humanity. Recalled a meeting in 1989 with Mr. Lodi Gyari, the legal adviser of His Holiness the Dalai Lama, who persuaded him to serve the cause of humanity and to share the same destiny. Says the UNPO was founded to take care of all human beings. Pleased by contracting Dr. Michael van Walt to the organization, who devoted himself to the UNPO. Expresses enthusiasm for the work of Deputy General Secretary Tsering Jampa and others as well for the work of the UNPO. Notes that despite difficulties and without distinguishing between ethnicity, race or colour, the UNPO team works together and stimulates each other. Changes have to be made, the struggle for democracy and self determination should be stimulated. Rules have to be followed, without accusing, blaming and undermining other members. The relations and brotherhoods should be strengthened. New blood and a new generation is needed. the UNPO is growing fast, changes have to be made, but with the same principles, and unity between the members. Advises close co-operation, effective lobbying within government and international organizations. Says that members come from North, East, South and West, and should work together effectively with equally shared power. Stresses that the members from the different geographical regions can learn from each other.

Appeals to the participants to have a close look at the nominations, to trust the nominations and elections. Urges the chairperson to be elected to work effectively and to be trusted by the members. Adds that the elections are not about power or prestige. Thanks the members for the support and confidence. Extends special thanks to Dr. Michael van Walt van Praag for his daily charge and commitment to the organization. Expresses gratitude for the extended financial resources Dr. Michael van Walt van Praag has made possible. Urges members to be careful with their finances, pay their fees and continue their spiritual, physical and financial support to the UNPO. Thanks everybody and wishes all the best for the new office holders to be elected. Calls the nominees in alphabetical order to the stage in order to present themselves.

[Break]

Mr. Erkin Alptekin, Chairman: Reopens session, reads the names of the nominees and invites the first candidate to step forward to present himself.

Mr. Atner Khuzangai, President of the Chuvash National Congress: Says he was born in the Chuvash Republic in 1948. Chuva People are of Turkic origin in language and culture and practice Orthodox Christianity or other local religions. States that he graduated at the Oriental Faculty of the Lenin State University in Moscow in 1972. Notes that he received a degree in the Arab language, majored in Arab philosophy and earned a post-graduate degree in International Law and International Relations. Speaks various languages; German, French, Turkish, English and Russian. Says in 1992 he was one of the founders of the Chuvash National Congress, and is highly esteemed by his own people. Notes that he was elected State Deputy of the Chuvash Republic in 1994. Adds he was Chairman of the Committee of International Language and Culture, which adopted various important international documents. Ends by referencing his experience with UNPO policies and problems.

[Nominee questioning takes place, and the second candidate steps forward.]

Mr. Akhyad Idigov, Chairman of the Parliament Committee of Foreign Affairs of Chechenia: Says he was born in 1948 in Kazakhstan. Notes that after growing up in the countryside, the family moved back to the city in their homeland. Attended a Russian high school. Graduated in Construction Engineering, worked with Italian and Bulgarian construction companies. States that he is one of the founders of the National Liberation Movement, then became Member of Parliament, Deputy Chairman of Parliament and Chairman of the Chechen Parliament. Says that until 1997 the Chechen Parliament had to work underground; difficult but good work was done. Notes that he acted as a representative of the Chechen Party in all the negotiations in Moscow. Stated that he was elected again in the parliament this year and is now Chairman of the Parliament Committee of Foreign Affairs, and also serves as a member of the National Court. Notes that he is married and has two children. Claims Chechenia is an example for all nations in the struggle for self-determination. Says Chechenia is ready to fight for all small states and unrepresented nations.

[Nominee questioning takes place, and the third candidate steps forward.]

Chief Germaine Tremmel, Head Hereditary Chief, Lakota Nation: Says her official name means "Lady seen by her nation" in her traditional language. Comes from the United States, in traditional language "Turtle Island". Started freedom struggle at a young age. At 19 took stand for massacres on women and children, defended the sacred site where the bodies were buried. Was arrested and jailed for four years. Notes that her husband and children had to live underground during the time of detention. Recalls that after jail, at age 26, she learned the English language to understand the oppressor and the treaties. Notes that she studied at the University of Colorado and graduated in Federal Indian Law. Returned home to represent her people legally. Founds the "Women of all Red Nations" to defend the rights of all indigenous women. Has nine children and fourteen grandchildren. States that she remains traditional in culture and language. States that she has a been legal representative of her people for the last four years and has been active in the international arena. Says the main reason to join the UNPO was the mutual respect for each struggle, to speak and act together to achieve their goals. Notes that she is the only female Head Heredity Chief, and has 70,000 members and covers a lot of territory. Believes in the principle of the UNPO that there is an equality between all nations and peoples. Stresses that she lives, as should all members, according to the Covenant of the UNPO. States that she is honoured to be nominated and that it is a milestone for her people. Stresses that she is not above other participants. Adds that wherever she will go she will represent the members of the UNPO and expects that wherever members go they will do the same.

[Nominee questioning takes place, and the fourth candidate steps forward.]

Mr. Seif Sharif Hamad, Vice Chairman, Civic United Front of Zanzibar: States that he was born in 1943 in Zanzibar. Notes that he has studied in Zanzibar and Dar es Salaam. Mentions that he graduated in Political Science and International Relations. In 1964, Zanzibar was occupied and the Zanzibaris planned a strategy to gain sovereignty. Penetrated the ruling party successfully. Became member of the Central Committee and Director of Economic Planning. Was elected Chief Minister of Zanzibar, then started to speak for the rights of Zanzibaris. Recalls that he was fired and jailed. Recalls that under pressure of international and human rights organizations, he was finally released and continued with the struggle. States that he founded the Civic United Front and became the Vice Chairman. In 1995 the first elections were held in Tanzania. Claims that he won the elections, but due to large riggings the Presidency was taken from him. Comments that through numerous diplomatic missions and meetings with prominent officials, he has gained a lot of useful experiences. Recommends strengthening the UNPO and developing new ideas as a necessary next step. Accepts the nomination because everybody else declined and nobody wanted to take the responsibilities. States that if elected, he will help and cooperate with all the members as much as possible.

[Voting takes place.]

Mrs. Chundak Dawa Koren, Chairperson of the Election Committee: Announces the results: Dr. Khuzangai 10 votes, Mr. Idigov 4 votes, Chief Tremmel 6 votes and Seif Hamad 18 votes. No candidate has more then 50% of the votes.

[Procedural discussion]

Mr. Erkin Alptekin, Chairman: Announces the three remaining candidates, Mr. Khuzangai, Chief Tremmel and Seif Hamad.

[New ballots are distributed and voting takes place.]

Mrs. Chungdak Dawa Koren, Chairperson of the Election Committee: Announces the results: Dr. Khuzangai 13, Chief Tremmel 4 and Seif Hamad 21.

Clarifies that the candidate of Zanzibar received more than 50% of the votes. States that the representative from Zanzibar has been elected as the new Chairman.

Mr. Erkin Alptekin, Chairman: Asks Mr. Seif Sharif Hamad if he accepts the election result. States that he is honored to present the new Chairman of the UNPO, Mr. Seif Sharif Hamad. Advises the new Chairperson to act fairly in regard to the organization and wishes all the best.

Mr. Seif Sharif Hamad, Chairman: Accepts the election as Chairman of the UNPO for the coming two years. Expresses gratitude for the given confidence and promises to serve to the best of his ability. Extends special thanks to Mr. Erkin Alptekin for his good work as a Chairman of the UNPO. Acknowledges successes of Mr. Erkin Alptekin and will continue his good work. Requests the delegates to work hard and cooperate closely to achieve the objectives and goals of the UNPO. Wishes to work in close co-operation with the Secretariat and hopes that Dr. Michael van Walt van Praag will be willing to teach and support him. Expresses gratitude towards the other nominees and states that only one person can win, but this does not mean that he is better than the others. Accepts because of the urge to serve mankind. Looking forward to work closely with the members of the UNPO. Stresses that members should be united and fight together to let the whole world know of the existence of the UNPO and to realise the shared objectives one day.

[Erkin Alptekin, the former Chairman, steps down and receives a standing ovation.]

Mr. Seif Sharif Hamad, Chairman of the General Assembly: Closes the session.

[Session adjourns]

General Assembly V: Wednesday, 16 July 1997

Afternoon session

Mr. Seif Sharif Hamad, Chairman: Convenes the General Assembly. Proposes the election of the two Vice-Chairs, and suggests that the same Election Committee be used. Clarifies that there remain two candidates: Mr. Göran Hansson, Representative of Scania, and Mr. Atner Khuzangai, Representative of Chuvashia. Calls Mr. Khuzangai to introduce himself.

Mr. Atner Khuzangai: Says he will do his best to improve the UNPO activities, especially in the former Soviet region.

Mr. Göran Hansson, Representative of Scania: Reads parts of his previous statement. Believes the UNPO is the most important organ to help the members to achieve shared goals. Commits himself to help the UNPO in every possible way. Stresses the importance of timely payment of membership fees, since all members depend on the income of the organization. States that he cannot refuse this nomination, and will do his best to satisfy all. Recalls Scania has been a member of the UNPO since 1993, and that he has been a member of the Steering Committee since January 1994, and also has headed and participated in other committees. Informs that he has built up the web-site of the UNPO since 1995. Believes people degenerate when they lose control over their own affairs, and that countries should recognize the peoples that live within their boundaries. Stresses that it is necessary for people to have the right of self-determination and to ensure their wishes are respected.

[Voting takes place.]

Mrs. Chungdak Dawa Koren, Representative of Tibet: Announces Mr. Khuzangai received 24 votes, and Mr. Hansson 13.

Mr. Seif Sharif Hamad, Chairman: Congratulates Mr. Atner Khuzangai on his victory, and asks him to give his acceptance speech.

Mr. Atner Khuzangai, First Vice-Chairman: Thanks the respect and the support given to him, and declares he will do his utmost to justify the trust and hopes of the members, so together all can reach their goals. Quotes Mr. Ismael Gaspari who stated: " In our thoughts, speech, and work we must be together." Thanks all.

Mr. Seif Sharif Hamad, Chairman: Moves to begin the election of the Second Vice-Chair. Informs that there are two candidates: Mr. Göran Hansson, Representative of

Scania, and Dr. Salav Alijev, Representative of Kumyk.

Mr. Göran Hansson, Representative of Scania: Adds to what he had said in his previous statements. Accepts the present nomination and considers it to entitle the same responsibility as any other to which he was nominated before.

Dr. Salav Alijev, Representative for Kumyk: Expresses that Kumyk is a multi-national country with more than 30 peoples. Adds that the Kumyk movement was a pioneer in the 1980s within the former Soviet Union, and that they have always worked hard to claim national rights for all peoples. Has worked in the Assembly for Turkish Peoples and in several congresses, and was one of the initiator of the North Caucasus peace initiatives. Participates every year in international fora and decided to join the UNPO, since it is an organization with similar goals as our people. Condemns violence as a means to solve conflict since it creates a blood-bath and highlights that they desire to solve their problems through political and thus non-violent means. Adds that he has taught Literature at university level for 24 years, first of different peoples of the former Soviet Union, and later of the peoples of Caucasus. Points out he is a Doctor of Science and has headed the national movement. Acknowledges he is old (more than 60) and that he speaks no English, even though he does speak other languages.

[Nominee questioning takes place, followed by voting.]

Mrs. Chungdak Dawa Koren, Representative of Tibet: Announces the results of the election: Mr. Hansson 28 votes, Dr. Alijev 9.

Mr. Göran Hansson, Second Vice-Chairman: Thanks everyone for their support and states that the UNPO is worth working for. Promises to do his best in his new position.

Mr. Seif Sharif Hamad, Chairman: Calls Senator Parris Chang, President of the Steering Committee, to deliver his report.

Senator Parris Chang, President of the Steering Committee: States that all present have witnessed UNPO democracy in action during these elections. Recalls how in the Taiwan Parliament some of its members have even fought on the floor and stresses the contrast of these peaceful and smooth elections. States that the UNPO, since its foundation, has always defended the rights of nations, indigenous peoples, and other unrepresented groups by reporting to and informing the international community and the media of their grievances. Explains the function of the Steering Committee and the election procedures of its members. Reminds that regional balance must be kept in mind. Informs that in 1996 and 1997 three sessions of the Steering Committee were held: In The Hague in February 1996, Geneva in October

1996, and in Bonn in March 1997, respectively. Notes that eight new members were admitted during this period and that observer members are under the same financial obligation as members. Emphasizes the decision to suspend Georgia, due to its actions contrary to the Covenant of the UNPO. Underlines Georgia attacked Abkhazia and supported Russia during the war against Chechenia.

Points out that the decision to hold the Fifth General Assembly in Estonia was taken by the Steering Committee because of the need to give a global character to the organization. Proposes Taiwan as the next host for the General Assembly meeting, and also for the next meeting of the Steering Committee to evaluate the conditions of the site. Comments that the election of the new General Secretary is a major task, especially in conjunction with the election of the Chairman and two Vice-Chairpersons. Explains that the Steering Committee created an Election Committee to consider applications for the new General Secretary. Stresses that in the past the Steering Committee has not functioned as well as desired, since it has been difficult to convene twice a year due to the great distances between members. Proposes the following measures to restructure the UNPO: a) alleviate the General Secretary and the Secretariat of excessive functions, also creating a structured decision making process, b) elect a Treasurer and a Fundraiser either by the General Assembly or by the Steering Committee, since the UNPO will require greater resources in the future, and c) empower the President of the Steering Committee to take greater responsibility in decision making and have larger executive powers as well, since the Steering Committee does not meet often enough to give appropriate guidelines. Requests members to think about the direction they want for the UNPO, which has grown dramatically in size during the past years. Concludes that the UNPO should consider how to consolidate its organs and efficiently use the limited resources. Thanks audience for their attention.

Mr. Atner Khuzangai, First Vice-Chairman (chairing the meeting): Asks if there are any questions on the Steering Committee report.

Mr. Erkin Alptekin, Representative of Eastern Turkestan: Advises that the Treasurer should be elected by the Steering Committee, which would permit his/her replacement in a timely fashion, without having to wait for a General Assembly.

Mr. Ledum Mitee, Representative of Ogoni: Asks for report of the Steering Committee to be submitted in writing to the members, in order to facilitate voting.

[Break]

Mr. Seif Sharif Hamad, Chairman: Reopens session. Asks the General Secretary to present his report.

Dr. Michael van Walt van Praag, General Secretary: Says his report can be found in the package that was handed out to all the participants. States that because the General Assembly is already behind schedule, he will not read his report as originally planned. Comments that the report summarizes the essential points that affected all individual members during the last two years and gives a general overview of the work the UNPO has carried out in the last two years. Remarks that the report also addresses the position of the UNPO in today's world. (Notes that the different seating of delegations in the conference room today has no political significance. Clarifies that this was done to prevent one delegation from constantly sitting in the back while others are always seated in the front). States that he will address the essential issues pertaining to the history, present situation and future of the organization as well as the failures and successes of the UNPO.

Explains the UNPO was born out of the frustration of nations, peoples and minorities who were excluded from the international community and unable to participate in decisions regarding their own destiny. The UNPO was founded to provide its members an international voice and to take their demands seriously. Reminds that the rights of indigenous peoples, nations and minorities need recognition in order to reduce and prevent conflicts. Says the UNPO started with 15 members and now consists of 50 members, it has grown from a club of friends to a political organization. Clarifies that he refers to the political quality of the organization in a positive sense: the organization is able to make decisions, take responsibilities and to represent the members. Reminds that this was the intention of the founding members. Adds that because of its evolution, the UNPO has become more complicated, members have different interests which may conflict at times. States that the UNPO must continue to learn to deal with such things. Informs that such a process is occurring now and is working well. States the Secretariat has grown as well, and must continue to provide services and representation to enhance its credibility. Adds UNPO is unique because it crosses borders of nations and religions and because the members run the organization themselves. States that this has a large psychological impact and makes existing governments and international organizations see the UNPO as a challenge to the current status quo. Adds that this challenge is also because the UNPO enables its members to speak openly, making governments uneasy. Continues with the achievements of the UNPO. Informs that recognition of the UNPO within the international community is growing and the members see and use the strength of the organization. States that the number of candidates for the position of chairman shows more members are willing to take responsibility.

Says that the General Assemblies and conferences which are organized by the UNPO serve as a way for the members to get their message out to the world. Reminds that media and intelligence agencies cover these events and make sure the message reach the parties involved. Adds that reports of the events are published and are included in the UNPO Yearbook. The UNPO Yearbook is published in the same series as the Yearbook of the United Nations and provides useful information to the outside world. Stresses the growing importance of UNPO missions. In the past, reports of these missions were neglected, but are now taken more seriously. One of the reasons is a report on the situation in Abkhazia in which the General Secretary of the UNPO warned against the danger of a possible war. Recalls that at first the report was neglected. Adds that after war broke out, some concerned governments turned to the UNPO for advice. States that this enhanced the credibility of the report of UNPO missions. Says the Media and Information Centre of the Secretariat publishes all important UNPO events and activities.

Emphasizes the importance of being taken seriously. Notes that representatives of nations, peoples and minorities are not always taken seriously by governments or the United Nations. Clarifies that they are often seen as too emotionally involved and to lack a clear view on the situation. Stresses that this is nonsense and that the leaders of the movements involved are generally in a better position to identify the problems and needs of their people than the so called experts, who have gained their experience from books and reports. States now the importance of the UNPO is growing, the organization is more often able to arrange meetings between member representatives and high government officials. Emphasizes that this also makes the UNPO more credible. Adds the credibility of the UNPO and the members depends on each other. Underlines that the legitimacy of the member representatives and the way they live up to the principles of the UNPO determine the credibility of the organization. Adds that the credibility of the members depends partly on the accuracy and quality of the work of the UNPO. Urges members to provide the secretariat with accurate information so the UNPO can carry out its task as efficiently as possible.

States the need to reduce conflict. Refers to the war in Abkhazia. Large number of international organizations, specialists in conflict prevention try to be objective and deny the emotional aspect of the problem. Reminds that the UNPO is not neutral but is involved, because of its commitments to the members of the UNPO. States that the UNPO acts with credibility and objectivity, while understanding the emotional aspects. Observes that positive and negative emotional aspects are present in political changes and conflicts. Emphasises the strength of the UNPO: the close working relationship and the trust between the secretariat and the members. Acknowledges the obligation to present and advise the members in the best possible way. Organises diplomacy and negotiation trainings available for all the members. States the need to participate is stimulated by the Effective Participation Program, which enables all members to participate in the UN and other international fora. States the need to reduce oppression. Remarks that members should learn from each others' experiences and share information. Reminds that no expert can know the actual situation better than the local people who have been through the difficulties within their homeland. Says a combination between individual and collective solidarity should be made. Advises that the Secretariat should be more effective in providing special methods to develop strategies. States that the UNPO has goals to achieve. States that each member and each case needs full attention to be provided with the best possible strategy. Says that attention should be paid on individual, regional and thematic problems. Gives the example of the lack of international laws on forced deportations. States that contact among the members should be built, strengthened and made successful. Says that the issue of self-determination has been brought to the attention of the United Nations by the UNPO. Normally self-determination is seen as the source of conflict. Clarifies that in fact it is the refusal of governments to deal with the issue of self determination that is the real source of the conflict.

Remarks that the UNPO has not achieved all its goals yet, otherwise all would not be here today. Reminds of the war in Chechenia. States that the UNPO helped the Chechen member in all possible ways but could not prevent the war. Calls this a failure. Adds that another failure is that the support between members should be more stimulated by the secretariat. Suggests that in case of an emergency with one of the members, the other members should be informed and be willing to provide their support and assistance to the member in need. Observes that other failures of the UNPO are the lack of a Legal Council, handling of the workload and priorities. States that these deficiencies in the organization should be discussed during this General Assembly. Says another failure is the inability to appropriately follow up on missions. Mentions that other problems surface and need direct attention undermining the following up of missions. Recommends better decision making processes and prioritizing. Emphasizes the Secretariat needs guidance from the members. Suggests that they should inform the Secretariat of the accurate situation in their regions and make clear requests for assistance in time of despair. Says that some members ask frequently and get a lot of attention from the Secretariat, while other members do not request anything and fail to provide the Secretariat with accurate information. Underlines that this attitude should change, members should keep the secretariat well informed on their situation. Says that more people representing the members should be working at the Secretariat. Adds that this would increase the emotional and historical knowledge of the regions. States that in order to achieve this, a list of vacancies should be sent to all members and they should provide potential candidates. Repeats that the above mentioned deficiencies of the organization should be addressed during this General Assembly.

Says that a memo by the General Secretary on the decision making structure was included in the information package that was distributed at the start of the Assembly. Urges members to read this before the elections of the General Secretary and the Steering Committee.

Introduces Deputy General Secretary Tsering Jampa, who runs the Secretariat in The Hague. Introduces the Assistant General Secretaries; Mr. Menelaos Tzelios (for UN Affairs and for the Americas), Dr. Linnart Mäll (for Eastern Europe Region and Director of the Tartu Coordination Office), Ms. Helen Corbett -in absentia- (for the Asia-Pacific Region), Mr. Victor Kasiëpo (for the Environment), Ms. Frieda Souhuwat (for Financial and Personnel Affairs) and Ms. Karen Onthank (Director Washington Office). Stresses that the UNPO members should use the knowledge and capabilities of the Assistant General Secretaries for information and support.

Introduces and thanks the staff from the The Hague and Tartu Offices. Thanks the Special Assistant to the General Secretary Ms. Julie Berriault (in absentia). Says that only three staff members are fully paid. Notes that the rest of the staff are volunteers. Hopes to be able to pay more staff members in the future.

Says that the work and procedures of the Peace Action Council will be explained tomorrow by Mr. Don Rodrigo Carazo Odio. Says that the UNPO should look at the possibilities of modern technology, such as Internet. Introduces Mr. Göran Hansson to show the participants a slide-show of the UNPO website he has made.

[Session adjourns]

GENERAL ASSEMBLY V: THURSDAY, JULY 17, 1997

Morning session

Mr. Seif Sharif Hamad, Chairman of the General Assembly: Convenes the General Assembly. Invites the General Secretary to make announcements regarding the nominations of the post of General Secretary and the new Steering Committee members.

Dr. Michael van Walt van Praag, General Secretary: States that according to the agenda, the opportunity for nominations for the post of General Secretary and the new Steering Committee members closes before lunch. Explains that the situation for the Steering Committee is as follows:: some members' terms have expired and some members' terms are still in effect, and need not be re-elected. Adds that the terms of the following members have expired: Mapuche, Chittagong Hill Tracts, Kosova, and Crimea. Proposes that a decision should be made according to the memo on restructure. Indicates that members of the Steering Committee should appoint an individual who should attend all Steering Committee meetings for the purpose of continuity. Moves on to say that members cannot have two positions of leadership within the organization. Explains that a member of the Steering Committee may not hold any other official office within the UNPO. Emphasizes the importance of regional balance within the Steering Committee, which needs to be reaffirmed by the General Assembly before a new General Secretary and Steering Committee are elected.

[Procedural discussion takes place, resulting a forwarded motion.]

Mr. Parris Chang, President of the Steering Committee: Informs that the motion of Senator Nimrod on the election procedure for the post of General Secretary should be voted upon, and that in future a new procedure on this issue must be worked out. Notes that there were several nominations for the function of General Secretary, without the proper procedure for the Steering Committee to process them. Points out that all nominees should be interviewed by Senator Nimrod, so he can give his final suggestion to the Steering Committee.

Mr. Seif Sharif Hamad, Chairman: Refers to Article 19 of the Assembly Rules of Procedure, which states that motions are voted upon in the order in which they are proposed, unless the Chairperson decides otherwise. Invites Senator Nimrod to repeat his motion.

Senator John Nimrod, Representative of Assyria: Presents his motion again on the procedure of the election of the General Secretary. Notes that if procedure is not approved by the General Assembly then it is necessary to go back to the rules as stated in the Covenant. Adds because the General Secretary is not up for re-election, the participants should consider carefully the candidates for the position of General Secretary. Emphasizes the candidates should be fully qualified and there is a need for a good job description, which states the basic duties of the General Secretary.

Kalon T.C. Tethong, Representative of Tibet: Calls for a more systematic way to address the different issues since the election of the members of the Steering Committee and the election of a new General Secretary are discussed simultaneously. Proposes to proceed with the point of the members of the Steering Committee, and that the procedure on the election of General Secretary should be discussed later.

Mr. Seif Sharif Hamad, Chairman: Estimates that if the question of double functions within the Steering Committee is resolved in the suggested way, a new member should be appointed from the same region. Stresses that the issue at hand is the question of the double functions in the Steering Committee.

Mr. Erkin Alptekin, Representative of Eastern Turkestan: Stresses that in the past the rule was followed that the President of the Steering Committee had the power to control the Steering Committee and the Secretary on behalf of the General Assembly. Adds that the Chairman and Vice Chairs of the General Assembly, therefore, have no right to vote in the Steering Committee since he/she would have to vote on himself. Indicates that it follows that he/she is automatically relieved of his/her function of member of the Steering Committee.

Representative unidentified: A proposal to finish the decision on the elections of members of the Steering Committee is forwarded. Comments are made that it is necessary to have the names of individuals who will represent the specific members in the Steering Committee, both for the ones to be elected and those remaining. The importance of having a list to see which regions are represented is stressed. It is further stressed that it is important to clarify that the President of the Steering Committee should be elected either by the Steering Committee or by the General Assembly. Members are requested not to belabor this issue too long, and it is recommended that a nomination list be made. An urge is made to leave the question of the election of new General Secretary for later.

[Procedural discussion takes place.]

Senator Parris Chang, President of the Steering Committee: Reminds all on the interview procedure for the post of General Secretary. Urges those that have not been interviewed to make an appointment with Senator Nimrod. Names nominees: Mr. Alptekin, Dr. Arakchaa, Dr. Mäll, Senator Nimrod, Chief Tremmel.

Ms. Frieda Souhuwat, Representative of the South Moluccas: Highlights that the nomination commission does not merely consist of Senator Nimrod. Indicates that there are also nominations outside of the UNPO. Proposes that the function of the General Secretary should be fully clarified, and that this should be done before the interview, so the nominee understands the scope of the function. Comments that Senator Nimrod is also on the list of nominees.

[Senator Nimrod withdraws his name and voting takes place.]

Mr. Seif Sharif Hamad, Chairman: States that 32 voted in favour of the proposal and that 9 were against, and that, therefore the motion is passed. Moves on to the second issue of the election of members for the Steering Committee. Indicates, after restating all considerations on the matter, that those members of the Steering Committee who have not yet finished their term should continue until the next General Assembly, or that all of them should resign. Underlines the remark made by the General Secretary for the need to preserve continuity in the Steering Committee. Recommends that those who have not yet completed their term should continue.

Mr. Menelaos Tzelios, Representative of the Greek Minority in Albania: Comments that the second issue is not a matter for discussion in the General Assembly, and that they should, therefore, only vote on the issue of expiring.

Mr. Akhyad Idigov, Chairman of the Parliament Committee of Foreign Affairs of Chechenia: Reminds all that the time has not yet elapsed for the remaining members of the Steering Committee, and that they should, therefore, stay in office. Stresses that the provision in the Covenant is not violated.

Mr. Seif Sharif Hamad, Chairman: States that Article 33 paragraph 2 of the Assembly Rules of Procedure is very clear, and that there are, therefore, 5 vacancies. Asks the General Secretary to inform the General Assembly on the current representatives of the Steering Committee.

Dr. Michael van Walt van Praag, General Secretary: Names the members who are currently on the Steering Committee: the Chechen Republic Ichkeria, Chittagong Hill Tracts, Crimea, Inkeri, Iraqi Turkman, Kosova, Mapuche, Taiwan, Tibet, Ogoni, Scania, South Moluccas. Adds that membership of the Steering Committee of Mapuche, Chittagong Hill Tracts, Kosova, and Crimea has expired, and remarks that Scania has ceased to be a member and, therefore, another position has become vacant. Highlights that regional balance should be maintained. Lists the current members that were elected on regional grounds: Ogoni, Iraqi Turkman, Mapuche, Taiwan, Scania, Inkeri, and the Chechen Republic Ichkeria. Observes that both Mapuche and Scania should be replaced by members of the same region, and that the others are open to all the members of the UNPO.

Mr. Seif Sharif Hamad, Chairman: Requests that the nominations for the members of the Steering Committee should be handed in after the break. Reminds that there are five vacancies, two of which require regional representation. Suggests that the same election commission as yesterday should be responsible. Invites the General Secretary to represent the proposal on restructuring UNPO organs.

Dr. Michael van Walt van Praag, General Secretary: Explains two points from the memo, regarding Structure and Governance, and what emerged from the Steering Committee. Suggests the memo should not be handled as a package, and points out that it is composed of elements based on the experience of the Steering Committee and the General Secretary. Informs that it offers a way to improve the UNPO, especially now that the UNPO has so many members. Assesses that the UNPO should be transparent in its procedures. Underlines that members of the Steering Committee should be appointed on an individual basis by the respective members, in order for the members of the Steering Committee to build up expertise through continuity. Proposes the consolidation of the Steering Committee with the Board of the Foundation of the UNPO in the Hague, which is responsible for managing finance. Points out that in the proposal, the Steering Committee automatically sits on the Board of the Foundation (Stichting). Recommends that a Treasurer should be appointed by the Steering Committee.

Observes that the lapse of time between General Assemblies is too long, and that in the proposed way a Treasurer could be replaced without having to wait for a General Assembly. Suggests that the Treasurer should be elected on the basis of individual capacity, rather than on the basis of being a member. Emphasizes that the proposals for restructuring have several reasons: 1) That it will alleviate the tasks of the General Secretary, since he has had to fulfil too many different functions, which has impeded his work. Finance has become increasingly important, and demands for proper accounting are called for, especially to have accountability towards members and funders; 2) That it is inappropriate for the General Secretary to have to make decisions daily, and, at the same time, to make decisions on the financial aspects, 3.) That it is crucial to have consultation, and not leave finance to one person, i.e. the General Secretary. That no matter how responsibly the General

Secretary acts, members may feel he/she is biased towards certain projects. Hopes that the members do not feel he has acted biased in any way. Moves on to the matter of decision making in the Steering Committee. Points out that the Steering Committee only meets every six months, for two days, in which all decisions need to be made. Claims that this is not feasible, and that, consequently, resources and time of the General Secretary are wasted. Requests that the General Assembly should decide on the formation of the Executive Committee, comprised of the Treasurer, the President of the Steering Committee, and the General Secretary. Explains that Dutch law requires that the individuals are fixed and are not changed all the time. Suggests that they meet frequently, approximately once every month. Indicates that the General Secretary up till now had to be invited by the Steering Committee. Suggests that the General Secretary should be a non-voting member in the future. Emphasizes that the role of the President of the Steering Committee must be strengthened without having to change the Covenant. Remarks that this will reduce the responsibilities of the General Secretary. Ends by stating that the Board of the Foundation will, under the proposal, have full control over finance of the UNPO.

[Nominee questioning takes place.]

Senator Parris Chang, President of the Steering Committee: Emphasizes the importance of restructuring the UNPO and improving decision making mechanisms. Informs that the Steering Committee has reviewed and approved some of the proposed changes by the General Secretary including: a)To elect a new treasurer who would be a non-voting member of the Steering Committee and in charge of the budget, fundraising and other financial responsibilities in order to lighten the General Secretary's burden; b) To form an Executive Committee consisting of three people, the General Secretary, the President of the Steering Committee and the Treasurer, which should meet at least once every two months and make all necessary decisions and policies while the General Assembly and the Steering Committee are not in session; c) To have the General Assembly give greater powers to the President of the Steering Committee.

Mr. Ledum Mitee, Representative of Ogoni: Comments that some of the proposals made by the General Secretary and by the President of the Steering Committee overlap, but that they should vote on them separately anyway. Clarifies there are several important issues on the table: a) To compose the Board of the Foundation with the members of the Steering Committee; and b) To name the Treasurer. Remarks that this is an issue with which he does not feel comfortable. Adds that the Covenant has imposed several duties on the General Secretary and that those should not be usurped by the Treasurer, since the Covenant states so. Reminds that the rules should not be violated. Considers the General Assembly should amend the Covenant to that purpose, for which the members would require a new proposal to be presented one month prior to any voting session. Admits it is necessary to alleviate the

General Secretary of all his burdens.

Mr. Khagi-Mourat Khatoukaev, Representative of Circassia: Thinks that the Covenant must be changed in order for the UNPO to function more effectively and supports the proposal of the General Secretary. Suggests to vote now on the suggestions of the General Secretary concerning the structure of the UNPO, and create a Committee which should include the General Secretary and the President of the Steering Committee in order to prepare concrete proposals.

[Procedural discussion takes place.]

Dr. Michael van Walt van Praag, General Secretary: Explains all his proposed changes can be made without altering the Covenant. States this could be done by naming the Steering Committee as the Board of the Foundation and by having the Treasurer appointed by the General Secretary and approved by the Steering Committee. Continues by saying that the Steering Committee is allowed to create sub-committees, and an Executive Committee would fall under this category. Adds this should be enough until the next General Assembly, when proper changes in the Covenant could be made.

[Procedural discussion takes place.]

Mr. Seif Sharif Hamad, Chairman: Clarifies the wording of the motion and requests a vote be taken.

[Voting takes place.]

Announces the results: In favour 28, Oppose 2, Abstain 3.

Dr. Michael van Walt van Praag, General Secretary: Advises the General Assembly to pass a resolution calling the General Secretary to appoint a Treasurer and for that to be approved by the Steering Committee.

Mr. Erkin Alptekin, Representative of Eastern Turkestan: Seconds the motion.

Mr. Seif Sharif Hamad, Chairman: Asks all to vote.

[Voting takes place.]

Results: In favour 36, Oppose 0, Abstain 2

Moves to create an Executive Committee composed of the President of the Steering Committee, the General Secretary and the Treasurer, since the General Secretary needs others in decision-making.

Dr. Michael van Walt van Praag, General Secretary: Adding to this, I propose that a motion be presented by which the General Assembly proposes for the Steering Committee to have a little group, called whatever the members want, composed of the President of the Steering Committee, the General Secretary and the Treasurer. Adds that this small committee would be a decision making body, during the periods in which there is no session of either the Steering Committee or the General Assembly. Adds the following motion would not imply an alteration of the Covenant.

Senator John J. Nimrod, Representative of Assyria: Understands by this that an outsider may become part of the Steering Committee if the Treasurer is not a member.

Dr. Michael van Walt van Praag, General Secretary: States that was not the meaning of the proposal and clarifies it would be a request for the General Secretary to meet with the Treasurer and the President of the Steering Committee regularly.

Mr. Ledum Mitee, Representative of Ogoni: Reminds members that the General Assembly is the highest organ and that it has already decided the Steering Committee should meet at least twice a year, leaving the possibility open for them to meet even more often. Adds that he does not see the problem in keeping it like that, which implicitly allows some members of the Steering Committee to meet as often as possible. Remarks the General Assembly should not interfere too much in the functions of the Steering Committee. Agrees with Senator John J. Nimrod, Representative of Assyria. Requests the General Assembly to vote in such a way.

Dr. Michael van Walt van Praag, General Secretary: States that there are three basic articles in the Covenant dealing with the Steering Committee: 1) One that deals with its composition, 2) a second that deals with its meetings at least twice a year and, 3) a third which states that the Steering Committee possesses all of the powers delegated to it by the General Assembly. Adds that if the General Assembly decides to delegate functions to the Steering Committee it would be correct for it to do so in light of article 18 of the Covenant.

Chief Germaine Tremmel, Representative of the Lakota Nation: Reads Article 31 of the Assembly Rules of Procedure: "Article 31 Creation of Committees: The Assembly, in consultation with the General Secretary, can create special bodies, such as committees or working groups. The Assembly shall specify the mandate of these bodies." Suggests the Steering Committee should prepare a better worded motion which would specify the mandate of this Executive Committee and present it to the General Assembly. Asks if anyone would second her.

Senator Parris Chang, President of the Steering Committee: Clarifies that article 31 of the

Assembly Rules of Procedure refers only to when the General Assembly is in session and asks what happens when there is no session.

Mr. Ledum Mitee, Representative of Ogoni: States he does not understand what has been said, and asks if, for example, the Election Committee chosen during this General Assembly is valid only in this session. Moves again that the Steering Committee to create a sub-committee.

Dr. Michael van Walt van Praag, General Secretary: Remarks that if what Mr. Ledum Mitee suggests is done, the Steering Committee could not appoint any one who is not its member, therefore leaving the President of the Steering Committee to meet with himself once a month. Requests the General Assembly to give concrete directives to the Treasurer and the President of the Steering Committee to meet with the General Secretary, since this is not prevented by the Covenant. Stresses that if such a decision is important for the decision making policies of the UNPO, then the General Assembly as its supreme organ should do it.

Mr. Ledum Mitee, Representative of Ogoni: Submits respectfully that the Steering Committee has power to invite the General Secretary to one of its sessions and that this should cover the need of a creation of a sub-committee.

Mr. Erkin Alptekin, Representative of Eastern Turkestan: Highlights what the General Assembly should do is lighten the load of functions now given to the General Secretary. Recalls how difficult it has been in the past for the Steering Committee to meet and stresses it is of utmost importance to provide a means for effective decision making within our organization.

[Procedural discussion takes place.]

Mr. Zacarias da Costa, Representative of East Timor: Requests an end of discussion on the issue and requests a vote.

Mr. Seif Sharif Hamad, Chairman: Answers this is not possible since the President of the Steering Committee has raised a point that has still not been dealt with. Suggests the Executive Committee should meet at least once a month since 'whenever possible' is too vague. Indicates the importance of giving this Executive Committee a mandate as well.

Dr. Michael van Walt van Praag, General Secretary: Understands what is being asked and emphasises that there is no intention to allow this executive body to usurp the powers of the Steering Committee. Underlines that it would be created to carry out the functions of the Steering Committee more effectively, when other bodies are not in session. Notes that the General Assembly has two choices: to leave things as they are, or to ask the General Secretary to consult with others before making important decisions.

Mr. Ledum Mitee, Representative of Ogoni: Expresses he would be more comfortable if the motion stated that in order to carry out his functions, the General Secretary should consult with the President of the Steering Committee and the Treasurer.

Mr. Salav Alijev, Representative of the Kumyk People: Requests the Chairman to please explain to him what the problem is, and the concrete proposals. Emphasizes the General Assembly should vote on the issue.

Mr. Erkin Alptekin, Representative of Eastern Turkestan: Recalls how during all these years the General Secretary has always tried to contact members of the Steering Committee and the Chairman, but there was often no prompt response, and he had to decide on important issues alone. Adds that sometimes those same people consulted would later reprimand the General Secretary for his decisions, and even accuse him of unaccountability. Proceeds by stating that therefore the General Secretary asked them to create a mechanism through which to make the UNPO transparent and effective. Invites the General Assembly to do something in that respect in order not to depend on only one person anymore.

Dr. Michael van Walt van Praag, General Secretary: Explains communication is not enough, since the General Secretary can use several means of communication to reach the President of the Steering Committee and the Treasurer and still not receive prompt response. Insists that a regular meeting by these officials is of extreme necessity for the UNPO.

Mr. Seif Sharif Hamad, Chairman: Suggests that the General Assembly direct the President of the Steering Committee, the General Secretary and the Treasurer to meet once a month in order to make important decisions. Asks for a second to the motion.

Chief Germaine Tremmel, Representative of the Lakota Nation: Seconds the motion.

Mr. Seif Sharif Hamad, Chairman: Orders the voting to begin.

[Voting takes place.]

Results: In favour 31, Oppose 0, Abstain 2.

[Session adjourns]

GENERAL ASSEMBLY V: THURSDAY, 17 JULY 1997

Afternoon session

Mr. Seif Sharif Hamad, Chairman: Convenes session. Asks Mrs. Chungdak Dawa Koren, Chairperson of the Election Committee to step forward to receive the last nominations for the Steering Committee. States that all draft resolutions should be handed over to the Resolution Committee.

Mr. Zacarias da Costa, Representative of East Timor: Stresses that regional balance should be kept in mind.

Mr. Seif Sharif Hamad, Chairman: Invites the General Secretary to make clear the procedure of electing the members of the Steering Committee.

Dr. Michael van Walt van Praag, General Secretary: Urges the participants to indicate precisely the name of the individual they want to appoint to the Steering Committee.

Mr. Seif Sharif Hamad, Chairman: Moves to the agenda. Proposes first to discuss the report of the General Secretary, followed by the report of the President of the Steering Committee. Invites the participants to make comments.

[Comments are forwarded]

Mr. Seif Sharif Hamad, Chairman: Asks if any participant wishes to comment on the report of the General Secretary. Invites Don Rodrigo Carazo Odio to the stage to deliver his account of the Peace Action Council.

Don Rodrigo Carazo Odio, Co-Chairman of the Peace Action Council: Expresses his joy to work with all members for justice. Explains the Peace Action Council was an initiative of the General Secretary, who invited him to join. Continues that the Peace Action Council consists of eminent men and woman from all continents. Adds that the Council was created to prevent violent conflict or end wars between states and peoples and minorities. Informs that the Peace Action Council is composed of an equal number of leaders from among the UNPO member nations and peoples, and from persons outside that membership who enjoy international recognition. Informs that together the Council members have broad access and credibility among both state and non-state actors. Points out that the Peace Action Council is an autonomous body. Notes that the Peace Action Council consists of six persons now, since two of the original members have passed away, namely Lord David Ennals and Dr. Abdul R. Babu. Adds the current members are, beside himself, Kasur Lodi G. Gyari, Ms. Mairead Corrigan Maguire, Dr. Michael Ghebernegus, Mr. José Ramos Horta and the General Secretary of the UNPO, Dr. Michael van Walt van Praag. Informs that when all positions are filled, the Peace Action Council consists of 25 internationally respected persons, of whom 12 Council members will be selected from among the UNPO members, and 12 from among eminent persons outside the UNPO. The 25th member is the General Secretary of the UNPO. Adds that an Executive Committee will be established which will be responsible for running the Council and for reviewing each request immediately, and deciding on action to be taken. Points out that the Peace Action Council is headed by two co-chairpersons. Remarks the Council will be assisted throughout by the Secretariat in the Hague. Invites members to talk with him about his work. Assures that he will be available for all members.

Mr. Seif Sharif Hamad, Chairman: Thanks Mr. Carazo for his short and clear presentation. Underlines that everybody understands and appreciates the work of the Peace Action Council. Asks if there are any questions regarding the Peace Action Council. Continues that the structure of the UNPO has been dealt with extensively, and that the organization of the Secretariat will be discussed during the presentation of the UNPO budget. Calls on member delegates to deliver comments on the report of the President of the Steering Committee.

Mr. Erkin Alptekin, Representative of Eastern Turkestan: Recommends that members should try to find ways for the Steering Committee to work more effectively. Points out that it is important that all members of the Steering Committee attend every meeting. Suggests that the formation of regional offices would be helpful.

Mr. Seif Sharif Hamad, Chairman: Agrees with Mr. Alptekin. Explains that the Steering Committee works on behalf of the General Assembly and that the Steering Committee has to do the work, because the General Assembly meets only once every two years. Adds that the Steering Committee should make decisions, which are now made by the staff in the Hague. Stresses that the members are the policy-makers of the UNPO. Re-emphasizes that members should always send the same representative to the Steering Committee, and that they, therefore, have to appoint a permanent delegate. Requests that the Assembly should propose how to make the Steering Committee more effective.

Mr. Ledum Mitee, Representative of Ogoni: Comments on the Report of the President of the Steering Committee. Wishes to discuss its recommendations separately, so participants will realize where the Steering Committee is heading and which points need to be clarified. Indicates that this would be helpful and that it would give the General Assembly a sense of direction in which the Steering Committee is heading.

Senator Parris Chang, President of the Steering Committee: Refers to the discussion of the recommendations made by the General Secretary, commenting that they are almost the same. Repeats his recommendations: 1) A Treasurer must be appointed by the General Secretary and should be approved by the Steering Committee; 2)

Establishment of an Executive Council, consisting of the General Secretary, the President of the Steering Committee and the Treasurer; 3) To empower the President of the Steering Committee, so he/she may act on behalf of the Steering Committee. Explains that the President of the Steering Committee now only has the authority to preside over the Steering Committee.

Mr. Ledum Mitee, Representative of Ogoni: Thanks the President of the Steering Committee for his explanation. Brings up the issue of membership. Considers that it is the right moment to expand the organization and calls the Steering Committee to proceed in this direction. Points out that the Steering Committee should not close the door for the brothers and sisters who wish to join the UNPO. Reacts to the suggestion of the President of the Steering Committee to increase the power of the President. Observes that this would be too revolutionary, and does not want to adopt this rule.

Mr. Seif Sharif Hamad, Chairman: Informs that the Steering Committee may delegate its power to the President, but that the General Assembly maintains control of the Steering Committee.

Mr. Erkin Alptekin, Representative of Eastern Turkestan: Observes that the UNPO is not a single nation, but that it consists of 50 different members. Warns that if the President of Steering Committee acts on his own, without prior consultation of the Steering Committee, the interests of some members could be jeopardized, which could endanger the regional character of the UNPO. Comments that on important and delicate issues the Steering Committee should be able to decide collectively, after which the General Secretary should carry out its policy. Advises the President of the Steering Committee and the General Secretary to work closely together.

Senator Parris Chang, President of the Steering Committee: Acknowledges that a decision on the establishment of an Executive Board already has been made.

Mr. Seif Sharif Hamad, Chairman: States that no more authority will be delegated to the President of the Steering Committee: Urges the members elected to the Steering Committee to appoint an individual to the Steering Committee who will attend all the meetings of the Steering Committee.

Mr. Ledum Mitee, Representative of Ogoni: Observes that many members are faced with a lot of problems in their own organizations, which can prevent them from attending the meetings of the Steering Committee. Suggests that two individuals per member should be appointed, so the second individual can fill in, in case the former should be absent. Assesses that this would secure continuity.

Mr. Erkin Alptekin, Representative of Eastern Turkestan: Suggests that the appointed individual could inform the Steering Committee that another person can fill in for him/her, should the appointed person not be able to come.

Dr. Michael van Walt van Praag, General Secretary: Stresses that the issue of appointing individuals was already agreed upon this morning, and that the agreement is now weakened. Remarks that if members cannot find an individual willing and able to serve properly in the Steering Committee, they should refuse to be nominated.

Mr. Reynaldo Mariqueo, Representative of Mapuche: Agrees that in principle only one individual should be appointed, but indicates that should any problems arise within the region of the member they should be free to send someone else.

Mr. Seif Sharif Hamad, Chairman: Acknowledges that this discussion had already been concluded this morning and that the General Assembly should move on to another topic.

41. *Dr. Michael van Walt van Praag*: Informs that after the break registration forms will be handed out for three Working Groups on Nonviolence as a preparation for the upcoming conference in Tallinn. Explains that the Working Groups will be based on the Conference Program: 1) Conditions for Effective Nonviolent Change; 2) Nonviolent Strategies; and 3) The role of the UNPO in relation to Nonviolence. Advises that large delegations divide themselves among the different Working Groups.

[Break]

Mr. Seif Sharif Hamad, Chairman: Re-opens session. Says the Election Committee has a problem with the nominations for Steering Committee, since nominations should be of individuals, not of participants. Clarifies the names of the nominees should be mentioned. Continues with the next topic on agenda: finances of the UNPO. Proposes a presentation and explanation of the budget, since members have already received the budget memo this morning. Remarks that the discussion will take place tomorrow morning, and allow more time to the members to study the numbers.

Dr. Michael van Walt van Praag, General Secretary: Invites Ms. Frieda Souhuwat, the Assistant General Secretary for Finances, to the floor. Explains the Financial Statements for the year ended December 31, 1996. Mentions the Statements contain three parts: a) the financial statement for the year 1996 of the Secretariat the offices in Washington and Tartu, which still has to be officially approved by the accountant, b) the budget and financial reports up to June 1997, which are also not final but give an idea of our present financial position to the members, and c) the budget for the General Assembly and the Conference on Nonviolence which shows the expected incomes and the expenditures. d) The fourth part shows the draft budget for 1998 which is before the General Assembly for adoption.

Explains the UNPO functions primarily due to fundraising, a small portion from member fees, a larger portion from governments and private or individual foundations. Mentions he has included a memo in the information package explaining potential sources for funding: contribution from members can be used for expenses for which other funders do not provide money. This, for example, includes salaries for staff. Foundations and governments provide funds for specific projects. States that we also have started experimenting with investing some money with a group with whom the South Moluccan government has close relations and with whom it has had very positive experiences. This will also give us more flexibility in the future if we can build up our own funds. Stresses that funds can only be raised for special objectives since governments and organizations do not give money for the free use of the UNPO. Comments that these donors demand the presentation of draft proposals for meetings, projects, programs, trainings or missions to be clear and accompanied by a detailed budget. Adds that governments and organizations only pay after having received a report and detailed budget of their sponsored activity. Says that the accountants of the donors sometimes check the financial books of the UNPO to verify how the money was spent. Explains there is only some flexibility in the way the UNPO can spend money.

Describes the two major programs of the UNPO: The Effective Participation Program and the Conflict Prevention Program. Highlights that these programs have proven to be popular and allowed the UNPO to receive good donations. Explains the sections of budget including those of fixed and variable costs. States that all he has stated should give members a clearer idea of the figures. Informs that during the last years there has been a steady increase in the funds raised. Observes that in 1997 the UNPO has been able to pay a few (4) of their staff members. Recalls how two years ago the UNPO almost ran out of money, and that this must be avoided in the future. Says the UNPO is careful in spending money. Clarifies the budget for 1998 is still in draft form since we are not certain to be able to raise the money. Requests the members to take all this information into account when reading the budget and accompanying memos.

Mr. Erkin Alptekin, Representative of Eastern Turkestan: Asks the General Assembly to consider the possibility of opening a small UNPO office in Moscow, since many members come from this region. Adds that this would facilitate communication.

Dr. Michael van Walt van Praag, General Secretary: Mentions there is already a UNPO Coordination Office in Tartu and explains that regional offices should be equally distributed through the different regions as should the funds and resources. Expresses that there are no UNPO offices in the Africa or the Asia Pacific region, and that an office in Moscow would give two regional centers for the CIS/Baltics region.

Mr. Khaji-Mourat Khatoukaev, Representative of Circassia: States that the members of CIS have difficulties communicating among each other because the region is underdeveloped. Emphasizes it is necessary to open an office in Moscow. Informs that the communication within Russia is easier and cheaper than with countries outside of Russia. Adds that Mr. Yuri Anchabadze, from Abkhazia, has prepared a concrete proposal which is still in an initial state and would even allow the office to be self-funded at the beginning, without aid from the UNPO.

Mr. Seif Sharif Hamad, Chairman: States that regional offices will be discussed later on during the General Assembly, and that the members should leave those topics for then. Moves to the topic of regional meetings, which will be held this afternoon. States that three points should be considered by all regional meetings: a) creating a regional office, b) sending a representative to work with the staff in the Hague office, c) how to improve communications between the members, and between the members and the Hague office. Adds that the regions can meet in the Assembly hall, upstairs or outside as they wish. Invites the Election Committee to step forward and announce the nomination list for the Steering Committee.

Mrs. Chungdak Dawa Koren, Representative cf Tibet: Reads nominees for the Steering Committee. Announces there are two candidates for regional seats: 1) Chief Germaine Tremmel, Head Hereditary Chief of the Lakota Nation, for the Americas, and 2) Mr. Menelaos Tzelios, from the Greek Minority in Albania. States that the nominees for the open chairs are: Mr. John J. Nimrod, Representative of Assyria; Mr. Pradhir Chakma, from Chittagong Hill Tracts; Mr. Erkin Alptekin from Eastern Turkestan; Mr. Zacarias da Costa, from East Timor; Mr. Menelaos Tzelios, from the Greek Minorities in Albania; Ms. Kealoha Pisciotta from Hawaii; Kosova (no name); Mr. Amin Ibragimov from Kumyk; Ms. Isak Chishi Swu, Representative of Nagaland; Mr. Renat Kharisov from Tatarstan; and Dr. Kara-Kys Arakchaa, Representative of Tyva.

Mr. Seif Sharif Hamad, Chairman: States that the nominees should accept their nominations.

[Procedural discussion takes place.]

Mr. Salav Alijev, Representative of Kumyk: Announces they nominate Mr. Amin Ibragimov, Representative of Kumyk, for the regional seat.

Mr. Seif Sharif Hamad, Chairman: Repeats that the Eastern European region should be allowed to fill the vacated regional seat. Adds that the only nominee has been from Circassia, but that it was presented by someone from a different region, therefore being invalid.

Dr. Michael van Walt van Praag, General Secretary: Notes that the Steering Committee is composed of twelve members, of whom five have vacated their seats. Reminds the General Assembly that out of those five seats, three were fixed regional seats: one for Europe, the second for Eastern Europe and a third for the Americas. Announces that the members that still remain in the Steering Committee are: Chechenia, Inkeri, Iraqi Turkman, Ogoni, South Moluccas, Taiwan and Tibet. Adds there are two additional seats open to members from any region, nominated by any region.

Mr. Seif Sharif Hamad, Chairman: Formally announces the vacancy of the regional seat for the East European Region in the Steering Committee. Asks members of the region if they have nominees. Asks all persons who had been nominated to state if they accept or not. Asks Mrs. Chungdak Dawa Koren, Representative of Tibet, to read the names again. Announces the lists of nominees will be distributed at the regional meetings.

[Session adjourns.]

General Assembly V: Friday, 18 July 1997

Afternoon Session

[A portion of this session was closed. Citation begins with resumption of the open session.]

Mr. Michael van Walt van Praag, General Secretary: States that one of the failures of last year was that the UNPO failed in the creation of a Legal Council, which will try to advise members, organize meetings, review the requests and establishment of ad hoc tribunals for members. Asks the Chairman to put a point, regarding the establishment of such a Council, on the agenda. Says that while all the members are here at the moment, the opportunity should be taken to discuss the issue together. Suggests that a body of jurists should be created with lawyers from inside and outside the UNPO. Refers to the relation with international and human rights laws. Urges members who are interested to meet tomorrow morning before the morning session to discuss the matter.

Mr. Atner Khuzangai, Vice-Chair: Asks if there are any questions. Stresses that this is an important commission for the UNPO and that the members should think and talk about this subject thoroughly. Moves on to the next point, the election of the members of the Steering Committee.

Mr. Ledum Mitee, Representative of Ogoni: Comments on the election procedure. Refers to the article 16 in the Covenant which states that the Steering Committee shall be composed of five to fifteen people. Reminds that there are now only twelve members on the Steering Committee. Suggests that three more candidates should be elected to increase the number of Steering Committee members to fifteen.

Senator Parris Chang, President of the Steering Committee: Admits Mr. Mitee is right. Remarks that coordinating fifteen people is even worse than coordinating twelve people. Adds that the United Nations has 168 members and a Steering Committing of fifteen persons and that the UNPO has fifty members so a Steering Committee of fifteen people is a bit too much. Adds that if the number of Steering Committee members increase, the budget should be adapted as well.

Mr. Ledum Mitee, Representative of Ogoni: Remarks that the UNPO should not be compared with the United Nations. Stresses that as many people as possible should be involved in decision-making. Wonders why at the time of the creation of the UNPO, the Steering Committee was reserved for fifteen members.

Dr. Michael van Walt van Praag, General Secretary: Observes that under Title II, Article II, paragraph II in the Steering Committee Rules of Procedure the Chairperson and the Vice Chairperson participate in the Steering Committee without the right to vote. Questions whether the number has already been reached by adding up the Chairs with the members.

Senator John Nimrod, Representative of Assyria: Underlines that it is good that members of the Steering Committee are chosen on an individual basis as it generates a certain degree of discipline and non-attendance should be sanctioned. Seconds Mr. Mitee's motion to increase the number of seats.

Mr. Aslambek Kadiev, Special Representative of the Chechen Republic Ichkeria to the UNPO: Points out that with more members on the Steering Committee the budget should increase. Requests that no sanctions are put into effect when members are simply not able to attend. Gives the example of Ken Saro-Wiwa being a Steering Committee member while arrested and, therefore, unable to attend Steering Committee meetings.

Chief Germaine Tremmel, Representative of Lakota Nation: Refers to the General Secretary's question. Asks if extra members are admitted they could serve alternately in order to make a quorum.

Dr. Michael van Walt van Praag, General Secretary: Is not sure if the Covenant provides for this, but should the General Assembly wish to amend the Rules of Procedure or even the Covenant they could decide to do so.

Mr. Atner Khuzangai, Vice Chairman: Says that yesterday the report of the President of the Steering Committee was adopted and that the possibility to nominate is closed and therefore, the proposal contradicts the agenda.

Senator John J. Nimrod, Representative of Assyria: Considers the motion to be valid and asserts that the Vice Chairman has no right to deny this, because it was not suggested to open the nominations list.

Mr. Atner Khuzangai, Vice Chairman: Recommends that the General Assembly should adopt a new item on the agenda.

Mr. Ledum Mitee, Representative of Ogoni: Stresses that the motion does not introduce anything new and that they should not be restricted from exercising their right within the mandate of the law. Adds that even if the possibility had not been in the Covenant, the General Assembly should be able to amend. Highlights that the Chairs are not members of the Steering Committee. Adds that to deny the motion would give a bad sign, especially since other members agree with the motion.

Mr. Erkin Alptekin, Representative of Eastern Turkestan: Notices that their is consensus on the motion and that it needs to be voted upon. Underlines, as a former Chairman, that should they refuse it would create a bad precedent for the future.

Mr. Atner Khuzangai, Vice Chairman: Suggests the motion from Mr. Mitee and seconded by Senator Nimrod and Mr. Alptekin should be voted upon.

Mr. Bata Bayartuev, Representative of Buryatia: Asks whether the increase of the members of the Steering Committee will be regionally based or should be open to everyone. Adds that if it should be regionally based, regions need to be redefined.

Mr. Atner Khuzangai, Vice Chairman: Refers to Article 16 of the Covenant, which stipulates that the Steering Committee shall be composed of five to fifteen persons but the discussion on composure should be left for later.

Mr. Ledum Mitee, Representative of Ogoni: Affirms that the new members should not be based on regional representation but rather on personal experience.

Senator Parris Chang, President of the Steering Committee: Asks Mr.. Mitee that should the motion be supported, the nominations would be opened again.

Mr. Ledum Mitee, Representative of Ogoni: Comments that there are already eleven nominees. Indicates that it might not be necessary to open the nominations again. Adds that this is for all members to decide. Suggests to proceed as is.

Mr. Atner Khuzangai, Vice Chairman: Proposes to vote on the motion.

[Voting takes place.]

Results: 12 in favour, 22 against and 5 abstained. Observes that the motion has been defeated. Moves on to the election of the new members of the Steering Committcc.

Dr. Kara-Kys Arakchaa, Representative of Tyva: Withdraws from the nomination list for the Steering Committee as she is also running for the post of General Secretary.

Mr. Atner Khuzangai, Vice Chairman: Invites Mr. Nadir Byekir of the Election Commission to step forward.

Mr. Nadir Byekir, Representative of Crimea: Reads the nominations for:

Regional seats: 1)Chief Germaine Tremmel (Lakota) for the Americas; 2) Mr. Menelaos Tzelios (Greeks in Albania), Kosova for Europe; 3) Mr. Teuvezh Kazanokov (Circassian) for CIS region;

Open seats: Senator John J. Nimrod (Assyria), Mr. Pradhir Chakma (Chittagong Hill Tracts). Mr. Erkin Alptekin (Eastern Turkestan), Zacarias da Costa (East Timor), Mr. Menelaos Tzelios (Greeks in Albania), Ms. Kealoha Pisciotta (Hawaii), Mr. Renat Kharisov (Tatarstan), Mr. Isak Chishi Swu (Nagaland).

Mr. Sertac Bucak, Representative of Kurdistan: Remarks that the same person has been nominated twice, for the regional and an open seat. Requests clarification on this issue.

Mrs. Chungdak Dawa Koren, Representative of Tibet: States that this is not allowed and asks if the Kosova nomination is allowed, because the delegation is not attending the General Assembly and no specific individual is named.

Dr. Michael van Walt van Praag, General Secretary: Answers the question of Mr. Bucak. Explains that it is possible to be nominated for two seats as long as there are two consecutive ballots cast. Adds that it is not possible to be nominated on two lists if the ballot is cast in one. Requests the General Assembly to decide on the fairer of the two.

Senator John J. Nimrod, Representative of Assyria: Declares that the General Assembly should pass a resolution that a nomination can only be on an individual basis and not be based on members. Adds that the Election Committee recommends that each region makes a selection. States that if a member is selected for a regional seat, the person should withdraw from the nomination from an open seat. Suggests that the Kosova nomination is removed from the nomination list since no individual has been nominated.

Mr. Atner Khuzangai, Vice Chairman: Accepts the motion and suggests voting takes place.

Mr. Menelaos Tzelios, Representative of Greeks in Albania: Withdraws his nomination for the open seat list.

Mr. Teuvezh Kazanokov, Representative of Circassia: Proposes to make two separate ballots, one for regional seats and one for open seats. Urges to begin the vote immediately.

Mr. Atner Khuzangai, Vice Chairman: Acknowledges that Mr. Menelaos Tzelios has been removed from the open seats list. Adds that Kosova is also taken off the list since no individual was nominated.

Mr. Nadir Byekir, Representative of Crimea: Comments that in the resolution regarding the individual basis of members, no set time is given when the individuals should be named. Suggests that they can appoint the individual after one month so the issue can be discussed on the home front.

Dr. Michael van Walt van Praag, General Secretary: Underlines that this debate on delaying nomination of an individual is not sound. Stresses again that for the members of the Steering Committee to sit on the board of the Foundation it is legally required to know the names of the individuals, commenting that it is merely a practical and legal question and not a political one.

Mr. Reynaldo Mariqueo, Representative of Mapuche: Expresses his discontent over the individuality requirement stating that it violates democratic principles.

Mr. Atner Khuzangai, Vice Chairman: Points out that the decision on the individuality requirement has already been made yesterday.

Mr. Qenan Sheji, Representative of Albanians in Macedonia: Wonders why Kosova can not be on the list, stating that it is in the law of the UNPO that the organization should defend those members, in this case Ms. Edita Tahiri, that are unable to join the General Assembly. Asks the General Secretary to explain. Claims to be representative of all the Albanians, i.e. also of Kosova, stressing that he sat in for the Kosova Steering Committee member during the last days. Recalls that the Albanians are not divided by choice. Agrees with Mr. Mariqueo that the followed procedure is undemocratic and that it does not matter which individual represents the region.

Dr. Michael van Walt van Praag, General Secretary: Remarks that he is not aware that the Albanians have ceased to be three separate members. Emphasises, however, that it is possible for members who are divided throughout different states to be regarded as one member if they should wish so. Points out that, in fact, a decision to this effect as made by the last Steering Committee. Adds that should they be one member, they could still consist of separate components. Repeats he is not aware that the Albanians have as yet reemerged as one member.

Mr. Qenan Sheji, Representative of Albanians in Macedonia: Acknowledges that the Albanians are indeed one member now.

Dr. Michael van Walt van Praag, General Secretary: Underlines that this decision has not been communicated to the Secretariat.

Mr. Atner Khuzangai, Vice Chairman: Recommends that the Assembly should now move on, stressing that the reemergence of the Albanians has to be supported by proper evidence.

Mr. Qenan Sheji, Representative of Albanians of Macedonia: Expresses his anguish by pointing out that due to difficulties at the Serb border that Kosova is unable to attend the General Assembly.

Ms. Frieda Souhuwat, Representative of South Moluccas: Expresses her confusion over the assertion by Mr. Sheji. States that he has no clear mandate, and that ,therefore, they must proceed with voting.

Mr. Ledum Mitee, Representative of Ogoni: Asserts that the nomination of Kosova is invalid since Mr. Sheji should have been nominated by the region. Wonders what the consequences are and asks whether the seat should be left open.

Mr. Atner Khuzangai, Vice Chairman: Adjourns the session.

[Break]

Mr. Atner Khuzangai, Vice-Chairman: Re-opens session and proceeds with the election of members for the Steering Committee.

Dr. Michael van Walt van Praag, General Secretary: Adds that if only one nomination has been made for a regional seat, then that person should be automatically elected.

Mr. Atner Khuzangai, Vice-Chairman: Asks someone to present the motion.

[Procedural discussion takes place.]
Dr. Michael van Walt van Praag, General Secretary: Explains there are three seats with

only one contestant, therefore an election is not necessary. Adds that since there were no objections to these nominees, then they are, in fact, elected.

Mr. Ledum Mitee, Representative of Ogoni: Objects and asks members to raise hands so the candidates will be supported by the General Assembly.

Mr. Atner Khuzangai, Vice-Chairman: Asks those who are in favor of automatically electing the nominees for the three regional seats to raise their hands. Announces the results: All in favour. Declares them elected.

Mr. Nadir Byekir, Representative of Crimean Tatar People: Explains the voting for the open seats will start and reads the list of nominees:

> Senator John J. Nimrod, Representative of Assyria;
> Mr. Pradhir Chakma, from Chittagong Hill Tracts;
> Mr. Erkin Alptekin of Eastern Turkestan;
> Mr. Zacarias da Costa of East Timor;
> Ms. Kealoha Pisciotta, Representative of Hawai'i;
> Mr. Isak Chishi Swu of Nagaland;
> Mr. Renat Kharisov representative of Tatarstan.

Mr. Erkin Alptekin, Representative of Eastern Turkestan: Notes that the delegation of Tatarstan left and asks what to do about the nomination of Mr. Renat Kharisov.

Mr. Atner Khuzangai, Vice-Chairman: Informs he has received an official letter from the Tatarstan delegation accepting the nomination and that there is no problem in including Mr. Kharisov in the ballot.

Senator John J. Nimrod, Representative of Assyria: Emphasizes it is not fair to include the delegate of Tatarstan in the ballot, since he was removed from the nominee list for Chairman because he was not present at that time.

Mr. Nadir Byekir, Representative of Crimean Tatar People: States that because it is not written in the Covenant that the nominee should be present, then it would be up to the General Assembly to interpret this provision. Adds he considers it is preferable to include Mr. Kharisov in the list.

Mr. Atner Khuzangai, Vice-Chairman: Comments that the representative of Tatarstan was here and had to leave, but that he did leave an acceptance of the nomination.

Mr. Ledum Mitee, Representative of Ogoni: Questions if it is possible to vote for a person who cannot vote himself.
Dr. Michael van Walt van Praag, General Secretary: Answers that there is no provision

which would clarify Mr. Mitee's question, but that it seems logical that it is not possible to vote for a person who cannot vote himself.

Mr. Reynaldo Mariqueo, Representative of Mapuche: Asks what the situation of the Assistant General Secretary is if he/she is elected in the Steering Committee.

Dr. Michael van Walt van Praag, General Secretary: Answers that the General Secretary would then choose another person accordingly.

Mr. Nadir Byekir, Representative of Crimean Tatar People: Explains that there are two approaches to the issue of having one nominee, depending on the type of legal system of a country. Suggests that those members who do not consider it appropriate for Mr. Kharisov to be included in the nominee list should not vote for him. Offers this suggestion as a practical approach to the problem.

Senator John J. Nimrod, Representative of Assyria: Asks the First Vice Chairman what the decision is regarding the nomination of Mr. Kharisov.

Mr. Atner Khuzangai, Vice-Chairman: Answers that he considers the nomination of Mr. Kharisov, Representative of Tatarstan, to be valid.

Senator John J. Nimrod, Representative of Assyria: States that in view of the decision made by the Chairman, he moves to remove Mr. Kharisov's name from the nominee list.

Mr. Atner Khuzangai, Vice-Chairman: Asks if anyone seconds the motion.

[Procedural discussion takes place.]

Mr. Atner Khuzangai, Vice-Chairman: Asks members to vote by raising their hands. Announces the results: In favour: 13, Against: 17, Abstained 4. Declares motion denied and that Mr. Kharisov will remain on the nominee list for the open seats of the Steering Committee.

Senator John J. Nimrod, Representative of Assyria: Asks the Chairman if a majority of votes is needed to be elected for the Steering Committee.

Mr. Atner Khuzangai, Vice-Chairman: Confirms that a majority is needed.

Dr. Michael van Walt van Praag, General Secretary: Explains the procedure of the election. Adds that there is one ballot per delegation, with each nominee having a box next to his/her name, and that the members must mark two boxes.
[Voting takes place.]

Mr. Nadir Byekir, Representative of Crimean Tatar People: Announces the resulting votes:

Senator Nimrod	(Assyria)	9
Mr. Pradhir Chakma	(Chittagong Hill Tracts)	5
Mr. Alptekin	(Eastern Turkestan)	22
Mr. da Costa	(East Timor)	11
Ms. Pisciotta	(Hawai'i)	9
Mr. Chishi Swu	(Nagaland)	15
Mr. Kharisov	(Tatarstan)	7

Declares that Eastern Turkestan has won an open seat because Mr. Erkin Alptekin received more that 50% of the votes.

Dr. Michael van Walt van Praag, General Secretary: Explains a second ballot, without the names of Mr. Erkin Alptekin, and the two persons with the least votes which are Mr. Pradhir Chakma of Chittagong Hill Tracts and Mr. Renat Kharisov of Tatarstan, will be handed out. Reminds members they must tick one box, and that each delegation has only one vote.

[Voting takes place.]

Mr. Nadir Byekir, Representative of Crimean Tatar People: Announces the resulting votes:

Senator Nimrod	(Assyria)	8
Mr. da Costa	(East Timor)	6
Ms. Pisciotta	(Hawai'i)	9
Mr. Chishi Swu	(Nagaland)	17

States no nominee received more than 50% of the votes, and therefore the election must be repeated.

Dr. Michael van Walt van Praag, General Secretary: Informs members the name of Zacarias da Costa, Representative of East Timor, will be removed from the list since he received the least votes.
[Voting takes place.]

Mr. Nadir Byekir, Representative of Crimean Tatar People: Announces the results:

Senator Nimrod	(Assyria)	5
Ms. Pisciotta	(Hawai'i)	11

Mr. Chishi Swu (Nagaland) 24

States that Mr. Isak Chishi Swu, Representative of Nagaland, has been elected into the Steering Committee.

Mr. Seif Sharif Hamad, Chairman: Congratulates the elected members of the Steering Committee on behalf of the General Assembly.

[Session adjourns]

General Assembly V: Saturday, 19 July 1997

Morning session

Mr. Seif Sharif Hamad, Chairman: Opens the meeting and requests the participants offer one minute silence to commemorate the people who have passed away since the last General Assembly. Honoured by the presence of Mr. Carl von Habsburg from the Parliament of the European Union and invites him to the floor.

Mr. Carl von Habsburg, Member of the European Parliament: Expresses his gratitude for the invitation to this General Assembly, allowing him to take part in a UNPO event. Stresses the important role the UNPO has, and gives the example of the UNPO's success story Estonia. Indicates that Estonia has entered into negotiations with the European Union for eventual admittance. Hopes more successes will follow for other UNPO members. Emphasizes that the UNPO's role in conflict prevention is commendable. Adds that the European Parliament has been developing a law on minorities and ethnic groups which would provide increased recognition for regions, not only conventional states. Encourages the UNPO to present a global view on this issue, which will be profitable in the future. Wishes success and thanks all.

Mr. Seif Sharif Hamad, Chairman: Thanks Carl von Habsburg and invites the General Secretary to give the qualifications that are necessary for his post.

Dr. Michael van Walt van Praag, General Secretary: Refers to the memo on the General Secretary's position written by Senator Chang, which was included in the information package. Urges all members to read the document carefully. Emphasizes that the most important requirement is that the General Secretary has full trust and confidence from all members. Explains that this is the reason for the requirement that any candidate must obtain a majority of votes of all members present in order to win.

Mr. Ledum Mitee, Representative of Ogoni: Proposes a motion on the position of General Secretary. Refers to the provision in the Covenant stipulating that the

General Secretary must serve three years from the day of his election. States that the General Secretary was elected at the fourth General Assembly in the Hague in 1995 and indicates that, therefore, the post of General Secretary does not become vacant until 1998. Underlines that the General Secretary must resign formally should he not wish to fulfill his time. Observes again that the UNPO as an organization must follow proper procedure if it wishes to be taken seriously. Acknowledges that nobody can force the General Secretary to continue in his post. Suggests that the item should be removed from the agenda.

Mr. Isak Chishi Swu, Representative of Nagaland: Seconds the motion.

Mr. Seif Sharif Hamad, Chairman: Suggests voting. Invites the General Secretary to give his reaction to the motion.

Dr. Michael van Walt van Praag, General Secretary: Questions if the intervention of Mr. Mitee is technically correct. Points out that he has made his formal resignation known to the Steering Committee. Adds that since the Steering Committee is representative of the General Assembly, this should be sufficient. Remarks that the members must have been aware of his intentions since the President of the Steering Committee had notified the members in January 1997. Agrees in principle to the three year term but comments that he has served the UNPO for more than six years which is the equivalent to two terms. Explains that he, therefore, does not wish to serve as General Secretary beyond August (to allow for transition). States formally that by August 30 he will no longer serve as General Secretary. Offers his services to the UNPO in another capacity.

Mr. Ledum Mitee, Representative of Ogoni: Repeats his request to have a formal resignation by the General Secretary. Expresses that the General Assembly should formally thank the General Secretary. Comments that the previous elections of the Steering Committee members were not in line with the rules. Re-emphasises the importance of following the rules strictly. States that this does not validate the resignation sent by the Steering Committee. Says that if there is no formal resignation before elections are held, he considers the organization primitive.

[Procedural discussion takes place.]

Mr. Seif Sharif Hamad, Chairman: Calls for a short break.

[Break]

Mr. Seif Sharif Hamad, Chairman: Reopens session. Calls the representative of Circassia, Mr. Khaji-Mourat Khatoukaev.
Mr. Khaji-Mourat Khatoukaev, Representative of Circassia: States that their people have

had the same problems the UNPO is suffering from now, which relate to the structure of the organization. Adds that their structure consisted of a Chair and Vice-Chairman with honorary functions, but no real decision making power. Remarks that after this structure was changed, the International Circassian Association managed to get more things done in a year than in the previous five years. Suggests a solution must be analyzed by the members in order to restructure the UNPO during the next General Assembly so as to create a more efficient organization. Remarks the importance of the continuity of work in the UNPO, and requests the General Secretary to remain in his post until the next General Assembly. Stresses the importance of solving the issue at hand today.

Mr. Seif Sharif Hamad, Chairman: Agrees with Mr. Khatoukaev completely, and states the General Assembly should give some thought to this issue in order to solve it in the future. Considers it is important to deal with the motion on the table.

Mr. Ledum Mitee, Representative of Ogoni: Requests the election of General Secretary to be suspended, because there is no vacancy of the post due to the fact that there has been no official resignation from the current General Secretary and his term is still running. Adds that if the General Secretary would resign as of now, he moves for an extraordinary session of the General Assembly to be held for the sole purpose of electing a new General Secretary.

Mr. Seif Sharif Hamad, Chairman: Requests a member to second the motion.

Mr. Isak Chishi Swu, Representative of Nagaland: Seconds the motion.

Mr. Seif Sharif Hamad, Chairman: Asks members to vote by raising their hands. Repeats that the motion is to have the election of General Secretary suspended; since there is no vacancy of the post due to the fact that there has been no official resignation from the current General Secretary, and his term is still running. Adds that if the General Secretary would resign as of now, an extraordinary session of the General Assembly should be held for the sole purpose of electing a new General Secretary.

Mr. Nadir Byekir, Representative of the Crimean Tatar People: Asks the General Secretary if he agrees with the motion.

Mr. Seif Sharif Hamad, Chairman: States that the General Secretary cannot speak out on a motion, since it is the duty of the General Assembly to decide. Requests members to vote.

[Voting takes place.]
Results: In favor 31, Oppose 5, Abstain 1. Declares the motion has been passed and

suspends the election of the General Secretary.

Dr. Michael van Walt van Praag, General Secretary: Resigns formally from his position as General Secretary of the UNPO. States that, therefore, there is no General Secretary of the organization. Adds that he has a solution for this problem. States that he will continue working with the Deputy General Secretary in order to keep the organization and the Secretariat running, until the end of the period for which he was elected, which is January 1998. Remarks that not having a General Secretary during these six months would not mean a catastrophe for the UNPO, since he and the Deputy General Secretary will continue performing their tasks and the Chairman and the President of the Steering Committee have greater responsibilities. Adds he does not wish to continue with the title of General Secretary, since he considers this could cause the matter to be taken less seriously and elections would then be likely to be postponed, as was the case during this Assembly. Agrees for an extraordinary General Assembly to be held in January 1998, but that he could not be present either then or in February 1998, since he will be away for two months. Requests the members to take this into consideration. Repeats he and the Deputy General Secretary will continue working together for six months and requests this General Assembly to give a guarantee that an extraordinary General Assembly will be held.

Mr. Seif Sharif Hamad, Chairman: Comments that this General Assembly must then make interim arrangements, like the acting General Secretary just said. States the General Assembly must choose a date before January 1998 or after February 1998 so Dr. van Walt van Praag can be present. Urges members to take this matter seriously, since an election of a General Secretary is of utmost importance for the UNPO and the General Assembly must have candidates. Proposes that the General Assembly should create a committee which would look for candidates. Adds that the Chairman should have the responsibility of this committee and that it should be based in the Hague. Presents the proposal to the floor for discussion by the members.

Mr. Salav Alijev, Representative of Kumyk: States he thinks highly of the General Secretary and that often he requested him to continue in his position as General Secretary. Comments that they are violating an individual's right to choose freely and that this is unacceptable for an organization like the UNPO which was founded to defend the rights of people. Adds that the General Assembly would be in violation of the Covenant if they delegate the right to elect a new General Secretary to a Committee.

Mr. Seif Sharif Hamad, Chairman: Answers he does not think they have violated the UNPO Covenant. Reminds the members that Dr. Michael van Walt van Praag has agreed to continue until January 1998. Clarifies there has not been an election for the General Secretary since the resolution was passed to postpone the item on the agenda to be dealt with by an extraordinary General Assembly.

Mr. Akhtar Buskunov, Representative of Bashkortostan: Reminds all members that nominees were presented three days ago, they were accepted and now there must be vote. Adds that they must vote to decide if the nominations have been declined or not, and that until this has been done the General Assembly will not be able to vote on Mr. Ledum Mitee's motion. Stresses this should be possible since the General Assembly is the highest decision-making body of the UNPO. Highlights that creating an extraordinary session of the General Assembly would, therefore, be a violation of the rules of the UNPO.

Mr. Seif Sharif Hamad, Chairman: Considers all procedures and rules have been followed correctly. Mentions Mr. Ledum Mitee had objected on the formality of the resignation of the General Secretary and that the General Assembly voted in favour of a motion calling for a postponement of the elections. Clarifies the issue is closed and there should be no further discussion.

Mr. Nadir Byekir, Representative of Crimean Tatar People: Asks for clarification as to what will happen to the current two nominees for General Secretary who properly followed all the procedures.

Mr. Seif Sharif Hamad, Chairman: States that the process must start anew and that these two candidates, if they accept, should be nominated again for the next elections.

Mr. Akhyad Idigov, Representative of the Chechen Republic Ichkeria: Comments having an extraordinary General Assembly would cost a lot of money for this organization. Insists the election should take place today.

Dr. Kara-Kys Arakchaa, Representative of Tyva: States she is one of the candidates. Adds that she has listened to the debates concerning the procedure and fully agrees with the proposal made by the representative of Ogoni, Mr. Ledum Mitee. Adds that the term for the current General Secretary has not ended. Suggests he should continue for six months, and that the extraordinary General Assembly be held at that time. Requests that the two current nominees should continue to be valid candidates for the next elections.

Ms. Nadejda Zolotariova, Representative of Udmurt: Comments that she understands why the election has been moved six months, but does not comprehend why new nominations are necessary since two are already on the list. Suggests that perhaps the members consider these two people insufficiently qualified for the job.
Mr. Seif Sharif Hamad, Chairman: Assures the members of the General Assembly

that has never been his intention, and apologizes for any misunderstandings. Adds he has a high respect for all the candidates. States that the protection of the rules and Covenant are the most important issue at hand.

Mr. Hamad Massoud Hamad, Representative of Zanzibar: Comments that a host country is necessary for an extraordinary General Assembly session. Adds that such an assembly would cost a considerable sum. Proposes members should send only one representative and that the session (which would only deal with the specific issue of the election of the General Secretary) should last for one day only. Suggests the next General Assembly should take place in Taipei, since we already have an invitation.

Mr. José Amorim Dias, Representative of East Timor: Requests clarification regarding whether the nominees for the General Secretary must be members.

Mr. Seif Sharif Hamad, Chairman: States there is no provision in the Covenant requiring the General Secretary to be a member.

Mr. José Amorim Dias, Representative of East Timor: Considers the General Secretary should be a qualified person, who is not a member and therefore could maintain a balance in the organization, catering to all members equally. Comments Dr. Michael van Walt van Praag is that kind of a person and requests all members to take this into account.

Representative unidentified: Considers the proposal to hold elections in six months is reasonable. Adds that members should consider electing the replacement now, in order to save funds for the UNPO, and determine who would take over after January 1998.

Mr. Salav Alijev, Representative of Kumyk: Asks the Chairman again about what would happen to the two currently running nominees. Asks if they would be left hanging in the air.

Senator John J. Nimrod, Representative of Assyria: Urges the General Assembly to take some action and moves for the Chairman to appoint a search committee which would start looking for candidates for General Secretary.

Mr. Seif Sharif Hamad, Chairman: Says that before the Assembly considers Senator Nimrod's motion, it must decide whether the current candidates will remain on the nomination list since they have been correctly nominated.

Mr. Seif Sharif Hamad, Chairman: Answers that elections were postponed due to the adoption of Mr. Mitee's motion and that they should move on.
Kalon T.C. Tethong, Representative of Tibet: Considers a decision has already been

made and that the Assembly should move to the topic of the next extraordinary General Assembly. Moves that the two current candidates are maintained on the nominee list.

Mr. Seif Sharif Hamad, Chairman: Asks for seconds.

Ms Frieda Souhuwat, Representative of the South Moluccas: Seconds the motion.

[Procedural discussion takes place.]

Mr. Seif Sharif Hamad, Chairman: Requests members to please listen. Clarifies that the General Assembly had decided earlier for a postponement of the election, and that now some members feel this motion should be revoked. Adds that this motion has been seconded and that we should vote on it. Repeats the motion and asks members to vote by raising their hands.

[Procedural discussion takes place.]

Mr. Seif Sharif Hamad, Chairman: Calls for a break in order to provide time for consideration.

[Break]

Mr. Seif Sharif Hamad, Chairman: Convenes the General Assembly. Invites the General Secretary to make a statement.

Dr. Michael van Walt van Praag: Apologizes for the confusion surrounding his resignation, but re-emphasizes that it is crucial that the UNPO should be governed by its own members. Adds that as a principle it is not right for a General Secretary to stay on for too long. Expresses his satisfaction over the past days, which clearly proved that this General Assembly is capable enough to elect its own leadership. Underlines that the object of this specific General Assembly is to consolidate and to unify. Explains that a transition from a small to a larger organization is as a rule hard and painful. Continues that it is important that loopholes in the Covenant are being discovered, and that we can learn from past mistakes. Regrets strongly that there are members, who believe that there are hidden agendas. Warns that such unfounded rumours can easily lead to serious feelings of mistrust. Stresses the need for unity among all members.Expresses his surprise that during the previous break a lot of people approached him to inquire whether the General Secretary did not wish to stay in his post. Emphasizes his determination to step down, and move to another position that would help him to be of more use to the UNPO, admitting that at present he has too many functions with which he is not comfortable. Introduces a compromise, which has been arrived at through thorough consultation. Suggests that the next six months be a transition period in which he will continue to serve the organization in a temporary administrative post, which should not be confused with the post of General Secretary. Proposes to convene an extraordinary General Assembly in March, 1998, solely for the purpose of electing a new General Secretary, by strictly following the rules. Re-emphasizes that the main criteria for a good General Secretary are having full support and complete trust from a very large majority of the members. Assures that all members will be able to send one delegate to this extra General Assembly. Urges the members to keep in mind the larger ideal, for which they are all striving, instead of arguing about petty details. Notes that a journalist suggested that the members from the CIS region had expressed their discontent with the UNPO, which they allegedly believed not to take a close enough interest in the region. Comments emotionally that there is no other region for which the organization, and himself personally, has taken so many risks, sent so many missions, or allocated more funds than to the CIS region. Proposes to start with a clean slate.

Mr. Seif Sharif Hamad, Chairman: Adjourns the session.

[Session adjourns]

GENERAL ASSEMBLY V: SATURDAY, 19 JULY, 1997

Afternoon Session

Mr. Seif Sharif Hamad, Chairman: Comments that Dr. Michael van Walt van Praag has clarified some of the issues concerning the position of General Secretary and has tried to find a solution. Announces an agreement has been made and calls Dr. van Walt van Praag to announce it.

Dr. Michael van Walt van Praag: States that many members discussed the issue during the break and agreed upon a solution, which is to vote on whether the elections for General Secretary would be held today, or not. Adds there could be several outcomes to this vote: a) To hold the elections today, with the two current candidates. b) To postpone the elections, which would mean an extraordinary General Assembly would be held for the sole purpose of deciding who the General Secretary would be; and the interim arrangement proposed earlier would be implemented. Adds that in such a case, the list of nominations would remain open, and that it would be understood for this time that the President of the Steering Committee, the Chairman of the General Assembly and the General Secretary must come from three different geographical regions. c) in case the elections are held today, but none of the candidates receive more that 50% of the votes of members present in the ballot, then the second option would take place and an extraordinary General Assembly would be summoned. Urges the members not to discuss on procedural issues anymore and vote.

Mr. Seif Sharif Hamad, Chairman: Asks the members to proceed with the vote on whether the elections for General Secretary will be held today.

Senator John J. Nimrod, Representative of Assyria: Asks for a point of clarification regarding the period of time for which the General Secretary would be elected, should the elections be held today.

Dr. Michael van Walt van Praag: Clarifies the period is from today for 3 years until an ordinary General Assembly takes place.

Senator John J. Nimrod, Representative of Assyria: Asks if the President of the Steering Committee, the Chairman and the Treasurer must come from three different regions, and if they should vote like that today.

Dr. Michael van Walt van Praag: Emphasizes no one is talking about the Treasurer, but that if they go on to an extraordinary General Assembly, the President of the Steering Committee, the Chairman, and the General Secretary would have to come from three different regions.

Senator John J. Nimrod, Representative of Assyria: Asks if it is then only for that election.

Dr. Michael van Walt van Praag: Answers that it is correct.

Mr. Seif Sharif Hamad, Chairman: Requests the motion: "That elections will be held today". Requests the Assembly to vote by raising their hands. Results: In favour 21, Oppose 15, Abstain 2. Declares the elections will be held today. Calls the Election Committee to come to the front. Announces the two candidates will give their presentation speeches, and calls on Dr. Kara-Kys Arakchaa, Representative of Tyva.

Senator John J. Nimrod, Representative of Assyria: Asks what would happen should the ballot be handed in blank.

Mr. Seif Sharif Hamad, Chairman: States that the winner must have over 50% of all votes, blank or not.

Dr. Kara-Kys Arakchaa, Representative of Tyva: Thanks the Steering Committee for allowing her to present her candidacy, and the delegates for letting the elections continue. States her candidacy was proposed by the Supreme Khural, by a representative of Tyva. Comments that now the world in no longer bipolar and believes that the creation of the UNPO is a politically important step to take. Thanks the founding fathers of the UNPO. States that members cannot only expect things from the organization, but that they must participate actively to support it. Points out there are between 3,000 to 5,000 peoples in the world, and only 200 States. Mentions she has worked in the United Nations Working Group on Indigenous Populations, where the problem of self-determination, property rights, environmental rights and other issues are discussed. Highlights that people have the right to develop their culture, traditions, education, and health in order to be part of the global community. Regrets that States have a negative approach toward peoples and nations, but that the world is made up of peoples, now heard through the UNPO. Acknowledges the aims of all nations are different; some want independence, some recognition, and others autonomy without secession. Adds that the UNPO must consider the problems of each of its members equally and promote solutions. Moves on to her curriculum. Mentions she graduated as a Doctor of Science in Chemistry from Moscow State University in 1950, and that after graduation she worked as university lecturer in the Science Research Institute. Adds that she served as a representative of Tyva in the Duma of the Russian Federation during the years 1993 to 1995.

Adds she was appointed as the head of the State Commission on Nationalities of the Russian Federation, where the problems of ethnic minorities and peoples of Russia were discussed. States she wrote three books concerning the rights of peoples, worked in the making of several conventions; in the promotion for the creation of an institute which would protect the peoples of Russia, and initiated parliamentary action in Russia on the ratification of ILO Convention 169. Adds she prepared the draft of the 1995 Law on Minorities, which was regrettably not supported by the Russian Duma. Comments that this draft has been now reconsidered for discussion, since fortunately the situation in Russia has changed and the question of minorities and indigenous peoples is again considered important. Comments that she is also part of the Working Group on the Draft Declaration of the Rights of Indigenous Peoples, and has brought up the issue of indigenous peoples in the European Parliament. Comments she lives in Moscow, where she currently serves as a member of the State Committee of the Russian Federation on Northern Regions, and the House of Nationalities of Russia. Adds that she is working towards a Ph.D. in international law dealing with minorities, indigenous and other peoples, and that in 1997 she was the only female candidate for presidential elections in Tyva. States that she has a daughter who is married and three grandchildren. Offers to answer any questions the audience might raise and thanks all for the attention given.

[Nominee questioning takes place and the second candidate steps forward.]

Dr. Linnart Mäll: Comments he is not happy to see Dr. Michael van Walt van Praag leaving, and would like him to continue with his work. States he has worked with Dr. van Walt van Praag since 1990, and has shared many words with him: good and bad. Says Dr. Michael van Walt van Praag is a wonderful man, with many bad sides and also many good. Adds that those good sides are enough to want him to stay in the UNPO. Comments he never thought he would be a candidate, but that since Buryatia nominated him and others also asked him to run, he could not decline. Affirms if he were elected he would continue with Dr. van Walt van Praag's line of work, especially since they worked together and know all about the UNPO. States he has also made some contributions to the UNPO, such as being the Chairman of the Preparatory Committee and the First Elected Chairman of the General Assembly (re-elected at the second). Regrets Estonia is no more a member of the UNPO, since it is part of the United Nations. Comments he has also worked as Assistant General Secretary for Eastern Europe and the former Soviet Union, and is the director of the Tartu Coordination Office which was hard to create but is now working well as members can see with this General Assembly. States he has also worked in Tartu University and is an historian specializing in East-Asian peoples. Adds he is the president of the Estonian Pan-European Society. Underlines that if elected he will resign from his current positions and move to the Hague, since as a General Secretary he would still be able to work in academia. Observes the General Secretary must be a working horse. Comments that the President of the Steering Committee and the Chairman are the most important men of the UNPO, and that he will be the working horse.

[Nominee questioning takes place, followed voting.]

It is announced that there are 39 ballots and that the results are as follows:

Dr. Kara-Kys Arakchaa, Representative of Tyva	5
Dr. Linnart Mäll	19
Abstentions	15

Declares no candidate received more than 50% of the votes, therefore, no new General Secretary has been elected.

[Break]

Mr. Seif Sharif Hamad, Chairman: States that the voting has taken place and that neither one of the candidate received enough votes. Underlines that according to the prior agreements, in case no candidate received enough votes an interim arrangement should be arranged. Says that some members did not agree with the results of the voting but have been persuaded during the break to accept the result. Thanks members for their acceptance. Thanks Mr. Linnart Mäll for his role in the persuasions and adds that he does not work for his personal interest but carries the UNPO in his heart.

Dr. Linnart Mäll: Thanks the members for voting; those who voted for him, for Dr. Kara-Kys Arakchaa and those who abstained.

Dr. Michael van Walt van Praag: Thanks the members for their patience. Informs the members that they will be notified on time for the next special General Assembly.

Requests members to write the exact name, address and telephone and fax number of the representative of the delegation on a piece of paper in order to avoid problems with the invitation and information for the next General Assembly.

Mr. Erkin Alptekin, Representative of Eastern Turkestan: Asks clarification on the number of candidates, and how people can add to the nomination list.

Mr. Seif Sharif Hamad, Chairman: Clarifies that nominations are open until election day. Explains a committee will be set up to encourage possible nominees. Expresses that a regional balance should be kept in mind. More details will be given before the end of this General Assembly. Asks the working groups if they can hand in their written recommendations for the Nonviolence Conference to the Secretariat. Announces the names of the member representatives elected to the Steering Committee and, therefore, to the board of the Stichting UNPO (the Netherlands foundation of the UNPO): Mr. Akhyad Idigov (Chechen), Mr. Teuvezh Kazanokov (Circassians), Mr. Erkin Alptekin (Eastern Turkestan), Mr. Menelaos Tzelios (Greeks in Albania), Mr. Alexander Kiryanen (Inkeri), Mr. Muzaffer Arslan (Iraqi Turkman), Chief Germaine Tremmel (Lakota), Mr. Isak Chishi Swu (Nagaland), Mr. Ledum Mitee (Ogoni), Ms. Frieda Souhuwat (South Moluccas), Mr. Parris Chang (Taiwan) and Ms Chungdak Dawa Koren (Tibet). Adds that the Chairman and the Vice Chairman will be non-voting members of the Steering Committee. Says that Mr. Parris Chang will be President of the Steering Committee until January 1998, when his term of presidency ends. Moves on to the resolutions. Announces that next the Resolutions will be presented for adoption by the representative of the delegation.

Senator John J. Nimrod, Representative of Assyria: Mentions having a problem with the procedure of adopting Resolutions. Says that when a Resolution is passed this does not necessarily imply that all members support the Resolution. Reminds the General Assembly that one member stepped out because of a Resolution. Wonders whether there was a special Resolution Committee which has reviewed and selected the Resolutions.

Mr. Atner Khuzangai, Vice Chairman: Admits that the Resolution Committee, consisting of Mr. Nadir Byekir (Crimea), Mr. Zacarias da Costa (East Timor), Mr. Ledum Mitee (Ogoni), Mr. Atner Khuzangai (Chuvash) and Ms. Inaria Kasiëpo (West Papua), has examined all the Resolution drafts, consulted with the members and finalized the draft Resolutions. Adds that Ms. Karen Onthank and other staff members have helped the Resolution Committee with the draft Resolutions.

Senator John J. Nimrod, Representative of Assyria: Asks if the Resolution Committee had received instructions, had consulted the General Secretary and if the Resolution is kept in a special framework so there is no problem.
Mr. Seif Sharif Hamad, Chairman: Answers in the affirmative. Invites the represen-

tative of Acheh to present his Resolution.

[Discussion of all Resolutions takes place, and voting is conducted. The following resolutions were adopted by the General Assembly.

1: Resolution on Acheh/Sumatra
2: Resolution on Albanians in Macedonia
3: Resolution on the Batwa People
4: Resolution on the Rights of the Chechen People
5: Resolution Concerning the Cabinda Enclave
6: Resolution on Chittagong Hill Tracts (CHT)
7: Resolution on the Present Situation of the Ingush of North Ossetia
8: Resolution on the Mapuche in Chile
9: Resolution on the Karenni State
10: Resolution on the Military Occupation and Colonization of the Shan States
11: Resolution on Zanzibar
12: Resolution on the Kumyk People
13: Resolution on the Situation of the Circassian Nation
14: Resolution on Smaller and Indigenous without any Form of Statehood]

Mr. Seif Sharif Hamad, Chairman: Repeats it is not possible and it would be unfair to others; and that the issue is closed. Asks Ms. Tsering Youdon Jampa, Deputy General Secretary, to address the Assembly.

Ms. Tsering Youdon Jampa, Deputy General Secretary: Apologizes for taking some time of the General Assembly. States she has been involved with the UNPO since its creation, both personally and as a Tibetan. Expresses her gratitude for the opportunity given. Says she could never compete with the General Secretary she worked for, but accepts the challenge given to her by this General Assembly. Says she is pleased to see how this General Assembly solved their differences and came out united and strengthened. States she is proud to be part of the UNPO and is more committed than ever to work on its behalf. Comments that in regard to her new position as Deputy General Secretary, now the highest office in the UNPO since there is no acting General Secretary for the next six months. States she will need instructions from the former General Secretary. Highlights all their work could not have been possible without the help the dedicated staff of the UNPO, past and present. Thanks them for their assistance and dedication, and for being there whenever the UNPO needed them. Thanks members who have nominated her for the position of General Secretary, but formally declines since she considers this exceeds her capacities. Hopes to be worthy of the members' trust and confidence in her new position.

Mr. Göran Hansson, Vice Chairman: Expresses his gratitude to the interpreters for doing such a good job. Comments he is certain the General Assembly shares his feelings.

Senator Parris Chang, President of the Steering Committee: States that coming from a Parliament known for fighting on the floor, he is pleased to see how this Assembly resolved differences in a civilized manner. Congratulates everyone on this achievement. States the UNPO has progressed a lot in the past 6 years, from 15 members to 50, protecting minorities, peoples and oppressed groups. Adds this organization would not be here without the talents and services provided by Dr. Michael van Walt van Praag. Proposes to pass a resolution of gratitude to Dr. van Walt van Praag. Assembly claps.

Mr. Seif Sharif Hamad, Chairman: States he understands by this clapping that the resolution has been adopted.

Senator Parris Chang, President of the Steering Committee: Continues. States that this General Assembly has restructured the decision-making process, the Steering Committee is more responsible and the UNPO will no longer depend on only one person. Urges members to be serious about the UNPO since it is the only way this organization will be successful. Announces that last night he had a phone call from a reporter in Taiwan who asked him why he devoted his time to the UNPO, having so many important issues back home. Comments he answered that he does so because Taiwan cares. Adds that even though he will be Taiwan's Foreign Minister in three years when his party wins the elections, he will work for the UNPO until then. Highlights that Taiwan cares because it has also been a victim of chauvinism, like Tibet, Eastern Turkestan, and other nations under the control of Russia and Indonesia. States that he needs the support of all members of the Steering Committee and that he will be in the Hague at least once a month in order to work with the General Secretary and Treasurer. Stresses that the UNPO is the only advocate for nations and peoples rights and that all should work hard for it.

Dr. Michael van Walt van Praag: Thanks everyone for the past six years, which were an inspiring but hard period. Adds that he has learned more during these six years than during the rest of his life, and that these years seem longer than all the others. Comments he could not have done this job if it had not been for the help of the dedicated staff in the Hague, United States and Tartu. Thanks them for helping him to do something he believes in, and help oppressed people wherever they may be. Thanks Ms. Tsering Jampa for leading the staff so well and wishes all of them luck after six months when he would leave. Hopes this time in Estonia brings us closer and makes the UNPO a more solid organization. Reminds all members he had cautioned against the formation of blocs, and that they can witness for themselves the negative consequences this could have. Stresses that members should always remember they have more similarities than differences, especially in their suffering and objectives. Expresses thanks for the honor of working with the UNPO.

Mr. Seif Sharif Hamad, Chairman: States he is happy to have completed the agenda brought before the General Assembly during the past five days; successfully solving the controversies that arose. Adds this was possible to achieve thanks to the cooperation, responsibility, and dedication of all the members, and their highest interest in the UNPO. Remarks what happened today should be considered as positive, since members from different backgrounds, cultures, languages and religions have been able to express their opinions and feelings freely. Highlights the achievement for unrepresented peoples and nations to be able to express themselves without fear. Considers it is worse to go home mumbling rather than freely stating what they think. Says the General Assembly was able to reach an acceptable conclusion for all. Wants to take this opportunity to thank all those who have made this General Assembly a success:

a) Mr. Erkin Alptekin, for leading the UNPO while in office, for being a committed member and now part of the Steering Committee;

b) Ms. Tsering Youdon Jampa for all her good work during the past six and a half years. Comments that most members know Ms. Jampa as a tireless, hardworking woman who is prepared to sacrifice herself for the organization. Expresses his satisfaction that she has accepted to serve for the next six months with Dr. Michael van Walt van Praag in the same team as before;

c) All Assistant General Secretaries for their contributions,

d) All members of the staff, without exception, for serving us well in the Hague, and during this Assembly. Notes one peculiar trait of the staff group is that it is dominated by the fair sex: women. Thanks again the ladies and few gentlemen that compose it;

e) The Coordinators in the United States and Tartu, who are both doing a wonderful job at our service;

f) Dr. Linnart Mäll, for his intervention and persuasive power to help all members reach an agreement and proceed with the Assembly;

g) Dr. Michael van Walt van Praag, who has been the soul and guiding torch of the UNPO. Adds that his services cannot be counted, and that sometimes he has even endangered his own life for the causes of the UNPO. Adds that his level of commitment is something to admire. Comments Dr. van Walt van Praag is never tired, never angry and reacts calmly without emotion, which makes him a true peoples' leader.

States that this General Assembly has chosen him to serve as its Chairman. Comments that the UNPO is a reputable organization and that what they have built should not be destroyed. Adds that members must start building on what has already been created and make it even more successful. Pledges to serve the General Assembly well, without making distinctions between members. Hopes that God will help all members, Inshallah. Requests all members not to hesitate to communicate with him whenever in need, and that he will be available for all. Adds that his address can be obtained from the Secretariat in the Hague and that he will try to get an e-mail account to facilitate communication.

Promises to do to the best of his abilities in order to help all members, honestly, dedicatedly and without favoritism. Thanks all.

Declares the Fifth General Assembly of the Unrepresented Nations and Peoples Organization closed.

NONVIOLENCE AND CONFLICT: CONDITIONS FOR EFFECTIVE PEACEFUL CHANGE

International Conference
Tallinn, Estonia
21–23 July 1997

Rapporteurs:
Julie Berriault with Sheri Jay

ACKNOWLEDGEMENTS

The rapporteurs are grateful to the following individuals whose writings and assistance have contributed significantly to this report:

Ms. Mililani Trask,

Dr. Gene Sharp,

Mr. Steven Whiting,

as well as all the indefatigable UNPO Secretariat staff.

The UNPO wishes to sincerely thank the following organizations for their invaluable support of the Conference on Nonviolence:

Interchurch Organization for Development Cooperation (The Netherlands),

Humanist Institute for Cooperation with Developing Countries (The Netherlands),

Danish Ministry of Foreign Affairs,

Bread for the World (Germany),

Highland Cottage Trust (United Kingdom),

International Centre for Human Rights and Democratic Development (Canada),

Heinrich Böll Foundation

MESSAGE FROM HIS HOLINESS DALAI LAMA

I am pleased to learn that the Unrepresented Nations and Peoples Organization, of which Tibet is a member, is organizing an International Conference on Nonviolence and Conflict from 21–23July 1997, in Tallinn, Estonia. On this occasion, I extend my greetings to the UNPO and all the participants at this conference.

Today, there is a growing global awareness of the meaning and importance of nonviolence. Although violence is still rife, I believe that the trend of world opinion is apparently in favour of nonviolence.

I have always strongly felt that the best way to resolve a problem or conflict is through nonviolent means. The path of nonviolence may take some time, but its result is more lasting and it does not have negative side effects.

The recent successes in resolving conflicts and achieving freedoms through nonviolent approaches have further convinced me of the efficacy of nonviolence. Moreover, I feel that nonviolence is also much closer to the human nature. It is with this conviction that I remain fully committed to the nonviolent Tibetan struggle for freedom and have been persuading my people not to abandon nonviolence as the appropriate form of struggle.

The UNPO's mission to uphold nonviolent means in order to advance the interest of the peoples that it represents is most encouraging. I am hopeful that the UNPO's International Conference on Nonviolence and Conflict will further promote the effectiveness and importance of nonviolence. I wish your conference and deliberations every success.

17 July 1997

EXECUTIVE SUMMARY

The UNPO International Conference, Nonviolence and Conflict: Conditions for Effective Peaceful Change was held July 21-23 in Tallinn, Estonia. It brought together representatives of indigenous peoples, minorities, and non-self governing nations, representatives of governments, multilateral organizations, non-governmental organizations (NGOs), and experts in the field of nonviolence, to discuss the contemporary, practical meaning and application of nonviolence, particularly in relation to conflicts between states and non-state entities.

The Conference sought to answer whether nonviolent action can be effective as a means to bring about change; and how such action can be made more effective.

In particular, it sought to identify those factors, both internal and external to a nonviolent movement, which are favorable for that movement's success, and to define nonviolent strategies which can be used by non-state groups.

The Conference was organized in response to a pressing need: as the incidence of conflicts waged within state borders increases, nonviolence as a viable alternative to armed struggle is progressively under pressure. In an interlinked world, how to promote nonviolence in these disputes is a question which concerns the entire international community.

The Conference was unique in that it directly involved the leaders of peoples and nations responsible for making decisions of whether to use armed force or nonviolence in pursuit of their goals; and for deciding how to respond to violence inflicted upon them by states.

Participants explored the relationships between nonviolence, violence, terrorism, conflict and limitations experienced by peoples as they attempt to exercise their right to self-determination. Self-determination was understood as the process by which a people or nation obtains any goal in a broad spectrum of possible objectives, from human, linguistic or cultural rights, to democracy, protection of the environment, autonomy, or, in some cases, independence. The limiting of the exercise of that right was identified, in many cases, as the cause of conflict.

The Conference fundamentally reaffirmed the use of nonviolence as an active means of promoting and achieving goals, while rejecting violence as an instrument for resolving political, social and economic problems. It condemned both unprovoked violence against nations, peoples and minorities and all forms of terrorism, regardless of the perpetrators.

It acknowledged that violence is not limited to the use of arms, but can include cultural genocide, forced assimilation and the destruction of the environment on which a people's existence and development depends. It reaffirmed the fundamental rights of nations and peoples to exist and develop as they choose, in accordance with their right to self-determination.

In relation to the use of self-defense, Participants recognized that in some cases nations and peoples feel compelled to use armed force to defend themselves against armed aggression, genocide and other prolonged or massive forms of violence against them; yet they remained aware that once begun, violence breeds violence and is difficult to control and contain.

Participants recommended several actions which could be undertaken by peoples and minorities as well as by certain sectors of the international community, including state governments and international organizations (including, specifically the UNPO), to support and foster nonviolence, particularly in conflicts of an intrastate nature.

SECTION ONE

A. Conference Objectives and Aims

The UNPO Conference on Nonviolence and Conflict: Conditions for Effective Peaceful Change, held in Tallinn, Estonia, from July 21 to 23, 1997 had as its principal aim to bring together representatives of minorities, indigenous peoples and nations, representatives of governments and international organizations, and experts in the fields of nonviolence and conflict management to examine:

- whether nonviolent action can be effective as a means to bring about nonviolent change; and
- how such action can be made more effective.

The above were addressed within the context of helping to prevent the outbreak of violent conflict.

The goals of the Conference were to:

- identify what conditions, both within movements and externally, contribute to making nonviolent action viable and effective;
- discuss practical strategies by which movements and peoples can nonviolently pursue their goals;
- make recommendations to governments and other members of the international community on how to contribute to establishing the conditions necessary for effective, long-term, peaceful change; and
- make recommendations to the UNPO for its continued work in encouraging and assisting the nonviolent prevention and resolution of conflicts worldwide.

B. Conclusions

The Conference:

- reaffirmed the use of nonviolence as an active means of promoting and achieving goals;
- rejected violence as an instrument for resolving political, social and economic problems;
- condemned all unprovoked violence against nations, peoples and minorities;
- condemned all forms of terrorism, regardless of the perpetrators;
- acknowledged that violence is not limited to the use of arms, but can include cultural genocide, forced assimilation and the destruction of the environment on which a people's existence and development depends;
- reaffirmed the fundamental rights of nations and peoples to exist and develop as they choose, in accordance with their right to self-determination;

- recognized that in some cases nations and peoples feel compelled to use armed force to defend themselves against armed aggression, genocide and other prolonged or massive forms of violence against them; and
- remained aware that once begun, violence breeds violence and is difficult to control and contain.

C. RECOMMENDATIONS

To Peoples, Minorities, Movements and Their Leaders

The Conference urged leaders of peoples and minorities to:

- develop effective strategies for peaceful change appropriate to their specific situations; and
- open themselves up for dialogue at all levels with the parties with whom they are in conflict.

And specifically recommended that the UNPO Members:

- make full use of the UNPO's facilities, services and training programs, including those relating to the United Nations.

To the International Community

The Conference called on governments, international organizations, NGOs and on their leaders to adopt clear and principled policies in order to reduce the use of violence. These must include:

- recognition of and respect for the equal rights of all peoples and minorities, regardless of their size, their culture or religion;
- taking the needs and views of unrepresented peoples and minorities seriously;
- speaking out and condemning all unprovoked acts of violence and gross violations of human rights against unrepresented peoples and minorities;
- recognition of the legitimacy of movements or governments which use peaceful and democratic means to achieve their objectives;
- engagement in open and sincere dialogue with all such movements and governments and rewarding their adherence to nonviolence; and
- encouragement and active assistance in the peaceful resolution of conflicts between State governments and nations, peoples and minorities over whom they claim authority.

To Corporations and Financial Institutions

The Conference called on corporations and financial institutions to:

- end the violent exploitation of those resources upon which peoples' survival depends; and
- cease from promoting violence through irresponsible arms trade and commercialization of violence in the media and in their products.

To the Unrepresented Nations and Peoples Organization

In the area of information dissemination, the UNPO was called upon to:

- more fully provide a conduit for information from the UNPO Members themselves to media outlets, governments, international organizations and others, to continue to change prevailing perceptions of nonviolence and Members' individual goals and aspirations;
- compile information briefs and analysis on Members for use with international organizations and the media;
- more widely distribute the UNPO Yearbook, UNPO News and other UNPO publications;
- distribute information among the UNPO Membership from the UNPO Members in order to provide knowledge of others' campaigns and to build solidarity;
- increase the number of documents translated into Russian, and to establish an information center located in a CIS country to assist in translation efforts; and
- direct more funds to media staff and efforts.

In the area of conflict prevention, the UNPO was requested to:

- act as an early warning system for conflicts by providing timely information on the situations of its Members to governments, intergovernmental organizations, and NGOs, with the purpose of preventing the outbreak of violence;
- organize fact- finding and diplomatic missions to areas of potential or actual conflict among its membership and to use reports of these missions in its work to prevent violence and promote nonviolence in these areas;
- respond to urgent requests of the UNPO Members and others who are faced with the imminent outbreak of violence against them, making use of the Peace Action Council;
- announce that the UNPO Members, and the UNPO on their behalf, are willing to begin dialogue and negotiations with governments, financial institutions, multinational corporations and other entities, to resolve conflicts nonviolently;
- provide other conflict prevention or resolution services such as mediation to the UNPO Members; and
- establish new forms of political co-operation between unrepresented peoples and independent peoples, as a model of co-operation and solidarity for the future.

To support self-help among its Members, the UNPO was called upon to provide:

- expanded trainings which take into account special circumstances of Members, such as regional placement. Further, it was recommended that these trainings not only train leaders of movements, but also other segments of the leadership and people, with a concentration on youth. Trainings should include those in nonviolence, effective use of the media, conflict resolution, diplomacy, mediation practices and leadership. Short-term seminars for new UNPO members on these subjects were also suggested;
- legal services through the creation of a legal council and by publishing an annual legal magazine with relevant topics to nations and peoples;
- opportunities for Members to join together to express their cultural characteristics, as in cultural gatherings which would reaffirm the unique and irreplaceable aspects of peoples, many of whom are threatened, or to address the special needs of Members in a particular region, such as the former Soviet Union;
- assistance in developing individual Member policies which suit the reality of their specific situations, particularly concerning the use of self-defense.

In the area of legal activities, the UNPO was encouraged to:

- work to preserve the integrity and scope of the right to self- determination in international law, and to prevent it from being weakened;
- strengthen existing conventions which protect collective rights, by bringing cases and violations before their monitoring bodies;
- widen its and its Members sphere of influence to forums other than the political or human rights bodies of the UN, for example those working in development, environment, and social and humanitarian arenas, as well as monitoring systems established by international and regional organizations.

Further recommendations included: The establishment of an exchange program between young Members; the publication of a set of international legal instruments relevant to the UNPO Members' concerns; providing assistance in the development of languages; the establishment of a permanent 'International Council for Peoples' Rights'; the establishment of a working group to address specific cases of Members who are faced with the decision of whether to use violence or nonviolence in their struggles; the development of analyses on the causes of conflicts.

UNPO Members were urged to provide the UNPO with:

- any information regarding developing situations whereby tensions are on the rise and violence is imminent.
- accurate and comprehensive ongoing information as frequently as possible, to assist the Secretariat in its work, which includes combating the tendency of the media to use misinformed and inaccurate information in its reporting.

D. CONTEXT OF THE CONFERENCE

The UNPO Covenant, the official Charter of the Organization, states:

> *It shall be the aim of the Organization by assisting its Participating Nations and Peoples to express their positions, needs and grievances in legitimate forums and by providing a community of support, to advance the fulfilment of the aspirations of Participating Nations and Peoples by effective nonviolent means.* (Article 1)

The Covenant also commits the Organization to provide:

> *. . .training in nonviolent strategies in the development of strategic plans and policies* (Article 2 (e)).

In Art 5 (d) it lists as a requirement for membership in the organization:

> *Rejection of terrorism as an instrument of policy.* (Article 5(d))

In August, 1991, the UNPO convened an International Conference on Preventing the Use of Force by States Against Peoples Under Their Rule, in The Hague. The official statement of the Conference, the UNPO Declaration of The Hague of 6 August 1991 stated:

> *Unprovoked use of all forms of violence by States against Nations and Peoples is to be condemned.*

In January, 1992, Participants in the UNPO International Conference on Population Transfer, also held in Tallinn, Estonia, acknowledged the close relationship between violent conflict and population transfer, which can destabilize regions and exacerbate tensions between distinct peoples and governments, while violating fundamental human rights, including the right to self-determination. The UNPO Conference, Self-determination in Relation to Individual Human Rights, Democracy and the Protection of the Environment, held in The Hague in January 1993 elaborated the connection between the denial of the exercise of the right to self-determination and human rights violations, and the outbreak of violence. The Conference affirmed the need for effective nonviolent preventive measures which do not attempt to deny the right or a peoples' exercise of it.

In 1994 and 1995 the UNPO organized a series of consultations on Conflict Prevention: the Post Cold War Challenge, in The Hague. Participants stressed the critical need for nonviolent methods to be utilized by the international community, including the UNPO, to prevent the outbreak of violence in conflicts involving minorities, peoples and nations. The Participants emphasized that these measures should be undertaken in full recognition of the rights of peoples, including the right to self-determination.

The above mentioned conferences have been organized during a time when internationally the practice of nonviolence, particularly in conflicts of an intra-state nature, is increasingly being put to the test. Over the past several years, events have shown that while the practice of nonviolence in conflicts between states and non-state groups is pursued by many peoples and minorities, some have taken up armed force in an effort to achieve their goals or to defend themselves. Others, while committed to the use of nonviolence, are questioning their choice, many in the face of severe repression. At the same time, several groups who have used armed force have been able to achieve results which attest, at least in the short-term, to its potency. Armed resistance prevented the Russian Army from establishing control in Chechenia in 1994 and 1995, the Georgian Army from extinguishing Abkhazian autonomy in 1992, and it was a protracted war which ultimately gave Eritrea its long-cherished independence.

This disaffection with nonviolence has been in large part due to the reluctance of the international community to pay attention to, or actively address the needs of peoples who are struggling to exercise their right to self -determination. As a result, peoples and minorities are hard pressed to find ways to gain international attention, or bring about change in their situations. Many peoples simply do not have the tools necessary to gain the attention and support needed from the international community. Examples include:

- Hostage-taking by members of the Free Papua Movement in early 1996, in an attempt to bring international attention to their environmental and human rights situation;
- Ongoing armed unrest in East Turkestan in reaction to increased Chinese government repression and international indifference
- Increased violent resistance in Kosova, which has until now used nonviolence against the repression of the Serbian government;
- Increased violence in the Great Lakes region of Africa, a region which drew little international attention before violence reached genocidal proportions; and
- Conflicts in the Caucasus.

The UNPO organized the Conference in response to what it perceived to be a strong need within this global context, to support the UNPO Members and others like them to use nonviolence. For this reason the participation in the Conference of the principal actors and decision-makers of the movements often faced with violence used against them or with the choice to use violence or nonviolence, was of central importance.

E. Place of Meeting and Participation

The two-day Conference was held in Tallinn, the capital of Estonia, six years after that country's successful nonviolent struggle for independence from the Soviet Union. Attending the Conference were representatives of the UNPO Members, representatives of nations, peoples and minorities not represented in the UNPO, representatives of governments, representatives from international organizations, and experts in the field of nonviolence.

F. METHODOLOGY

On 19-20 April 1997, the UNPO in cooperation with the Heinrich Böll Foundation convened a Preparatory Seminar on issues of nonviolence, in Bonn, Germany. The main objective of the seminar was to examine the conditions necessary for effective nonviolent change in preparation for the UNPO's International Conference on Nonviolence and Conflict. Participants, who included representatives of the UNPO Members, parliamentarians, and experts in the field of nonviolence, helped to identify key issues to be addressed at the Conference. The Conference discussion paper, developed with input from the Bonn Seminar, identified and explored several issues in depth, in order to prepare the Participants and focus the discussion. The issues included:

- What is nonviolence?
- How effective is nonviolent action?
- Is nonviolent action contributing to the creation of violence?
- What is violence?
- Can we distinguish violence from terrorism?
- What should the UNPO's position be regarding violence?
- Conditions necessary for effective nonviolent change.
- The UNPO's role in the promotion and implementation of nonviolent change.

A questionnaire with detailed queries concerning several aspects of the discussion was used parallel to the Conference. Three workshops were held prior to the Conference in order to further focus the discussion, on:

(i) Conditions Necessary for Effective Nonviolent Change;
(ii) Nonviolent Strategies; and
(iii) The UNPO Role in Promotion and Implementation of Nonviolent Change.

G. LIST OF PARTICIPANTS

Panel Members and Chairs:

Dr. Gudmunder Alfredsson, Co-Director/Professor, Raoul Wallenberg Institute of Human Rights and Humanitarian Law, University of Lund, Sweden;
Venerable Prajnalana Bhikkhu, Chittagong Hill Tracts;

The Hon. Audrius Butkevicius, MP., Member of the Seimas, and former Defense Minister, Lithuania;
The Hon. Nadir Byekir, MP, Mejlis of Crimean Tatar People, Parliament of Crimea, Republic of Crimea, Ukraine;
Senator Parris Chang, Member of the Senate, Taiwan, Professor Emeritus, Political Science and International Relations, Pennsylvania State University, USA;
Mr. Kenneth Deer, Mohawk Nation Council of Chiefs;
Mr. José Amorim Dias, CNRM (East Timor) European Representative;
Ms. Michelle Ernsting, International News Producer, Radio Netherlands;
Kasur Lodi Gyaltsen Gyari, Special Envoy of His Holiness the Dalai Lama, former Minister of International Relations of the Government of Tibet, Washington, DC;
Mr. Seif Sharif Hamad, Chairman of the General Assembly, UNPO, Vice Chairman, Civic United Front (CUF), Zanzibar;
Mr. Atner Khuzangai, President, Chuvash National Congress, Chuvash Republic, Vice Chair of the UNPO General Assembly;
The Hon. Akhyad Idigov, Chairman, Parliament Committee of Foreign Affairs, Chechen Republic-Ichkeria;
Ms. Inaria Kasiëpo, Foundation for the Study and Information of Papuan Peoples, West Papua Peoples Front, The Netherlands;
The Hon. Tunne V. Kelam,Vice President, State Assembly, Estonia;
Dr. Linnart Mäll, Professor of Oriental Studies, University of Tartu, Estonia;
Mr. Fèlix Martí, Director, Centre UNESCO de Catalunya, Spain;
Mr. Ledum Mitee, Acting President, Movement for the Survival of the Ogoni People (MOSOP), London;
Senator John Nimrod, General Secretary/Special Advisor, Assyrian Universal Alliance, USA;
Don Rodrigo Carazo Odio, President Emeritus, University of Peace, former President of the Republic of Costa Rica;
Venerable Samdhong Rinpoche, Chairman, Assembly of Tibetan People's Deputies, Tibetan Government in Exile, India;
The Hon. Arnold Rüütel, M.P., State Assembly, Estonia, former President of Estonia;
Dr. Gene Sharp, Senior Scholar, The Albert Einstein Institute, Cambridge, USA;
Mr. Isak Chishi Swu, Chairman, National Socialist Council of Nagaland;
Mr. Hans Thoolen, Regional Representative, United Nations High Commission for Refugees, Sweden;
Chief Germaine Tremmel, Head Hereditary Chief, Lakota "Hunkpapa" Nation;
Mr. Menelaos Tzelios, General Secretary, International Federation for the Protection of the Rights of Ethnic, Religious, Linguistic and other Minorities, Representative to the UNPO of the Greek Minority in Albania, USA;
Dr. Michael van Walt van Praag, former General Secretary, UNPO, The Hague, The Netherlands.

UNPO Member Delegates

The Hon. Ramzan Ahmarov, Chairman, Parliament Committee of Information and Publishing, MP, Chechen Republic-Ichkeria;

Mr. Imran Akhaev, Representative, Chechen Republic-Ichkeria in Estonia;

The Hon. Khizir Akhmadov, Minister of Foreign Affairs, Chechen Republic-Ichkeria;

Mr. Anguita Aldisson, General Coordinator, Mapuche Interregional Council, Temuco, Chile;

Mr. Salav Alijev, President, Kumyk People's Movement "Tenglik", Dagestan Republic;

Mr. Erkin Alptekin, Chairman, Eastern Turkestan Union in Europe, Germany;

The Hon. Dokka Amagov, MP., Chechen Republic-Ichkeria;

Dr. Kara-Kys Arakchaa, Supreme Khural of the Republic of Tyva , former MP of the Russian State Duma, Republic of Tyva;

Dr. Muzaffer Arslan, Turkman Co-operation and Cultural Foundation, Ankara, Turkey, Iraqi Turkman;

Mr. Nigmet Baazakov, Chairman, Uighur Union in Kyrgyzstan;

Mr. Joel Batila, Special Counsellor, Front de Libération de L'Enclave du Cabinda;

Mr. Bata Bayartuev, Vice-President, All-Buryat Association of the Development of Buryatia;

Mr. Pavel Bikmurzin, Chairman of the Board, Mari Public Center "Mari Ushem", Bashkortostan;

Mr. Sertac Bucak, Socialist Kurd Party (PSK), Initiative for Human Rights in Kurdistan, Bonn, Germany;

Mr. Francisco Xavier Builo, Free Cabinda Foundation, Representative, Front de Libération de L'Enclave du Cabinda, the Netherlands;

Mr. Akhtar Buskunov, Chairman of the Board, Bashkirian Public Center "Ural", Bashkortostan;

Dr. Robert Gyula Cey-Bert, International Ambassador of Karenni State, Hungary;

Mr. Pradhir Chakma, Jana Samhati Samiti, Chittagong Hill Tracts;

Mrs. Shirley Chang, Taiwan;

Mr. Zacarias da Costa, East Timor Permanent Representative to the European Union, Brussels;

Mr. Dashi-Nima Dugarov, President, All-Buryat Association of the Development of Buryatia;

The Hon. Sacita Gairbekova, Chairwoman, Committee of Social Affairs, Chechen Republic-Ichkeria;

Ms. Tsybenova Gatchjidma, Translator of Chuvash Congress, Chuvash Republic;

Mr. Jacques François Gieskes, Deputy Representative, Front de Libération de L'Enclave du Cabinda, the Netherlands;

Mr. Hamad Massoud Hamad, Director - Human Rights, Civic United Front, Zanzibar;

Mr. Göran Hansson, Stiftelsen Skånsk Framtid- Foundation for the Future of Scania, Sweden;
The Hon. Lin Hongtsung, M.P., Legislative Yuan, Taiwan;
Ms. Bi-khim Louise Hsiao, Department of International Affairs, Democratic Progressive Party, Taiwan;
Mr. Amin Ibragimov, Kumyk People's Movement "Tenglik", Dagestan Republic;
Mr. Omarjan Ibrahimov, Representative, Uighur Cultural Association in Uzbekistan;
Mr. Rahmetullah E. Inayetullah, Representative, Eastern Turkestan in Saudi Arabia, Director of the Studies Department, Muslim World League, Saudi Arabia;
Mr. Vilkhelm Iosifov, Vice President, Laros/Assyrian Universal Alliance, Moscow;
Ms. Tsering Youdon Jampa, Assistant General Secretary, UNPO, The Hague, the Netherlands, Tibet;
Dr. Aslambek Kadiev, Special Representative, Chechen Republic-Ichkeria to UNPO in The Hague, the Netherlands;
Mr. Mugudin Kahrimanov, Kumyk People's Movement "Tenglik", Dagestan Republic;
Mr. Zéphyrin Kalimba, President, Association for the Promotion of Batwa, Rwanda;
Mr. Teuvezh Kazanokov, Member of the Executive Committee, International Circassian Association, Karachay-Cherkess-Republic;
Mr. Nurshat Khasanov, Chairman, Uighur Youth Association in Kyrgyzstan;
Mr. Khaji-Mourat Khatoukaev, General Secretary, International Circassian Association, Karachay-Cherkess-Republic;
Mr. Aleksander Kiryanen, Vice-Chairman, National Movement "Inkerin Liitto", Russian Federation;
Mr. Wladimir Kokko, National Movement "Inkerin Liitto", Russian Federation;
Mrs. Chungdak Dawa Koren, Representative of His Holiness the Dalai Lama in Geneva;
Mr. Dilmurat Kuziev, Chairman, Uighur Trade Association in Almaty, Kazakhstan;
Mrs. Livia Laks, Sweden;
The Hon. Alexei Leontyev, Deputy of State Council, Chuvash Republic;
The Hon. Nikolai Lukianov, Chairman, Chuvash National Party, Chuvash Republic;
The Hon. Abubakar Magamadov, Chairman, Parliament Committee of Defense and Public Security, Chechen Republic-Ichkeria;
Mr. Reynaldo Mariqueo, International Coordinator, Mapuche Inter-regional Council, England;
The Hon. Shih Ming-te, M.P., Legislative Yuan, former Chairman of the Democratic Progressive Party, Taiwan;
Mr. Th. Muivah, General Secretary, National Socialist Council of Nagaland;
The Hon. Azamat Azievich Nalgiev, M., Republic of Ingushetia;
The Hon. Anastasia Nikolaeva, Member of the Presidium, Chuvash Congress, Chuvash Republic;
Mr. Antonio Mbemba N'Zita, Diplomatic Counsellor, Front de Libération de

L'Enclave du Cabinda;
Mr. Henriques Tiago N'Zita, President, Front de Libération de L'Enclave du Cabinda, Head of the Provisional Government of Cabinda;
Mr. Pisanh Paladsingha, Director, Mon Information Services, Bangkok, Thailand, Mon State;
Ms. Kimberly "Kealoha" Pisciotta, Representative, Ka Lahui Hawai'i;
Ms. Zhanetta Proshutinskaya, Member of the Komi National Revival Committee, Komi Republic;
Drs. Fathi Radjab, European Representative, International Circassian Association, The Netherlands;
Ms. Rosemary Roe, Association for the Defense of Black Rights, Aboriginals of Australia;
Ms. Grace Roembiak, West Papuan People's Front, The Netherlands;
Ms. Aminat Saieva, Representative, Chechen Republic-Ichkeria in Lithuania;
Mr. Yasin Samedi, Representative, Uighur Youth Association in Kazakhstan;
Mr. Qenan Sheji, Academic, UNPO Representative for the Albanians in Macedonia, Amsterdam;
Mr. Sunthorn Sripanngern, Secretary, Mon Unity League , Bangkok, Thailand, Mon State;
Mr. Manut Srisuwan, Shan State Representative, Thailand;
Mr. Youra Tarverdi, Advisor - Assyrian Universal Alliance, California, USA;
Kalon T. C. Tethong, Minister of Foreign Affairs, Tibetan Government-in-Exile, Dharamsala, India;
Ven. Phra Mai Thanomklin, Mon State, Chairman, Mon National Relief Committee;
Mr. Sao Thura, Shan State Representative, Germany;
Mr. Cham Toik, Representative for Mon State, Mon Unity League, Vancouver, Canada;
Mr. Chope Paljor Tsering, Representative of His Holiness the Dalai Lama, Budapest, Hungary, Tibet;
Mr. Muradin Urchukov, World Congress of Abkhazian People, Abkhazia;
Mr. Gennadi Verblyudov, Representative of the Chuvash Republic;
Mr. Myo Win, Representative of the Shan State to UNPO, Germany;
The Hon. Musa Yandiev, MP, Republic of Ingushetia;
Ms. Nadejda Zolotariova, Member of All Udmurt Association "Udmurt Kenesh", Udmurt Republic.

Guest Participants:

Mr. Heino Ainsoo, former Director, UN Division of the Estonian Foreign Ministry, Estonia;
The Hon. Dr. Toomas Alatalu, MP, State Assembly, Estonia;
Ms. Iris Almeida, Director of Programmes, International Centre for Human Rights and Democratic Development, Montreal, Canada;

Doña Estrella Zeledón de Carazo, Costa Rica;
Mr. Yevgeni Chetvergov, Member of the Erza National Movement "Erzian Mastor";
The Hon. Algirdas Endriukaitis, MP., Member of the Seimas, Lithuania;
Pastor Avo Kiir, Estonian Evangelical Lutheran Church, Estonia;
The Hon. Rytas Kupcinskas, M.P., Member or the Seimas, Lithuania;
The Hon. Albert J. F. Lin, MP., Legislative Yuan, Taiwan;
Mr. Werner Lottje, Secretary for Human Rights, Diakonisches Werk der Evangelischen Kirche in Deutschland, Stuttgart, Germany;
Chief Edward Moody (Quatsinas), Hereditary Chief, Nuxalk Nation;
H.E. Bernd Mützelburg, Ambassador of the Federal Republic of Germany, Estonia;
The Hon. Viktor Niitsoo, MP., State Assembly, Estonia;
Ms. Catharine Perry, Nonviolence Trainer, Quaker Peace & Service, London;
Chief Lawrence Pootlass (Nuximlayc), Head Hereditary Chief, Nuxalk Nation;
Mr. Michael Roekaerts, Pax Christi International, Brussels;
Ms. Christine Schweitzer, Institute for Peacework and Nonviolent Settlement of Conflict, Wahlenau, Germany;
Mr. Alexander Shipontak, Representative of Podkarpatian Russins in the Baltic States;
The Hon. Enn Tarto, M.P, State Assembly, Estonia;
The Hon. Lauri Vahtre, MP, State Assembly, Estonia;
Mr. Stephen Whiting, Nonviolence Programme Coordinator, Quaker Peace & Service, London;
Ms. Christel Willenbrock, Embassy of the Federal Republic of Germany, Estonia;
Mr. Rainer Willert, Resident Representative to the Baltic States, Friedrich Naumann Foundation;

Others present included members of the public and press

SECTION TWO

A. INTRODUCTION

Throughout the world today increasing numbers of indigenous peoples, minorities, non-self governing nations, and other non-state groups are attempting to exercise their right to self-determination as provided for in the Charter of the United Nations, the International Covenants on Human Rights, as well as the Covenant of the Unrepresented Nations and Peoples Organization. Their goals range widely, from independence or forms of autonomy, to cultural, religious, social and economic rights, as do the methods by which they seek to achieve them.

Though the right to self-determination is enshrined in fundamental international instruments, there exist no internationally accepted legal mechanisms with which to address claims to it. Instead, the legitimacy of the claim, and the correct response to it, is left largely to the state in which it occurs, which by its nature cannot be an impartial judge. State governments and multilateral organizations have shown great reluctance to intervene in these cases, citing the need to uphold the territorial integrity of fellow states. The result is conflict, the root causes of which are not destined in the near future to diminish or disappear. How those conflicts are conducted, whether violently or nonviolently, is of paramount importance to an increasingly interdependent world.

A principal objective of the Unrepresented Nations and Peoples Organization is to provide effective alternatives to violence for its member nations, peoples and minorities, in their efforts to achieve their objectives. However, among unrepresented peoples, nonviolent approaches are often viewed with scepticism. In recent years, many movements and peoples who have chosen and pursued nonviolent strategies have been met with extreme violence or have been effectively ignored. Examples include the Ogoni of Nigeria who were successful at bringing world attention to the environmental devastation caused to their land by oil companies, as well as human rights abuses and social and economic inequities perpetrated by the Nigerian military government. Once their campaign had been internationalized, the Nigerian military responded with force to crush the movement and execute Ogoni leaders.

Likewise, the Chechen independence movement was nonviolent from its beginnings in 1991. In that year it successfully and nonviolently repelled Russian special forces who had parachuted into Chechenia. From 1991 to 1994, it continued to keep Russia out of Chechen territory without violence. However, in December 1994, Russia used massive military force in its attempt to recover its hegemony in the area which resulted in hundreds of thousands of lives lost, on both sides.

At the same time, nonviolent movements such as that in Sanjak in Yugoslavia, the Tibetans and the Albanians in Kosova have been successful in raising international attention and support but have not achieved their goals, while the anti-apartheid movement in South Africa and the Solidarity movement in Poland did.

Questions which the Conference was to address stemmed from these examples and others like them: Why do some movements succeed while others fail? What are the conditions needed for nonviolent action to be effective? How should the effectiveness of nonviolent action be judged? How can nonviolence be encouraged on all sides?

B. WHAT IS NONVIOLENCE?

The term nonviolence is complex and has varied meanings, among which it is important to draw distinctions. In general, the term has been interpreted as in the negative - an absence of violence. However, nonviolence, both in theory and practice can and should be viewed as a positive, an active and potent force for attaining certain goals.

Two categories of definition can be named: principled and pragmatic. In their application, these categories are not necessarily mutually exclusive, and some movements have utilized both concurrently to significant effect.

Principled nonviolence is often rooted in traditional or religious beliefs and customs, or in moral principles alone. It is based on a moral stand, an ethical code which disallows the practice of violence, often throughout all actions of life. Principled nonviolent practitioners do not necessarily utilize nonviolent actions and strategies, though they at times have. For practitioners of principled nonviolence, the aim of any nonviolent endeavour is, as the Venerable Samdhong Rinpoche, Chairman of the Assembly of Tibetan People's Deputies, Tibetan Government in Exile stated," the establishment of truth and removal of injustice. It does not aim to eliminate or defeat anyone. For a true nonviolent activist, there is no enemy. It aims to end injustice by making the perpetrator of injustice see reason and undo the wrong done by him."

A significant question which principled nonviolence seeks to answer is: Is there a unity of ends and means; are the means of attaining goals, particularly those based on ideals such as equality, justice or peace, in concert with the ends?

Principled nonviolence includes such diverse beliefs as pacifism, a generally non-active form of resistance to violence; Tibetan Buddhist practitioners who eschew all forms of violence; and the commitment of the Quakers, a religious group, to use their deeply held belief in a nonviolent way of life to effect change, not only within themselves as individuals or in their immediate sphere of influence, but also in the world at large.

Pragmatic nonviolence is best understood as the decision to use nonviolence based upon practical strategic considerations. It does not rely on a fundamental commitment to nonviolence which extends to all situations; it may be limited only to the situation at hand. Pragmatic nonviolence is based upon the use of proactive, positive nonviolent strategies and actions. It seeks to change the status quo, ranging in individual cases from specific policies which affect a specific group to the overall dynamics of power in a society.

With pragmatic nonviolence, a people or a movement can choose not to use violence even if there is no traditional or religious basis for that choice in their culture. For example, the Crimean Tatars, traditionally a warrior culture, have chosen to use nonviolence because of its practical worth in their struggle for their rights following their return to the Crimea after decades in exile. Likewise, the Native Hawaiians chose to use nonviolence when the Americans took over Hawai'i a century ago. At that time, Queen Liliu'okalani, the Hawaiian ruler, counselled her people not to use violence and suffer certain devastating defeat.

In other cases peoples who are traditionally nonviolent have used arms: the Buddhist Mon people of Burma have chosen to use armed force in their struggle with the dominant Burmese military government.

Some peoples employ both principled and pragmatic approaches. The Tibetan struggle for independence, which is deeply influenced by the nonviolent philosophy of Tibetan Buddhism, is also quite pragmatic in its approach. The Tibetans have used international diplomatic and public relations campaigns, and nonviolent resistance within Tibet, in their struggle for independence from the Peoples Republic of China. These nonviolent activities are linked to very pragmatic considerations: Tibetans are few and the Chinese are many, and perhaps more importantly, the Chinese are neighbors with whom the Tibetans must live into the future.

The question is raised of whether nonviolent movements are more effective if there is a traditional cultural base for them in a society. Some traditionally nonviolent groups, including the Tibetans, have been very successful at remaining so in the face of severe repression. At the same time, others, such as the South African anti-apartheid movement, do not possess such a penetration in their culture of nonviolence as a principle, yet have been successful at attaining their goals. It is notable that many indigenous cultures also possess traditional methods of conflict prevention and resolution which can be sources of strength when nonviolence is threatened. It would appear that the presence of a nonviolent tradition can support nonviolent action within a society, yet it is not a required prerequisite for success.

At the same time the question arises if a group, when pressed, will abandon nonviolence more readily if it does not possess a principled commitment to it. If nonviolence is seen only as a tactic, will not a people or movement drop that tactic when and if it is no longer expedient to pursue? As a tactic alone does it have the roots to sustain a long campaign?

The Conference raised these and similar questions about the nature of nonviolence, but did not seek to answer them definitively. It did concur that in general nonviolent campaigns can be at least as effective as violent ones, but they require sacrifice, patience and discipline, and more courage.

Regardless of the source of a people's or movement's choice to use nonviolence, it is in most cases nonviolent action which manifests that decision. Nonviolent action can be divided preliminarily into

(i) 'conflictual' actions used to wage conflict and;

(ii) actions which are 'nonconflictual'.

Conflictual actions can be considered to include mass public mobilizations, such as economic and political noncooperation; civil disobedience, such as strikes, hunger strikes, demonstrations, and vigils; grassroots mobilization such as letter writing campaigns; and campaigns designed to build political awareness among the people. In this sense, nonviolent action can be employed not just for defense, but also for offense.

Nonconflictual actions can include such activities as negotiations and conciliation, which are carried out once the dynamics of power have shifted, and the group conducting the campaign has been successful in acquiring enough legitimacy with which to negotiate.

Although a people may engage in purely nonviolent actions, these actions can be and often are met with violence in return. In recent years, governments have responded militarily to perceived threats posed by nonviolent movements. In some cases, overt acts such as economic embargoes, political isolation, military action, imprisonment, judicial murder, and attacks in the media have been used to quell nonviolent movements. Death squads and other means of covert repression have also been used against populations seeking change within states and societies.

Governments are often reacting to a perceived loss of political and economic power, including profits from natural resources or access to foreign aid, when they respond violently to nonviolence. Using power and violence to maintain power is a traditional response, yet one which can lead to spiralling conflict.

In many cases, using violence, whether covert or overt, against groups does not destroy the movement. It can instead make the group stronger and more committed to its goals. It can also encourage the group to use violence, thus beginning a cycle of violence which, once begun, is difficult to stop.

This was evident in the Abkhazian response to the use of military force by Georgia in 1992, following the former's proposal for an equal federative relationship between Abkhazia and Georgia. Once military force was used, Abkhazia successfully defended itself in-kind, while developing internal political structures, holding elections, and otherwise asserting itself as an increasingly sovereign entity. This conflict has required the intervention of peacekeeping forces.

In another example, Chechenia's armed response to the Russian incursion galvanised disputing factions of the nation. Once united, this resistance ultimately defeated the Russian military, though not without huge combatant and civilian losses, and ongoing instability in Chechenia and the Caucasus region as a whole.

Some violent conflicts which began nonviolently have continued for decades, costing lives and consuming resources, without addressing the root causes of the dispute. The armed conflict between Nagaland and India which began with an attempt to solve the problem by political means - of Nagaland's claim to its original independent stature before it was forcibly annexed into the Indian state - has lasted 50 years and claimed thousands of lives.

The Conference discussed methods of conducting conflicts nonviolently which do not invite a violent response. The example of Estonia was presented as an example of a bloodless revolution, in large part due to external factors, such as the strategic use of international opinion and to internal conditions, such as broad-based citizen support. Estonians used the break in the status quo caused by the 1991 attempted coup d'état in Moscow, to make their decisive move for independence, literally, as one Estonian representative stated, "under the guns of the tanks which had rolled into Tallinn." The Conference emphasized the need for careful planning, based on in-depth analyses of the government's pressure points, to judge if and when it will react violently, and how to discourage such violence. In a larger sense, the development of democratic systems with built-in minority rights protection mechanisms were also proposed as a deterrent to violent response.

At the same time, some Participants pointed out, in many cases little can be done to prevent a government from responding violently to what it perceives as a threat, whether the threat is violent or nonviolent, and this should be anticipated when planning nonviolent campaigns. In fact, they argued, a violent response exposes what is violent in the power structure, and is a necessary component to any process of change. Because nonviolent action is aimed at changing the status quo, the nonviolent activist becomes a lightning rod drawing this inherent violence upon his or herself. Yet this need not dissuade a movement from continuing to pursue its goals without violence; movements should not engage in nonviolent campaigns without expecting to be hurt.

Often the nonviolent group is named as the instigator of the violence, despite the presence of overt or covert violence in the society or government itself. Thus it is important to consider the context within which the struggle is occurring before placing blame for violence.

C. What is Violence?

The Conference spent some time defining the term violence. To many Participants, violence was not limited to the use of armed force, but extended to other policies and actions which threaten the well-being of a whole people, including their cultural and social continuity and survival.

Many Participants identified powerful governments and economic interests as being the chief initiators of violence, as they react to perceived threats to their control. Some Participants questioned whether it was possible to change the process by which power becomes linked to violence. This was brought up in relation to current regimes who fought for and attained independence from colonial powers earlier in the century, only to, once in power, impose repressive "internal colonial" rule on smaller peoples within their own borders.

Forms of violence identified can be categorized into four broad areas:

(i) armed violence, whether overt or covert, which can include rape;

(ii) cultural violence, such as assimilation of smaller peoples into the dominant culture or the injection of foreign, at times violence-based values, into a society through the media. When these actions endangered the survival of the people as a whole, they were termed cultural genocide;

(iii) tactical unarmed violence, or acts calculated to oppress peoples through mechanisms other than armed force, such as starvation, embargoes, dispossession and exploitation of resources which sustain a population, levying of unfair taxes on particular populations, extortion, confiscation and destruction of property; and

(iv) socio-economic violence, as in the actions of industrialized and consumer states to access the natural resources of others. The concentration of wealth in the hands of a few, and the globalization of world markets were mentioned in this context.

Participants highlighted several violent practices which deserved special attention. They rated the destruction of the environment as a particularly prevalent and dangerous form of violence visited upon peoples, because of the dependent and complex relationship between the people living in that environment and the land.

Forcing populations to act against their will, or against their own interests was also named as violent, in particular forced labor, whether for military uses or development projects. Population transfer, particularly when done without the consent of the population being transferred or the population to whose territories they are transferred was also identified in this context.

The Conference was divided on the trafficking of drugs with some contending that the use of drugs was a personal choice and therefore could not be considered an act of violence perpetrated upon another, and others who saw as violent the deterioration of society and individuals caused by the consumption of drugs. It was also pointed out that historically drugs have been used to subvert and control populations, such as the Chinese citizenry by the British during the Opium Wars, and that revenues from drug trafficking have been used to fund covert military activities, as in the Contras and Nicaragua.

Terrorism is generally violent, or relies on the threat of violence, whatever form it takes. Either it directly employs an act of violence, or invokes fear of an act. Fear is the objective of terrorism. Terrorism is not necessarily restricted to the use of armed force. UN General Assembly Resolution 40/61 adopted December 8, 1995 unequivocally condemns all acts of terrorism and defines terrorism as acts "which endanger or take innocent lives, jeopardise fundamental freedoms, and seriously impair the dignity of human beings."

Examples of terrorism provided by the Participants included hijacking, kidnapping, torture and killing of non-combatants as well as combatants outside the battlefield, destruction of infrastructure, bombing of public places or means of transportation, and death squad activities.

Distinctions have been drawn between state terrorism and "liberation terrorism." The Conference was asked to examine if the act of terrorism was to be judged differently dependant on who perpetrates it. Participants pointed out that who the perpetrator was made no difference, that the act of intimidating a population through violence and terror was always to be called terrorism and was to be condemned.

D. Self-Defense

Many Participants questioned whether peoples should be expected to choose nonviolence when subjected to violence which threatens the survival of that people. In particular, they argued, if nonviolent avenues had been exhausted, it was understandable if the choice was made to defend themselves with violence. Nonviolence, it was felt, while indispensable as a principal means for dealing with conflict, might not be the most realistic strategy for severely threatened peoples.

Others stated that nonviolence was a way of life from which there was no derogation. Further, defense could be carried out nonviolently, as in Civilian Based Defense Systems now being developed and used positively during the Baltics' struggle for independence. It should be kept in mind, they argued, that oppressor groups, better equipped for violent conflict, often try to draw nonviolent groups into violence, in order to defeat them.

In general, it was felt, self-defense was legitimate. It was argued that not responding at all to acts of aggression was not acceptable; there needed to be a correct response to violence. At the same time, the Conference was careful to acknowledge that once begun, cycles of violence are difficult to break. "Responsive violence" while understandable, should not be encouraged.

E. Conditions for Effective Nonviolence

It is difficult to measure the effectiveness of nonviolence. One way is by looking at how well a movement has been sustained at a particular level. In this case, both Tibet and Kosova could be judged effective. Another is to judge the ability of the movement to bring attention to an issue. The Ogoni of Nigeria clearly were able to meet this criteria. Yet how these achievements actually effect change in their situations is debatable. Or nonviolence can also be judged by whether the movement has been able to meet its goals, such as the South African anti-apartheid movement, and Poland's Solidarity movement.

With nonviolence there remains no clear and generally accepted measurement for effectiveness and judging efficacy remains a largely subjective undertaking. It was recommended that a study be done of nonviolent movements and their achievements as a first step in developing a framework by which to judge them. Still, some Participants argued, simply engaging in the struggle and reaping benefits such as dignity, courage and solidarity with others should be judged as part of the success of the movement.

The Conference was asked to identify and discuss favorable conditions for effective nonviolent change. Two sets of conditions were identified: (i) internal, or conditions within movements, peoples, minorities; and (ii) external, or the behavior of actors outside the movements which affect them.

Many Participants noted that both internal and external conditions are interdependent and necessary for a successful campaign. In this sense, every internal action should be viewed not only for its internal relevance and strategic importance, but also its external logic and value; how it will be judged by impartial and friendly governments, NGOs, the media and others.

At the same time, some cautioned that while "third party" support was important, each movement or people must rely upon itself, and not upon outside actors. Often, if not fully committed and without full understanding of the people who are engaged in the conflict, outside forces can prove unreliable.

What could reasonably be expected of the United Nations and other world bodies was also raised in this context. Outside of monitoring compliance with human rights instruments, the real willingness of the UN to respond in more proactive ways, such as intervention, is limited. This was emphasised with the example of Cabinda which has forwarded to the United Nations, the Organization of African States (OAS), and other intergovernmental organizations letters asking for an investigation of Angola's forced annexation of the territory, to which there has never been a response.

F. Internal Conditions

The Conference identified several internal conditions which contribute to effective nonviolence, including (i) strong and responsible leadership; (ii) dedicated, educated and disciplined populace; (iii) cohesive organizational structure; (iv) resources; and (v) strategies.

The most high profile and successful nonviolent movements in recent memory, the Indian Independence Movement and the US Civil Rights Movement, had in common strong, charismatic and committed leaders. It is difficult to consider the success of either movement without attributing it in large part to the ability of these leaders to galvanise their people and world opinion in favor of their cause, and to have the strength and discipline to adhere strictly to nonviolent means. Both Mahatma Gandhi and the Reverend Martin Luther King Jr. were exceptional individuals, without whom these movements might never have been effective. Contemporary examples of such leaders include His Holiness the Dalai Lama of Tibet, Daw Aung San Suu Kyi of Burma, Dr. Ibrahim Rugova of Kosova, Mr. Mustafa Jemilyev of the Crimean Tatars, the late Ken Saro-Wiwa of the Ogoni, and Dr. Sulejman Ugljanin of Sanjak.

However, corrupt or disingenuous leadership can be detrimental to a movement, and power struggles within it can damage its credibility and ability to survive. Additionally, there is a danger in over-reliance on a particular leader or leaders, particularly if they are suddenly absent, either through assassination, imprisonment or exile. Still, some leaders continue to be influential while in prison, while serving as living symbols of the movement. Xanana Gusmao, the imprisoned leader of the East Timorese liberation movement and Nelson Mandela are two well-known examples.

Not all groups rely on strong individual leaders, some have built organizational systems with diffuse or revolving leadership. Still, there is a definite need for leadership, whether as individuals or as a collective, which can strategize, organize, inspire and represent the movement to the opponent and to the outside world.

Qualities identified for strong responsible leadership included dedication, the ability to think strategically, diplomacy, honesty, patience, incorruptibility, determination, and courage. Leaders trained in nonviolent processes were judged as having more options to pursue in conflicts. Leaders must, the Conference agreed, be good examples by embodying the principles of nonviolence, in order to serve as inspiration not only to those within the movement, but also to the outside world.

The strength of a movement also lies in its people as a whole. To be effective as a nonviolent force, they must share common values and moral principles, and agree on the means to achieve their goals. As an example, it was suggested that democracy is a contemporary principle around which people can coalesce and organize, and one which outside agents, such as governments, can join with in solidarity. To build internal solidarity, education and training programs developed within movements were suggested.

In addition, the population should be prepared for struggle. Logistical concerns, such as internal communications, provision for the population's physical necessities, including medical assistance for injured resistors, and establishing communications to the outside world were listed.

In a nonviolent campaign, one segment can discredit an entire movement if it uses violence or otherwise acts in contravention to the policies of the larger group. Thus, cohesiveness is essential to an organization. Participants highlighted the need for democratic structures as a means to address dissension. Democracy was also seen as one way to mitigate potential or actual damaging monopoly by leaders.

A nonviolent movement depends in large part on the resources available to it. Financial resources, material resources, technical resources, human and time resources are very important, and should be included in strategic planning. At the same time, several Conference Participants questioned from what source these resources could be made available.

From the principled view, the use of strategies in nonviolent struggles was acknowledged as anathema: in essence, it was explained, nonviolence has no battles to win, yet the use of strategies implies the defeat of an enemy. Still, within this context, there are many actions which can be employed to implement the principle of nonviolence.

At the same time, many Participants strongly emphasized that, from the pragmatic point of view, if nonviolent campaigns are to be effective it is imperative they, much like violent campaigns, have well-developed strategies. Strategies need to be developed on the macro as well as on the micro levels, with both long and short-term goals developed from clear objectives. They must be based on in-depth analyses of the situation. The strengths and weaknesses of opponent, of the nonviolent movement, and other internal and external conditions must all be considered.

Strategies should be revisited frequently as the conflict unfolds. At the same time, it was suggested, it is important to allow improvisation and unscripted actions. Further, it is important to remember that each strategy is relative to its context and cannot be duplicated from situation to situation.

It was also pointed out that in some cases, despite the importance of strategies, improvised nonviolent struggles have been successful.

G. External Conditions

All conflicts exist within a larger context, both regional and global, though some are more geographically or politically isolated than others. Thus, those involved in conflicts are not limited to primary parties. Situations may be influenced by others with a stake in international economic, political, social and cultural relations. For example, former colonial powers can have significant interests in conflicts in former colonies or present spheres of influence, such as France in Rwanda, and Portugal in East Timor. Nonviolence is not solely the responsibility of the people, minority or movement who is engaged in a nonviolent struggle. It is shared by all those with a stake in the conflict.

The Conference discussed the roles and responsibilities of several international agents of influence, including: (i) governments, (ii) multilateral organizations such as the United Nations, (iii) transnational corporations, (iv) the media, and (v) NGOs.

In general, international attention can be beneficial to a movement. On one level, there is the confidence of knowing that attention is turned to the conflict, and that the injustices and repression which have instigated the movement, are exposed. This in and of itself can encourage the continuation of nonviolence. It also can serve to allay, even if only temporarily, those parts of a movement who are impatient with the pace at which change is occurring. If the leaders of a movement can show that they are being listened to and taken seriously, that their situation is being discussed outside of the narrow theatre of conflict, and that there are others who are concerned about its outcome and who are perhaps working to assist them, it can help keep the movement cohesive and nonviolent.

The international community is not always so obliging however, and nonviolent movements do not, generally, draw the kind of attention and concern that violent conflicts do. In conflicts of an intra-state nature, governments have shown themselves to be generally reluctant to intervene even diplomatically where movements are perceived as threatening the territorial integrity of other states. This reluctance has led to some of the most violent and devastating conflicts in the past decades, including those within the former Yugoslavia and Chechenia. There is, in addition, the judgement that as long as movements are nonviolent, governments need not worry about them, it is only when they turn violent that there is a need for intervention or action. This short- sighted perception actually encourages the use of violence and contributes to further instability.

To encourage nonviolence and discourage violence, governments must find methods to interact with, or even at times, support nonviolent movements, which also take into account their own strategic and political concerns. Positively rewarding nonviolent movements for using nonviolence, whether or not the government agrees with the particular issue of dispute, would go far to encourage the use of nonviolence in general. Promoting dialogue between the parties would help to deter the outbreak of violence. Governments need to be convinced to clearly and openly recognize leaders of nonviolent movements, and show support for the nonviolent approach to issues, and by doing so, foster respect, both internally and externally, for a responsible leader and the movement. A cohesive movement is a better partner for dialogue and problem-solving than a fragmented and uncontrolled one, thus it is in governments' best interest to promote cohesiveness within movements.

International organizations, such as the UN, the OSCE, OAS, OAU and others can be highly influential in conflicts. It is increasingly imperative that these organizations develop policies which support nonviolent rather than violent change. The UN, as the most powerful international instrument for effective nonviolent change, is largely, as one participant stated, a "club of states" (or of governments in power.) As such, it functions largely to protect its members at the expense of the rights of smaller peoples and nations.

The Conference called upon the UN to establish mechanisms to address claims to self-determination. One suggestion was to restructure the Decolonization Committee of 24, established to apply self-determination in the colonial context of past decades, for this purpose. It was stressed that any body charged with investigating or possibly adjudicating these claims, in order to be fully effective, would have to include the full participation of the claimant peoples themselves.

Current legal instruments for the protection of human rights, monitored by the UN, are severely limited in their ability to address issues pertinent to peoples and minorities. Despite the establishment of international tribunals, lack of accountability and punishment for gross and systematic violations of human rights endangers the credibility of the system as a whole. Human rights regimes by and large are protective of individual human rights, not the rights of groups. Implementation of instruments is slow, and hampered by political manoeuvring and bureaucratic policies. As a result instruments are inadequate in their protection of cultures and identities, the destruction of which is a primary source of conflict internationally.

The double standard applied by governments and international organizations which protects sovereignty and territorial integrity of states at all costs, even through violence, yet is reluctant to address the protection of communities and peoples, creates great frustration among the latter, and can ultimately lead to the use of violence if no redress is offered.

Participants stressed the need for international instruments for the protection of group rights, as in the current Draft Declaration on the Rights of Indigenous Peoples, and further ratification of existing treaties, as in the International Labor Organization's Convention 169 Concerning Indigenous and Tribal Peoples in Independent Countries. The UN Declaration on the Rights of Minorities is still limited in its scope and application as it addresses only the rights of individuals belonging to minorities, rather than the group as a whole.

Still, minorities and peoples were encouraged by some to bring their claims under existing mechanisms, despite their drawbacks, and to seek wider support for their goals, for example through the specialized agencies of the UN. They were also urged to use the coming year, 1998, declared as the International Year of Human Rights, as an opportunity to press for broader protection of collective rights.

The UN and other multi-lateral organizations were called upon to support nonviolence and nonviolent movements. In resolving conflicts of an intra-state nature, which are often long-lived and complex, it is important for the UN to address the root causes of the conflict, and not be satisfied with only a cessation of violence. Likewise, when brokering peace agreements, it is imperative that all parties, including non-state actors, are called to the table for negotiations. Failure to do so can result in complications and further conflict.

Transnational corporations must also bear responsibility for the occurrence, escalation and continuation of conflicts. When the economic interests of corporations conflict with or cause harm to an indigenous people or local community, it is imperative that the transnational be held accountable. Often, corporations are complicit with governments in oppressing peoples from whose traditional land the corporation seeks to extract resources, and from which the government and government elites will profit. Mechanisms do not exist to hold corporations accountable for irresponsible or oppressive actions which lead to conflict when the people attempt to defend the land upon which their culture, their physical survival and their identity, depend. Corporations, though protected by opaque and diffuse structures, must be held accountable and mechanisms put into place for greater transparency and monitoring of their activities. The case of Shell and other oil companies in Nigeria, particularly in relation to the Ogoni, Freeport's mining activities in West Papua, and UNOCAL in Burma are examples of how a transnational's activities can cause and influence conflict.

Arms manufacturers and dealers also bear direct responsibility for the easy availability of arms, particularly small arms, used in violent conflicts around the world.

In its coverage, the international media shapes perceptions of all facets of a conflict. In choosing what to cover, it decides what movements, violent or nonviolent, will receive attention and how. In these ways it is an extremely powerful influence on individual nonviolent struggles and on the use of nonviolence generally around the world.

Many nonviolent struggles need the support of the media and access to the conscience and attention of the outside world in order to be effective. Nonviolent campaigns, including those by NGOs, such as Greenpeace with Shell's Brent Spar, and peoples, such as the Baltic States, the Ogoni, and the Tibetans, have in recent years made use of the international press as part of their strategies, to very successful effect. While good press coverage does not guarantee success, it goes a long way in encouraging the movement and its supporters to continue on nonviolently, as well as presenting nonviolence in general as a viable path.

A media outlet's motivations for covering or not covering a situation or a movement can be complex, including the value of the story in terms of financial benefit (will it sell copy?), the value of the story vis a vis other current events and trends, the staff time it takes to research and present the story, and the outlet's perception of what will be of interest to its readership. Journalism produced with undue concern for the bottom line can choose to cover violent conflicts and actions and ignore nonviolent ones, which by and large require more in-depth, well-researched coverage, and do not necessarily have the immediate impact, or "tension" that violence does. As Ms. Michelle Ernsting, International News Producer, Radio Netherlands commented, "...the violence, and how to deal with it becomes the story. The real issues of human rights and repression, get lost along the way." By choosing to focus on violence as pervasive, unsolvable and without alternatives, the media is complicit in its perpetuation.

Some Participants felt that in various cases the media is subject to control by large financial interests and governments, who have the power to influence, control and manipulate it resulting in coverage of peoples, nations and movements' situations contrary to their interests.

To strengthen respect for nonviolence and promote its institutionalisation the media must expand its coverage of nonviolent struggles. It must portray nonviolent action as an alternative to violence, to begin to alter public perceptions. The real people, their personalities, histories and goals must be put in the public view rather than dismissing them as "ethnic fundamentalists, warring factions, rebels or separatists".

Peoples and minorities were encouraged to include media outreach and relations as part of their overall strategies, and to learn how to work with the international press to promote their true stories.

At the same time, some Participants expressed frustration with media practices exercised by oppressive governing bodies. Often, they felt, the media is subject to control by monied interests and governments, who have the power to influence, control and manipulate it, resulting in coverage of their situations contrary to their interests.

Over the past decades the role and influence of non-governmental organizations has grown considerably. Many NGOs monitor compliance with international standards in human rights, provide training and education in nonviolent action, offer mediation and conciliation services, publicize the struggles of isolated peoples faced with environmental or other crises, and otherwise support nonviolence and nonviolent action.

At the same time, NGOs must be careful not to project their own strategies onto or otherwise overlook the peoples they seek to assist. They should look carefully at the situation of the affected peoples and seek guidance from those involved in the struggle to see where they can be most useful.

It was suggested that NGOs be trained by peoples and minorities, in how to provide assistance to them and others like them. In this way, the affected peoples would have an opportunity to help NGOs understand how to be most effective in their situations.

The limitations and overload of NGOs was also raised as well as the inability of many organizations to answer the growing volume of requests for assistance from nations and peoples. In this respect, nations and peoples were urged to learn how NGOs function, and to get their attention.

Building alliances with other movements including those within a state which are also working for nonviolent change, friendly governments, NGOs and others with sympathetic or similar goals, is an important strategic device for nonviolent movements. Estonia built alliances with governments who never recognized its annexation to the Soviet Union, and with the other Baltic countries who were similarly working for independence. The East Timorese movement has built up alliances with international organizations and governments and has developed relations with citizens groups within Indonesia who are agitating for democratic change within the country at large. It has also developed solidarity with Tibet. These types of alliances encourage and sustain nonviolent movements. At the same time, Participants pointed out that building alliances can be difficult under very repressive regimes.

H. CONCLUSIONS

The Conference agreed that nonviolence, whether principled or pragmatic, is to be promoted as an active method for dealing with conflict, particularly those between states and non-state groups.

Because any one conflict has wide and profound affects beyond the principle antagonists, all concerned have a role in helping to promote nonviolence. At the same time, there is a more global need to promote nonviolence and peace in a heavily populated and increasingly volatile world. Responsibility lies with governments, international organizations, the media, corporations, as well as nations and peoples. It is not limited to efforts to prevent nonviolence in individual situations, but extends to reform of the very structures which maintain the current international status quo.

In today's world, the unrealized exercise of the right to self-determination, impunity for gross and systematic human rights violations including genocide and an increasingly polarized and deregulated global economy lead to conflict, and particularly affect peoples, nations and other non-state groups. Attention must be paid to and substantive action taken on these and related issues to reduce the growing number of conflicts, and hence the threat or practice of violence.

Participants rejected violence as an instrument for resolving political, social and economic problems, and further condemned the use of unprovoked violence against nations and peoples. They extended the definition of violence well beyond the use of arms, to those practices which endanger the survival or well-being of whole peoples, including cultural genocide, forced assimilation and the destruction of the environment on which a people's existence and development depends. Careful to delineate terrorism from other forms of violence, they condemned its practice, regardless of the perpetrators.

While many minorities, indigenous peoples and others remain in principle committed to nonviolence, the Conference recognized that in some cases they may feel compelled to use armed force to defend themselves against armed aggression, genocide and other prolonged or massive forms of violence. Without condemning these actions, the Participants acknowledged that once begun, violence breeds violence and is difficult to control and contain.

The Conference was an important step in bringing the practical discussion of the use of nonviolence into the international arena. It helped to more fully distinguish those issues which are of critical importance to the use of nonviolence and the rejection of violence. It helped to identify those areas where more research and investigation must be done in order for there to be concrete methods for supporting nonviolence.

It was, overall, a step in the process of creating a more peaceful and just world.

SECTION THREE
SUMMARY OF COMMENTS FROM PARTICIPANTS

A. Day One (21 July 1997)

Opening Statements

1. *Mr. Seif Sharif Hamad, Chairman of the UNPO General Assembly, Vice Chairman, Civic United Front (CUF), former Presidential Candidate, Zanzibar.* Thank you to the UNPO Founding Member Estonia, who has not abandoned or forgotten the UNPO after attaining independence, for hosting this Conference. I am the newly elected Chairman of the UNPO. This is a great honor bestowed on me by the Members of the UNPO. With the honor goes heavy responsibility which I humbly accepted because of my people's and my own conviction that the UNPO stands on firm and internationally accepted principles.

The Members of the UNPO are united by their aspirations and beliefs in creating just societies where all people will have equal opportunities regardless of their ethnic origins, cultural and traditional variations and the sizes of their peoples or nations. In many countries from which the UNPO draws its Members these noble principles are ignored with impunity. The minorities face different kinds of violence: marginalization as a result of immigration and emigration policies of the government in authority; extermination; treatment as second class citizens; and in some cases their environment is being destroyed. Minorities are denied their fundamental right of self-determination. Facing different types of atrocities, Members of the UNPO have chosen to fight for their rights by nonviolent means. Even when violence is applied, on examination it would be found that the use of violence by some movements is a response to long-time use of violence by the respective governments towards those peoples or nations.

Members of the UNPO believe in applying nonviolent means in attaining their goals. This is yet another factor which brings together peoples and nations in the UNPO. Therefore, it is very proper for the UNPO to take the initiative in organizing this Conference whose main objectives are:

- To offer an opportunity to different people to share experiences and provide expert opinions on this very important subject which has impact on all countries;
- To search for the definitions and interpretation of violence vis a vis nonviolence; and
- To examine whether nonviolent action can be effective to bring about change and how such action can be made more effective.

In particular this Conference will have made a great contribution if it can identify and examine the conditions both within our movements and without which contribute to make nonviolence visible and effective.

The search for the meaning of nonviolence is very important. It is the responsibility of all the world community to apply nonviolence in solving their conflicts. If we are not clear about what is actually meant by nonviolence or nonviolent actions then parties to any conflict may employ violent methods while claiming their actions are nonviolent. In order to have peace, which is a prerequisite for economic, social, political and moral development in any society, violence must be prevented. Governments, movements, NGOs and the media all have roles to play in supporting nonviolent action to resolve conflicts.

All of us owe it to our respective future generations to develop a culture of nonviolence to effect desired political, social and economic changes. We have an enormous task before us which must be undertaken by everyone who is committed to making changes, so as to make the world a more peaceful place.

2. *The Honorable Tunne V. Kelam, Vice President, State Assembly, Republic of Estonia:* Human rights, minority rights and the right to self-determination are clearly stipulated in UN documents, which are signed by most states, but often not implemented. Even large states postpone the introduction of democracy, alleging that the time will be ripe for it only after several generations.

In 1972, under Soviet occupation, different underground resistance groups sent a secret memo to then-UN Secretary General, Kurt Waldheim, requesting the UN to help evacuate the Soviet occupation troops from Estonia and to organize free elections under UN supervision. As a result many were arrested by the KGB just for trying to implement their democratic rights. It was a signal that the UN cannot do everything, and so the UNPO was founded. Estonia was one of the Founding Members of the UNPO. In the same year that the UNPO was formed, Estonia re-attained independence.

It was the goal of Moscow to populate Estonia with a non-native population, so that even if the situation changed, restoration of an independent republic would be impossible. So it was a dramatic race against time to regain independence before this happened. It was a surprise that the potential conflict, which could have resulted in violence, was solved peacefully with no bloodshed.

It is worth studying why this happened. Important were the different political forces working closely together with different tactics who were nonetheless in critical moments able to unite their forces. Also there was the ability to form and elect an independent non-Soviet body, the Congress of Estonia, which would create a counterbalance to existing Soviet bodies. Third was very clear moral and political support of leading world democracies who never recognized the annexation of the Baltic States to the Soviet Union as legal.

It is our duty to be grateful for what has happened to us, that we are able now to exist once again as an independent nation and one which is in a good position to be included as an equal member in the European Union and other international organizations. It is our duty to render moral courage to those nations who have not been able to achieve national aims, and who have to suffer under discrimination.

Nonviolence is a peaceful alternative in the contemporary world. If we succeed in making it a leading model in coming decades it will mean saving tens of thousands of human lives, not to speak of torture and suffering.

3. *Venerable Samdhong Rinpoche, representing His Holiness the Dalai Lama of Tibet*: (Reading the statement of His Holiness the Dalai Lama of Tibet) I am pleased to learn that the Unrepresented Nations and Peoples Organization of which Tibet is a Member, is organizing an International Conference on Nonviolence and Conflict from July 21-23, 1997, in Tallinn, Estonia. On this occasion, I extend my greetings to the UNPO and all the Participants at this conference.

Today, there is a growing global awareness of the meaning and importance of nonviolence. Although violence is still rife, I believe that the trend of world opinion is apparently in favor of nonviolence. I have always strongly felt that the best way to resolve a problem or conflict is through nonviolent means. The path of nonviolence may take some time, but its result is more lasting and it does not have negative side effects.

The recent successes in resolving conflicts and achieving freedoms through nonviolent approaches have further convinced me of the efficacy of nonviolence. Moreover, I feel that nonviolence is also much closer to the human nature. It is with this conviction that I remain fully committed to the nonviolent Tibetan struggle for freedom and I have been persuading my people not to abandon nonviolence as the appropriate form of struggle.

The UNPO's mission to uphold nonviolent means in order to advance the interests of the peoples that it represents is most encouraging. I am hopeful that the UNPO's International Conference on Nonviolence and Conflict will further promote the effectiveness and importance of nonviolence. I wish your conference and deliberations every success.

4. *Dr. Michael van Walt van Praag, former UNPO General Secretary*: Welcome to distinguished speakers, delegates and guests. I mean distinguished not only in terms of the titles and careers which the Participants bear, but also of their service to human kind, to the causes for which the Members of the UNPO and the organization stands.

When we first proposed the subject for this Conference, the reaction was often, 'why discuss nonviolence?' For many people nonviolence is perceived as a philosophy, and in some cases interpreted as a negative, i.e. " if it is not the violent path, what is it, then?" This Conference seeks to tackle nonviolence from the other side.

The Members of the UNPO and other peoples are faced with serious struggles for the survival of their entire peoples, cultures, religions, traditions, languages, for the environment in which these peoples and cultures survive, and for humanity as a whole. In those struggles peoples and their leaders have faced difficult choices: what tactics, actions, instruments will they use to attain their goals.? Having justice on your side does not ensure the realization of that justice. There is a need for action and strategies, and often a philosophy behind those strategies and tactics. This Conference has been called to discuss how it is possible to make such nonviolent action effective.

There are too many examples of peoples who have for a long time adhered to the principles and practice of nonviolence and yet have been attacked with brutal force, have been repressed, and have had to defend themselves with the use of arms at some point. How can you expect peoples who are oppressed and have their backs to the wall to use nonviolent means to attain their goals? As long as a movement is not violent it is not taken seriously by the international community. Once sufficient violence is used the international community responds. This is the wrong message. Those who consistently use nonviolence should be listened to, taken seriously and encouraged. If not, the violence that occurs in self-defense is only the logical consequence of the mistakes for which we are all responsible.

The Conference is designed to ensure that some conclusions are reached, and proposals for action are produced, which can be implemented by Participants and the UNPO.

PANEL 1: The Meaning and Significance of Nonviolence in Action

The first panel sought to explore nonviolence as action, in particular its relevance to and importance in current global conditions. Practical examples of nonviolent campaigns were presented, and the significance of nonviolence was discussed in these individual cases and in the larger international context.

Panel Chairperson

Kasur Lodi Gyaltsen Gyari, Special Envoy of His Holiness the Dalai Lama of Tibet

Panel Members

Don Rodrigo Carazo Odio, President Emeritus of the University of Peace, former President of Costa Rica

Mr. Seif Sharif Hamad, Chairman of the UNPO General Assembly, Vice Chairman of the Civic United Front of Zanzibar

The Honorable Arnold Rüütel, MP, State Assembly, Republic of Estonia, former President of the Republic of Estonia

1. *Kasur Lodi Gyaltsen Gyari*: The topic of nonviolence is neither new nor something of which the Participants are unaware. Nonviolence is an important issue for the UNPO, since it is one of its founding principles. The UNPO was conceived in Estonia, and later established in The Hague, and has reached a level of maturity, and I am inspired by Estonia's leaders and those who took part in the struggle for free-

dom. I visited the country with Dr. van Walt van Praag while it was still under Soviet occupation, sneaking in from St.. Petersburg (former Leningrad) almost illegally since the Soviet government would not grant us visas to visit the Baltic states. I later came to Estonia in spring, when it emerged as an independent nation. Even a few years before independence came, nobody believed it could come true. The Baltic struggle for independence was nonviolent, and a good example to other nations and peoples of the world.

2. *Don Rodrigo Carazo Odio*: I come from a small piece of land in the center of Central America. My land is a special area with specific problems. Costa Rica is subject to the special circumstances of living as a poor country together with a rich and powerful nation.

Since the beginning of Indo-American culture, our community has learned to condemn violence, but today we are being affected by a culture of violence, coming not only from direct acts, but from all modern and sophisticated means of communication. People are taught how to practice violence by an endless education coming from the television screen.

Costa Ricans abolished slavery even before becoming independent from Spain, capital punishment in 1882, and declared armed forces unconstitutional in 1948. Thanks to this, my land is that part of the globe in which a woman about to give birth knows that her child will never be a soldier.

For us, "terrorism is terrorism" and therefore we do not make any distinction between types of this kind of violence or between those who perpetrate these acts. We do not make any distinction between different ways of terrorism or terrorists. Costa Rica is in total accord with the 11 February 1991 the UNPO Declaration of The Hague which states that all perpetrators of terrorism should be condemned.

The American continent, all the way from the North to the South is being affected by terrorism with the most active forms of violence: from the migration of millions and millions of people looking for food and shelter from the South to the North and also within the South to the severe threats of forced transfer of these people to their areas of origin. From drug trafficking to the concentration of wealth in the hands of the few, violence is spreading crime and poverty as the most serious problem in the region, and migration is creating minorities.

In my country, in which tradition has made peace a way of life, and dialogue an instrument of peace, we are very seriously concerned about the problems which could destroy the aforementioned tradition. Education for nonviolence, which is something Costa Ricans had been considering as an instrument to be applied in other areas of the planet, is now beginning to be badly needed at home. We have learned that violence is not only caused by political factors, but by social events, economic policies and greed.

Next year, 1998, will be the Year of Human Rights and this should be a positive occasion to educate the people in charge of the existing instruments and mechanisms which work for human rights, not to address all of their interest to individual human rights, both locally and globally, but to pay real attention to the protection of the rights of peoples, including particularly minorities, their cultures, and identities.

Our time has come to be an era of globalization, but the real and factual powers of our time have been struggling only for one kind of globalization: the one of merchandise, which bears crime, lack of justice and violence.

Let us work, and hard, to educate ourselves and as many people as possible on how to translate the word globalization into globalism, in which we could give the real meaning of the preaching of creating a global village for human beings living together in solidarity, harmony and peace.

Conflict prevention and conflict resolution, through nonviolent means, are the only positive instruments; let us work to develop them, beginning from a positive change of ourselves spreading from our attitude and from our behaviour.

3. *Mr. Seif Sharif Hamad*: Zanzibar is an archipelago located off the East Coast of Africa, in the Indian Ocean. The most prominent of the islands are Unguja and Pemba which have a total land area of 1,651 sq. km, and are inhabited by about 800,000 people. Zanzibar attained its independence from British Colonial rule on December 10, 1963 and became a member of the UN on December 16 of that same year.

On January 12, 1964 there was a popular revolution led by Abeid Karume, who was not born in Zanzibar. On 26 April, 1964, acting alone, President Karume and Julius Nyerere of Tanganyika united the two countries into one sovereign state later to be known as the United Republic of Tanzania. On a stroke of a pen Karume, without consulting anyone in Zanzibar, surrendered the sovereignty of the people of Zanzibar to Nyerere's Tanganyika. The second day Nyerere acted promptly to notify the Secretary General of the UN that Zanzibar was no longer a sovereign state and so did not deserve to be a member of the UN. Hence, only 132 days after being admitted to the UN, Zanzibar was stripped of its membership from the organization. Since then the people of Zanzibar have been struggling to recapture their rightful place in the UN.

The recent history of Zanzibar has been characterized by violence. In 1961 while Zanzibar was still under colonial rule, violence broke out in June elections where more than ten people were killed, and many hundreds were injured. Again during the 12 January, 1964 revolution, more than 13,000 people were killed, thousands were maimed and many thousands were forced to seek refuge in different countries.

When we started the struggle to win back our seat in the UN we, the leaders, had to identify our objective. It is not to cut out all relations with Tanzania, because we are very small and cannot afford to have a giant as an enemy. Our objective was to maintain the identity of Zanzibar which was gradually being eroded. We made a decision that in fighting for our rights we shall apply all means, provided that in the application of such means we shall not be the cause of any loss of life, incapacitation of anyone or loss of property. Hence it is obvious that for us when we speak of violence we mean an act or action that brings death to innocent people, the injury or maiming of innocent people and loss of property belonging to innocent people. To us nonviolence is any act or action that is meant to avoid consequences that are brought by employment of violent actions.

We used several methods for accomplishing our purpose: i) To make people aware that their sovereignty was robbed from them, and the identity of Zanzibar being gradually lost; ii) To infiltrate the ranks of the ruling party so as to know its objectives, its strategies and its strengths. This we did successfully; iii) At the right time, when people had been sensitized sufficiently, to demand that the identity of Zanzibar should be preserved. We knew that this would infuriate the powers that be and knew the consequences. At that time no one was expected to say anything wrong about the Union. We prepared the people for the consequences.

We were expelled from the ruling party in 1988, put in prison in 1989-91. But the struggle continued. People were distributing leaflets demanding the rights of Zanzibar and that leaders be released without conditions. 10,000 people signed a memorandum to President Julius Nyerere and his puppets demanding a referendum. With the collapse of communism and introduction of multi-partism in East Europe we changed tactics. Now we claimed for multi-partism in Tanzania, to have a party which would legally fight for the rights of the people of Zanzibar. We were successful

June 1992 the authorities introduced multi-partism and we founded CUF, which gained much popularity. October 1995 the first multi-party election was held in Zanzibar. I, on behalf of CUF won the presidential election. But the ruling party refused to acknowledge this victory. At that time, violence could have broken out, but we spoke to the people to stay calm, but not to co-operate with the illegally installed government, our MPs boycotted sessions. We were successful. We carried out a diplomatic offensive with the UNPO's help. As a result:

- Donors do not deal with the Zanzibar government and cut development aid.
- Pressure was put on the Union government.
- Now it is publicly acknowledged that there is a conflict which must be solved sooner than later.

I do not think that nonviolence can bring violence. In the case of Zanzibar, despite the fact that people do not subscribe to violence and heeded our advice to remain calm and refuse to be provoked, the government used and continues to use violence to acquire submission: imprisonment, torture, demolition of houses, expulsion from government service, discrimination in education opportunities and in other citizen's rights, have been employed.

People are losing their patience. If no action is taken violence will break out any time. If no solution is found before 26/10/97 when Dr. Salmin Amour who was installed as President celebrates his second anniversary, the possibility of the outbreak of violence is very high. The security organs and the ruling party youths will use the occasion to humiliate the majority of Zanzibaris who have warned us that enough is enough. The international community must act before it is shocked into a response of supplying tents, blankets, medicines and food for the victims of the violence which could be prevented if the world had the will to act earlier.

Such violence would be a natural response to state provocation, oppression, humiliation and other violent acts. Such responsive violence cannot be the same thing as terrorism and cannot by any means be equated to it. Terrorism is a predetermined action whose instrument is the use of force with the intention to kill, or at least harm, others. To my mind responsive violence is not pre-determined while terrorism is a predetermined action of violence and which those who use it believe that it is the only way to effect change.

Even when violence is used, there is no way of predicting the result, i.e. as in South Africa, where they fought more than 20 years for freedom, and Rwanda, and Somalia. People should avoid resorting to violence, for these are clear examples of its consequences. The UNPO Members should use diplomatic offensives. For example there is the tremendous diplomatic pressure by other nations against Tanzania. People should never lose their rights. Nonviolence needs patience, time, work, and outside support in order to be successful.

4. *The Honorable Arnold Rüütel*: The concept of self-determination originated from the understanding that small nations with no statehood also have the right to exist and the need to defend their rights, culture and individuality in the international arena. Minorities express the diversity and richness of the world and its cultures. The problem of unrepresented peoples is a struggle which illustrates the intellectual and material heritage of colonialism in the present democratizing world.

Estonians know how it feels to be a minority within a large state, because they were forcibly joined to the former Soviet Union and could not stand or speak up for their rights. It was natural in this situation that Estonia was one of the founders of the UNPO. As an independent nation, as well, Estonians wish to eliminate the colonial-political results of the Soviet annexation, and to mitigate their influence in their national and political life. Nowadays the Estonian government is accused of not defending the rights of the immigrants that came during the Soviet era. Estonia has never carried out a policy of national oppression or discrimination, but rather one of tolerance.

Estonia has always had common interests with the unrepresented peoples in their struggle against colonialism. Today, due to NATO and the European Community, there is much talk about human rights and democracy in the world. It is regrettable that the individual rights of people are considered more important than the collective rights of minorities.

Formerly (with the creation of the collective security system in Europe) the idea of an indivisible peace was considered vital, but today a different approach should be taken, upholding justice as indivisible. If states really wish to found a world which is dominated by peace, stability and justice, they will have to build their policies upon the principle of consistency and understanding justice equally applied to all. Peace and stability in the world depend more on the consistency of implementing democratic principles than on the hypocritical moral lectures given to small unrepresented peoples. Democracy must mean the right for peoples to decide their own business as nations, and not dissolve them into lots of individuals.

It may be considered that Estonia has got some experience to share with other peoples still struggling for their independence, recognition or representation in the world family of states and nations. However, Estonia's way to recognition and representation was possible only for Estonia. Regardless, I believe that there is also something in the Estonian experience that may be considered by other peoples striving for freedom. One of the necessary factors was a complete unanimity in the goal, not only of the Estonian people but all three peoples of the Baltic countries. This was expressed by the "Baltic Chain", a 600 kilometre-long living chain of people joining the peoples of three Baltic states demonstrating our will to restore our independence.

Though the political leaders of that time had different opinions in some matters, these were more concerned with tactics than with principles. To some extent these different views were of use to the independence movement, dispersing attention and counteracting the central authority of Moscow. These different views were balancing each other and competing among themselves, they made our leaders look for possibilities to initiate.

The attempts to create a counterbalance to the political national movement — in the form of an empire-minded mass movement, Interfront—was a complete failure. The Baltic states did not accept the movement. Interfront, based on the population brought in and immigrated mainly in realisation of Soviet colonial policy, could not mobilize any noticeable part of the numerous, foreign-language-speaking mass of immigrants who knew nothing about Estonian life or history. It was not caused by the support of the immigrated population for the restoration of the independence of Estonia as far as the reform and the democratization policy of the central authority, politically splitting the immigrated population into supporters of democracy and an empire-minded camp. These camps in their turn were internally divided into antagonistic forces, the merging of whom in the past had not been possible.

A relatively small part of the foreign population supported the restoration of independence. In percentages it nearly corresponded to the Russian minority in Estonia before World War II. This support, despite its small weight in proportion of forces, shows that a great part of the one time Russian minority of the Republic of Estonia also supported the restoration of Estonian statehood. In those days independence was opposed only by the so-called civil garrison of the Soviet colonial power. Now one part of this population is protesting against the non-existent national oppressing in Estonia. The other factor which cannot be underestimated in the peaceful formation of our struggle for freedom was its overwhelmingly parliamentary character. The reasons for this can be observed on three different levels: psychological, historical and political.

On the psychological level our nation is characterized by steadiness and avoidance of premature emotional actions that could provoke a reaction to aggravate the real situation. On the historical level it should be considered that Estonia had once struggled for its independence, had been acknowledged winner and its statehood had been internationally recognized. In 1940, breaking the concluded treaties, the Soviet Union occupied Estonia and violently merged it with itself. Publicly declaring that Estonia had voluntarily entered the Soviet Union, the political leadership of the empire, to say nothing of the international community, knew very well that the incorporation had been for Estonia a brutal violation of international law. Being aware of that, it was most probably somewhat braking to suppress our independence movement with force.

On the political level it was important that the Soviet empire, wishing to manifest itself as a high-class democracy, could not prevent the native population from participating in the economic, administrative and political structures. The general opposition and armed struggle with the Soviet regime dominating in Estonia after World War II and in the following decade, became gradually softer in the second half of the 1950s and the first half of the 60s and was gradually replaced by the participation of the representatives of the native population in the work of the Soviet organs of power. Certainly this caused a certain political unreliability and a split in the society.

This split was a basis for the formation of two national movements in the course of the restoration of independence: i) the Citizens' Committees movement, initiated by dissident forces, publicly and in principle opposing the Soviet regime and openly striving for the restoration of the independence of Estonia and ii) the Popular Front, formally supporting the reform movement of the Soviet regime. The Popular Front joined the most different political trends, beginning from the democratic socialism to the ideology of national rebirth. The most important difference between those movements was trust in or unreliability towards the official organs of the government of Estonia of that time.

Although the participation of natives in the Soviet organs of government politically split the society, it still gave an opportunity to defend national interests before the central authority in Moscow. Therefore the central authority could not successfully realise all its plans that could have undermined the bases of the Estonian national existence.

The last example of their plans was to start a large-scale production of phosphorite in Estonia. If this plan had been realized, the major part of Estonian cultural landscape could have been devastated, many important ecological problems would have been produced, and a new wave of immigration of a work force would have changed the Estonian nation into a minority in its historical homeland, facing the possibility of physical destruction, as has happened to many other small nations in the former Soviet Union.

While the crisis situation in the empire was growing deeper, the existence of the native staff in the economic, political and administrative structures of the state became an important factor. Although the central authority tried to use them as an instrument of its policy, the government of Estonia and the Supreme Council in the new conditions emphasized their formal right to pass independent decisions in matters concerning Estonia. So the resolution on the superiority of the Estonian laws was adopted, the right for political activities was given to public movements (that politically paralyzed the one-party Soviet system), the use of armed formations against public demonstrations prohibited, the referendum on the restoration of independence of the state was proclaimed and after receiving the positive answer, a period of transition to independent statehood was promulgated.

All those steps, paralyzing the activities of the Moscow central authority in Estonia, remained within the framework of normal parliamentary practice. So the central authority, having declared the programme of democratization, was deprived of the possibility to use force against the independence movement. Therefore it may be said that the positive attitude and activities towards independence of the organs of state power of Estonia of that time had a remarkable role in the nonviolent struggle for independence.

In this situation the only opportunity of the central authority to maintain control over the development of events (that were clearly aimed at the breakup of the empire) was a large-scale use of force. All attempts to stabilize the situation by local power demonstrations had had no results. It was rather pouring oil on the fire, pointing out the need to democratize society and to end the totalitarian past. In August 1991 the attempt of that kind was made: the empire-minded removed Mr. Gorbachev from office and with the help of military forces tried to establish control over the state. But they had made a mistake in their calculations, the process of democratization had already developed too far to stifle it only with the demonstration of violence. The use of arms against the people would have easily turned against the organizers of the coup d'état itself or even developed into a civil war.

For Estonia the coup in Moscow was a unique chance. The legal central authority was replaced by the self-appointed, but to subordinate their regulations was not in accordance with the laws of the Soviet empire itself. Though the development of events was not promising, the highest organ of state power in Estonia, the Supreme Council, made a resolution to restore the national independence of Estonia that had been demolished in 1940 by the Soviet occupation and the following annexation. It was practically a unanimous decision. No votes were against it, only some representatives of the Soviet military forces did not take part in the voting. Figuratively speaking, the decision to re-establish independence was practically made in front of the muzzles of guns of the tanks arriving in Tallinn.

To summarize, it may be said that in the bloodless restoration of the independence of Estonia, the political factors mentioned before had an essential role. But the fact that the use of force mentioned was not responded to with the use of force was also of much importance. It is problematic what could have been the further developments of events in Estonia if the tanks sent to Estonia had fallen under fire. Maybe it is inappropriate to compare with, but one could draw a parallel between the events in Czechoslovakia in 1968, in Estonia and in Chechenia. But not only the clever option was involved. This option was made also due to the fact that at this moment Estonia had been completely unarmed. However, this example gives occasion to once more consider the chances of armed or peaceful struggles and drawbacks in defending national goals in fighting for recognition.

And finally, the Estonian experience of the peaceful restoration of national independence can hardly be copied by anyone else. But there is something in it that can be considered by unrepresented peoples. They will have to decide it themselves.

5. *Senator Parris Chang*: Historically the white man referred to the "white man's burden" when describing colonialism and the spread of Christianity, but nowadays the reality is another: colonization exists in the form of black men against black men, and yellow men against yellow men, making violence and colonization no longer the privilege of white men.

Taiwan has been practicing nonviolence throughout its struggle. July 1987 was a crucial moment in Taiwan's history, when the ruling party Kuomingtang (KMT) was compelled to lift martial law. Before this, anyone who conducted political actions against the government was accused of treason. Instead of resorting to violence, the KMT had to compete with other parties in the ballot box. The people of Taiwan have made the government open up through nonviolent means, and Taiwan has transformed into a multi-party democracy.

Should we differentiate between just violence and unjust violence? Most of us believe that all violence is wrong. Many countries believe that there are just wars. Last year, China tried to intimidate Taiwan when Taiwan was undergoing presidential elections. Fortunately, the United States came to Taiwan's aid. How does a nation like Taiwan deal with China's intimidation and its claim that it has the right to start a war to colonize Taiwan? No other country supported Taiwan, nor did the UN even discuss the issue, although they state that their policy is to preserve peace and security. Peace is achieved through everyone's actions which bring forth the respect of human rights, true change and nonviolence as a reality.

6. *Kasur Lodi Gyaltsen Gyari*: Dr. Chang has brought up many important issues, including colonialism. The world witnessed the end of colonialism in Asia with the Hong Kong hand-over. However it was given to China, currently perhaps the most powerful colonizers of the world, which is now contradicting its own history of rejecting colonialism. What might the meaning of nonviolence be, if some forms of violence might be justified?

7. *Mr. Ledum Mitee, Acting President, Movement for the Survival of the Ogoni People (MOSOP)*: I would like panelists to discuss the definition of justifiable violence. The US will not sell Taiwan defensive weapons, yet cannot the MIG fighters which they sold to Taiwan be used for offense? We must be careful what we are saying. When

does the right of self-defense come in? If there is one isolated attack is it an excuse to go forward with full-scale war?

8. *Mr. Salav Alijev, Representative of Kumyk*: This conference is very important, since the world is experiencing a period of decolonization and may be on the way to a third World War. Peaceful resolution of conflicts is more important now than ever, especially since nations and mankind depend on it.

There could be two interpretations of peaceful means: i) narrow, benefiting some nations and peoples; and ii) a wider sense, where these peoples are considered to be of international and global importance. International organizations such as the UN do very little to help peoples and nations in their struggle for human rights.

I represent Kumyk, where we fight for the reunification of our state, which was divided between Dagestan and Azerbaijan in the collapse of the former Soviet Union. While Kumyk was a part of the Soviet Union, we did enjoy some sort of administration powers, but that is not the case anymore. Kumyk is one of the oldest cultures in the Caucasus, and has a long history of division. In Azerbaijan the Kumyk people are facing genocide, have no rights, no means of communication, and a colonial situation; and our people in Dagestan are now in the minority. It is not easy for our people to talk about self-determination when we are being exterminated. The Chechen Republic-Ichkeria is facing similar problems, since they were devastated in the war against the Russian Federation.

The Kumyk people are aware they should not use violent means, but we must take into consideration that people waiting for independence are under pressure and may resort to violence. We are starting negotiations with the Russian Federation to discuss the issues. When there is oppression by big states, people might easily turn to violence, i.e. people within the Russian Federation where the federal status of the different republics is not respected. The Kumyk people are still facing a colonial situation, and no one pays attention to our problem since we are a small nation. Sometimes national movements have no experience with nonviolence and it is important for them to learn more about it.

9. *Mr. Seif Sharif Hamad*: Regarding justified violence: think of the situation of a cat that has been placed in a room with no possibility to escape. After being placed in this room the cat is hurt, in this case the cat would surely try to scratch its offender. Sometimes a nation is put in a situation where there is no alternative other than to respond with violence, therefore the term 'responsive violence.' This sort of violence should not be encouraged, but if it happens it should be tolerated.

10. *Don Rodrigo Carazo Odio*: Violence is experienced by people in many ways, from armed and financial violence, to the absorption of identity and the possibility of being disappeared by a controlling neighbor. Violence consists of different problems and attitudes. In our part of the world we think the best way to struggle against violence is to be yourself, not an object of change, but a subject of existence. This is a

philosophy of life, through which you are yourself no matter what surrounds you. We oppose the sale of arms, but Chile is now trying to purchase fighter airplanes, each worth US$ 25 million, when it could be using that money to help support the many people in Chile who live in poverty. It is important for people to keep a balance, and to know where and how to struggle for peace. Circumstances may vary, but if you are sure about yourself and what you are, the possibilities of survival are real.

11. *Kasur Lodi Gyaltsen Gyari*: The justification given by Mr. Hamad on his concept of responsive violence is interesting, and this Conference would probably need a whole panel to analyze the topic. Not responding at all is not equal to nonviolence. Nonviolence should be the most active and courageous response possible. People who practice nonviolence are even more courageous than those who use force. Even when one is in the position of the cat in Mr. Hamad's example, the violent response in itself would contradict the principle of nonviolence. Nevertheless, if one is in the cat's position, one should not sit in the room, but rather do something. Violence should not be justified even in that case. For some of us nonviolence is a life experience, and the issues differ as situations differ therefore making each group react in a different way.

PANEL 2: Internal Conditions for Effective Nonviolent Change

Panel Two discussed conditions, such as leadership and organizational structures within movements, peoples and minorities which are favorable for the effective implementation of nonviolent action.

Panel Chairperson
Mr. Ledum Mitee, Acting President, Movement for the Survival of the Ogoni People (MOSOP)
Panel Members
Mr. Audrius Butkevicius, Member of the Seima of the Republic of Lithuania, former Defense Minister of Lithuania
Reverend Prajnalankar Bhikkhu, Representative of the Chittagong Hill Tracts
Chief Germaine Tremmel, Vice President of the UNPO Steering Committee, Head Hereditary Chief, Lakota "Hunkpapa" Nation

1. *Mr. Ledum Mitee*: Welcome to the second section of the Conference, Internal Conditions Necessary for Successful Nonviolent Change.

2. *Mr. Audrius Butkevicius*: When speaking about nonviolent change I adhere to the concept of civilian based defense (CBD) used by Professor Gene Sharp: "CBD rests on the theory that political power, whether of domestic or foreign origin, is derived from the sources within each society. By denying or severing these sources of power

populations can control rulers and defeat foreign aggressors."

I believe that CBD fits perfectly well in the war theory concept of psychological defense or psychological operations, which, according to NATO definition, are "planned psychological activities in peace and war directed to enemy, friendly and neutral audiences in order to influence attitudes and behaviors affecting the achievement of political and military objectives."

I consider it is wrong to separate external conditions from internal ones. In effective nonviolent change it is necessary to create a complex of external and internal conditions, only such a complex allows for the possibility of CBD. We cannot rely solely on internal conditions necessary for effective nonviolent change. Drawing from my own experience which I acquired when using the CBD method in Lithuania in 1987-93, I can state that to achieve an effect a nonviolent strategist should plan his activities in three fields simultaneously:

(i) in his territory and society;
(ii) in the territory and society of the adversary; and
(iii) in the territories and societies of neural and friendly states.

Nonviolence as a method is effective only because we, the people, are guided by the same or similar values, and because most cultures share the same moral principles. Nowadays some of these values like democracy or human rights have become the levers of international politics which no member of the international community can afford to ignore. Thus, today as never before nonviolent actions can be exceptionally effective if their strategists rely on these universal human values in the three fields mentioned above.

Therefore, the main condition for effective nonviolent change is a complex assessment of nonviolent action and the situation, an ability to plan and execute the activities in one's territory as well as in the enemy's and neutral territories, and an ability to lean on fundamental human values which affect international politics, to force international opinion and the international community to react. Even nonviolent action taking place "internally" should be based on "external" logic, viewed not only from the point of view of one's own, but also from the enemy's society, as well as from neutral and friendly states.

Other "internal" conditions for effective nonviolent change are connected with this main condition. The first condition is the availability of a leader or leaders who are capable of turning the idea of nonviolence into a universal ideology as well as the availability of a strategic planning group to prepare for nonviolent change. Effective nonviolent change can only be brought about by deliberate and well-planned long-term activities. Nonviolent action demands a much greater and deeper preparation than an ordinary military operation. Nonviolent action always requires a much more sophisticated set of instruments of social psychology and is based on the analysis of attitudes, values and myths that prevail in a society. It also utlilizes ideas and ideologies. An individual participating in the action is not a depersonalized and unified soldier who blindly obeys commander's orders, but a full-blooded "civilian" driven by his emotions, crowd instinct and the impulses of the subconscious. Here it is important to ensure very precise planning and organization.

The second condition is the creation of an organizational structure which can organize CBD actions. This structure performs several very important functions without which nonviolent change is impossible:

(i) teaches the society the CBD methods and behavior during a nonviolent action;
(ii) ensures the organizational and technical support for the CBD action, for example, vehicles to carry people, hot tea and fires in wintertime;
(iii) receives voluntarily the blow when the enemy attacks during the CBD action, gives cover to the other participants of the action, sacrifices themselves intentionally and if necessary will die to attract the attention of the international community to the developments, inciting guilty consciences among one's people who are not participating in the action and a feeling of guilt among the enemy;
(iv) neutralizes instigators who can damage the idea of nonviolence; and
(v) controls the situation by preventing the adversary from using against the organizers of nonviolent action other groups of the society like national or religious minorities, social groups, etc.

I can assure you that today an adversary who knows the possibilities of application of CBD can ruin nonviolent actions if the latter are not supported by an organizational structure far superior to that of the enemy.

The third condition is the preparation of the society for a nonviolent change. The strategists of nonviolent action must find a way to destroy the legitimacy of the enemy's authority and create within the society the principles of legal justification for its own activity. For instance, in the Baltic states this was done by explaining to the public the consequences of the Ribbentrop-Molotov pact to the Baltic states and by forcing the adversary, in this case the Soviet Union, to admit in public this act as unlawful. To create this condition the actions mobilizing the society and oriented towards national self-esteem and universal human values are of crucial importance. In Lithuania such actions were the return of the remains of deportees and political prisoners who were deported by the Stalinist regime to Siberia—practically every Lithuanian family was affected by the Stalinist repression. The public defense of the Parliament as a symbol of democracy and freedom during the January events in 1991 turned into a particularly powerful mobilizing action. This action predetermined the possibility of nonviolent change in Lithuania.

The fourth condition is the possibility of the organizers of nonviolent action to control their resources:

(i) human resources and a necessary number of CBD experts to create organizational structures in key parts of the country;

(ii) time resources are necessary, minimal period of time until the beginning of a conflict during which an organizational structure will be put in place, the public prepared for the ideas of nonviolence, and interests of the leaders of different public groups coordinated;

(iii) material and financial resources. These are necessary for the survival of the participants of the nonviolent action: food, shelter, heating, etc. In the case of a protracted conflict, resources should be planned in such a way as to ensure a sufficient standard of living. Resources should be planned in advance and distributed according to their importance to various stages of the struggle;

(iv) resources necessary to organize CBD include:
  a) communications, as many communications channels as possible;
  b) vehicles and fuel reserves;
  c) information resources.

Organizers must conduct regular, impartial and operational assessments of the situation within their own society, and that of the enemy as well as friendly or neutral states. This should be a continuous monitoring to determine the trends. Here you cannot do without public opinion polls. On the other hand, this is also an opportunity to exert influence over the mass media, to provide it with timely, interesting and unbiased information, in appropriate language and manner, so as to make it understandable and psychologically acceptable to the societies of friends and foes. In this regard modern means of communication, satellite links and television play a crucial role. These means were among the most important factors which forced the US and Soviet governments to stop wars in Vietnam, Afghanistan and Chechenia.

The fifth condition which is crucial is the desire of the society to carry on the struggle. The organizers of nonviolent action have to perceive their action as a well-staged show. It must be interesting for both actors and spectators. We like games. It is necessary to plan both tragic and comic sides of the struggle. And always keep a rabbit in a hat which will be pulled out when the attention of "spectators" is beginning to subside and the "actors" are beginning to tire of playing.

You should remember that an enemy will always do something which people fear most, but you can always exploit it.

And yet another condition which cannot be ascribed to internal, is the necessity to ensure the support of various forces abroad. However, it can only be created "internally." The most important thing is to show to the world that our resistance is continuous, long-term and universal; that even if we do not achieve our goals the world will not find spiritual peace and will not be able to discuss comfortably the issues of democracy and human rights. Therefore, it is necessary to present every nonviolent action as an expression of a common strategy, to create a mechanism to register every unlawful action of the enemy and disseminate information across the world. It is necessary to agree with the leaders of the neighboring states of favorably inclined social groups on such issues as a possibility of a respite for the leaders of resistance, training of volunteers, and supplies of immediate necessity.

Having implemented these conditions the price the enemy will have to pay to retain authority and political control will be too high. Then as Napoleon said, the big power will die of indigestion.

3. *Reverend Prajnalankar Bhikkhu*: Violence cannot be extinguished by violence, it can only be extinguished by nonviolence. An act of violence gives birth to many violent activities. So violence is a matter of relativity. The growing violence in different parts of the world makes a peace-loving person consider some sort of institution that could manufacture specific nonviolent strategies to ensure peace in the world.

Scholars interpret the term nonviolence in different ways. I am not a scholar, but as a peace-loving Buddhist monk I am here stating my feelings about nonviolence. To me nonviolence means a unique way that leads one to his or her ultimate goal. In other words, nonviolence is an instrument that makes one acquainted with reality, peace and a solution. As an instrument, nonviolence should pertain though not be limited to the following internal conditions:

(i) mutual trust, respect and recognition;
(ii) refraining from using means of violence;
(iii) negotiation; and
(iv) realistic approach.

The conflicting groups must have the feeling of mutual trust, respect, and recognition to create a conducive atmosphere for a nonviolent solution. This will lead them to realize the necessity of cease-fire, i.e.,: refraining from using violence, and the use of negotiations. If a genuine and long lasting solution to a conflict is really sought the conflicting groups must come to the negotiation table. All conflicts ultimately come to an end at the negotiating table. It provides room for both sides to discuss different aspects of the problem.

Sometimes these internal conditions do not suffice for an effective peaceful change, because a strong group is trying to impose its idea on a weak group. The Jana Samhati Samiti (JSS), the political party in Chittagong Hill Tracts, declared a unilateral cease-fire in 1992, and since then has been using peaceful means to enter into a peace agreement with the Bangladesh government. The JSS has drastically modified its demands from provincial autonomy with its own legislative council, to regional council. However, the government is not ready to fulfil these modified demands which also include general administration and law and order within the framework of the regional autonomous council, traditional land rights, withdrawal of the settlers from the CHT and demilitarization. There is no progress even after the fifth round of peace dialogue which ended on 18 July. Our experiences in CHT lead me to identify external conditions for an effective peaceful change in our problem:

(i) international pressure on Bangladesh authorities for an international facilitator in the peace process;
(ii) ensuring that the government will accept the financial offer of the European Parliament for rehabilitation of the settlers outside Chittagong Hill Tracts, with international monitoring;
(iii) financial aid from Japan, Australia, some European countries and donor agencies should be conditional on whether human rights improve in CHT;
(iv) involvement of UNHCR in rehabilitating Jumma refugees now being repatriated from India; and
v) UNPO's dedication to work on solutions for its Members.

4. *Chief Germaine Tremmel*: The Lakota People have to abide by unseen laws. It is important to understand the philosophy of the Lakota: circles within circles, a matter of cause and effect. You must come from your inner circle, which is you, keeping in mind that the consequences of your actions and words will eventually come back to you. I come from a warrior society and I was taught ways to conduct myself, in manner and language. One of the first things I was taught was: to ask where my intentions are. I looked inside to see where those intentions were, if they included everyone. This process is called a transformational vision. One is an active part in the web of complex inter-dependencies, which obligates one to seek all connections and relationships which affect one, and understand their dynamics and how they work together. It is important to accommodate yourself to everything and everyone. There are four steps to this process, including thinking the highest thought of ones self and community and environment with respect and compassion, as this influences the actions of individuals and community. Different types of thought in this process are:

(i) Relating to one's physical place, forming the recognized boundaries of one's land and home, each indigenous group's territory;
(ii) Relating to relationships with people, plants, animals, natural elements and phenomena, to understand the difference and similarity between ourselves and other life forms;
(iii) Involving reflective contemplation, the application of the capacity to think, i.e. be thorough and make wise choices, which has to do with respect, ethics, morals and proper behaviour, and which leads to the development of humility;
(iv) Wisdom, founded on accumulated experiences, using the realm of the elders and advisory societies; and
(v) A visionary experience, a place of sacredness, seeking directly a solution to complexities.

The Lakota are a warrior society, but we do not need to kill our enemy. We can count coup on the spirit of that person, and they can live. It is hard to practice our way of life in modern America. We are now bringing it back.

5. *Mr. Ledum Mitee*: The panel has identified strong leadership and structure of organization as an internal condition. Most speakers said that internal and external conditions overlap. Resources were also named. Speakers mentioned how cultural and traditional influences influence the implementation of nonviolence, and the environment of where the action is taking place.

6. *Mr. Menelaos Tzelios, General Secretary, International Federation for the Protection of the Rights of Ethnic, Religious, Linguistic and other Minorities, Representative of Greeks in Albania*: During the Bonn Preparatory meeting, it was raised that violence starts at home. Does this relate to internal nonviolent solutions?

7. *Mr. Henriques Tiago N'Zita, President, Front de Libération de L'Enclave du Cabinda, Head of the Provisional Government of Cabinda*: The Cabinda people were forced to accept violence. How can we put an end to violence in Cabinda by using nonviolent means? Women, children and old people suffer tremendously due to the fact that their villages are burned down. The Cabinda people have to fight the military with peaceful means.

8. *Chief Lawrence Pootlass (Nuximlaye), Head Hereditary Chief, Nuxalk Nation*: The Nuxalk Nation is experiencing genocide and ethnocide. In the past settlers were welcomed and helped by the Nuxalk. There is only one village left with 200 Nuxalk inhabitants, where there were in the 1860's 160 towns and thousands of Nuxalk. Despite this, my elders, chiefs and people believe in nonviolence, as we continue to protect our forests, land and sacred areas. We have many sacred areas, one is Ista where the First Lady descended. I was imprisoned for a month in 1995 for protecting a sacred area, from which I was forcibly removed. They are using monies and our own people to oppress us.

9. *Chief Edward Moody (Quatsinas), Hereditary Chief, Nuxalk Nation*: The teaching of nonviolence has touched a lot of our people. We will continue to use nonviolence to protect our land and our forests and our way of life. The forests have been stripped, which threatens our way of life, which I consider a force of violence against my people. Because we are using our own laws and culture to protect our land we have been criminalized and imprisoned. But our own laws which were given to us by our Creator give us our responsibility to look after our land, which in turn gives us our life.

10. *The Hon. Akhyad Idigov, Chairman, Parliament Committee of Foreign Affairs, former Chairman of the Parliament, Chechen Republic- Ichkeria*: Over 1 million people lost their lives during the Chechen war against Russia, a lot of people were disabled, and the Chechen economy stopped functioning properly. Nonviolent means are too difficult at the moment, but they will have a principle role in the future. Nonviolent

measures should be registered in our Constitution, to help our nation to survive. The European Union did not help in the conflict. Practical help is needed in order to make laws to avoid conflicts.

11. *Senator Parris Chang, Member of the Senate, Taiwan*: The history of nonviolence is exemplified by Gandhi's effective nonviolent struggle against the British. An internal condition in that movement was leadership, the charisma of Gandhi, but also his ability to convince his colleagues and followers to adhere to nonviolence. Also the Reverend Martin Luther King's nonviolent fight for civil rights, in which he was supported by people of all ethnicities, and which brought about laws on equal rights for all Americans. Martin Luther King's ideals may not have yet been fully realized, but the environment has been created for more nonviolent changes.

12. *The Honorable Nadir Byekir, MP, Mejlis of Crimean Tatar People, Republic of Crimea*: Psychological and institutional conditions are necessary for hope for success of nonviolent activity. The size of the people relates to the success of the movement. There are, unfortunately, many examples of unsuccessful nonviolent movements, many are small minorities who do not have a choice of either violence or nonviolence. In some cases there is a traditional background for nonviolence, in some cases there is not. Unlike Buddhists, the Crimean Tatars are a warrior nation, yet are practising nonviolence. Discipline and control is very important as an internal condition. All sectors of the movement must support nonviolence. A small group of terrorists may discredit the nonviolent intentions of the whole movement. Nonviolence takes more planning and resources than military action. Usually nonviolence takes a long time. Where will resources for nonviolent action be found?

13. *Ms. Kimberly Kealoha Pisciotta, Representative of Ka Lahui Hawai'i*: Regarding cultural influence on nonviolent solutions, the Native hawaiians adopted nonviolence ten years ago, bearing in mind the nonviolent stance Queen Liliu'okalani took when she submitted to the US when it took over Hawai'i. The Queen was strong and hoped that the US would do the correct thing. She asked us to yield because there were not many of us left. Today, there are 6,000 pure-blooded hawaiians. The elders want to fight for their land, since the land created the Kanaka Maoli. If you destroy the environment, you destroy the people. It is an affront to the Creator and creates unbalance and sets creation unravelling. Our cultural background stresses our commitment to all people; if we do not fight for the environment and peace, everybody in the world will die. We are also a warrior society and understand there is a need for a nation's self- defense. We must try nonviolence first, and if that does not work, we must see what comes next.

14. *Mr. Göran Hansson, Stiftelsen Skånsk Framtid, Foundation for the Future of Scania*: To stage nonviolent resistance costs money. One way to limit opposition from states' points of view is to starve the opposition so that they cannot carry out activities. How

can people obtain the financial means under violent repression, to promote nonviolent activity?

15. *Mr. Hamad Massoud Hamad, Director, Human Rights, Civic United Front, Zanzibar*: Without committed leadership, the policy of nonviolence cannot work. Within nonviolent movements collaborators can damage the nonviolent system, and are used by the oppressing system. When they are expelled they may become troublemakers. Unless people are educated about nonviolence the system will not work, but what about when the oppressors will never allow demonstrations or seminars which will allow for this type of education? If people are provoked, they can be arrested, in these cases lawyers should represent the oppressed.

16. *Dr. Gene Sharp, Senior Scholar, The Albert Einstein Institution*: I am concerned about the formulation "conditions necessary for effective non-violent change" since "necessary" implies that without them you cannot use nonviolence, which is not true. I recommend the use of another word, such as "favourable" or "unfavourable" conditions. I am also concerned with the statements dealing with the need for charismatic and strong leadership, since those leaders can be removed, assassinated, or make a mistake. There are some few struggles that have such a leader. One can make up for the absence of a charismatic leader in other ways, such as by diffusing the concept of nonviolence throughout the society, and by creating diffuse leadership and strategic sophistication on how nonviolence is used pragmatically. We should not exclude possibilities by the way we formulate our questions.

17. *Mr. Th. Muivah, General Secretary, National Socialist Council of Nagaland*: If a leader of a people can do to his opponent what he wants the opponent to do to him the basis for nonviolence is there. If he cannot do that, nonviolence is meaningless. The change must start with the leader's approach to the problem. We must have a philosophical basis for nonviolence, from there everything follows. Without this there can be no internal changes.

18. *Chief Germaine Tremmel*: The Lakota people denounced going to war against the Untied States, and we struggle with the fact that this may have ended our people. In 1990 the Lakota Nation declared ourselves independent on one of our sacred mountains. Leaders of nations and peoples have an obligation to be among their people. We come from a warrior society of which we are very proud. It does not mean necessarily going to war. It took the Lakota about 200 years to be able to say that we believe in peace. Part of the process was to implement a protocol, to commit ourselves to nonviolence, and to educate our people on that stand. Next, the decolonization process had to be in place, by educating our people and restoring our cultures and societies. It is important to understand and know the environment around you and have accountable leadership within each nation's cultural context.

19. *Rev. Prajnalankar Bhikkhu Chakma*: A collective effort is necessary since both sides are an essential part of the process of achieving nonviolence. We must respect, trust and recognize each other. Nonviolence (ahimsa) is the ultimate way to realize reality and peace and to obtain a solution. The people of the Chittagong Hill Tracts believe in this principle and we strive for a nonviolent solution.

20. *The Honorable Audrius Butkevicius*: When we speak about nonviolent change, we have different understandings. I mean the ability to use power in society in order to defend it. For this method to be effective, one must be active spiritually, mentally and physically. For this I am speaking about a social and psychological violence, not physical violence. Co-operations between human beings are based on conventions of all kinds and this method is to use these conventions to defeat your enemy. This very concrete method starts with the organization. Leaders do not necessarily have to be charismatic, but at least enough to break old stereotypes. There are 243 methods of the Civilian Based Defense. Dynamite might destroy a building, but Civilian Based Defense can destroy a state. But it is necessary to know how to use it.

21. *Mr. Ledum Mitee*: Conditions "favorable" for nonviolent change is more appropriate to this discussion than "necessary." Leadership may be important, but we should consider why some leaders are more effective in nonviolent movements than in other kinds of movements. A leader should be ready to sacrifice himself, this distinguishes the leadership. Cultural and geographical factors can be favorable for enhancing nonviolent strategies. For example, in the Tibetan case, violence is not an option, because the geography does not support it.

B. Day Two (22 July 1997)

Opening Statement

1. *Dr. Linnart Mäll, First Chairman of the UNPO General Assembly*: Today we will address the issue of external conditions for effective nonviolent change. My friends will speak today about our struggle for freedom in every part of the world. The UNPO must be the most democratic organization in the world, without violence, physical or moral.

PANEL 3: External Conditions for Effective Nonviolent Change

Panel Three sought to define and discuss conditions external to movements, such as the behavior of governments, international organizations, the media and others, which influence the efficacy and encourage the use of nonviolent action.

Panel Chairperson

Mr. Kenneth Deer, Mohawk Nation, Council of Chiefs

Panel Members

Mr. José Amorim Dias, CNRM (East Timor) European Representative

The Honorable Akhyad Idigov, Vice President of the UNPO Steering Committee, Chairman, Parliament Committee of Foreign Affairs, former Chairman of the Parliament, Chechen Republic- Ichkeria

Mr. Hans Thoolen, Regional Representative of the UNHCR for Sweden (speaking in a personal capacity)

1. *Mr. Kenneth Deer, Panel Chairperson*: I come from the Mohawk people, part of the Six Nations Iroquois Confederacy in North America. It is my duty to bring you greetings from our chiefs, our clan mothers, our men, our women and our children and to those yet unborn, to yours. We mention the unborn because our unborn will one day meet your unborn in the future. As Chairman, I will try to find the balance between the time allotted for the panel and the importance of the issue of nonviolence. Yesterday we discussed the internal conditions for nonviolent change, and some speakers noted that they are inseparable from external conditions.

2. *The Hon. Akhyad Idigov*: Nonviolence is an old theory, which can be found in the Bible and the Koran. It is characteristic of humankind to solve conflicts with military weapons, and without adherence to human principles. Co-operation between nations and peoples is necessary to solve conflicts in a nonviolent way. All conflict should be resolved in a peaceful way, but this requires the will of all parties involved.

Chechenia has followed all the rules of international law and the constitutions from the Soviet Union and Russia from the beginning of its existence. Chechenia has never voluntarily joined another country. The Chechen Republic used nonviolent means during its presidential and parliamentary elections. This is the way the Chechens built up statehood. Before 1995, many negotiations took place with the Russian Federation on the future relationship between the two countries. The Russians nevertheless started a war in which 30 percent of the Chechen population was killed, of which 30,000 were children. Many children, women and old people still suffer from injuries, but Chechenia lacks the medical resources to help its war victims, since the Russians destroyed many hospitals. This is a fact although it is not known by many people.

The Chechen delegation fully supports nonviolent methods as the best way to solve problems. The Chechen Republic wants to have peaceful relations with all the nations in the world, because external relations are of great importance, and all nations should express solidarity against an aggressor. The Chechen people have been victims of genocide for centuries but effective action has never been taken to stop the oppressor. All Participants should consider things that happen in another part of the world as if they were happening to themselves, instead of ignoring them. Participants and the UNPO should unite and solve the problems together and send missions to the hot spots of the world.

3. *Mr. José Amorim Dias*: Nobel Peace Prize winner José Ramos-Horta is unfortunately not able to address the Participants, he has other obligations and is currently busy in Lisbon, Portugal.

The people in East Timor suffer the same problems as many of the Participants and the people inside our countries cry for freedom and peace. Although I look young, I have been involved in the East Timorese resistance for more then ten years. I was 11 years old during the Indonesian invasion, and when I was 15, I started my involvement in the East Timorese resistance. Besides organizing peaceful demonstrations I collected information on human rights violations in order to inform the international community. I continued this work while in university and got arrested; after my release I finished my study alongside my struggle for East Timor and left for Indonesia in 1986. I tried to raise awareness among the Indonesian people about the struggle of East Timor. I established contacts with students, intellectuals and activists. The movement in Indonesia has grown since then.

This movement also strives for democratisation in Indonesia, a country that has suffered under the dictatorship of General Suharto for more than 30 years. We explain to the Indonesian people why we fight for East Timor and that it is similar to the struggle for independence Indonesia fought against the Dutch colonial rule. The support for East Timor in Indonesia has become greater, especially among young people, and they have set up solidarity groups. We gather all supporters of East Timor, both in Portugal, and inside and outside of Indonesia into solidarity groups so we can discuss the problems. We also contribute to the Indonesian people by raising awareness of their situation internationally.

In the past five years, as a sign of our success, the Indonesian regime has become more oppressive and many of the East Timor supporters are in prison now, serving sentences from five to ten years. I am talking about external conditions within Indonesia, i.e.,: building solidarity with Indonesians. We try to build trust among young people in Indonesia; in the future they will build a democratic regime and I hope that it will lead to a solution of the problem of East Timor.

We have support from NGOs and even friends within the Indonesian government, with their help we go to the UN and try to make friends who will help our struggle. The leader of East Timor, Xanana Gusmao, is still in prison in Indonesia, and through his cell tries to reach all levels of the Indonesian society and to bring the message of peace to the Indonesian government, to understand that East Timor is not a threat to Indonesia and the solution of the problem of East Timor will help save Indonesia's national integrity. During the last 22 years the East Timorese resistance achieved some success: the world has been informed about the issue of East Timor and the continuing human rights violations, and the awareness within Indonesia has been increased. The armed resistance in East Timor represents only a symbol of the whole resistance because we are a small people we cannot count on our forces to defeat Indonesia. We changed our strategy to peaceful means, during these more than 20 years.

4. *Mr. Hans Thoolen*: While discussing external conditions for nonviolent change, the focus should be on three factors:

- Nonviolence should be recognized and (with more difficulty) rewarded.
- Respect for human rights should be enforced even handedly, even in the case of big nations.
- There should be more understanding that prevention is better than cure and that real solutions require long-term work.

To what extent can the 'international community' influence these factors? To clarify since the international community is all of us, it therefore could mean nobody. Often people when they speak of the international community seem to have in mind some regional or international organization, but actually identifying a particular organization, such as the UN and the OSCE is out of fashion, perhaps not so surprising after some serious failures by the UN and a decade of UN-bashing in the media of several countries. By using the vague international community, speakers do not have to be too realistic about matching resources and expectations. Still, it should be possible to address some of these aforementioned factors, especially in the less ideological world of the post-Cold War.

Nonviolence should be recognized, upgraded and rewarded by international organizations. The UN itself is based on the concept of nonviolent change. The monopoly of the legitimate use of force in the UN Charter clearly points in that direction. Although the maneuverability of the UN organization is small, there are certainly possibilities to demonstrate, more than before, that nonviolence pays, and at least that certain forms of violence, even if committed under the cloak of sovereignty, do not. The recent creation of international tribunals is a case in point, but also in the conduct of peacekeeping, conflict resolution and technical assistance activities, international organizations could seek to privilege nonviolent counterparts and defend their legitimate right to seek a change to the status quo.

It would appear at first glance that the UN would be the best place to address issues of peoples rights, to a lesser degree group rights and would not be effective in the many cases of individual rights. The reality is the other way around. Individual rights are handled more easily by international organizations than group rights. The question of self-determination is in many respects a no-no. However, even effective protection of individual rights, including the individual rights of persons belonging to minorities and peoples, should go a long way in making the option for nonviolence a more realistic and fruitful one. In this regard, I call your attention to an excellent article by Mr. Menelaos Tzelios in the recent edition of the UNPO News.

Regarding prevention and long-term commitment, the UN and other international organizations have made some progress at the conceptual level, but in the implementation there is still a lot lacking. It is not realized enough that a typical feature of conflicts involving minorities and peoples is their longevity, and too often a return to normalcy and simple cessation of armed conflict is proclaimed as a definite solution. Even a relative success story such as Cambodia seems to be unravelling. The fire brigade mentality is not helpful in the search for long-term policies applicable to minorities and unrepresented peoples. For this reason alone, seeking better and sustained co-operation with external, non-traditional actors seems to be the least that the UN and other international organizations could do.

International rules on self-determination, particularly outside the colonial context, are narrow, and certainly so when applied and interpreted by a body composed of states. Efforts to change the situation with regard to the right of self-determination should not be abandoned but tempered with the realization that progress will be slow. Getting the UN to support a wider self-determination approach is only one out of the many tools and methods you have at your disposal. According to Martin Ennals, "Nowhere is there a procedure of arbitration, no definition of terms, no UN body which will entertain about self-determination as such. It is a right which creates expectation without fulfilment. People are dying for that right which is known to exist but nowhere defined (1991, preparing for the conference of self-determination held in Saskatoon, Canada)."

5. *The Hon. Akhyad Idigov*: Everybody speaks about the outcome of conflicts, but not about the causes. Conflicts are models of force. It should be examined who produces and proliferates weapons; the big nations are responsible for this. Big countries can kill people without any punishment, e.g. the Russians killed 100,000 people in Chechenia, but Russia is a member of Security Council, the body that governs morality in the world. There is human rights monitoring in the Baltic States, but not in Russia, Chechenia or in Tibet, all because Russia is a member of the Security Council of the UN. President Clinton said that the problems in the Chechen Republic have to be solved with as little blood as possible. Any blood is too much. This attitude is also to be found in the UN bodies, otherwise there would be no need for the UNPO.

The UN is an organization that only serves the interest of the big nations at the expense of all peoples and nations. Everybody looks up to the UN and its branches all over the world, but no one dares to say the king is naked. We should sit down with the big nations to make them aware about the fate of small nations, because the people with power have all the resources but they have lost their hearts. Otherwise the good work of the UNPO will have little effect. The UN should enlarge the Commission on Decolonalization and this Commission should also represent the UNPO. Members should visit embassies of Russia, the United States and China to deliver this message.

6. *Kalon T. C. Tethong, Minister of Foreign Affairs, Tibetan Government in Exile*: External conditions apply to both parties, not only to the party seeking resolution. They are also the responsibility of the dominant power and the international community. Regarding the clarification given by Mr. Thoolen about the international community as all and nobody, this is the crux of the problem, wherein nobody is

responsible for the problems of unrepresented nations and peoples.

Both parties must show will and courage to settle and negotiate, the absence of which can lead to violent conflict and the loss of lives, such as in Chechenia and East Timor. This comes from the frustration and desperation of the people who are struggling for their freedom and fundamental rights. It is the primary responsibility of the parties involved to create the external conditions for the peaceful resolution of conflicts. However, international bodies are equally responsible; it is not good enough to say, as many dominant countries do, as they exploit the resources and the peoples of weaker nations, that they do not want to intervene in the internal affairs of another country.

For example the People's Republic of China, which uses the excuse that Tibet is an internal affair of China. If that is so, then China can violate international human rights law and claim it is written that within the boundaries of China's sovereignty they can violate international law. I use the word responsibility, because all conflicts affect neighbouring environments, and once regional, conflicts become international problems, i.e. Tibet affects the whole of the sub-continent of India and Central Asia. The favourable conditions for nonviolence must be created on both sides of the conflict.

7. *Representative of the Organization to Maintain the Erzyan Language*: I was born in the town where the first atomic bomb was made, in the country of Mordva. The Mordvan people are not even given the right to be identified as such (since they are only known as Erdzyan), and 600,000 of them cannot speak their mother tongue anymore. We cannot teach Mordvian in school and are denied practice of our religion. We must use self-defense, by peaceful means or we are doomed to perish as a people. We cannot be a member of the UNPO which is a symbol for peace.

8. *Mr. Werner Lottje, Secretary for Human Rights, Diakonisches Werk der Evangelishen Kirche in Deutschland*: Much hope is placed on international human rights organizations in the struggle for human rights and self-determination. Organizations involved in struggles should know how human rights organizations function and that their scope of action is limited, compared with what is needed. Human rights organizations, though, can make an important contribution by removing the veil of legitimacy of violence used against just causes. Today, the international human rights community cannot grow fast enough, in answer to the growing number of organizations seeking their help. Organizations involved in struggles should not be frustrated if human rights organizations inform them that they do not have the time to help them.

9. *Rev. Prajnalankar Bhikkhu Chakma, Representative of the Chittagong Hill Tracts*: The UN is the most powerful instrument for effective nonviolent change in conflicts. Under the UN, the world is characterized as having peace, security and justice. Many human rights organizations all over the world defend human rights, yet there are

many human rights violations recorded at the UN Human Rights Commission. For example, on June 12 1996, Ms. Kalpana Chakma, Secretary of the Hill Women's Federation was kidnapped by an armed military group led by Lieutenant Ferrous, and is still missing. The main human rights organization in CHT reported her disappearance to the UN, yet to this date we still don't know her whereabouts. How effective is the UN in contributing to effective peaceful change to a conflict? I question whether the UN can take any initiative for a solution to an internal conflict or human rights violations.

10.*Mr. Zéphyrin Kalimba, Association for the Promotion of Batwa*: I come from Central Africa where conflict and violence have been present for a long time. These acts are influenced by foreign countries like the United States and France. Genocide occurred in Rwanda, and the Batwa pigmy minority suffered greatly as well, and could not take real actions against the regime. The international community did nothing to help Rwanda until it was too late. A nonviolence campaign should start to provide information to governments and international organizations on the problem, which would not only prevent conflict but also acts of violence.

11. *Mr. Henriques Tiago N'Zita, President, Front de Libération de L'Enclave du Cabinda, Head of the Provisional Government of Cabinda*: The people of Cabinda are committed to applying nonviolence principles to solve problems, since we are peace loving people. A commission must be formed by the UN, the UNPO and the Organization for African Unity (OAU) to investigate the human rights situation in Cabinda and the refugee camps in the Democratic Republic of Congo and Congo Brazzaville. This commission should see how violence is applied by the Angolan forces in the Cabinda territory. The leaders of Cabinda have written many times to the UN and OAU, but all these appeals met no success. I hope that the UN, OAU and the UNPO will take serious steps this time to find out about the human rights situation in Cabinda.

12. *Mr. Reynaldo Mariqueo, International Co-ordinator, Mapuche Interregional Council*: The Mapuche Nation live in the southern part of Chile and Argentina. Our nation fought a war of more than 300 years against colonial invasion, but this was an act of self-defense and not of aggression. Self-defense in this context is a fundamental principle adopted by the UN. Today the Mapuche face cultural genocide and ethnocide. Our culture has never been recognized by the dominant nations. Therefore we are dying out as a nation, our language is not recognized and land is taken away from us, and our environment destroyed. Another threat is the economic development of Chile, e.g. the construction of highways and of six hydroelectric dams in the Bio-Bio River will affect many indigenous families. Participants should think about the problem of cultural ethnocide, because many indigenous peoples around the world are facing assimilation and non-recognition of our fundamental rights as peoples. As the next millennium approaches, a gathering should be organized, perhaps by the UNPO, where nations could bring their culture and music and tell the world we exist and will continue to exist in the future.

13. *Dr. Robert Gyula Cey-Bert, International Ambassador of Karenni State*: I agree with the statement made by Mr. Mariqueo that cultural violence is the most dangerous form of violence. It is more difficult to resist cultural violence than physical violence because the former attacks the national and cultural values, your soul. If you are destroyed culturally, your nation will disappear. There are many forms of cultural violence: when children cannot be educated in their own language and about their own history and national traditions. The invasion of the Coca Cola, hamburgers and Marlboro culture, and religious missionaries are forms of cultural violence. The only way to resist this influence is to protect the nation with cultural and psychological strength and to defend tradition. Nonviolent resistance should be psychological and cultural.

14. *The Honorable Rytas Kupcinskas, MP, Lithuania*: The media has a strong influence on international developments, since they cover the whole world. For example the extensive media coverage of the killing of the famous fashion designer Versace, while the killing of hundreds of people in Tibet and East Timor almost gets no media attention at all. The UNPO has the authority and moral force to support national liberation movements. The UNPO is well informed and will grow and achieve more authority in the future. Finances are extremely important and the UNPO should try to obtain a clear picture of how conflicts are financed, especially when a big power is involved. The respect for the organization will be based on the support it can give to its Members.

15. *The Hon. Akhyad Idigov*: The UNPO plays an important role in the world today. It depends on the Members to influence which direction the organization will go: a passive or an active one. The future of the UNPO also depends on financial resources. I welcome the presence of Mr. Thoolen, a representative of UNHCR, since this organization has difficulties protecting the rights of refugees, especially when big powers are involved. The big powers try to make the problems of small countries invisible, and the smaller nations will face many problems in the future. The UNPO and Participants should defend the rights of peoples. I propose a resolution which includes such points as to obtain influence through mass media and to raise the importance of the situation of the UNPO Members. We could refer to the problems in Chechenia and ask the UN to recognize the independence of the Chechen Republic. I propose a commission be set up, which would study the situation in Chechenia. The UNPO should call on other international organizations, like the UN and the European Parliament, to impose concrete measures instead of just words. In this way situations like Chechenia could be avoided. This commission should also investigate the death of the Chechen leader General Dzhokhar Dudaev. The active position of the UNPO could be used every time we need to solve problems.

16. *Mr. Hans Thoolen*: It is worthwhile for the UNPO Members as much as for other

groups to educate oneself about NGOs, the UN and other intergovernmental regional bodies. The UN is not as complex as many people think. It is sad that some comments including those made in the debate here, continue to show confusion regarding factual issues. For example, the UN does not monitor the Baltic States at all, the OSCE does monitor two out of three of the countries. Russia tried to have the UN monitor the Baltic States, but their attempt failed last year. This shows the opposite of what has been said here, that even big countries sometimes fail to have their way at the UN. Big countries do have extra weight in the UN, but this is necessary for the effectiveness of the UN: a Security Council consisting only of small, peace-loving nations would not have the same impact. You need to have a compromise between what you want the UN to do and how you want it composed.

The arguments of internal jurisdiction and territorial integrity are not only invoked by big countries. This is a problem UNHCR faces everywhere even with the Nordic and Baltic States. However, it is completely passe´ to use that argument when there are gross and systematic violations of human rights; the UN recognizes control over domestic jurisdiction, but this principle cannot be invoked so a country is free to do whatever it wants within its borders. Many countries support this view nowadays, and this is an enormous step forward compared to the situation only a decade ago when most countries argued against it.

The UN procedure for solving the disappearance of an individual is in many cases inadequate. It functions largely due to the input of non-governmental international human rights organizations. The structure of the UN is not obsolete and the UN is not too big. The budget of the UN is the same as that of the New York City fire brigade, and the budget is small compared to the expectations people have of the UN. For example the budget of the UNHCR (US$ 1.2 billion in 1996) is not that much, considering the 26 million people who need care by the UNHCR.

PANEL 4: Nonviolent Strategies

Panel Four addressed the role and relevance of strategies in nonviolent campaigns. Participants stressed the central requirement of strategic planning for successful nonviolent action and named those elements which need to be considered in planning strategy. Concrete examples of strategies used by particular nations were presented.

Panel Chairperson

Senator Parris Chang, President of the UNPO Steering Committee, Member of the Senate, Taiwan

Panel Members

The Honorable Nadir Byekir, MP, Mejlis of Crimean Tatar People, Republic of Crimea

Ms. Michele Ernsting, International News Producer, Radio Netherlands

Venerable Samdhong Rinpoche, Chairman, Assembly of Tibetan People's Deputies, Tibetan Government in Exile

Dr. Gene Sharp, Senior Scholar, The Albert Einstein Institute

1. *Senator Parris Chang, Chairperson*: The era of revolution is over. Leaders who used armed struggle brought suffering to their own and other people. We have seen the reversal of the trend. In the past decade the international community has honored statesmen and human rights leaders who practice nonviolence. The rewarding of people who practice and preach nonviolence is an external condition which promotes nonviolence. Successful strategies have included those used in Gandhi's struggle, and the US Civil Rights Movement.

The revolution which occurred in Taiwan ten years ago went largely unnoticed by the international community. Before martial law was abandoned at that time, more than 25 of the current Members of Parliament were imprisoned for their activism. Taiwan is trying to maintain its freedom and independence from China. To cope with China's threat, Taiwan businessmen infiltrate the Chinese market. If China invades Taiwan, the mainland economy and people will suffer the most. We are trying to induce peaceful evolution in China. We try to persuade China that one nation could organize many states, just like Germany at one time; we could form a separate state. An independent Taiwan would not be hostile towards China.

The Chinese colonization practices should be condemned and resisted by the international community. We have not been so successful in this area: when China intimidated Taiwan in 1996, the UN did nothing. The international attitude was that China should solve its own internal affairs. We want the international community to accept that the use of force against people is an international issue, not the internal affair of that country. The Taiwanese cannot be pacifist, we must defend our freedom and independence and save our sovereignty. We only possess defensive weapons.

2. *Venerable Samdhong Rinpoche*: My statement is based on my own individual ideas; it concerns the topic of the discussion and in this capacity I do not represent the Tibetan community. I am not a strategist and feel that the word 'strategy' belongs to the vocabulary of generals, armed forces and defense establishments. Nonviolence is neither a matter of strategy nor does it contain any strategic dimension, because it has no battles to wage and no wars to win. 'Strategy' implies use of all possible means to gain victory without any consideration for right or wrong. It aims at winning a war and hence it implies defeat of the enemy and victory for one's own side.

The aim of nonviolence is the establishment of truth and removal of injustice. It does not aim to eliminate or defeat someone. For a true nonviolent activist there is no enemy. Nonviolence aims to end injustice by making the perpetrator of the injustice see reason and undo the wrong done by him. In the end the nonviolent activist and the wrong-doer should have no bitterness left between them. They may even become friends. Uprooting or weakening violence is the ultimate aim of nonviolent action. It does not aim to eliminate the wrong-doer.

The roots of violence are embedded in hatred, greed and egotism that seeks domination over others, and the search for glorification on the part of a person, group, a race or a nation. From the nonviolent point of view all of these are mental defilements that go against truth, justice and human dignity. As nonviolence is rooted in truth, love and compassion, its practitioners see the world in a way which is entirely different from the world-view of a person taking recourse in violence. Once the wrong-doer starts seeing reason the roots of violence start drying up. As violence is based on untruth it cannot be sustained in the long run. Being based on truth nonviolent endeavor is sustainable and despite serious setbacks, hurdles and slow progress, it is bound to weaken the roots of violence. The only condition is that the practitioners of nonviolence do not forsake steadfastness, patience, and above all, their commitment to truth.

To persons like me nonviolence in its general form has no strategic use. If we take it as a strategy it implies that one is making use of if because of certain compulsions. It may be so because under the given circumstances the means or resources of violence are not available to him. It may also imply that no sooner one feels he is strong enough to use violence he may easily replace 'strategic nonviolence' by truly 'strategic' violence. For a true nonviolent practitioner, nonviolence is not a matter of convenience, it is a matter of conviction.

I suggest finding ways and means to implement the principle of nonviolence in different situations and propose two essential principles:

(i) Unity and purity of ends and means. The means employed for the application of nonviolence in concrete situations should be chosen very carefully. If the end to be achieved is truthful and just, then without exception, the means should be pure and unassailable likewise.

(ii) Skillfulness in the choice of means and methods. The practitioner of nonviolence has to use all his skills to determine the most effective way or ways of action. Skillfullness in choosing and using the right means is a rare quality and that is why a nonviolent movement needs a highly principled as well as a highly skillfull cadre and leadership.

It is difficult to enumerate the methods of nonviolent action. There are more than 200 methods identified by Mr. Gene Sharp. Which methods are to be employed when and where can only be decided by its practitioners on the basis of the nature and needs of the actual situation, which may differ from case to case. In many cases well-tried methods like nonco-operation or civil disobedience can be easily adopted but there may also be situations where it is difficult to use these methods. Existing or old methods may have to be suitably revised or new methods may have to be evolved. Therefore, the choice of methods depends upon the nature of the specific situation.

Factors concerning the decision on the method to be used should include:

(i) time and duration;
(ii) place;
(iii) levels and scales of action;
(iv) tempo of action;

(v) tackling violence;
(vi) facing suppression; and
(vii) degree of assertiveness.

I belong to that category of practitioners of nonviolence who, according to their tradition, believe that nonviolence is one of the noblest ideals of human society which must be practice d and upheld not only during the course of a national or human rights struggle, but should be practice d throughout one's life. People like us may be considered outdated in the modern world of ever-changing ideas, practices, techniques and technologies.

The views expressed reflect my personal belief. I am of the firm opinion that anyone who considers nonviolence as a noble value and tries to see it being practice d in a non-traditional way, is a person of noble intentions and of high moral commitment. If anyone endeavors to conceive nonviolence as a 'strategy' and sincerely desires to resolve conflicts through nonviolence is a hundred times superior to one who preaches or uses violence in any form. What is most important in the present age is to bring nonviolence at the top of the agenda.

3. *Dr. Gene Sharp*: Clear thinking in this area is currently still impeded by inadequate use of clear concepts and terminology. Major confusion is introduced by accepting the widely used term 'nonviolence.' The word is variously used to refer to ethical or religious nonviolence ('principled nonviolence'), nonviolent action or nonviolent struggle (usually on a pragmatic basis), inaction or passivity, and any activity that is not violent. Those various beliefs or behaviors can be extremely different from each other, and need to be given different names. Otherwise we cannot discuss the various phenomena with any clarity. My recommendation is that we drop the word 'nonviolence,' except for a very restricted use. Instead, we should call the different phenomena by separate names.

This discussion is on 'nonviolent action'— a technique of conflict without violence that uses methods of symbolic protest, nonco-operation and intervention to gain objectives. There is also a conceptual problem. It is understandable that many people will see it natural and correct to group together at one end of a continuum the forms of action and beliefs that are without use of violence. These may include negotiations, conciliation, conflict resolution, pacifism, nonviolent action, and others. On one level that makes sense.

However, the grouping can lead to lack of clarity and confusion. A different perspective is, first, to separate beliefs (as the various types of pacifism or principled nonviolence) from types of action. Then, second, within the category of types of action to place nonconflictual types of action that do not involve violence (such as negotiations, conciliation, and others) at one extreme and, at the other extreme, means of waging conflicts. The means of waging conflicts would then be divided in two parts (at least), violent conflict and nonviolent conflict. Nonviolent action is in this view parallel with violent conflict. Both share some similar characteristics (being means of applying pressures and of fighting) and also are separated by some sharp differences (the means of action and types of pressures used, whether violent or nonviolent methods). It is therefore understandable that warriors and others who have used violence bravely can switch to the use of nonviolent struggle without immense problems.

Nonviolent action includes three classes of methods:

(i) symbolic protests;

(ii) nonco-operation (including social boycotts, economic nonco-operation, as economic boycotts and labor strikes, and many forms of political nonco-operation); and

(iii) nonviolent intervention (including sit-ins, hunger strikes, and parallel government). Attention is called to the list of 198 methods that has been distributed.

The effective use of nonviolent action has requirements. These include nonviolent discipline and persistence, as well as other important ones. Both those who might otherwise choose to use violence in other circumstance and believers in principled nonviolence can use this technique.

In the conference program attention has focused on 'necessary' internal and external conditions for the use of nonviolent action. In my view there are favorable and unfavorable internal and external conditions but these are not absolute requirements. At times groups may compensate for specific unfavorable conditions by increasing the strength of other existing favorable conditions. There are many factors that determine the outcome of a nonviolent struggle. Many of these are listed in the distributed reprint. This includes four factors in the social situation, nine in the opponent group, four in third parties, and seventeen in the nonviolent group. The nonviolent group can influence most of these. However, as with the use of violence, not every attempt to apply nonviolent struggle succeeds. Skill, strength, discipline, wise strategy, numbers, persistence, and other factors are needed. Nonviolent struggle can be made more effective than it has been in the past by deliberate efforts to do so. The available resources for making future applications more effective include the past experience of many groups in many parts of the world. This history is often little known and its importance minimized. Yet it has frequently been powerful.

Historically, nonviolent action has been widely practiced. This includes its application here in Estonia, as well as in neighboring Latvia and Lithuania, against the Soviet Union. It has been used in many other conflicts in the Americas, Africa, Asia, Europe, and Australasia. Nonviolent struggle has been waged, sometimes successfully, against all types of political systems, including extreme dictatorships and empires. Improvised and unprepared nonviolent struggle has been more effective in a large number of cases than has been generally recognized.

The whole phenomenon of nonviolent action has long suffered from limitations. Past cases were often improvised or had only minimal planning and preparations. There were only limited scholarly studies available. The phenomenon was plagued by misconceptions and confusion. Many of the popular conceptions of what is required to make nonviolent action work are not valid. Such misconceptions include the ideas that success requires a democratic, or even nonviolent, opponent; or that success requires world support; the aid of the media; a much longer time span to succeed than does violence; or a 'climate of nonviolence.' Those views are not accurate.

The view has been expressed that if a group is using nonviolent action, the opponents should be expected to respond nonviolently also, and that if the response is instead violent repression there is something wrong. That view is not in accordance with reality. The opponent group often depends on violence to maintain itself and its practices. When challenged nonviolently, violent repression is a sign that the nonviolent movement is threatening the status quo. It is not true that the opponent side must respond nonviolently or the movement has failed. Nonviolent action is a technique for combating violent opponents.

It is also not true that the right of self-defense requires a shift to violence. A switch from nonviolent struggle to violent struggle can lead to the defeat of the previously nonviolent resistors. The opponent group is almost always very well equipped to fight violence by superior violence. Indeed, in many cases the opponent group often attempts to provoke the nonviolent resistors to apply violence instead in order to help defeat them.

Self-defense can be conducted with nonviolent struggle to the advantage of the resistors. (Indeed, such a defense policy has been developed that is called 'civilian-based defense.' Writings on it were used in planning the 1991 defense against the Soviet Union in Estonia, Latvia, and Lithuania.)

The technique of nonviolent struggle, applied skilfully, is able to withstand violent repression and still succeed. The casualty rates are almost certainly much lower than with violent resistance. Against violent repression, in addition to the impact of nonco-operation and other resistance, this technique employs 'political jiu-jitsu' which makes the violent repression of the opponents rebound to weaken the opponent group and to strengthen the resistance.

Nonviolent struggle can operate through four mechanisms: conversion of opponents (unlikely), accommodation (involving compromise), nonviolent coercion (the opponents have no choice), and disintegration (the opponent regime falls apart). These are described in the distributed monograph "The Role of Power in Nonviolent Struggle." (It needs to be read very slowly, as each sentence covers the content of several pages of The Politics of Nonviolent Action.) As mentioned previously, despite the unprepared earlier practice of nonviolent action, there have been more successes in the past than might reasonably have been expected. Very importantly, there has also been a growth of politically significant cases in the twentieth century in various parts of the world. It is now possible to increase the effectiveness of nonviolent struggle in the future through careful analysis, planning, and preparations. I suggest the following twelve steps in that direction that a group considering the use of nonviolent action might take.

1) Conduct an in-depth study of nonviolent struggle as a political technique, including its methods, dynamics, and mechanisms. The dynamics will show how the technique operates against violent repressive opponents.

2) Determine in clear terms the group's objective(s). These need to be more precise than 'freedom,' for example. The objective(s) should be formulated so that it can be easily measured whether or not it/they have been gained. Examples might be de jure independence, autonomy, federal status, minority rights, or other.

3) Conduct an analysis of the nature of the problem. What maintains the unwanted domination? What makes liberation possible?

4) Learn how to think and plan strategically. Attention is suggested to the distributed article on the importance of strategy in nonviolent action.

5) Prepare a strategic estimate of the conflict. What are the strengths and weaknesses of both the opponents and the potential nonviolent resistors? Attention is especially drawn to identification of weaknesses of the opponents, how to aggravate them, and how to weaken the opponents' strengths. Attention is also required on means of strengthening weaknesses of the dominated group and how to capitalize on that group's strengths.

6) Prepare a grand strategy — a master plan for the whole coming struggle to achieve the identified objective(s). It must be well done.

7) Plan individual campaigns for identified, more limited, specific goals. Using identified strategic principles of nonviolent action, prepare a strategic plan for achieving such specific limited goals.

8) Aim for maximum self-reliance, but plan for third party nonviolent assistance if possible.

9) Strengthen one's own institutions, and possibly create new ones to serve the needs of the population that is to resist. Some of these may also serve as resistance organizations during the conflict.

10) Prepare one's own population for struggle. A variety of means will be required, including among others spreading knowledge of nonviolent action, preparing layers of leadership, arranging communications, assisting provision of the population's physical necessities and medical assistance for injured resistors, and establishing communications to the outside world.

11) Learn how to calculate and make gains despite setbacks that may be encountered. Setbacks are not permanent defeats. Lessons should be learned from them such as how to improve the development of strategies, increase the solidarity of the resistors, maintain discipline, increase the capacity to continue resistance despite repression, and other factors. Weaknesses need to be identified and efforts made to strengthen the population and the resistors, while undermining the opponents. Gains and accomplishments need to be recognized and the resistors given credit.

12) Consolidate limited victories in individual campaigns to achieve specific goals short of the full objective(s). Resistors and the general population need to recognize when they have won achievements, and to learn how to follow those successes with further efforts in the next stages of the conflict.

13) When the declared objective(s) is/are won, protect them from being stolen by internal or external forces (as by a coup d'état) and take steps to ensure consolidation of a new democratic system.

These are among the steps that can increase the effectiveness of future applications of nonviolent action. This technique is already a major tool of liberation. It can be made still more powerful.

4. *The Honorable Nadir Byekir*: Nonviolent strategies vary a lot, and I'm not ready to draw any conclusions from all the different possibilities. I will suggest to you some observations made on the basis of the peaceful struggle of the Crimean Tatar National Movement. The main qualities of our strategies are:

- Universality, trying all possible measures of nonviolent actions.

- Legality, using all existing legal opportunities, in four capacities:

  a) the Constitution and other Ukrainian legislature;

  b) International law, especially obligations of the Ukraine, using precedents in the practices of democratic foreign states that are known to be critical of the position of the Ukrainian government;

  c) using legal procedures (court procedures, administrative complaints, etc), both internal and external, like parallel reports to the responsible UN agencies, communications to human rights-protecting institutions; and

  d) drafting legal proposals for the Ukrainian government which could be used to find a just solution to the problem of the Crimean Tatars. Government experts avoid public and free discussions with our representatives because they are not sure of their own legal arguments.

- Pro-activism, such as blocking railways and damaging buildings of the local parliament or restaurants and shops belonging to the Mafia, but always under the strict condition that no personal harm is inflicted. We try to keep political initiatives in our own hands. We would be happy if the government could work on proposals acceptable to my people. Unfortunately this is not the case. So we need to force the government into political dialogue.

- Co-operation with the international community in the broadest sense, including UN agencies like UNDP, UNHCR, UNESCO, ILO, IOM, OSCE and others, especially those that are concerned with the protection of human rights, like the Sub-commission, CERD, etc., international NGOs; and seeking understanding with other, weaker indigenous peoples of the Crimea, the Karais and Crimchaks.

- Scientifically-based approach, obtaining relevant analyses from all disciplines including sociology, psychology, political science, legal and economic issues.

- Planning, i.e. developing an overall strategy. Serious strategy needs to be structured in a real 'step by step' manner in all possible directions with variants for urgent circumstances. It is very important that a policy keep space for improvisation and unexpected actions, which may be the most effective in the struggle with the bureaucratic machinery.

5. *Ms. Michele Ernsting*: I would like to react to the media section in the discussion paper on nonviolence. I believe this presents a much worse picture of media's motives than actually is the case.

The paper says that 'half-truths are reported to enhance sensationalism' and entertainment value. I think more often than not half-truths are reported because journalists like myself simply don't have time to gather the adequate information before a deadline; often journalists simply do not know whole truths. Radio Netherlands broadcasts 24 hours a day, and we have relations everywhere. I work for 'Newsline', a current events news program. What we do is look at relations between countries or of opposing groups within countries. The issues or incidents which affect these relationships are important to us.

We assessed media coverage of both violent and nonviolent actions. At first glance, it seemed to most of us that violent actions were more effective in terms of getting media attention. But on closer inspection we realized that our coverage of specific nonviolent campaigns was in the end more thorough than our coverage of violent ones. For example the Ogoni struggle in Nigeria, and the mass rallies in Serbia last winter.

Though objectionable, a high degree of tension is of interest to the media. When a violent action occurs, we often do spot coverage; who, what, when, where and why. Because we have to cover the act of violence, and explain the reasons for it in three minutes, our coverage of violent issues can be superficial. Many violent events become 'same old stories,' as has become the case with Northern Ireland where most attention is given to the peace process, rather than to terrorist attacks. It's not as interesting to us anymore because we make the assumption that it is no longer interesting to a listener. Also, we tend to wait for a 'news peg' before we look at a particular subject. If we know there will be a violent action to peg the story to, we are far less likely to cover the same issue during peaceful periods. In other words, the violence, and how to deal with it becomes the story, The real issues of human rights and repression get lost along the way.

On the other hand we found our coverage of specific nonviolent campaigns to have more depth. A successful nonviolent campaign can be very compelling for the media. In the case of the Serbian opposition demonstrations in Belgrade, the coalition became expert in the art of brinkmanship. The tense stand-off between the opposition and the Serbian government was extremely compelling from our point of view, because it seemed that at any moment the Serbian leadership could have resorted to violence to quell the protests.

During this campaign, we looked at the characters involved in the stand-off, we examined the background issues, such as human rights, workers rights, and post-war democracy in the region. In a sense we were forced to do this because there were no 'easy' violent actions to focus on, we had to dig deeper for story angles. As a result we made many contacts in the region. In this case, a nonviolent campaign produced more thorough coverage, something which is good for the groups involved and for the media.

The fact is from our experience, there are few campaigns which successfully create the amount of tension necessary to attract international attention. Many of the successful campaigns involve well-known dissidents or powerful governments or corporations. So how do you get an issue on the media's agenda? This is difficult to answer effectively, but we did come up with some possible media strategies.

1) Remember coverage is a two-way street, in that the media outlet has to get something out of it as well: good information, access, contacts, a quality interview that is interesting to listeners. Think about what you're offering.

2) Having several articulate spokespersons is essential, and they must be fluent in English, and be able to voice the aims of the people in a clear concise way e.g. Hanan Ashrawi, spokesperson of the Palestinian authority.

3) Good background information from reliable, not necessarily supportive, sources, which the UNPO has provided in the past.

4) Try to make a link between the immediate situation and a more universal issue, such as environmental issues, e.g. Shell in Ogoniland.

5) Try to link issues to other events in the news, which already have the public's attention.

6) Get to know the international journalists in your area, and develop a trustworthy relationship with them.

7) Use available technology, such as the Internet.

8) Conduct active rather than passive campaigns, i.e. do not victimise yourself but show initiative.

6. *Mr. Salav Alijev, Representative of Kumyk*: I appreciate the problems some UNPO Members are facing while dealing with China, but I want to stress the problems the Kumyk people face with Dagestan. The Kumyk people are divided up. I am a doctor of genealogy. My people are vulnerable, and have a right to assistance, since they advocate nonviolence.

7. *Mr. Akhtar Buskunov, Chairman of the Board, Bashkirian Public Center "Ural", Representative of Bashkortostan*: Bashkortostan, as a sovereign republic, should have the right to participate in international organizations. My people first lived in tribes, and then became a nation. They were first subjected to Tatar and Mongol rule, and later were taken over by Russia, and suffered serious repression. They are separated into various provinces. There is an artificial border between Bashkortostan and Kazakhstan. All imperial states will disintegrate, and small nations will survive. Bashkortostan will try to be a trustworthy UNPO Member.

8. *Chief Lawrence Pootlass (Nuximlaye), Head Hereditary Chief, Nuxalk Nation*: I am grateful to the Creator for this Conference, and congratulate the President of Estonia. When I first came to this land we felt the pain in our hearts for the many years of suffering you have had. Our people are very anxious to learn what has happened in such a short time in this part of the world.

Our people over the past 150 years have been oppressed and persecuted. I am grateful to the Founding Members of the UNPO; all the flags that represent so many different nations. I am honored to give recognition to Dr. Michael van Walt van Praag. I am not very educated but I speak from my heart and spirit. I am honored to give him the name LaQuaymiis, which means "he who gives feast by the sea," also on behalf of Chief Germaine Tremmel of Lakota Nation and Ms. Pisciotta of Hawai'i, with whom the Nuxalk share so much history. I endow Dr. Michael van Walt van Praag with an eagle feather, which gives him the right to come to our territory.

PANEL 5: UNPO's Role in the Promotion and Implementation of Nonviolent Change

Panel Five solicited recommendations and discussion on how the UNPO can be more effective in promoting nonviolence generally, and assisting its Members to implement nonviolent change.

Panel Chairperson

Ms. Inaria Kasiepo, Representative of the West Papuan Peoples Front

Panel Members

Mr. Fèlix Martí, Director, Centre UNESCO de Catalunya

Mr. Menelaos Tzelios, UNPO Assistant General Secretary for Relations with the UN and the Americas; General Secretary, International Federation for the Protection of the Rights of Ethnic, Religious, Linguistic and other Minorities; Representative of the Greek Minority in Albania

Mr. Isak Chishi Swu, Chairman, National Socialist Council of Nagaland

1. *Ms. Inaria Kasiepo, Panel Chairperson*: The promotion and implementation of nonviolence link us to the international community. It is important to recognize, identify and strengthen groups with a history of nonviolence, in particular women's groups.

2. *Mr. Fèlix Martí*: Catalunya, an unrepresented nation, through peaceful means has reached a good level of self-government and recognition within the Spanish kingdom, and we are trying to become a recognized nation member of the European Union. I work with the UNESCO Secretariat in several international programs in order to promote a culture of peace and the promotion of language diversity.

Peoples, minorities and nations are not the main sources of conflict in the world, conflict is often instigated by big powers: political, economic and the mass media. When nations and peoples want to work for an effective peaceful change they should develop strategies in order to act in the fields of these main players. The UNPO could be active in three areas:

1) Information: nations, minorities and peoples do not have a strong presence within the mass media, and suffer from silent or secret violence. When peoples' struggles appear in the media they are presented as being violent. It is important to present objective information about our realities and our movements and pass it on to the media, in order to influence public opinion. This might not be easy at the local level, but the UNPO could be very effective at the international level. The UNPO Yearbook should be used not only as an internal report, but also as a report for others.

2) The UNPO should become a specialized organization for conflict resolution in the specific field of collective rights. The UNPO can have the moral authority to act as mediator and negotiator in the conflicts of people, nations and minorities. There are conventions and courts that deal with individual human rights, but there is nearly nothing for the protection of peoples' or collective rights. The UNPO could establish, for example, a permanent 'International Council for Peoples' Rights' for that purpose.

3) The UNPO should fight against political marginalization, and try to reform the UN system into a mechanism in which all peoples in the world can effectively participate. The UN is based on a state system that frequently ignores the reality of these peoples and it would be positive for the UNPO to help international organizations establish peace and security, on the basis of the recognition of collective rights. Some states are open to establishing a new international democratic system without exclusions and fully accepting the right of self-determination. The UNPO can also establish new forms of political co-operation between unrepresented peoples and independent peoples. The UNPO should not be a ghetto of second class nations, but rather a model of co-operation and solidarity for the future.

The UNPO can be a space of co-operation between nations that agree on three basic principles:

(i) protection and promotion of cultural and linguistic diversity;
(ii) respect for collective rights, including the right of self-determination; and
(iii) the adoption of nonviolent methods of conflict prevention and conflict resolution.

3. *Mr. Menelaos Tzelios*: Since its establishment over six years ago, the UNPO has been actively involved in promoting nonviolence to resolve conflicts between its Members and state governments. Although six years is a very short time for any organization of this nature to produce dramatic results, the UNPO has been able to establish itself as a serious and reputable organization. This is due mainly to the fact that the organization deals with the peoples and movements who are often at the center of controversial issues involving the rights of peoples and to the fact that the UNPO was able to provide credible and accurate information to the international community regarding impending conflicts involving one or more of our Members.

The current question is what the UNPO can and should do to capitalize on this reputation and move to the next stage where our warnings to governments and international community will not only be taken seriously, but also motivate them to intervene before conflicts reach the uncontrollable stage with catastrophic and unpredictable results for all parties concerned. To achieve these objectives, the UNPO should concentrate its efforts, strategy and financial support to:

(i) governments, the international community, financial institutions, multinational corporations, and the international media that our Members and the UNPO on their behalf, are prepared to begin dialogue and negotia- tions for conflict resolution through nonviolent means;
(ii) activate the Peace Action Council as soon as possible;
(iii) prepare Members by providing training on how to effectively use the media, conflict resolution and nonviolence, and leadership training; and
(iv) select one or two cases and devote all our efforts and energy until satisfactory results are achieved. This could have a tremendous impact and will increase the powers and effectiveness of the UNPO among our membership and the international community.

For the UNPO to be strong and effective, Members must do their share to support the organization by providing the necessary funds and the most accurate and credible information possible on their situations. Every organization is as strong as its Members want it to be, and the UNPO is no exception.

4. *Mr. Isak Chishi Swu*: It is difficult to define nonviolence. If it has to do with the doctrine of love, to understand its meaning may not be that intractable. Resorting to force when dealing with problems that could be solved without it is an act of violence, and when violence is used, man's rationality is relegated to the background. How effective can nonviolence be when countering violence? Nonviolence is indispensable for resolving conflicting issues, especially if higher values, such as life, are involved. Therefore, commitment to nonviolence is a necessity.

But the assertion that nonviolence is unreserved and total is against the laws of creation. It is a principle whose application may be restricted due to the nature of the issue concerned. Violence often begets violence. It is not clear to what extent nonviolence can prevent bloodshed, especially in certain instances of conflict. Therefore, generalization of violence or nonviolence as a means to deal with conflicting problems is without much basis. In the ultimate analysis it is basic human nature that needs to be taken into practical consideration to make violence or nonviolence a realistic means to solve problems.

Commitment to nonviolence must be one's principle and that of the organization he belongs to. It should never be an expediency. Any ideal principle must have strategy. Otherwise it is only a mere piece of untenable idealism. It tends toward passivity; it is also apt to be superseded by interests. Without the initiations of correct strategy for the realization of ideal values, it is impossible to make the nonviolent principle a living force or a living reality. In other words, without a correct approach to the problem it is simply not possible for one to prove himself with the principle.

Nonviolence is not only a defensive law but it is also a means to take initiative to be on the defensive. A principle is vulnerable when there is no strategy for its defense. A principle is dead or dormant when initiative for its fostering or realization is absent. The leaders who are committed to the principle must see that they have the initiative always in their hand to enable them in the first place to uphold the principle; secondly, to enable them to create a suitable situation whereby high values of the principle are proved through; thirdly, to enable them to solve the situation in the light of the principle. Only then can people be persuaded to the effectiveness of the nonviolent principle. This is the way violence can be effectively replaced by peaceful means.

But this issue has also much to do with the leadership in many respects. Idolization of the leadership or the temptation of the leaders to raise or place themselves above the organization, above the principle and even above righteousness, sometimes marked the chapters of history. When an organization or a people cannot check or halt such tendency, things turned out disastrous, affecting the principle as well. In order to prevent the organization from degenerating into irresponsibility, the working principle of the organization must be democratic and leadership must always be on a collective basis. Only in this way, can there by coherency and transparency in the working system of the organization.

5. *Ms. Iris Almeida, Director of Programmes, International Centre for Human Rights and Democratic Development, Montreal, Canada*: The organization I represent was created by the Canadian Parliament to promote the application of the International Bill of Rights. We have the privilege to support the UNPO's work and I am proud to discuss the theme of strategies of nonviolence. When we look at the world today, we see an escalation of war, civil strife and conflict, which will multiply. The UNPO can make significant contributions to this situation. There are several important factors that should be taken into consideration:

(i) globalization and the concentration of land and wealth in the hands of the few;
(ii) the increase of arm trafficking, especially of small arms, sometimes more accessible than a piece of bread; and
(iii) impunity, that is lack of punishment and accountability for massive, continued and systematic violations of human rights.

It is very important to have a concrete and deep analysis before acting, which the UNPO could conduct. Humanitarian action can never replace political action. Rwanda received millions of dollars after the genocide had happened, but its conflict was never prevented. The strategies of nonviolence must be seen in the political sense, because we are talking about power, the power to decide on the lives of peoples and their destinies.

There is a need for local action, and for the dialectic between local and global struggles. The UNPO can bond East with West, North with South and collaborate with the achievement of peace.

6. *Mr. Erkin Alptekin, Chairman, Eastern Turkestan Union in Europe, Germany,*

Representative of Eastern Turkestan: I am a Uighur from Eastern Turkestan. In the UNPO Covenant it is stated that in order to become a Member, a people must adhere to nonviolence. If so, the UNPO has to develop trainings and research to support Members to carry out nonviolence. Some live on territories and carry on struggle inside countries, others live outside and try to be the voice for the people in foreign countries.

Uighurs learned from our history to carry out nonviolence, use of violence gave an excuse to the People's Republic of China to slaughter us. The Chinese have killed at least two-and-a-half million Uighurs, injured 500,000 and imprisoned another 500,000. At home, Uighurs are forced to choose between two ways: do nothing, be assimilated and appear as cowards or rise against the Chinese and die like a hero.

How can I convince the people back home about the benefits of nonviolence? My adherence to nonviolence here is no help. This is especially difficult since we do not have an outstanding leader, like H.H. the Dalai Lama, to pacify them, and people are gradually losing their patience.

7. *Mr. Menelaos Tzelios*: The UNPO denounces terrorism, not violence, not that we encourage violence. The UNPO's purpose is to teach and train Members to achieve their goals without violence. Quite a few Members are engaged in violence, for example East Timor; UNPO has been trying to convince the government of Indonesia to start dialogue with East Timorese. The UNPO is also training Members in nonviolence.

8. *Mr. Alexander Shpontak*: My nation has existed as such for more than a millennia, when we were first called White Croatians and then Russins. In 1918 the Russins wanted independence, and in October of that year they were recognized as an independent people with self-determination. The Paris Treaty recognized our autonomy, although this was never reconfirmed by the Czech State of which we are a part at the moment. After that time, the Vienna Arbitration took the decision to give part of the Russian land to Hungary. I am not a UNPO Member and have not had the possibility to state my people's case in other fora, and our problems are not covered by mass media. Ukraine has kept us under suppression and does not want to give our autonomous status back.

9. *Mr. Cham Toik, Representative, Mon Unity League*: This is the first time the Mon have attended a UNPO function. I have been involved with nonviolence since my student years, because of repressive military regime I was a victim of violence, and worked in the resistance movement. Nonviolence is a complex issue and I request the UNPO to define its issues clearly. We are living in similar situations as other the UNPO Members, under suppressive states and are being assimilated. It is important to define nonviolent strategy, violence and cultural genocide, and how to reach the media. Many people living in Burma are dying every day and this remains unknown to many in the world.

10. *Heino Ainsoo, former Director, UN Division of the Estonian Foreign Ministry, Estonia*: For the UNPO to be more effective in nonviolence one must recognize that the world order is established by the UN, which is a collection of states. Recent violent events in the former Yugoslavia have given self-determination a bad reputation. Self-determination is under attack and its importance is deteriorating while the principle of territorial integrity is being made more supreme. The UNPO should concentrate to preserve the strength of the right to self-determination in international law. With such action, nonviolence will stand a chance.

11. *Mr. Aleksander Kiryanen, Vice-Chairman, National Movement "Inkerin Liitto", Representative of Inkeri*: The UNPO can do several things for the promotion and implementation of nonviolent change, such as aiding in the development of languages. It would be a great achievement if the UN passed a declaration on the rights of minorities. It is important to deal with the right for the preservation of mother tongues; the main role of the UN should be to provide mechanisms for people to defend this right. The UNPO should exercise control so this right is adhered to, and Members should help the organization for this purpose.

12. *Mr. Th. Muivah, General Secretary of the National Socialist Council of Nagaland*: When we analyze nonviolent strategy, we must consider whether it is realistic to practice nonviolence. Even Mahatma Gandhi told a woman to scratch British soldiers if attacked by them. Those committed to nonviolent principles should make strategies realistic. If it is only a principle, it will not solve any problems.

13. *Mr. Salav Alijev, President, Kumyk People's Movement "Tenglik"*: When I go back home, I am faced with the problem of telling the young Kumyk people what I have learned. Young people are always asking about ways to deal with the colonizers, and they, and other Kumyk people in general, have tried many peaceful methods like strikes, blockades of airstrips, to no avail. They are convinced nonviolence is the best way to solve conflicts. I hope the UNPO paid attention to the fact that some representatives from the former Soviet region are not prepared to take part in the discussion. This is due to the different types of thought, the mind of the old world, versus that of the developing countries. We understand all about nonviolence, but when we go back home it seems impractical and unrealistic; especially since the young are so desperate. Some of us say taking up arms is the only solution. The UNPO should have a special training or conference on nonviolent struggle, devoted to the questions of nations and peoples of the former Soviet Union.

14. *Dr. Kara-Kys Arakchaa, Supreme Khural of the Republic of Tyva, former MP of the Russian State Duma, Republic of Tyva*: I hope that in 2004 the UNPO will be active in entering agreements with states, holding negotiations and mediation proceedings and have a higher standing on issues. The International Labour Organization (ILO)

has a stand regarding indigenous peoples and nations, and on the preservation of their land and languages. Even in the ILO case the issue does not get enough attention at the state level. UNPO could serve as a preventive organization to help avoid misunderstandings between peoples and states. It should also produce a legal document which could be ratified by these states, and remind the UN of the importance of collective rights.

15. *Ms. Kimberly Kealoha Pisciotta, Representative of Ka Lahui Hawai'i*: The pursuit of peace requires a complete commitment to nonviolence. Global peace should be our ultimate goal. The reality of some Members is more difficult and it should be recognized that self-defense is sometimes an appropriate response to attack. The UNPO should adopt policies which reflect reality. Situations should be analyzed very carefully, because the situation for every Member is different. Examples of possible principles governing the use of violence in self-defense are: violence is an option of last resort after all other options have been exhausted; its use should be strategic and used in a defensive manner only against military personnel; the UNPO should never condone indiscriminate attacks against civilians or the use of weaponry designed for use against civilian populations. The UNPO could facilitate a working group to begin to address specific Member's cases in this regard.

16. *Ms. Inaria Kasiepo, Panel Chairperson*: There are no black and white situations, and all experiences are different. Kealoha's comments are very helpful: the UNPO should be very realistic in its policies. The UNPO Covenant states that the promotion of nonviolence as a solution is a principle, which does not mean that Members who have to resort to violence as a form of self-defense are excluded, but it is the principle which is most important. As an organization we have to clarify definitions even more.

17. *Mr. Isak Chishi Swu*: From the Nagas' own perspective, nonviolence is a tough problem covering both theory and its practical application. The Nagas pursued nonviolent policy for seven years, after which Nagaland made the Nine-Point Agreement with India, but it was abrogated unilaterally by India whose armed forces massacred more than 150,000 of our people in a ten-year period. At the end of this period we came to a cease-fire agreement. The Naga people were never deterred from the principle of nonviolence. Therefore we never entered into India's territory to attack Indians; we never eliminated innocent civilians. At the end of ten years we participated in six rounds of talks with the Indian Prime Minister, but the cease-fire was again unilaterally abrogated.

In 1995 several generals admitted that a military solution was not possible in Nagaland. This was because the Nagas were firm in the principle of nonviolence. Finally, the Indian government has agreed to a nonviolent solution. In the beginning we met Mahatma Gandhi, who said the Nagas should be independent, and when presented with the fact that the Indian government would use force on the Naga people, said: "If they do so, I will go to Nagaland and let them shoot me first." India has now realized that nonviolence is the only way, and are going to have dialogue with us. Nonviolence may take a long time and be costly, but it is the only choice.

18. *Mr. Fèlix Martí*: I am concerned on hearing people say they have no power. The only way to find a political solution is by mobilizing our nations and involving some independent state members of the UN. Some Participants have presented the need for strategy, acting alone with no power or recognition. I recommend that the UNPO gives us the opportunity to act together for greater power in the pursuit of self-determination. We need training in this respect. Last year 100 NGOs approved the Universal Declaration on Linguistic Rights, which is not yet law, but the start of the process of getting a convention on linguistic rights.

19. *Mr. Menelaos Tzelios, UNPO Assistant General Secretary for Relations with the UN and the Americas; General Secretary, International Federation for the Protection of the Rights of Ethnic, Religious, Linguistic and other Minorities; Representative of the Greek Minority in Albania*: I agree with the delegate of Kumyk on the issue of young people, and hope to see more young persons in the next General Assembly. I will propose to the Steering Committee to hold a training program or workshop given by a small team who would visit all parts of the former Soviet Union, in order to carry on the important task of training in nonviolence.

PANEL 6: UNPO Policy on Nonviolence (UNPO Resolution on Nonviolence and Conference Statement)

Panel Six examined the UNPO's policy on nonviolence, and how that policy could be refined and implemented to more effectively promote nonviolent change.

Panel Chairperson

Dr. Michael van Walt van Praag, former UNPO General Secretary

Panel Members

Dr. Gudmunder Alfredsson, co-Director / Professor, Raoul Wallenberg Institute of Human Rights and Humanitarian Law, University of Lund, Sweden

Mr. Atner Khuzangai, President, Chuvash National Congress, Chuvash Republic,Vice Chair of the UNPO General Assembly

Senator John J. Nimrod, General Secretary / Special Advisor, Assyrian Universal Alliance

Venerable Samdhong Rinpoche, Chairman, Assembly of Tibetan People's Deputies, Tibetan Government in Exile

1. *Dr. Michael van Walt van Praag, Panel Chairperson*: Our task is to reach some consensus on the issues that have been raised and the opinions that have been stated,

and how we are to move on from here: what should the UNPO's stand be in respect to nonviolence, in regards to both its Members, and to the international community.

2. *Mr. Atner Khuzangai:* UNPO represents social, cultural and political conditions of nations and communities and freely defines strategies. Internal and external conditions have changed since the UNPO's founding and the number of Members have increased from 15 to 50. The General Assembly is the highest organ in the organization, and in between their sessions the Steering Committee takes over responsibilities. The Steering Committee unites different nations, speaks about the pain and sufferings of the Members and should be a platform for Members. Members come from all over the world, each region has conditions, difficulties, cultures, struggles and ideas. Many people can express their opinions and worries at the UNPO. The UNPO gets proper information and stimulates the information exchange between Members. Members should get more acquainted with each other.

A combined final proposal should be written, instead of internal reports for each separate Member. Education for delegates should be given on a regional basis, such as with the co-operation of the Tartu Office. The former Soviet way of thought should change. Through the UNPO, attention at the UN has been attracted to national minorities as in Ingushetia, Kosova, Nagaland and South Moluccas. Truthful information on the UNPO and its Members should be sent to the public. The UNPO sends missions to investigate critical situations and observe elections, such as to Chechenia, Abkhazia and Chuvash. In the former Soviet Union the UNPO is hardly known and little information on nations and peoples is available. Each Member should try to get the UNPO in the media, such as Chuvash has been trying to do with UNPO resolutions, and General Assembly and regional meetings reports.

Some delegates in the former Soviet Union received a letter from the Ministry of Foreign Affairs before leaving for the General Assembly, which recommended they not attend the General Assembly. The authorities did not know the UNPO fights for human rights. Peaceful development is the principle of the UNPO.

3. *Dr. Gudmunder Alfredsson:* Several thousand nations, peoples and minorities are competing for the attention of international and regional organizations. Most of the time actual facts on minorities are unknown to UN policy makers. Much greater effort must be made to inform them. The UNPO is the right organization to provide adequate information, but it is not getting world-wide attention yet. The UNPO publications, i.e. Yearbook and reports should be distributed worldwide, maybe even commercially. Organizations need to be approached with information about nations and peoples, and also about their policy, particularly nonviolent policy.

The Raoul Wallenberg Center has published a compilation of regional and international minority rights standards in international law. It has 140 pages, drawing on 38 instruments, and is only a selection of standards. There is also information on indigenous and peoples' rights. In these, the emphasis is on individual rights, but group and community rights are also addressed. In some cases the groups themselves are given access to pursue these rights through monitoring procedures. The problem is these are not being used.

Regional monitoring or implementation procedures established by international and regional organizations some of which are available to groups and are accessible without registration are not much used. For example the International Convention on Elimination of Racism and Racial Discrimination has been ratified by 140 States, about 30 of whom have granted jurisdiction to the UN Committee on Elimination of Racial Discrimination (CERD) to hear complaints about its violation. Complaints can be submitted by individuals and groups. Not a single complaint has been filed under this procedure. If concrete violations of the convention can be shown, there is a good chance make you point. Racism in the convention expressly includes ethnic and national origin.

There are a multitude of forums available in these organizations, e.g. on the environment and on human rights, but humanitarian, development and other fora are also important. These other fora feed into ECOSOC and General Assembly where the overall policy of the UN is decided. It is time-consuming and costly to work in these fora, however, the UNPO and NGOs with UN Consultative Status can be helpful in this regard.

Training is available in instruments and diplomacy. Besides leaders, all membership of peoples and movements should be included in training courses, as well as individuals from national governments, donor organizations, and the media. It is important for all these international actors to be trained regarding these standards, and the trainings can become forums for discussion and useful work. The Raoul Wallenberg Institute offers a Masters program and intensive trainings on human rights, and trainings in more then thirty countries, in, for example, criminal justice, human rights for women, parliamentarians and minorities. All costs will be paid.

4. *Senator John J. Nimrod*: It is good to establish what should be done, but it is more important to find what is a workable policy. The UNPO is diversified, its Members have differing needs. There is no such thing as 'a' policy which can meet all these needs. The UNPO has practiced and expanded its policy on nonviolence over these previous six years, keeping to its Covenant, which promotes nonviolence, and condemns terrorism. The UNPO has developed definitions and policy, through workshops, seminars and conferences. The UNPO policy puts a limit on Member's violence and nonviolence in pursuit of their aims and goals.

5. *Venerable Samdhong Rinpoche*: I am new to the UNPO and have not participated in any of its deliberations before. My perception of nonviolence is a bit different from other Member's and the organization's. I will try to make a few points which have come to my mind during this Conference.

1) Nonviolence is, besides an instrument for solving conflicts, essential for human survival. Instruments of violence have developed to an excessively dangerous and powerful level, and can no longer be used for solving social and other problems.

2) People still feel that nonviolence is not effective, which hinders the development of nonviolent means. Therefore, it must be taught that nonviolence is most powerful, if requirements, such as faith, courage and wisdom, are met.

3) People think that if the adversary is violent it is impossible to respond in a nonviolent way. This is a limited view. Nonviolence is very effective in response to violence, otherwise it has no use. Nonviolence is the most powerful response to violence.

4) Today nonviolence is discouraged, violence is encouraged. Today the financial value is the only human value left. The arms trade is profitable, and those who trade in arms are trying to encourage violent conflicts, so that they will profit. This approach must be opposed. Unless there can be opposition to this structural violence, nonviolence has no meaning.

5) Nonviolence must be used in a practical manner, otherwise it should not be kept as a principle. If we accept that it is a good principle, that means we accept it as practical. This must be promoted through education and consolidation of nonviolent actions all over the globe. We have to improve faith in nonviolent action. The UNPO has contributed quite a deal in this respect. Too often emphasis is put on individual rights, and the duties and responsibilities of individuals and groups are overlooked, these should be promoted.

6. *Dr. Michael van Walt van Praag, Panel Chairperson*: The report of this Conference will be sent out to the public. From the discussion we have been hearing in the past two days, we can distil the following important comments which will be reflected in the report of the Conference:

(i) Confirmation of the UNPO Member's commitment to nonviolence, as an active instrument;
(ii) Reaffirmation of fundamental rights of peoples, nations, minorities to exist and develop according to their own way of life, i.e. the right of self-determination;
(iii) Condemnation of terrorism, both by oppressors and the oppressed;
(iv) Acknowledgement of unprovoked violence against nations and peoples;
(v) Recognition that some peoples or nations feel the need to use armed force to protect themselves against genocide;
(vi) Recognition that violence breeds violence;

(vii) Nonviolent action can be effective even in cases of severe repression, but that in order for this to be possible strategies, skills, external and internal instruments must be used to the best advantage;
(viii) It is vital for organizations to have effective and proper tools to conduct nonviolent campaigns;
(ix) International organizations, governments, NGOs, etc., need to be convinced of the effectiveness of nonviolence and must take action to support and promote nonviolence;
(x) The spread of accurate and objective information is imperative;
(xi) Recognition of the linkage of violence and human rights violations, and need for promotion of respect versus sensationalization and commercialization of violence; and
(xii) Training proposals, including workable methods.

7. *Mr. Menelaos Tzelios, General Secretary, International Federation for the Protection of the Rights of Ethnic, Religious, Linguistic and other Minorities, Representative of the Greek minority in Albania*: Financial institutions should be addressed when they support governments which violate human rights. The statement adopted tomorrow by the Conference should be called 'The Tallinn Statement.'

8. *Mr. Th. Muivah, General Secretary, National Socialist Council of Nagaland, Nagaland*: How to be realistic in our approach to nonviolence? The nature of the problem demands an objective approach, especially on practicalities much remains to be discussed. When we are confronted it becomes no longer theoretical but practical. The UNPO must never appear to be obscure about this issue.

9. *The Honorable Musa Yandiev, MP, Republic of Ingushetia*: All texts of the UNPO reports should be translated into different languages.

10. *Mr. Aleksander Kiryanen*: A clear definition should be adopted by the UNPO on the matter of how the UNPO can support non-Member unrepresented nations or peoples.

11. *Mr. Werner Lottje, Secretary for Human Rights, Diakonisches Werk der Evangelischen Kirche in Deutschland*: It is important to involve young people. An exchange program between young UNPO Member-representatives should be established.

12. *Mr. José Amorim Dias, CNRM (East Timor) European Representative*: There should be a broadened dialogue with governments; as well as making demands of governments Members should also have something to offer them. People within nations that suppress can also be mobilised, in particular the young generation can help. This can offer some hope for the future.

13. *The Honorable Nadir Byekir, MP, Mejlis of Crimean Tatar People, Republic of Crimea*: The UNPO should develop a legal council which could be set up with help of lawyers among the Members and from outside supporters. This council could advise Members on relevant legal topics. The Steering Committee and the General Assembly should install the council. The UNPO should publish a special legal magazine, which would b devoted to the special legal problems of unrepresented nations and peoples.

14. *Mr. Bata Bayartuev, Vice-President, All-Buryat Association of the Development of Buryatia*: The UNPO now consists of 50 Members, with a population of over 100 million. As a whole, the UNPO has more subjects than France, England, or Germany. Legal consequences of the UNPO membership need to be explained better. The UNPO membership means de jure recognition. Nonviolence is important, especially since most Members do not possess weapons. It is therefore important that the substance of nonviolent principles should be elaborated upon. For most Members it is difficult to get access to international legal procedures, and it would be vital to have a set of the UNPO legal documents to show that they are represented. All Members should bring their local legal documents to the next General Assembly, so the UNPO's work can be more effective.

15. *The Honorable Mr. Rytas Kupcinskas, MP, Lithuania*: The UNPO should act as an early warning system for conflicts to be predicted and for violence to be prevented. There is a need for an assessment of who the perpetrators are, who is committing genocide, who commits the crimes.

16. *Mr Heino Ainsoo*: In the final document the need for self-help should be sufficiently stressed.

17. *Mr. Atner Khuzangai, President, Chuvash National Congress, Chuvash Republic*: In Chuvash there is a lack of young blood, which jeopardises continuity. The UNPO should found a legal council.

18. *Dr. Michael van Walt, Panel Chairperson*: Thank you to all the speakers and all the Participants. Please return in the morning for the discussion and adoption of the Tallinn Statement.

C. DAY THREE (23 JULY 1997)

On the third day, Conference Participants adopted the Tallinn Statement, and a press conference was held.

Closing Speech

1. *Mr. Seif Sharif Hamad, Chairman of the UNPO General Assembly, Vice Chairman, Civic United Front (CUF), former Presidential Candidate, Zanzibar*: In our religion there is an angel who is called Michael, who is responsible for taking care of all the human beings who pass away, in the North, East, South and West. This angel continues to do so until one person is left, who is God himself. I would like to thank Michael van Walt for being the force behind this Conference and for his guidance and leadership.

During the last two days some very interesting points and issues have been raised. I hope all Participants have learned a lot and will leave with a richer knowledge on nonviolence. The Conference report and the Tallinn Statement will be published and considered seriously by governments, NGOs and other international organizations, in order to make this world a better place.

TALLINN STATEMENT

INTERNATIONAL CONFERENCE ON NON-VIOLENCE AND CONFLICT: CONDITIONS FOR EFFECTIVE PEACEFUL CHANGE

Tallinn, Estonia, 21–23 July 1997

Leaders of some fifty nations, peoples and minorities, members of the Unrepresented Nations and Peoples Organization, met in Tallinn from July 21-23 1997 with representatives of other international organizations, NGOs and governments to discuss ways of preventing the outbreak of violent conflict and of making non-violent action effective.

The UNPO policy on nonviolence has been developed, expanded and practiced for the past six years since the founding of the UNPO. The Covenant of the UNPO, which is signed by all its members, provides for the "promotion of nonviolence and the rejection of terrorism as an instrument of policy."

The UNPO Member nations and peoples reaffirm their commitment to non-violence as an active means of promoting and achieving their goals and reject violence as an instrument for resolving political, social and economic problems. Conference participants condemn all unprovoked violence against nations, peoples and minorities and all forms of terrorism, regardless of the perpetrators. Violence is not limited to the use of arms, but can include cultural genocide, forced assimilation and the destruction of the environment on which a people's existence and development depends.

Conference participants reaffirm the fundamental rights of nations and peoples to exist and to develop as they choose, in accordance with their right to self-determination. They recognize that in some cases nations and peoples feel compelled to use armed force to defend themselves against armed aggression, genocide and other prolonged or massive forms of violence against them. At the same time they are well aware of the danger that violence breeds violence and is difficult to control and contain.

Conference participants explored both the philosophical and the pragmatic basis for the use of non-violent action and stressed the need for realistic approach to the subject. They concluded that effectiveness of non-violent action — even in the face of a violent oppressor—is dependent in large part on the internal conditions of each specific movement as well as on the attitude and actions of actors outside the movements. Good internal organization, coherent strategies, and the skillfull use of existing tools are essential for non-violent movements to be effective. Responsible leadership can be an important factor in this regard. At the same time, the conference participants are convinced that the behaviour of actors outside the movement, especially that of international organizations, State government, non-governmental organizations (NGOs) and the media affect —sometimes in a decisive way— the ability of a movement to successfully develop or maintain a non-violent strategy.

Conference participants believe that the inadequate internal organization, internal divisions, or lack of responsible leadership can be factors contributing to the outbreak of violence. The violation of human rights, both collective and individual, is a major factor. The conference participants are convinced that the absence of moral or political response to non-violent movements by international organizations (such as the UN), State governments and NGOs and insufficient or misinformed attention by the media not only contribute to the outbreak of violence and armed conflict, but also make it difficult for a movement to sustain a non violent approach.

Fundamental to the conduct of non-violent action is the availability of credible and complete information to all actors whose policies and actions can have an influence on the situation. The training in the use of available international mechanisms and the development of appropriate skills for non-violent action should be an important objective. The importance of developing programs for youth was emphasised. A number of concrete activities were proposed for the UNPO and for its Members, which will need to be examined and, where possible implemented. These will be included in the Report of the conference to be published this summer.

The conference participants call on the UNPO to strengthen its capability to assist its Members to improve the effectiveness of their non-violent movements and to inform the world policy makers and public of the plight, aspirations and realities faced by its Members. When needed, the UNPO should send missions to investigate the situation on the ground. The UNPO is urged to continue to speak out in support of its Members and against injustice, wherever it may occur.

The conference participants urge leaders of peoples and minorities to develop effective strategies for peaceful change appropriate to their specific situations and to open themselves up for dialogue at all levels with the parties with whom they are in conflict. They recommend that the UNPO Members make full use of the UNPO's facilities, services and training programs, including those relating to the United Nations, and recommends that the UNPO and other organizations work together closely to improve and broaden these services and programs.

The conference participants call on governments, international organizations, NGOs and on their leaders to adopt clear and principled policies in order to reduce the use of violence. These must include:

- recognition of and respect for the equal rights of all peoples and those of minorities, regardless of their size, their culture or religion;
- taking the needs and views of unrepresented peoples and minorities seriously;
- speaking out and condemning all unprovoked acts of violence and gross violations of human rights against unrepresented peoples and minorities;
- recognition of the legitimacy of movements or governments which use peaceful and democratic means to achieve their objectives;

- engagement in open and sincere dialogue with all such movements and governments and rewarding their adherence to nonviolence;
- encouragement and active assistance in the peaceful resolution of conflicts between State governments and nations, peoples and minorities over whom they claim authority.

The conference participants call on corporations and financial institutions to end the violent exploitation of resources which sustain peoples, and to end the promotion of violence through irresponsible arms trade and the commercialization of violence in the media and in their products.

SELECTED AGENDA OF UNPO ACTIVITIES IN 1997

January 20	A conference on the situation of the Ingrian Finns was held in St. Petersburg, Russia and attended by Dr. Linnart Mäll, Assistant General Secretary for Eastern Europe.
January 22–30	The UNPO sent a mission to monitor the elections in the Chechen Republic Ichkeria.
January 31	A delegation from Nagaland visited the UNPO Office of the General Secretary.
February 6	Bishop Paul Moore hosted a dinner in honor of the UNPO in New York.
February 11	Sixth anniversary of the UNPO was celebrated by Members and Secretariat staff.
February 17–21	UNPO Members participated at the UN and an Experts Seminar on Population Transfer in Geneva.
February 22–23	The Government of the Republic of Ingushetia and the UNPO co-sponsored an international conference on 'Refugees and Deported People: Problems and Solutions' in Nazran, Ingushetia which examined ways of responding to the refugee problem in Ingushetia by comparing it to situations in other regions.
February 23–26	The UNPO participated in an International Peace Conference on the Chittagong Hill Tracts in Bangkok, Thailand.
February 24–25	The Vice Chairman of the General Assembly visited the Chechen Republic to meet with President Maskhadov to discuss cooperation between the UNPO and the Chechen government.

February 26–27	The UNPO General Secretary visited Dhaka, Bangladesh to discuss the situation in the Chittagong Hill Tracts.
February 27–28	The Dutch National Committee for International Cooperation and Sustainable Development organized a two-day European Conference on Conflict Prevention (focusing on Africa). The conference took place under the Dutch chairmanship of the European Union and was held in Amsterdam on the eve of the informal Council of Ministers for Development Cooperation. UNPO representatives attended the conference.
March 3–21	UNPO provided assistance to Members at the UN Committee on the Elimination of Racial Discrimination's 50th session.
March 10	Demonstration commemorating the 38th anniversary of the Tibetan National Uprising Day in Geneva. The UNPO General Assembly Chairman, Erkin Alptekin, addressed the demonstrators.
March 10	UNPO provided assistance to Acheh/Sumatra, Bougainville, Chittagong Hill Tracts, Circassia, East Timor, Eastern Turkestan, Ingushetia, Ogoni, Nagaland, South Moluccas, Iraqi Turkman, Kurdistan and Tibet at the UN Commission on Human Rights (53rd session) in Geneva.
April 17–18	The 14th UNPO Steering Committee meeting was held in Bonn, Germany. Three new members were admitted to the UNPO Membership: Cabinda, the Shan States and Kumyk.
April 19–20	In cooperation with the Heinrich Böll Foundation, the UNPO organized a two-day seminar on nonviolence.

April 23–24	The UNPO General Secretary participated in the Third World Parliamentarians Convention on Tibet, held in Washington DC. The Convention adopted the Third World Parliamentarians Convention on Tibet action plan in support of His Holiness the Dalai Lama and the people of Tibet.
April 25	The UNPO Secretariat joins in the celebration of the Independence Day of the Republic of South Moluccas.
April 26–30	UNPO provided assistance to Members at the 3rd session of the UN Working Group on Minorities.
April 27	The UNPO and the Tibet Support Group (The Netherlands) jointly organized a fact-finding mission to Tibet.
April 28–29	The UNPO hosts the 1996 Nobel Peace Prize Laureate, José Ramos-Horta, during his visit to The Netherlands. The Secretariat assisted in arranging a series of meetings with the Dutch Foreign Minister, Dutch parliamentarians, NGOs and UNPO Member representatives. Dr. Ramos-Horta delivered the 1997 Müller Lecture at the Peace Palace in The Hague.
April 30	Ms. Edita Tahiri, Secretary of Foreign Affairs for the Democratic League of Kosova, and Mr. Anton Kolaj, Member of the Kosova Parliament, visited The Netherlands.
May 1–7	Representatives from Nagaland visited The Hague and briefed the UNPO staff on the present situation in Nagaland.
May 4–7	The UNPO organized a four-day training session on negotiation skills for UNPO Member leaders in The Hague. Representatives from Nagaland, Bougainville and East Timor participated.

May 22	The Conference on North Caucasian Peoples visited the UNPO Office of the General Secretary.
May 26–30	The UNPO provided assistance to Members at the 3rd session of the UN Working Group on Minorities.
June 21	Lakota Nation leaders hosted the third annual World Prayer for Peace Day.
July 15–23	The 5th UNPO General Assembly and an International Conference on 'Nonviolence and Conflict: Conditions for Effective Peaceful Change' was held in Otepää and Tallinn, Estonia.
July 26–August 2	The UNPO provided assistance to Members at the UN Working Group on Indigenous Populations (WGIP). Prior to the WGIP, the UNPO organized an introductory seminar for delegates new to the UN system. During the Working Group, the UNPO published the daily UNPO Monitor in Spanish and English.
August 2–30	The UNPO provided assistance to Members at the Sub-Commission on the Prevention of Discrimination and Protection of Minorities. In cooperation with the International Service for Human Rights, the UNPO conducted a training on the effective use of international human rights procedures.
August 8	A Sanjak delegation headed by Dr. Sulejman Ugljanin, President of the Muslim National Council of Sanjak, visited The Netherlands, Luxembourg and Strasbourg. The UNPO coordinated the visits.
August 25	*'China's Tibet: The World's Largest Remaining Colony'* was presented by Cees Flinterman, the head of the mission, during a briefing on Tibet organized by the UNPO at the UN, in coordination with Worldview International Foundation.

August 23 — The monthly meeting of the UNPO Executive Committee was held in The Hague.

August 27 — A delegation of the Iraqi National Congress led by Dr. Latif Rashid, representative of the Patriotic Union of Kurdistan, was received at the UNPO Secretariat by the Acting General Secretary and the Councillor on Political Affairs. The delegation was in The Netherlands seeking support for a campaign to set up a tribunal for Iraqi war crimes.

September 18 — Mr. Khizar Akhmadov, Foreign Minister of the Chechen Republic Ichkeria, visited The Netherlands. Mr. Akhmadov was in Europe seeking international support for the recognition of Chechenia, as well as humanitarian aid. The UNPO Acting General Secretary and the Coordinator of the Conflict Prevention Program met with Mr. Akhmadov who briefed them on the current situation in Chechenia and requested UNPO assistance in fundraising efforts.

September 23 — A delegation from Cabinda visited the UNPO Secretariat and met with the Acting General Secretary, the Counsellor on Political Affairs and the Coordinator of the Conflict Prevention Program. The delegation briefed the UNPO officials on the current situation in Cabinda and related issues.

September 25 — The Acting General Secretary, Councillor on Political Affairs and Coordinator of the Conflict Prevention Program attended the opening of an exhibition on Tibet in Leiden, The Netherlands.

October 8 — The monthly meeting of the UNPO Executive Committee was held in The Hague. Additionally, Dr. Parris Chang, President of the Steering Committee, briefed the UNPO staff on the current situation in Taiwan.

October 26–November 27	The UNPO provided assistance to Members at the UN Commission on Human Rights' Intersessional Working Group on a Draft Declaration on the Rights of Indigenous Peoples. Prior to the commencement of the Working Group, the UNPO organized preparatory training on the Draft Declaration for new delegates. As in previous years, the UNPO published the UNPO Monitors in English and Spanish.
November 28–December 1	The UNPO co-organized a training with the Movement for the Survival of the Ogoni People for Ogoni leaders and human rights activists.
December 5–7	The 16th Steering Committee meeting was held in The Hague and the Election Committee interviewed candidates for the position of UNPO General Secretary.
December 10	The Acting General Secretary and the Councillor for Political Affairs received representatives of the Radical Party (European Parliament) in The Hague. Discussions focused on ways of strengthening cooperation between the Radical Party and the UNPO.
December 15	A Chechen delegation headed by the Speaker of the Chechen Parliament visited the UNPO Secretariat and briefed the staff on initiatives to obtain international support for the situation in the Chechen Republic Ichkeria. The delegation was accompanied by a Lithuanian Member of Parliament.

Selected UNPO New Releases for 1997

January 30	Respect the Will of the Chechen People, the UNPO Urges
February 12	Eastern Turkestan in Crisis. the UNPO Urges International Community to Issue 'Stern Warning' to China
February 21	UNPO Expresses Hope for Change Following Death of Chinese Leader
February 26	Concrete Measures for Peace Put forward for Chittagong Hill Tracts
March 12	Bombings Will Be Used as Pretext for Severe Repression in Eastern Turkestan
April 21	Chechen Envoy Commemorates the Death of Former President with Appeal for Aid
April 22	1996 Nobel Peace Prize Laureate Visits the Netherlands
April 28	Three New Members for the UNPO
April 28	Energetic International Intervention Called for in Kosova
May 6	Military offensive Threatens Negotiated Solution in Nagaland
June 10	World's 'Unrecognized' to Meet in Estonia
July 15	UNPO Meets in Estonia for Fifth General Assembly
July 17	Peoples, Nations and Minorities Can No Longer Be Ignored. New Members Speak Out Against International Silence On Their Issues.

July 18	The UN and State Governments Must Take UNPO Member Issues Seriously
July 21	Effectiveness of Nonviolence Questioned at International Conference on Nonviolence and Change
July 30	Tensions Rise in Sanjak Region of the Federal Republic of Yugoslavia as Police Ban Meetings and MP is Arraigned on Charges of Secession
August 21	China Accused of Colonialism in Report of Tibet Fact-Finding Mission
November 10	Ogoni Suffering Continues Two Years After Brutal Executions

INDEX